INTRODUCTION TO BUSINESS

ASSIGNMENTS:

1 APR TS Ch. 1, 2
3 APR TH 3, 4
7 APR MON 5, 6
9 APR WED 7, 8
11 " FRID, 9, 10
17 " THURS, EXAM 1-10

21 APR-MON 11, 12, 13
24 APR-Thurs. 18, 19
29 " TUES 20, 21 ← EXTRA QUESTIONS
1 MAY. Thurs. EXAM 11-21
6 MAY TUES 23
7 " WED 24, 25
12 " MON 28, 29
14 " WED 30,
16 " FRI FINAL

McGRAW-HILL New York
BOOK St. Louis
COMPANY San Francisco
Düsseldorf
Johannesburg
Kuala Lumpur
London
Mexico
Montreal
New Delhi
Panama
Paris
São Paulo
Singapore
Sydney
Tokyo
Toronto

INTRODUCTION TO BUSINESS

SECOND EDITION

PAUL G. HASTINGS

School of Business Administration
California State University, Sacramento

INTRODUCTION TO BUSINESS

Copyright © 1968, 1974 by McGraw-Hill, Inc. All rights reserved.
Printed in the United States of America. No part of this publication
may be reproduced, stored in a retrieval system, or transmitted, in
any form or by any means, electronic, mechanical, photocopying,
recording, or otherwise, without the prior written permission of
the publisher.

1234567890   VHVH   79876543

Library of Congress Cataloging in Publication Data

Hastings, Paul Guiler, date
   Introduction to business.

   Includes bibliographies.
   1. Business.   I. Title.
HF5351.H32 1974   658.4   73-13801
ISBN 0-07-027020-1

This book was set in Univers by Allen Wayne Technical Corp. The
editors were Thomas H. Kothman, Harriet B. Malkin, and Annette
Hall; the designer was Joseph Gillians; and the production supervisor
was Bill Greenwood. The photo editor was Roberta L. Guerette.
New drawings were done by John Cordes, J & R Technical
Services, Inc.
Von Hoffmann Press, Inc., was printer and binder.

CONTENTS

PREFACE

The introductory course in business is taken mostly by freshmen and sophomores, some planning a major in business, others planning nonbusiness majors, and still others uncertain as to what their majors will be. This text is intended to be useful to all three groups. To this end the application of good management to various human activities is shown, from the use of budgeting by a college student to control his finances to the intelligent management of the world's resources. The study of business is as useful as the study of mathematics, and the application of its techniques is almost as universal.

The book begins on a positive note—what business has done for society. It ends by exploring what remains to be done—the needs facing society now and in the future, and what business can do to meet the challenge.

To ensure that the student remains interested throughout the course, the relevance of the subject matter to his daily life is noted. As each subject area is explored, its impact on daily life is shown. Where possible, the similarity between business operation and household operation is indicated.

Introduction to Business provides a broad but firm foundation in business on which more advanced business courses can be built. It is written in nontechnical language and, it is hoped, a stimulating style, and draws examples from the business world. The book aims at the following objectives:

1 To help the student understand the business world and how it functions
2 To clarify for the student all the many aspects of business, such as management, organization, production, labor, accounting, data processing, marketing, finance, and ethics
3 To outline for the student the philosophy, objectives, and responsibilities of business in its relation to its environment
4 To help the student acquire a good comprehension of how the free enterprise system works in a self-imposed context, serving society while benefiting itself

5 To familiarize the student with business vocabulary, thus encouraging him to read further in the field—as well as to gather information from newspapers and television—and in this way continually to increase his knowledge and deepen his understanding

6 To introduce the student to statistics, inventory systems, forecasting, research, and administration—in brief, all the skills that enter into the decision-making process

7 To give the student direction and motivation in making his vocational choice as wisely as he can

In pursuing these objectives in a way that would have meaning to the student, the text inquires into all the rich complexity of the business world. But it does not unduly emphasize any one aspect of business. Rather it attempts to survey the field swiftly and succinctly. Furthermore, each chapter is self-contained, to enable the instructor to organize his course according to the students' needs and to afford him the opportunity to enrich the text with his own knowledge and experience. Yet if he follows the text as structured, the instructor will be providing his students with a complete, logical, and general orientation to the business world and all its concerns, without oversimplification or superficiality.

Most students in an introduction to business course have taken no economics. Some understanding of economics is needed to understand business. Although not attempting to substitute for a principles of economics text, this book provides a stronger foundation in economics than other introductory business books do.

The problems of small business management and the character of small business operations differ in significant degree from those associated with large corporations. A large proportion of students will devote their talents in later years to small-scale enterprises. For these reasons this edition presents a chapter on small business management.

In this edition the important function of leasing is explained in the section on finance. In addition to a discussion of the instruments of short-term and long-term finance, the financial aspects of management of current assets are also treated.

Business is dynamic. This is emphasized in two ways. An early chapter traces the development of business to the present. Also, wherever appropriate, there is a discussion of probable trends of business in the future. This book emphasizes that those who want to train for management should prepare for business as it is operated not only today but also as it is likely to be operated 20 years from today.

Because of the increasing recognition of the larger constituency of business (society as a whole rather than stockholders, customers, and employees), the last chapter includes sections on (1) responsibilities toward individuals and groups and (2) responsibilities toward society as a whole. The latter develops the concept of interdependence in a crowded world and emphasizes the importance of intelligent management of the resources of the globe.

The exercises at the end of each chapter help the student master the subject and provide the basis for classroom discussion. The student can use these for review purposes. As an alternative, the instructor, by personally selecting questions and problems, can give the course the different emphases he may feel desirable for his particular classes. Such supplementary materials provide a flexibility that permits this book to be used for widely different teaching styles.

I am indebted to the many persons who have aided in numerous ways to bring this edition into being. To them I wish to express my deepest gratitude.

PAUL G. HASTINGS

TO THE STUDENT

The materials at the end of each chapter are intended to help you understand the subject matter and to fix it in your mind more firmly. For each chapter the text and the study materials complement each other. Furthermore, you should add to what you learn from the text what you learn from experience. Your business activity does not begin with your first full-time job after leaving school or college. Most students have borrowed money, made goods and sold them, and worked for pay. Obviously the business experience of most students at the time they enter college is very limited. But you have undoubtedly had some experience on which to draw for a better comprehension of the information and ideas in this text.

Follow whatever instructions have been given you in class with respect to chapter assignments, written materials to hand in, outside readings, and so on. Your instructor will tell you how to use the study material. After completing the assignment, fill in the name, section number, and date in the spaces provided at the top of the page; remove the pages, and hand them in to your instructor.

If you are "on your own," however, here are some suggestions that will help.

1 Read the terms at the beginning of each chapter to get a rough idea of what the key elements are.
2 Read the chapter. Be sure you understand any new words you meet. Business terms you are likely to be unfamiliar with are explained in the text, but for any serious student in this or any other course of study a dictionary is essential. Jot down the principal points of each section in the margin or other convenient place as you read.
3 Take the completion sentences one at a time. Supply the missing word and go to the next one. When you finish this section, check the words you supplied against the chapter text. If you have written a synonym of the correct word, it is acceptable. Use your judgment on this. Now add the number you have right. Is this 80 percent of the total? Ninety percent? What is your goal? Remember that what you get out of the study of business depends on the time and effort you put in. For those completion sentences you marked incorrectly, review the relevant sections in the chapter.
4 Now complete the true-false section and complete the exercises. End-of-chapter review questions are also provided.

PAUL G. HASTINGS

PART 1
THE BACKGROUND OF BUSINESS

The three chapters in this part form the foundation on which the others rest. The economic philosophy of a nation affects every aspect of business life. In the United States the dominant philosophy is capitalism, defined on page 7. Capitalism, of course, is a philosophy, not a religion. It has been necessary, during the course of our national history, for our concept of capitalism to undergo considerable change. If we did business today the way our ancestors did in 1800, the United States would still be a primitive, underdeveloped country. But while we have modified our application of capitalistic principles, we still subscribe to capitalism.

The survey of business development shows how our history has shaped our present business structure and our attitudes. Business is not static—it is dynamic, ever striving for improvement.

Economics is the necessary theoretical base on which to build an understanding of business. The millions of business transactions occurring daily are given coherent meaning through understanding economic principles.

CHAPTER

1

THE CHARACTER OF ENTERPRISE IN THE UNITED STATES

Generally the first chapter of a book is introductory. This chapter acquaints you in a broad way with business activity. Notice the distinction between business and economics, two studies that are closely associated. Note that the study of business emphasizes the more practical aspects of business activity. In contrast economics emphasizes theory. This distinction should be kept in mind when reading this chapter and succeeding chapters. It should also be kept in mind when taking courses in economics.

Chapter 1 contains a number of words that are probably unfamiliar, such as "entrepreneurship." Others, such as "land," "labor," and "capital," are familiar but are used in business and economics in a special sense. You should understand the meaning of each word you read and should use a dictionary to define those that are unfamiliar.

Although many economic systems have appeared in history, the ones that exist at present are variations of two major forms: capitalism and socialism. These are contrasted in this chapter. Be sure you are aware of the characteristics of each.

Man lives not just in the world but in society; not alone, but as a member of a group. His needs are more than emotional; they are material as well. Indeed, before man can do anything else, he must first survive. Survival in our complex society depends upon business providing man with those things that he wants or needs. Life as we experience it would be inconceivable without business.

Much of our brief existence on this earth is spent in making things, directly or indirectly, or in providing services such as entertainment, transportation, and education. We not only produce, we also consume; and we consume in larger quantities each decade. We are constantly striving for means of improving production, as our rising expenditures for research indicate. We are also striving constantly to stimulate increases in consumption, as our rising expenditures for advertising indicate. In both we have been eminently successful. If the function of business is to produce and stimulate consumption, we are better businessmen than our fathers were; and we would have to add that our children will be better than we.

What is business? It is the human activity concerned with material things—

manufacturing airplanes, erecting buildings, and producing paper boxes; lending money, trading stocks, and selling insurance policies; operating a railroad, managing a shoe store, and distributing goods. Business is essential to civilization. It is found in all societies except the most primitive. *Business*, then, is the activity of producing and distributing goods and services. *Economics* is the science that investigates production, distribution, and consumption of goods and services. It differs from business in its approach to the subject matter. Economics emphasizes theory. Business emphasizes practice. Each is useful—in fact, necessary—to the other.

In our study of business, as in the study of economics, it is necessary to understand the four basic factors of production: land, labor, capital, and entrepreneurship.

BASIC FACTORS IN BUSINESS

The production of things requires the use of land. *Land* is used here in its broadest sense to include the surface of the earth, everything beneath that surface, and everything above. All the raw materials of production come from the ground, the air, and the oceans. Economists worry increasingly about the growing scarcity of raw materials in general. Businessmen worry about scarcity of particular raw materials. World population is steadily increasing, and the earth is not getting bigger. The demand for raw materials of all kinds is increasing even more rapidly than the population.

LAND

Can we continue to find the materials we need? Probably we can, but we will have to search in places as yet unexplored. Business is presently devoting much effort to the search for new sources of materials. Oil wells have been drilled more than 30,000 feet below the earth's surface, as well as through the ocean floor under coastal waters. The frozen areas of Canada and the steaming jungles of Brazil are being explored for ores of all kinds. Magnesium is being extracted from the waters of the Gulf of Mexico, and salts are being recovered from ocean water. Machines are now being designed to explore and mine the ocean floor. Men have walked on the moon and research craft have landed on Venus and Mars. A hundred years from now will we bring back scarce raw materials from the planets and dispose of dangerous wastes in interplanetary space?

Labor is the use of brain or muscles in the production of things. Most labor converts raw materials into finished goods and distributes the products to consumers. The trend in the United States and in other industrial countries is to use more mental and less physical effort. Machines are taking over more and more of the backbreaking work formerly done by unskilled workers, and are doing many of the routine activities formerly done by skilled workers as well. This trend undoubtedly

LABOR

will continue, but labor will always be needed. Human intelligence created these machines, and human intelligence will guide them, no matter how complex they become. Machines have no imagination—as yet—and the source of inspiration, essential to progress, is still the human mind.

CAPITAL   Capital has a variety of meanings in everyday language. As one of the basic factors of production, however, *capital* is all of the things that workers use in production and distribution: tools, machinery, warehouses, factories, trucks, and anything else made by man to aid production and distribution. In the United States each passing decade witnesses more capital than before, as can be seen from Figure 1-1. The result is constantly increasing production. In some industries the investment per worker is very high, as shown in Figure 1-2.

ENTREPRENEURSHIP   The first three factors, land, labor, and capital, must be combined in such a way as to produce something of value. The activity of controlling and directing the other three factors is *entrepreneurship.* One way to show the relationship is illustrated in Figure 1-3. The entrepreneur does not produce things with his own hands, unless he is also a laborer. His role may be compared to that of the conductor of an orchestra. The conductor, who does not make a sound, is the most important person in the orchestra. The musicians play at the tempo he directs, play loudly or softly as he indicates, and play together by following his beat. Without the conductor, a hundred musicians playing at once would produce noise, not music. In a business, the workers take their cue from the entrepreneur. They follow his directions, and they work together as a team under his leadership.

However, the entrepreneur is more than a director of activities. His functions comprise the following:

1 *Initiation* He initiates business activity by bringing together the other three factors so that business activity can take place.
2 *Management policy* He determines the broad policies under which the business will operate.
3 *Innovation* He seeks new products, new production methods, new channels of distribution, and new services to render. This is not merely a process of discovering new products and services. Skill is involved in recognizing new ideas that have value in business and in rejecting those that do not. The entrepreneur must be able to judge the worth of what others invent, whether it be a new toy, a new filing system, or a new approach to advertising.
4 *Risk bearing* Business risks are shared by everyone connected with the business. When a company becomes bankrupt, the employees suffer, customers lose a source of supply, and creditors usually recover less than the amount lent. But the major risk falls on the entrepreneur. He purchases the raw materials, buys or leases the factory and machinery, and hires the workers. To put it another way, he pays those who furnish the other

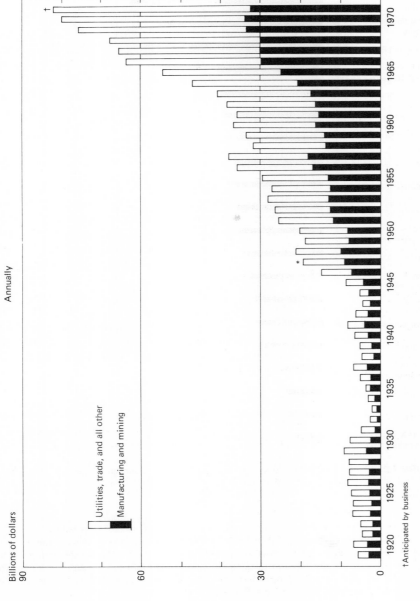

Annually

Billions of dollars

Utilities, trade, and all other

Manufacturing and mining

1920 1925 1930 1935 1940 1945 1950 1955 1960 1965 1970

†Anticipated by business

FIGURE 1-1   Business expenditures on new plant and equipment. *Source: Historical Chart Book,* Board of Governors of the Federal Reserve System, 1971.

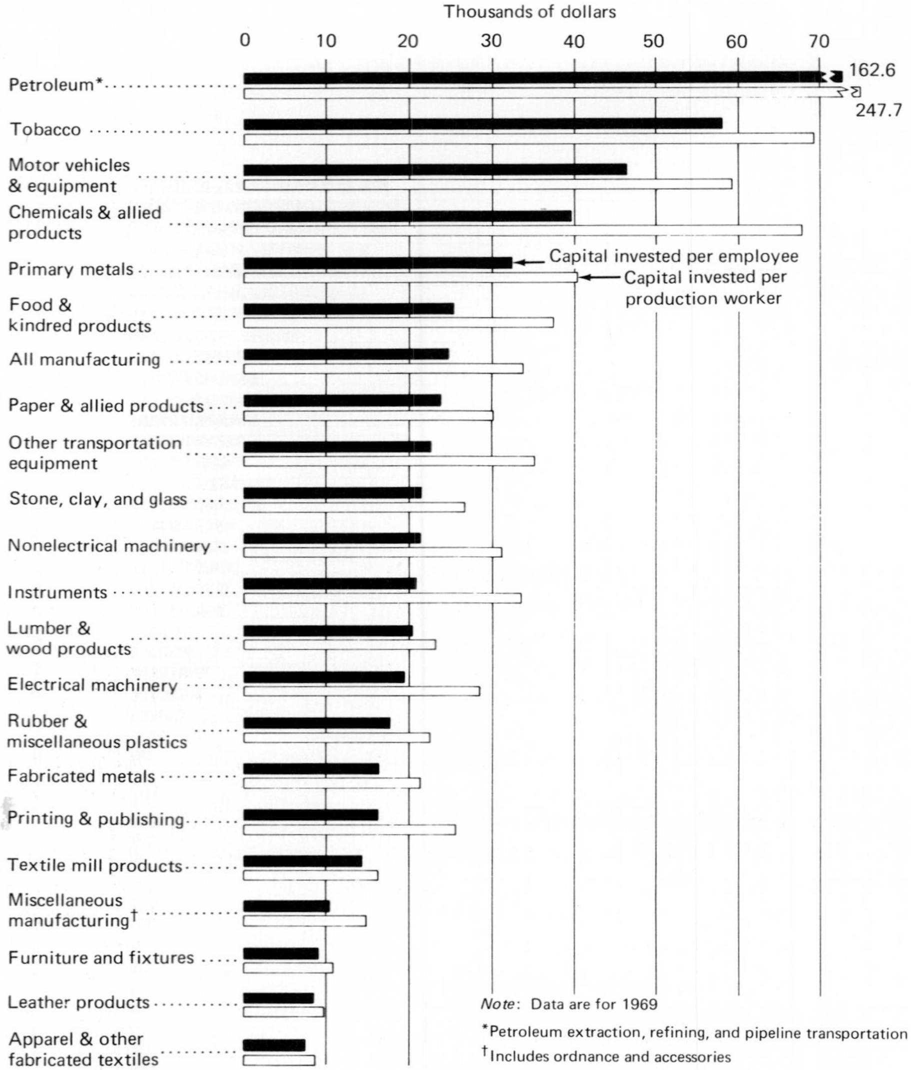

Thousands of dollars

FIGURE 1-2 Capital invested per employee in manufacturing. *Sources:* Bureau of Labor Statistics; Department of Commerce; Internal Revenue Service; The Conference Board.

three factors of production, whether the venture is a success or a failure, up to the limit of his ability to pay. If he is skillful—and lucky—the income of the business venture will pay for the land, labor, and capital used and still leave something for the entrepreneur. The amount remaining is *profit*. If the money brought in is not enough to pay all of the costs, the difference is *loss*. Naturally, the entrepreneur endeavors to make as large a profit and to suffer as little loss as he can.

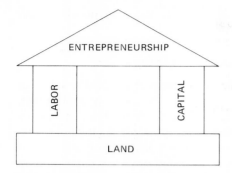

FIGURE 1-3 The Economic System. Land is the foundation, labor and capital are the pillars, and entrepreneurship holds everything together.

Who is the entrepreneur? In a small grocery store, employing four clerks, two delivery boys, a bookkeeper, a butcher, and a general utility man, it is usually easy to recognize the entrepreneur. He is the owner-manager. He started the store, decides operating policies, seeks improvements in operation, enjoys the profits, and suffers the losses. He orders the groceries that stock the shelves, hires the employees, and pays the rent. If the business succeeds, he lives well. If it fails, his losses may bankrupt him.

Generally, in a large corporation no one person can be identified as the entrepreneur. The function of entrepreneurship is divided. The stockholders, who own the corporation, bear the risks of failure, and to them belong any profits. But most stockholders do not participate in the organization or management of the business. These actions are the responsibility of the board of directors and the officers of the corporation. In small corporations those who own (stockholders) and those who manage (directors and officers) are often the same persons. But in large corporations 50,000 stockholders may own the company and 9 directors operate it. One of the unsettled problems of modern business is the result of the separation of ownership from control in corporations with many stockholders. How can 50,000 scattered stockholders exercise control? Even if such a large number could exercise control, how much authority over management policy *should* be exercised by 50,000 owners ranging from persons who know a lot about management to those who know nothing? We do not now have the answer.

The economic system of the United States is founded on *capitalism*, a system that has the following characteristics: private ownership of property, freedom of enter-

THE AMERICAN BUSINESS SYSTEM

prise, production for profit, free markets, competition, extensive use of capital, and limited government.

PRIVATE PROPERTY   In the United States, people and corporations may own property, either a little or a lot. Not all property, however, is private. There are public schools, public roads, and public parks. Furthermore, even privately owned property is not completely free from restrictions on its use. An owner of a piece of land in a residential community may not build a gasoline station on it, dig a deep hole in it and leave it uncovered, or use it as a garbage dump. A mining company is not free to bore tunnels that endanger miners' lives, even though the company owns the mine. An airline may not overload its airplanes. The use of property affects others besides the owners. We have considerable freedom to use our property as we see fit, but experience has shown that absolute freedom is unwise.

FREEDOM OF   Freedom of enterprise includes the following:
ENTERPRISE

> Free choice of a profession.
> Freedom to start any business anywhere.
> Freedom to produce any amount.
> Freedom to sell anywhere, any time, to anyone, and in any manner.
> Freedom to set price.
> Freedom of operation.

We have a larger measure of freedom of enterprise in the United States than is found in most other countries. However, we have never had complete freedom of enterprise. We have strict licensing laws governing the practice of medicine, pharmacy, and the law. Patents and copyrights restrict freedom of production. Import duties restrict the freedom to buy and sell. "Blue" laws restrict the times sales may be made to the public.

PRODUCTION   The driving force of capitalism is the struggle for personal gain. The successful
FOR PROFIT   operation of a capitalistic economy depends on everyone, in his striving for personal gain, guiding his actions toward the best interests of society. It assumes that the way to accumulation of wealth is through producing better quality, selling at lower prices, whenever conditions permit, and giving more service than competitors. It assumes that competition is primarily in the form of price, quality, and service. It assumes that competition is strong and is not diluted by collusion among competitors. Finally, it assumes that consumers have enough information and training to judge the differences in quality and service of competing businesses.

Markets bring buyers and sellers together. It is the instinct of buyers to pay as low a price as possible and for sellers to try to get as high a price as possible. In pure capitalism the market is free: there are no restraints by government. Neither do buyers conspire to force prices down nor sellers conspire to force prices up.

FREE MARKETS

If there are many sellers of each product or service and they do not act in concert, there will be competition. Similarly, if there are many buyers acting independently, there will be competition. In capitalism, competition is the force people depend on to prevent sellers from taking undue advantage of buyers and to prevent buyers from taking undue advantage of sellers. Capitalism assumes that competition exists at all levels—among producers, wholesalers, retailers, physicians, barbers, farmers, carpenters, and others; and it assumes that competition is in the form of price, quality, and service. In capitalism, competition is an essential ingredient of production for profit and free markets.

COMPETITION

A capitalistic society is one in which production and distribution are accomplished by extensive use of machinery, as illustrated in Figure 1-4. Although tailor-made clothing and other handmade goods are produced in a capitalistic society, their production is limited to a small proportion of total production. As we saw in Figure 1-1, the amount of capital (machinery, buildings, trucks, tools, and those goods that are used to produce other goods) added to our nation's supply has increased rapidly in recent years.

EXTENSIVE USE OF CAPITAL

In a capitalistic society, government activity in business affairs is limited. Consumers depend on competition as the chief protection safeguarding their interests. Capitalism also assumes that government does not support business through price supports, subsidies, and tariffs.

LIMITED GOVERNMENT

In discussing capitalism, one feature is uniformly present. It is business freedom. The ultimate of business freedom is known as *laissez faire capitalism*, which is the complete absence of government regulation and support of business. The United States is closer to laissez faire capitalism than are most other industrial nations. But neither the United States nor any other industrial nation has known complete business freedom. Nevertheless, there is now more government regulation and support of business than our great-grandfathers knew. This is largely the result of the increasing complexity of business operations and of the increase in population with each passing decade.

Some of the restrictions are the result of demand from certain industries—

This farmer raised only enough food for his own use.

This farmer raised enough food for three families.

This farmer raises enough food for about ten families.

FIGURE 1-4   The use of capital in production.

for example, subsidies, price-fixing laws, and tariffs; some are the result of demands from organized workers—for example, minimum wage laws; and some result from demand by consumers—for example, pure food and drug laws, anti-monopoly laws, regulation of electricity and gas rates, and laws against false advertising.

Some restrictions are obviously necessary. Others are just as obviously unnecessary. Some are harmful both to business and to consumers. Which are the necessary ones and which are the unnecessary ones? Put such a question to a mixed group of individuals, and a discussion will ensue that will probably become very heated. We all agree that some restriction on business freedom is necessary. But we disagree as to the amount and types of restrictions needed. Since the vast majority of Americans subscribe to the philosophy of capitalism, we should strive to maintain as wide an area of individual freedom as possible. We should accept each restriction only after we are reasonably certain it is necessary.

In the United States, capitalism has been molded to meet our needs as we see them. As the years pass, as our experience grows, and as our environment changes, we modify our business system, always striving to make it satisfy our needs better. Probably the most noteworthy features of our capitalism are specialization, mass production, and mass distribution. These are not unique to the United States, but their development has been greater here than elsewhere.

THE CHARACTERISTICS OF BUSINESS IN THE UNITED STATES

Our business system carries specialization to a very high degree. Our workers in factories, offices, and stores are specialized. The tools and equipment they use are also specialized. This specialization permits each worker to concentrate his energy in a narrow field, where his ability and training enable him to become expert. Specialization permits equipment to be designed for a specific job for maximum efficiency for that job. Geographical specialization permits North Carolina to concentrate on tobacco products, Akron on rubber goods, New York on finance, and Idaho on potatoes. Specialization enables us to put our labor, equipment, and geography to their most productive use.

SPECIALIZATION

Specialization allows us to produce in large volume. Producing in large volume allows us to use assembly lines and other mass-production techniques, which are aspects of specialization. Mass production of standardized goods is a characteristic of production in the United States, enabling us to produce more per worker than any other nation produces.

MASS PRODUCTION

MASS DISTRIBUTION   Mass distribution is essential to mass production. Our transportation system has developed to permit rapid transport of goods in large volume by rail, highway, pipeline, airplane, and water transport. Warehouses, wholesale distribution centers, and retail outlets are designed to move the large volume of goods from producer to consumer. Our superb distribution system complements our mass production and gives the average American far more material benefits than his parents had.

ALTERNATIVE
ECONOMIC SYSTEMS   We stated earlier that the economic system of the United States is based upon capitalism. Are there other systems? As a matter of fact there are several, some differing slightly, some sharply, from capitalism. Some systems, such as mercantilism, occupy an important place in history but have disappeared. Others, such as fascism and communism, are more political in their emphasis than economic. We shall confine our discussion of alternative systems to the major alternative to capitalism, developed largely during the present century. This system is socialism. It is the economic system on which the political system of communism is based, a system practiced in the Soviet Union, China, and several other countries.

Socialism is an economic system based on government ownership of the means of production and distribution, government control of prices, and government planning rather than competition determining what shall be produced, where it shall be produced, and how much shall be produced. The contrasts between the two systems of capitalism and socialism are summarized below:

Capitalism	Socialism
Private ownership of property	Government ownership of property
Production for profit	Profit motive eliminated
Prices set by demand and supply forces in free markets (see Chapter 3)	Prices set by government authorities
Competition determining which producers survive and which fail	Periodic government review of performance of various productive facilities
Extensive use of capital	Extensive use of capital (often more of a goal than a reality)
Strict limitations of government intervention in business decisions	Almost total government control of business decisions

The terms *capitalism* and *socialism* have become involved in the post–World War II struggle for political influence between Russia and the United States. "Socialism" is a pejorative term in the United States; "capitalism" is the pejorative in Russia. The economic system in the United States is not pure capitalism, although it comes closer than other industrial nations. There are elements of capitalism in Russia, although mostly in the agriculture and service industries and only on a small scale. In Great Britain, Sweden, and other Western European nations, railroads and other major industries are nationalized (government-owned and -operated). Thus the nations of the world occupy various positions on the spectrum between pure capitalism and pure socialism.

Change is a most important characteristic of business in the United States, and an essential ingredient of continued progress. The goods we produce, the way we make, store, and transport them, the conditions under which we work, the way we finance business, and other aspects of our economic life have changed considerably during our history. Progress requires change. Part of the explanation for the high level of economic activity in the United States is that the business system is dynamic. With some individual exceptions, it is receptive to change. This does not mean, however, that all change is progress. More people are killed each year on the highways than were killed 50 years ago. A dollar will buy less than half what it did for our grandparents. Of course we hope that the types of change that are injurious will be reversed and those that are beneficial will not be delayed by vested interests.

THE ATMOSPHERE OF CHANGE

Change can be painful, however. A valuable skill may become obsolete, as when glass blowing is supplanted by machine-made bottles. The sales of an industry may be reduced almost to the vanishing point, as in the case of harness and carriage making after the production of the automobile. We should not be surprised that people resist change that affects them painfully. Labor unions may respond to change by demanding that particular skilled workers be retained by employers even when the skills are no longer needed. Businessmen may respond to change by demanding subsidies, price supports, and restrictive laws. Resistance to change is found in all countries, but in this country it is less intense in industry than it is in other countries. Mostly because of this, business progress has been rapid in the United States.

Business is the activity of producing and distributing goods and providing services for material welfare. The study of business emphasizes practice while that of economics emphasizes theory.

SUMMARY

The four basic factors of production are land, labor, capital, and entrepreneurship. Entrepreneurship is necessary to coordinate the other three factors.

The business system of the United States is founded on capitalism, which has the following characteristics: private property, freedom of enterprise, production for profit, free markets, competition, extensive use of capital, and limited government. In addition, the American business system has developed a high degree of specialization, mass production, and mass distribution. Furthermore, with some exceptions, businessmen in the United States are more receptive to change than are businessmen in most other countries. While not all change is progress, all progress does require change.

Socialism is the major alternative economic system contrasting with capitalism. Socialism is based on government ownership and control of the means of production and distribution.

QUESTIONS FOR REVIEW

1 Define business. What is the difference between business and economics?
2 All raw materials are derived from land, water, and the air. What foods and raw materials do we get from the sea? From the atmosphere?
3 In the United States and other industrial nations, the trend is to use more mental labor and less physical labor. Do you see any problems this might create?
4 Can a cabinet shop or a small factory, with 10 or 12 workers, operate successfully if all are equal and no one is the "boss"? Explain your answer.
5 What are the functions of the entrepreneur?
6 Describe the differences between socialism and capitalism.
7 If a person owns a piece of land in a residential area, he is not free to use it in any way he wants. Should he be allowed to? Discuss.
8 "Striving for personal gain results in the public good." What assumptions underlie such a statement?
9 How do we benefit from specialization in production? What types of specialization do we find in industry?
10 "Change is necessary to progress, but not all change is progress." Explain this statement.

SELECTED READINGS

Chapman, Elwood N.: *Big Business: A Positive View*, Prentice-Hall, Inc., Englewood Cliffs, N.J., 1971.

Du Pont, The Autobiography of an American Enterprise, Charles Scribner's Sons, New York, 1952.

Ford at Fifty, Simon and Schuster, Inc., New York, 1953.

Galbraith, John K.: *The Affluent Society*, Houghton Mifflin Company, Boston, 1958.

James, Marquis, and Bessie R. James: *Biography of a Bank*, Harper & Row, Publishers, Incorporated, New York, 1954.

May, Earl C., and Will Oursler: *The Prudential*, Doubleday and Company, Inc., Garden City, N.Y., 1950.

U.S.A., The Permanent Revolution, by the editors of *Fortune*, reprinted by Prentice-Hall, Inc., Englewood Cliffs, N.J., 1951.

Walton, Clarence C.: *Business and Social Progress: Views of Two Generations of Executives*, Fredrick A. Praeger, Inc., 1970.

Name	Section	Date
C. Patte	*1*	*6 Apr 70*

COMPLETION SENTENCES

1 In our business activities we constantly strive to _*improve*_

production and to _*increase*_ consumption.

2 Business may be defined as the activity of _*producing*_ and

*Distributing* goods and services.

3 _*World Pop.*_ is steadily increasing.

4 Magnesium is extracted from _*the waters of G. of mex.*_

5 Profits are the reward of risk. In a corporation profits belong to

*Stockholders.*

6 Business expenditure on plant and equipment from 1961 to 1971 has more

than _*doubled*_ .

7 In an economic system _*Enterprise*_ holds everything together.

8 One characteristic of capitalism is _____*Private*_____ ownership of property.

9 Capitalism assumes that business competition is primarily in the form of *Price, Quality & Service*

10 The ultimate in business freedom is known as *Laissez faire* capitalism, in which there is absence of *Gov't* interference in business.

11 Specialization permits us to put our labor, equipment, and geography to *their most productive* use.

12 Some restrictions on business freedom are the result of demands from certain industries. Examples are *Subsidies*, *Price Fixing Laws*, and *Tariffs*.

13 Mass *Dist.* is essential to mass production.

14 Not all *Change* is progress, but all progress requires *Change*.

15 Markets bring *Buyers* and *Sellers* together.

TRUE OR FALSE STATEMENTS

/ **1** Man's needs are both emotional and material.

F. **2** Businessmen are constantly striving to stimulate increases in production, but they are more apathetic about stimulating increases in consumption.

Name   Section   Date

T 3 Economics emphasizes theory. Business emphasizes practice.

F 4 The demand for raw materials increases as rapidly as the increase in population.

F 5 Labor is the use of muscles rather than brains to produce things.

T 6 Capital is all the things that workers use in production and distribution.

F 7 The function of the entrepreneur is confined to the directing of business activities.

T 8 It is easier to identify the entrepreneur in a small business than in a large corporation.

F 9 Corporations may use property, but they do not own it.

F 10 Privately owned property is completely free from restrictions on its use.

T 11 The system of capitalism assumes that consumers are well informed on what they buy.

T 12 The driving force of capitalism is the struggle for personal gain.

T 13 Extensive use of machinery is a characteristic of a capitalistic society.

F 14 The form of capitalism in the United States is laissez faire capitalism.

F 15 Progress does not require change.

1 The business system in the United States carries specialization to a very high degree. List activities around the home that are specialized for father, mother, and children.   **EXERCISES**

Father   Mother   Children

2 We do not have complete freedom to use our property in any way we see fit. Write a brief report giving arguments in favor of permitting either (*a*) every farmer complete and unrestricted use of his farmland or (*b*) the owner of a house and lot complete and unrestricted use of his property. Then give arguments in favor of restricting the use of property, indicating the types of restrictions you think necessary.

    a   In favor of restricted use.

    b   Against restricted use.

    c   Types of restrictions necessary.

Although you have studied history in grade school and high school and possibly in college, much of what you retain probably consists of battles and political intrigues. This is partly because wars and changes in government have always been more extensively reported through the centuries than have other changes in human life, and partly because wars and political upheavals create more excitement and are more easily remembered by both those going through the experience and those reading about it afterward. But the aspect of history considered in Chapter 2 is the development of business.

Although this may not be as exciting as the study of military campaigns, it is probably more important to the development of our present standard of living. In reading this chapter, you should be impressed with the common characteristics of early and modern business, but you should recognize the differences. It would be easy for a historian to emphasize the common characteristics of old and modern cultures and thus create the impression that very little change has occurred over the years. Another historian could emphasize the differences and thus show that change through the centuries has been radical. You should recognize that very important changes have taken place but also that there are many elements of similarity between present business activities and older business activities.

Historical developments rarely occur suddenly, particularly in the area of social developments. When changes take place, they generally have roots in the past. Appreciation of this fact should make it easier for you to understand the reason for many of the historical developments that have taken place, and to understand why they have taken place. You should also understand that you are not living "in the last chapter of the world's history." The world has existed for a long time and changes in the future will very likely be as great as they have been in the past.

The reason we study history as a separate subject and include history in the study of business is to appreciate the fact that we are living in a changing world. The future will be different from the present, but the seeds of future change are planted in the here and now. This does not mean that what you study in your business courses will become obsolete by the time you have to earn a living, but it does mean that the process of learning is a continuous one—it does not end with your receiving your college diploma. What you learn in this course in general and in Chapter 2 in particular will serve as a basis for a better understanding of the development of business institutions during your later years.

This chapter deals with the nature of constant change characteristic of an economy in a process of rapid development. The United States was and still is a young nation, which has helped it accept new ideas and new techniques more readily than they are accepted in some other parts of the world. *The atmosphere of receptivity to change is the most important single point to be gained by reading this chapter.*

When we contemplate world history, we must admit that the United States is a young nation. During its brief existence, it has made some important contributions to mankind. Most of them, however, have not been entirely original: they have been built on the wealth of experience that centuries of human development in the Eastern Hemisphere have provided. Our money system has its roots in ancient Phoenicia. Our philosophy of government and our word *democracy* originated in Greece. Anyone who attempts to work simple arithmetic problems by using Roman numerals will be grateful for the Arabic numerals we use today. Our basic system of business, brought to a high degree of perfection by American genius, is built on European foundations. From the time that man first learned to use tools, each generation has passed on its contribution to the next. Each age has taken the ideas, institutions, and techniques of the past, modified them—sometimes for the worse but usually for the better—and given them to the future.

THE RISE OF CAPITALISM   At what point shall we begin our study of the development of American business? An appropriate point would be the beginnings of modern capitalism. The origins of American capitalism lie in European history, in the period of the Industrial Revolution and the expansion of commerce to worldwide scope. One of the important changes making possible modern capitalism was the gradual social and moral acceptance of interest on money. Dante in the *Divine Comedy* assigned moneylenders a special place in hell. The changed social attitude of the Industrial Revolution is shown in the following observation on Dante's attitude toward interest: "He who takes it goes to Hell; he who does not goes to the poorhouse." Another change in social attitude fostering the development of capitalism was the shift from considering merchants socially inferior to landowners to accepting them as influential members of society.

Both the development of capitalism and the Industrial Revolution were well under way when the United States emerged as a nation. The most celebrated book on *laissez faire* capitalism, Adam Smith's *Wealth of Nations*, a landmark in economic history, was first published in 1776, the year of our Declaration of Independence. The new nation began its existence without having to combat prejudices against commerce that were still strong in the older countries of Europe. The United States began its history with the following advantages:

A wealth of natural resources of all kinds
A philosophy of individual freedom
A willingness to accept new ideas
A belief in the dignity of work

FOUNDATIONS OF BUSINESS IN THE NEW NATION

FINANCE

The first sessions of the Congress of the United States saw the passage of several laws to foster the growth of business. The American dollar, divided into 100 cents, was created to replace the variety of currencies then in use. The Bank of the United States was chartered to provide loans to government and business, with one-fifth of the capital subscribed by the federal government. To encourage new manufacturing enterprise in this country, Congress placed a tariff on importers bringing foreign wares into the United States.

The stocks of the Bank of the United States, of insurance companies, and of other institutions were bought and sold by investors in the larger cities on the Atlantic. Commerce in these certificates was carried on in coffeehouses, in auction rooms, in stores, and on street corners. When the United States government issued debt certificates in 1790 in the amount of $80 million, the market for securities expanded greatly and trading became more active. It was natural that this activity should be centered in New York City, the first capital of the United States. In 1792, two dozen businessmen decided to meet regularly under a tree in lower Manhattan Island to buy and sell securities for themselves and their clients. This was the origin of the New York Stock Exchange. Trading continued outdoors regardless of the weather at first. Soon the group moved their activities to a nearby coffeehouse. This was the first of many buildings housing the Exchange, each one being larger than the last to accommodate an increase in activity. The growth of the New York Stock Exchange has reflected to a remarkable degree the expansion in the size and diversity of businesses in the United States.

INDUSTRY

Until the Civil War, the United States was largely an agricultural country, a source of food and raw materials from farm, forest, and ocean. A few manufacturing and other industries developed early, however. Iron smelting, shipbuilding, and lumbering were active industries during the colonial period. After tariff obstacles were placed in the path of imported European manufactures, cotton and woolen mills were erected, gunpowder production expanded, and other wares in great variety were made. Production was mostly in small factories and shops. It was not until the end of the century that mass-production techniques made the United States one of the foremost manufacturing nations.

TRANSPORTATION

From the time that the first colonists landed in Virginia and Massachusetts until the American Revolution, travel between settlements had been largely along the Atlantic coast and up the navigable rivers as far as boats could go. The many rivers served as convenient avenues of commerce between inland cities and the coastal ports. Unfortunately, the rivers mostly flowed east from the Appalachian Mountains to the Atlantic. Direct north-and-south commerce was slow in developing because of the lack of natural waterways. Some canals were built, but they were costly and limited in capacity compared to the rivers.

Land transportation was slower in developing. There were trails through the forests from the time the first settlers landed, and packhorses could move goods over these trails. But the cost was high and restricted severely the variety of merchandise that could be transported. The need for roads was serious. State and local governments built a few roads, and the federal government built one highway, the Cumberland Road, across the mountains and as far west as Illinois. Most of the roads built before 1820, however, were built by private companies for profit: tolls were charged for their use. Because bars were set up at toll stations, they were called "turnpikes."

Commercial railroads were first developed in England but were quickly introduced into the United States. The first American railroad was the Baltimore and Ohio line, which began service in 1830. From then until the end of the century, railroad building expanded rapidly, while canals and highways declined in relative importance. Railroads were constructed and operated as private companies. They were financed by individual investors, by state and local governments, and by extensive grants of land from the federal government to railroad corporations.

As the scattered cities were being connected by rail, Samuel F. B. Morse, a portrait painter whose hobby was electricity, was experimenting with devices to transmit messages by wire. He secured a patent on a successful device in 1837, but was unable to get private investors to risk money in its development. After years of unsuccessful efforts to secure private backing, Congress gave him $30,000 to construct a test line from Washington to Baltimore. In 1844, Morse demonstrated the capability of the telegraph by tapping out the message "What hath God wrought" from Washington to an associate at the other end of the line in Baltimore. This demonstration proved the commercial profitability of the invention, which Congress then permitted private companies to exploit.

With the development of better transportation and communication, industry expanded in size and variety. Communities, no longer isolated, specialized in the production of items that, for one reason or another, they could produce at an advantage over other communities. With this growth of specialization, a shift of population from the country to towns and cities began which has continued to the present day and is still continuing. This shifting pattern of production permitted fuller utilization of natural and human resources. It also resulted in an ever increasing volume of production per person, permitting a rising standard of living.

THE EMERGENCE OF THE UNITED STATES AS A WORLD POWER

THE CIVIL WAR

The decision of the Southern states to form a new nation precipitated a war that split the industrial North from the agricultural South. The conflict began in 1861 and continued for 4 years. When the shooting stopped in 1865, 620,000 of the 3 million men in uniform lay dead. It was the bloodiest war in our history, and rare was the family not touched by personal tragedy.

This war marked the emergence of the United States as a world power. The unity of the nation was preserved, although at a frightful price in human suffering. The tradition of strong central government able to attack national problems was established. The speed of industrialization was accelerated. The scars of war were quickly obliterated, although bitterness between the peoples remained for many years. In short, the nation recovered rapidly from the struggle and was economically stronger after the war than before.

TRANSPORT

The movement of men and materials in fighting the Civil War considerably increased the traffic on the railroads. After the end of hostilities, many veterans moved to the Western territories to start a new life. The demand for transportation, rather than declining, continued to expand. In 1860, there were 30,000 miles of railroad; in 1900, there were more than 200,000. Railroad construction in the sparsely settled plains of the Midwest and the mountains of the West was aided by grants of federal land more generous than had been given before the war. The lines crept further west each year until, in 1869, they stretched from the Atlantic to the Pacific.

Of equal importance to the expansion in total mileage was the consolidation of small railroad companies into large units. This expansion permitted more efficient use of equipment and better scheduling of trains. A standard gauge for rails was adopted, so that fewer changes were required in travel. Trains went faster, and passenger accommodations became more luxurious. Finally, the air brake, block signals, and other safety devices took the adventure out of train travel and made it a matter of routine.

STEELMAKING

Prior to the Civil War, steel was expensive and the quantities produced were small. Its use was confined mainly to knives, tools, weapons, and similar articles. During the war, steelmaking processes were developed that soon brought the price of steel down sharply and enabled large quantities to be produced.

In the growth of the steel industry, one name stands out sharply: Andrew Carnegie. There were, of course, many powerful figures that shaped the direction of industrial development in our country. We cannot study them all in this brief survey, and it is hard to pick one name as representative of the whole group. The characteristics common to this group—ambition, willingness to accept risks, adaptability to change, personal drive, keen judgment of human character, and ruthlessness in business transactions—are found in the personality of Andrew Carnegie. It is perhaps too easy to forget that industries are molded by individuals. To emphasize this point, a look at the life of Carnegie is useful.

As techniques for making steel cheaply were being developed, entrepreneurs sought to take advantage of the profit possibilities found in these processes. Andrew Carnegie was one of these men, a Scot who had immigrated to America and found a job as messenger on the Pennsylvania Railroad. He rose rapidly in the company and became chief of the Western Division. Experiments with iron bridges to replace wooden ones on the Pennsylvania Railroad convinced him that ironmaking would be a rapidly growing industry and that the quickest path to fortune in iron was in bridge building. He organized a bridge company, then a company to furnish iron for his bridge company. The rest of his business life was one of organizing companies, expanding their capacity, getting control of competitors, and adopting improved methods for making iron and steel. In 30 years, he dominated the industry. His success lay in his skill as an organizer, his perception of the probable future course of business, and his willingness to act decisively and without hesitation. Having become one of the greatest industrial giants of all time, he renounced the life of business by transferring his properties (valued at around $500 million) to the newly organized United States Steel Company in 1901. The remaining years of his life were spent giving away his fortune by setting up educational and charitable foundations.

EVOLUTION OF THE
MODERN
CORPORATION

The increase in population and the expansion of the railroad network permitted businesses to expand their markets extensively. In most industries, companies became large units with operations ranging over many states. The process of creating large concerns was made difficult before the Civil War (partnerships are unwieldy for large organizations and the granting of corporations charters was a privilege given infrequently by state governments). The Civil War brought the industrialist into a position of power in political and community life, however, and gradually the laws of the states and the nation reflected this power.

After the Civil War, states competed to attract business concerns: taxes might be forgiven for the first 10 years, land and buildings might be offered free or at low rental, and direct financial aid might be given. A more important form of competition was the changing of corporation laws to make them more attractive than those of neighboring states. Each state treated corporations with out-of-state charters on approximate parity with those having domestic charters. Companies doing a nationwide business could be chartered in whichever state offered charters most favorable. This increased the possibilities of abuse of the privilege of incorporation, and business regulation was made more difficult. The requirement of federal incorporation of corporate enterprises in interstate trade might have helped, but movements in this direction were stifled. New Jersey was foremost during most of the years of the post-Civil War period in changing its laws to conform to the desires of corporation promoters, but in the present century, Delaware—the second-smallest state and largely agricultural—has managed to attract a third of all industrial corporations listed on the New York Stock Exchange.

THE UNITED STATES AND TWO WORLD WARS

War is destruction. It is the scattering of steel and lead, the sinking of ships, the mutilation of fields and forests, the demolition of buildings, bridges, and highways. And it is the killing of men, women, and children. The cost of war is incalculable. Although billions of dollars in property and thousands of lives were lost to the United States in the First World War, the losses were confined to material and men sent abroad.

WORLD WAR I

During World War I, to furnish the materials needed to fight, production plants of the United States were expanded. The variety of goods produced was increased also, as optical goods, dyes, and other items replaced those that had been imported from Germany. The United States became the "arsenal of democracy" during the war, and emerged from it the foremost industrial nation of the world.

A DECADE OF RAPID GROWTH

The conversion from war production to peaceful production was accomplished fairly soon after the fighting stopped in November 1918. Several young industries grew into giants during the decade following the war. Automobiles were luxuries before the war. But Henry Ford's assembly-line techniques brought the price of cars down and the volume of production up, so that during the 1920s, cars became commonplace in the United States. Motion pictures (silent) brought drama to villages as easily as to cities. For those who stayed at home, the radio offered news, music, comedy, commercial messages, and, for the persistent listener, even a few educational features. In most other nations, radio was partly devoted to public enlightenment, but over most of the United States, the airwaves were used almost entirely for advertising.

Transportation had depended heavily on the railroads before the First World War. During the 1920s, the domination of railroads began to decline noticeably. The rapid increase of automobiles sparked a tremendous program of highway construction. The new highways permitted heavier loads and higher speeds. Buses, trucks, and automobiles cut deeper into the railroad's share of traffic each year. The airplane also emerged as a form of transportation. Subsidized heavily by the government, as the railroads had been decades earlier, airlines began to take passengers and even freight from the railroads. Thousands of miles of track were abandoned during the 1920s and 1930s.

A DECADE OF DEPRESSION

The front page of the *New York Times* for October 30, 1929, reporting the news of the previous day, contained the following headlines:

> STOCKS COLLAPSE IN 16,410,030 SHARE DAY
> 240 ISSUES LOSE $15,894,818,894
> SLUMP IN FULL EXCHANGE VASTLY LARGER

Stock prices had kept rising during the 1920s. At first this reflected the growth of business and the profits of this prosperous period. As the decade drew to a close, however, stock prices rose to fantastic heights, as measured by the values of the companies they represented. A drop was inevitable, but when the collapse came in 1929, it took most people by surprise. The nation began its slide into the worst depression in its history, with production, employment, and prices dropping continuously for 3 years. But this fact—that depression was setting in—was not realized for many months.

The extent of the Depression was measured in unemployment, rising to 14 million persons, and in the decline in national production, from $80 billion in 1929 to $36 billion in 1933.[1] But the pain and suffering imposed during those years cannot be appreciated by persons who have never experienced physical want. Tuberculosis increased its toll of lives as families doubled up to save rent and ate less nourishing food. In some localities, half the children ate their only solid meal in school. Apple vendors, shivering in the cold, appeared on the street corners of the larger cities. Oppressive fear of what the morrow might bring took the place of the buoyant optimism of the previous decade. In the 1920s, people had faith in the existence of permanent prosperity. In the 1930s, they began to wonder if the existence of idle factories and millions of idle workers might, after all, be normal.

Depression is a complex economic malady. Its causes are not completely known, and doctors of economics disagree about its cure. What is generally

---

[1] The latter figure represents production in terms of dollars with higher purchasing power than in 1929. The decline in real production was less than the dollar figures indicated, but was nevertheless very substantial.

accepted is that no simple cure exists, and that a successful treatment must contain a number of different ingredients. The situation was difficult for the government. Depressions had previously been allowed to run their course without political interference and, like fevers, had eventually subsided. The most recent one, however, was far more intense than any before, and many feared that the nation might be close to collapse.

People demanded action. But what kind of action? In the search for a means of effecting recovery, the basis of business operation was not changed. It remained a capitalistic, free enterprise system, which businessmen of today, as before, proudly compare with the economic systems of less productive parts of the world. But, although the basis was not changed, a number of important modifications were made, reflecting people's demand for governmental responsibility in maintaining prosperity. The administration in Washington, under Herbert Hoover until March 1933 and then under Franklin Roosevelt, responded with a variety of aid for all groups.

It would be beyond the scope of this book to discuss all of the agencies established during the Depression. Basically, the difference between Hoover and Roosevelt was that the former attempted to restore production and employment by giving financial aid to producers, hoping that they would thus be encouraged to produce more goods and employ more people. The Roosevelt administration continued financial aid to producers but added aid to the unemployed and low-income groups under the theory that an increase in consumer spending would stimulate orders for production of goods, which in turn would increase demand for workers and decrease unemployment. Roosevelt continued the program of loans to bankers, farmers, railroads, industrial corporations, and cities. In addition, his administration provided work for part of the unemployed millions, low-cost housing, gifts of food to schoolchildren, and aid in other forms.

Activities to develop the country were also initiated or expanded by the federal government. Flood control, irrigation, soil reclamation, electric power generation and distribution (particularly in rural areas of small farms and towns, which had been neglected during the expansion of private electric power), and research were among those emphasized. Government services to the people increased in both quantity and variety.

The spirit of reform was not confined to governmental activity. The philosophy of business was changing also. The intense and sometimes irresponsible individualism of the pre-Depression era slowly changed to an acceptance of responsibility to society. For example, the New York Stock Exchange, by voluntary action of its members, imposed restrictions on the conduct of members on and off the Exchange that were more severe in many respects than the restrictions imposed by Congress. Management came to be regarded by businessmen more as a profession, like the law and medicine, and the beginning of standards of ethical conduct gradually appeared. Corporation directors in the larger companies began to encourage the attendance of stockholders at the annual meetings of their corporations and to promote more active interest by stockholders in the affairs of the companies whose securities they owned.

THE SECOND
WORLD WAR

Barely 20 years after the end of the First World War, a second major conflict erupted in Europe and spread to include all the major powers of the world. The first war had been so frightful that many persons thought a second one would end European civilization. But another war was fought, and civilization, though changed, survived. The second war was worse than the first. Starting in 1939, it lasted 6 years, spread hostilities to all continents and oceans, and spread death and destruction on a scale beyond the worst nightmares of human imagination.

The demands of the Second World War on United States production were greater than before. Factories operated around the clock. Teenagers, housewives, and retired workers were added to the labor force. The challenge of the enemy called forth the supreme effort of the men in the front lines, to which they responded magnificently. But, to a considerable degree, the war was won in the factories and farms. The enemy was unable to match the tremendous production of the United States.

**BUSINESS
DEVELOPMENT
AFTER WORLD WAR II**

With the coming of peace in 1945, many businessmen expected a depression. Both the Civil War and the First World War had been followed by depressions. Some companies followed a policy of careful avoidance of debt wherever possible and were reluctant to expand. Others expanded their operations, going into debt if necessary, and made their plans on the belief that there would be no depression following this war.

RECOVERY FROM
THE WAR

Although there were slight dips in production during the 20 years after World War II, there was no depression. The continuance of large governmental expenditures for war goods to counter the menace of Russian and then Chinese military power cushioned occasional declines in private spending, as did unemployment insurance, social security, and other federal programs. Under both Democratic and Republican presidents, the stated policy of the federal administration was to use governmental power to combat any developing depression. The means of countering declines in business activity developed during the Roosevelt administration may have contributed to maintaining prosperity. Whether the experience of the Great Depression has provided the government with the powers necessary to make depressions a thing of the past cannot be determined yet. But a depressionless era for the future is at least a possibility.

And what of the future? Many problems exist for which the coming years will have to provide a solution. The world is smaller in terms of communications and transportation, and the people living on it are more dependent on each other. Life is more complex. The answers to economic problems are more difficult than they appeared to be in an earlier and simpler age. Some of the problems that the young people of today will have to face during the remaining years of the century are the following:

Can a high level of production and employment be maintained every year?

What dangers lie in the existence of a high government debt? And an even higher private debt?

How can inflation of prices be effectively controlled?

Should the role of the government in the economy be more or less than at present?

To what extent should international trade be encouraged?

What will be the effect on the economy of new industries, such as satellite communication, ocean-floor exploration, computer technology atomic energy, and space travel? To what extent should the government encourage, by subsidy or otherwise, the development of these industries?

Are we depleting our natural resources too rapidly for long, sustained industrial growth? Can business find substitutes for those resources becoming scarce?

Can the increasing pollution of the atmosphere, rivers, land, and oceans be reduced to a level that the earth's natural processes can absorb?

Can new sources of energy, such as hydrogen, be developed to provide the rapidly increasing power needs of people and industry?

The development of business in the postwar period has taken place in an atmosphere of international tension, rising population pressure on depleting natural resources, and growing concern for the quality of the human environment. How will this affect business, and how will business react to it? Nobody can be sure, for there is no precedent to guide us. Our knowledge of the past can help us create a better future, but such knowledge will not of itself provide us with the answers we seek. We must discover new solutions. Indeed, adaptability to new conditions and the ability to solve new problems are essential to survival. This is true of a family, of a business, and of a nation. Perhaps, for the first time, it is also true of the human race.

SUMMARY

The beginnings of capitalism and the development of the factory system were under way when the United States became a nation. The United States escaped the disruption of commerce and society experienced by the nations of Europe during the shift from feudalism to capitalism.

From 1790 until 1860, the United States was mainly an agricultural country. Industry was carried on in small firms; transportation was by water; and although commercial banking expanded rapidly, individual banks were mostly small. The participation of the federal government in economic life was limited to curtailing imports, minting coins, and giving away land.

After 1860, industry grew rapidly. Steel, oil, coal, railroads, the telegraph, natural gas, and electricity were examples of new or rapidly developing industries. Aiding the rapid expansion of companies was the increased ease with which promoters could get corporation charters from state governments and the competition among states in attracting business by granting charters.

After World War I, there was a decade of prosperity followed by a decade of depression, the worst in our history. In an effort to end this Great Depression, the federal government increased its activity in business life. Government regulation and government services increased in quantity and variety.

To meet the demand for war production during World War II, industrial capacity expanded considerably. After the end of the war in 1945, production declined briefly, and then there was a period of sustained increase in production. There have been minor dips in national production, but there has been no depression such as followed the previous major wars.

QUESTIONS FOR REVIEW

1 What changes in people's attitudes toward business occurred during the Industrial Revolution?
2 What advantages did industry in the United States have over European industry when the United States began its existence as an independent nation?
3 Describe the origin of the New York Stock Exchange.
4 Which manufacturing industries were found in the United States before the Civil War? Suggest reasons why these industries were developed rather than others.
5 Why was the development of overland transportation in the United States slower than that of water transportation before the Civil War?
6 How did the Civil War affect industry in the North? In the South?
7 What changes in railroading followed the Civil War?
8 What were the qualities that made Andrew Carnegie a wealthy industrialist?
9 By what means did states and cities compete with each other to attract business firms?
10 What is a business depression? Illustrate, by describing the Depression of the 1930s.

SELECTED READINGS

Allen, Frederick Lewis: *The Big Change, 1900–1950*, Harper & Row, Publishers, Incorporated, New York, 1952.

Degler, Carl N.: *Out of Our Past*, Harper & Row, Publishers, Incorporated, New York, 1959.

Galbraith, John Kenneth: *The Great Crash, 1929*, Houghton Mifflin Company, Boston, 1954.

Groner, Alex: *The History of American Business & Industry*, American Heritage Publishing Co., Inc., New York, 1972.

Landes, David S.: *The Unbound Prometheus*, Cambridge University Press, New York, 1969.

Rozwenc, Edwin (ed.): *The New Deal*, D. C. Heath and Company, Boston, 1949.

Smith, Adam: *The Wealth of Nations*. There are many editions of this classic work, first printed in 1776 in England. Although it is not necessary to read the whole of this work, every serious student of business or economics should become acquainted with it.

Snyder, Louis L., and Richard B. Morris (eds.): *They Saw It Happen, Eyewitness Reports of Great Events*, The Stackpole Company, Harrisburg, Pa., 1951.

Soule, George, and Vincent P. Carosso: *American Economic History*, Holt, Rinehart and Winston, Inc., New York, 1957.

Studenski, Paul, and Herman E. Krooss: *Financial History of the United States*, McGraw-Hill Book Company, New York, 1952.

Tawney, R. H.: *Religion and the Rise of Capitalism*, Harcourt, Brace & World, Inc., New York, 1926.

Name   Section   Date

COMPLETION SENTENCES

1 Our _Money Sys_ has its roots in ancient Phoenicia, and our

word "democracy" originated in _GREECE_ .

2 Adam Smith published a book called _Wealth of Nat_ in the year

_1776_ .

3 To encourage new manufacturing enterprise in the new nation, Congress erected

Tariffs .

4 Turnpikes were _Private_ roads built for

Profit .

5 Samuel F. B. Morse, a portrait painter, invented the

Telegraph with $30,000 given by

Congress

6 After the Civil War, small railroad companies were

Consolidated.

7 The principal individual in the growth of the steel industry was

Carnegie.

8 A third of the corporations listed on the New York Stock Exchange operate

under charters issued by the state of _Del_.

9 During the decade of the 1920s, several young industries grew into giants.

Two examples are _Autos_ and

Motion Pic.

10 During the 1920s stock prices rose, reflecting the growth of

Economy.

11 In the depression of the 1930s, Roosevelt's administration provided financial

aid to _the unemployed_.

12 In the search for a cure for the depression of the 1930s, the economic system

of the United States remained as a _Capitalistic free enl._

13 Both the Civil War and World War I had been followed by an economic

Depression.

14 Under both Republican and Democratic presidents following World War II,

government policy was to combat a developing depression through

Gov. Aid.

Name	Section	Date

15 The development of business in the post-World War II period has taken place in an atmosphere of _____ .

TRUE OR FALSE STATEMENTS

F **1** The economic system of capitalism is an American invention.

T **2** The Bank of the United States was chartered with capital provided partly by the federal government.

F **3** The first capital of the United States was Philadelphia.

T **4** The shipbuilding industry in America originated before the American Revolution.

T **5** Production prior to the Civil War was mostly in small factories and shops.

F **6** Commercial railroads were first developed in the United States.

F **7** The first railroads in the United States were government-owned.

T **8** Samuel F. B. Morse was a portrait painter.

T **9** One of the consequences of the Civil War was the tradition of a strong central government.

F **10** Although railroad construction proceeded rapidly after the Civil War, it was not until 1889 that rails spanned the continent.

F **11** The United States Steel Company was organized around the beginning of the twentieth century.

T **12** The Civil War brought the industrialist into a position of power in political and community life.

T **13** Corporations doing business in interstate trade must operate under federal charters.

T **14** During the 1920s the dominance of railroads in transportation began to decline noticeably.

T **15** In 1929 the stock market dropped sharply.

16 During the period of the Depression, in which unemployment increased sharply and production declined, prices actually rose.

17 The purchasing power of the dollar was higher in 1933 than it was in 1929.

18 Prior to 1930 there was little interference by government in combating depressions.

19 No aid was given by the Hoover administration to stimulate the economy in the depression.

20 Declines in economic activity in the United States have been less severe since World War II than they were before World War II.

EXERCISES

1 Most states have laws permitting the formation of corporations by a relatively simple process of applying for a corporation charter to the secretary of state of that state. What might have been the development of business in the United States if all corporations operating in interstate trade had been required to secure certificates of incorporation from the federal government? What are the advantages and disadvantages of such a requirement? After preparing this report, keep it until the end of the term. Then read your report again in the light of your study of the later chapters of the text. When rereading your report, you should be aware of any changes in your opinions. Have any occurred? Explain.

a List advantages of federal incorporation of interstate businesses.

b List disadvantages of federal incorporation of interstate businesses.

c End-of-course changes or modifications in a and b.

Name   Section   Date

2 Suggest what might have been the trend of business in the United States and in the confederate states if the South had succeeded in its rebellion.

3 Select one of the economic problems facing the United States during the last of this century (from the list toward the end of this chapter). From the library or some other source of information, find at least two different suggestions for solution to the problem. Identify your source of information. Summarize the suggestions. Add any ideas of your own.

3

THE ECONOMIC BASE FOR BUSINESS

There are two major divisions of economic study: *macroeconomics* and *micro-economics*. The former deals with national economic problems, such as taxation, inflation, combating depressions, the government debt, and others. Taxation and combating depressions, and their effect on business, are discussed in Chapter 29. Other national economic problems are touched upon in other chapters. The latter term refers to the study of the behavior of businessmen as individuals, and it is sometimes called *economics of the firm.* This chapter deals with microeconomics.

Review the definition of economics in Chapter 1. Keep in mind that material things are scarce and that economics is a study of economizing. We have to make choices, as businessmen and as consumers. Having more of one thing generally means having less of another.

There are questions interspersed in the text of this chapter. Consider these questions when you read the chapter. Think out answers in your mind—or write them down on paper. It will help you understand the economic concepts discussed.

Study the charts and the tables carefully. Each chart describes in a diagram one of the principles discussed in the text. Each table accomplishes the same. For some students an explanation by a diagram is easier to understand; for others the use of a table is clearer. If you can learn through both methods, it will help you to learn not only in this course but in others as well.

In Chapter 1 we defined economics as the study of the production, distribution, and consumption of goods and services. Every serious student of business finds it necessary to study economics as part of his business program. Although a prior knowledge of economics is not needed to understand an introduction to business, an explanation of some of the basic elements of economics will enhance your grasp of business principles. In this chapter we shall not take up the problems of society as a whole—inflation, unemployment, taxation, government debt, and the nation's supply of money. Rather we shall discuss the economic problems faced by the business firms—scarcity, demand for goods and services, prices, and competition.

Business firms form an essential link in the chain of production, as is shown in Figure 3-1.

SCARCITY   Suppose you are one of a small number of inhabitants living on an island in the Persian Gulf, an island that produces a fabulous amount of oil yearly. Assume that the revenues from the sale of oil are such that everybody lives like a millionaire. Food, clothing, shelter, luxuries—everything is available for the asking. There is no need to work; all labor services are provided by foreigners. In such a Garden of Eden the principal ingredient of economics is missing. There is no scarcity.

Unfortunately, we live in a society in which our wants exceed our resources. All of us cannot have everything we want. Therefore, we must *economize*. We must choose between our wants, deciding which ones to satisfy first. The need to economize, to recognize scarcity, is found in practically every decision a business-man makes, as well as in the decisions consumers make. This means more than economizing on the money we spend. It means economizing on everything of value. If we want more of one thing, we must accept less of another. Three examples of choice involving scarce resources are shown in Figure 3-2.

Another example of choice forced by scarcity is illustrated in Figure 3-3 and Table 3-1. Assuming a farm of limited acreage, the limiting factor is land. If all the cultivable land is devoted to the production of wheat, 500 bushels of wheat can be produced. If all the land is devoted to the production of rye, 800 bushels of rye can be produced. Or the farmer can produce some of both crops; for example, he can produce 400 bushels of wheat and 250 bushels of rye or 200 bushels of wheat and

FIGURE 3-1   The economic system.

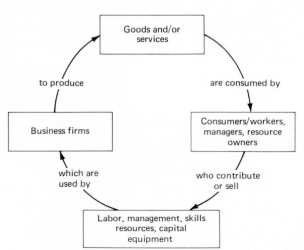

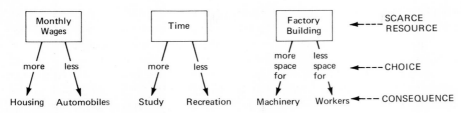

FIGURE 3-2 Choices forced by scarcity.

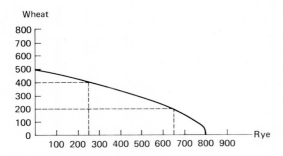

FIGURE 3-3 Production curve of a farm.

TABLE 3-1 **PRODUCTION SCHEDULE OF A FARM**

Wheat (bushels)	Rye (bushels)
0	800
100	760
200	640
300	500
400	250
500	0

640 bushels of rye. Because the amount of land available to the farmer is limited, he must sacrifice wheat to increase rye or sacrifice rye to increase wheat. Choices of this nature must be made whenever one deals with scarce factors.

If you were asked, What is your demand for theater tickets, you would probably answer with a question: What is the price? If the price is high, probably you would go to the theater infrequently; if the price is low, you would probably go more

DEMAND

often. Demand is a relationship between price and quantity. It can be defined as the schedule of amounts that will be bought at a corresponding schedule of prices.

Suppose you are the owner of a motion picture theater. You would certainly be interested in estimating the demand for theater tickets in your area. Suppose you set a price of $4.50 per ticket and hold to that price for one week. At the end of the week you find you have sold an average of 50 tickets per showing. The demand for theater tickets at a price of $4.50 each is 50 tickets per showing. The second week you cut the price to $4 and find you have sold an average of 100 tickets per showing. Each week you cut the price by 50 cents, and each week you sell more tickets per showing. At a price of 50 cents per ticket you are sold out for each performance. If you cut the price per ticket still further, you cannot sell more tickets per showing, because you have only 450 seats. Now you can estimate the demand for tickets to your theater. You can also recognize the nature of demand. Let us restate for emphasis: demand is the quantity of an item or service that is bought at each price of a range of prices.

It is important to distinguish between demand and quantity demanded. "Demand" is the relationship of price and quantity over a range of prices and quantities. Demand is shown by a schedule (Table 3-2) or by a curve on a graph (Figure 3-4). "Quantity demanded" is any point on the demand curve or schedule. Thus at a price of $3 the quantity demanded is 200 tickets per showing.

Of what value is this to a businessman? Suppose you are a businessman; in this instance suppose you are the theater owner. You have two showings per night and no matinees. At $4.50 per ticket you sell 50 tickets per showing, collecting $450 per night. At 50 cents per ticket you sell 450 tickets per showing, collecting $450 per night. The only difference is that you have a bigger crowd at 50 cents per ticket than you do at $4.50 per ticket. If your costs of operation (lease payments on the building, maintenance, utility bills, salaries for projectionist, ticket clerk, and manager) are the same amount regardless of the number of tickets

TABLE 3-2   DEMAND SCHEDULE FOR
               THEATER TICKETS

Price per Ticket	Number of Tickets Sold per Showing	Receipts per Night (two showings)
$4.50	50	$450
4.00	100	
3.50	150	
3.00	200	
2.50	250	
2.00	300	
1.50	350	
1.00	400	
.50	450	450

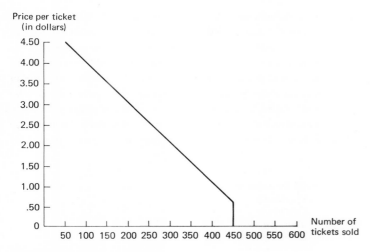

FIGURE 3-4   Demand for theater tickets.

you sell, what price would you set for tickets? Complete the last column of Table 3-2. What is your decision?

We have discussed above the amount of theater tickets that are demanded at different prices. That is a demand schedule. What is a supply schedule? *Supply* is the schedule of amounts that are offered by the producer of an item or service at different prices. Like demand, supply is represented by a supply schedule or a supply curve. What is your supply schedule as the theater owner in the above example? Since your theater has 450 seats, you offer 450 tickets regardless of the price you post on the ticket window. At a price of 50 cents, you offer 450 tickets for each showing (and sell them all). If you set a price of $4.50, you still offer 450 tickets per showing (but only 50 are bought, and you have 400 empty seats). Once your theater is built with a capacity of 450 seats, your supply is set until you change the dimensions of the building.

SUPPLY

However, many producers of goods and services can vary the amount they offer for sale. Let us examine the case of a college student, John Jones, who is considering working during the school year. If the price offered for his labor services (the wage rate) is low, he decides not to work at all. If the price is high, he decides to reduce his academic load of courses and work full time. Between these extremes he is willing to work longer hours if the price is attractive, and shorter hours if the price is less attractive. The supply schedule for his labor services is shown in Table 3-3 and his supply curve in Figure 3-5.

Many different supply schedules can be constructed and many different supply curves drawn. If you are a college student, your supply curve is likely to be quite different from that of John Jones. Perhaps your course schedule is so demanding or your income from your parents so generous (or both) that no amount of money can induce you to spend some time on a job. If that is your supply schedule, you are fortunate (and rare). Some students are in a position to offer to work a certain number of hours a week (say, 15) at whatever wage is offered. If George Brown, college student, has 15, and only 15, hours a week to spare and wants very much to work and will accept whatever wage he can get, from $1 an

TABLE 3-3 **SUPPLY SCHEDULE OF LABOR OFFERED BY JOHN JONES**

Hourly Wage Offered	Number of Hours per Week John Jones Is Willing to Work
$10	50
9	45
8	40
7	35
6	30
5	25
4	20
3	15
2	7
1	0

FIGURE 3-5 Supply curve of labor offered by John Jones.

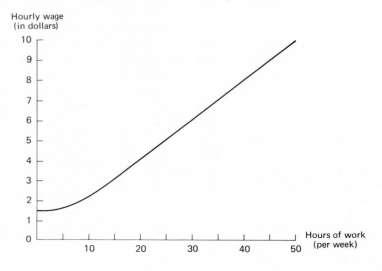

hour to $10 an hour, his labor supply curve will be quite different from that of John Jones in Figure 3-5. What will it be? Can you draw it on Figure 3-5?

Rather than examining the supply schedule of labor of an individual, consider the supply of labor of a group. Suppose we consider a college of 10,000 students (and, for simplicity, no minimum wage laws). How does this group react to different wage rates for unskilled student labor? If the college offers a standard wage of 50 cents an hour, how many hours of labor per week will be forthcoming from the student body? Probably not many. If the college offers an hourly wage of $1, the number of students willing to work will rise. At a wage of $1.50 an hour the number of students and the hours worked will rise still further. At each increase in the wage rate the number of students willing to work and the number of hours they offer to work will increase. The supply curve of student labor rises as the price (the hourly wage rate) rises. The curve will look like Figure 3-5, perhaps steeper, perhaps shallower. If the college business office has estimated accurately the supply of unskilled student labor, the office can determine what wage rate must be offered to get the amount of student labor the college needs. So also can a businessman analyze the supply of factory labor, raw materials, or other resource to estimate how much he will have to offer for greater or smaller quantities of each.

PRICE ELASTICITY

"Price elasticity" refers to the increase in supply offered relative to an increase in price (elasticity of supply) and to the increase in offers to buy relative to a decrease in price (elasticity of demand).

PRICE ELASTICITY OF SUPPLY

George Brown, referred to in the previous section, wanted very much to work 15 hours a week and was willing to accept any wage he could get. Since the available supply of his labor was 15 hours a week regardless of the pay scale, the supply was not affected by price. *Price elasticity* is the term used to describe the effect of price on supply (also on demand, as we shall see later). If supply is sensitive to changes in price, supply is called elastic; if supply is insensitive to changes in price, it is called inelastic. George Brown's supply of labor is completely inelastic (completely insensitive to changes in price). The supply of theater tickets in the example earlier in this chapter is also completely inelastic. What is the dividing line between elastic and inelastic? If a 1 percent increase in price is coupled with *less* than a 1 percent increase in quantity supplied, we call supply inelastic; if a 1 percent increase in price is coupled with *more* than a 1 percent increase in quantity supplied, we call supply elastic.[1]

What good does it do a businessman to know the elasticity of supply—for

---

[1] A 1 percent increase in price coupled with a 1 percent increase in quantity supplied is called *unit elasticity*. Economists examine the relationship of supply and demand not only to changes in price but also to changes in other factors, such as consumer income.

example, raw material for his factory? If the supply is inelastic, he will have to offer more than a 1 percent increase in price to increase the quantity available to him by 1 percent. If the supply of a second raw material is elastic and the business-man offers an increase in price of 1 percent, he will find more than a 1 percent increase in the supply of the second raw material offered to him. If he needs more raw material and can substitute the second raw material for the first in some appli-cations, obviously he can save money by increasing his purchases of the second raw material (elastic supply) rather than increasing his purchases of the first raw material (inelastic supply).

PRICE ELASTICITY OF DEMAND

The concept of price elasticity applies also to demand. If demand is sensitive to changes in price, it is elastic; if demand is insensitive to changes in price, it is inelastic. Your demand for table salt is probably completely inelastic in the range of prices between 5 cents and 30 cents a pound. Would you or your family increase your purchases of table salt if the price were cut to 5 cents a pound (not a temporary sale price at one store but a "permanent" reduction)? Would you or your family decrease your purchases of table salt if the price rose to 30 cents a pound? If the answer is "no" to each question, your demand for table salt is completely inelastic at prices between 5 cents and 30 cents a pound. Should a family decrease slightly its purchases of table salt if the price rises and increase slightly its purchases if the price falls, the family's demand for table salt is rela-tively inelastic. To be more precise, if an increase of 1 percent in price is related to less than a 1 percent decrease in quantity demanded, the demand is inelastic; but if an increase of 1 percent in price is related to more than a 1 percent decrease in quantity demanded, the demand is elastic. Figure 3-6 shows elastic and inelastic demand and supply curves.

How does a businessman apply demand elasticity to his business decisions? If the demand for his product or service is highly inelastic, a reduction in his selling price will increase sales very little. By the same token, if he raises his price, the decline in his sales will also be very slight. If demand for his product or service is highly elastic, a slight reduction in price would result in considerable increase in sales; but a slight increase in price would result in a substantial, perhaps disastrous, decline in sales. If a businessman can make the demand for his product more inelastic, it is usually to his benefit to do so. He might accomplish this by adver-tising, by using a trademark, or by making his product distinctive from its com-petitors in color, shape, or design.

THE RELATIONSHIP OF DEMAND, SUPPLY, AND PRICE

A demand curve, as shown in Figure 3-4, is typically downward-sloping to the right, with prices on the vertical scale and quantities on the horizontal scale. A supply curve, as shown in Figure 3-5, typically slopes upward to the right. What happens if

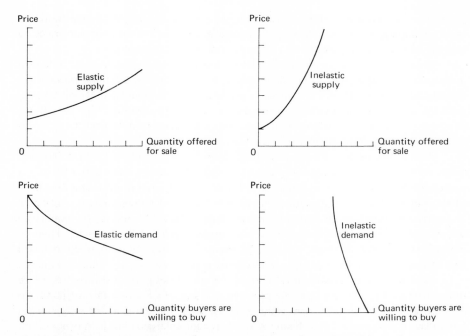

FIGURE 3-6 Graphical representation of elastic and inelastic supply and demand.

we combine the two? That is what we shall examine now. We shall use milk as an example, although steel, corn, or almost anything else would serve equally well.

Table 3-4 gives the demand schedule and supply schedule for milk. Let us assume that the schedule is the result of research for a dairy county in the Midwest done by the dairy department of a state university, and that the prices represent bulk (wholesale) prices and are expressed in cents per quart. As is to be expected,

TABLE 3-4 DEMAND AND SUPPLY SCHEDULES FOR MILK

Quantity Demanded (in 1,000 quarts daily)	Price per Quart (in cents)	Quantity Supplied (in 1,000 quarts daily)
1,175	50	1,800
1,300	45	1,700
1,400	40	1,600
1,500	35	1,500
1,600	30	1,400
1,700	25	1,200
1,800	20	800
2,000	15	300

at high prices people will buy less milk; at low prices they will buy more. In contrast dairy farmers will increase their milk production if they expect prices to be high, but will curtail production if they expect prices to be low.

If the milk price is 20 cents, the amount buyers want to buy daily is 1,800,000 quarts. But at that low price some small dairy farmers stop milk production entirely and other farmers curtail their production. The amount that will be produced is only 800,000 quarts. The situation is obviously unstable. Milk is sold out at stores as fast as it is put on the shelves, and bulk buyers of milk find they cannot buy all they want. What happens? Prices rise.

If the milk price is 45 cents a quart, dairy farmers produce 1,700,000 quarts daily. Milk buyers, however, will buy only 1,300,000 quarts daily. Now there is a surplus of 400,000 quarts of milk daily. Prices fall. At what point is stability (also called the "point of equilibrium") reached? Table 3-4 shows that at a price of 35 cents per quart dairy farmers will produce 1,500,000 quarts. At that price buyers will buy 1,500,000 quarts. Daily supply equals daily demand. There is neither surplus nor shortage. Looking at Figure 3-7, you notice that the demand and supply curves meet at a price of 35 cents and a quantity of 1,500,000 quarts.

How long does stability last? Usually for very brief periods. In the first place it is difficult to estimate demand precisely. If you are a dairy farmer about to increase your herd of cows, you want to know what the demand for milk will be, not today, but several months from today when your enlarged herd is in production. How do you measure future demand? You make a guess, or you depend upon the

FIGURE 3-8   Shifts in supply of milk.

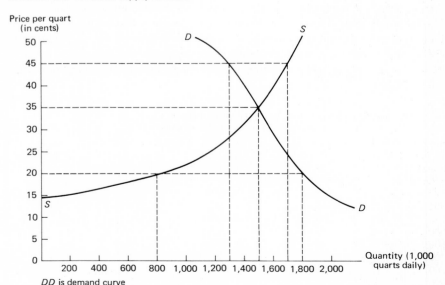

DD is demand curve
SS is supply curve

informed guess of a government agency or dairy association (probably published as a scientifically prepared market forecast).

   In the second place consumer tastes change, and often these changes are not anticipated. Also, the cost of cattle feed may rise, or some other cost of producing milk may go up. In a dynamic economy like that of the United States consumer tastes are constantly changing, sometimes slowly, sometimes rapidly; and costs of production, as well as methods of production, keep changing. The point of equilibrium keeps changing, because the shape and position of the demand and supply curves keep changing. If the price of tea is above the equilibrium point, packages of tea sell slowly, and grocers find themselves overstocked with tea. If the price of tomatoes is below the equilibrium point, buyers snap up tomatoes as rapidly as grocers put them on display, and tomatoes are usually out of stock at most stores. When price is substantially above or below the equilibrium point, both buyers and sellers are aware of it; but to determine the **precise** equilibrium point is generally beyond the accuracy of information available to buyers and sellers.

Suppose dairy farming becomes less attractive than it has been in the past—perhaps because of an increase in the cost of feed or a decrease in the amount of pasture land. At each level of prices less milk would be produced than before. The supply curve shifts to the left, as is shown by the new supply curve S_1 in Figure 3-8. At the old equilibrium price of 35 cents per quart there is now a shortage of milk.

SHIFTS IN DEMAND AND SUPPLY

FIGURE 3-8 Shifts in supply of milk.

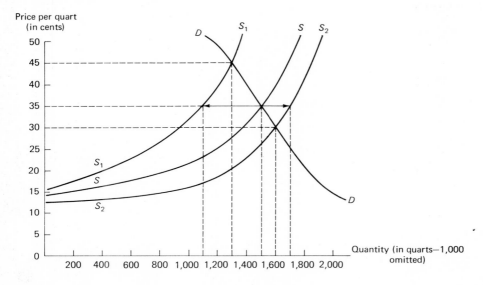

How much is the shortage? Draw a line *horizontally* from the intersection of the old demand and supply curves at 35 cents to the new supply curve at 35 cents. The length of the line indicates the shortage at 35 cents. Since the new supply at 35 cents is 1,030,000 quarts and the previous supply at 35 cents was 1,500,000 quarts, the shortage is 470,000 quarts.

As is usual when shortages develop, the price of milk tends to rise. And as usual when prices rise, producers tend to produce more. But, as you can see from the S_1 curve, dairy farmers increase their production at higher prices less than they did before. The new equilibrium is reached at the intersection of the S_1 and D curves. The new equilibrium price is 45 cents and the new equilibrium quantity is 1,280,000 quarts.

What happens if dairy farming becomes more attractive? At each price more milk is produced. The supply curve has shifted to the right, as shown by the new supply curve S_2 in Figure 3-8. At the old equilibrium price of 35 cents there is now a surplus, measured horizontally along the line between the S and S_2 curves at the level of 35 cents. There is now more milk produced than can be sold at 35 cents, and (assuming no government or dairy association interference) prices go down. The new equilibrium is shown by the intersection of the D curve with the S_2 curve at a price of 30 cents and production at 1,600,000 quarts.

Let us now consider a shift in demand. Perhaps publicity has been given to a report that suggests a correlation between the consumption of milk and an increase in heart attacks. At each price for milk, less milk will be bought. The demand curve shifts to the left, as shown by D_1 in Figure 3-9. The supply of and demand for milk, formerly in equilibrium at a price of 35 cents a quart, are now

FIGURE 3-9   Shifts in demand for milk.

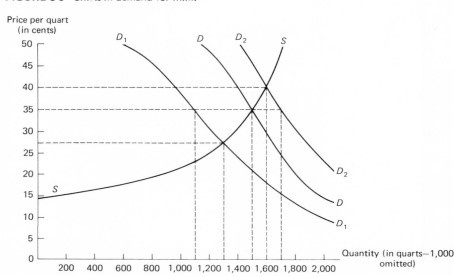

in disequilibrium. At 35 cents only 1,120,000 quarts will be bought daily. Prices will tend to drop. At lower prices, dairy farmers produce less milk, but buyers tend to buy more. The new equilibrium is shown at the intersection of the S curve with the D_1 curve in Figure 3-9. At 27 cents a quart dairymen will produce 1,300,000 quarts daily and buyers will buy 1,300,000 quarts daily.

Instead of unfavorable publicity, suppose there is favorable publicity for milk, possibly the result of a heavy advertising campaign by the dairy industry. Demand for milk increases—that is, the demand curve shifts to the right. At 35 cents there is now a shortage of milk. At 35 cents buyers want 1,720,000 quarts but dairymen produce only 1,500,000 quarts. The advertising campaign has obviously succeeded. Prices rise. At higher prices more milk is produced and milk buying declines. Equilibrium is reached where the S curve intersects the D_2 curve. At 40 cents dairymen will produce 1,600,000 quarts and buyers will buy 1,600,000 quarts. Once more there is stability.

COMPETITION

Nearly everybody favors competition in business. But what is competition? Basically, competition is the effort of two or more parties, acting independently, to gain the same goal. If the price for gasoline is identical at 10 service stations on a street, does that indicate the absence of competition, or does it indicate intense competition? There are different kinds of competition and varying degrees of competition. When you run a race, you are engaging in competition, as you are when you are hunting a job or trying to impress your neighbors by buying a new car. However, since this is a book about business and since a businessman is a member of an industry, we shall examine the competition between firms in an industry. Also, to simplify our examination of competition, we shall emphasize price competition.

The two extremes of competition are perfect competition (sometimes also called "pure competition") and pure monopoly. Although the extremes exist only in theory, like a perfect vacuum, they are useful to examine, inasmuch as the extremes provide a standard against which differences from the extreme can be measured. Indeed, the intensity of competition or lack of it has approached the extreme in some industries. We shall also give some attention to the area between the extremes, which we shall call imperfect competition.[2]

PERFECT COMPETITION

Perfect competition is competition in which the following conditions are found:

1 No firm has any measurable influence over the price at which it sells. Each firm accepts whatever is the market price for its products. Each firm is a "price taker" rather than a "price setter."

[2] In economic textbooks such designations are used as "oligopoly," "monopolistic competition," and "administered pricing."

2 The product sold by each firm is indistinguishable from the product sold by other firms in the industry.

3 There is no collusion among firms, nor any "understandings" or agreements to reduce competition.

4 There is no barrier by government action or industry action to restrict entry of new producers into the industry, nor is there any price control or price support. Also, there is no aid given by government or the industry to keep existing members from "giving up" and leaving the industry.

Let us examine each of these characteristics of perfect competition. Since each producer cannot control the price at which he sells, he tends to produce as much as he can, so long as any increase in his production does not cost more than the price at which he has to sell. If total industry production increases while demand does not, the industry price will fall, and individual firms will begin cutting back on their production. Each firm strives to reduce its costs of production rather than trying to influence price (which it cannot).

If each firm's product is similar but differs slightly from products of other firms, price differences are apt to appear. Even if the differences are more apparent than real, prices tend to differ, since buyers will prefer one firm's product over that of another firm. Is there any difference between the gasoline of one major brand compared with another major brand if the octane rating is the same? There may be none, but the average motorist probably feels that there is, and his preference for one brand over another permits some differences in gasoline prices to exist. In perfect competition each firm's product is indistinguishable from that of other firms. In perfect competition it does not pay to advertise your brand or even to brand your product. In perfect competition each firm acts independently of others. If firms agree, formally or informally, in secret or in the open, to keep prices up or production down, competition is diminished.

It is natural for a businessman to feel that new firms entering his industry make it harder for him to make a living. After all, he argues, he has enough trouble keeping up with existing competitors without having to worry about additional competitors. It is also natural for him to welcome any impediments to the entry of new firms. If a government license is required to enter an industry and the license is difficult to get, the existing members of the industry, already having licenses, welcome the licensing requirement. A license, or any other impediment, however, is a departure from perfect competition.

An example of nearly perfect competition was wheat farming before World War I, when there were no price supports, acreage limitations, export subsidies, or similar interferences in the market. If the wheat farmer thought the price of wheat too low, what could he do? If he cut his wheat production in half, what effect would 200 or 300 fewer bushels have on the price of wheat when total production in the nation was millions of bushels? If he tried to get a higher price for wheat because it was Farmer Jones Brand, he would be laughed at. Wheat was bought according to grade, not label, and each grade commanded a uniform price regardless which farm produced it. Nor would it do any good for an individual farmer to advertise. Finally, there were no government price supports or production controls. Farmers improved the quality of their wheat to the best of their ability (to get a higher grade), reduced their costs of production as much as they could, and sold at whatever price existed in the market at the time of sale.

The nearly perfect competition in wheat and other farm products ended during the Depression of the 1930s. Because in perfect competition there is no concerted action among producers to restrict production when there is a decline in demand, prices fell steeply from 1930 to 1933. Competition is not comfortable for the competitors, and the closer that competition comes to being perfect, the less comfortable it is for the competitors. Price competition, of course, keeps prices down and benefits consumers. Through its influence over Congress, the farming industry moved sharply away from perfect competition, and this condition has existed ever since. Most other industries never were close to perfect competition.

The opposite of pure competition is pure monopoly. **Pure monopoly** is a market in which only one firm produces a good or provides a service. Pure monopoly is approached in such examples as the postal service, local telephone, gas, water, sewer, and electric power, and a single hospital serving an isolated community. How close to pure monopoly the above examples are depends on how narrowly you define the product or service. If you want electricity brought to your house, your choice is limited to one electric power company. However, you could buy a small electric generator, gasoline-powered, and generate your own electricity. If you want running water in your house and you live in a city, you are limited to buying water from the single company or city agency that runs pipes along your street. However, there is an alternative—you could buy a tank truck and haul water to your house. Can you think of alternatives to telephone service, gas service, sewer service to residents of a city, or hospital service in an isolated community? How attractive or convenient are these alternatives?

PURE MONOPOLY

In the absence of government regulation a monopolist can set any price he wants for his service or product. Of course, if he sets a very high price, he will find his sales declining. Conversely, if he sets a low price, he can expand his sales. The demand for his product is the same as the demand for the industry's product, because the monopolist is the industry. Thus, before World War II there was only one company producing aluminum from ore in the United States. Aluminum Corporation of America was the aluminum industry.

The monopolist estimates the demand for his product or service (and probably draws a demand curve) in deciding upon his price. The demand curve will show the monopolist how much he can sell at different prices. If the demand is inelastic (as explained earlier in this chapter), a cut in price will expand sales relatively little and an increase in price will curtail sales relatively little. If demand is elastic, an increase in price will lead to a considerable decline in sales but a cut in price will expand sales considerably. The monopolist can set his price wherever he chooses (unless restrained by government); but whatever price he sets, he is forced to take the volume of sales determined by demand at the price set. If the monopolist wants to operate at a given volume of sales, he can look at the demand curve and see what price he must set to achieve the desired volume. The monopolist can choose a price or a volume of operations and sales, but he cannot dictate both. He is naturally happy to be faced with an inelastic demand for his output, since he can increase his price with little loss in sales.

IMPERFECT COMPETITION   Between the extremes of competition and monopoly there are many types of markets exhibiting varying degrees of competitiveness. Some examples of these are shown in Table 3-5. Each industry has its own unique characteristics, which makes any classification attempt difficult. Some industries are close to being monopolies. For example, there are only four producers of ingot aluminum in the United States, and entry into the industry by another competitor would be very costly, because a large investment is necessary. Some industries are closer to perfect competition. For example, auto repair shops are very numerous—often quite small—and offer almost identical services. But they are not as close to perfect competition as wheat farming was before government price supports and production controls were enacted.

As we saw before, the essential characteristics of perfect competition is that each producer has virtually no control over the price at which he sells his product or service. In the case of perfect monopoly, we saw that the monopolist does have complete control over the price of his product (but having chosen his price, his volume of sales is determined by the demand for his product). The in-between industries have varying degrees of control in setting their prices. If you drive on a city street or on a highway, you will notice some variation in prices for gasoline at service stations. Does this indicate complete freedom on the part of oil companies

TABLE 3-5   IMPERFECT COMPETITION—TYPES AND EXAMPLES

Characteristics	Examples
1 Small number of producers, all large; products similar but different	Auto manufacturing, cigarettes
2 Large and small producers; some products identical, some products similar	Steel manufacturing
3 Many producers, large and small; some products identical, many products different	Pharmaceutical drug manufacturing
4 Many producers, large and small; most products identical, a few products different	Lumber
5 Very many producers, all small; products similar but different	Barber shops

in setting gasoline prices? No. If one station sells regular gasoline at 50 cents a gallon while competing stations sell the grade at 36 cents, the station will get very few customers; if it prices its gasoline at 20 cents a gallon, the station may get many customers but will probably be selling below cost. A variation of a few cents per gallon between stations permits all to get customers. People are willing to pay a slightly higher price for gasoline from one station than for the fuel from another because the higher-price station may be more convenient, look cleaner, have more cheerful attendants, or sell gasoline that customers think (perhaps erroneously) is superior in quality. As a generalization, the closer an industry is to perfect competition, the less is the control that firms have over setting their prices. The closer an industry is to perfect monopoly, the greater is the control that firms have in setting their prices.

It is natural for owners of a business firm to prefer a condition close to monopoly over one close to perfect competition. There are some things that firms can do to move their products or services in the direction of monopoly. One is to strive to make their product more distinctive from competing products. One refrigerator manufacturer might offer revolving shelves, a second might offer automatic ice-cube making, and a third might offer an ice-water faucet. If the distinctive feature is successful in attracting customers, the company will usually find it has increased latitude in setting its prices. Generally, however, the introduction by one company of any distinctive feature does not give the company an advantage for very long. Other companies soon copy it. As a result, in many industries the introduction of new features is never-ending. Can you name some new features introduced (and then copied) by companies in automobile manufacturing? In radio and television manufacturing? In the cigarette industry?

We saw earlier that it would be foolish for a wheat farmer to advertise his brand of wheat. A monopolist frequently advertises, but the emphasis tends to be more on the product than on the brand (because the customer has no choice of brands). "Better cooking with gas" and "Live better electrically" illustrate the type of advertisement a monopolist uses. Industries in the in-between area often make heavy use of advertising. Where companies introduce new features to their products constantly, these features must be announced to the public. Whether the new feature is important or trivial, useful or not, makes little difference. For a company to move in the direction of monopoly, the important factor is that it makes the customer *think* that a particular brand is different and that the difference is important.

SUMMARY

Economics is the study of the means by which a society allocates and distributes its scarce resources to meet man's unlimited wants. Ignoring a few rare cases, all businesses and all consumers practice economizing to a greater or less degree because neither businesses nor consumers can get everything they want. Thus businessmen and consumers are faced with varying degrees of scarcity and must decide what they want more in contrast to what they want less.

An individual's demand for an item is the schedule of amounts he is willing to buy at a series of prices; the demand for a company's (or an industry's) product is the schedule of amounts of the product customers are willing to buy at various prices. For almost all products or services, the amount bought increases with lower prices and decreases with higher prices. If the amount of a product customers are willing to buy declines slowly as prices increase rapidly, the demand for the product is inelastic; if the amount of a product customers are willing to buy decreases rapidly as the price increases slowly, the demand for the product is elastic.

A businessman's supply is the schedule of amounts of a product or service he is willing to offer for sale at various levels of price. Industry supply is the schedule of amounts all firms in the industry together are willing to offer for sale at various prices. Normally, the amount offered for sale rises with higher prices and decreases with lower prices. If the amounts offered for sale increase relatively less than the increases in price, the supply is inelastic; if the amounts offered for sale increase relatively more than the increases in price, the supply is elastic. The equilibrium price for a product is that price at which the amount customers are willing to buy is just equal to the amount producers are willing to offer for sale. For most products, however, the equilibrium price is constantly shifting upward or downward and is difficult to predict in advance.

When a decline in demand occurs, the amount customers are willing to buy at each of a series of prices is less than before; when an increase in demand occurs, the amount customers are willing to buy at each of a series of prices is greater than before. If a decline in supply occurs, the amount producers are willing to offer for sale is less at each of a series of prices than it was before; if an increase in supply occurs, the amount producers are willing to offer for sale is greater at each of a series of prices than it was before.

The concept of perfect competition includes the following:

1 No producer in the industry has any measurable control over the prices at which he sells.
2 There is no collusion among firms.
3 There is no barrier to entry of new firms in the industry and no government interference in prices or production.
4 The products sold by each firm are indistinguishable from the products of other firms.

The concept of pure monopoly is a market in which there is only one producer of a product or service and there is no competition whatever. A monopolist can set his price at whatever level he selects, but then he is faced with whatever volume of sales customers are willing to buy at the price set.

The types of markets between the extremes of perfect competition and pure monopoly are characterized by imperfect competition. The closer an industry is to monopoly, the greater is the degree of control the firms in the industry have over the prices they set for their products. The closer an industry is to perfect competition, the less is the control firms have over the prices they set. There is a natural tendency for producers to make their services or products move toward monopoly if they can, so as to gain greater latitude in setting prices. A means of trying to accomplish this is for a firm to introduce distinctiveness into its products and to use advertising that emphasizes the distinctiveness in the minds of customers.

QUESTIONS FOR REVIEW

1   "If everybody has everything he wants, there is no need to study economics." Criticize.
2   What is a demand schedule? How can a businessman determine the demand schedule for his product?
3   Explain how preparing an estimated schedule of supply of student labor will help a college in deciding how many hours to hire students to work per week.
4   What is meant by price elasticity? Give examples, other than those in the text, of elastic and inelastic demand.
5   What is meant by the point of equilibrium between the demand for and the supply of an item? Why does this point tend to change position constantly?
6   What might cause a shift in demand, either an increase or a decrease, for beef? For airline travel? For cameras?
7   What is pure competition? What is pure monopoly? Since each exists only in theory, why study it?
8   A monopolist can set either his price or a desired level of sales but not both. Explain.
9   If there are four gasoline service stations on a corner, with each selling gasoline at the same price, is this evidence of lack of competition? Why or why not?
10 List some types of competition in business other than price competition. Name the industries in which you find them.

SELECTED READINGS

Abbott, Lawrence: *Economics and the Modern World*, Harcourt Brace Jovanovich, Inc., New York, 1972.
Brandis, Royall: *Principles of Economics*, rev. ed., Richard D. Irwin, Inc., Homewood, Ill., 1972.
Hailstones, Thomas J.: *Basic Economics*, 4th ed., South-Western Publishing Company, Cincinnati, 1972.
Lynn, Robert A.: *Basic Economic Principles*, 2d ed., McGraw-Hill Book Co., New York, 1970.
McConnell, Campbell R.: *Economics: Principles, Problems, and Policies*, 3d ed., McGraw-Hill Book Company, New York, 1972.
Samuelson, Paul A.: *Economics*, 9th ed., McGraw-Hill Book Company, New York, 1973.

Name	Section	Date

COMPLETION SENTENCES

1 The need to _Economist_ is found in practically every decision

a businessman makes.

2 Demand is the relationship between _Price_ and

Quantity .

3 Demand is the _Quantity_ of an item or service that is

Bought at each _Price_ of a range

of prices.

4 Quantity demanded (in economic analysis) is _Any Point_ on

the demand curve.

5 Supply (in economic analysis) is represented by a _Supply_

schedule or a _Supply_ curve.

6 Typically, as price rises for an item, the supply offered

increases .

7 If supply is sensitive to changes in price, supply is called

elastic .

8 If the supply of raw material for a factory is inelastic, buyers wanting the material will have to offer ___more___ than a 10 percent increase in price to induce suppliers to offer a 10 percent increase in supply offered.

9 The demand for table salt is ___inelastic___ in the price range between 5 cents and 30 cents.

10 If a businessman can make the demand for his product or service more

___inelastic___ , it is usually to his benefit to do so.

11 The point of intersection between the demand curve and the supply curve is

___point of equality___ between the amount demanded and the amount supplied.

12 The two extremes of competition are _Pure Comp_ and

Pure monopoly .

13 If competition is perfect, no producer has any measurable influence over

___The Price___

14 A producer established in an industry prefers that his market be closer to

___Monopoly___ than to ___Competition___

Name   Section   Date

15 In general it is less important that the product of a producer be distinctive than it is that his customers _~~think they~~_ it is distinctive.

TRUE OR FALSE STATEMENTS

F **1** Demand means the amount of an item that will be bought at a specific price.

T **2** If the price rises for an item, the amount sellers offer on the market generally rises.

T **3** If demand is sensitive to changes in price, it is elastic.

T **4** If the demand for a company's product is highly inelastic, a 10 percent increase in price will reduce sales by less than 10 percent.

F **5** A demand curve is typically upward-sloping to the right.

T **6** In a competitive market prices are generally unstable.

T **7** The two extremes of competition are pure competition and pure monopoly.

T **8** In perfect competition a firm is a price taker rather than a price setter.

F **9** Under perfect competition it pays to advertise your brand, so as to distinguish it from your competitors'.

T **10** Price competition in general benefits consumers.

F **11** A monopolist is in the happy position of being able to set both his price and his volume of sales, unless he is regulated by government.

T **12** Companies in the category of imperfect competition make extensive use of advertising.

T **13** The advertising of a monopolist often emphasizes the product rather than the company brand.

F **14** Wheat farming is at present an example of an industry having the characteristics of almost perfect competition.

T **15** In an effort to increase a company's sales, it is less important that significant differences distinguish the company's product than that customers think that significant differences exist.

EXERCISES

1 The monopolies discussed in this chapter are not pure monopolies, since there are alternatives available, even though expensive or inconvenient. Typical monopolies are listed below. Suggest alternatives, and give the disadvantages or inconveniences in each case.

Monopoly	Alternative	Disadvantages or Inconveniences
Telephone (local)		
Telephone (long-distance)		
Natural gas		
Sewer service		
Police protection		
Hospital service in isolated community		

2 Table 3-5 (page 54) is a list of types and examples of imperfect competition. See how many other examples you can add to each of the five characteristic types listed on that page.

Characteristic type	Example
1	
2	

Name   Section   Date

Characteristic type	Examples
3	
4	
5	

3 The effort of companies in the category of imperfect competition to give their product or services distinctive features is intense. Indicate distinctive features found in the two industries listed below. Add two other industries of your choice to the list.

Industry	Distinctive Features
1 Automobiles	
2 Television sets	
3	
4	

4 Below is a production schedule indicating the various amounts of wheat and corn that can be produced on a given piece of farmland. Assume the costs of producing corn and wheat on the land are the same. If wheat is selling at $2 a bushel and corn at $1 a bushel, determine the amounts of receipts from both corn and wheat at the different levels of production. Which is the most profitable division of production between wheat and corn? If the price of wheat remains the same but the price of corn rises to $1.20, does this change your answer?

Wheat (bushels)	Cash Receipts (at $2 per bushel)	Corn (bushels)	Cash Receipts (at $1 per bushel)	Total Cash Receipts
0		900		
100		780		
180		620		
260		470		
340		270		
400		140		
450		0		

PART 2
ORGANIZATION AND ADMINISTRATION

The next five chapters examine the different forms of business, the problems of management, internal organization structure, and office procedures. However, an organization suitable to a gasoline service station or a barber shop would not be suitable for a large manufacturing company. The techniques of management would also differ. Because the problems of small business differ significantly from those of large business, a chapter is devoted to small business.

The particular phases of management dealing with production, labor, distribution, and finance will be discussed in later chapters. We are here concerned with the structure of firms of different sizes and types, how businesses are brought into being, and how they are managed once they are in existence. With the framework of business in mind, you can understand better the phases of management treated in later parts.

CHAPTER
4

FORMS OF BUSINESS ORGANIZATION

The number of forms of business organization expanded during the Industrial Revolution as business became larger and more complex. The variety of forms available makes it possible for the organizer of an enterprise to choose a form that most closely meets his requirements as to financing, control, and tax benefits. You should become familiar with the characteristics of the forms discussed in this chapter.

Pay particular attention to the summaries of the advantages and disadvantages of the three most common forms of business organization. Read these carefully and review them from time to time. Notice the differences between the limited partnership and the general partnership. Notice also the differences between the business corporation and the cooperative and the mutual company. Keep in mind that, because business changes in character as time passes, forms of business different from those that exist today may be developed in the future.

Although it is not necessary to study in detail the example of the certificate of incorporation of the Summerton Oil Company, it is useful to look at this as a typical example of a charter of a corporation. As a matter of fact, this certificate is taken directly from an actual business corporation, with only the names and the incorporators changed. It is possible to get model certificates of incorporation to suit the demands of the average small company, and to modify these to suit the particular needs of a small corporation.

The description of the stockholders' meetings is intended to show the human characteristics of this aspect of corporate management. If you have an opportunity to attend a stockholders' meeting, you would find it not only educational but also interesting.

Suppose you are considering starting a weekly newspaper aimed at readers between the ages of sixteen and thirty. What form of business would you choose in organizing such an enterprise? Your choice would depend on many factors. Do you want to be the sole boss, having complete ownership and control? Or do you need the money and management help that a partner could bring, or two partners, or three? Perhaps you plan to raise money from 200 or 300 persons but do not want that many people running the business. Fortunately, there are many forms of business from which you can choose.

The variety of forms of business organization available today reflects the complexity of business activity in the modern world. The range of choice is considerable, and it is the purpose of this chapter to describe the most frequently used of these forms, which are listed below:

Sole proprietorship	Corporation
General partnership	Cooperative
Limited partnership	Mutual company

The **sole proprietorship** is a business firm owned and controlled by one person, who is known as the proprietor. This is the most commonly used form of business, as is shown in Table 4-1. It is also the simplest. To bring a proprietorship into being, a person simply "opens his doors for business." No legal red tape is involved. However, if you want to open a restaurant, a certificate from the local board of health may be required. If you want to open a barber shop, a convalescent home, a funeral establishment, or one of many other types of enterprise, very likely you will be required to get a license to operate. Such certificates are required for a person to perform a particular service regardless of whether the enterprise is a proprietorship, partnership, or corporation.

SOLE PROPRIETORSHIP

If you decided to start a weekly newspaper as a proprietorship, you would have to depend on whatever money you had to invest and what money you could borrow. Perhaps you would hire an experienced newspaperman to manage your weekly. If so, you would be an exception, because nearly all proprietorships are managed by the proprietor. More likely you would act as publisher, editor, circulation manager, and advertising manager. The success of the paper would depend largely upon your talents, because you would be making the major decisions. You would be liable for payments of wages of employees you hire, payments on any money borrowed, and all expenses of operation. If the paper proves to be a success, the income from advertising and subscriptions will be sufficient to meet all the expenses and provide an income to you for your efforts. If the paper is not a success, you are still liable out of your pocket for all payments as they fall due. In short, if the business is profitable, you alone take all the profits; if the business is a failure, you alone bear the losses, even if it bankrupts you. J. C. Penney, Eastman Kodak, and F. W. Woolworth all started as proprietorships and through profitable operation became giant firms.

TABLE 4-1 PERCENTAGE OF COMPANIES ORGANIZED AS SOLE PROPRIETORSHIPS, PARTNERSHIPS, AND CORPORATIONS

	Proprietorships			Partnerships			Corporations			Total
	A	B	C	A	B	C	A	B	C	
Agriculture, forestry, fisheries	93.0	1.7	0.7	3.0	0.5	0.3	0.4	0.1	0.3	100
Mining	50.0	3.1	3.1	18.8	1.6	3.1	9.4	3.1	7.8	100
Construction	69.9	5.7	4.8	4.0	1.3	1.5	3.4	1.8	7.8	100
Manufacturing	37.0	4.4	4.2	4.7	1.5	2.5	8.9	4.7	32.1	100
Transportation, communication, electrical, gas, and sanitary services	74.1	2.9	2.1	3.5	0.8	0.8	7.0	2.4	6.4	100
Wholesale and retail trade	53.0	10.8	9.5	4.2	2.0	3.2	3.6	2.5	11.2	100
Finance, insurance, and real estate	43.8	1.3	0.7	19.0	1.2	0.9	24.2	3.8	5.1	100
Services	81.0	4.0	1.0	4.3	1.0	1.3	3.8	1.3	2.3	100

Note: *A* = less than $50,000 gross income
B = $50,000 to $99,999 gross income
C = $100,000 or more gross income

Source: Statistical Abstracts of the United States, 1968, p. 475.

A summary of the advantages and disadvantages of the sole proprietorship is below:

SOLE PROPRIETORSHIP

Advantages	Disadvantages
Owner receives all profits	Unlimited liability of owner for all business debts
Ease of organization	
Freedom in making management decisions	Limited financial resources
Minimum legal restrictions	Short duration—business ends with death, incapacity, or decision of proprietor to terminate
Maximum incentive to succeed	
Business income and proprietor's income taxed as one	Growth is slower than with other business forms
Ease of dissolution	May be difficult to hire competent employees in slow-growing, impermanent business

PARTNERSHIP

The uniform Partnership Act, adopted by 40 states, defines a partnership as "an association of two or more persons to carry on as co-owners a business for profit." Like the proprietorship, a partnership is simple to create and is well adapted to small businesses. It is particularly well suited to businesses that sell personal services rather than goods. Partnerships are very common in the fields of law, medicine, and accounting. Montgomery Ward & Company, Procter & Gamble, and the brokerage firm of Merrill Lynch, Pierce, Fenner & Smith all started as partnerships (and all later became corporations).

Almost three-fourths of all partnerships consist of two partners, and less than one-tenth of the partnerships in the United States have more than four partners. However, in accounting, brokerage, and law firms the number of partners sometimes runs to 20, 50, or more than 100. For such large numbers the limited partnership form is used.

A partnership can be created by a simple oral agreement among two or more persons. An oral agreement is very unwise, however, because of the likelihood of misunderstanding later on. A written agreement may be short or lengthy, simple or complex. A typical agreement, often titled "Articles of Partnership," contains the following items:

Name of partnership firm

Names of partners, and amount of investment of each

Partnership address

Description of business activity of firm

Duration of partnership

Responsibilities of each partner

Addition of new partners, withdrawal of partners, and dissolution of firm

Preparation of financial statements

Salary and other compensation for each partner

Distribution of profits and sharing of losses

THE GENERAL
PARTNERSHIP

The most common form of partnership is the **general partnership**, also known as the **simple partnership.** In this form all partners share in operating the firm. More important, the personal property of all partners is subject to call if needed for payment of partnership debts. The principal advantages and disadvantages of the general partnership are outlined below:

GENERAL PARTNERSHIP

Advantages	Disadvantages
More financial resources than proprietorship has	Unlimited liability for business debts
More managerial talent than proprietorship	Existence ends with death or withdrawal of any partner
Better credit standing than proprietorship	Restricted transfer of ownership
Few legal restrictions	Possible uncertainty among employees as to who is "boss"
High degree of personal incentive	
Freedom from tax on business income	

A partnership is similar in some respects to a marriage. In a typical partnership the partners spend much of their working day in company with one another. A clash of personalities can strain any working relationship. If the clash becomes severe, the partnership may have to be dissolved, just as a strained marriage may end in divorce. It follows that when a person takes a business partner or a marriage partner, he or she should do so with the utmost caution. In most cases it is easier to dissolve a business partnership than a marriage partnership. Nevertheless, it is probably true that persons enter into a marriage contract with less investigation than in entering into a partnership contract. The moral in both cases: look before you leap!

THE LIMITED
PARTNERSHIP

To form a limited partnership it is necessary to follow the procedures required by the law of the state. Practically all of the states have laws providing for the formation of limited partnerships. Thirty states have virtually the same law, known as the Uniform Limited Partnership Act. A **limited partnership** is a firm that has at least one general partner, with unlimited liability for debts of the firm, and one or more limited partners. The limited partners may invest a sum of money in the firm and be free of general liability for the debts of the firm. If the firm fails to pay its debts, the limited partner may lose his investment, but that is the limit of his loss.

The limited partnership agreement must be in writing, signed by all of the partners, and filed with a public officer designated by state law, usually the county clerk or recorder of the county where the partnership was created. Limited partners do not participate in the management of the firm. Their share of the profits is specified in the partnership agreement. One attraction of the limited partnership is that the death or withdrawal of a limited partner does not end the partnership agreement. This feature is particularly useful in forming a partnership with 50 or 100 partners, since the turnover in membership among limited partners does not affect the existence of the firm.

The limited partnership has enjoyed an increase in popularity recently. Long used in oil well drilling, cattle feeding, equipment leasing, and real estate, it has been applied during the 1970s to motion picture production, cable television, apartment houses, and hotels.[1]

A *corporation* is an entity legally separate from the persons owning it. Government (sometimes the federal, more usually the state) creates the corporation, regulates its activities, taxes it, gives it authority to enter into contracts and to sue and be sued in its own name, and dissolves it. The distinction of a corporation as a being separate from its owners has been part of our legal heritage for generations. The classical definition of a corporation is contained in the 1819 decision of the United States Supreme Court in its finding on *Trustees of Dartmouth College v. Woodward:*

CORPORATION

> A corporation is an artificial being, invisible, intangible, and existing only in contempla-
> tion of law. Being the mere creature of law, it possesses only those properties which
> the charter of its creation confers upon it, either expressly or as incidental to its very
> existence. These are such as are supposed best calculated to effect the object for which
> it was created. Among the most important are immortality, and, if the expression may
> be allowed, individuality; properties by which a perpetual succession of many persons
> are considered the same, and may act as a single individual. They enable a corporation
> to manage its own affairs, and to hold property without the perplexing intricacies, the
> hazardous and endless necessity of perpetual conveyance for the purpose of transmitting
> it from hand to hand. It is chiefly for the purpose of clothing bodies of men in succession
> with these qualities and capacities that corporations were invented, and are in use. By
> these means, a perpetual succession of individuals are capable of acting for the promo-
> tion of the particular object, like one immortal thing.

In the United States, the corporation was sparingly used prior to the Civil War. Where it was used, the federal (rarely) or state (more often) government issued charters through a separate bill enacted by the legislature for each corpora-tion. The legislatures confined such acts to the creation of companies either owned or controlled by the government or having some public purpose, such as toll roads, railroads, banks, and canal companies. After the Civil War, state incorporation laws were passed to provide easily secured charters to incorporate a wide variety of businesses. During the past 100 years, the corporation has become an increas-

---

[1] An example of a limited partnership is the organization of Calidad Vineyards in 1971. The promoters offered 2,000 limited partnerships to investors at $2,500 each to develop 1,175 acres in Santa Barbara, California, for wine grapes. No profit was expected from this venture until 1975 at the earliest. *Business Week*, Dec. 11, 1971, p. 90.

ingly popular form of business organization, particularly where the size of the business is large or the organizers expect rapid growth.

Unlike the proprietorship and the partnership, the corporation can exist only through governmental authority. It is an entity separate from its owners. Government brings it into being, and government can end its existence.

The corporation is a very flexible type of organization, adaptable to many different needs. Nearly all large businesses are corporations. Nevertheless, many small businessmen choose the corporation form, particularly if they anticipate rapid growth. Most states have laws providing for the organization of hospitals, colleges, and other charitable organizations as nonprofit corporations, with no stockholders.[2] Municipal governments are also organized as corporations. The advantages and disadvantages of the corporation compared to partnerships and proprietorships are summarized below:

CORPORATION

Advantages	Disadvantages
Limited liability of stockholders	Tax on business income
Very large financial resources possible	Must follow state law in organizing firm
Ease of transfer of ownership	Extensive legal regulations and restrictions
Long or perpetual life	Possible limited personal incentive
Facilitates rapid growth	
Legal entity distinct from owners	

ORGANIZATION AND CONTROL OF THE CORPORATION

If three persons, the minimum permissible in most states, decide to form a corporation for the purpose of prospecting for oil, for example, their first step would be to determine in rough outline the type of provisions they would want to include in the charter of the prospective corporation. They would then retain the services of a good corporation lawyer, who would draw up a *charter* (also known as a *certificate of incorporation*) complying with all of the provisions of the state laws and interpretation of the laws of the state from which the charter is being requested.

ORGANIZATION   A charter must usually contain the following:

The name of the corporation
The purpose for which it is formed

[2] The board of directors or trustees are named in the original corporation charter. When a replacement is needed, generally the remaining directors or trustees elect a new member. Sometimes, as in the case of some colleges, the alumni or other groups are given the privilege of electing one or more trustees.

The place or places where its business is to be transacted

The term for which it is to exist

The number of directors or trustees, and the names and residences of those appointed for the first year

The amount of its capital stock and the number of shares into which it is divided

An example of a certificate of incorporation follows. The certificate has to be notarized and sent to the secretary of state of the state issuing the charter. If this official finds nothing contrary to law, he files one copy of the certificate and sends another with the seal of the state back to the incorporators. The clerk of the county in which the company has its principal office also receives a copy.

The incorporators hold an organizational meeting of stockholders, at which time a board of directors is elected. Bylaws are adopted, as are any other actions necessary for commencement of business. The bylaws contain the detailed rules under which the corporation is to be managed. They will, for example, set the time and place of the stockholders' meetings and of the directors' meetings, indicate the number constituting a quorum, and state what standing committees of the directors shall be created and what their duties shall be. The stockholders are usually called into meeting only once a year, but the directors meet as frequently as they deem necessary.

The stockholders are the sole owners of a corporation. They do not participate in the management of their property, but delegate the management to the directors, as shown in Figure 4-1. Some corporations issue two (or, more rarely, more than two) classes of stock, distinguished by the designations "preferred stock" and "common stock." **Preferred stock** is a class of stock that is given priority over the   CONTROL

FIGURE 4-1 Diagram of a corporation.

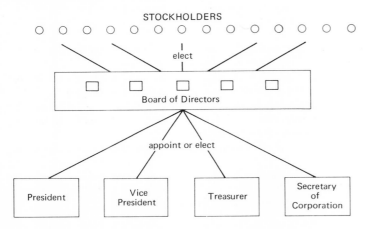

common stock in the payment of dividends and has any other preferences stated in the corporation charter, as explained in Chapter 24. The preferred stockholder is not usually given the right to vote for directors of the corporation. This right is given to the common stockholder, who votes usually by proxy, as explained below.

The authority and responsibilities of the board of directors are contained in the charter and bylaws of the corporation, as the Certificate of Incorporation of the Summerton Oil Company illustrates. In addition the directors are bound by the corporation laws of the state under which the corporation was formed. State laws vary, but the important features are summarized below:

Directors are responsible to the stockholders for managing the corporation in the best interests of the stockholders.

Directors must use prudence and good judgment in making decisions. The "prudent man" rule of law applies here, as it applies to the executor of an estate and in other cases where a man is entrusted with the property or welfare of others. In this application of the prudent man rule, the directors must manage the corporation with the same degree of care a prudent man would use in managing his own business affairs.

The day-to-day management of the corporation may be (and usually is) delegated to officers chosen by the directors. But the directors remain responsible for supervising and checking the performance of the officers.

TYPES OF CORPORATIONS

Since the corporation form is adaptable for many uses, identifying names are given to these uses. The more commonly used designations are given below:

Private corporation: Organized by private citizens to earn a profit. Also known as *business corporation* or *profit corporation.*

Public corporation: Organized by federal, state, or local government for the purpose of providing a public service. Examples are each of the Federal Reserve Banks, the Commodity Credit Corporation, and the United States Postal Corporation. Also known as *government corporation.*

Nonprofit corporation: A hospital, university, or other organization operated for the benefit of persons using the facility. Any excess of income over expenses is used to improve the facility.

Open corporation: A private corporation with stock bought and sold freely by many investors. All corporations on the stock exchanges are open corporations.

Closed corporation: Stock is closely held, usually by only a few people, often members of one family. Not traded among investors. Also known as *family corporation.*

Domestic corporation: A corporation operating in the state of its incorporation. A corporation chartered under Illinois law is known as a domestic corporation in Illinois; in all other states it is known as a foreign corporation.

Foreign corporation: A corporation operating in a state other than the state that issued the charter.

Alien corporation: A corporation operating in a nation other than the one in which it was incorporated. Volkswagenwerk AG is an alien corporation in the United States; General Motors, Inc., is an alien corporation in Germany.

Certificate of Incorporation of Summerton Oil Company

We, the undersigned, in order to form a corporation for the purposes hereinafter stated, under and pursuant to the provisions of the General Corporation Law of the State of Delaware, being Chapter 65 of the Revised Code and the acts amendatory thereof and supplemental thereto, do hereby certify as follows:

1 The name of the corporation is

Summerton Oil Company

2 The principal office of the corporation is to be located in the City of Dover, in the County of Kent, in the State of Delaware. The name of the resident agent is the United States Corporation Company, whose address is No. 19-21 Dover Green in said city.

3 The nature of the business of the corporation and the objects or purposes proposed to be transacted, promoted, or carried on by it are as follows, to wit:

To mine, dig for, or otherwise obtain from the earth petroleum, rock or carbon oils, natural gas, other volatile mineral substances, and salt; to manufacture, refine, prepare for market, buy, sell, and transport the same in the crude or refined condition; to acquire for these purposes gas and oil lands, leaseholds, and other interests in real estate and gas and oil and other rights, to construct and maintain conduits and lines of tubing and piping for the transportation of natural gas or oil for the public generally as well as for the use of said corporation; to transport such oil and gas by means of such pipes, tank cars, or otherwise, and to sell and supply the same to others; to lay, buy, lease, sell, and operate pipes, pipe lines, and storage tanks to be used for the purpose of transporting and storing oils and gas, and of doing a general pipeline and storage business:

To do all and everything necessary, suitable, and proper for the accomplishment of any of the purposes or the attainment of the objects or the furtherance of any of the powers hereinbefore set forth, either alone or in association with act or acts, thing or things incidental or appurtenant to or growing out of or connected with the aforementioned business or powers or any part or parts thereof, provided the same be not inconsistent with the laws under which this corporation is organized.

4 The total number of shares which may be issued by the corporation is TEN THOUSAND (10,000) all of which shall have no nominal or par value. The corporation will commence business with ONE THOUSAND (1,000) shares.

5 The names and places of residence of each of the original subscribers to the capital stock and the number of shares subscribed by each are as follows:

Name	Residence	Number of Shares
J. J. Hunt	Mason City, Iowa	400
M. Q. Bruehn	Des Moines, Iowa	300
R. L. Johnson	Hastings, Nebraska	300

6 The corporation is to have perpetual existence.

7 The private property of the stockholders shall not be subject to the payment of corporate debts to any extent whatever.

8   The number of directors of the corporation shall be fixed and may be altered from time to time as may be provided in the Bylaws.

The directors shall also have power, without the assent or vote of the stockholders, to make and alter bylaws of the corporation; to fix the times for the declaration and payment of dividends; to fix and vary the amount to be reserved as working capital; to authorize and cause to be executed mortgages and liens upon all the property.

In addition to the powers and authorities hereinbefore or by status expressly conferred upon them, the directors are hereby empowered to exercise all such powers and do all such acts and things as may be exercised or done by the corporation; subject, nevertheless, to the provisions of the statutes of Delaware, of this certificate, and to any bylaws from time to time made by the stockholders; provided, however, that no bylaw so made shall invalidate any prior act of the directors which would have been valid if such bylaw had not been made.

IN WITNESS WHEREOF, we have hereunto set our hands and seals the 14th day of December, 1967.

In presence of: *C. H. Jarvis*
        as to all

J. J. Hunt	(L.S.)
M. Q. Bruehn	(L.S.)
R. L. Johnson	(L.S.)

STOCKHOLDERS' MEETINGS

While attendance at stockholders' meetings of small, locally owned corporations is frequently high, attendance at the meetings of large corporations with widely scattered stockholders is quite low. A resident of San Francisco who owns 10 shares of General Motors Corporation common stock would hardly consider it worthwhile to travel to Wilmington, Delaware, to attend the annual meeting. If he happened to be near Wilmington at the time, he might find chartered buses waiting at the stations to meet trains on which stockholders were expected, so that the owners of the company could be taken to the meeting in comfort and convenience. He might find that the meeting was to be held in a specially cleared area of one of the buildings in which General Motors cars were being assembled, and that as many as 3,000 stockholders (of a total of over 500,000 stockholders) were expected to attend. Conducted tours of the plant would probably be arranged and a complimentary lunch provided. At the meeting itself, which might last an hour or two, he would find most of the directors and some of the officers on the speakers' platform ready to answer questions from the floor. While the election of directors for the coming year would be the main feature of the meeting, questions from stockholders would probably take up most of the time. The following questions and comments, selected from the reports of the annual meetings of stockholders of the Standard Oil Company of New Jersey, show the type of statements, both of a business and nonbusiness nature, that are made by stockholders:

"I want a woman on the Board . . . and I am going to ask you please not to give us the old saw about no woman having enough sense to be on the Board."
"Isn't it expensive to produce and sell three grades of gasoline?"

"How much did we spend on advertising last year and how did it compare with the prior year?"

"I would like to voice my opposition to outside directors . . . to take a university president, for example, would not serve any useful purpose."

"Since the success of this great oil company depends on strong, robust employees, I suggest . . . that the management and the shareholders of this company set an example in public health by refraining from smoking at this meeting."

"Is [the Standard Oil Company of New Jersey] planning to enter the field of uranium in any way?"

From the standpoint of maintaining order and providing necessary facilities at a meeting, the directors of large corporations are probably thankful that, although attendance at meetings is encouraged, only a small fraction attend in person. There are about 4 million shareholders of the American Telephone and Telegraph Company. If only 1 of every 10 were to attend, the 400,000 persons could not be accommodated in our largest stadium. Those who do not attend in person, however, can be represented by proxy, a sample of which is shown in Figure 4-2. A proxy form signed by a stockholder authorizes the holder of the proxy to vote the stockholder's shares on any question put to a vote at the meeting. The stockholder may indicate on the form how he wants his shares voted on any issue he knows will be brought up at the meeting. Because so few stockholders attend in person, because the directors already on the board are usually the only ones sending out proxy forms to the stockholders, and because the costs of sending the forms are charged to the company, the directors of large companies with scattered stockholders are a virtually self-perpetuating body.

COOPERATIVES

Cooperatives are organized as corporations with those duties, rights, and privileges accorded to business corporations. They are treated under law equally with corporations, except where the law makes a special provision for cooperatives. A cooperative begins existence when its charter is approved. Stockholders are usually referred to as members rather than as stockholders. Dividends on stock are limited, usually to 6 percent of the amount paid for the stock. Voting is generally limited at members' meetings to one vote per member rather than one vote per share of stock, thereby preventing control of the enterprise through purchase of a majority of the outstanding stock. The profits are distributed among the members in accordance with the amount of business each member transacts with the cooperative. A cooperative retail store generally charges the same price to members and nonmembers alike.

Periodically, the cooperative declares a *patronage dividend*. This is stated as so many cents per dollar of purchases by each member, and the larger the amount of total purchases for the period, the larger is the patronage dividend for the member. Cooperatives are accorded certain legal privileges not given to corporations. An example is the treatment of patronage dividends as a refund of part of the

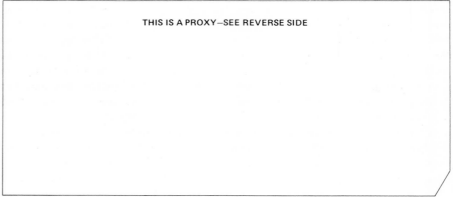

FIGURE 4-2   A proxy card, front and back (*Kellogg Company*).

purchase price of goods bought by each member, and not as a distribution of company profits, thereby exempting the amount of such payments from the corporation income tax.

There are two types of cooperatives in the United States, the ***consumer cooperative*** and the ***producer cooperative***. The former, of which the retail store is an example, has never been as popular in the United States as it has been in Northern European countries. Possibly the reason has been that competition at the retail level of distribution in the United States has been more intense than in other countries and, as a result, there has not been much room for further reduction of retail costs to consumers through the organization of consumer-owned stores. Possibly, too, in the United States the standard of living is so high compared to other nations that the savings in retail costs expected through the cooperative store are not a sufficiently compelling motive to organize many stores.

Producer cooperatives, however, have been organized in considerable numbers among farmers. An example is a cooperative creamery, buying milk from members and nonmembers alike and paying the same price as other creameries. The patronage dividend in such a case gives the member dairyman an additional payment for each hundredweight of milk sold to the cooperative, dependent on the amount of net income earned by the cooperative.

Unfortunately for the organizers of some cooperatives, they have discovered that a business enterprise, regardless of the form of organization, is not always successful, that the problems of management are not always easy to solve, and that bankruptcy is the rude awakening for many dreams of financial success. Inexperienced or incompetent management is the cause of a large proportion of the failures of cooperatives. On the other hand, some cooperatives have become big business. The California Fruit Growers Exchange rivals in size and extent of business operations many of the larger corporations in the United States.

MUTUAL COMPANIES

Mutual companies are found in the financial field of operations. The two largest and many of the smaller insurance companies in the United States are organized as mutual companies. There are mutual savings banks, mutual loan societies, and mutual savings and loan associations. About 75 percent of the sales of life insurance sold by nongovernmental companies is sold by mutual companies. However, this type of business organization has been largely ignored by businesses other than insurance and savings.

Similar to the cooperative, the mutual company is owned by its members; it begins its existence with a charter granted by the government, and is treated as a corporation by law except where the law provides for separate treatment. In a *mutual savings bank*, the depositors are the owners. In a *mutual insurance company*, the policyholders are the owners. There are no stockholders as such. Sometimes stock is sold to provide the initial funds to begin business. Where this is done, the charter provides a limited dividend and a program of retirement of the stock until there is none remaining. Profits are used to build up reserves of the company or are paid out as dividends in the manner of patronage dividends in cooperatives.

The member-owners do not usually have any voice in management policy because they do not vote for the directors or trustees of their company. Practically all mutual savings banks, for example, have boards that are self-perpetuating. When a vacancy occurs, it is filled not by an election by members but by the remaining board members' appointment of a replacement.

CHOOSING A FORM OF BUSINESS ORGANIZATION

The choice of the form of business organization is one of the most important decisions that the promoters of a new business are called on to make. The forms of business organizations should be examined carefully so that the one most suited to the needs of the promoters of the enterprise may be chosen. Each form has certain advantages and disadvantages, and these must be carefully weighed. Although a change in the form of business organization can be made during the later life of an enterprise, a poor original selection may inhibit the growth and development of the business during its early existence.

The following points should be considered in making a choice of business organization:

Ease and speed of accomplishing the organization

Amount of capital required to commence operations

Legal considerations restricting the free choice of a business form in particular cases

The effect of taxation on the choice of the form of organization

Liability of owners

Size of the business and the expected rate of growth

Expected stability of earnings

The importance, or lack of it, of maintaining control by a small group of persons

Frequently, one form of organization will appear suited to the needs of a particular enterprise but will later prove to be unfavorable because of changed circumstances. For example, high rates of personal income taxation were responsible for the change of many proprietorships and partnerships to the corporation form during the 1930s and the 1940s. However, the more recent increase in corporation income taxes, coupled with the decrease in the effective personal income taxes resulting from the tax laws of the early 1950s, caused a shift of closely held corporations (those having few stockholders) to the proprietorship or partnership form of organization. The goal of business is profits. Because the choice of the form of organization affects profits for a long time in the future, care in making the choice is an important factor in business success.

SUMMARY   The major forms of business organization are the sole proprietorship, general partnership, limited partnership, and the corporation. The first two have the advantages of ease of formation, simplicity of structure, less regulations, and that the income is not subject to corporate income tax. The limited partnership is subject to more regulation but it limits liability for the limited partners. The corporation allows limited liability for owners, is well suited to ownership by many persons while allowing ease of transfer of ownership, and can have perpetual existence. On the other hand, it is subject to the corporate income tax and greater regulation than other business forms, and it cannot be formed as easily or as quickly as the proprietorship or partnership.

With few exceptions, corporation charters are secured from the state government, but not necessarily from the state where the principal business is conducted. Although the stockholders are the owners, the directors and officers conduct the affairs of the corporation. The directors must report to the stockholders at least once a year and are usually elected by the stockholders to 1-year terms.

Cooperatives are corporations of a special type. Voting for directors is usually limited to one vote per stockholder, and dividends are distributed on the basis of both the ownership of stock and the amount of patronage each stockholder gives to the cooperative.

Mutual companies are similar to cooperatives in organization, but the customer-members are the owners. There are no stockholders. Dividends are distributed on the basis of the amount of business each members does with the company. Mutual companies are found mostly in the insurance and savings fields.

QUESTIONS FOR REVIEW

1 Proprietorships are nearly always small enterprises. Why is it difficult to operate a large enterprise as a proprietorship?
2 Why is it advisable to have a partnership agreement put into writing?
3 Compare and contrast the rights and responsibilities of a limited partner with those of a stockholder in a corporation.
4 Why was the corporation form of business little used before the Civil War but used with increasing frequency after that war?
5 What types of information are found in the charter of a corporation?
6 Who owns a business corporation? Who manages the corporation? Is the distinction useful or not, in your opinion?
7 Should attendance at stockholders' meetings be encouraged? Why or why not?
8 What information is found on a typical proxy form?
9 Explain the difference between a stockholder in a corporation and a stockholder in a cooperative.
10 What rights do you have as a member of a mutual company?

SELECTED READINGS

Anthony, Edward L., and A. Barr Comstock: *Choosing the Legal Structure for Your Firm*, Small Business Administration, Management Aid no. 80, 1957.

Bogen, J. I. (ed.): *Financial Handbook*, 3d ed., The Ronald Press Company, New York, 1952.

Hastings, Paul G.: *The Management of Business Finance*, D. Van Nostrand Company, Inc., Princeton, N.J., 1966.

Lasser, J. K.: *Business Management Handbook*, sec. 1, McGraw-Hill Book Company, New York, 1952.

Name	Section	Date

COMPLETION SENTENCES

1 The most common form of partnership is the _general_

partnership.

2 In a limited partnership there may be any number of

limited partners, but there must be at least one

general partner.

3 In a limited partnership the agreement among partners must be

written and must be drawn up according to

state law .

4 Over 90 percent of all partnerships in the United States consist of no more

than _four 4_ partners.

5 Each corporation is created by _government_ .

6 Municipal governments are organized as ___*City,*___ .

7 A business corporation is owned by its ___*stockholders*___ .

8 Only the ___*directors*___ of a corporation have the authority to declare dividends.

9 If a person cannot attend the annual meeting of his corporation in person, he can be represented by a ___*proxy*___ .

10 Cooperatives are organized as a special form of ___*Corp.*___ .

11 In a cooperative the patronage dividend is given to each member in proportion to his ___*purchases from / sales to*___ .

12 Producer cooperatives in the United States are confined chiefly to the ___*farming*___ industry.

13 In a mutual insurance company the ___*policy holders*___ own the company.

14 In practically all mutual savings banks the ___*board of direct*___ are self-perpetuating.

15 Most life insurance is sold by companies that are ___*mutual*___ .

TRUE OR FALSE STATEMENTS

T **1** The sole proprietorship is a business owned and controlled by one person.

T **2** No legal "red tape" is involved in the organization of a proprietorship.

T **3** If you organize a proprietorship, your investment in the enterprise depends upon what money you can put in and what you can borrow.

Name   Section   Date

T 4 The limited partnership is the most common form of partnership.

F 5 In a limited partnership the liability of each partner is limited.

F 6 The corporation was a common form of business prior to the Civil War.

F 7 For businesses operating in interstate commerce, a federal charter is usually used.

T 8 A corporation is an entity separate from its owners.

T 9 "Corporation charter" and "certificate of incorporation" are terms referring to the same document.

F 10 A person may not be a director and an officer of the same corporation at the same time.

T 11 In large corporations with many stockholders only a small percentage attend annual meetings in person.

F 12 At stockholders' meetings questions from the stockholders are confined to such matters as management and finance.

T 13 Stockholders not attending an annual stockholders' meeting in person may be represented by proxy.

F 14 The patronage dividend in a cooperative is based on the number of shares each member owns.

T 15 Consumer cooperatives have never been as popular in the United States as in Northern Europe.

EXERCISES

1 From your library or other source list the steps necessary in your state to organize a corporation. Cover the following points:
  a Minimum number of incorporators
  b Minimum capitalization
  c Limitations, if any, on business activity, or lines of business prohibited to corporations
  d Is a license required to sell stock? What agency issues such a license?

2 After reading the description of annual stockholders' meetings, can you suggest any changes to improve such meetings? In outline form suggest what changes you would make and why.

3 Case problem for written report or class discussion. The case that follows has been prepared from an actual business. Read the case carefully. Then consider the three alternatives at the end. Next, prepare a report criticizing the alternatives from the point of view of the parties involved. Which plan or organization do you recommend? Why?

In 1945, H. B. Stuck returned to civilian life after serving 4 years with the United States Army in Europe. His first employment was with the Armour Company, where he worked as a laborer in the meat packing division. When an opening in the sales department was offered him, he accepted. A short time later, he was promoted to the head of the Adhesive Products Department of the Fort Worth plant of Armour and Company. In 1948, the Armour Company, for legal reasons, decided to close down its adhesive operations in Fort Worth. Although Stuck could have accepted a position with Armour in another location, it occurred to him to form his own manu-facturing company, and to try to sell adhesives to the customers he formerly served as salesman for Armour.

Pursuing his idea, he began looking for the equipment and building space necessary to begin operations. His conversations with ex-classmates and friends led to the discovery of a kettle and other equipment, used to make dog food, which was suitable for manufacturing adhesive. He bought the kettle for $100 and rented a space 10 by 33 feet for his manufacturing operations.

At this point is was necessary for Stuck to determine the capital re-quirements of the new business and to decide on the form of business organization. He estimated that an investment of $5,000 would be necessary to get the business started. Unfortunately, his savings were small. He found that he could borrow not more than $4,000 from close friends, relatives, and other sources. The possibility of a loan of $1,000 secured by a lien on personal property was considered as a means of securing the additional funds needed.

In discussing with business acquaintances the plans for the new com-pany, Stuck found two men who were interested in investing money in the new enterprise. One, J. D. Jones, was willing to invest $1,000 and another, I. P. Kirkland, was willing to invest $100. Both suggested that Stuck form

Name   Section   Date

a corporation and obtain the needed $5,000 by the sale of stock. Upon further investigation, however, Stuck found that Kirkland and Jones were apparently the only ones who would be willing to purchase stock in the company. If the corporation were formed, it would apparently be necessary for Stuck to subscribe to $3,900 in stock to furnish the $5,000 deemed necessary, unless he could persuade his close friends and relatives to purchase stock rather than lend money directly to him. Neither Jones nor Kirkland was familiar with the business of manufacturing and selling adhesives, but both were successful businessmen in the community.

The other possibilities for organization that Stuck considered were a general partnership and a proprietorship. He was uncertain which form of organization would be best. He wanted to retain control of his company, but he was aware of the importance of other considerations, such as taxes, the hazard of starting a new business on a shoestring, and the need for considering the future expansion of the company if successful.

The alternatives available were as follows:

1 Form a corporation in which $5,000 would be raised by issuing stock in exchange for Stuck's kettle and $4,900 in cash. Stuck would finance the purchase of his shares by borrowing on his own signature. The balance sheet of the company upon organization would appear as follows:

Assets		Capital stock	
Cash	$4,900	Jones	$1,000
Kettle	100	Kirkland	100
	———	Stuck	3,900
	$5,000		———
			$5,000

2 Form a partnership with Jones and Kirkland as general partners and borrow $3,900 from friends and relatives.

3 Organize his business as a proprietorship.

Even though large businesses may get most of the publicity, it remains true that most enterprises are small business. There are rewards in operating one's own small business, but the rewards are not always monetary.

This chapter discusses what distinguishes small business from large business. The pitfalls of entering the field of small business operation and the requisites for success in small business are intended, not to discourage, but to make a person entering such an enterprise wary. The requisites for success in small business are not always the same as for success in large business. For example, to succeed in a large corporation a person can be, perhaps must be, a specialist—in finance, production, selling, or research. In small business, a person should be a generalist rather than a specialist.

Buying a franchise is one of the simplest ways of becoming a businessman. But notice that in exchange for the aids of various types the franchisor provides, the franchisee surrenders some of his independence. (If franchising is of particular interest to you, read "Franchising's Troubled Dream World," *Fortune*, March 1970, p. 104.)

No small businessman should be unfamiliar with the Small Business Administration. Take particular note of the wide variety of services the agency offers, who is eligible to receive them, how and where one can get the services, and their relatively low cost.

How can you become a millionaire? There are several pathways to this goal, of which the chief ones are listed below.

1 Work your way up the ladder of executive positions of a large corporation.
2 Become a star entertainer in music, professional sports, comedy, or acting.
3 Inherit a fortune.
4 Marry into a rich family.
5 Start a business of your own.

The first path is generally a long one, with the goal reached at age fifty or sixty. The second requires a degree of talent and luck that is given to a very few. The third you cannot control, unless you can choose the family you are born into. The fourth raises the choice of marrying for love or money. That may be a difficult choice to make, but very few have such a difficulty to face. Of all the choices the last one seems to beckon most invitingly. An article in *Time* magazine, "Millionaires under Forty—How They Do It,"[1] described the careers of several persons who became wealthy in a relatively few years. Nearly all of them chose early in life to be their own bosses. They felt that the big corporation was no place to get rich—competition among executives was too rugged and the rate of advancement too slow. So they went into business for themselves, and at the start their businesses were small.

WHAT IS SMALL BUSINESS?

The Small Business Administration, described later in this chapter, defines small business in terms of number of employees and volume of sales. For example, a manufacturing business is small if it employs no more than 250 employees, a retail business is small if annual sales do not exceed $1 million, and a wholesale business is small if its sales do not exceed $5 million. Although any definition of small business is apt to be arbitrary, for this chapter it is probably better to define small business in terms of its operating characteristics rather than of rigid dollar limitations. We shall define small business according to the following characteristics:

Size: Not dominant in its field. The actions of a small unit in an industry have little influence on the large units; the actions of a large unit have considerable influence on the small units.

Area of operations: Generally local, although some small, specialized mail-order companies distribute catalogs nationally.

Financing: Investment is generally from one or a few persons, usually local residents.

Management: Independent of other firms in the industry. However, franchise operations are typically controlled to some extent by the franchising company.

In large businesses the corporation form is used almost exclusively, with owners (stockholders) generally delegating management to directors and receiving reports once a year on company operations. In a small business the owners typically manage the business themselves. Although it is true that in a limited partnership and in a small corporation (see Chapter 4 for a description of these business forms) some owners do not manage, generally such "silent" owners contribute less capital to the small business than do the active managers.

[1] *Time*, Dec. 3, 1965, pp. 88–97.

At the end of World War II, Ewing L. Kaufman invested $4,300 to start a drug company, making pharmaceuticals in the basement of his house. In 1972 the company, Marion Laboratories, had after-tax profits (after payment of federal corporation income taxes) of over $6 million.

ATTRACTIONS OF BEING A SMALL BUSINESSMAN

In 1955 at the age of sixty-five Harland Sanders, restaurant operator, was bankrupt. However, he still had ambition. Existing on monthly Social Security checks and driving a 10-year-old Ford, he tried to sell franchises of his newly created Kentucky Fried Chicken Corporation. In two years he sold only five franchises. Eight years later he had sold 700. In 1964 he relinquished control of the corporation in exchange for $2 million.

In 1965 Robert Guccione, aged thirty-two, borrowed $1,170 and founded a new magazine, *Penthouse*. His pretax profits for the year 1972 were in excess of $7 million.[2]

The above examples suggest one of the powerful attractions of starting your own business: the vision of money and lots of it. To tell the stories of fortunes made on small investments during just the last 10 years would take many days. Opportunity still knocks for those able to listen. Nevertheless, it should be added that the odds in favor of getting rich quickly are very small. To avoid frustration a person aspiring to operate a small business should be motivated by more than a desire for wealth.

Do you want to be your own boss? If so, a small business can make it possible. You will not have to ask permission to leave work early or make excuses if you arrive late. You decide how to run your business, what persons to hire, how much to advertise and where, and whether to spend all of the profits or to reinvest for expansion. You are the boss, and in most cases your decision is final. If you want maximum independence, organize your business as a proprietorship or as a corporation with you as sole stockholder. If you have partners or fellow stockholders, you will lose some independence but will gain additional investment and probably business talents different from your own.

Do you want prestige? This is difficult to measure. However, if you are the owner of a retail store, your standing in the community is usually higher than if you are the manager of a store that is one unit in a chain of stores. If an independent businessman and an executive or employee of a corporation have approximately the same responsibility or authority, the independent businessman generally is given a higher social recognition.

[2]This figure represents profits earned in the United States alone. Substantial additional profits were earned on sales of the magazine in other countries and on other operations related to the magazine. *Business Week*, Aug. 19, 1972, p. 23.

Do you want to try out new ideas? It is certainly not true that large enterprises discourage new ideas from their employees and executives. But it is true that new ideas often tend to get lost in the shuffle or compromised in a large organization. Bureaucracy and inertia are not confined to big government: they are found in big business as well. With your own small business you are free to try out your ideas.

Do you enjoy the sense of accomplishment? In a large organization, particularly at the lower levels of employment, it is often difficult for a person to identify his contribution to the success of the whole. Work in a large company is highly specialized, and workers sometimes feel that whether their work is mediocre or superior, nobody will notice. In your own small business the quality of your performance is visible to you—painfully so if it is bad, but with a feeling of pride when it is good.

PITFALLS AND DISADVANTAGES   Balancing the attractions of small business, there are several disadvantages. Among these are the threat of bankruptcy, uncertain income, heavy responsibilities, long hours of work, and difficulty in attracting good employees.

BANKRUPTCY   In 1966 in a small California town a corporation was formed by three men to sell a line of imported automobiles under an exclusive dealership. The men, who were sole owners of the corporation, invested $30,000. Amid high hopes the agency opened for business. Eight months later a total of six cars had been sold. Expenses exceeded income each month, even though the three owners worked without pay. The agency closed its doors, the corporation ended in bankruptcy, and the three men went their separate ways. One of the three was divorced by his wife at the time the agency closed.

Wealth is the dream—bankruptcy the reality—for many small enterprises. The rate of failure is higher for small businesses than for large ones, and higher for the first five years of operation than for later years. Competition is frequently intense among small businesses, and one consequence is failure for some. Two reasons in particular contribute to the higher failure rate among small firms. First, small business is generally local. If a decline in economic activity occurs in a locality, the independent businesses feel the full effect. Branch units of a larger business are more apt to survive, because large business is not usually dependent upon the economic fortunes of a single locality. Secondly, a small business is generally confined to a single industry. If there is a depression confined to that industry, small firms are less likely to survive than those larger firms that have activities in two or more industries.

When you seek a job with a company, one of the factors you will very likely consider is steadiness of income. Particularly if you are an office worker or an officer in a corporation, you are likely to have a relatively high degree of job security, and with it steadiness of income. You may not get rich, but you know where your next pay check is coming from. If you are a salesman working on a commission, your pay may fluctuate substantially; but if you are a regular salesman, you can generally depend on a basic minimum. To you the peace of mind that comes with steady employment with a large employer may be more important than the possibility of high income in a business of your own. For many people this is so.

UNCERTAIN INCOME

If you were the owner-manager of a small business, you very likely would be the sales manager, the production manager, the purchasing agent, the personnel director, the advertising manager, the treasurer, and possibly the chief accountant. If your business grew, you could hire specialists to shoulder some of these responsibilities. But as chief executive of a small firm, most of the important policy decisions would be yours. Furthermore, you would be making decisions with the knowledge that with each important decision you made, the existence of your firm might be at stake, particularly during the early life of the enterprise. To some people this brings exhilaration; to others, insomnia and ulcers.

HEAVY RESPONSIBILITY

Among owners of small businesses long hours of work are common. An 80-hour workweek is not rare, particularly when a new business is started. Even at home the owner generally has his business on his mind. Often his wife and children work in the business also. Boredom rarely kills a small businessman, but exhaustion sometimes does.

LONG HOURS

Usually it is more difficult for a small businessman to find and retain capable employees than it is for large businesses. The small businessman does not have the interviewing or testing facilities found in the personnel department of a large corporation. He is also apt to be at a disadvantage in training new employees.[3] For example, the training given by the owner of a quick-order lunch counter to a new assistant is apt to be brief, informal, and haphazard. By contrast, a new operator of a McDonald hamburger franchise spends several weeks in carefully planned classes at the McDonald "Hamburger University" in Chicago. Wages and

DIFFICULTY OF ATTRACTING GOOD EMPLOYEES

[3] A recent study showed that only 7 percent of small businesses had a formal training program of any kind. Most provided informal on-the-job training or none at all. Paul G. Hastings and Constantine Danellis, "The Finance Function in Small Business Firms," *Journal of Small Business Management*, April 1967, p. 12.

fringe benefits are usually lower in small businesses, and assurance of long-term employment is less. In some cases a small businessman can hire and retain ambitious and capable employees by offering part ownership of the business, but such a lure cannot be offered to more than a very few in a small business.

REQUISITES FOR A SUCCESSFUL SMALL BUSINESS

It doesn't take a fortune to make a fortune, nor does it take a college education, or family connections, or youth, or experience. But it helps.

Success in a business of your own comes in so many different forms that it is difficult to establish a pattern. Nevertheless, the common ingredients of starting a profitable enterprise include the following:

> Willingness to take financial risks
> Long hours of work
> Powers of persuasion
> Recognizing opportunity
> Experience
> Good health

WILLINGNESS TO TAKE FINANCIAL RISKS

Persons have started small businesses entirely with other people's money, but this is rare. In most cases a person starting a small business commits his own savings to the enterprise. If successful, the profits are his; if unsuccessful, some or all of his savings are lost.

LONG HOURS OF WORK

As mentioned earlier, long hours are to be expected. A person preferring regular hours of work should probably become an employee for somebody else.

POWERS OF PERSUASION

The owner of a small business deals constantly with customers, suppliers, employees, and others. In most of these contacts he is seeking to persuade. Persuasiveness is useful in any line of endeavor; it is essential in the success of small business operation.

RECOGNIZING OPPORTUNITY

Businessmen, large and small, are constantly looking for profitable opportunities. At any time and place undoubtedly there are opportunities for profitable business as yet unrecognized. Who will discern these opportunities? If you can recognize a real opportunity before others do, your chances of success are good. However, often what appears to be a profitable opportunity turns out to be a mirage and traps not only small entrepreneurs but managers of large corporations as well.

According to Dun & Bradstreet, Inc., the leading business credit agency, the four most frequently identified causes of business failure are the following:

EXPERIENCE

> Incompetence
> Unbalanced experience
> Lack of managerial experience in general
> Lack of experience in the specific field of business

Notice the emphasis on lack of experience in the above list. Even incompetence is associated with or results from lack of experience. Before starting your own business, if possible you should work for someone else, becoming familiar with the product or service, the characteristics of the customers, the suppliers, the way the business is operated, and the common pitfalls to avoid.

Most small businesses are one-man operations, in the sense that the major decisions and supervision are the responsibility of one person. If he is unable to manage, the business often goes to pieces. Even if a business is managed by two or three partners, the illness or death of one may cause severe management difficulties.

GOOD HEALTH

The financing of a business is of two types: equity and debt. *Equity* represents ownership. In a small business the equity is confined chiefly to the money invested by the owners plus the profits retained in the business. Equity can be measured by subtracting the total business liabilities (what the company owes) from the total assets (property, money, and other items of value the company owns). The original financing of nearly all businesses, particularly small businesses, is equity financing. A person opening a restaurant, retail store, or repair garage invests his savings to start the business.

FINANCING SMALL BUSINESS

A method of obtaining the use of goods, that is neither equity nor debt, is *leasing*. A *lease* is essentially a long-term rental contract. Almost anything that is durable can be leased. Stores, factories, and other buildings are very commonly leased by the users. Machinery, equipment, trucks, office furniture, typewriters, and similar items are often leased. Leasing is particularly attractive to small businesses. If the small businessman's financial resources are stretched thin, a common condition of small enterprises, he can conserve his funds by leasing rather than buying. On the other hand leasing is apt to be more expensive in the long run than purchasing an item. Leasing is taken up more extensively in Chapter 24.

Debt is created when money is borrowed or goods and services received for which payment is to be made in the future. At the start of a new business it is usually difficult to borrow. Lenders are reluctant to extend loans unless there is a strong probability of repayment. After a business has operated successfully for a few months and has established a credit rating, lenders are more willing to lend.

The principal sources of debt financing for small firms are the following:

> Commercial banks
> Wholesalers and suppliers
> Finance companies
> The Small Business Administration
> Small business investment companies

COMMERCIAL BANKS

Commercial banks are primarily a source of short-term loans (repayment due in 1 year or less). However, banks also extend loans for periods longer than a year. The variety of credit available at commercial banks has earned them the label "department store of credit." As a matter of fact most small businesses depend almost entirely upon commercial banks for the cash loans they need.

A small businessman should choose a commercial bank carefully. Once having chosen, he should maintain his association with the bank indefinitely, making a change only for compelling reasons. A bank aggressively promoting its services, with eager and accommodating officers, can be very useful to a small business. Such a banker, unable to grant a request from one of his customers for a loan, will often spend considerable time in an effort to locate another source of funds. The banker will provide credit references and financial counseling, and in many other ways will act as a financial godfather to the small businessman.

WHOLESALERS AND SUPPLIERS

When a businessman orders $1,000 of goods from a company under terms permitting payment to be made 30 days later, he is receiving credit from the company. Often a retailer can purchase goods from a wholesaler on 30- or 60-day payment terms, sell the goods to his retail customers, and with the cash received make payment to the wholesaler before the due date for payment. Because the credit extended by wholesalers and manufacturers is tied to the sales made by them, the credit is generally extended on more generous terms than is the case with cash loans. A new business, struggling for existence, may be refused loans from banks and other sources of cash but will often be granted credit from wholesalers and manufacturers.

Finance companies primarily finance the purchase of automobiles and other consumer durable goods. Many finance companies also extend credit to small businesses. A small businessman may turn to a finance company if he is refused a loan from a bank. The interest rates charged are generally higher than bank rates.

FINANCE COMPANIES

The lending activities of this agency of the federal government are discussed with its other services later in this chapter.

SMALL BUSINESS ADMINISTRATION

In 1958 Congress passed a bill providing for the establishment of a new type of privately owned lending institution called a "small business investment company" (SBIC). Companies organized under this act raise money by selling their own stock to investors, raise more by borrowing from the Small Business Administration, and extend long-term financing to small businesses. They are permitted considerable latitude in their operations. Small businesses can get funds by borrowing from an SBIC or get equity capital by selling stock to it (if the small enterprise is a corporation). Most loans run from 5 to 15 years.

SMALL BUSINESS INVESTMENT COMPANIES

In 1969 the Commerce Department of the federal government launched a program to organize SBICs specifically to finance small firms organized and run by minorities (blacks, Mexican-Americans, and American Indians). Called Minority Enterprise Small Business Investment Companies (MESBIC), these companies make loans mostly to small enterprises located in the older areas near the centers of large cities.

During the decade of the 1960's there was a rapid growth in franchising. By 1970 about 1,000 franchise companies were in operation and over 600,000 outlets had been franchised.

FRANCHISE BUSINESS

What is a franchise? It is a contract between a company making a product or creating a service and a businessman distributing the product or furnishing the service locally. The company, called the *franchisor*, provides the product that the local businessman, called the *franchisee*, agrees to sell, usually within a territory reserved to him. The franchisor engages in national advertising, establishes standards of operation, and promotes the common business of franchisor and franchisees.

In the usual franchise agreement the franchisee pays the franchisor an initial fee (sometimes as low as $1,000, sometimes $50,000 or higher, either in one lump sum or in installments), for the privilege of obtaining the franchise. In addition the franchisee pays a monthly percentage of his receipts. He is also required to purchase certain products and supplies exclusively from the franchisor and is usually forbidden to handle competing products. In exchange the franchisee receives the right to sell the product or service within the territory allotted to him. He also receives management advice, bookkeeping forms, and occasional local promotions.[4] In most cases the architecture of the outlet, location, design of interior, and other details conform to a uniform design. A few franchisors provide no training in operating the business. Most provide some training, and some provide intensive training. Among the better-known franchisors are the major oil corporations, automobile manufacturers, Midas Muffler, Hertz Rent-A-Car, Holiday Inns, McDonald's (hamburgers), and Kentucky Fried Chicken.

To many a person with some money to invest in a business, a franchise is a welcome proposition. The franchisee receives help in getting started and continuing assistance while operating, the product already has an established name, and there is no competition (from the brand-name product) within a stated area. Some franchisees have become millionaires.

Nevertheless, as in any business, there are hazards, and a person considering buying a franchise should proceed with caution. Among the points to consider are the following:

Long hours
Badly run franchisors
Large investment
Lack of independence
Competition

LONG HOURS   Unless your are willing to work long and hard, managing any small business, franchised or independent, should be avoided.

BADLY RUN FRANCHISORS   In 1966 two brothers formed a company seeking to establish a chain of fried chicken distributors, exploiting the fame of country-style singer Minnie Pearl. By early 1969 more than 1,600 franchises had been bought by eager entrepreneurs. But very little help was given the franchisees in site selection, organization, record

[4]According to an executive of one franchisor, the bookkeeping forms, manual of instructions, and operating equipment are designed "to create fail-safe equipment and simple management techniques so that not even the dumbest franchisee will be able to misuse them." Charles G. Burck, "Franchising's Troubled Dream World," *Fortune*, March 1970, p. 104.

keeping, and training. Supervision was spotty. By the end of 1969 only 263 outlets remained in operation.

Although more spectacular than most, the collapse of the Minnie Pearl Chicken franchises was not isolated. Among the franchise operations promoted during the 1960s were quite a few that were hastily organized, often using the name of a famous actor, singer, or athlete. They were aggressively sold but poorly managed. Most quickly disappeared—along with the money deposited by the franchisees.

LARGE INVESTMENT

Some franchises require no direct payment to the franchisor. Some cost tens of thousands of dollars. It is not true that the former are invariably worthless, but it is true that the franchises offering the highest probability of success generally require a considerable cash investment by the franchisee.

LACK OF INDEPENDENCE

A franchisee is required to conform to whatever degree of standardization the franchisor requires. In most cases this means that all outlets must appear similar to the public. It can also mean standard hours of operation, methods of operation, advertising, reporting finances, purchasing, and hiring of employees. This can be a boon to the person with limited business experience, but it can be a deadening influence on a man with imagination. One franchisor sums it up in these words:

> That independent businessman idea is misunderstood. Maybe in Samoa you can find one. A man becomes a franchisee because he wants to belong. If he tells me he wants a franchise because he doesn't like to take orders, I don't care if he's the President's brother; I won't sign him on.[5]

COMPETITION

When a franchisor gives a franchisee an exclusive territory, the only competition that is barred from the territory is that of another outlet of the same franchisor. If you should be granted a Ford dealership exclusively for a town, you would be the sole Ford dealer in that town. But you would have competition from Chevrolet, Plymouth, American Motors, and others.

Competition from outlets of competitive franchisors can be strenuous. This was particularly true of the luncheonette, drive-in eating industry in the late 1960s. And it has been true for many decades among gasoline service stations. Even with a franchise from a well-established franchisor with a popular product, the franchisee must constantly keep on his toes.

[5] Ibid., p. 105.

THE SMALL BUSINESS ADMINISTRATION

The Small Business Administration (SBA), an agency of the Department of Commerce, was created by act of Congress in 1953 for the purpose of aiding small businesses. The aids include the following:

Improving access to equity funds and loans
Providing information
Offering advice and counsel on management problems of all kinds
Help in obtaining government contracts and orders
Help in recovering from natural disasters

Anyone who is a small businessman or who aspires to become one should get acquainted with the SBA. The regional offices of the Department of Commerce, located in the major cities of the United States, provide bases for the activities of the SBA in each of the regions served by the cities.

IMPROVING ACCESS TO EQUITY FUNDS AND LOANS

A small business needing funds should apply to a commercial bank or other non-government source of credit. If a loan under reasonable conditions is not available from private sources, an application can be made to the SBA for a direct loan. The amount requested can be less than $1,000 or as high as $350,000. The time period of the loan can be as long as 10 years.

The policy of the SBA is to encourage small businessmen to seek funds from private sources wherever possible. Sometimes a bank or other lending institution agrees to extend a loan but in an amount less than that requested by the borrower. In such cases the SBA may participate in the loan agreement by lending the difference. The SBA is permitted by law to make a loan jointly with a private lender (such a loan is called a "participation loan") where the SBA participation is not in excess of 90 percent of the joint amount. Also, the SBA share of a participation loan may not be more than $350,000 and the maximum period of the SBA share is 10 years.

One of the indirect means of SBA financial aid is by lending money to SBICs, which in turn lend to small business borrowers. The financing activities of the SBICs were discussed earlier in this chapter.

If a flood, earthquake, windstorm, or other act of nature strikes a city or region and the President declares the region a disaster area, residents of the area are eligible to borrow from the SBA at 3 percent per annum—for periods of as long as 30 years. On disaster loans the limit of $350,000 to one borrower does not apply. The stated purpose of disaster loans is to permit businessmen to repair or rebuild damaged buildings and other property so that the economy of a ravaged region can recover more rapidly than would be possible through private enterprise alone. Persons in regions affected have welcomed federal money made available by the SBA under the generous terms of the disaster program.[6]

PROVIDING INFORMATION

The SBA publishes a wide range of booklets, pamphlets, and other printed material. The pamphlets and some of the booklets are available free from the field offices of the SBA or from the head office in Washington. The publications are in simple, easy-to-understand language and cover every conceivable management problem that might confront a businessman. Representative titles are given below:

> Term Loans in Small Business Financing
> Loan Sources in the Federal Government
> Sales Forecasting for Small Business
> How to Reduce Your Operating Costs
> Judging Your Purchasing Efficiency
> Materials Control for Small Plants

OFFERING ADVICE AND COUNSEL

If a small businessman has a problem for which a solution is not apparent, he can take his problem to the SBA. A letter to the regional office describing the problem will bring a response. It is better, if the distance is not too great, to arrange a visit to an office of the SBA.

The SBA sponsors seminars, lectures, and instructional programs designed to help businessmen in the operation of their firms. These emphasize practicality rather than theory. Frequently they are held on college and university campuses, with the educational institution acting as co-sponsor. When there is a fee for attendance, it is nominal.

HELP IN OBTAINING FEDERAL GOVERNMENT CONTRACTS AND ORDERS

The law creating the SBA states, "It is the declared policy of Congress that the Government insure that a fair proportion of the total purchases and contracts for supplies and services for the government be placed with small business enterprises."[7] The SBA furnishes businessmen with information on purchases and contracts that agencies of the federal government plan to make. The SBA counsels businessmen

[6] The willingness, perhaps eagerness, of the SBA in distributing money to disaster areas has become a matter of controversy in recent years. Following a flood in Fairbanks, Alaska, in 1967, low-interest rate disaster loans made by the SBA included these (from *The National Observer*, June 30, 1969, p. 1):

> The Fairbanks Daily News-Miner suffered $70,000 in damages; the SBA extended a loan of $665,000.
> The Golden Nugget Motel sustained damages of $140,000; the SBA extended a loan of $894,000.
> The owner of a house appraised at a market value of $31,000 before the flood received a loan of $42,500 to repair it.

[7] Public Law 163, 83d Congress.

in the preparation of bids and explains the steps necessary in meeting contract specifications.

SUMMARY   A small business is one that is not dominant in its field, is generally local in its operations, is financed by one or a few persons, and is managed by one or a few persons. The proprietorship and partnership forms are most frequent in small businesses, although the corporation is also used. The common reasons why people go into small business for themselves are the dream of making money, the desire to be "one's own boss," prestige, to try out new ideas in business, and the pride of accomplishment.

Disadvantages of operating a small business include the risk of failure, uncertain income, heavy responsibilities, long hours, and the difficulty of attracting and keeping good employees.

To hope for success in running a small business, a person should be willing to take financial risks and to work long hours, be skilled in the arts of persuasion, be alert in recognizing opportunities for profit, have some business experience or training, and enjoy good health.

The principal source of funds for small enterprises is the investment of the owners. Supplementary sources of funds, chiefly in the form of loans, are commercial banks, wholesalers and suppliers, finance companies, the Small Business Administration (SBA), and small business investment companies (SBIC).

A franchise allows a businessman (the franchisee) to operate one unit of a chain of units organized by a firm (the franchisor) operating regionally or nationally. The franchisee receives the benefit of national advertising, management counsel, assistance in operating, and usually exclusive rights to the franchised operation within a specified area. A person with limited business experience often finds operating a franchise less risky than operating an independent business, and is willing to trade independence for the management guidance and established style of operations of a franchise.

The Small Business Administration was created by Congress to aid small enterprisers in securing equity financing and loans, to provide information and education to small businessmen, to offer advice and counsel on management problems, and to help small firms in obtaining contracts and orders from agencies of the federal government. The SBA also makes loans at low interest rates to businesses suffering damage from natural disasters.

QUESTIONS FOR REVIEW

1 Define small business in terms of size, area of operations, financing, and management.
2 What are the attractions of becoming a small businessman?
3 Is it true that new ideas tend to have a better chance of being tried in small business than in large? Why or why not?

4 The failure rate among small businesses is generally higher than among large businesses. Why should this be so?

5 In a small business it is sometimes difficult to attract and keep good employees. Why? Suggest ways that the difficulties can be met.

6 The requisites for success in a small business are listed on p. 96. Are each of these equally important in the success of a service station? A bookstore? Give your reasons.

7 Financing the start of a small business is done mostly through equity rather than debt. What are the reasons for this?

8 What are small business investment companies? How do they help finance businesses?

9 Explain the attraction of a franchise to a person with little experience in business who wants to be "his own boss."

10 What are the services offered by the Small Business Administration to small businessmen?

SELECTED READINGS

Broom, H. N., and J. G. Longenecker: *Small Business Management*, 3d ed., South-Western Publishing Company, Cincinnati, 1971.

Bunn, Verne A.: *How to Buy a Small Business*, Boston Technical Publishers, Cambridge, Mass., 1970.

Mason, Joseph G.: *How to Build Your Management Skills*, McGraw-Hill Book Company, New York, 1971.

Petrof, John V., Peter S. Carusone, and John E. McDavid: *Small Business Management*, McGraw-Hill Book Company, New York, 1972.

Small Business Administration: *Annual Report*, Small Business Administration, Washington, D.C. (Published annually. Write to U.S. Government Printing Office.)

Name	**Section**	**Date**

COMPLETION SENTENCES

1 The area of operations of a company defined as small business is generally

local .

2 In a small business _the owner_ typically manage the company.

3 The odds in favor of getting rich by starting a small business are

very small .

4 To achieve maximum independence of action, organize a business as a

proprietorship .

5 Bureaucracy and inertia are not confined to _big gov_ .

6 The rate of failure is higher for _small_ than for

large firms

7 In a small enterprise most of the policy decisions are made by

owner / manager

8 In a small business _The owner_ takes the profits and absorbs the losses.

9 _Lack of Exp._ is a very important factor in the failure of a small business.

10 Before opening a small business of your own, you should, if possible, _work for someone else_

11 The equity of a company can be measured by subtracting the _liabilities_ from the _assets_.

12 Most small businesses depend almost entirely upon the _comm. bank_ for the cash loans they need.

13 If a small businessman is refused a loan from a bank, he can sometimes get a cash loan from a _finance_ company.

14 In general the franchises that offer the highest probability of success require the highest _cash invest._.

15 Anyone who is a small businessman or who aspires to become one should get acquainted with the _SBA_.

TRUE OR FALSE STATEMENTS

F **1** A small retail business is one that has annual sales of not more than $50,000, according to the definition of the Small Business Administration.

F **2** To be classified as a small business a retail firm cannot qualify if it has sales on a nationwide basis.

T **3** In large businesses the corporation form is used almost exclusively.

Name   Section   Date

T **4** A person aspiring to operate a small business should be motivated by more than a desire for wealth.

F **5** Large businesses discourage new ideas from their employees.

T **6** One result of intense competition is bankruptcy for some businesses.

F **7** A typical small business operates in more than one industry.

F **8** If there is a depression in an industry, the larger members are less likely to survive.

T **9** In a typical small business the owner works longer hours than he would as an employee of a large firm.

T **10** Lack of business experience is one of the leading causes of failure in a small business.

T **11** Equity represents ownership.

F **12** Banks do not make loans to businesses for periods longer than 1 year.

T **13** Generally credit is extended by wholesalers and manufacturers to their customers on more generous terms than are available from banks.

T **14** Loans from a small business investment company usually are for terms of several years.

T **15** The franchisee is required to conform to whatever degree of standardization the franchisor requires.

EXERCISES

1 The requisites for success in operating a small business are:

Willingness to take financial risk
Long hours of work
Powers of persuasion
Recognizing opportunity
Experience
Good health

a Arrange the above in descending order of importance in operating (1) a service station, (2) a bookstore, (3) a small company making furniture, (4) a local weekly newspaper. For each of the four cases, write a brief statement indicating the reasons for your ranking.

b Appraise your own capability in each of the six requisites listed above for the four businesses listed in the table. Is it high or low? Explain briefly.

Service station	Bookstore	Furniture manufacturer	Newspaper

2 From your library or other source secure the following information:
  a Titles of at least five pamphlets or booklets recently published by the Small Business Administration (SBA)
  b The address of the SBA field office nearest you
  c The steps for preparing an application for a loan from the SBA
3 Select a business in which you are interested (such as a bakery, bicycle shop, TV repair shop, or restaurant). After investigation, write a report answering the following questions:
  a Where would you locate the business?

Name   Section   Date

b How would you get experience in the business?

c How much competition is there already?

d How much money would it take to get started?

In modern society everyone belongs to organizations. Some are formal, some informal, some complex, some simple. Think back over the past year. Try to identify the organizations you have belonged to. Note the elements of an organization, as discussed in this chapter.

Although *systems analysis* may appear to be a formidable-sounding term, the principle is not difficult to grasp, and once you have grasped it, you can apply it in many different contexts. Read this section carefully.

Examine the organization charts of this chapter. Compare them, and try to pick out in your own mind the advantages and disadvantages of each for different types of business activity. Bear in mind, however, that these organization charts indicate the characteristics of official or formal organization. Regardless of the form of business organization, individual human beings are involved. And, because human beings are gregarious animals, there will be many informal organizations within the structure of any corporation or business firm. The lines of authority indicated in these charts, therefore, are never the exclusive means of communication between different levels in any organization.

In Chapter 4 forms of business organization were discussed. These were legal forms, such as proprietorship, partnership, and corporation. This chapter takes up internal forms of organization. The two meanings of organization are different. Thus, a partnership and a corporation, although differing in their legal organization, might have the same form of internal organization. By the same token, two firms with the same legal form, such as a corporation, might have different types of internal organization.

An organization is a system of related elements operating in concert to achieve a common goal. Organization results from the need for cooperation. Without organization a group of people is a mob; with organization the group can become an efficient, effective force.

**NATURE OF
ORGANIZATION**

Organization comes into being when members of a group share a common goal, agree to work toward the goal, and are able to communicate with each other. Each person has his assigned task and is responsible for doing it at the proper time. If any person fails to perform his task, the total effort will suffer. Take football, for example. If 11 players take the field in a haphazard manner, positioning themselves wherever their fancy strikes, the opposition will score easily. Now have the players organize into a team with each player responsible for a specific position. With no increase in individual athletic ability, the team is more effective than the disorganized individuals were previously.

Organization has become so much a part of human life that it affects to greater or less degree almost all of our relationships with other people. A car pool is an organization. A family is an organization. The organization may be very formal, very rigid, and very complex; or it may be informal, loose, and simple. An organization such as a national government may exist for hundreds of years; or an organization may last no longer than it takes to play a game of doubles on a tennis court.

An organization contains the following elements:

Unity of purpose
Delegation of responsibilities
Coordination of effort
Control

The members of an organization must work toward the same goal. Each member should know how his efforts will contribute toward the goal. In some cases this is obvious. In an eight-oared scull each oarsman is aware of his contribution toward moving the craft through the water. In a large factory each worker's contribution is not so obvious; but if it is explained to him, he is more likely to work better.

Each member must know what is expected of him in the organization. If he is unclear about what his responsibilities are, he cannot direct his effort effectively toward the common goal. The importance of clear division of responsibilities varies with the type of organization. If one member of a family is uncertain whether today is his turn to feed the cat, the cat may go hungry, but it will not starve. But if a crew member of a spacecraft orbiting the earth is uncertain in the slightest what his responsibilities are, disaster may result. In a small business each worker might be told his responsibilities verbally; in a large organization job responsibilities are typically in writing.

It is not sufficient for a member to know what he is expected to do; it is just as important that he know when, where, and how long he is supposed to do it. Coordination of effort is vital to any organization. A team of horses may pull, but if they do not pull together, the wagon may not move.

For organization to be effective, there must be control. In an informal organization control may not be visible, or the degree of control may be very low.

If three women are preparing a joint meal in a kitchen, it is not necessary that one give orders to the other two. But in such a situation it usually develops that one of the women controls the joint effort, usually through suggestions, so that the various parts of the meal will be ready at the proper time. In a large, complex organization control is formalized. There are numerous levels of authority, and at each level the authority is divided among numerous officers or executives. To make a group of several hundred or several thousand individuals operate as a unit requires a division of authority both vertically among different levels and horizontally at each level. The organization chart of a business illustrates this, as is seen in Figure 6-1.

The nature of groupings of people has long been a subject of analysis. From these studies a body of knowledge has developed, known as *organization theory*, which seeks to explain and illuminate the nature of human organization. Theories of organization have used not only the disciplines of business administration but those of psychology and sociology as well. We cannot delve into this subject deeply in this book. However, we shall take up one facet of modern organization theory: systems analysis.

ORGANIZATION THEORY AND SYSTEMS ANALYSIS

Systems analysis, particularly that which treats of business organizations, is based on the assumption that the logical way to study an organization is to study it as a system. This approach can be framed in the form of questions such as the following:

What are the parts of the system?

How does each part depend for successful operation upon the other parts of the system?

What are the processes by which the parts of the system are linked together, so that the parts form a cohesive whole?

What are the goals of the system, and how do the efforts of each part contribute to the goals?

To appreciate how systems analysis might be used in studying a business corporation, consider the corporation as a system and apply the above questions to it. In the paragraphs to follow we shall expand on the concepts raised by the above questions. Although each researcher on organization theory has his own special emphases or innovations, there is one concept unifying nearly all: that systems analysis must consider the organization in its totality.

The basic part of any system is the individual person. His relationship to others is determined by the organization structure, which can be most easily illustrated by an organization chart. A chart shows each individual whom he supervises, who

THE PARTS OF THE SYSTEM AND THEIR INTERDEPENDENCE

FIGURE 6-1 Organization chart of a large corporation.

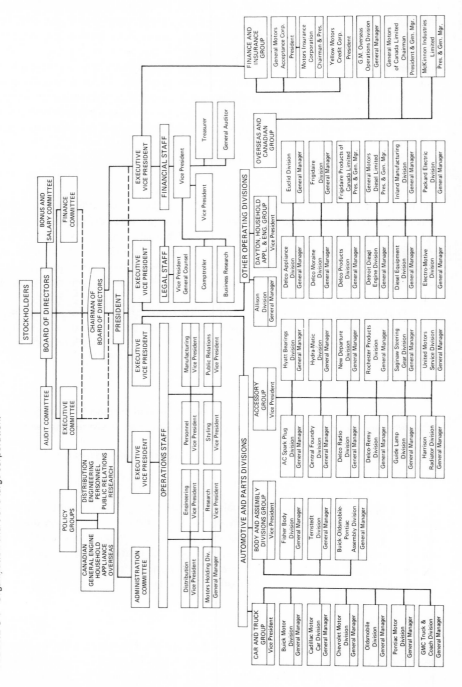

supervises him, and who is at the same level as he. The organization structure also indicates the nature of his responsibilities (sales, production, finance) and the relationship of these responsibilities to the system as a whole.

The relationships between individuals in a system are not defined by the formal organization chart alone. Because systems analysis emphasizes totality, the informal organizations of any system must be considered. An informal organization is any pattern of relationships between individuals not included in a formal organization. In systems analysis all the paths of contact between one individual and another, between individuals and groups, and between one group and another are examined.

INFORMAL ORGANIZATION

The physical setting has a bearing on the relationships between individuals in a system and on the effectiveness of the system. For example, the relationships between officers will be different when each has a private office from what it is when two or three officers are placed in each office. If workers are crowded together, their attitudes toward the other parts of the organization will probably be less cooperative than if they have plenty of room. Similarly, noise, temperature, and attractiveness of furnishings will affect the organization through their effects on the individuals. It is in treating these and similar problems that the disciplines of psychology, sociology, and physiology are useful to the systems analyst.

PHYSICAL SETTING

Communication is what holds any organization together. Much of systems analysis is devoted to study of the communications network of an organization. There are numerous means of communication in any system: written memoranda, spoken directions, the shrug of shoulders, the raising of eyebrows, and many others. The usefulness of systems analysis to business is in finding ways to improve communications.

THE LINKING PROCESS

Finally, in systems analysis the purpose for which an organization exists is studied. Each part of the organization contributes to the organization's goals or detracts from these goals. Analysts examine the effectiveness of various types of organizational structures in achieving goals. They also examine how communications, the physical setting, and other factors promote the desired objectives.

THE GOALS OF THE ORGANIZATION

The internal organization of a firm may develop as a result of careful study and analysis of the operations to be performed so that a form of organization may be selected that will best serve to carry out these operations. In other instances,

PURPOSE OF ORGANIZATION

the organization may be the result of haphazard growth over a period of years with no thought given to developing the most efficient type of organization. Yet whether conscious attention is given to the development of the form of organization or whether it is unplanned, each business firm will develop an organizational pattern following one of several general forms. These general forms will be explained in this chapter.

The organizational structure provides the means by which control of the business activity may be exercised by the top management down through the various levels of the organization. The form of organization selected for a particular business should thus be one that facilitates effective control of the operations and permits free communication of information downward from the top level as well as upward from the lowest level.

The organizational framework can be best visualized by referring to an organizational chart such as the ones illustrated in this chapter. The chart is a diagrammatic representation of the relationship of different staff members and employees. Such charts can be compared to the diagrams used in representing football plays. Just as football plays may be executed from one of several basic formations, the operations of a business may be carried on with one of several types of organizational structure.

Furthermore, as different football formations are developed to meet varying situations and no one of these formations is perfect for every need, there are various types of business organization, no one of which is ideal for every type of business activity. Each organization has its peculiar advantages and disadvantages. The selection of a particular form of organization should take into consideration the requirements of that particular business activity. Even in a single firm, it might be advisable to organize some departments along different lines from others, in response to the particular needs of the departments. Indeed, although the organization forms discussed here are considered as separate and distinct types, in actual business operations we might find various combinations and modifications of these basic types.

In any organizational structure of a medium-size or large business or institution, the levels of authority may run to 10, 20, or more. Nevertheless, these may be grouped into four categories, as shown in Figure 6-2. Top management is primarily concerned with major decisions that concern the business as a whole. The scope of middle management is more limited, being concerned with interpreting and administering the directives of top management. At the lower levels of operating management, authority is even more restricted, the latitude in interpreting directives "from the top" is less, and more time is spent in direct supervision of subordinates. In general the lower the level on an organization chart, the greater is the proportion of time spent in direct supervision, in following directives, and in filling out reports, and the smaller is the proportion of time spent in "thinking out" new ideas. Conversely, the higher the level on the organizational ladder, the greater is the proportion of time spent in reviewing reports from below, attending committee meetings, preparing plans, and determining policy.

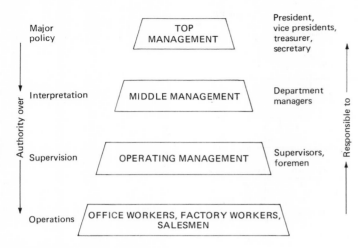

FIGURE 6-2 Levels of authority.

The *line organization* is also called the *military organization*. This form is used in business as well as in the military, but down through the years it has been identified as the typical army form despite the fact that it is no longer followed closely by military groups.[1] The principal characteristic of the line organization is the direct flow of authority from the top executive officer down through the various levels to the lowest, as is shown in Figure 6-3. The number of *echelons*, or levels of authority, in such an organization depends on the number of people and the limitations imposed by the span of control for the particular activity involved.

> As an illustration, consider the organization structure required for a group of 100 soldiers whose activities require only a small amount of supervision. In such a situation, 10 privates might be organized into a squad commanded by a sergeant, and two or three squads might be formed into a platoon commanded by a lieutenant. These, in turn, might be organized into a company of two or more platoons commanded by a captain. The line of authority flows in a direct line from the captain to the lieutenants to the sergeants to the privates.

> If the activities require closer supervision, fewer privates would be supervised by each sergeant. The number of squads would have to be increased, with a resulting

LINE ORGANIZATION

[1] The evolution of organizational patterns has depended greatly on military organization. The triumphs of Alexander the Great and Julius Caesar over more numerous and frequently better-equipped soldiers were due in large measure to the superior organization and tighter control of the Greek and Roman armies compared to the loose organization of the opposing hordes. The raids of the Mongols under Genghis Khan and his successors crushed Christian and Moslem forces through superior organization and mobility. Gibbon reports in *Decline and Fall of the Roman Empire* that "It was wonderful how punctually and effectually the arrangements of the [Mongol] commander were carried out in operations extending from the Lower Vistula to Transylvania. Such a campaign was quite beyond the vision of any European commander."

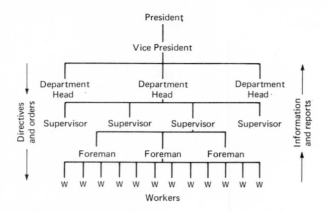

FIGURE 6-3   A line organization.

increase in the number of platoons and companies. Thus, if the span of control is smaller, the number of echelons or intermediate levels of command will be increased, with the result that the flow of authority from the top to the lowest level will have to pass through a greater number of intermediate officers.

In a business, the work of several employees may be directed by a foreman who, in turn, is under the supervision of a section chief, who is supervised by a department head, who is supervised by the top executive of the company. Until the beginning of the present century, this form of business organization was, for the most part, borrowed from the military. Oddly enough, in recent years, the Army, Navy, and Air Force have adopted some of the other organizational structures developed in business corporations.

Before we turn to these other forms, let us consider some of the advantages and disadvantages of the line organization. The first advantage resides in the unity of command it achieves. Each individual is responsible to only one superior, and the flow of authority from the top to the bottom is accomplished by a single line: There can be no confusion as to who is the "boss." Each individual receives his orders from the officer immediately above him in the chain of command.

This advantage of unity of command is reduced to some extent since this type of compartmentalization of the individual units makes communication among the various lower levels difficult. The primary means of communication among the lower units is up through the line of authority of one unit and down through the line of authority again until the other lower unit is reached. Some direct communication is permitted between two units at the same level, of course, but for the most part communication is restricted to the established lines of authority. Such direct communications among the lower units can be only of an informal nature rather than an order, since orders can be transmitted only along the established lines of authority.

Another weakness is that the communication lines tend to be lengthy. Formal communication follows the established lines of authority from top to bottom and from bottom to top. This is illustrated by the saying that the general tells the colonel, the colonel tells the major, the major tells the captain, and so on down the line until finally the order reaches the privates.

But the cumbersome procedure of transmitting orders through each level of authority is necessary for effective operations. This can be seen if we consider what happens when, for example, a general gives an order directly to a private without the intermediate officers' being aware of the order. A captain may then, unaware, assign duties to the private and, as a result, the unity of command has been destroyed, because the private now has conflicting orders from two superiors and is in the difficult position of choosing which to obey. It might appear logical for him to obey the orders of the highest ranking officer, but to do so would mean disregarding the orders of his immediate superior, to whom he is directly responsible, both now and in the future. Whatever choice the private makes is difficult. The usual solution is for him to inform the captain of the general's order. Even if this explanation is made and accepted by the superior, the problem does not end. It is still necessary for the immediate superior to pass the explanation on up the successive levels of authority in order that those who have been bypassed may be eventually informed of the action taken.

In the line organization, each level of authority is merely a subdivision of the level immediately above it. At any level the executive is responsible for all activities of the employees under his supervision. This means that all supervisors and executives have general rather than specialized authority and must, as a result, be familiar with all the activities of the organization. In a pure line organization, the operations of any one of the subdivisions are identical with the operations of any other subdivision at the same organizational level, since the basis of the line organization is the repeated subdivision of the operations into identical units as the size of the company increases. As a result, there is little if any specialization, and all management officials must have a broad, general knowledge of the operations. This is an advantage to the extent that when an executive is promoted to a high position of authority, his duties are similar but broader in scope. The line form provides excellent training at the lower levels for future top management officials. However, it is difficult to find enough executives with broad talent to fill all of the executive positions at the various organizational levels. This is, perhaps, the greatest weakness of the line organization.

FUNCTIONAL ORGANIZATION

It was the difficulty of securing a sufficient number of people who possessed all the qualities of leadership required by the line organization that led Frederick Taylor[2] to experiment with what he termed the *functional* form of organization,

[2]Taylor, sometimes called the father of *scientific management*, exerted considerable influence over the development of techniques of production and control.

a chart of which is shown in Figure 6-4. He held that it was almost impossible to find all of the executive qualities in a single individual. The person possessing sufficient technical ability might lack the ability to communicate his ideas to others or lack the ability to motivate those working under him to do their best. Taylor felt that it would be much easier to find several individuals, each of whom possessed some of the qualities required of a good supervisor, and to divide the work of a superior or foreman among as many as eight different individuals. Thus, an individual who was technically proficient would be responsible for the technical phase of the foreman's job. The record-keeping duties of the foreman might be assigned to another individual, who would not be required to exert personal leadership or technical supervision over the employees—and so on.

It is obvious that this plan of organization destroys the unit of command which was the greatest advantage of the line organization. For now, instead of each worker having a single "boss," each worker has as many as eight persons giving him orders. As a result, although the work of the foreman has been simplified, the worker has been placed in a difficult position. If he is to know what to do, it is necessary for all of these eight foremen to coordinate their work so that they will not give conflicting orders. Although the problem of securing good foremen has been simplified, an even more difficult problem may have been created. While the separate foremen may coordinate their activities, it is almost impossible for the average worker to understand this division of authority and to know when he is expected to take orders from one or another of the various bosses. Besides, each worker is subjected to the emphasis or interest of each of his bosses, as shown in Figure 6-5, making it difficult for a worker to satisfy all of his bosses.

LINE AND STAFF ORGANIZATION

The division of authority of the functional organization prevented any one of the foremen from exercising overall leadership and made it almost impossible for the average worker to understand what was expected of him. For this reason, Taylor's functional plan was never widely adopted in industry and was in use only for a short period of time in the few instances in which it was adopted. Its only

FIGURE 6-4   A functional organization.

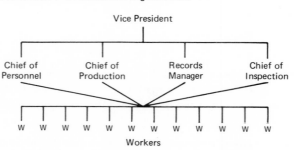

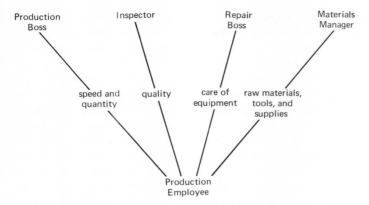

FIGURE 6-5 Division of emphasis in a functional organization.

importance was that it formed the basis for a form of organization that has become widely adopted today: the *line and staff* organization. Shown diagrammatically in Figure 6-6, it maintains the unity of command and the clear line of authority of the line organization. Added to the line organization at various levels are staff officers whose duties are specialized much as were the duties of the various foremen under the functional plan.

The functional organization divides the supervisory responsibility among several individuals, none of whom can be considered as the boss. The line and staff form maintains the clear-cut authority of a single individual who is clearly recognized as the boss. This is accomplished by giving authority (as in the pure line form) to one executive at each level. However, at any level there may be, in addition to the line executive, one or more staff executives.

Although the *line executive* has general responsibility for the operation of the entire department or branch, the *staff executives* have specialized duties limited to a particular phase of the work of the department or branch. The staff

FIGURE 6-6 A line and staff organization.

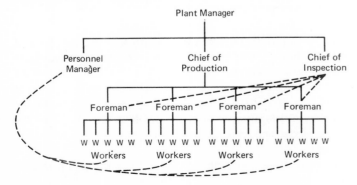

executives, as specialists, are not required to possess a broad knowledge of all phases of the operation, and since they do not usually exercise authority over the personnel in the department or branch, they are not required to possess as high a degree of leadership ability as are line executives. Through this division of work, the greatest advantage of the functional form of organization is achieved. In contrast to the functional form, however, one executive has prime authority, while the other (staff) executives exercise limited authority and are frequently responsible to the line executive much as any other employee. The function of a staff executive is to advise the line executive and to recommend possible courses of action. To the extent that the final action taken by the line executive is based on the advice of the staff officer, the latter may exert considerable influence on the operations of the department or branch. However, this influence is exerted through the line executive, and only with the consent of the line executive. The strengths and weaknesses of the line organization compared with the line and staff organization are summarized below:

LINE ORGANIZATION

Pro	Con
1 No confusion as to who is boss. 2 Simplicity. 3 Easier to fix responsibility. 4 Decisions can be made quickly.	1 Each boss must administer various aspects of supervision. 2 Too much concentration of power in each boss. 3 Eliminates specialization of management.

LINE AND STAFF ORGANIZATION

Pro	Con
1 Utilizes specialized management skills. 2 One boss has authority in most functions of management. 3 Combines most advantages of line and functional organizations.	1 Possible friction between line and staff officers over authority. 2 With staff specialists to be consulted, sometimes delay in making decisions. 3 Possible uncertainty in fixing responsibility.

In connection with the authority of staff and line officials, it might be well to consider two types of authority. The first is known as *authority of position*, which indicates the control over others that an individual exerts as a result of his position in the organization. All line executives possess such authority as a result of the positions they hold. The second type of authority is known as *authority of situation*; it is derived not by a delegation from above but from the ability of the individual, through his knowledge and ideas, to influence others to accept his plan of action in a given situation.

The distinction between these two types of authority is important in considering the relationship between line and staff officials. Line officials derive authority as a result of their line positions. This does not mean that they do not possess authority of situation, for since most line officials demonstrate knowledge and ability to their staff, they will also be respected for their ability as well as for their positions. Staff officials, on the other hand, have very limited authority as a result of their position in the organization and, for the most part, derive their authority from their ability to provide the line official with satisfactory solutions to special problems that confront him.

The line and staff organization requires that a delicate balance be maintained in the relationship between line and staff executives. In theory, the specialized ability of the staff officer should complement the broad, general ability of the line officer and permit a division of work that will provide the best solutions to the problems encountered in the administration of a business activity. Although we do not encounter the definite division of authority that was found in the functional organization, there is always the possibility that a staff officer may assume line authority whenever a line officer is reluctant to exercise the authority delegated to him.

Strictly interpreted, the line and staff organization provides that the staff officer exercise authority only through a line officer. Often, however, such a procedure is time-consuming. As a result, staff officials are generally given authority by line officials to exercise direct supervision in specific areas of management. As an example, we might refer again to the similarity of the business organization to a football team. The trainer, who is responsible for keeping the players in good physical condition, occupies the position of the staff official of the organization. His position is distinct from that of the assistant coaches, who exercise authority over the players only as directed by the head coach. The trainer's duties are specialized and different in nature from those of the head coach and assistant coaches. In addition to looking after the physical welfare of the players, he is responsible for advising the coaching staff at all times of the physical condition of the team and he makes recommendations about their fitness to participate in games and practice. Strictly speaking, it is up to the head coach, acting on the advice of the trainer, to make the final decision as to whether each player should play. However, the coach may delegate authority to the trainer to order a player to miss a practice, if, in his opinion, the physical condition of the player is such that it would injure his health. Authority in this case is limited and does not allow the trainer to excuse a player for any reason other than health.

The nature of the authority of a staff officer is limited in its scope to a particular field of activity, and it may be revoked or countermanded by the line officer. The weakness of the functional organization is a result of the employee's difficulty in determining who is his boss. This problem is not acute in the line and staff organization, but it can develop. In the above illustration, a problem might arise if a player excused by the trainer from a practice session is later told by the coach to play. The player is faced with a conflict of orders because of the failure of the first order to be channeled through the coach. When staff officials exercise direct authority on behalf of a superior officer, it is necessary that they keep the line officer informed of their actions. This policy will avoid most conflicting orders.

While line and staff organization possesses some of the advantages of the line and the functional form, it also has some of the disadvantages of these forms. It provides a degree of specialization not possible in the line organization and avoids, for the most part, the lack of unity of command which is the chief disadvantage of the functional organization. Yet the line and staff organization, being a compromise, cannot provide the full advantages of either the pure line or the pure functional types. At its best, it is superior to either of these other two forms. At its worst, it may have all of the disadvantages of the functional organization without the advantages of the line organization. If it is to be effective, it is necessary at all times that careful attention be given to the maintenance of the proper balance between the line officials and the staff officials.

COMMITTEE ORGANIZATION

The chief distinction of the *committee* form of organization is that, instead of a single individual, a group of officials makes decisions directing a department or section. The use of a committee rather than an individual enables the organization to make use of the training and judgment of all of the members of the group before an important decision is made. This may mean that the decisions reached are better, since they are a result of the thinking of several persons. The process, however, is time-consuming and means that it is almost impossible to arrive at an immediate decision on any matter. Delay is the chief disadvantage of the committee. Furthermore, it requires the time of several executives at each meeting, time which could be devoted to the individual responsibilities of each member. In the line organization, responsibility for decisions (good or bad) can be easily determined, since they are made by individuals. The committee organization does not permit pinpointing of responsibility.

Because of its weaknesses, the committee system is sparingly used. When it is employed, it is most often used to make decisions establishing broad policy. It is also used occasionally as a temporary replacement of a line executive until his successor is selected. Sometimes the committee form is established to provide training for minor executives who will in the future be given individual authority and responsibility. In such a case, the committee can provide experience in making decisions. The use of the committee to train management candidates is usually limited to a few areas within an enterprise where rapid expansion is anticipated and where a larger number of supervisors is expected to be necessary in the near future.

FLAT ORGANIZATION

The *flat organization* differs only slightly from the line organization. The difference results from stretching the span of control until each executive exercises supervision over many more departments or employees than are found in the line organization. This permits fewer echelons or levels of authority in handling large numbers of employees than in a line organization of similar size, and the lines of communication between top and bottom are shorter. On the other hand, the amount of attention each employee receives from his supervisor is less than is possible with the line form. Thus, the flat organization is suited only to those lines of activity in which the work is comparatively routine in nature and can be performed for the most part without constant supervision. In contrast the **tall organization** reflects the need for greater supervision by providing a small number at each level of the organization. These two forms are illustrated in Figure 6-7. An instance in which the flat organization might be effective is the mail-order business. Here the procedures for filling orders can be established in advance, most of the work can be reduced to a set pattern, and supervision can be limited to the handling of the relatively few orders of an unusual nature. The distinction between the flat organization and the regular line organization, however, is largely one of degree.

An organizational chart presents the **formal** organization of a business. Of equal importance are the many **informal** organizations that develop within any organization. While these are subject to constant change, some develop into more rigid patterns, in a few cases as rigid as the formal structure. Although they are not pictured on the organizational chart, their existence must be recognized and consideration be given to them.

INFORMAL ORGANIZATIONS

FIGURE 6-7 Diagrams of flat and tall organization structures.

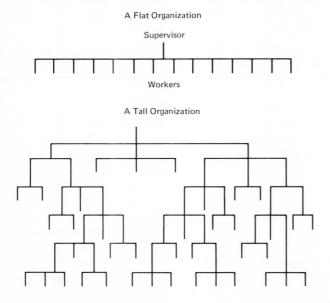

A Flat Organization

Supervisor

Workers

A Tall Organization

Examples of informal organizations are so numerous and their pattern is so varied that it is difficult to describe them briefly. Perhaps they can best be discussed by comparing them with formal organizations. Formal organization provides a relatively long-lived pattern of communication and authority, established by deliberate plan. The position of each individual in the formal plan is known and his relationship to other individuals within the plan is definitely established.

Informal organizations include any patterns of relationships among individuals outside the established organizational structure. In any business of moderate or large size there are hundreds of informal organizations, some existing for a short time, some becoming almost permanent. Examples could include a group of executives meeting together each morning for a coffee break, a group of workers forming a car pool to furnish transportation to and from work, or a weekly session of bridge or any other more or less regular social meeting involving the same individuals. The common characteristic of all of these is that they provide a means of communication in addition to the formal lines of communication, and that they place the individuals in a relationship that may differ from the relationship of the same individuals in the formal organizational structure. The conversation or activity of these groups may have little bearing upon their work within the organization. Yet to the extent that some conversation concerning their work is inevitable, such groups constitute an additional line of communication in the organizational pattern within the company.

If due notice is not given to the existence of informal organizations, executives will find themselves at a loss to explain many attitudes and actions of their employees. News often travels more quickly by the grapevine than by the established channels of communication. This is usually considered unfortunate by executives. But, if an executive has knowledge of the informal organizations that exist, he can often utilize them to advantage in supplementing the normal lines of communication. Or, if he feels it necessary, he can take steps to break up an informal organization if he feels it is responsible for leaking information before a formal announcement. Denying the existence of informal organizations prevents an executive from using them when desirable or curbing their activities when they appear detrimental to the company.

An executive should realize that great care must be taken in any attempt to disturb or break up these informal groupings, because such actions might be construed by employees as unwarranted interference with their freedom as individuals. In most companies, it is inevitable that some informal organizations develop that are incompatible with the formal organizational structure and that might disturb the effective operation of the firm. An extreme example might be the publication of a picture of a company president playing tennis with a newly hired office clerk, since this might have an unfavorable effect on the other clerks. But, for the most part, informal organizations develop among individuals with similar positions and social standing in the organization. An efficient executive will keep informed of the existence of informal organizations in his firm, will disturb them only when necessary, and will use them from time to time as a means of communicating with his employees.

SUMMARY

A group of persons acting without coordination is no better than a mob. The purpose of organization, whether in the military, a business firm, or a hunting expedition, is to have each person's actions complement those of others, so that the group acts together as a team. Different types of organization have developed to meet different needs, since no single type will satisfy the requirements of all organizations. Each business firm should shape its own organization to gain the maximum benefit from the efforts of its officers and employees.

In systems analysis an organization is studied as a (whole) system. A change, for the better or for the worse, in one part of the system affects other parts of the system. Each part of a system must be given careful consideration—for systems analysis emphasizes that no part of a system can be ignored without possible damage to the whole.

The line organization, also called the military organization, gives full authority in all areas of management or command, at each level, to one boss. There is no question as to who is in command over any individual. Authority and responsibility flow in a direct line from the top executive down to the lowest rank of employees.

The functional organization gives each executive authority over only one aspect of the subordinates' activities. One executive may have authority over scheduling of work and assignment of duties; another over hiring, firing, and promotion; a third over inspection of work produced; and a fourth over health and safety. This form permits the use of specialist managers, each expert in one aspect of management. But there is difficulty in making the lines of authority distinct, and there is often confusion as to who is the boss in particular situations.

The line and staff organization is a compromise between the pure line and the functional organization. It aims to combine the best features of each, but it is unable to avoid all of the weaknesses of the line or the functional organization. To get as many of the advantages while minimizing the disadvantages, the line and staff organization uses the basic structure of the line, but gives the line officers a staff of experts or assistants to provide information and advice to the line officers.

In addition to any formal organization of officers and workers, a number of informal organizations always develop. Some have a brief existence, others last a long time. Some include only a few individuals, others have many. They will come into being regardless of encouragement or discouragement by management. Whether "used" by management or not, their existence must be recognized.

QUESTIONS FOR REVIEW

1 What are the elements necessary to make any organization succeed?
2 Communication is what holds any organization together. Explain.
3 Why is the line organization particularly suited to the military? What are its advantages? Its disadvantages?
4 Distinguish between legal forms and internal forms of business.
5 Why is it advisable in most cases in a line organization for communications to go through channels of the line structure rather than bypass intermediate levels in the chain of command?

6 Compare the possible problems and advantages of the single boss of the line organization with several specialized bosses of a functional organization.

7 How does the line and staff form of organization compare with the functional form and with the line form?

8 In the line and staff organization the line executives have prime authority and the staff executives have limited authority. Explain what this means.

9 Distinguish between authority of position and authority of situation.

10 What are the advantages and disadvantages of the committee as a decision-making body? Give examples of questions that might be decided better by a committee than by an individual. Give examples of questions that might be better decided by an individual than by a committee.

11 Why do informal organizations develop in an office?

12 Should management encourage or discourage informal organizations? Give reasons pro and con.

SELECTED READINGS

Baker, Frank: *Organizational Systems*, Richard D. Irwin, Inc., Homewood, Ill., 1973.

Leavitt, Harold S., William Dill, and Henry B. Eyring: *The Organizational World*, Harcourt Brace Jovanovich, Inc., New York, 1973.

Luthans, Fred: *Organizational Behavior*, McGraw-Hill Book Company, New York, 1973.

Scott, William G., and Terence R. Mitchell: *Organization Theory*, Richard D. Irwin, Inc., Homewood, Ill., 1972.

Summer, Charles E., and Jeremiah J. O'Connell: *The Managerial Mind*, Richard D. Irwin, Inc., Homewood, Ill., 1973.

CHAPTER

6 REVIEW ACTIVITIES

Name	Section	Date

COMPLETION SENTENCES

1 Without _____*organ.*_____ a group of people is a mob; with

_____*organization*_____ the group can be effective.

2 The basic part of any business system is the _____*individual*_____ .

3 _____*Communication*_____ is what holds an organization together.

4 A sole proprietorship, a partnership, and a corporation, although differing in

their legal form of organization, might each have the same form of

_____*internal*_____ organization.

5 The _____*line*_____ organization is no longer used by present-

day military organizations.

6 In the line organization, each level of authority is merely a

_____*sub-division*_____ of the level of authority immediately above it.

7 In the line organization, there can be no confusion as to who is the

boss .

8 At any level of authority in the line organization, the executive is responsible

for all activities of the employees under his _supervision_ .

9 The two types of authority of staff officials are known as authority of

ideas and authority of _situation_ .

10 Line officials derive their authority as a result of their line

position .

11 The line and staff form of organization requires that a proper balance be

maintained in the authority and relationship between

line executives and _staff_

executives.

12 The line and staff organization provides that the staff officer will exercise

authority only through his superior line officer.

13 When staff officials exercise direct line authority on behalf of a superior

officer, it is necessary that they keep the line officer _informed_

of their actions if conflicting orders are to be avoided.

14 The chief disadvantage of the committee organization lies in its

slowness to act.

15 The committee organization does not permit pinpointing of

responsibility .

Name   Section   Date

TRUE OR FALSE STATEMENTS

T **1** In a large organization job responsibilities are typically in writing.

F **2** In an informal organization control is absent.

F **3** In systems analysis an organization is studied piecemeal. In organization theory it is studied as a unit.

T **4** The relationship between two officers in a corporation is affected by whether the officers share the same office or have separate offices.

T **5** The line organization is also called the military organization.

F **6** The line organization is at present used extensively by military groups.

T **7** An advantage of the line organization is the unit of command it achieves.

F **8** In the line organization there is some confusion as to who is the boss.

F **9** Communications and cooperation between different groups at the same level of the organization are made easier by the line form.

T **10** In the line organization, each level of organization is merely a subdivision of the level immediately above.

F **11** There is considerable specialization of duties in the line form of organization.

T **12** Frederick Taylor is sometimes called the father of scientific management.

T **13** In the functional organization each worker has several different bosses giving him orders.

T **14** In the line and staff organization, the line executive has general authority while the staff executives have no authority.

F **15** The line and staff organization requires a delicate balance of power between the line and staff officials.

EXERCISES

1 Analyze (1) an automobile and (2) a human body as a system. Treat the following aspects:

   a The "goal" or "purpose" of the system.

b Results of failure in coordination of elements of the system. How coordination is achieved.

c How "directives" are transmitted from the "control center" to the operating elements of the system.

d How the malfunctioning of one element affects the operation of other elements in the system.

Automobile

Human body

2 Select a club, fraternal organization, student organization, instructional department, or other organization. Analyze the organizational structure. From what sources do the officers derive their authority? How are they selected? What improvements can you suggest in the structure of the organization to improve its performance?

3 The manager of an office in which 160 clerks and supervisors work has noticed that for coffee breaks and lunches people go out in the same groups day after day. He wonders if he should discourage this kind of informal organization. He asks your opinion. Outline for him the potential dangers in the indefinite continuation of such groupings, as well as the dangers in interfering with them. Suggest how these groups might be used for the benefit of the company, if they can be used.

Management is a form of leadership, providing direction and order to the operation of business and nonbusiness units alike. As you read this chapter, refer from time to time to Figures 7-1 to 7-5. They will enable you better to understand your reading and to retain the essentials of management in your mind.

Note that to prevent haphazard operation, it is necessary for business managers to align their decisions with specific goals. Although it is axiomatic to accept profits as the primary goal of nearly all businesses, it is not true that profit is the goal of all activities in our economic life. For example, in nonprofit organizations, which are mostly either charitable or government organizations, the goal is obviously something other than profit. Even in some businesses there may be secondary goals almost as important as profit. It is important to determine what these goals are, so that business actions can be guided thereby. To recapitulate, this chapter deals with the formulation of business goals and the means by which these goals may be most efficiently achieved.

Management may be defined as the activity of organizing the work of groups of people so as to achieve a desired objective. Management may also be defined in terms of its functions, as described below. Management requires the willingness and ability to make decisions affecting not only the welfare of the company but perhaps its existence as well. Management is a form of leadership, with activities diagrammed in Figure 7-1 and functions diagrammed in Figure 7-2. The functions of management can be considered as beginning with planning, proceeding to organizing (to implement the plan), directing (to achieve the goals of the plan), and controlling the operations (to keep track of progress and assign responsibility for success or failure). The information from organizing, directing, and controlling in turn provides data on which existing plans are modified and new plans laid. Although a manager, while he is managing, does not directly engage in production, selling, or other similar activities, his contribution is vital to an organization. To repeat our analogy, the manager's role may be compared to that of the conductor of a symphony orchestra.

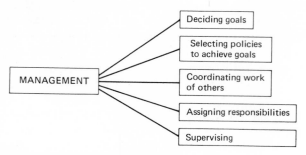

FIGURE 7-1 Activities of management.

FIGURE 7-2 The functions of management.

The conductor plays no instrument and makes no sound, but he is the most important single individual on the concert stage.

Although our primary concern in this chapter is with business organizations, the principles discussed in this and later chapters have validity and utility for other organizations as well. Good management in a hospital is as vital as it is in a furniture factory—perhaps more so. Sound management principles can and should be applied to the operation of colleges, government departments, religious institutions, and even family units. This does not mean that a father should treat his children in a boss-employee relationship or that a minister or rabbi should lecture his congregation the way a corporation president addresses a meeting of department heads. Not all characteristics of business enterprise can be applied to nonbusiness enterprises. But good business management techniques can be adapted, selectively and judiciously, to nearly all endeavors in which groups of people work together toward a common goal.

OWNERSHIP, CONTROL, AND AUTHORITY

The most direct means of control of a business enterprise is through the proprietorship form of organization. The legal ownership of the enterprise and its control are in the hands of a single individual. Even though the owner elects to have someone else take over the day-to-day management of the company, he still may resume the actual direction of the business at any time he desires.

Similarly, in the partnership form, the legal ownership and the control of business activity are usually in the hands of the same few individuals. Legal ownership and control, however, may be separated to some extent. A partnership, though owned by two or more individuals, may be controlled in its day-to-day operations by only one partner, with the other partners remaining inactive. In the partnership as in the proprietorship, legal ownership and control remain in the hands of the same individuals.

In the corporation, we find control separated from ownership by the nature of the organization. The stockholders own the corporation, but the corporation assets are owned by the corporation, not by the stockholders. The control of the corporation property is held by the directors, who are elected by the stockholders. Thus, the assets are owned by the corporation, the corporation is owned by the stockholders, and the directors control the corporation—even though some directors (in rare cases, all) may own no stock.

The board of directors meets periodically (once or twice a month, for example) to receive information from the top company officers. On the basis of this information plus any relevant data from outside the corporation, the directors establish policies and guidelines for the officers. The top officers in turn receive reports from lower officers and issue guidelines to the lower ranks in conformity with the policies adopted by the board of directors. The lower officers make decisions and issue orders to their subordinates and gather information from them for the reports to be submitted to higher management levels. At each lower level of management there is generally less emphasis on "thinking" or "creativity" and more emphasis on "doing" or "activity." This does not mean that persons at the lower levels of an organization are not encouraged to "think" or be "creative"; it is a matter of emphasis and availability of time. These subtle shifts in emphasis are shown diagrammatically in Figure 7-3.

OBJECTIVES OF OWNERS AND MANAGERS

The separation of ownership and control in a corporation has brought about the development of an entirely new group of individuals known as *management*, or sometimes *top management*. The management group is not always separate and distinct from the owners, since some members of the management group may also be members of the owner group. As the size of business units increases, the investment necessary to establish a new business enterprise involves the pooling of the capital of many individuals. Thus, although the managers of the corporation may also be part owners of the corporation, more and more frequently the ownership of stock by the management group represents only a small part of the total.

THE INTERESTS OF MANAGEMENT

Where management has little or no stock in the corporation, the question arises as to whether the interests and objectives of management coincide with the interests of the owners. The simple answer is that the objective of both groups is to operate

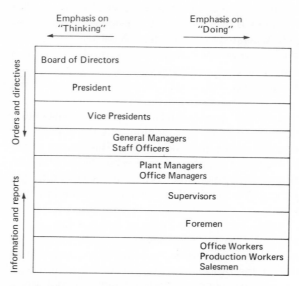

FIGURE 7-3 Management emphasis at various levels of authority.

the firm profitably. But this cannot be achieved if it is the sole objective blindly pursued, since it is only through rendering a service desired by others that any business activity can continue profitably.

DIVERGENCE OF INTERESTS   Where the owners do not actively participate in management, they usually judge the success of the enterprise on the basis of the income received on their investment and usually do not appreciate the importance of long-range development of the business. They may also want the company to pay as large dividends as earnings permit, while management may prefer to keep earnings in the company to expand the enterprise.

Divergence of interest is perhaps best illustrated by the early years of the Ford Motor Company. Although Ford was only one of several owners initially, he was the only one actively participating in management. As a manager, he sought to expand the company rapidly by retaining the earnings of the company and plowing them back rather than distributing them as dividends to himself and the other owners. This eventually led to legal action by the other owners in an effort to force the payment of dividends. Ford then bought the stock held by the other owners, gaining complete ownership and control. The accumulated earnings of many years brought the other owners a return of many times their original investment. Had the earnings been paid out in dividends, the other owners would have received much less.

Although Ford's policy of reinvestment of earnings benefited the owners, the management group is not always motivated by the desire to build a more profitable business for the company owners. Individuals are driven to act by many urges, and the profit motive may not always dominate. Some managers succumb to the ambition to increase their prestige at the expense of increasing the company profits. Some build larger and finer offices than the company can afford. Some engage in "empire building"—hiring more assistants than are needed, which increases the manager's feeling of importance.

COMMUNITY OF INTERESTS

Despite some difference in objectives, the management group must ultimately satisfy the desires of the owner group if it is to continue in office. It must also satisfy the customers of the business if it is to remain in successful operation. In addition to the owners and customers, management must be concerned with the welfare of a third group: the employees of the firm. By respecting the interests of the employees, management can expect to retain their services. The reverse is also true. By serving the interests of the company and its customers, employees can expect the demand for their labor to continue.

The identity of ultimate interest of management and employees exists despite the fact that the income of the employee, which he seeks to maximize, is an item of expense to the company, an expense management seeks to minimize. In spite of the resulting clash of interests, each is necessary to the welfare of the other. Production cannot be achieved without workers, and work cannot be effective unless it is organized and directed in an efficient manner. Thus, the owner group, the management group, and the employee group are necessary to each other, and their company is most successful when the common welfare of all is placed above the separate interests of each.

> **FEELING THE PRESSURE**: Middle-level managers suffer the greatest job stress of all employed groups, reports the Health Insurance Institute. And the situation is getting worse, the institute warns. One reason: The middle managers frequently must follow policies in which they have no confidence. *The Wall Street Journal*, Sept. 5, 1972, p. 1.

INPUT-OUTPUT ANALYSIS IN MANAGEMENT

In Chapter 6 the concept of a business firm as a system was introduced. Here we apply the systems concept to managing a firm, with the firm as a system, and viewing the firm as a processing unit, as illustrated in Figure 7-4. The inputs are materials, supplies, heat, power, labor, and supervision—everything that is needed to produce a finished product or service. It is the responsibility of management to schedule, coordinate, and supervise the flow of inputs so that the desired outputs will be produced most efficiently. For example, in a factory the management must

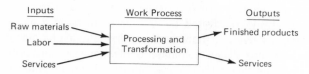

FIGURE 7-4 A business system in operation.

schedule the flow of sheet metal to a stamping machine so that the machine is not idle for lack of material. Labor of the proper amount and skill must be provided and supervised. Maintenance and repairs on the machine must be scheduled when needed. These are just a few of the things management must do to blend the inputs smoothly and thus produce the outputs as planned.

The science of management emphasizes the importance of providing not only those inputs of a tangible nature, such as materials, labor, and electric power, but also those of an intangible nature. Worker motivation (interest in the job, attention to detail, and pride in workmanship) may be as important an input as raw materials.

To simplify a complex business system, a series of subsystems may be identified. A subsystem may be analyzed as a function, such as a technical subsystem (machinery, floor layout), or as a personnel function (number and types of workers, wages, hours of work, incentives). A subsystem may be analyzed as a department, such as a marketing department, as diagrammed in Figure 7-5. Responsibility for management of a subsystem may be given to a department manager, personnel manager, or other executive. However, coordination of the various subsystems, blending their inputs and outputs so that the whole system operates as a unit, is the responsibility of the highest levels of management.

It must not be forgotten—and this is the essence of systems analysis—that a decision involving one element in the system, or in a subsystem, affects to some degree the other elements of the system. Thus a decision to change the hours of work in a factory affects the attitude of the workers and their quality of work; and their attitude in turn affects quality and quantity of output, which in turn affect costs of production, which in turn affect sales, and so on.

EXERCISING CONTROL

SPAN OF CONTROL   In establishing the mechanism through which control may be exercised, it is necessary to consider the **span of control**. This term refers to the limitations on an individual's capacity to exercise effective control over the work of others. A supervisor may have little difficulty in checking the effectiveness of two employees. If a third is added, he is able to give less attention to each. As the number of employees is increased, the direct attention given to each diminishes until a point is reached at which effective supervision vanishes. This point varies with the nature of the work being done.

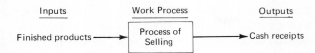

FIGURE 7-5 Marketing subsystem of a company system.

As the number of people in a business increases, additional levels of supervision must be added in order that effective control over their actions may be maintained. In any but the smallest firms, it is impossible for the manager to exercise direct control over all of the employees. A business employing 100 people will usually find it necessary to utilize several levels of supervision. Effective control may have to be maintained through indirect means regardless of the increasing difficulty of this task as more and more levels of supervision are added.

THE EXCEPTION PRINCIPLE

The management technique called the **exception principle** illustrates how business operations may be effectively controlled by indirect methods. This term is used to designate the practice of top management in allowing decisions regarding the usual day-to-day operations to be made by subordinate officials within the policies established at the top level. Under such a plan, most of the decisions can be made by persons at the lower levels of the organization without consulting their supervisors, since most business operations are routine in nature and specific directions for handling them may be established in advance of their occurrence.

If each decision regarding the operation of the business is made at the lowest possible level within the organization, then only the decisions concerning unusual situations must be brought to the attention of the higher levels of management. The release of top management from the time-consuming task of making decisions of a routine nature gives it more time for the careful consideration of exceptional problems.

AUTHORITY, RESPONSIBILITY, AND ACCOUNTABILITY

The exception principle is based on the maximum delegation of **responsibility**, authority, and accountability from top management down through the various intermediate and lower levels. It is important to understand the concepts of responsibility, authority, and accountability. If the three are not kept in proper relationship, the control of business operations by top management through indirect means is rendered difficult.

It would be impossible to find an employee who did not have some responsibilities delegated to him, even though they may be very limited. Some employees may have heavy responsibilities, even though they are not exercising supervision over other employees. They may, for example, be responsible for the proper use of equipment worth thousands of dollars. Responsibility is more demanding, however, when it involves supervising others. The relationship between the delegation of responsibility and the delegation of authority is evident when we consider that a supervisor, who is responsible for the employees under him, cannot effectively discharge his responsibilities unless he is given sufficient authority over the employees to ensure their compliance with his directions.

Thus, responsibility must be accompanied by an equal delegation of authority. There is an important distinction, however, between the delegated responsibility and the delegated authority. The authority to carry out an undertaking may be delegated from an executive to a subordinate, but the executive is not thereby relieved of the ultimate responsibility for the proper completion of the undertaking.

The relationship between the delegation of responsibility and the delegation of authority is not complete unless those to whom such delegation is made are also made accountable for their actions. Accountability requires that a person take the consequences of his actions. It also means that he must be prepared to explain and defend his decisions. To sum up, the relationship is complete only when accountability is required by the superior from whom the subordinate received his delegation of responsibility and authority.

POLICY FORMULATION   It is evident that although policy making is guided primarily by the desire to maximize profits, other objectives of management must be considered, such as health and safety of workers, company reputation, or mere survival (during a depression, for example). It is not always possible to distinguish these objectives, since some of the seemingly nonprofit objectives may in the long run bring about a greater profit than would complete preoccupation with immediate profits. The policies developed by a business enterprise to guide its future actions should then be designed to achieve these broad objectives.

The formation of business policies is as important a part of business as is designing the organizational framework and the process of control. An example of such policy is the selection of supervisors and executives from the employees of the company (promotion from within). Another example might be a foreman's prohibiting smoking to reduce the hazards that might result from matches and cigarettes in dangerous areas. The policy of promotion from within is usually established by top management. Policy formulation is primarily the responsibility of executives in the higher levels of the organization, but it is necessary on many occasions for officers at lower levels to formulate policies, too. Often these are interpretations or applications of companywide policies. In effect, the junior officers and supervisors establish precise policies to fit specific situations in accordance with the broad policies determined at the top executive levels. The chief distinction between policies formed at low supervisory levels and policies established at the top lies in the breadth of influence of the policy.

Executives at the top should try to establish broad policies to serve as guides to decisions to be made by officers at lower ranks. The keynote in forming any policy is to establish it before it is needed in order that it may be carefully formulated rather than hastily contrived to meet a problem requiring immediate solution.

When a policy is established, it helps reduce the time required in making separate decisions each time the same problem occurs. This advantage is diminished, however, by the fact that two situations are rarely exactly alike. Care must be taken to be certain that a particular policy is applicable to a specific situation. If there is doubt, the policy may have to be examined to determine if it should be applied. A junior supervisor may have to consult an officer at a higher level. In such a case, the decision of the officer can serve to clarify the policy and serve as a guide for future decisions of the junior supervisor.

Although broad policy is determined by top management, to be effective it must be based on information gathered from all levels of the organization. In theory—although not always in practice—there should be a two-way flow of ideas within the organization. Information gathered at lower organization levels can form the basis for determining policy by top officials. These policies are then explained to the men at the lower echelons of management to form the framework for their decisions. But often the two-way flow of information, ideas, and guidance becomes one-way. If there is no upward flow of information, decisions made at the top will be based on ignorance, not facts. If there is no sufficient downward flow of ideas and guidance, persons at the lower organizational levels may have to make decisions without sufficient knowledge of overall operations to guide them in coordinating their decisions with those of other departments within the company.

It is not sufficient to develop policies with care; it is also necessary that they be communicated effectively to the persons involved. This communication may be oral or in writing. If a firm is small, few policies may have to be in writing; if it is large, most policies will probably have to be written. A written policy is less likely to be misunderstood or ignored but it still has disadvantages. First, a tendency may develop to consider written policies as the only ones that must be followed. Second, while the operations of most firms change from time to time, written policies tend to lag behind changed conditions and to outlive their usefulness. The advantages and disadvantages of written policies must be balanced before communicating them to the members of the organization.

MANAGERIAL ABILITY

There is more than one way to develop the skills necessary for successful business operation. Skills may be developed by formal study of the elements of business, as in various courses in business administration; they may also be developed by observation and experience—perhaps bitter experience. There is not as wide a gap between study and experience, or between theory and practice, as some think. The difference lies more in the manner that business principles and techniques are learned than in the content. The important consideration is not the way persons gain their ability but whether they have mastered principles and developed abilities required for efficient business management.

Business has become increasingly complex, and the combination of formal training and practical experience has become increasingly important. Formal training permits future businessmen to use the knowledge compiled by hundreds of businessmen of the past and present. Such breadth of knowledge could not be encountered in a lifetime of practical experience. Yet formal training cannot completely substitute for actual experience. It enables a person to gain more from his practical experience in less time than he otherwise could.

THE FUNCTIONS OF MANAGEMENT   Previously, we considered the objectives of management. Now we consider the functions of management necessary to achieve the objectives. These functions are: planning, organizing, directing, coordinating, and reviewing and controlling.

PLANNING   The function concerned with preparations for the future operation of the business is *planning*. It involves the consideration of future demands for the company's product, its supply of raw materials, and other resources required in its operations. Planning must also take into consideration the future actions of competitors and the outlook for the general level of business activity.

Planning requires forecasting the future. Regardless of how difficult it is to predict future events, and despite the reluctance of some businessmen to do so, it is impossible to avoid prediction. Every business must arrive at some decisions concerning the future as a basis for planning its operations. If the executives refuse to forecast the future in laying their business plans, they are operating on the assumption that conditions in the future will be the same as those in the present. In today's rapidly changing world, such an attitude spells disaster.

ORGANIZING   The preparation necessary for putting plans into action is *organizing*. It involves establishing the procedure, developing the organizational structure, and providing the factors necessary to carry out company plans. It is also an essential function. If top management does not perform the organizing function, it will be undertaken by someone in the lower levels of management, and the result is likely to be unwieldy and haphazard. If nobody undertakes this function, the result' is chaos—like an orchestra with each musician playing at a different tempo or a football team with each player operating on the principle of "every man for himself."

Putting the previously drawn up plans of operation into effect is *directing*. This function is built on the first two functions of planning and organizing. Directing operations is undertaken at all levels of authority, but is particularly important as a function of lower-level management. It is difficult to separate these functions of management, and such separation is done here for the purpose of describing them: Planning, organizing, and directing are in practice carried on simultaneously.

DIRECTING

The *coordinating* function brings together the elements necessary to achieve a common objective by utilizing teamwork to gain the maximum effectiveness of the various talents of individuals in a firm. It is important where the complexity of a business requires close coordination of all activities to produce desired results. For example, a repair shop employing three men requires less precise coordination than an automobile manufacturing plant where subassembly lines must be coordinated with precision so that fenders, engines, wheels, and so on will be brought at the precise rate to the precise points on the main assembly line.

COORDINATING

Examining performance to determine whether actions are being carried out in accordance with plans is *reviewing*. Controlling consists of three parts: supervision, comparison, and corrective action. Supervision seeks to ensure that the company plans are properly carried out. Comparison involves comparing results with previously established standards. Corrective action changes operating procedures after determining the reasons for any divergence of actual performance from planned performance.

REVIEWING AND CONTROLLING

The principles of good management, although developed principally in business firms, are useful to any type of organization. However, nonbusiness organizations should modify the principles of business management so as to make them adaptable to nonbusiness uses.

SUMMARY

A business can be viewed as a processing system. Inputs are materials, power, labor, supervision, and anything else that is needed. The function of business management is to coordinate the flow of these inputs so that each input is used with maximum effectiveness. The outputs resulting from the processing of the inputs are whatever goods or services the business firm is organized to produce.

Although management and ownership may be separate, as they are in a corporation, the goal of both is to operate a profitable enterprise. In pursuing this goal, however, the interests of management and the interests of the owners may diverge in some respects. Similarly, the interests of management and employees may diverge in particulars, even though both want to be associated with a profitable company.

A supervisor's capacity to direct others is limited by his span of control (the number of persons he can supervise effectively in any given situation). Effective management permits routine decisions to be made at the lowest level possible, so that only unusual problems are brought to higher levels of management for decision. Confining managers' decisions to the unusual problems is known as the exception principle.

Each level of management must have a degree of authority. Within this latitude of authority, the manager is responsible for the results of his command and must account for the performance of the department or division he directs.

A policy is a broad guide within which decisions are made. Policies made at top management levels are broad indeed. Those made at lower levels are narrower, but even at the lowest level of a company, policies are made.

Managerial skills can be learned to some degree by study, but study must be supplemented by experience. Management can be made more effective by recognizing the functions constituting management. They are planning, organizing, directing, coordinating, reviewing, and controlling.

QUESTIONS FOR REVIEW

1   Good management in a hospital or university is as important as good management in a steel mill. Why should this be so? How do you measure good management in a hospital? In a college or university?

2   At each descending level of management there is generally less emphasis on "thinking" or "creativity" and more emphasis on "doing" or "activity." Explain what is meant by this.

3   Do the interests of management and those of the owners always coincide? When might they differ?

4   The interests of management and employees usually differ with respect to wages. On what other matters do the interests of these two groups diverge? On what matters do they coincide?

5   How does the span of control determine the number of subordinates an executive can effectively supervise?

6   Explain the exception principle. How can it be applied to increase management efficiency?

7   What is the purpose of establishing policies in business?

8   Policy making takes place at all levels of a company. What policies might the manager of one store of a chain of retail stores make?

9   What are the dangers in making a policy too rigid? Too flexible?

10   Why is it essential that there be a two-way flow of communications from the top level of management to the lowest level?

11   If a business is efficiently run, will it be profitable? Are inefficiently run businesses always unprofitable?

12   Since the future cannot be predicted exactly, why plan for the future?

Dale, Ernest: *Management: Theory and Practice*, 3d ed., McGraw-Hill Book Company, New York, 1973.

Jennings, E. E.: *The Mobile Manager: A Study of the New Generation of Top Executives*, McGraw-Hill Book Company, New York, 1971.

Johnson, Russall J.: *Executive Decisions*, South-Western Publishing Company, Cincinnati, 1970.

Jucius, Michael J., Bernard A. Deitzler, and William E. Schlender: *Elements of Managerial Action*, Richard D. Irwin, Inc., Homewood, III., 1973.

Koontz, Harold, and Cyril J. O'Donnell: *Principles of Management*, 5th ed., McGraw-Hill Book Company, New York, 1972.

SELECTED READINGS

Name	**Section**	**Date**

COMPLETION SENTENCES

1 The role of a manager in a business can be compared to that of a

conductor in a symphony orchestra.

2 Good _management_ is as vital in a government agency or

hospital as it is in a factory.

3 The most direct means of control of a business organization is through the

proprietary form of organization.

4 In a corporation, unlike a partnership or proprietorship,

control is separated from _ownership_.

5 The initial delegation of control in a corporation is from stockholders to

directors.

6 Corporation stockholders may want to receive _as large div,_ as earnings permit, while management may prefer to keep _earnings_ to expand the enterprise.

7 The limitation on an individual's capacity to exercise effective control over the work of others is called _Span of control_

8 If top management is released from making routine decisions, more time is available to devote to _exceptional_ problems.

9 In theory, although not always in practice, there should be a _two-way_ flow of ideas within an organization.

10 It is necessary to develop policies not only to guide the business in its operations but also to _communicate_ them to the various levels of an organization.

11 _Planning_ is the function of management concerned with preparation for the future operations of business activity.

12 Planning requires _forecasting_ the future.

13 _Organizing_ may be considered as the preparation for putting plans into operation.

14 The _Directing_ function of management is the actual putting into operation of the previously agreed upon plan.

15 The _coordination_ function of management involves bringing together the various elements necessary to achieve a common objective.

Name   Section   Date

TRUE OR FALSE STATEMENTS

F **1** Not all characteristics of management in a business can be applied successfully to nonbusiness organizations.

F **2** Generally persons at the lower levels of a large organization are encouraged to be creative.

F **3** In a corporation the stockholders discuss and control operations through frequent stockholders' meetings.

T **4** The objective of both management and owners is primarily to operate the business at a profit.

T **5** Divergence of interests between owners and managers of a business is illustrated by the early history of the Ford Motor Company.

F **6** The span of control refers to the vigor with which a supervisor controls his subordinates.

T **7** In spite of some clashes of interest between management and workers, each is necessary to the welfare of the other.

F **8** The exception principle allows usual day-to-day decisions to be made by subordinates; exceptional problems are decided by subordinates but decisions are immediately reported to supervisors.

T **9** It is impossible to find an employee without some responsibility delegated to him.

T **10** To be effective, responsibility must be accompanied by authority equal to the responsibility delegated.

T **11** Policy formulation is not primarily the responsibility of executives in the higher levels of the organization.

T **12** Policies are developed at all levels of an organization.

F **13** To be effective, it is necessary that company policies be communicated to employees in writing.

T **14** Organizing, as one of the functions of management, is the preparation necessary for putting plans into action.

F **15** A repair shop employing three men requires just as much coordination as an automobile assembly plant.

EXERCISES

1 Select an organization within your school or college. What policies, if any, are determined by the entire membership meeting in a body? What policies are determined by the chief officer of the organization? What policies are determined at lower levels? Are the policies clear or vague? What improvements can you suggest?

2 What qualities are important in a successful executive? Divide these qualities into two groups: those that can be achieved by study and training and those that are "part of a person's nature" or are inherited.

Achieved	Inherited

3 In the Jones factory, Joseph Smith, the factory supervisor, as part of his overall power, has the authority to order certain workers to be assigned to particular jobs. However, his power is limited by the authority of Robert Johnson, the safety director, who has the power to veto work assignments for reasons of safety. When a dispute arises between Johnson and Smith over whether "reasons of safety" are being used too often by Johnson, how would you settle it? What kinds of additional information would you want, if any, before settling such a dispute?

CHAPTER

8 OFFICE ADMINISTRATION

To some persons, office work is a dull routine of filing papers, adding columns of figures, typing letters, answering phones, and filling out forms in quadruplicate. Such persons would much rather be outdoors or in a laboratory or workshop. Other persons picture office work as higher-status than production or sales work, as an opportunity to work with executives, and as the best route to promotion to top management. Some office work is dull; some is exciting. Some office jobs offer little chance of promotion; others are designed as trainee positions for executive posts. But, however one looks at office work, it is essential to business operation.

In reading this chapter, try to appreciate the revolution in office equipment that has been under way since World War II. Routine and dull jobs are being done more and more by machines as the years pass. Mechanical office skills—typing, adding, copying, preparing payrolls—are becoming relatively less important than the ability to make decisions involving exceptions to the routine. Office skill is becoming a management skill rather than a mechanical skill.

Most persons asked would say that office work is simply the paper work of a company. It is writing letters, filing forms, issuing checks, recording sales, answering the telephone, preparing charts and reports, and doing scores of other similar jobs. Office work in itself does not create income. But without office services, neither production nor sales could continue.

Office work in a bank differs from office work in a factory, and it is different in a hospital from that in a college. The office serves the company, and the nature of office activities depends on the nature of the company's activities. We cannot discuss all of the activities found in a typical office, although a few will be treated as representative. The purpose of this chapter is to provide a sampling of office functions to give the reader an appreciation of office work—its importance and its position in the business world. The importance of office work basically is twofold: it involves storing information and providing information. It is the application of these two functions in different situations that provides the great variety of office work.

THE NATURE AND IMPORTANCE OF OFFICE ADMINISTRATION

ACTIVITIES OF AN OFFICE

COMMUNICATIONS

One of the features distinguishing a civilized society from a primitive one is the refinement of communications. A primitive tribe depends on human memory to store information, and it usually uses word of mouth to communicate. The development of early civilizations paralleled the introduction of writing in some form. Until the last century, letter writing was the only way of communicating at a distance, with the exception of such methods as Indian smoke signals and African drums.

Although faster means of communication have been developed in recent years, letter writing is still of prime importance. In fact, the volume of business letters has increased in spite of the telephone and telegraph. The ability to compose a good business letter is therefore just as important now as it was in previous decades. The gift of expression of a William Shakespeare or an Ernest Hemingway is not necessary—although it may help. What is needed by a good letter writer is the ability to organize his thoughts logically and to express them with clarity.

A good letter or memorandum should contain the following:

1 *Good organization:* A person writing or dictating a letter should organize it beforehand. It is useful to jot down the points to be covered, and to arrange them in logical sequence. If something of importance is forgotten until the end of the letter, a postscript can be added, but generally this indicates a hurried letter. A postscript, however, is sometimes used intentionally for the sake of emphasis. The organization of a letter depends on its purpose. For example, a sales letter is often not read to the end by the person receiving it, particularly if it is a form letter duplicated by the thousands. In such a case, the most important information should be in the first one or two paragraphs, and the paragraphs should be short. If the interest of the reader is not captured in the first few sentences, the letter probably will be tossed into the wastebasket.

2 *Clear writing:* Sentences should usually be short and words should be simple. Technical language should be used only as necessary. If diagrams or illustrations will help, they should be enclosed on separate sheets of paper.

3 *Conciseness:* Nearly all letters contain excess words. Some, like *Dear Sir* or *Yours truly*, are not essential to convey the message, but are used for the sake of tradition. Sometimes a letter is longer than necessary for the sake of politeness, and sometimes it is shorter: In responding to a request, a college president once sent a letter containing the following:

> Dear Mr. . . . . :
>   No.
>   Yours truly,

Although a good business letter is concise, it is possible to be too concise. Most letter writers, however, should be on guard against being too wordy rather than being too concise.

4 *Attractiveness:* The appearance of a letter, especially a sales letter, is almost as important as what it says. It should be properly centered, clean, and uncluttered. Erasures, if any, should be neat. A business letter reflects the image of the company, and this image must be favorable.

Largely because of the expense of typist salaries, the average short business letter costs a company more than $2. Because many letters are written in a typical office, care should be taken that this cost is not wasted. This caution applies to interoffice memorandums as well as to letters sent through the mails.

Mail represents one of the most important contacts between a company and its customers, suppliers, and others. A letter lost may result in a customer lost. Incoming mail must be carefully sorted so that each letter reaches the proper person to handle it. Outgoing mail requires equal care. Letters and enclosures should be properly folded, inserted into the envelopes, and the envelopes securely sealed. It is vital to address all envelopes correctly. Machinery (envelope-stuffing machines, postage meters, and addressing machines, for example) can increase the accuracy and speed of preparing letters for mailing, particularly where thousands of pieces are handled.

A telephone is a necessity for virtually every business. The rules of politeness that apply to face-to-face conversation apply equally to telephone conversation. Furthermore, because persons do not see each other (except in experimental telephones), the voice must convey the full message. Some persons find it difficult to talk without gestures. Probably such habits cannot be cured but, with practice, any person can improve his telephone technique.

The telegraph is not used as much (in relation to other means of communication) as it was in the last century. For rapid communication at a distance, the telephone is used. Telegrams can be useful where a person cannot be easily reached by phone, where rapid verification of telephone terms is needed, and for other special uses. The general rules for a good telegram are simple: Make it brief, accurate, and clear.

RECORDS

Information about a company is stored in *records*. Old records show the history of the company and are useful in indicating the progress of the company over the years. Recent or current records form the basis for decisions regarding a company's operations. They can settle disputes, and are necessary for tax returns and other reports required by government. Records provide the information on which projections into the future can be made.

Much of the time spent in an office is used in preparing, storing, and recovering records. Two essential policies regarding records must be made by each company, usually at the executive levels of the company. These concern what information to record and how long to keep the records. Of course, extremes must be avoided. Only a businessman acting alone can keep his business "under his hat." Certainly, records should be extensive enough so that the death or illness of an employee will not interrupt operations. But, on the other hand, should every telephone conversation be recorded? A copy of every letter be kept? A memorandum of every decision be made? Records can be so sketchy and incomplete that executives do not know where their company stands. Or they can be so detailed and voluminous as to drown office workers in a sea of paper.

How long to keep a record depends on the nature of the record. The corporation charter must be kept for the entire life of the corporation. If an executive gives an order in writing, a copy should be kept at least until the order is carried out. Financial records are generally kept for a long time; interoffice memorandums are usually kept for relatively brief periods. Modern devices permit records to be kept for longer periods than would have been feasible a few years ago. Banks, for example, record on microfilm the face and reverse of every check they handle. Some companies use microfilm to record for permanent storage letters and other documents that would have been destroyed under the record-keeping policies of a generation ago. Nor is microfilm the last word in compact record keeping. Vast quantities of information can be stored in the "memories" of electronic computers, to be brought forth when needed by the mere flick of a switch. The capacity of modern devices for record keeping is a boon as well as a hazard. Like an old woman who hates to throw away a letter, however old it is, a company can accumulate too much data. Just as every attic and storage room in a house should be cleaned out periodically, it is wise policy for a company to weed out obviously unneeded information from its files once in a while.

OFFICE EQUIPMENT

An office contains many types of equipment: filing cases, typewriters, adding machines, duplicators, telephones, etc. Many high schools and colleges teach the handling of office machines, but it is difficult to keep current with the new machines coming into use continually. A revolution is taking place in the office that is comparable to the revolution in the factory. In a modern factory, machines make the products, with workers watching dials to check on the performance of the machines and to take care of occasional situations beyond the capabilities of machinery. In today's office, increasing use is made of machines to do the routine work formerly done by semiskilled workers, mostly young women. A bank of 20 years ago, for example, had checks sorted, charged to depositors' accounts, and otherwise handled by girls given brief training in this work. The work was dull, it took little intelligence, and the girls kept their jobs for only a few months while seeking something better—often marriage. Machines are now used in larger banks to sort checks (using magnetic ink) at the rate of thousands an hour, post them automatically to the right accounts, place them in envelopes, and do other operations required in check handling. More and more, drudgery in the office is being shifted to machines.

The office worker of the future will not be a person whose skills are confined to taking dictation, typing, answering the telephone, and sealing envelopes. Greater skills will be needed as routine chores are done by machine. Office machines will never replace office workers, just as automatic machinery has not eliminated the factory worker. In both the office and factory, however, the future will require better-trained and more resourceful workers. These will handle exceptional or emergency situations. Consider the handling of checks as described above. No machine can process a check embroidered on cloth, carved on the side of a watermelon, or written on a football—and these are just some of the more dramatic cases of actual checks cashed by banks. Office work of the future, while requiring more training, will also be more interesting, provide greater variety, and (best of all) pay higher wages.

A secretary in a business firm usually works with one executive. She (or he) acts as receptionist, answers the telephone, types letters and reports, files papers, and does other chores for the executive. A good secretary does more, however. She can relieve the executive of nearly all of the detail work of his position, so that he can turn his attention to decisions that require concentration. Some of the decisions she can make herself. She has enough knowledge of the executive's work so that he can attend committee meetings, go to conventions, and work away from his office when necessary, secure in the knowledge that she is taking care of the routine of his office. If the executive authorizes it, she may issue orders to his subordinates and sign his name to letters. She may be asked to meet a customer at the airport or to entertain a client at lunch. An executive may become so dependent on his secretary that he finds it almost impossible to function if she is away from the office for a few days. Some executives find it necessary to take their secretaries with them on some of their business trips or to attend committee meetings.

It is obvious that a good secretary is more highly trained than a stenographer. A college degree in office administration is useful, as is training in the special field of the secretary's employer, such as law in a law office, bookkeeping in an accounting office, retailing if the executive is the owner of a store, and so on. She must have tact, initiative, good grooming, and a pleasing personality and be willing to work long hours when necessary.

QUALIFICATIONS OF A GOOD SECRETARY

Office work is a service function: the function of receiving, storing, rearranging, retrieving, and presenting information. Since information on paper is more likely to be accurate and less likely to be misunderstood, most office work is paper work.

Much of the paper work of an office consists of writing letters. A good business letter is well organized, clear, concise, and attractive.

Since much business is transacted by telephone, the telephone must be used properly. A person must speak clearly and use the rules of politeness required in conversation. But to avoid misunderstanding, a telephone agreement is often confirmed by letter. Frequently, to save time, a telegram is used instead of a letter.

The keeping of records is essential to a business. Some records, such as the corporation charter, are kept permanently. Others are kept for varying lengths of time. Here judgment must be used. Important records are kept for long periods while unimportant information is kept briefly, then destroyed so as not to swamp the storage facilities of the office.

In a modern office, many types of equipment are found. Their chief purpose is to permit a larger amount of information to be handled faster and more accurately

SUMMARY

than could be done without machines. Using machines effectively requires knowledge of the capabilities and limitations of office machines.

With a good secretary, an executive can handle much more work than he could alone. A secretary handles the details that would otherwise distract an executive. If she (or he) is capable and shows good judgment, she can take over some of the responsibilities of the executive and can make decisions on her own.

QUESTIONS FOR REVIEW

1 Describe the differences in communications between a jungle tribe and a modern urban society.
2 What are the steps in preparing a well-organized letter?
3 Give the characteristics of a good sales letter.
4 What costs other than postage are incurred in writing a business letter? What is the rate for postage of a letter at present by regular mail? Air mail?
5 What are the elements of etiquette in telephoning?
6 Why is a telegram relatively less important as a means of communication now than formerly? For what reasons are telegrams used today?
7 Give examples of records that should be kept relatively long, and examples of records that should be kept a short period and then destroyed. On what basis do you make the distinction?
8 The capacity of modern devices for storing information is tremendous. Why is this both a benefit and a hazard?
9 "Drudgery in the office is increasingly being shifted to machines." Explain this statement.
10 Office machines are becoming rapidly more sophisticated and versatile. Does this contribute to unemployment? Discuss.
11 Describe the qualities of a good secretary.
12 Distinguish between the duties of a stenographer and those of a secretary.

SELECTED READINGS

Haney, William V.: *Communication and Organization Behavior*, 3d ed., Richard D. Irwin, Inc., Homewood, Ill., 1973.

Krey, Isabelle A., and Bernadette V. Metzler: *Effective Writing for Business*, Harcourt Brace Jovanovich, Inc., New York, 1972.

Neuner, John J. W., B. Lewis Keeling, and Norman F. Kallous: *Administrative Office Management*, South-Western Publishing Company, Cincinnati, 1972.

Stutsman, Galen, and Elfreda M. Rusker: *Secretaries on the Spot*, The National Secretaries Association, Kansas City, Mo., 1961.

Terry, George R.: *Office Management and Control*, Richard D. Irwin, Inc., Homewood, Ill., 1970.

Whalen, Doris H.: *The Secretary's Handbook*, Harcourt Brace Jovanovich, Inc., New York, 1973.

Zelko, Harold P.: *The Business Conference: Leadership and Partipation*, McGraw-Hill Book Company, New York, 1969.

CHAPTER

8 REVIEW ACTIVITIES

Name   **Section**   **Date**

COMPLETION SENTENCES

1 The purpose of office work is basically twofold: *storing*

information and *providing* information.

2 A primitive tribe depends upon *human memory* to store infor-

mation.

3 What is needed in a good business letter writer is the ability to

organize his thoughts logically and express them with

clarity .

4 If the *interest* of the reader is not captured in the first

few sentences of a sales letter, the letter will probably be tossed into the waste-

basket.

5 Sometimes a letter is longer than necessary, for the sake of _____.

6 A business letter reflects the image of the _____ , and this image must be favorable.

7 A letter _____ may result in a customer _____.

8 Because in telephone conversation gestures cannot be seen, _____ must convey the full message.

9 For rapid communication to distant points, the _____ is usually used.

10 Old records show the history of the company, and are useful in conveying _____.

11 Records should be extensive and detailed enough so that the death or illness of a key employee will not _____.

12 The corporation charter must be kept for _____.

13 Vast quantities of information can be stored in the _____ of electronic computers.

14 _____ jobs in offices will require greater skills, as routine and repetitive chores are done by _____.

15 A good secretary is more highly trained than a _____.

Name   Section   Date

TRUE OR FALSE STATEMENTS

T **1** Office work in a bank differs from office work in a factory.

T **2** Office work in itself creates work for a company.

F **3** The volume of business letters has decreased with the invention of the telephone.

F **4** A postscript is indicative of a poorly organized or hastily written letter.

T **5** A good business letter does not contain excess words.

T **6** The appearance of a sales letter is almost as important as what it says.

T **7** With practice practically anyone can improve his telephone technique.

F **8** Communication by telegram is more frequently used in the 1970s than it was a century ago, in relation to other means of communication.

T **9** In most businesses very little office time is devoted to preparing, storing, and recovering records.

F **10** How long to keep a particular piece of information does not depend upon the nature of the information.

T **11** Banks make a copy of the face and reverse of the checks they handle.

T **12** More and more office drudgery is shifted to machines.

T **13** Greater skills will be required of the typical office worker of the future than are required of the worker of today.

F **14** A secretary in a business firm usually works with several executives.

F **15** A secretary may be authorized to issue orders to subordinates of an executive, but the secretary is never permitted to sign his name to letters.

EXERCISES

1 Prepare from sources in the library or by visiting a company a report on office jobs that can be handled by computers. Indicate types of office work that cannot as yet be done by computers. Are there office jobs done by computers that in your opinion should be handled by people? Explain.

Jobs Done by Computers	Jobs Done by People

Comments:

2 Telephones that can transmit visual images on a screen (as in closed-circuit television) as well as the voices of the speakers are technically possible and may be common in the future.

   a Prepare a report on what changes, if any, would probably result if office telephones transmitted pictures as well as sound.

   b Would the advantages outweigh the disadvantages? Explain.

3 Collect a dozen business letters. Try to get examples that you consider poor and examples that you consider good. Be able to explain (in a report to class, if necessary), by using the letters as examples, the differences between a good letter and a bad letter.

PART 3
PRODUCTION

Production involves men, machines, and materials. The next two chapters concern ways they can be combined for maximum efficiency.

Before production can begin, a location must be chosen. The arrangement of machines, materials, offices, doors, loading docks, and other physical facilities must also be made so as to aid production, not hinder it. The problems of location, layout, and inventory management are discussed in Chapter 9, which also discusses location and layout of stores and offices, where "production" is not in goods but in services.

Production requires that goods be stored and moved. Materials and supplies must be purchased, stored until needed, and moved to the machines (or, in the case of stores, to the counters and shelves). When goods are manufactured, the finished goods must be again stored until time for delivery. Then they must be packaged or otherwise prepared for shipment, loaded, and dispatched to the customer.

Goods can be produced by separating a raw material into finished parts, as in petroleum products. Goods can be formed by combining materials, as in making bread. Or goods can be made by shaping, stretching, or cutting a material, as in making wire, saw blades, or aluminum foil. These are the *basic production processes*. A complex article, like a television receiver, requires many variations and combinations of these processes before the final product is ready for use.

CHAPTER

9 LOCATION, LAYOUT, AND INVENTORY MANAGEMENT

Location is of extreme importance in most business endeavors. Examine carefully all the factors involved in the selection of a location. Remember that some of these factors are of decisive importance for some industries and unimportant for others. Furthermore, the importance of some factors of location changes as time passes. For example, climate and availability of water might be vitally important to a particular industry at one time but less so when air conditioning and long-range transportation of water become available. Similarly, location on a railroad was essential for many businesses 40 years ago but is now unimportant for many of these same industries. Business decisions applicable in the past do not necessarily apply today.

The purpose of layout within an organization is to facilitate business operations. Layout is the arrangement of desks in an office, of machines in a factory, or of counters in a store to expedite the operation of a business. In reading the section on layout, you should remember that the ideal is to attain as large a flow of work as can be done with existing equipment. You could generalize and say that assembly-line techniques can be used wherever they promise increasing efficiency. Even though assembly-line techniques were first developed in manufacturing, they have since been adapted to office routines and even to retail store operations. In some businesses, of course, assembly-line layout cannot be used at all. Nevertheless, the placement of machinery in a factory and the filing cabinets, desks, counters, and other work aids in an office can help facilitate the daily routine of work.

You should consider inventory control as a means of regulating the flow of goods so as to keep costs at a minimum, reduce the hazards of damage to merchandise, and reduce the possibilities of theft. Inventory can be thought of as a flowing stream: raw materials and supplies enter the plant, are held for resale or for processing, and then are distributed to customers. Running out of raw materials is similar to a river running dry. Having too much inventory on hand can be compared to a river overflowing its banks. In either case the results can be disastrous. The ideal inventory is like a river that neither rises too high nor falls too low but flows at a steady rate.

Retailers in many cities of the South have noticed that stores located on the shady side of the street get more business, other things being equal, than competing stores across the street. A gasoline service station is almost always located on a street corner, where it attracts more motorists than do stations in the center of a block. A motel on a quiet street may be more restful than one on a busy highway, but the location on the busy highway draws more travelers.

These examples illustrate the importance of *location*. Careful selection of location is important to the success of any business. In some industries, it is the difference between profits and bankruptcy.

What is a good location? It depends on the characteristics of the business. A good location for a warehouse is a poor one for a hat store. The expected *rate of growth* is also a factor. If rapid expansion is forecast for a factory, the availability and cost of neighboring land are considered in the choice of location. *Centralization* or *decentralization* may also be important. Some companies bring their operations as close together as possible. Others have a policy of small plants or offices scattered throughout a state or nation. These needs and desires are the background against which the factors of geography and community must be considered. No location is perfect. Favorable factors are balanced against unfavorable ones. What makes the task difficult is that the company must live with its selection usually for a long time. The future, as well as the present, must be weighed in making the selection.

The more important geographic factors in location are distance to raw materials and to customers, climate, power, water supplies, and transportation, as illustrated in Figure 9-1. In some cases, a single factor will be decisive. A retail store, for example, must locate where the customers are. A sawmill, where trees are. In other cases, several factors must be given approximately equal importance.

In many cases, it is necessary for a plant to be located close to the raw materials it uses. If the raw materials are heavy and the finished products light, transportation costs can be reduced by selecting a location close to the source of raw materials. In mining, crude-oil extraction, and logging, the operations must obviously be undertaken where the ores, oil, and trees are found. Vegetable and fruit canneries are situated where the foods are grown to minimize damage to fruit and vegetables through transportation to the cannery. Iron and steel furnaces generally are located near the source of the raw materials they use. If not, they are placed near deep-water channels to take advantage of low-cost water transportation. Let us take iron production as an illustration. Three main ingredients are needed in abundance to smelt iron: iron ore, coal, and limestone. Approximately 3 tons of coal are needed to process 1 ton of iron ore. The iron furnaces of Pittsburgh are favorably

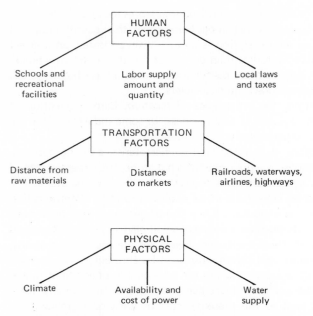

FIGURE 9-1 Factors in site slection of a manufacturing plant.

located because Pittsburgh is close to plentiful supplies of coal and limestone. In spite of the fact that for decades the iron ore fed into the Pittsburgh furnaces has been brought from Minnesota, Pittsburgh iron and steel have competed successfully with steel mills closer to Minnesota. An additional advantage of Pittsburgh is its location on the Ohio River, a natural waterway.

For some industries, distance from raw materials is a negligible factor. Examples are jewelry manufacturing, dressmaking, precision instruments, camera production, and the manufacture of electronics.

For industries falling between the two extremes described above, raw materials constitute a factor varying in importance. In such cases, the plant is located on the basis of relative advantage, with the cost advantage of location close to raw materials measured against the cost advantage of location close to customers, power supplies, or skilled labor.

CUSTOMERS   Many manufacturers find it advantageous to choose a site close to the principal market for their products. For companies making bakery goods or other perishables, location close to the market is almost essential. Where the principal raw material is plentifully distributed over the country and the finished product is heavy, as in bricks or concrete blocks, location close to the market reduces transportation costs and perhaps permits a lower delivered price. If rapid delivery is necessary, a competitive advantage can be secured by a location close to the market. Suppliers selling to automobile manufacturers are mostly located in Michigan and neighboring states, for example.

If the market for a company's products is nationwide, company management may decide plant location without respect to market considerations, particularly if prompt delivery is not vital to sales. If the market is national, however, management might undertake decentralization of production, since different areas of the country can be served from branch plants more rapidly than from a single source. The decision to decentralize would have to take into account many other factors, of course, such as the relative efficiency of small-scale and large-scale production.

CLIMATE

England became the leading textile producer of the world in the nineteenth century partly because of her damp climate. A humid atmosphere is favorable for spinning cotton into thread and weaving thread into cloth because cotton fibers are less likely to break when slightly moist. Textile manufacture in the United States developed first in New England, which also has a moist climate.

The photographic film available in the early days of motion pictures required a lot of light. The transfer of the film industry from the Atlantic coast to southern California occurred primarily because the generous amount of sunshine in that area permitted more days for filming outdoor action than had been possible around New York, where the industry was born.

Climate is not as important a factor in location as it was previously. It is still important to people who work for industry, but less so for industry itself. Humidity in textile plants can be maintained within whatever limits are considered ideal. Photographic film is now so sensitive that pictures can be made under light conditions considered impossible a few years ago. An extreme example of climate control is a mile-long building constructed during World War II in Fort Worth, Texas, to manufacture bombers and used since the war to produce a variety of planes and parts. The building has not a single window, depends entirely on artificial illumination, and is air-conditioned. Working inside the structure, a person is completely unaware of temperatures outside (which may vary from 15 to 110 degrees), of rain or sunshine, or even whether it is day or night.

POWER

Electric power is needed in quantity to produce aluminum, chemicals, and fertilizers, to name a few products. Water power has been the cheapest producer of electricity in the past. Thus, companies needing large amounts of cheap electricity have located close to hydroelectric generators. In the future, however, electricity may be produced more cheaply by atomic energy than by falling water. Also, recent progress in the transmission of electric power over very long distances has reduced the variation in electric power costs in different localities.

WATER   Water is necessary to nearly all industries, and some require large amounts. One example is paper making; water is needed to wash the logs, to transport the wood pulp, to accomplish the matting process, and to eliminate impurities. High-quality paper requires clean water. About 50,000 gallons of water are used to make each ton of paper. Therefore paper mills are located where clean water is available in large quantities at low cost.

The continued rise in population in the United States has made water a critical resource in many communities. The use of water by industry has often rendered it unfit for further use downstream by other industry—to say nothing of rendering it unfit for wildlife and human beings. Pure water for those industries requiring it has become increasingly scarce, and locating supplies of naturally pure water has become increasingly difficult. Many companies find it necessary to purify local water before using it in the plant. In a few cases where wells are the main source of water, excessive pumping relative to the natural rate of water accumulation has so lowered the water table in an area that some plants are forced to relocate.

TRANSPORTATION   Adequate transport facilities are essential. Adequacy, however, varies from one industry to another, and also from one company to another. For a company manufacturing small items marketed over a limited area, access to good highways over which trucks can be used constitutes adequate transportation. If the same company expands its market area and ships in large volume, rail transportation would probably be required. A company using heavy raw materials brought from a distance and selling in a nationwide or worldwide market probably requires water transport facilities. Oil refineries, steel mills, and companies in other heavy industries are generally located where water transport is available.

If a company chooses a location at a distance from its principal market. possibly to take advantage of cheaper power or more abundant labor, it must absorb part of the freight costs to enable it to meet the price of competitors closer to the market. If freight rates increase, the cost of doing business for a company distant from the market will rise more than for a nearby company. The same will be true for transportation costs of raw materials. For example, an increase in freight and parcel post rates tends to make it more difficult for a distant mail-order house to compete with local retail stores. If freight rates fall, local retailers tend to feel the competition from mail-order houses more keenly. In other words, high freight rates insulate a local market from distant competition; low rates open a local market to distant competition. Consequently, communities that have high inward and outward freight rates will attract businesses of a strictly local character and will be shunned by companies with a regional or national scope of operations.

Until the 1960s it was accepted as an axiom by practically all communities that population growth was a good thing and that the amount of industry a municipality should strive to attract could be answered by a single word: More. In the 1970s there has developed a countertrend, small but growing, that questions the desirability of increased industry for a community. More industry brings more jobs and more local tax revenues; but it also brings more urban density, more street traffic, perhaps more smoke and industrial wastes, and more pressure on local services such as schools, public safety, and recreational facilities. The arrival of new industries may transform a town into a city. Some will welcome the change; others view it with regret.

COMMUNITY FACTORS

As our grandparents approached the twentieth century, growth was synonymous with progress. As we approach the twenty-first century, we begin to ask, How much longer can growth continue unchecked? An increasing number of communities no longer provide special inducements to attract new industries and new residents. A few discourage the arrival of new residents and place obstacles to the establishment of new industry. Nevertheless, neither industries nor individuals stand still. People move from place to place. Companies also change their location. And as some companies disappear in one area, others appear in another. The importance of careful selection of sites for companies remains. There are so many factors involved in the selection of a business location that the decision must be based on the relative importance of each factor to the particular business.

There are three aspects of availability of workers that should be considered in appraising a town: adequate supply, cost, and skill. If workers with a particular skill are required, it is advisable to determine the availability of each type of skill before deciding on a location. In some cases other characteristics of a location may be so attractive that a company may be willing to overcome a lack of workers with a needed skill by bringing in such workers from other areas.

SUPPLY OF WORKERS

If unskilled workers can be used, a company has a much wider geographic area from which to choose. Then cost and availability will probably be the determining factors. One reason the states of the South have recently attracted industry is the availability of plentiful labor, mostly unskilled, willing to work at wage rates below those of the North. In addition to regional differences in wage rates, there is frequently a difference in wage rates between urban and rural areas, with higher wages found in towns than in villages.

The laws of some states are more restrictive than the laws of others, and in some industries this may be important. For example, the size and weight limits imposed on trucks vary considerably from one state to another. This is important to a

LOCAL GOVERNMENT AND BUSINESS FACILITIES

company using trucking extensively in its operations. Some states have taxes on income, some on sales, some on both income and sales, and some on neither. Some have taxes on specific industries, such as the tax on petroleum in Texas. Corporation laws of the states also vary, for both local corporations and out-of-state corporations.

Nearly all city governments try to bring in new industries, and will make their laws and taxes attractive to business. This does not mean that the most desirable city is the one with low taxes and few regulations. Low taxes may mean inadequate municipal services, and regulations may be so few as to make property and persons unsafe. Company officials must consider taxes and regulations along with extent and quality of city services.

A good location usually requires a variety of retail stores, banking facilities, hospitals, schools, and recreational opportunities. Many of the services provided by a community will be used by businesses as well as by people. Even those services, such as schools and parks, that are not used directly by businesses benefit industry indirectly by the advantages they give employees. Site selection committees for large companies give considerable weight to the quality of schools, recreational facilities, and other city services. They know that not only do individuals suffer from an unpleasant place to live but businesses do too, principally because of increased labor turnover and the probability of future tax increases. It is obvious that it takes more tax money to raise the level of community services than to maintain them after they have been raised.

INDUCEMENTS OFFERED BY CITIES
Cities compete with each other in trying to secure new business. To a considerable extent this is done by advertising the natural advantages of a town with respect to geography, climate, population, transport, and so on. In addition, many towns offer specific inducements, such as a gift of land for a factory or reduced taxes for several years.

It is difficult to determine the success of specific inducements in bringing in new business. Opinions differ, and statistical studies made on the subject are inconclusive. The businessman considering such inducements should remember that at best they are generally of temporary benefit and that if the inducement involves much financial sacrifice by the city, it may generate resentment against those companies taking advantage of the inducement.

FACTORS IN LAYOUT
Layout is the arrangement of facilities such as rooms, desks, machinery, and doors within a building. The goal of a well-planned layout is to arrange the facilities so that there will be an orderly flow of work and a minimum of confusion. A good layout for a grocery market would make selection of groceries as easy and pleasant as possible, with storage facilities, loading dock, check-out

stands, and manager's office located for maximum efficiency. A bank layout should provide a smooth flow of checks, cash, and other items between the tellers' cages and the bookkeeping department, transit department, and the money vault, with convenient locations for the officers' desks, and an adequate lobby area.

Efficient layout promotes coordination between departments. In planning a layout, the office managers or plant foremen and the workers should be consulted. It is much better to take time to plan a good layout than to have to change a poor one after it has been established.

PLANT LAYOUT

There are two general types of production layouts: group and line. *Group layout* is generally found in small plants, where lathes may be grouped in one area, presses in another, and drills in a third. The number of machines can be kept low with such a layout because the material to be processed may be brought back to the same machine several times during the manufacturing process.

Large factories nearly always use the *line* (also called *straight line*) *layout*. The line is not usually straight in such a layout, but it is continuous and it eliminates the backtracking of material found in the group layout. Hence the flow of work is smoother, and bottlenecks are less frequent than in group layout. Because a larger number of machines is required, compared to group layout, the line layout needs a larger output to be profitable than does the group layout. Some common types of line layouts are shown in Figure 9-2.

FIGURE 9-2   Line-type flow diagrams.

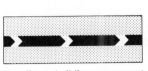
"Line" type building arrangement

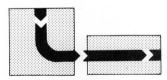
"L" type building arrangement

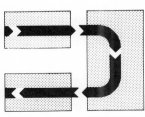
"U" type building arrangement

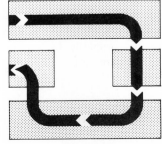
"Quadrangle" type building arrangement

Plant layout must take into consideration many factors. Some common ones are the following:

Possible need for expansion of production volume

Time required to complete various subassemblies to provide a smooth flow of work to the main assembly lines

Proper spacing of machinery

Sufficient space for materials handling equipment

Provision for changing locations of machines if the pattern of production must be re-arranged because of changes in product design

Safety and comfort of workers

The plant layout will determine to some extent the type of machines used and vice versa. To illustrate, if the line layout is used, specialized presses, cutting tools, and other special-purpose machines will be used, each designed for maximum efficiency for a single type of operation. And, where special-purpose machines are available, the layout selected can be of the line type. Conversely, if general-purpose machines that can adjust to a variety of operations are used, the group layout probably will be used. This is because general-purpose machines are associated with relatively small-scale production—and small-scale production, in turn, generally is best handled on the basis of group layout.

The type of building, like the type of machinery, interacts with the layout. If the building is already in existence, the layout must be planned to fit the building. On the other hand, if the building is not yet constructed, the layout can be planned with relative freedom to meet such demands as proper spacing of machinery and comfort of workers. The building is then designed to suit the layout.

Factory design has changed considerably in the past 40 years. The old factory buildings were located generally in cities, were several stories high, dingy and for-bidding, and were surrounded by slums they helped to create. Newer factories are frequently located at a distance from the old industrial sections of cities, are surrounded by grass, shrubbery, and parking lots, and are designed to be pleasing to the eye. Improved transportation has freed factories from crowded urban locations and placed them where there is room to spread. And spread they have, with one-story construction common.

Although modern factories have windows, they are not as dependent on the uncertain illumination from the sun as were the old factories. Some buildings use glass extensively, but primarily for esthetic reasons. A few modern buildings are completely devoid of windows.

RETAIL STORE LAYOUT   In the layout of a retail store, attractiveness and convenience to customers are of prime importance. As far as is possible, shopping in the store must be made a pleasant experience for the customer. Nevertheless, costs must be kept in mind.

Most retail stores are in locations where rent is high. Therefore the retailer must strive to attain the most efficient use of his floor space.

Factors that must be considered in retail store layout are: customer characteristics, customer traffic, type of store, placement of merchandise, and flexibility.

Obviously, a store that does not attract customers does not sell. **Customer characteristics** are therefore a vital consideration in planning layout. This necessitates studying the type of customers the store seeks to attract. Are they rich or not? Are they men, women, or both? Are they mostly teen-agers or adults? Are they housewives or office workers? The answers to these questions will enable layout to be planned with a better understanding of the customer's viewpoint.

The **customer traffic** through the store must be planned with the same care as if the store manager were in charge of streets and highways. Doors should provide easy access and exit. The arrangement of aisles, counters, and cashier stands should facilitate a smooth flow of people. Wide aisles can be used where traffic is dense or where shoppers are likely to linger, thus slowing traffic. Narrower aisles are permitted where traffic is light. The layout of a large store may provide one or two broad "main thoroughfares," with "side streets" leading to sections or departments, all arranged according to a careful study of traffic patterns in the store.

If there are several floors in a store, the traffic flow to and from the elevators must be considered. When escalators are also used, because each escalator normally connects only two floors, the system should be arranged to permit passengers to move from one escalator to another with a minimum of walking. Frequently, escalators will be placed near the center of the store, with elevators along a wall on the side of the building.

The type of store will determine the layout to a considerable extent. Furniture stores require space for proper display of chairs, tables, sofas, lamps, and related items. If there is sufficient space, the items can be grouped into several sample arrangements suggesting their use in a home. A grouping of contemporary chairs, tables, and lamps enhances the attraction of each, as similar groupings will do for other styles.

A men's clothing store will generally have suits toward the back where they can be tried on in some privacy, and where there are convenient dressing rooms. There must be space for suit racks and for such items as neckties, socks, underwear, and accessories.

Grocery stores plan the traffic flow from entrances, along the aisles, through the check-out stands, and out to the parking area. Since grocery stores are mainly self-service, they place the check-out stands at one spot in the store. Small items such as cigarettes, candy, and gum are frequently placed there too, where they are less likely to slip into pocket or purse, unnoticed and unpaid for.

The placement of merchandise also depends largely on the type of store. However, some other considerations apply, depending on the class of merchandise. Merchandise can be divided into three classes as follows:

1 *Convenience goods:* These are goods bought frequently, where the choice is made by habit rather than by comparison with other goods, and where the price is low. Examples are candy, cigarettes, toothpaste, and, to a lesser degree, men's socks and handkerchiefs.

2 *Shopping goods:* These are goods that require more time in selection, where the customer shops around before making a decision, and where the price is higher than for convenience goods. More selling effort is usually required on the part of sales people to make a sale. Examples are clothing, furniture, appliances, and luggage.

3 *Specialty goods:* These are goods that appeal to a particular clientele, rather than to the average shopper. Examples are high-quality cameras, shortwave radios, antiques, gourmet foods, and oil paintings. Customers for such goods are generally skilled in appraising quality and performance, and they make their choice with care.

If the customer cannot quickly and easily purchase the convenience goods, the sale may be lost. Such goods should be placed where the store's largest traffic volume passes, or, sometimes, at several places in the store.

Because shopping goods take longer to sell than convenience goods, they should be placed where customers can comfortably browse without interfering with the flow of traffic. Dressing rooms should be provided for clothing, and chairs for trying on shoes. These goods should generally be placed farther from the store entrances than convenience goods. If a store has several floors, convenience goods predominate on the street floor and shopping goods on other floors.

Specialty goods, like shopping goods, take time to sell. They are usually placed by themselves, away from the main customer traffic. In a department store, each class of specialty goods is sometimes placed in a secluded section of the store, creating the impression of a separate specialty shop.

Flexibility in store layout permits a retailer to modify the layout to meet changing needs. During the Christmas season, those items suitable as gifts—every store has some items it features for the holiday trade—need more display space. The toy department, for example, will need more room. Studies of sales volume and customer traffic in different departments or sections of the store may warrant changes in floor space or location assignments. Or, if a sale is advertised, the featured item may require special consideration in placing it in the store, perhaps far from its usual location. In a classic example, when Gimbel Brothers department store in New York City advertised in October 1945 the first sale in the United States of a ball-point pen, the following happened when the sale started:

. . . five thousand people were waiting to swarm through the doors, and fifty extra policemen were hastily dispatched to restrain the throng. Inside the store, where ball-point pens lay heaped in gleaming piles on the counters of two aisles running almost the entire length of the Thirty-second Street side, buying quickly reached the proportions of a stampede. In an attempt to break up the jam, Gimbels hurriedly set up emergency counters, and during the day, as fresh supplies of pens were rushed here by plane, placed them on sale in other departments. "We took over Umbrellas, we knocked out Clocks, and we went into Silver," a Gimbels' man recalled recently. "Ball-point pens all over the place."[1]

A good layout should increase store sales. Since sales depend on customer satisfaction, retail layout should be planned from the point of view of the customer. But costs should also be considered. In sum, the best layout is the one that achieves a maximum of sales with a minimum of expense.

OFFICE LAYOUT

An office does not manufacture goods and does not have the volume of customer traffic of a retail store. Nevertheless there are similarities between office layout and store or factory layout. A plant must plan a smooth flow of goods in process of manufacture, a store must plan a smooth flow of customer traffic, and an office must plan a smooth flow of paper work from one desk to another and from one room to another. The flow of office work should proceed with a minimum of interruption and delay through the departments of the office. The locations assigned to desks, filing cabinets, typewriters, calculating machines, and other office paraphernalia must facilitate the flow. Private offices must be so located as to support the movement of paper work, or at least not to hinder it. If the office is large, adding machines, typewriters, accounting machines, meter mailing machines, and the workers using them can be placed as in the line type of layout of a factory. In some offices, conveyor belts are used to transport papers from one desk to another.

Paper work requires the keeping of records of all kinds, from canceled checks to carbon copies of letters. This creates a problem of storage. Cabinets to file papers must be provided in convenient places, and shelves, boxes, or other containers must be available. Recent records, or those referred to frequently, must be kept where they can be quickly reached. Old or infrequently used papers may be put in a room out of the way. "Dead records" may be stored in a separate building. Valuable documents can be kept in a safe in the office or in a safe-deposit box at a bank.

LAYOUT PROCEDURES

Proper planning of layout can save time and money. Several steps may be undertaken in a proposed layout:

Ask department heads, foremen, office managers, or others concerned with the new interior arrangement to submit ideas.

[1] *The New Yorker*, Feb. 17, 1951, p. 39.

Have those in charge of the layout put their ideas on paper. These are then criticized, modified, or radically changed through consultation with all parties participating in the layout.

When a rough plan is achieved that appears to be satisfactory, reproduce it in miniature through use of three-dimensional models. By this means the executives can see the machines, desks, counters, walls, and other items in a better relationship to each other than would be possible by means of a diagram on paper. Such a model is particularly worthwhile in a factory layout because heavy machinery, pipes, and overhead conveyors, once placed in a building, cannot be changed except at great cost.

Layout procedures may be costly. But they are used to avoid mistakes that may be even more costly. Good layout planning anticipates problems in interior arrangement and permits changes to be made while they can be done with a minimum of cost and delay in work.

NATURE OF INVENTORY CONTROL

In all except the service industries, the handling of raw materials, goods in process of manufacture, finished goods, supplies, and merchandise demands considerable attention. The quantity of each of these goods on hand is called the *inventory*, and is classified as raw materials inventory, supplies inventory, and so on. The management of these inventories is called *inventory control*. If careful management is not exercised, the inventories tend to get out of control. The result will be increased expense and reduced profits.

It is equally bad to have too large an inventory or too small an inventory. Too small an inventory causes delays; too large an inventory ties up company funds and increases the risk of loss due to declining prices—particularly important in style goods or seasonal merchandise. The inventory must be well balanced in each division, model, or classification of items. The size of the whole inventory of hand tools, for example, may be satisfactory, but there may be an oversupply of wrenches and an undersupply of screwdrivers.

Inventory control must take into consideration price trends. If the movement of prices is upward, it is well to increase inventories beyond immediate needs, thus meeting part of the future requirements with goods and supplies bought at earlier, lower prices. If the price trend is downward, stocks should be kept sufficient to meet immediate needs only. If state or local taxes are levied on inventories, it may be wise to reduce stocks at the time when inventories are valued for tax purposes.

INVENTORY CONTROL RECORDS

A sound system of inventory control will provide the necessary information on which inventory decisions can be based. The information required includes the following:

Description of each item in stock
Amount of each item in stock

Point at which stock must be replenished

Length of time between placement of order and delivery

Rate of use of each item daily, weekly, or monthly

Goods on order but not received

Sources of supplies of goods to replenish inventory

The simplest way to keep a record of inventory is for a person to take a physical count from time to time. This is essentially what a housewife does in controlling her kitchen inventory. She will determine perhaps once a week what she has on hand in fruits, vegetables, bread, canned goods, coffee, and meat. Those items that are low or used up will be put on the shopping list. If the family runs out of an item before it is replenished, due to an oversight in taking stock, the inconvenience is usually slight. If there are no eggs for breakfast, pancakes or cereal can substitute. If the coffee can is empty, the family drinks tea or cocoa. There is little need for formality in managing inventory. In some small business establishments, inventory control is essentially of the kitchen type. The manager goes through the stockroom occasionally and sees what needs to be replenished. He works out in his mind or on a scrap of paper the amount of various items he is likely to need for the week or month ahead, the number of each item he has in stock, the probable length of time required to get delivery on an order to replenish depleted items, and the amount to order. Where a factory or store is operated by a few people, this method of inventory management may be satisfactory. It may also work where the source of supply to replenish inventory is close at hand. Neighborhood grocers or automobile repair shops located in cities can usually replace depleted items from wholesalers located in the same city, with delivery, if necessary, on the same day.

The method of controlling inventory described above is, of course, out of the question for a large company. A firm having many employees and a substantial inventory depends on written records of every different item in the inventory. Receipts, reductions in stock, and supply in store are recorded. Such a method is sometimes called the *perpetual inventory control* because the written records tell what is in inventory at all times.

If conditions were ideal, the inventory of each item would fall to zero just at the moment a shipment to replenish the stock arrived and was being unloaded. Obviously one cannot count on such perfect coordination. In most manufacturing and selling operations it is necessary to prevent the stock of an item from falling to zero. To do this a manager must ascertain how long it takes to get a refill order delivered, and how rapidly the item is used up. If, for example, the assembly line of a radio manufacturer requires an average of 1,000 tubular condensers daily from inventory and it takes 12 days after placing an order before the shipment is received, then the time to order another shipment might be placed at the point where the inventory falls to 12,000 condensers. But this leaves no margin for delays. A safety margin of 5 days' supply might be decided. Then the minimum reorder point would be set at 17,000 condensers.

The safety margin must take into consideration the consequences of "running out." If the lack of tubular condensers would shut down the assembly line, the safety margin probably would be set high. The safety margin on office pencils, on the other hand, would usually be set low. A graphic representation of a reorder schedule is shown in Figure 9-3, which illustrates a full replacement of stock with each reorder.

PHYSICAL INVENTORIES

The exact amount of each item in inventory is shown on the inventory record. However, it is necessary occasionally to verify the records, in spite of the time and effort it takes. Many things can happen to make the actual number of units of an item in inventory differ from the number indicated in the accounting records. Materials might get mislaid on the shelves or in the bins; more or less might be issued than is recorded by the stock clerk; and incorrect items might be issued.

Still another reason for discrepancy is theft. It is estimated that more than half a billion dollars is lost yearly because of the dishonesty of employees, executives, and customers.

In some businesses, particularly small, family-held ones, the owners will take company property for personal use, usually to evade paying their share of income taxes. As one writer put it, in a pamphlet addressed to owners of small businesses: "If you want others to respect your property, you must show an equal respect for

FIGURE 9-3   Reorder schedule under inventory control.

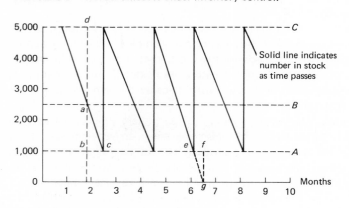

	C (5,000 units)	Maximum inventory
	B (2,500 units)	Reorder point
	A (1,000 units)	Minimum inventory expected
bd	(4,000 units)	Usual order quantity
ab	(1,500 units)	Units used up while order is filled
fg	(1,000 units)	Safety factor in event of delays
ef	(about 3 weeks)	Safety factor in terms of time

it . . . . If they see you slip, they will find little reason for remaining upright themselves."[2]

The taking of a physical inventory requires careful planning where many items of different kinds are involved. Inventory sheets or cards must be prepared. Employees detailed to taking inventory must be briefed on their duties. Shelves, bins, or other containers must be identified or tagged when the contents are counted. The count must be concluded in as short a time as possible because additions to stock and withdrawals from stock complicate the process of counting.

INVENTORY CONTROLS IN MANUFACTURING

INTERMITTENT MANUFACTURING

Most manufacturing is done on a *job-order* basis. This is particularly true in small companies and in large companies where the volume of production of a particular item is insufficient to make use of mass-production techniques. In job-order manufacturing, an order to produce 40 coffee tables is the signal for production of coffee tables to start. When the job is done, no more coffee tables are made until another job order is received.

Materials for coffee tables, to continue the illustration, must be available to permit production to begin soon after customer orders are processed. This requires maintaining inventory levels even during nonproducing periods, in anticipation of future orders.

MASS PRODUCTION

Mass production is on a continuous basis in contrast to intermittent, job-order production. Production is standardized and assembly-line methods are used. Purchase of materials is coordinated to production as far as possible, and inventories of raw materials are maintained largely because the receipt of ordered materials cannot be perfectly synchronized with production schedules. If perfect synchronization could be achieved, there would be a steady flow of raw materials from suppliers to the machines in the plant and a steady flow of finished goods from the machines to the delivery trucks. The difference in inventory management between job-order and mass-production manufacturing can be summarized as follows:

Job-order inventory policy—maintaining an available reserve of materials to permit production to start without delay.

Mass-production inventory policy—maintaining sufficient inventory to prevent work stoppages due to delay in receipts of materials.

[2] George C. Webster, *Reducing Stock Shrinkage in Small Firms*, Small Marketers Aids, no. 40, Small Business Administration, Washington, 1959.

INVENTORY CONTROLS IN MERCHANDISING

It is self-evident that when a store keeps its inventory low, its costs will fall. It is equally self-evident that when a store does not have an adequate selection of goods, its sales will fall.

Most stores carry a large variety of goods in stock. Some items move fast, some slowly, and some not at all. In some stores, 20 to 25 percent of the items account for 75 to 80 percent of the sales. A close control of inventory will identify the slow-moving items and show how slow each is. Steps can then be taken to reduce the number carried in stock for each item and to stop carrying those that move very slowly.

A periodic physical check is required in most stores as part of the inventory control system. In recent years, the tendency in retailing has been to take physical inventories more frequently. Rather than once a year, which used to be typical, semiannual, monthly, and even weekly counting of stock is becoming more common. Different inventory dates for each department or division of the store are sometimes used.

MATERIALS HANDLING

Good inventory practice requires not only care in handling inventory records but care in handling the inventory itself. This means proper storage facilities and adequate equipment for moving materials. Machine handling of materials in a plant has to a large degree supplanted moving and lifting by men. Conveyor belts lift goods up an incline. Rollers or slides safely convey goods from a higher to a lower level. Where goods have to be weighed as well as moved, a scale with rollers on its weighing platform can be set in the line of rollers, thus eliminating an extra handling.

A skid box, or pallet, permits a fork truck to lift heavy boxes for stacking or moving. To save time and labor, a fork truck will remove a loaded pallet from the stock room, carry it to the shipping dock, and load both box and pallet on a van. On the receiving dock at the end of the journey, another fork truck can unload the van much more quickly, since the pallets are already in place. The pallets can be marked with identifying marks for return to the owner if they are reusable. Often the van company will agree to return the pallets to the owner free of charge, since this method of loading and unloading reduces the amount of time a van is idle.

PACKAGING

Modern materials handling requires not only quick and safe methods of stacking and moving but also inexpensive yet secure packages for the goods. The technology of packaging has progressed rapidly during the present century. In fact, the mass production and mass distribution of today would not have been possible with the packaging techniques of a half-century ago.

The containers used in industry prior to World War I were largely made of wood, metal, glass, or sacking. Wooden crates were necessary for bulky and heavy items such as machinery. Metal and glass were used where the containers required sealing, and most granular materials were packed in sacks. These materials are still used, but they do not have the same dominance they once had. While metal and glass are very important in packaging, the use of wood and sacking has become less so. Paper and plastics, relatively little used before World War I, have grown tremendously in packaging and to a considerable degree have supplanted other materials. This is particularly true of wood, which has become more and more expensive as our lumber resources have become scarce relative to our rising population. The post-World War II years saw a tremendous increase in the use of man-made materials.

Packaging of goods for retail distribution has also undergone considerable change during the past 50 years. Carbonated beverages, once found only in bottles, are now found in cans. Milk is now packaged in plastic containers. The pickle barrel is no longer seen in grocery stores, having been displaced by bottles, and wooden crates are used much less than before. Heavy consumer items, such as furniture, washing machines, and television sets, are packaged in fiberboard containers.

In packaging consumer items, as in packaging industrial products, strength, ease of handling, ease of stacking, and economy are essential. In addition, however, packaging of consumer items requires *displayability*. The package provides a means by which the product can be advertised at the point where it is sold. Also, the package may be designed to be used by the consumer after it is empty. Jellies are sometimes packed in glass containers shaped as drinking glasses. Packages in the consumer field are required to sell as well as to protect, and, in some instances, the former requirement is paramount in package design.

Location may make the difference between success and failure in a business. A good location for one business, however, may be a poor one for a different type of business. To select a good location, one must consider the following factors and determine how important each is to the business under consideration: **SUMMARY**

Proximity to raw materials
Proximity to customers of the business
Climate
Availability and cost of power
Availability and cost of water
Transportation facilities
Supply and cost of skilled and unskilled labor
Local government restrictions on business
Local government inducements to attract business

Layout is the arrangement of machinery and equipment in a factory and the arrangement of desks, cabinets, and similar equipment in an office. Good layout will speed the flow of work, whether in an office or factory. New buildings are designed to permit efficient layout. In existing buildings, layout is adapted to the structure to make the best use of the available space. In retail stores, layout must take into account the convenience of the customer as well as the needs of display and storage of merchandise.

In a manufacturing plant, inventory is the supply of raw materials, goods being processed, finished products, and supplies used by the firm. In a wholesale or retail firm, inventory is the stock of merchandise carried to fill the orders of customers.

Keeping track of inventory is one of the functions of inventory management. Other functions are handling and storage of inventory. Tight control of these functions will make the best use of the materials on hand. The goal of inventory management is to keep enough of each item on hand so that the firm will not run short, but to keep no more than this amount.

The primary purpose of packaging is to protect the contents. Other purposes are to make items easy to transport, handle, and store. For consumer items, an important function of packaging is to attract the eye of the customer.

QUESTIONS FOR REVIEW

1 What is a good street location for a service station? A motel? A grade school? Give reasons for your answers.

2 Why is climate not as important a factor in the selection of a location for manufacturing as in previous decades?

3 What products need a lot of electric power for their manufacture?

4 Which industries are usually located near deep-water transport? Why?

5 What considerations apply in determining the adequacy of the labor supply of a town?

6 "A business should choose a city for its operations where the state and local taxes are the lowest that can be found." Discuss this statement critically.

7 Why is it of any concern to business companies whether schools, parks, and residential areas are of high quality?

8 In designing a layout, what factors should be taken into consideration where factory operation is intended?

9 Why are factory buildings that were constructed in recent years usually wide, long, and of only one or two stories?

10 Name some important considerations in planning the layout for a retail store.

11 Distinguish among convenience goods, shopping goods, and specialty goods.

12 In a store stocking both convenience goods and shopping goods, where should the convenience goods be placed? The shopping goods?

13 Show by using an example, such as a department store or a grocery store, why flexibility in layout is important.

14 Proper record handling is important in the layout of an office. Explain why this is so.

15 Why should a business avoid too large an inventory? Too small an inventory?

16 Suggest how a business manager should react to an anticipated increase in prices with respect to inventory management.

17 "In some businesses, inventory management is essentially of the kitchen type." What does this mean?

18 Explain the process of perpetual inventory control.

19 If a businessman keeps a written record of items in inventory, why is it necessary to take a physical count of items from time to time?

20 "If a businessman is sole owner of a business, it makes no difference if he takes articles from his business for personal use." Do you agree? Why or why not?

Buffa, Elwood S., and William H. Taubert: *Production Inventory Systems*, Richard D. Irwin Inc., Homewood, Ill., 1972.

Mallick, Randolph W., and Armand T. Gandreau: *Plant Layout and Practice*, John Wiley & Sons, Inc., New York, 1951.

Moore, J. M.: *Plant Layout and Design*, The Macmillan Company, New York, 1962.

Robichaud, Beryl: *Selecting, Planning, and Managing Office Space*, McGraw-Hill Book Company, New York, 1959.

SELECTED READINGS

Name	Section	Date

COMPLETION SENTENCES

1 Textile   manufacture   in   the   United   States   developed   first   in

New England , partly because its climate was conducive to

textile manufacture.

2 In recent years climate has become _less_ important

as a factor in site selection.

3 The   continued   rise   in   population   of   the   United   States   has   made

land a critical resource in many communities.

4 High freight rates insulate a local market from _distant_

competition.

5 The size and weight limits imposed on _trucks_ vary con-

siderably from state to state.

6 Low taxes may mean _____ *fewer* _____ municipal services.

7 It takes more money to _____ *raise* _____ the level of municipal services than to _____ *maintain* _____ them after they have been raised.

8 Good layout promotes _____ *coordination* _____ among departments.

9 There are two general types of production layout: _____ *group* _____ and _____ *line* _____ .

10 _____ *specialty* _____ goods are those that appeal to a particular clientele rather than to the average shopper.

11 Inventory control must take into consideration _____ *price* _____ trends.

12 The simplest way to keep a record of inventory is for a person to take a _____ *physical count* _____ from time to time.

13 Keeping track by means of written records of every type of item in inventory is called _____ *perpetual inventory* _____ .

14 Two reasons for the inventory records and the actual numbers of items counted being different are _____ *theft* _____ and _____ *incorrect entries* _____ .

15 It is estimated that more than a half-billion dollars is lost yearly because of the _____ *dishonesty* _____ of employees, executives, and customers.

Name	Section	Date

TRUE OR FALSE STATEMENTS

F **1** Since many factors are involved in the selection of a site, no one factor is decisive.

F **2** Iron and steel furnaces are usually located near the market for their products rather than near the raw materials.

T **3** The making of paper pulp requires a lot of water.

T **4** Oil refineries and steel mills are generally located where water transportation is available.

F **5** If freight rates rise, local retailers tend to feel competition from mail-order houses more keenly than before.

F **6** One reason Southern states have attracted industry has been the availability of plenty of labor.

F **7** Because of legal restrictions, cities compete with each other in attracting new businesses only by emphasizing the natural advantages of each city.

F **8** To avoid needless friction the managers but not the workers should be consulted in planning a layout.

F **9** Factories seldom use the line type of layout.

T **10** Factory windows are now designed largely for esthetic reasons rather than to provide illumination.

F **11** Wide aisles should be planned in a store in areas where customers are likely to linger in shopping.

F **12** Using three-dimensional models in planning layout is more important for an office than for a manufacturing plant.

F **13** Although inventory control is concerned with handling inventory, it is not concerned with price trends.

F **14** If inventory records are carefully kept, taking a physical count of inventory is unnecessary.

T **15** Relatively little of the total manufacturing in the United States is done on a job-order basis.

T **16** In mass production, assembly lines are used.

T **17** If a store keeps its inventory low, its costs will be kept down.

) **18** Machine handling of inventory has largely supplanted lifting and moving by men in the larger plants.

F **19** The use of cloth sacks in packaging has increased since the end of World War I.

T **20** In consumer goods the package is often designed to increase the salability of the item packaged.

EXERCISES

1 Each region or locality has certain attractions or advantages and certain unfavorable characteristics or disadvantages for certain types of industry. Examine the region (or locality) in which you live (choose either your state or your town or city). What are its attractions to industry? What are its unfavorable characteristics? Can any of these be overcome? How? What types of industries would be most likely to be attracted to your area?

Attractions	Unfavorable Characteristics

Types of Industries Likely to Be Attracted	How the Unfavorable Characteristics Might Be Overcome

2 Suggest methods of improving the layout of your college library, the college bookstore, the cafeteria, or an office. List improvements you feel would make better use of layout and make service more efficient.

a Deficiencies in present layout.

b Suggestions for improvement.

3 Bring to class four or five packages. Be prepared to describe the good and bad points of each package. Where a package is deficient in some respect, be able to suggest improvements.

4 Case problem for written report or class discussion.

Although he has a very tight inventory control, George Wankel, a wholesaler, finds that he is missing a substantial number of small, expensive items every week. He doesn't know how this could happen. The goods are locked up, and each order sent out for delivery is carefully checked by Wankel or his son. He also finds that he has a fairly constant surplus of inexpensive inventory items on hand. Finally he asks you for help in solving the mystery.

What can you suggest as a possible explanation? What can you offer as a a means of reducing "disappearances of inventory items"?

10 PRODUCTION MANAGEMENT AND PURCHASING

Production is concerned with making things. The methods used fall into one or more of four basic processes. As you read, think of as many examples as you can of each type of production process, drawing from your own experience or reading. Basically, there are two types of production: intermittent and continuous. The United States has become famous for continuous production, although in the 1970s Japan, West Germany, and other industrial countries have adopted production techniques pioneered in the United States. Probably the most dramatic example of continuous production is the assembly line. Try to think of examples where continuous production has been applied to each of the production processes you thought of earlier.

From the standpoint of business management, the importance of production control can hardly be overestimated. In reading the section on organization for production control, distinguish the different problems that must be met as the size of production facilities increases. Notice that as the volume of production in a plant increases, problems become more complex and new problems appear. Be aware also that as the volume of production increases, certain efficiencies of production appear.

The problem of controlling quality in production is an ever-present one. In this connection a review of the concepts of statistical quality control will help you.

Be aware of the existence of change as it applies to the science of production. The future will see a greater use of automatic machinery and electronically regulated production. Do not assume that the production methods with which you may be familiar in a particular industry will continue without change. In the area of production, change has been rapid in the past and undoubtedly will be rapid in the future.

In the section on purchasing, follow the mechanics of the purchasing process. Although not all these mechanics will be found in every type of purchasing activity, you should understand the place of each and be able to see its relationship to the others.

PRODUCTION PROCESSES   Production is the process of creating something of value. In its broadest sense, production includes the creation of anything that people are willing to buy. It includes haircuts, tonsillectomies, motion pictures, bus rides, and night club entertainment. It also includes making airplanes, diesel locomotives, and toys. The term is used in this chapter, however, in its narrow definition as the concentration of materials, machinery, and men to produce goods. By changing the form of materials, production increases their value. A sheet of steel becomes a tin can or an automobile fender. A block of wood becomes a fence post. A lump of clay becomes a brick or a flower pot. The materials have become more valuable through the process of production.

The *production process* is the method by which materials are changed in form. These processes can be classified into four types: analysis, synthesis, extraction, and fabrication.

ANALYSIS   The process of breaking down a raw material into a number of products is *analysis*. A log might be cut into boards; the scrap pieces made into pencils, toothpicks, and matchsticks; the sawdust pressed into pieces for burning in fireplaces; and the bark used on floors. In petroleum refining, oil is broken down into gasoline, kerosene, fuel oil, asphalt, and many other products. A large meat packer will reduce a hog into many cuts of meat, use the bone and blood for fertilizer and the hide for leather, and prepare the bristles for brushes.

SYNTHESIS   The process of combining two or more raw materials into a single finished product is *synthesis*. Glass results from the fusion of sand with lime, soda, potash, and other chemicals. Solder is the combination of tin and lead. The chemical and drug industries use the process of synthesis to a considerable degree, as does the steel industry.

EXTRACTION   The raw materials used in production come from the land, the sea, or the air. The process of drawing out these materials is *extraction*. Mining, quarrying, and petroleum production extract substances from the earth. Fish and minerals such as magnesium, sodium, chlorine, and bromine are extracted from the sea. Nitrogen and oxygen are extracted from the air. Farming might be called an extractive industry, since the cultivated plants draw materials from the ground and the air.

FABRICATION   The process of making products of greater value from already manufactured materials is *fabrication*. The materials may be cut, machined, woven, knitted, shaped, or combined with other materials. For example, thread is woven into cloth; diamonds are cut into gems; and steel is shaped into plows. Automobiles are fabricated from steel sheets, plate glass, rubber mats, spark plugs, and a hundred other items already manufactured either by the automobile company or by independent suppliers. The process of fabrication is very widely used in a highly industrialized economy such as ours.

Production is basically carried on in either of two ways: continuously or intermittently. The problems of inventory management for each of these types were discussed in the previous chapter. Here, we shall examine the production techniques of each.

TYPES OF PRODUCTION

In intermittent production, a number of articles are produced of one type. Production of that type then ceases, and production of a different article is undertaken. Labor and equipment are applied to materials for a relatively limited period, either in response to an order from a customer or in anticipation of such an order. Machinery is set up and adjusted for the particular job and, upon completion, is dismantled or reset for a different job.

INTERMITTENT PRODUCTION

In continuous production, labor and equipment are applied continuously to materials over a long period of time. Specialized machinery is purchased or existing machinery is adjusted for a production run that is likely to continue for months. The products must be highly standardized and the volume large. One example is the making of steel tubing, as illustrated in Figure 10-1. The assembly-line method of manufacture is an application of continuous production. The necessity of coordination is greater in continuous production than in intermittent production, since an interruption at any stage may stop the entire process.

CONTINUOUS PRODUCTION

Continuous manufacturing generally is less flexible than intermittent manufacturing. Because standardization is necessary to achieve the maximum benefit from the continuous process, the number of models, sizes, and designs must be kept low. Or, to put it another way, if the number of models and styles of a product is increased, production volume must also increase if the continuous process is to be used efficiently. The tremendous volume of output of the major automobile manufacturers has made it possible for them to manufacture a variety of body designs, engine sizes, and style series while still using the continuous process of manufacturing.

In addition to automobile manufacturing, continuous production is found in many factories producing consumer appliances and in cement production, paper making, sugar refining, petroleum refining, textile production, and flour milling.

The deciding factors in determining the type of production employed in a

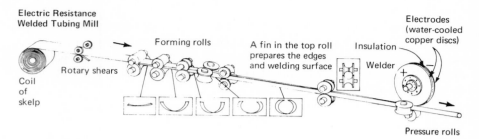

FIGURE 10-1 Continuous production of steel tubing by electric welding.

plant are volume and variety of models or designs. If volume is low or the variety of designs is high, intermittent production is indicated. If volume is high or if the variety of designs can be kept low, continuous production can be used. Frequently, a company will begin its existence as a job-lot producer, using the intermittent type of production. As it grows in size and expands its volume, a point will be reached at which it becomes more efficient to use continuous production.

STANDARD GOODS
AND CUSTOM GOODS

Closely associated with the type of production is the type of product. Because intermittent production permits greater flexibility of design and style, a larger variety of goods can be produced. Design can be easily altered to suit each customer. Where goods are produced to customer specifications, they are called *custom made*. Because only one, or at most only a few, of each specification are produced, less use can be made of automatic machines and more dependence must be placed on labor in production. Custom-made goods are, of course, more expensive. However, one of the reasons why custom goods are popular is that they *are* expensive and that their possession is evidence of their owners' wealth.

In some products, the distinction provided by custom manufacture is unimportant. This is true of lawnmowers, outboard motors, portable radios, and toothpaste. In other products, distinction is very important and custom manufacture is more widely used, as in women's dresses and hats. Because custom manufacture is more popular, "custom features" or "personalized" touches are often added to standard goods. Mass-produced houses, all with identical floor plans, are differentiated by different exterior trim, inside and outside colors, and location of cement walks and garages. Pencils, pens, and other items are "personalized" by printing the owner's name in gold letters. Even an automobile can be made distinctive by the addition of bits of chrome here and there.

Standard goods are those produced to the manufacturer's specifications rather than to the customer's. In order to sell goods, it is necessary to design products that customers will buy, but, in the case of standard goods, the design is not made to suit a particular customer but a group of customers. It might be said that standard design is a compromise of customer tastes or that it caters to the average taste. Where a large volume of each design is produced, it is practically necessary that common desires be given preference. This does not mean that all television sets will look alike, for there are many standard models. But it does mean that a television set that is to be enclosed in a bookcase and is to match the color and grain of the wood will require a custom-made cabinet rather than a standard one.

Standard goods are generally manufactured by the continuous type of production process. They usually carry the manufacturer's brand and are usually widely advertised.

In producing goods for industry, both standard production and custom production are found. Surprisingly, where the continuous type of production is used by a company manufacturing consumer goods, the company will generally require custom-made tools and machinery; and where a company produces custom-made goods, it will generally use standard tools and machinery. Lathes, planers, and milling machines designed for a variety of products and for flexibility of operation can be used for custom manufacture. Because of their adaptability they can be used in many factories and can be produced in quantity according to a standard design. But when a factory produces its own branded consumer product in large volume by continuous manufacturing, it may need specially designed (custom-made) lathes, planers, and milling machines.

PRODUCTION CONTROL

IMPORTANCE

Production control is a well-defined set of procedures for integrating labor, machinery, and materials to achieve maximum economy in the process of production. It makes possible better inventory control. It makes promised delivery dates easier to achieve, and so contributes to customer satisfaction. It permits better scheduling of employee working hours, thus contributing to employee morale. And it reduces cost.

All plants, big or small, must use some production control. The problem is in determining whether the type of control used is adequate. To determine the adequacy of production control in a plant, a manager should seek the answers to the following groups of questions:

What is the output capability of the plant? What is the capacity of each machine? How many men are available? Are double or triple shifts possible if needed? Are there any existing or potential bottlenecks in the chain of production?

What is the backlog of unfilled orders? Are these firm orders, or are they likely to be canceled in the event of a slight downturn in business activity? How much work, in terms of daily production, is required to complete the orders on hand?

What is the forecast of sales for the future? How dependable have past forecasts been? Is the sales pattern seasonal?

What is the inventory of materials, supplies, and tools? How readily can replacement be made of these items when needed?

The actual form of control depends on the product made, the variety of designs, the type of production process, and the volume of production. A company making a single size of concrete block has a relatively simple problem in production control. A company making a large variety of foods or Christmas decorations has a much more difficult problem. Precision increases the problem of production control, making control more difficult in the manufacture of camera lenses than in the making of toys. If the production process requires many subassemblies and parts, as in television manufacture, control is that much more difficult.

ORGANIZATION

In a small factory, the manager or his foreman would assemble the necessary information for controlling production. He would schedule customers' orders so that they would be ready on the promised dates. He would keep in constant touch with the daily production in the plant, and know which machines were being used and which were standing idle. He would keep checking on the supply of materials, to make sure of their availability. He would assign work to employees to bring out the best use of their capabilities and their time.

He probably would make little use of paper records, issuing his orders in person. He would spend most of his time in the shop rather than the office, and probably would do grudgingly the paper work that could not be avoided. He would know at first hand the condition of the machines, the talents and temperaments of his men, and how much of the output was not up to standard. He would make decisions on the spot to meet the minor crises that are bound to occur daily. If a machine were out of order, he would arrange for repair and reschedule production and employee assignments until the machine could resume production. If a key employee were absent or extra work needed to be done in the shop, the manager would hire another worker or do the work himself.

With a change in production, the manager would have to determine the effect of the change on existing production techniques. He would decide which machines would have to be retired or altered and how many new machines or tools would be needed. He would assign the men to their new jobs and explain to them the nature of the changes in production. He would see that they understood their new assignments and were fulfilling them capably. He would check particularly closely on the quality of production until the new assignments were mastered by the men.

Thus, in a small plant, the effectiveness of production control generally rests on one man. He needs a working knowledge of the machines in his plant and a good grasp of figures to control inventories and costs; he must be adept in the art of employee relations, plan his work carefully, and have the mental discipline to make decisions and accept responsibility.

As the size of a factory increases and the number of men working on the machines increases from 10 to 20, to 40, to 70, to 100, and higher, the control of production by one man is impossible. The manager will have to spend more and more time in his office and will delegate the actual supervision of the men working in the plant. He will have to hire a full-time inventory clerk, and will probably need an office assistant. His orders will no longer be given in person to the men at the machines, but will be relayed through foremen or posted on the plant bulletin board. Contact will be less direct, less personal, and misunderstandings will be more frequent. To make sure orders are understood, they will tend more and more to be written.

As the plant continues to expand and its products become more diversified, the plant manager will have to delegate much of the authority he exercised in the simpler days of small production. He will now issue broad orders, leaving to subordinates the detailed decisions necessary in following his orders. He will, for example, schedule the production of each shop in the plant so as to coordinate the production schedule as a whole. But he will leave to the shop foremen the discretion to schedule the work among the employees in each shop, as long as the production of the shop meets the plant schedule.

The plant manager in a large plant requires assistance in making decisions. He does not have the time to keep his working knowledge of machines always up to date. Probably, he will have to depend on an expert mechanic or chief engineer or the foreman of each shop for this knowledge. The inventory clerk of the small plant will probably become a materials manager as the plant expands, and will have the responsibility of maintaining an adequate inventory for scheduled production.

The plant manager, of course, will no longer be able to inspect the output to determine its quality. This responsibility will be assigned to inspectors or to a division of quality control. The function of maintaining satisfactory employee relations will be given to a personnel director. And the keeping of records will now require more filing clerks, more typists, more office personnel of all types; and an office manager will be needed to supervise their work. As the plant grows, the manager will realize that the following developments have taken place: rather than controlling production, as he did when the plant was small, he has become a coordinator of production-control activities exercised by others; control has become impersonal; and whatever the rate of growth of production in the plant, the rate of growth of paper work has been far greater.

In most production departments, both the line and staff types of organization are used. The line organization proceeds from the plant manager or vice president in charge of manufacturing to the production manager, the foremen, assistant foremen, and production employees. Staff functions are exercised by the personnel director, materials manager, and chief engineer. The organizational chart of a production department is shown in Figure 10-2.

Although the plant manager has specialists to give him information, he will probably try to watch the actual production in the plant as often as he can get away from his office—or his home. A vivid description of a plant manager is contained in the following:

Maintaining the enormous flow of U.S. production requires an enormous variety of workmen-sweepers, mechanics, toolmakers, vice-presidents. But if one job may be

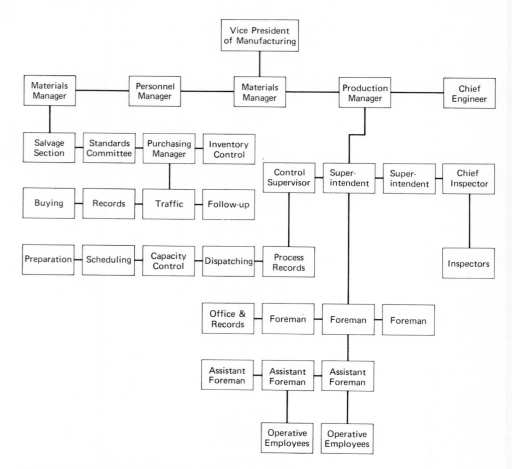

FIGURE 10-2 Organization of a production department.

singled out as the most vitally important, it is almost certainly that of production man. His title may be works manager, plant supervisor or vice president in charge of operations. But his job is always the same: to deliver goods and at a cost that will make the whole venture profitable. To accomplish this he must set up a production line, keep it moving, schedule its supplies and subassemblies, maintain quality, see that the machines work efficiently—and in between—plan retooling for the next model. This requires a type of man which, produced in the U.S. in comparative plenty, may itself be regarded as one of the notable achievements of American production.

Usually they are college graduates, although some learned the correspondence-school way. They often wear their hats even in the office, a habit acquired during years spent "in the shop," for a good production man almost always started at the bottom and knows his company's every little operation better than his own scarred palm. He has worked hard and has an instinct for leadership which makes others work hard without resentment. He is aggressive yet friendly, imaginative yet practical, and he fervently believes that a fast-moving production line is the most beautiful sight on earth. One was recently asked why he seldom took time off. "Well," he said, "it's like this. First you're tooling for your new models and you work night and day for weeks without sleep, hardly. You just get your line working and a bug develops, and you can't rest until it's ironed out. Then, when it's finally going, you don't like to take a day off because it's such a pleasure just to stand there watching and listening to the thing hum."[1]

Production control, basically, is of two kinds: order control and flow control. *Order control* is based on the control of a job lot or "batch" of work through the various processes required in transforming raw material into a finished product. Each order is controlled so that it arrives at the proper time. Figure 10-3 illustrates the sequence followed by two orders through a factory. Production control records the location of each order or job lot as it progresses, schedules the routing so that sufficient machine capacity is available at the right times, and makes tools, materials, and men available as needed. Order control is the type found in intermittent production.

PRODUCTION-CONTROL PROCEDURES

Flow control, used in the continuous type of production, regulates the rate of flow of materials to each work area or shop and to each machine in the shop. Figure 10-4 illustrates the sequence followed by work in process under flow control. The material must flow to the machines at a constant rate. To achieve a uniform rate of flow, the machine capacity available at each station must be adequate to permit a steady rate of progress.

Many small companies engage only in intermittent manufacturing, and therefore use order control. Many large companies produce only on a continuous basis, and use flow control. A large number of companies apply flow control to high-volume products and order control to products manufactured in low volume.

[1] *Life*, Oct. 4, 1948, p. 72.

FIGURE 10-3 Order control.

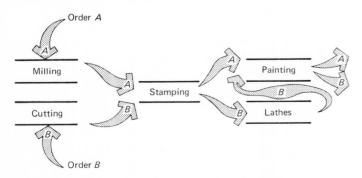

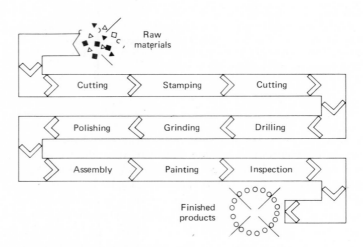

FIGURE 10-4 Flow control.

PRODUCTION MANAGEMENT

The management of production entails performing those functions of planning, organizing, and supervising that are found in any area of management. Production objectives are established, and production management must attempt to gain the objectives. The objectives must be integrated with the overall objectives of the enterprise. Production is not an end in itself but is part of the broader goal of expanding sales and profits. If, for example, the production manager sets quality standards too low in order to reduce costs, it may interfere with the marketing goal of attracting sales by stressing quality.

In small plants, production management is apt to depend on "feel" or intuition to a considerable extent. In larger plants, study and analysis are often undertaken before decisions are reached. To state it another way, in small plants, management is an art; in large plants, it is a science.

SCIENTIFIC MANAGEMENT

One of the striking developments in management in the present century is the concept of *scientific management*, although the idea of applying the disciplines of science and mathematics to production did not originate in the present century.[2] Nevertheless, the application of the idea and its growth is a twentieth-century phenomenon. Frederick W. Taylor is generally credited with starting the trend in scientific management. He experimented with various work techniques in an attempt to eliminate waste motions, reduce the time required for various operations, and increase worker output. One of the principles he emphasized was that planning

---

[2]Charles R. Babbage, an English mathematician, suggested in *On the Economy of Manufactures*, published in 1832, that the methods of science and mathematics could be applied to the operations of factories.

for production should be divorced from its execution. On this point he wrote as follows:

> Under the old type management success depends almost entirely on getting the "initiative" of the workmen, and it is indeed a rare case in which this initiative is really attained. Under scientific management the "initiative" of the workmen (that is, their hard work, their goodwill, and their ingenuity) is obtained with absolute uniformity and to a greater extent than is possible under the old system; and in addition . . . the managers assume new burdens, new duties and responsibilities never dreamed of in the past. The managers assume, for instance, the burden of gathering together all of the traditional knowledge which in the past has been possessed by the workmen and then of classifying, tabulating, and reducing this knowledge to rules, laws, and formulae which are immensely helpful to the workmen in doing their daily work. In addition to developing a *science* in this way, the **management** takes on three other types of duties which involve new and heavy burdens for themselves.
>
> These new duties are grouped under four heads:
>
> *First.* They develop a science for each element of a man's work, which replaces the old rule-of-thumb method.
>
> *Second.* They scientifically select and then train, teach, and develop the workman, whereas in the past he chose his own work and trained himself as best he could.
>
> *Third.* They heartily cooperate with the men so as to insure all of the work is being done in accordance with the principles of the science which has been developed.
>
> *Fourth.* There is an almost equal division of the work and the responsibility between the management and the workman. The management takes over all work for which they are better fitted than the workmen, while in the past almost all of the work and the greater part of the responsibility were thrown upon the men.[3]

Taylor believed that efficient management required the study of each task performed in a plant. Rather than assigning a job to a worker and letting the worker determine how it was to be done, Taylor declared it was the function of management to tell the worker exactly how the job should be performed. This involves deciding what tools should be used, how they should be used, and the rate at which each worker should perform. Rather than permit workers to work at the same task in different ways and at different speeds, management should standardize on the methods and rate of production for each worker and for every step of the production process.

Work simplification is one of the goals of scientific management. Taylor approached this goal by observing a worker for a given task and analyzing his actions. Each task was observed in detail, and waste motions noted. When the best sequence of movements was determined, instructions were prepared, and all workers were instructed to use the same motions. By observing the loading of coal, for example, Taylor calculated that by adopting the most efficient sequence of motions, a good man could load 47 tons during a working day, compared to the average of 12½ tons loaded per man at the time.

While the term "scientific management" is not as commonly used now as it was in Taylor's day, the methods he pioneered have been refined and advanced,

[3] F. W. Taylor, *Scientific Management*, Harper & Row, Publishers, Incorporated, New York, 1947, pp. 36–37.

and form the basis of many management principles in current use. Modern management is concerned with improving production methods through: simplification of tasks, better work surroundings, improved tools and machines, and better control of production processes.

1   Simplification of tasks: This was given prime importance by Taylor. By and large, the methods he used are in use today, and his aversion to wasted motion is shared by modern managers. However, today there is greater understanding of human factors such as mental fatigue induced in some persons by unchanging, repetitive actions.

2   Better work surroundings: These affect not only a worker's morale but his output. Good light, shielded machinery, reduction of noise, and correct working temperatures can reduce rejects and raise output. Well-planned layouts will provide easy access to supplies, tools, materials, and facilities for worker comfort.

3   Improved designs in machines and tools: These can increase production and reduce costs. During his stay at the Bethlehem Steel Works, Taylor found workers shoveling with a wide variety of shovels, usually owned by the men. The same shovel was used by a man to shovel 38 pounds of iron ore per load and to shovel 3½ pounds of rice-size coal. By using small-capacity shovels for heavy material, and large shovels for light material, the work capacity of each man was greatly increased. Similarly, the shape and location of control knobs, dials, and levers are given as careful consideration as the other parts of machines.

4   Production-control processes: These processes, such as routing, scheduling, and dispatching, were studied by Taylor and are the subject of continued study today.

MOTION-AND-TIME STUDY

One of the tools Taylor used to analyze tasks was a stopwatch. While working in the machine shop of the Midvale Steel Company, he decided "it was simpler to time with a stopwatch each of the elements of the various kinds of work done in the place, and then find the quickest time in which each job could be done by summing up the total times of its component parts, than it was to search through the time records of former jobs and guess at the proper time."[4]

Timing work routines has grown into an important tool of management. The main purpose is to achieve uniformity in the performance and measurement of work, but such studies also provide management with accurate information on the time required for each task in the chain of production. This information permits production schedules to be set up with greater precision. The accurate measurement of work aids in estimating and controlling costs, and permits the establishment of time standards for completing tasks. Output of individual workers can be measured against these standards and reasons for deviations investigated.

A recent adaptation of time-and-motion study is *micromotion* study. A high-speed motion-picture camera photographs an operator at work. The camera might be set at 4,000 frames per minute. After the film is developed, it is run through the projector at the normal speed of 960 frames per minute, so the sequence of

[4] *Ibid.*, p. 148.

actions can be analyzed in slow motion. When the motions used in a task are too rapid to be followed at normal speed, micromotion study is helpful. It also permits a much greater accuracy in measuring the time for each element in a task. The main drawback is expense.

Production is not measured by volume alone; it is measured by quality of product as well. Goods that are defective cannot be sold or, if they are sold, the reputation of the producer suffers. It is therefore necessary that care be used in production, that standards of quality be established, and that output be up to standard. The success of a company in maintaining high standards will in considerable measure determine its success in competition with other producers. But quality alone does not ensure the success of a company. A raising of quality may be achieved only at prohibitive cost. There is a market for Rolls-Royce cars and for Steinway concert grand pianos, but it is limited because of price. In producing for a mass market, quality standards must be set in relation to the costs involved in maintaining the standards set.

INSPECTION AND QUALITY CONTROL

After standards have been set, steps must be taken to ensure that the products meet the standards. *Inspection* determines whether the product is up to standard, or, if not, why it is substandard. The amount of inspection required depends on the nature of the product. A company making drugs for hospitals must provide a considerable amount of inspection. During the first year of production of polio vaccine in the United States, several batches of vaccine from one producer contained live viruses, causing rather than preventing polio in persons vaccinated. It was painfully evident that in this instance the amount of inspection was not enough. In the production of medicines, precision tools, gauges, and similar products, it is common to inspect every item. Where it is necessary to keep costs down and a high degree of precision is not essential, sampling, discussed below, is used.

INSPECTION

The methods of inspection vary according to the production process and the article produced. In the case of drugs, a small amount from each batch might be subjected to chemical analysis or microscopic examination. Inspectors may listen to car engines through a doctor's stethoscope. Sometimes, adequate inspection requires that an assembled machine be run for a period, disassembled, and then an examination be made of the parts, replacing those seen to be defective. Inspection of this type is obviously expensive. Some products can be tested only by destroying them, such as a test of the bursting strength of a paper container. Obviously, such a test can be used only on the basis of sampling.

METHODS OF INSPECTION

Many scientific aids are available to facilitate inspection. In addition to the microscope and stethoscope mentioned above, inspectors use stroboscopes, photo-electric cells, high-speed cameras, x-ray machines, and other devices. For example, a photoelectric cell may scan a line of nuts moving along a conveyor belt. If a defective nut passes the light beam, the photoelectric cell will actuate a mechanical arm that automatically knocks the defective nut off the belt. Another example is the use of x-rays to detect flaws that cannot be seen with the eye.

Inspection is generally divorced to some extent from production. While inspectors could be put under the jurisdiction of production foremen, for example, it is better to keep the inspectors independent so they can use their judgment and report their results more reliably.

Inspection is done either **on the floor** or **centrally**. If it is done centrally, all inspection for a division or shop is done at one place. The advantage is that central inspection clearly separates inspection from production and permits the use of inspection devices or techniques that might interfere with production if used on the production floor. A disadvantage is that it involves movement of materials from the production line to the central inspection station, which may slow down production. **Floor inspection** is done on the spot where the item is produced.

SAMPLING

As mentioned above, where defective products cannot be tolerated, every unit of production will be inspected. But this is costly, and is not necessary for many products. Where "100 percent inspection" is not used, a sample is taken to test for quality. The sample may be 1 out of every 10 units, 1 out of every 100, or 1 out of every 1,000. If a machine produces 8,000 units between adjustments, the first and last few may be examined to determine the accuracy of adjustment of the machine, and 80 others may be selected at random for quality testing. The maximum permissible number of defects in the sample of 80 may be 4. If less than 5 are defective, the batch is approved. If 5 or more are defective, the entire batch may be rejected or the balance of the batch may be inspected. The size of the sample to be inspected and the disposition of substandard batches are decisions of considerable importance for management.

STATISTICAL QUALITY CONTROL

Statistical quality control applies the discipline of statistics to the problem of controlling quality. If 10,000 bolts are produced under a set of specifications, they will not be identical. There will be variations in dimensions, perhaps so small as to be negligible. A few, perhaps, will vary so much from the standard that they will have to be scrapped. The variations from the standard, if presented statistically, will form a **frequency distribution**. The distribution will indicate what percentage of the 10,000 bolts falls within acceptable limits and what percentage of the total is unacceptable. By taking samples from the output of bolts, measuring the bolts in the sample, and recording the measurements on a statistical chart, it can be seen whether the variations of the bolts in the sample fall within tolerable limits. If so, the batch from which the sample was taken is also assumed to be within tolerable limits. Statistical methods can determine the size of the sample that must be taken to be confident that the sample adequately represents the whole. As long as the samples taken periodically from production indicate the output is within the tolerance limits imposed by management, no corrective action is indicated. But if the tests indicate that the samples exceed the tolerance limits, the machinery will have to be adjusted, production methods changed, or other steps taken to improve the quality of the product.

AUTOMATION

The word *automation* came into general usage shortly after World War II. Apparently it was coined by an official of the Ford Motor Company, which established an Automation Department in 1947. Although definitions of the term vary, one of the definitions is as follows: "[Automation is] continuous automatic production, largely in the sense of linking together already highly mechanized individual operations. Automation is a way of work, based on the concept of production as a continuous flow, rather than processing by intermittent batches of work."[5]

Automation transfers to machines the work, both physical and mental, formerly undertaken by men. Automatic production is not an invention of the present century; flour milling, for example, was done automatically from the unloading of grain at one end to the sacking of flour at the other end as early as 1790. The concept of automation, however, goes further. It involves the use of machines to control machines. Furthermore, the material is passed from one machine to another without human aid, making a complex series of operations automatic. And the machines are automatically adjusted to correct for deviations from the standard.

The characteristics of automation can be described as: automatic machinery, coordinated handling of materials and processing, feedback, and electronic computers.

AUTOMATIC MACHINERY

The development of automatic machinery continues to transfer worker functions to the machine. These functions are primarily the repetitious ones, which are considered routine and drudgery for most persons. Even the tasks of service and inspection are being taken over by machines. The reduction in the work force in some cases has been spectacular. One company, for example, was able to assemble 1,000 radios a day on automatic machines guided by two workers. Former assembly methods had required 200 workers.

[5] Ralph J. Cordiner, *Testimony on Automation before the Subcommittee on Economic Stabilization*, Joint Congressional Committee on the Economic Report, Washington, Oct. 26, 1955, p. 3.

COORDINATED HANDLING OF MATERIALS AND PROCESSING

Where machinery is used to cut, grind, or otherwise change materials, the work done by the machine operator is the job of picking up a blank piece of metal, for example, putting it into the proper position on the machine, holding it in place while the machine cuts, bores, or shapes the piece, and setting the completed piece aside. In factories using automation, the machines are fed automatically and the flow of material through the machines is coordinated.

FEEDBACK

"Feedback" is used to describe the process of automatic adjustment of machinery whenever any variation from production standards reaches the maximum allowable. A simple example is a thermostat, which may be set to turn a furnace on when the room temperature drops 3 degrees below the setting on the dial and turn the furnace off when the temperature rises 3 degrees above the setting. Oil refining and chemicals use feedback extensively. In the steel industry, strip mills are adjusted as to speed and roller setting by feedback, so that the machine corrects itself to maintain uniform quality of output.

ELECTRONIC COMPUTERS

The electronic computers, developed after World War II, reduce much of the drudgery in mathematical computation. The speed with which they operate is fantastic compared with the time required by the human brain. One example is determining the best nozzle and bucket angles for a steam turbine, which takes 15 to 60 minutes by computer and 1 to 3 years for a trained human being.

The extent of computer application in the manufacture of turbine blades is described in the following excerpt from *Business Week*:

> A computer system controls every step from the receipt of an order to the shipment of the finished product. A computer sends an assignment to a production worker via a teletypewriter. The message includes the location of material, operator instructions, and a list of tools he will need along with the location. A central computer that controls 32 machine tools gives directions for tool setup to produce a specified turbine blade design. Once the operator completes the setup, he merely pushes a button and the computer controls the entire machining job.[6]

The advance in computer applications to production make many existing production techniques rapidly obsolete. What will future production techniques based on the computer be like? One publication gives this answer: "It's as difficult to guess today where the computer world is going as it would have been for 18th century man to foresee the industrial civilization that has grown out of James Watt's little steam driven pump."[7]

[6] *Business Week*, Sept. 9, 1972, p. 89.
[7] "Computers," a special report, *Business Week*, June 21, 1958, p. 68.

Materials and supplies are needed by every business, whether it be manufacturing, distribution, or service. They must be made available at the proper place, at the proper time, in the proper quantity, with the proper quality, and at the proper price. In many businesses, purchasing has an importance equal to production and selling in creating profits. Successful purchasing requires training and judgment, and in large businesses it is done by specialists. In a small business, it may be the part-time responsibility of an executive. In any case, it is a function that must be exercised with care.

IMPORTANCE OF PURCHASING

Purchasing can be defined as the obtaining of materials, supplies, and equipment for use by a company or for resale. It involves more than merely buying, although that is the most important activity of a purchasing department. Broadly speaking, purchasing includes testing of samples to aid in choosing between competing products, following up orders that have been placed but not yet delivered, and examining delivered items to verify quality and quantity. Some writers prefer the term *procurement*, since it is broader. However, the officers or departments responsible for the functions described above are usually called *purchasing departments* or *purchasing agents*; we prefer the term *purchasing*.

One of the fundamental decisions with respect to obtaining required materials is whether to buy or to make. Such a decision is properly made at the top executive level of the company in most cases, because it involves the production department, the finance department, and perhaps other departments as well. Nevertheless the decision is based largely on the same considerations that guide the purchasing department in its choices: cost, quality, quantity, and dependability.

THE DECISION TO BUY OR TO MAKE

If a businessman calculates that an item can be made by the company more cheaply than it can be purchased, he might save money by producing the item rather than buying it. It is important, however, that the calculations be carefully made. Production may involve investment in plant and machinery, which cannot be liquidated except at a loss if the company should ever want to return to the policy of buying rather than making. But often, after careful consideration of all the risks involved, the decision is frequently made to produce rather than to buy. In other cases, such study often provides valuable data that can be used to bargain with a supplier to reduce his price. A large retail grocery chain, for example, can use the threat of going into the business of making jam or baking cookies to secure price reductions on these items.

COST

If no supplier is making a product of sufficiently high quality to meet the specifications of the company, the company may have to make the item itself. However, the explanation may be one of the following:

QUALITY

There has been no previous demand for such high quality.

The quality specifications demanded by the production department are unrealistic.

It is not possible to meet such high standards without adding excessively to costs.

Before undertaking production to assure quality, the possibilities listed above should be considered. If suppliers specializing in a particular item do not make it of sufficiently high quality, there is usually a reason.

QUANTITY One of the reasons for producing rather than buying is that the needed quantity of an article of special rather than standard design is so small it would not interest a supplier. Before deciding to make the article, management should consider simplifying or standardizing the design, or determining the cost of placing an order large enough to interest a supplier, and keeping the quantity not immediately needed for future use. Also, if production of an item is unprofitable for a supplier, production might be equally unprofitable for the company using the item.

At the other extreme is the need for quantity so large that it is not within the productive capacity of any supplier. Dividing the order among several suppliers would multiply the work of the purchasing department in keeping track of deliveries from different suppliers and in assuring uniformity of product. For these reasons, a company requiring a large quantity of an item will often make the item itself. However, the possibility of interference with existing production by adding production in large quantity of a new item may deter management from producing the item.

DEPENDABILITY If a company buys an item from a supplier, it is dependent on the stability of production of the supplier. The supplier might be shut down because of a labor-management dispute, a breakdown of machinery, or for other reasons. If a company makes rather than buys, it might be assured a more dependable supply. Furthermore, if an item requires servicing, it might in some instances be better to make the item rather than to buy, since the workers who produced the item would be available to service it without delay.

OTHER CONSIDERATIONS If a company wishes to safeguard a secret process or design, it may wish to make most or all of the components of the finished article in its own plant. For example, a newspaper was once able to publish rough sketches of the new automobile models of the major car manufacturers before the models were introduced. The sketches were not gotten from the manufacturers but from information pieced together from suppliers to the automobile companies.

The existence of unused plant capacity will frequently dictate a decision to make rather than to buy. A company strives to keep its work force and plant operating at as near capacity as possible. To do this, a company will sometimes shift from buying an item to making it.

If there appears to be collusion among suppliers to keep the price of an item high, a company might decide or at least threaten to make it. Collusion among producers is a violation of antitrust laws, but proof is difficult and enforcement spotty.

ELEMENTS OF PURCHASING

In a small firm purchasing might be handled as a part-time function by one man. In a large company the function of purchasing is handled by a purchasing department, with an organizational structure similar to Figure 10-5. The purchasing department exists to meet the needs of other departments in a company. It is therefore essential that cordial relations and an attitude of mutual helpfulness prevail among departments. The production department, for example, is naturally interested in maintaining a stock of materials and supplies sufficiently large to meet all possible needs and of a quality as high as can be secured. The purchasing department must be concerned with costs, however, and must temper the demands of the production department to keep costs down to reasonable levels. On the other hand, in an effort to make a good showing by keeping costs down, the purchasing department might be tempted to order from suppliers whose prices are low but whose delivery schedules are undependable and whose product quality is variable.

FIGURE 10-5   Organizational structure of a purchasing department.

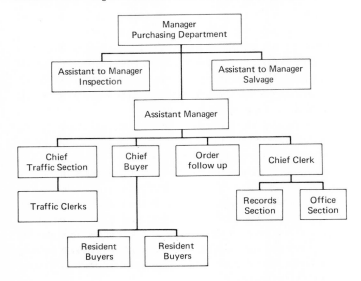

Each department must understand the other, and must recognize that compromise is often necessary for the welfare of the company as a whole.

The production department must keep the purchasing department informed as far in advance as possible of its future materials requirements and about its production schedule. Whenever changes in production schedules are necessary, they must be communicated to the buyers of materials so that changes in purchase orders may be made where necessary. Emergency orders for materials to be rushed to the plant cannot always be avoided, but the production department should endeavor to keep such requests to a minimum.

The purchasing department, for its part, must keep the production department informed of materials ordered, expected arrival dates, and any delays that might occur. Delays in the delivery of ordered materials might interfere with production schedules. The purchasing department is sometimes obligated to prevent production delays by securing deliveries from alternate sources, if possible. Buyers frequently discover new products, materials, or other items in their contacts with sources of supply. Some of these might be of interest to the production department. Buyers receiving samples from visiting salesmen pass them on to the production department if it appears that the samples might be useful. Sometimes the advertisement of a new material will sound so promising that the production manager might request one of the buyers to order a sample for testing. Because the file of catalogs, price lists, material specifications, and so on in a purchasing department will be quite extensive, the production department and other departments should frequently refer to the file before making a request for materials or supplies.

PURCHASING IN THE MERCHANDISING FIELD

In industry, purchasing is done to facilitate production. It must therefore be closely geared to production schedules and specifications. In industry, the purpose of production is to create sales, and the purpose of purchasing is to facilitate production. Purchasing, then, is only indirectly concerned with sales. But in merchandising, no production is present, so purchasing is *directly* concerned with sales. For that reason, the responsibility for purchasing and sales is generally given to the same individual for each division or department of the store.

The elements of purchasing are almost the same for both industrial purchasing and purchasing in the field of merchandising. Some additional comments on the purchasing function in the field of merchandising are necessary.

In merchandising, the goods bought are the goods sold. Successful buying requires familiarity with the store's customers, their income status, their level of taste, their age, and other characteristics. The majority of the buying decisions are therefore made by the department managers, usually called *buyers*, who are responsible for selling what they buy. However, in some types of merchandising, there are exceptions. Some department stores or fashion houses employ *resident buyers*. These buyers are specialists who spend their time in New York, Paris, or other centers of fashion, placing orders for stores, but not having responsibility for selling. However, their judgment is obviously measured by their success in selecting items than can be profitably sold, and they, like department managers in a store, must keep in touch with changing consumer desires. Another exception is the buying pattern of chain stores. Chain stores centralize almost all of their buying, thus separating the buying from the selling responsibility. Even here, though, the buyers are closely concerned with the salability of what they buy even though they are not responsible for its sale.

In small stores, buying is generally done by the owner or manager. His buying procedures will roughly parallel those of buyers in a large store but will be less formalized.

PURCHASING POLICIES

There are certain aspects of buying that affect the decisions of the purchasing department. They are: speculation, reciprocity, personal considerations, and bribery.

SPECULATION

When prices of materials fluctuate, profit can result from purchasing in larger quantity than needed when prices are low, in order to buy less when prices are high. The prices of many raw materials fluctuate up and down over a wide range, and it is in the buying of these that speculation is largely concentrated. Where a purchasing agent is authorized to speculate in the purchase of the raw materials used by a company, he must be given wide latitude of action. He must be free to buy in excess of immediate needs, and he must be free to act quickly. Needless to say, such a man must be shrewd, experienced, and daring. It is not the type of responsibility for a man who worries or is subject to ulcers. If he is successful, he can save his company a lot of money.

Speculation, however, can turn sour. Poor judgment or bad luck can cost a company all of its profits from production and more. In order to avoid losses by speculation, some companies have followed a policy of "hand-to-mouth" buying. This was particularly prevalent during the Great Depression. By purchasing only what is needed when it is needed, the risk of ownership of raw materials that might drop sharply in price is shifted to the supplier. However, such a policy forces a company to pay whatever the market price might be at the time the materials are needed. The materials costs of the company would fluctuate constantly, and the company would have to change its selling prices constantly or suffer losses when raw material prices were high. Furthermore, hand-to-mouth buying invites work stoppages caused by delays in materials deliveries.

For commodities such as grain and cotton, which are bought and sold on commodity exchanges, a means exists by which the risk of fluctuating prices can be minimized. This is called *hedging*. Commodity exchanges and hedging are discussed in Chapter 26.

RECIPROCITY   When the opportunity arises, it is natural for a company to buy from those suppliers that in turn buy the products of the company. If a company places orders with a supplier *because* the supplier buys from the company, the practice is called *reciprocity*. For example, the X Office Furniture Company might buy paint from the Y Paint Company only as long as the Y Paint Company bought its office furniture from the X Company. Sometimes reciprocity is more complex. The X Office Furniture Company might buy paint from the Y Paint Company because the Y Company buys chemicals from the Z Chemical Company, which in turn buys its office furniture from the X Company.

The extent to which reciprocity is practiced by industry varies from company to company. It is a rare company, however, that does not practice it in any degree. Often, reciprocity is urged by the sales department to hold an old customer or to secure orders from a new customer. In many cases, no urging is needed. It is natural for a purchasing agent to buy from friendly suppliers, and one of the best ways for a supplier to show friendship is to buy from the company employing the purchasing agent. Where the price of the customer's products is high, or the quality and service poor, it is of dubious merit to buy from the customer. In the example above, if the quality of Y paint was low, delivery undependable, or prices high, it would probably be poor policy for the purchasing agent of the X Office Furniture Company to buy Y paints just to secure the continued patronage of the Y Paint Company. The gain from the sale of office furniture would have to be balanced against the loss from the purchase of inferior or overpriced paint.

Each case has to be decided on its merits. Where the volume of business at stake is large, the decision for or against reciprocity would be decided not by negotiations between the sales manager and the chief purchasing officer but at the top level of management. If the sales department is forced to use reciprocity as an inducement in making sales, there might be suspicion that the company's products or prices were not competitive. As a generalization, it can be said that efficient companies use reciprocity in buying less than inefficient companies do.

PERSONAL   Personal considerations are always present to some extent in influencing buying
CONSIDERATIONS   decisions. A salesman might be a close friend or relative of the owner of the firm employing the purchasing agent, or of a high-ranking executive of the firm. It might be suggested to the purchasing agent that other things being equal, he should favor this salesman in placing his purchase orders. The suggestion might be mild, or it might be strong. Perhaps no suggestion would be made at all, but the mere knowledge of the relationship might influence the decision of the purchasing agent.

Most salesmen are friendly, have pleasing personalities, and are pleasant to be with. In fact such qualities are almost necessary in selecting salesmen. Some, however, are more pleasant than others. Some purchasing agents might place an order because the salesman has an attractive personality rather than because the product is superior to its competitors. On the other hand, purchasing agents hold their jobs because they are expert buyers. A buyer who is noticeably influenced by personalities in his buying decisions may not last long as a buyer. Purchasing agents are much less influenced by personal considerations than are consumers. A consumer, who finds it hard to distinguish quality among a dozen brands of washing machines, will frequently make the choice on the basis of the "friendliness of the store."

Any company officer who is in a position to influence buying policies is a potential target for a bribe. The bribe may be cash, but more often it is something other than cash, and may range in value from ball-point pens to expensive household appliances. While the National Association of Purchasing Agents and practically all companies condemn the acceptance of bribery, it is difficult to determine the extent to which a prohibition against receiving gifts from salesmen should be enforced against company personnel. Is the receipt of a desk calendar from a supplier a bribe? Should a purchasing agent refuse the gift of a pencil with his name in gold, worth possibly a half-dollar? When Christmas approaches, gift giving between companies is at its greatest. How much this giving is a token of appreciation for past orders and how much a subtle effort to win future orders is impossible to measure.

BRIBERY

Efforts of companies to prevent gifts from influencing buying decisions vary from prohibition against accepting *any* gifts to efforts to control the receipt of gifts. Some companies permit employees to accept pencils, calendars, and other items of small value. Others draw the line in terms of money, prohibiting the acceptance of any item valued at more than $1, or perhaps $5. A few companies require all personnel receiving gifts from suppliers to turn the gifts over to a specified company officer. This officer then raffles off such gifts at a company party so that all employees may benefit and so that the gifts will not remain the property of those company officers who might be influenced in their business decisions by the receipt of the gifts. If it is known that company rules prohibit or severely restrict the receipt of gifts, a salesman or supplier might send a bottle of perfume to the wife of a purchasing agent, or a case of beverage to the home address of the agent. The acceptance of such gifts is harder for a company to control.

Company managements prohibit or control the acceptance of gifts because it tends to reduce the independence of judgment of the recipient of the gifts. Two other reasons against gift giving should be mentioned. One is that gifts cost money, and must be reflected in the prices of the company giving them. The second reason is that gift giving becomes competitive with respect to value. If one salesman gives a pencil to a client, a competitor may give a pen. On the next occasion, the first salesman may give a pencil-and-pen set, while the competitor may give a dozen golf balls. As the gifts increase in value, they are no longer mere expressions of goodwill, but bribery. Nevertheless, as long as the gifts are accepted by the purchasing agent of a company, no supplier feels he can afford to stop giving or even to stop increasing the value of his gifts.

Similar to gift giving is the problem of entertaining. The acceptance of excessive entertainment by buyers is frequently prohibited by their employers. But what is "excessive" entertainment? There is considerable disagreement as to where the line should be drawn. Usually the acceptance of a lunch is permitted, even though the cost of a meal can vary from $1 to $10 or more. The acceptance of a dinner is also generally permitted. However, a trip to a theater after dinner is sometimes considered excessive.[8]

In recognition of the influences brought to bear on industrial buyers, the National Association of Purchasing Agents has formulated a code of principles, excerpts from which are given below:

> To consider, first, the interests of his company in all transactions and to carry out and believe in its established policies.
>
> To buy without prejudice, seeking to obtain the maximum ultimate value for each dollar of expenditure.
>
> To subscribe to and work for honesty and truth in buying and selling and to denounce all forms and manifestations of commercial bribery.
>
> To avoid sharp practices.
>
> To cooperate with all organizations and individuals engaged in activities designed to enhance the development and standing of purchasing.

SUMMARY   The function of production is to change the composition or form of materials to increase their value. Basically, there are four ways by which this can be done:

> Analysis—breaking down a raw material into a number of products.
>
> Synthesis—combining two or more raw materials into a finished product.
>
> Extraction—bringing forth materials from the ground, water, or air.
>
> Fabrication—shaping, cutting, and otherwise changing the form of materials, and then assembling them into finished products.

Production is carried on intermittently or continuously. In intermittent production, machinery and labor are applied to the production of first one type of article, then to a second type, perhaps then to a third, and back again to the first. The volume of production is small relative to the variety of products. In continuous production, men and machines are assigned to a particular job which is infrequently changed. This requires many men and machines to produce a variety of products, since each man and each machine is given a specialized task. Production is therefore large relative to the variety of products. Custom-made goods are usually made by

---

[8] The Public Affairs Department of the Columbia Broadcasting System produced in 1958 a broadcast entitled "The Business of Sex," showing a widespread practice by businesses, in which call girls were used to entertain buyers and executives of client corporations.

the intermittent process; standardized goods are usually made by the continuous (mass-production) process.

Production control in a small plant often can be accomplished by one man, the plant manager. In a large plant, control must be delegated to specialists, with one undertaking scheduling, another the control of inventory, another the supervision of workers, another inspection and maintenance of quality, and another the maintenance of machinery. These activities must, of course, be coordinated, and coordination becomes the vital responsibility of the plant manager.

By examining and timing the movements of workers (motion-and-time study), wasted effort can be avoided. By applying scientific methods and mathematical analysis to the problems of production management, the efficiency of men and machines can be increased.

The goal of production is rarely quantity alone. Each finished product must pass standards of quality. Inspection and quality control are intended to accomplish this.

Production has become much more automatic since World War II. Increasingly, machines guide and control operations, inspect for quality, make adjustments when necessary, and undertake other tasks formerly requiring human effort. This development, automation, is rapidly reducing the number of workers needed to produce a given quantity of goods.

Purchasing is the activity of business having to do with making materials and supplies available to a business at the times needed, in the proper quantities, with correct specifications, and at a price that is reasonable.

QUESTIONS
FOR REVIEW

1 What are the four chief production processes? Give some examples of each other than the ones mentioned in the chapter.

2 What are the advantages of intermittent production over continuous production? What are the disadvantages?

3 Name some examples in which intermittent production is effective and some examples in which continuous production is effective.

4 If a factory makes standard goods, it is likely to require custom-made tools and machines; if it makes custom-made goods, it is likely to require standardized tools and machines. How do you account for this?

5 In a small plant how is production generally controlled?

6 As a plant becomes larger, what changes in the character of production control are likely to take place?

7 What is the difference between order control and flow control? For what types of production is each suited?

8 What is "scientific management"? Is it a new principle?

9 Who was Frederick Taylor? What were some of his contributions to the art of management?

10 "Work simplification is one of the goals of scientific management." In general terms, how can this problem be tackled?

11 Explain how the surroundings in which a person works affect his efficiency on the job.

12 For what purpose is a person in a factory or office watched to analyze his motions while doing a job? Why is a stopwatch used in such observations?

13 What is the advantage of micromotion study over the use of the stopwatch?

14 What is the purpose of inspection in production? What scientific aids are used in inspection of production?

15 Explain the technique of sampling in inspecting products for quality.

16 What is meant by "automation"? Why are electronic computers increasingly used in applying automation to production?

17 Is it possible to demand too high a quality standard in determining specifications for products purchased by a company? Why or why not?

18 What are the advantages in using reciprocity as a policy in purchasing? What are the dangers?

19 It is important that a salesman have a pleasing personality and an attractive appearance. Should these factors be given similar importance in the selection of a purchasing agent? Explain your answer.

20 Why are purchasing agents more likely to be the recipients of gifts from salesmen than are other company officers? Is there any danger in this?

SELECTED READINGS
Garrett, Leonard J., and Milton Silver: *Production Management Analysis*, 2d ed., Harcourt Brace Jovanovich, New York, 1973.

Mayer, Raymond R.: *Production Management*, 2d ed., McGraw-Hill Book Company, New York, 1968.

Moore, Franklin G.: *Production Management*, 6th ed., Richard D. Irwin, Inc., Homewood, Ill., 1973.

Niebel, Benjamin W.: *Motion and Time Study*, 5th ed., Richard D. Irwin, Inc., Homewood, Ill., 1972.

Name	Section	Date

COMPLETION STATEMENTS

1 _Synthesis_ is the process of combining two or more raw materials into a single product.

2 Production is basically carried on in either of two ways:

continuous or _intermittent_.

3 _Order Control_ is the control of a job lot or batch of work through the process required in making the finished product.

4 Frederick Taylor is generally credited with starting the trend in _scientific_ management.

5 Work _simplification_ is one of the goals of scientific management.

6 _Motion and time Study_ is the application of timing to the production process.

7 The main drawback of micromotion study is _*expense*_ .

8 _*Inspection*_ determines whether the product is up to standard and, if not, why it is substandard.

9 The purchasing department exists to meet the needs of other _*departments*_ in a company.

10 _*Mass*_ production is on a continuous basis, in contrast to intermittent, job-order production.

11 When a store keeps its inventory low, its costs will _*be lower*_ .

12 When a store does not have an adequate selection of goods, its sales will _*drop or fall*_ .

13 In recent years the tendency in retailing has been to take _*physical*_ inventories more frequently.

14 _*Purchasing*_ can be defined as the obtaining of materials, supplies, and equipment for use by a company or for resale.

15 One of the fundamental decisions with respect to obtaining necessary materials is whether to _*buy*_ or to _*make*_ .

TRUE OR FALSE STATEMENTS

1 Buying is one, but not the most important, activity of a purchasing department.

2 Synthesis is the process of making an artificial product to replace a natural one.

3 Extraction is defined as bringing materials up from the ground.

Name   Section   Date

T **4** Broadly speaking, farming is an extractive industry.

T **5** Fabrication is a process that takes materials already manufactured and makes them into products of greater value.

F **6** The term "purchasing" is broader than the term "procurement."

T **7** In continuous production specialized machinery is used.

F **8** Custom-made goods are usually manufactured by the continuous production method.

F **9** Standard goods are made to the customer's specifications rather than to the manufacturer's.

F **10** In producing goods for industry uses, standard goods are produced but not custom goods.

T **11** All plants, big or small, must use some degree of production control.

T **12** As production in a company expands from small- to large-scale, the paper work necessary to production control grows at a more rapid rate.

T **13** Production control is fundamentally of two kinds: order control and flow control.

F **14** Even in small plants production management is not dependent on "feel" or intuition.

T **15** A large retail company may use the threat of making some items it sells, rather than buying them, to cause the supplier to reduce his price.

F **16** Part of Frederick Taylor's management principles was the belief that the experienced worker should be given the responsibility for determining how his individual job should be performed.

T **17** The purchasing department exists to meet the needs of the other departments of a company.

T **18** One of the most important tools in scientific management is the stopwatch.

F **19** The management function of inspection determines whether a product is up to standard, but does not determine the reason the product is not up to standard.

T **20** The amount of inspection required depends on the character of the product.

EXERCISES

1 The techniques of efficient production can be applied to one's individual activity just as effectively as they can to factories. The preparation of meals, working in a garden, making articles from wood or other materials, and even preparing for exams can be made more efficient by application of the techniques mentioned in this chapter. Because habit obscures any inefficient actions, it is difficult for a person to realize the existence of poor methods in his daily routine. Examine carefully any action you undertake frequently, preferably on a daily basis. You might select preparing breakfast, washing dishes, dressing, or washing a car.

a What waste motion can you discover?

b What changes can you suggest to reduce the time involved and increase efficiency of operation?

2 To appreciate production techniques and problems, nothing you read can substitute for a visit to a production plant, whether it is a small furniture or machine shop or a large factory. If possible, visit a factory near you. This is best done if the factory arranges organized tours for visitors. If you plan to visit a small shop, a phone call requesting permission is advisable. After your visit, report what you saw. Cover the following points:

a Kind of production (analysis, synthesis, etc.).

b Extent of machinery used, and whether special or multipurpose machinery is used.

Name   Section   Date

c If time and motion studies are used.

d Whether order control or flow control is used.

e List the methods of controlling quality used.

PART 4
HUMAN
RESOURCES

Every business enterprise is an organization of people. No matter how much use is made of labor-saving devices, people are still needed to operate factories, railroads, and banks. The completely automatic factory, operated without any human direction, may come into being—but at present it is still a dream in the minds of engineers.

A one-man enterprise does not have the problems of labor that cause concern in larger enterprises. Where groups of people work together in a business, labor problems arise. How shall the income of the enterprise be shared? How long shall each person work each day and each week? How shall persons be hired, and under what conditions shall they be discharged? Who shall be the "boss," and how shall he be selected? What rights of organization shall the workers be permitted? How shall they be trained? These and associated questions comprise the subject matter of the next three chapters. In earlier decades, many businessmen thought the answers to labor problems were simple, and that the problems could be solved in the manner of solving problems of machinery use and maintenance. Human engineering is now recognized to be more complex than mechanical engineering. The emotions, fears, ambitions, and pride of human beings are considered much more than they were formerly by thoughtful managers. In reading these chapters, therefore, keep in mind that officers and workers are beings with minds as well as muscles, that each one is an individual, and that the successful boss is the one who tries to understand human nature.

CHAPTER

11 LABOR ORGANIZATION IN THE AMERICAN ECONOMY

Probably the most important industrial resource of any nation is its labor resource, especially its supply of skilled labor. The success of any business enterprise is dependent to a considerable degree on the capability and efficiency of the workers in the plant and office. The management of employees is one of the most important aspects of business activity. You will probably be required at some point in your career to supervise in some measure the work of others. An understanding of the problems involved will aid greatly in improving your supervision. Obviously, you cannot become a capable supervisor just by reading—you must have experience, patience, and understanding of human nature as well. Nevertheless, a familiarity with the aspirations of workers and the development of organizations of labor will help. This chapter attempts to give you an awareness of the development of relations between workers and employers and the need for appreciation of each by the other.

It is necessary, when supervising workers, to be aware of them as individuals and as members of labor organizations. Workers as individuals frequently react differently from the way they do as members of an organization. Employers must deal with both—organized workers and individuals.

In reading the section on labor legislation, attempt to understand the direction of legislation more than the details of individual laws. It has been said by some writers in the field of labor legislation that such laws follow the swings of a pendulum. A period of legislation favorable to unions is followed by a period favorable to management. See if you can determine any evidence for such swings of a pendulum.

THE SUPPLY OF LABOR In 1973 about 90 million persons were working or were available for work, not counting those in the armed forces. This is the *labor force* of the United States. The number has been growing each year, as Figure 11-1 shows. Every year approximately 2 million persons are added to the labor force as children grow up and become available for work, and roughly 1 million persons leave the labor force, through death or retirement.

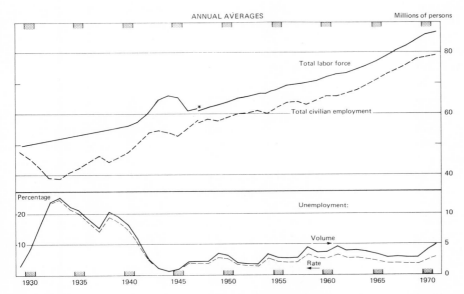

ANNUAL AVERAGES   Millions of persons

FIGURE 11-1 Labor force, employment, and unemployment. (Federal Reserve Chart Book,
Board of Governors of the Federal Reserve System, 1972, p. 78. Data from
Bureau of Labor Statistics.)

The labor force is what we depend on to run the machines in the factories,
run the machines to plant and harvest crops on the farms, to run the railroads, to
teach in schools, and to work at all of the other jobs that contribute to our well-
being. The labor force is not the same as the population of the United States; in
fact, it is less than half the population. It does not include babies, children
attending school, housewives, retired people, and persons in institutions such as
prisons and hospitals.

Figure 11-1 shows a great bulge during the years 1941 to 1946. How was it
possible to expand the labor force so rapidly? Many persons not included in the
labor force took jobs in industry to replace workers joining the armed forces and
to take the additional jobs that the expanded production for war required. These
new workers were housewives, retired people, and teen-agers. Their efforts contributed to the production of goods and services that overwhelmed Germany and
Japan during World War II. At the end of the war, most housewives returned to
their kitchens, teen-agers to their classrooms, and older people to retirement. In a
future emergency, the labor force could again be expanded. In fact, it would be
possible, although probably not desirable, to expand the labor force considerably
beyond the level achieved during World War II. This potential labor supply is sometimes called the *labor reserve*, and includes all persons over the age of fourteen
who are not already counted in the labor force and are not in institutions.

The labor force and the labor reserve together constitute the *labor potential*.

Many persons who went from the labor reserve to the labor force during World War II did not go back to the labor reserve at the end of hostilities. This resulted in a permanent shift in the labor potential. During the 1920s and the 1930s, the labor force varied from 52 to 55 percent of the labor potential, but after World War II it held steady at about 60 percent.

Traditionally the man has worked at a job for pay while the wife has worked in the home. It is natural, therefore, that a larger proportion of the male population than of the female population should be counted in the labor force. At the height of World War II 89.9 percent of the male labor potential was in the labor force, and 36.8 percent of the female labor potential was similarly occupied. In 1970 about 85 percent of the male labor potential and about 33 percent of the female labor potential were found in the labor force. During the present century, the proportion of females in the labor force has shown a rising trend. The number and variety of job openings for women have increased constantly. At the same time, women have enjoyed an increasing degree of independence, and a career of work has become socially acceptable. On the other hand, the proportion of males in the labor force has shown a downward trend since 1900. The reason for this has been largely that, besides the influx of women, males spend a longer time at school than in earlier times and live more years in retirement than before. The longer years in retirement are made possible by the greater life expectancy at present compared with 70 years ago, more widespread and more generous pensions, and compulsory retirement rules in many jobs.

As stated earlier, the labor force in 1973 was about 90 million. Should the number in the labor force have been higher or lower? This raises a question that is not easy to answer: What is the ideal proportion of working population to total population? This in turn raises a number of other questions: Is the rising proportion of women in the labor force a good or a bad trend? To what extent should children be permitted to work before finishing high school? Should the compulsory retirement age found in many jobs be raised, lowered, or abolished? Should a shorter workday or workweek be encouraged? Should annual vacations be made longer? Should farm workers from Mexico or skilled technicians from Europe be permitted to take jobs in the United States when there are many persons unemployed in our country? These questions touch on issues that are being seriously debated. They are questions broader than the field of business administration, involving the disciplines of psychology, sociology, and government policy; and there is obviously no simple answer to any of them. Developments in the areas of these questions, however, will be watched closely by business management during the balance of the century. Management's concern is with the supply of labor, and all of these questions affect the supply of labor.

THE CHANGING AMERICAN LABOR FORCE

Some significant changes have taken place in the American labor force since World War II. Jobs in manufacturing have steadily become a smaller proportion of total employment. From 1960 to 1970 the decline was from 27.1 percent to 24.4

percent, as Figure 11-2 shows. Women are now 40 percent of the labor force, with a considerable increase in the number of mothers working in factories, shops, and offices. In 1970 over 30 percent of the women with children under age six were working outside their homes. The Census Bureau has noted a sharp increase in the number of women who leave a job briefly to have a baby and return to the same job they held before.

Workers in Europe organized to improve their economic position long before the American colonies became an independent nation. Even in colonial days, although industry was less developed than in England, American workers joined together in organizations called "benevolent societies." The primary purpose of these societies was to aid member families suffering illness, debt, or death of the wage earner. They were not primarily concerned with improving wages or working conditions. Most societies were weak. Occasional efforts to present a united labor front in dealing with employers were repulsed by refusal of employers to recognize labor organizations as bargaining agents and by failure of the courts to give them legal status.

DEVELOPMENT OF LABOR ORGANIZATION

FIGURE 11-2 Employment by major industry, 1960–1970. (AFL-CIO, *American Federationist*, November 1972, p. 17.) Source: U.S. Department of Commerce, Bureau of the Census.

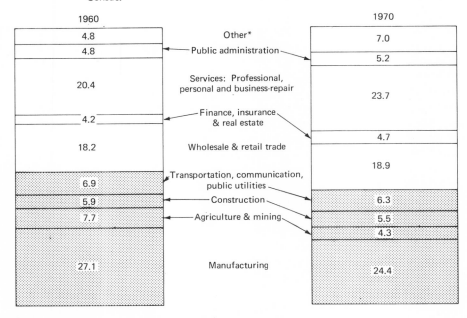

*Includes entertainment-recreation and those not reporting in the census.

In 1833 the Parliament of Great Britain enacted a law to improve the working conditions of the young in textile factories, particularly to prevent factory owners from requiring as long hours for children as for adults. For children under age twelve the work week was *reduced* to 48 hours and for children from age thirteen to age eighteen the work week was reduced to 69 hours. These shorter working hours did not apply to adults.[1]

In spite of obstacles, however, labor organizations grew in size and number during the 1800s. By 1865 more than 30 national labor organizations had been formed. A few, such as carpenters, bricklayers, and other construction crafts, date their origins to the period before the Civil War.

The growth in size of business units that characterized the period after the Civil War had a profound effect on the workers in the mines, railroads, and factories. As the factories became larger and larger, an ever widening gulf separated the owners and workers.

The owner's primary concern was earning a maximum return on his investment. The worker, on the other hand, no longer owning his tools, making only a small part of the finished article produced by a factory, and rarely seeing or dealing with a customer, often took little pride in his work. His chief concern was with the money in his pay envelope.

The sharply disparate goals of employer and employee evolved after the Civil War into bitterness and bloodshed. In the wealth flowing from the factories, the worker and his family shared little. Wages of $2 to $4 for a working day of 10 to 16 hours were what the adult male could expect.

In contrast to the skilled workers, the condition of the unskilled workers was untouched by successful union activity until the present century. Organization on a craft basis (membership restricted to workers of a single craft or skill, such as cigar makers) became one of the earliest means used by workers to try to secure improvement. Workers in the same craft, such as hatmakers, cigar makers, and hod carriers, found a common basis for association. Some of these associations held a tenuous relationship of descent from the craft guilds of the medieval period. By the time of the post-Civil War period labor organizations had become unions with the primary purpose of advancing the economic interests of members. These unions pitted their power against the growing strength of the large employers and employers' associations. The beginning of the modern labor movement may be dated in the year 1869, with the founding of the Noble Order of the Knights of Labor. This organization began as a union of garment workers in Philadelphia. Membership soon spread to other cities and to other crafts. In 1886 nationwide membership of the Knights passed 700,000. Internal conflict—one faction wanting to engage in political activity, another wanting the organization to confine its efforts to collective bargaining with employers—split the Knights, weakened their power, and led to the disappearance of the union.

---

[1] Arvel B. Erickson, and Martin J. Havran, *England, Prehistory to the Present*, Doubleday & Company, Inc., Garden City, N.Y., 1968, p. 403.

In 1881 a number of craft unions banded together in a loose organization called the Federation of Organized Trades and Labor Unions. In 1886 members of several crafts broke away from the Knights of Labor to join the young federation. In that year (1886) the organization adopted the name American Federation of Labor (AFL). The member unions remained autonomous, with the AFL having little more authority over a member union than the power to expel it from the AFL. However, the AFL did bring cooperation between member unions, so that each union supported other member unions in disputes with employers. Under the leadership of its first president, Samuel Gompers (who was reelected president every year but one from 1886 until his death in 1924), the AFL largely ignored political action and social goals such as better housing and improved medical care. Instead the AFL fought for economic goals: higher wages, shorter working days, pensions, and the like.

Almost all employers, large and small, resisted the development of unions. Their methods varied. One was to employ labor spies to learn the identity of union organizers and the plans of labor organizations, some of which strove to maintain secrecy in order to combat employer reprisals or government prosecution. Local and state police were used to break up labor meetings. Court injunctions were obtained by employers to end strikes or boycotts through expansion of the legal definition of the word *property* to include the right of uninterrupted business operation by employers but not the right of uninterrupted employment by workers. Thus courts ordered an end to strikes by labor but not lockouts (the closing of a plant by an employer to force concessions in a labor dispute).

THE AMERICAN FEDERATION OF LABOR

A few unions were established on the basis of industry rather than craft prior to the 1930s. The United Mine Workers, for example, included carpenters, electricians, and muleteers in addition to those who wielded pick and shovel in the mines. But the big rise in industrial unions did not take place until 1935, in which year eight unions withdrew from the American Federation of Labor to create a new federation. This was called the Committee for Industrial Organization, later renamed the Congress of Industrial Organizations (CIO). The CIO brought union organization to automobile manufacture, steel making, electrical goods, rubber manufacture, and other industries. Unlike the AFL, the CIO welcomed semiskilled and unskilled workers into its ranks, undertook more aggressive tactics to gain recognition, and engaged in political activity.

THE CONGRESS OF INDUSTRIAL ORGANIZATIONS

After a separate existence of 20 years, the AFL and the CIO combined into one federation called the AFL-CIO. This brought "under one roof" most of the organized workers in the nation. In 1972 the AFL-CIO comprised 121 unions, each of which bargained with management on behalf of its members. Each union

MERGER OF THE AFL AND THE CIO

is free to leave (or may be expelled from) the AFL-CIO. The AFL-CIO engages in community affairs, political action, such as voter registration and lobbying in Washington and the state capitals, and promoting the image of organized labor before the American public and the world.

During the struggle, first for existence and later for acceptance, some abuses by labor unions against workers and against management appeared. Workers refusing to join a union might be harassed, intimidated, or worse. Strikes and picketing, described later, instead of being peaceful, sometimes erupted into violence. Sabotage of machinery occasionally occurred.

With the right of workers to organize and bargain collectively with management secured by federal law in the 1930s, national labor unions became powerful. They used their power to promote legislation, support political candidates, and influence public opinion. Sometimes power was used responsibly, sometimes irresponsibly. Although the structure of unions remained democratic, elections were usually uncontested, particularly for high offices in national unions. The collection and handling of dues from workers and the investment of union pension funds were sometimes dishonest. The salaries, perquisites, and pensions of top union officials often compared favorably with those of corporation executives, while retired or injured workers of the same unions might live in poverty. The passage of the Labor-Management Reporting and Disclosure Act in 1959 (discussed later) attempted to correct the worst abuses found in some union operations. Wherever there is power, there is temptation to abuse it, and organized labor is no exception.

INDEPENDENT UNIONS   There are several national unions not affiliated with the AFL-CIO. The International Brotherhood of Teamsters left the federation in 1958 and the United Automobile Workers withdrew in 1968. Other unions independent of the AFL-CIO are the United Mine Workers, the United Federation of Electrical, Radio, and Machinist Workers, and the railroad brotherhoods (locomotive engineers, firemen, trainmen, and conductors).

There are also many small independent unions. These are mostly local unions, restricted in many cases to a single company or a single plant. Some were formed on the initiative of management rather than of the employees and have been dominated in varying degrees by management. These are called *company unions*. Other small unions have been formed on the initiative of the workers. The number of workers belonging to independent unions is about 4 million.

In recent years attempts have been made to unionize office workers and other "white-collar" employees. The union appeal has generally been based on the evidence that production workers have increased their wages more rapidly than office workers. For example, from 1939 to 1959 the average weekly earnings of production workers in manufacturing rose from $25 to $95, while earnings of clerical workers only doubled. In spite of this record, "white-collar" workers have not joined unions in great numbers. They resist "standardization" to a greater degree than do production workers, more of them hope to advance to managerial positions than is true of production workers, and there is some feeling that union membership entails loss of social status. Union efforts have met with some success among retail store clerks (where rate of pay is frequently very low) and among employees of the federal government.

The present status of unions is a result of the efforts of workers to organize together to secure better working conditions and higher wages. It is also the result of the endeavor of employers to prevent unions from using their power to a degree considered dangerous by employers. We will discuss below the types of unions and the degree of recognition accorded to union organizations in bargaining between labor and management.

UNION STATUS

The degree of recognition given by an employer to a union takes different forms. Four of the more important are described below:

EMPLOYER
RECOGNITION

Only those workers who are already members of the union may be hired by the employer. Unions may maintain hiring halls where workers are hired by union officials and furnished to employers in the number requested.

Closed Shop

Employers are permitted to hire union or nonunion workers. If nonunion workers are hired, they must join the union within a stated period after being hired.

Union Shop

When a contract is signed between the union and the employer specifying maintenance of membership, all employees who are members of the union or who become members after a specified date must remain members for the balance of the term of the contract.

Maintenance of
Membership

The employer makes no distinction between union and nonunion workers when hiring. Each employee is hired and dealt with on an individual basis. In effect, the employer ignores the union.

Open Shop

Most of the labor force is not unionized, and never has been. Membership in labor unions increased unsteadily until the end of World War I, at which time it reached roughly 4 million persons, but that was less than 20 percent of nonfarm workers. During the 1920s and the first part of the 1930s, union membership declined, reaching a low of slightly above 2 million in 1933. The legal protection given to union workers and organizers by legislation during Roosevelt's administration, however, resulted in a rapid expansion of union membership. Organized workers increased as a proportion of all workers, rising above 30 percent during the 1940s. Since the end of World War II, union labor has increased only at the same rate as the total labor force. In terms of percentage, union membership has remained steady since 1945 at about 32 to 34 percent of nonagricultural labor.

TYPES OF UNIONS

There are basically two types of unions in the United States: the **craft union** and the **industrial union**. The craft union is organized on the basis of the skill of the worker. Examples of such unions are those that include, respectively, barbers, plumbers, carpenters, screen actors, and airline pilots. Membership in some of the craft unions is not easy to obtain. The apprenticeship requirements, standards for admission, and initiation fees in some cases are used to restrict the available supply of certain skills. The **industrial union** admits members regardless of skill or type of work being done by the member. These unions recruit their members on the basis of the industry in which they work. Examples are the United Automobile Workers, the United Steel Workers, and the International Ladies Garment Workers Union.

INDUSTRIAL CONFLICT

Most of the contacts between managers and workers are friendly. Minor disagreements and misunderstandings occur, but are resolved with a minimum of friction. Both groups are in agreement on basic objectives. The workers are interested in expanding company sales and income. Management is desirous of having contented workers. But within the framework of basic goals, the particular interests of management and labor can be in sharp disagreement. Management's efforts to expand sales and increase profits involve controlling costs and increasing efficiency of operations. These efforts are frequently in conflict with the desires of workers for higher wages and seniority rights. When disputes arise, they can usually be settled by consultation between management and workers. Occasionally, however, no common ground can be found on which to base an agreement. It is then that conflict may become a matter of concern not only to management and labor, but to the public and government as well.

To understand the seeds of industrial conflict, one must be familiar with the fundamental objectives of organized workers. In summary they are as follows:

1 Higher wages
2 Shorter hours

3 Satisfactory means for handling on-the-job grievances
4 Satisfactory rules of work
5 Seniority rights
6 Safer and more pleasant working conditions
7 Union recognition
8 Pensions
9 Paid holidays and vacations
10 Fringe benefits, such as hospitalization, medical care, and company-paid insurance
11 Promotion of legislation favorable to organized labor
12 Support of political candidates friendly to labor
13 Efforts to influence public opinion

In trying to secure higher wages or better working conditions, the lessons of history have shown workers that as individuals they have very little power, but in union with fellow workers their power is greatly increased. When a disagreement between management and a single employee cannot be resolved by negotiation, the fact that the employee loses his job is usually of minor consequence to management but of grave consequence to the employee. On the other hand, when a disagreement between management and a strong union supported by most or all workers in a plant results in workers leaving their jobs, the consequences can be serious to both. Unions give workers economic power, and the exercise of this power brings concessions from management that action by individual workers would not.

THE WEAPONS OF LABOR

In a labor-management conflict, there are certain weapons that may be used by each side (illustrated in Figure 11-3). Labor's chief weapons are the strike, boycott, and picketing.

STRIKE

A *strike*, also called a *walkout*, is the refusal of laborers to work on their jobs. If the demands by the union are reasonable, the rejection of these demands by a company places the responsibility for a strike on management. If union demands are unreasonable, the responsibility for the work stoppage is clearly the union's. Because the initiative in calling a strike rests with the union, the public generally blames the union for the work stoppage. In such cases, making a judgment without knowledge of the facts is an exercise in prejudice rather than reason. It is easily within the power of a strong union or a strong company to create conditions so intolerable that the other party will resort to a work stoppage. Causes and responsibilities aside, strikes are a resort to power. Victory generally goes to the party with the most power, not necessarily to the party whose demands are most deserving.

THE WEAPONS OF LABOR

Form	Means Used
Strike	Refusal to work
Boycott	Refusal to do business with
Picketing	Discouraging patronage

THE WEAPONS OF MANAGEMENT

Form	Means Used
Employers' Association	Cooperative dealing with problems; public relations
Blacklist	Barring persons from employment
Injunction	Action (e.g., strike) stopped by court order
Lockout	Refusing entrance of workers to plants

FIGURE 11-3 Industrial conflict.

And because strikes interrupt production, the general public is usually injured to some degree.[2]

The immediate injury of a strike is borne by the company and the workers. Unless a company has a large inventory of unsold goods, the stoppage of production will result in lost sales, and some customers may be lost permanently to competitors. Workers on strike lose their pay checks, and these may or may not be offset by the gains won from a successful walkout. Injury is also suffered by other companies and workers whose production is dependent on the uninterrupted operation of the company at which the work stoppage occurred. A work stoppage in the steel industry, for example, may cause layoffs of workers in automobile plants, shipyards, coal mines, and railroads. Work stoppage caused by a strike may

[2]Sometimes a strike occurs in an industry operating at considerably below capacity and suffering from excessively high inventories. In such cases, a strike, if it is of short duration, may not be unwelcome to management because in the absence of a strike-induced cut in production, management might be forced to curtail production by other means.

have the same results as work stoppage caused by a depression. In either case, it is to be avoided if possible.

Causes of Strikes	Percent
1 Wages and hours	50
2 Other working conditions	25
3 Union organizations	15
4 Intraunion issues	5
5 Combination of union organization and wages and hours	5

Source: Adapted from U.S. Department of Labor statistics

BOYCOTT

A *boycott* is a refusal to do business with a company. If a company is operating with nonunion workers while a union is on strike against it, union officers will likely urge the union members, their families, neighbors, and friends to boycott the company. By the use of placards or other means of advertising, the union members may appeal to the general public to stop patronizing the company. If other unions participate in the boycott, the business of the company may be seriously affected. Whenever the boycott is confined to the members of the particular union in dispute with the company, it is termed a *primary boycott*. Where attempts are made to enlist the support of other groups, generally other unions, a *secondary boycott* results. Generally, primary boycotts are ineffective. Secondary boycotts, however, have proven to be strong weapons in the past.

PICKETING

When the persons are stationed at the entrances to a factory, store, or office for the purpose of persuading workers not to enter and the public not to patronize a place of business, the action is called *picketing*. Placards are carried announcing that a strike is in progress and giving general complaints of the workers against the management. Picketing depends for its effectiveness on the degree of sympathy aroused in the public. Probably its greatest success is in enlisting the aid of members of other unions in not dealing with a picketed company. Some union workers as a matter of principle will not cross a picket line, regardless of the merits of the union arguments.

THE WEAPONS OF MANAGEMENT

Management has used a number of techniques in its conflicts with organized workers. The most important of these techniques are: the employers' association, the blacklist, the injunction, and the lockout.

EMPLOYERS'
ASSOCIATION
Employers associate together for a variety of purposes, such as securing the passage of favorable legislation, promoting the prosperity of a particular industry or of business in general, promoting business in a particular city or state, curtailing "destructive competition" between companies, or dealing cooperatively with labor problems. These associations, generally termed *employers' associations*, are usually broad in purpose, covering many aspects of business activity. One of the most important areas of activity is labor-management relations, particularly with respect to relations with unions. The existence of employers' associations has promoted a trend, of minor importance at present, toward bargaining with unions on a multi-company basis. In Europe, it is quite common for a labor union representing workers in an industry to sign a contract with an employers' association representing all of the companies in the industry. Industrywide negotiations between companies and workers are not prevalent in the United States, but local contracts involving several companies and a union in a city or region do frequently occur. The formulation of local associations to present a united employer front to union bargaining agents has been fostered by businessmen's associations such as the National Association of Manufacturers.

Probably the main effort of employers' associations is directed toward the public and the government. By the use of propaganda, public support is sought for the point of view of management rather than that of the union. Advertisements, public speakers, radio programs, and "educational" films are used to influence the public. Union tactics, such as strikes and picketing, are more direct, while management gives more attention to indirect tactics such as influencing public opinion and legislation. Employers' associations seek to introduce and secure the passage of laws at the local, state, and federal level favorable to employers. Unions are now devoting more attention to cause passage of laws enabling them to add to their strength.

BLACKLIST
Persons aiding in the organization of a union within a plant may be discharged from their jobs and their names put on a *blacklist*. Such a list serves as a means of preventing such "troublemakers" from securing employment elsewhere. Generally, the person discharged for union activity is told he is being discharged for inefficiency or some other reason, and the blacklist to which his name is added is distributed in secret to members of an employers' association. Employers have used labor spies to uncover union activity in a plant and to secure the names of the union organizers. These spies, secured from detective agencies or other sources, provide names for the blacklist by infiltrating unions and sometimes even become officers in the unions. But they pass on information about union plans to management.

INJUNCTION
A court order directed at one or more persons requiring that certain action be taken or that certain action be stopped is called an *injunction*. Between the Civil War and World War I, injunctions were issued rather freely by courts on the request

of employers to restrain almost all types of strike activity. During the past 30 years, however, their use has been limited mostly to prevent damage to company property, to restrain violence, and to restrict picketing.

The *lockout* is the reverse of a strike. The employer institutes a lockout by closing the gates to his plant and refusing to permit workers to enter. Both management and labor seek to avoid blame for a lockout or a strike. However, as pointed out in the discussion of strikes, the blame for a lockout may rest with an unreasonable union, just as the cause of a strike may be an unreasonable stand by management.

LOCKOUT

The welfare of employers and the welfare of employees are bound up together. The income of both derives from the same sources. Both welcome an increase in sales, a reduction in costs, or an improvement in production techniques. Both, in short, want to work with a prosperous company in a prosperous industry. The methods by which the common goal is achieved, and the division of company income among owners, managers, and employees, however, cause disagreements. Workers wish to see costs reduced, but not through a reduction in wages or worker benefits. They welcome improvements in techniques, as long as they do not result in a layoff of workers. Differences between management and workers are inevitable with respect to details, but the existence of goals common to both serves as a lever in resolving differences. By far the majority of disputes are settled before a strike becomes a reality.

SETTLEMENT OF DISPUTES

When there is no union in a plant, the individual worker is left to deal alone with his employer on such matters as wages, hours, working conditions, and vacations. When a plant is organized by a union, the workers *bargain collectively* with their employer. The union representatives meet with the representatives of a single company or of several companies to negotiate contracts under which union members will work. Collective bargaining usually brings contracts more favorable to workers than would be possible by workers acting individually, for the obvious reason that workers collectively are more powerful. In addition, collective bargaining makes it possible for workers to use expert negotiators to represent them in their dealings with management. When a labor contract is negotiated between union representatives and those of the company, the deliberations may last for many days or many weeks. If agreement cannot be reached, negotiations may be broken off, to be resumed at a later period. If the differences appear to be irreconcilable through negotiation, a strike may be called. Considering the vast number of agreements negotiated in a year, it is rare for negotiations to break off completely. The vast

COLLECTIVE BARGAINING

majority are settled at the bargaining table without a strike being called and, therefore, with nothing newsworthy to be reported.

CONCILIATION

Frequently, the settlement of a difference between management and labor can be promoted by a third party. The process used is either conciliation, mediation, or arbitration. In conciliation, the participation of the third party is kept to a minimum. In effect, the conciliator's efforts are directed only at bringing management and labor together. Negotiations on a new labor contract might have broken down, and attempts by both sides to resume negotiations have failed. With the impasse drifting toward a possible work stoppage, a conciliator, having the confidence of both company management and union officials, might be able to bring about a resumption of talks. He also might arrange the time, place, and agenda for the meeting.

MEDIATION

Mediation goes beyond conciliation. In addition to bringing the parties together, the mediator will participate in the negotiations, generally in the role of a compromiser. He will attempt to define the issues in terms that can form the basis for give and take on both sides. He will suggest concessions one side can make in exchange for concessions by the other side. One of the most important contributions of a mediator probably is in finding means of saving face for both parties. To encourage the use of conciliation and mediation, the Federal Mediation and Conciliation Service was established in 1947. While this federal service is available and its use is encouraged, neither labor nor management is required to use it. There is no compulsion in accepting either the service or the recommendations of a mediator.

ARBITRATION

When there is no prospect for settlement of a dispute, a work stoppage appears to be inevitable. To avoid such an action, arbitration is frequently used. This places the authority to settle the dispute in the hands of a third party, either a single arbitrator or a board of arbitration. In submitting a dispute to an arbitrator, both management and union agree to accept the decision rendered. An arbitrator must be impartial to be acceptable to both sides. A board of arbitration is frequently composed of one member representing the union, one the company, and one independent. The third member is usually designated chairman. He may be a government official or a private individual. In either case, he must maintain a reputation for impartiality. The two most important sources of impartial arbitrators are the Federal Mediation and Conciliation Service and the American Arbitration Association. The latter was founded in 1926 and is the most important private organization furnishing arbitrators for labor disputes.

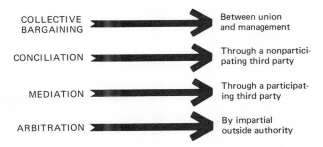

SETTLEMENT OF DISPUTES

COLLECTIVE BARGAINING → Between union and management

CONCILIATION → Through a nonparticipating third party

MEDIATION → Through a participating third party

ARBITRATION → By impartial outside authority

FIGURE 11-4

In a number of states, work stoppages caused by labor disputes are forbidden by law in such activities as hospitals, electric power, water, law enforcement, and fire fighting. In case of disputes between employer and employee in these areas, state law may require that the dispute be submitted to arbitration and that the decision of the arbitrator be binding on employer and employee. This is *compulsory arbitration*.

When management and union voluntarily agree to submit a dispute to arbitration, the action is called *voluntary arbitration*. Where strikes are prohibited by law, compulsory arbitration may be used to resolve major issues, such as wage rates, hours, and general working conditions. Where arbitration is voluntary, the issues submitted to arbitration generally concern interpretations of the labor contract and relatively minor matters.

LABOR LEGISLATION

Most of the laws concerning labor organization passed before World War I were directed toward weakening unions. Most labor laws passed during the Depression were aimed at strengthening unions. Labor legislation passed since World War II has generally sought to control actual or possible abuses of power by unions or officials of unions. To these generalities there are, of course, exceptions. The major laws concerning labor are discussed below.

NATIONAL INDUSTRIAL RECOVERY ACT

One of the first acts passed by Congress under the presidency of Franklin Roosevelt was the National Industrial Recovery Act (NIRA), signed in 1933, which sought to reduce unemployment and eliminate "unfair" competition. This law declared it to be the right of workers to "organize and bargain collectively through representatives of their own choosing," and to be "free from interference or coercion of employers of labor or their agents in the designation of such representatives or in self-organization." This was the first legislative guarantee of labor's right to organize and bargain collectively with employers. Following passage of the act, union membership began to increase. A large number of complaints of alleged interference with union organization impelled Congress later in 1933 to create the National Labor Board for the purpose of investigating labor disputes. However, the NIRA was declared unconstitutional by the Supreme Court in May 1935.

NATIONAL LABOR RELATIONS ACT

Soon after the NIRA was declared unconstitutional, Congress passed in 1935 the National Labor Relations Act, also known as the Wagner Act. This act restored the organizing and bargaining rights of labor contained in the NIRA, since the court decision invalidating the NIRA had not specifically ruled on the constitutionality of the labor provisions. The basic features of the Wagner Act are the following:

Labor-management disputes in all industries operating in interstate commerce are declared the concern of the federal government, since such disputes create unrest and strife and therefore obstruct the flow of interstate commerce.

Five employer actions are declared unfair labor practices prohibited by law. They are: (1) interference with, and restraint or coercion of, employees in their attempts to organize a union; (2) the domination of a union by an employer or any financial support of a union by an employer; (3) discrimination against an employee because of his support of a union or because of his engaging in union activity; (4) the discharge of an employee or discrimination against an employee for having filed a complaint against an employer for alleged violation of the law; (5) refusal to bargain collectively in good faith with the representatives of the workers.

The National Labor Relations Board (NLRB) replaced the labor board dissolved with the invalidation of NIRA. This board has the responsibility of investigating reports of violations of the law, of protecting the organization of workers into unions, and of issuing orders to cease and desist from unfair labor practices.

The constitutionality of the Wagner Act was upheld in 1937 in a case appealed to the Supreme Court. Union organization spread rapidly, particularly with the vigorous activity of the Congress of Industrial Organization (CIO) in industrial unionization. The Wagner Act, however, covered only companies engaged in interstate trade; those that engaged in trade wholly within the borders of one state were not covered. State legislation applied in intrastate trade. Eleven states passed laws modeled after the Wagner Act in the years after 1935, but the others did not.

FAIR LABOR STANDARDS ACT

In an attempt to set up minimum standards for wages and hours, Congress passed in 1938 the Fair Labor Standards Act. This established a maximum workweek of 40 hours and a minimum hourly wage of 40 cents for employees of businesses operating in interstate commerce. Employees could work beyond 40 hours a week if they were paid for the overtime work at least 50 percent above their regular hourly wage (called time-and-a-half pay). Employees in two industries, however, were left unprotected by law. Farm laborers and clerks in retail stores were exempt from the provisions of the law. In addition, those companies doing business entirely within a state were again not covered by federal wages and hours legislation.

Although the federal minimum hourly wage and maximum workweek do not apply to companies in intrastate trade, their existence serves as a level to push up wages in exempt industries. The better workers generally seek employment where wages and hours are more favorable, leaving poorer workers available for companies paying below the federal minimum wage. Unions use the federal standards as models in striving to improve working conditions in intrastate trade. To enlist the support of the general public, unions equate minimum decent wages and hours with federal minimum wages and hours.

During World War II, both employers and employees recognized in all but a few instances their responsibilities in maintaining production for the war effort, and work stoppages were few. After the war, however, the pent-up grievances in labor-management relations were released. It was a period of turmoil: prices rose rapidly after the elimination of price controls, goods of all kinds were scarce, workers changed jobs, and companies shifted from war to peacetime production.

In that first year after the war, unions presented management with a series of demands that workers felt represented the accumulation of reasonable wage increases and working improvements that they had foregone during the war. To management, these demands appeared excessive. Both management and unions were unbending. As a consequence, the year 1946 witnessed a larger number of strikes and more man-days of labor lost than any previous year in American history, even larger than the previous record year of 1919. Public sympathy had shifted against organized labor after World War I, and it shifted against unions again after World War II. In this atmosphere, the Labor Management Relations Act, also known as the Taft-Hartley Act, was passed in 1947.

The main features of this act are as follows:

1 *Union unfair labor practices:* The Wagner Act identified certain unfair labor practices of employers; the Taft-Hartley Act added unfair practices on the part of unions. These included: the failure of unions to bargain in good faith; secondary boycotts; featherbedding (the demand by a union that an employer hire workers even though they are not needed); and jurisdictional strikes except where certified as legitimate by the NLRB.
2 *Union security:* The Wagner Act permitted labor contracts to contain a closed-shop clause, requiring an employer to hire only workers already members of the union. Taft-Hartley prohibited the closed shop. The Wagner Act permitted state law to be more favorable to unions than federal law but made invalid state laws that were less favorable. Taft-Hartley made invalid state law more favorable to unions than federal law but yielded to state laws less favorable to unions. Taft-Hartley permitted union-

LABOR MANAGEMENT RELATIONS ACT

shop contracts, which provided that an employer could hire nonunion workers on the understanding that they would be required to join the union to keep their jobs. Nevertheless, about a third of the states in the 1950s passed "right-to-work" laws prohibiting both the closed shop and the union shop, leaving employers free to employ nonunion workers whenever they were available.

3 *Union responsibility:* Taft-Hartley cleared the uncertainty concerning the legal responsibility of unions by declaring that unions may be sued in federal courts for breach of contract, illegal boycotts, and other matters. This was objected to by labor leaders on the ground that the Taft-Hartley Act so weakened union security that a union could not easily discipline workers. Particularly, they felt that with the law making it easier for workers to leave unions at will and forbidding unions from expelling a member for any reason other than nonpayment of dues, the union could not be responsible for damaging actions of individual workers.

4 *Employer opinions:* The right of employers to express themselves in any manner on union actions, union membership, and similar matters was guaranteed, so long as the employer did not use threats in his expressions of opinion.

5 *Disclosure of financial affairs of unions:* Reports of income and expenses and the financial standing of unions were required to be disclosed to union members and to the NLRB.

6 *National emergency strikes:* If the President of the United States declared that a pending or imminent strike threatened the national health or safety, the Attorney General could petition a federal court for an injunction to halt the strike or to prevent one from starting. The injunction could be for 80 days or less. Before the end of the period, union members must, by secret ballot, vote on the most recent offer of the company.

7 *Changes in the NLRB:* The National Labor Relations Board was increased from three to five members. The general counsel of the board was given much broader authority.

8 *Fact-finding boards:* In a labor dispute of nationwide importance, the President of the United States was authorized to appoint a fact-finding board. Such a board would hear the arguments of each side, ascertain the facts in the case, and give publicity to the issues involved. The law, however, provided that no recommendations be made by the board. The function of the board appointed for each dispute was to gather information, not to render a judgment.

LABOR MANAGEMENT REPORTING AND DISCLOSURE ACT

During the late 1950s, a committee of the United States Senate disclosed corruption and embezzlement on the part of certain union officers and collusion between irresponsible employers and irresponsible union officers, which caused injury to workers and the public. Out of these disclosures came an act called the Labor-Management Reporting and Disclosure Act, better known as the Landrum-Griffin Act. This law was passed in the fall of 1959, and it:

Tightened restrictions on secondary boycotts and jurisdictional picketing.

Required that employers disclose spending for the purpose of influencing workers.

Required regular elections of union officers by secret balloting.

Prevented a person from holding union office for five years after conviction of a felony or membership in the Communist Party.

Held union officials accountable for union funds and property.

Made embezzlement of union funds a federal offense.

Placed restrictions on loans from union treasuries to union officers and members.

Guaranteed protection to all union members at union meetings exercising their rights to participate and vote.

SUMMARY

The potential supply of labor includes all persons over the age of fourteen who are not in institutions and who are physically and mentally capable of working. Those holding jobs or actively seeking work constitute the labor force, which has held fairly steady in the United States at about 60 percent of the potential labor supply.

Since the beginning of American history, part of the labor force has been unionized. Since World War II, about one-third of nonfarm workers have belonged to unions. They have been organized according to the craft of the worker or according to the industry in which he is employed. Workers join unions to achieve power they would not enjoy as individuals. To achieve their aims unions exercise their organized power in various ways. The most dramatic way is the strike. Employers also exercise power in various forms to counter the demands of unions. But by far the greatest number of disputes is resolved by negotiation rather than violence, and perhaps for that reason go unreported in the press.

Of the many laws that have been passed by Congress on labor matters, probably the two most important are the National Labor Relations Act (Wagner Act) and the Labor Management Relations Act (Taft-Hartley Law). The first act sought to guarantee to labor the right to organize and bargain in good faith with employers. The second sought to eliminate some of the abuses Congress felt were being perpetrated by irresponsible labor leaders.

QUESTIONS FOR REVIEW

1 What is the difference between the labor force and the labor reserve? What is the significance of this for national emergencies such as war?

2 For what reasons has the proportion of females in the work force risen since 1900? Do you expect this trend to continue? Why or why not?

3 Account for the widening gulf between the interests of workers in factories and the owners of factories during the last century.

4 What activities does the AFL-CIO engage in in addition to organizing workers and bargaining with management?

5 Why has unionization of "white-collar" workers been less successful than unionization of "blue-collar" workers?

6 Distinguish between the closed shop, union shop, maintenance of membership, and open shop.

7 What is the difference between the craft union and the industrial union? Why was union organization on the basis of craft developed earlier than organization on the basis of industry?

8 What is picketing? What is its purpose in labor-management disputes? Is it ever used where no labor dispute is involved?

9 What does the Labor Management Reporting and Disclosure Act seek to accomplish?

10 What are the benefits to workers in bargaining collectively with management?

11 Distinguish between conciliation and mediation. What benefits does labor receive from each? What benefits does management receive from each?

12 For what types of work should compulsory arbitration be required in settling disputes? Justify your selections.

13 What are the main features of the National Labor Relations Act?

14 What were the economic conditions following World War II under which the Labor Management Relations Act was passed?

15 What are the main features of the Labor Management Relations Act?

SELECTED READINGS   Brody, David W.: *The American Labor Movement*, Harper & Row Publishers, Incorporated, New York, 1971.

Fisher, Malcolm R.: *The Economic Analysis of Labor*, St. Martin's Press, Inc., New York, 1972.

Galloway, Lowell E.: *Manpower Economics*, Richard D. Irwin, Inc., Homewood, Ill., 1971.

Perlman, Richard: *Man as a Human Resource*, McGraw-Hill Book Company, New York, 1973.

U.S. Department of Labor: *A Brief History of the American Labor Movement*, U.S. Government Printing Office, Washington, D.C., 1970.

Name   Section   Date

COMPLETION SENTENCES

1 Since the end of World War II the size of the labor force has held steady at

about ___*4,5 – 5,6*___ percent of the labor potential.

2 Jobs in manufacturing have steadily become a ___*major*___

percentage of total employment.

3 Organization on a ___*benevolent association* SOCIETY___ basis became one of the earliest

means or paths toward unionization.

4 Unlike the AFL, the CIO welcomed ___*unskilled*___ workers in

their member unions.

5 A union organized on the initiative of management is called a

___*company*___ union.

6 _____Office_____ workers resist "standardization," and have not joined unions as readily as factory workers.

7 In a _____Closed Shop_____ only those workers who are already members of a union may be hired by the employer.

8 In a _____Open Shop_____ employers make no distinction between union and nonunion workers when hiring.

9 The _____Craft Union_____ is organized on the basis of the skill of the worker.

10 The American Federation of Labor developed as a grouping of _____Craft Unions_____ unions.

11 A _____strike_____ is the refusal of laborers to work on their jobs.

12 A _____Boycott_____ is a refusal to do business with a company.

13 A _____Picket Line_____ seeks to impose a human barrier preventing access to a place of business.

14 The number of persons, excluding the armed forces, working or available for work is called the _____Labor Force_____

15 In submitting a dispute to _____Arbitration_____, both management and union agree to accept the decision rendered.

Name	Section	Date

TRUE OR FALSE STATEMENTS

T **1** During the present century, the number and variety of job openings for women have increased.

F **2** In the American colonies associations of workers were not primarily concerned with improving wages or working conditions.

T **3** In 1970 jobs in manufacturing dropped to a smaller percentage, compared with 1960, of total employment in the major industries.

T **4** Nationwide labor organizations did not exist before the Civil War.

F **5** Unionization of unskilled workers began in the 1800s.

F **6** In the last century most employers welcomed union organization.

T **7** Of the major unions comprising the AFL-CIO, none has so far withdrawn.

F **8** Labor force minus labor reserve equals the labor potential.

T **9** There are basically two types of unions in the United States: craft unions and industrial unions.

T **10** A strike is also called a walkout.

T **11** Picketing and striking often go on at the same time.

F **12** The main effort of employers' associations is directed toward gaining the sympathy and support of the public and the government.

F **13** A blacklist is not intended to serve as a means of preventing a worker from securing employment.

F **14** Between the Civil War and World War I, injunctions to restrain strikes were sparingly issued by the courts.

T **15** The vast majority of labor agreements are reached without a strike being called.

T **16** Arbitration is not resorted to as a means of avoiding a strike, but as a means of speeding negotiations.

F **17** Most of the labor laws passed before World War I were directed toward strengthening unions.

T **18** The National Labor Relations Act of 1935 is also called the Wagner Act.

F **19** During World War II, there were many work stoppages by unions.

F **20** The Taft-Hartley Act prohibited the closed shop.

EXERCISES

1 Select a trade union for study, either a local union or one of the national unions. Prepare a report on this union, covering the following:

  a Brief history

  b Membership dues (amount and how collected)

  c Principal officers (names and how selected)

  d Variety of skills or crafts covered by the union

2 *Case Problem for report or class discussion.*

Roger Tripp became a salesman for a toy manufacturer after graduation from college. He was very successful during his first year. As a matter of fact, his work brought him to the attention of the top management of the firm, and he was recognized as having executive possibilities. He was invited to lunch by the executive vice president of the company, Ward Browne. Browne said he had heard the workers in his factory considering union organization. While he was not violently opposed to having a union in the plant, he thought that it was unnecessary for the protection of the workers. He also thought that if management could anticipate the desires of the workers and give them any reasonable demands they might make as members of a union, then union organization could be avoided. After lunch he asked Tripp to think over what he said and report back to him any ideas he had on the subject.

Prepare a report for Browne giving the reasons, both economic and non-economic, for union organization. Also state any opinions you might have regarding why, in a company where management strives to safeguard the welfare of its workers, the workers still are attracted to union organization. Finally, state what you think should be the position of management regarding union organization: should it be for, against, or neutral? Give reasons to back up your stand.

CHAPTER

12

SELECTION AND TRAINING OF EMPLOYEES

To some extent, selecting employees is similar to buying something. When you buy a thing, you try to get the best for your money. You examine the commodity carefully, try to discover if there are satisfied users, and try to decide whether the price is reasonable or not.

In selecting an employee, it is necessary to exercise as much care as in buying something that costs a lot of money. A great change has taken place between the haphazard method of selecting employees during the first half of the century and the careful, systematic selection procedure used by most employers today. Try to understand why this development has taken place, and how it can be compared with the increased use of scientific methods in other phases of business management. Notice also, in selection of employees, the increasing emphasis on mental ability and education rather than physical strength. And notice the increased employment of women in jobs for which they would not have been considered a few decades ago.

In selecting employees for a position, two points should be emphasized. It is sometimes said that you cannot put a square peg in a round hole: an employee must be suited to his job, and the job must be suited to the employee. Therefore, it is essential that the job and the applicant both be analyzed to see that each is suitable to the other. Not so long ago, the attitude of employers was that applicants should seek the job, and employers should merely announce available openings. Today, more and more employers are actively recruiting employees. The employer who merely waits for applicants to come to him will probably not hire the most capable workers available. It is important for the employer to seek the best available workers for his openings, and it is important for the employee to seek the best positions.

Most of you will start your career as employees. Therefore, it would be wise for you to read this section of the book with care. Some topics in this chapter will undoubtedly be of considerable help to you in applying for jobs and in conducting yourself at the job interview.

Many college students, particularly freshmen and sophomores, feel that the receipt of a diploma after 4 years of study marks the end of their education. This is far from true. It is wise to bear in mind that the occasion of receiving a diploma is called a commencement exercise. The end of your college career is more like the beginning of your education than the culmination of it. You will find that after you begin your career, you will need to continue both formal and informal study to get ahead in your work. In almost every career, it is necessary to keep up with changing methods.

Part of this chapter covers the training of employees. Continual education is necessary for the most effective use of human energy. Wherever you work, you will probably find an opportunity for more study. From the employer's standpoint, a new employee must in most cases be trained for the particular job for which he is chosen, and his training must continue even after he has gone beyond his original job.

In this, as in other aspects of management, you will notice from your reading that there is a greater emphasis on mental training than on training of physical skill. Finally, never overlook the fact that employees are not machines. They are human beings subject to worry, ambition, and emotion. They should be treated as human beings and not as numbers.

During the nineteenth century, a common method of hiring workers was to post a notice outside the factory gate stating that the following morning three workers would be hired. The notice might specify a skill, such as carpentry, or it might not specify any skill. Persons interested in the job would present themselves at the gate at the designated time. If jobs were plentiful, only one or two might appear. If unemployment were heavy, a large number would crowd the gate. In such a case, the method of selection might be haphazard. Perhaps the first three in line would be chosen. Or possibly the employer would select the men that appeared to be the strongest, youngest, or healthiest.

Training of employees was apt to be as primitive as the selection. Much of the work in early factories was physical, and little training was needed. Training was usually given on the job, with an experienced employee explaining the work as it was being done. Almost never was there any attempt to measure the aptitude of workers or place them in jobs where their capabilities and interests lay. Haphazard methods of selection and training are still found, particularly in such fields as agriculture, but they are much less common today. In modern factories, physical effort has been largely replaced by machines, and unskilled labor is not as much in evidence. Intelligence and judgment rather than brute strength are sought by employers. As production methods have been refined, so have methods of selection and training of employees.

ANALYZING THE JOB   The first step in selecting an employee is job analysis. Before new workers can be recruited, it must be known what type of work they are being recruited for. In other words, the job must be analyzed to determine the worker qualifications needed to fill it satisfactorily. This can be done by observing an employee on the job, by interviewing the employee and his immediate supervisor, or by having employees fill out questionnaires concerning their jobs. Whatever the method used, the information about the job should be classified to enable the personnel department to match the specifications of the job with the qualifications of the applicants. The following information about the job is needed:

The job title
The names of the departments containing this job
The number of workers employed by the company or plant at this job
The relation of the job to other jobs
The promotion prospects
Equipment used on the job
Detailed description of duties and responsibilities of the job
Experience and education requirements
Age, sex, and physical characteristics required
Salary and hours of work

After the information about a job has been compiled, a job specification should be prepared. This lists in detail the requirements needed by an applicant for the job. It will be classified according to the kind and degree of skills and experience required, education requirements, maximum age limits, and personality characteristics desired. The job specifications reduce the possibility of misunderstanding between the department placing the requisition for a new worker and the personnel department; it aids the interviewer in screening applicants; and it also indicates what deficiencies an otherwise promising candidate must correct or overcome in order to qualify for the job. Since each human being is different, it is unlikely that an applicant will be found who fits exactly the job specifications in every respect. For this reason, the people in the personnel department must exercise good judgment in their selection of employees. Some deficiencies of an applicant may be minor, and can be ignored. Other deficiencies can be corrected, such as deficiencies in education or training, if the applicant is impressive in other respects. What has been stated in other connections can be applied here: job specification is a necessary guide to good judgment but not a substitute for it.

RECRUITING

The larger the number of candidates that can be rounded up for a job, the better will be the prospects for getting a capable worker. If he wants the best workers available, the employer cannot wait for them to come to him. He must actively seek candidates for the positions he wants to fill. The chief sources of new workers are state employment services, private employment agencies, advertisements, schools, and recommendations of employees and friends.

STATE EMPLOYMENT SERVICES

With the aid of federal funds, state employment services provide employers with lists of available workers. Because unemployed workers must register with state agencies to qualify for unemployment compensation, these agencies serve as an important source of available workers. Unemployed persons are interviewed by state agencies, tested, and classified according to skills and type of work. The preliminary screening, in other words, is done for the employers for most kinds of production and routine office jobs. Requisitions from employers are matched against the available labor supply, and suitable prospects are sent to employers for interviewing.

PRIVATE EMPLOYMENT AGENCIES

The private agencies provide the same type of services to employers as the state employment services do. Skills of a higher type are more likely to be located through a private employment agency than through a state agency. Supervisory and executive talent may be located with the aid of a private agency, for example.

ADVERTISEMENTS IN NEWSPAPERS, RADIO, AND OTHER MEDIA

The classified advertisement sections of the large metropolitan newspapers carry employment advertisements placed by employers and by persons seeking work. This is one of the most important means of locating new employees. Trade magazines also have classified advertisements in many cases.

SCHOOLS

Employers sometimes send company recruiters to visit schools and colleges at graduation time. Generally, the types of positions for which school graduates are sought are career positions with opportunities for advancing to management levels.

RECOMMENDATIONS OF EMPLOYEES

It is common practice for employees to suggest friends, acquaintances, or relatives when an opening occurs. This can be a very useful source of new employees, particularly in small firms. This source has its disadvantages, however. An employee cannot be completely free of bias in recommending a friend or relative. Furthermore, the personnel department may feel under pressure to hire a person recommended by an officer in the company, particularly if the person is a relative of the officer. Because of these disadvantages, some companies make it a rule that not more than one member of a family may work in one department or even in the company. Some do not permit wives of employees to be hired. Where relatives and friends of officers are given obvious preference in filling desirable job openings and in receiving promotions, the effect on employee morale is damaging.

The selection of employees involves the following steps: application forms, interviewing, references, and testing. In some cases, all steps are followed; in others, one or more of the steps may be omitted.

The purpose of using an application form filled out by a job applicant is twofold. It permits unqualified applicants to be rejected before time and money are spent in bringing them to the company for an interview. It also permits the interviewer to ask questions of a more searching nature than would be possible without the information provided by the form. Although application forms of companies vary, they generally require the following information: name and address; age, education, and work experience; position sought; height, weight, marital status, number and age of children; physical defects, if any; and references.

APPLICATION FORMS

The purpose of the interview is to gain information about the applicant that cannot be gotten from the application form. The interview can precede or follow the filling out of the application form, but most companies use an application form first, following it with an interview if the candidate merits further consideration. Some companies grant a brief interview to all job applicants, have the more promising ones fill out an application form, and, on the basis of the application forms, select a few for final interviewing.

INTERVIEWING

Successful interviewing demands a good deal of tact and judgment on the part of the interviewer. The way that the applicant answers questions is judged as well as the answers he gives. If the primary purpose of the interview is to get additional information about the applicant, the conversation should be guided by the interviewer. The specific information can then be drawn from the applicant with a minimum expenditure of time. If, on the other hand, the interviewer seeks to test the initiative and poise of the applicant, the casual, unplanned conversation is most useful.

Frequently, information can be gotten from an interview that cannot be secured easily from an application form. For example, the following items of information might make an employer hesitate before hiring an applicant:

Weak reason for leaving previous position
Frequent shifting from one position to another
Application for a job at considerably less salary than the previous job
Serious domestic difficulties
Obnoxious mannerisms

An interviewer must remember that most applicants are under some strain during a job interview. He should put the applicant at ease if he can. He should be considerate of the applicant's feelings. To a considerable degree, the "interviewer is the company" in the minds of many applicants. It is therefore poor public relations for an interviewer to be brusque. In some companies, it is the policy to state the reasons for the rejection of an applicant. In others, the process of rejection is to tell the candidate that his application will be considered, and then never contact or write him. Most companies reject an applicant by telling him that his qualifications are not precisely what the company needs at this time, or by saying that there are several persons being considered for the opening and that the one chosen will be notified within 4 or 5 days.

REFERENCES

Letters of recommendation used to be much more common in the hiring process than they are now. Occasionally, a person will be asked to submit letters of recommendation along with the application form. More usually the application form will provide space for the names and addresses of three or four references to whom the employer may write, requesting confidential information about the character, reliability, and personality of the applicant. A person seeking a job will naturally list the names of those individuals likely to praise him. Because of this, an employer often discounts favorable statements in reference letters. On the other hand, a critical or lukewarm letter of recommendation can be damaging to an applicant. References from friends are considered least valuable in securing dependable information about an applicant. References from a former employer, however, are often given considerable weight. Companies may send the former employer a form to fill out asking for information not contained in the application form or for the purpose of verifying statements made by the applicant as to salary earned, length of service with former employers, and reasons for leaving.

TESTING

Tests are more likely to be used to screen applicants for jobs in large organizations than in small ones. They are most likely to be used for jobs for which vacancies occur frequently. The large company generally prepares its own tests, or has them specially prepared. Small employers may request the United States Employment Service to set up tests for the employers' use. Tests can be divided into the following classifications:

Intelligence Test

When American men were being drafted into the Army during World War I, large-scale use of intelligence tests was made to determine the qualifications of soldiers for military duties. Their use has spread to industry since that time, and the tests have been refined and improved. These tests do not measure the direction of mental ability but rather the extent of native intelligence. As such they are useful to those employers of large numbers of men and women in separating the dull from the bright.

Aptitude and Proficiency Tests

These tests attempt to measure the talent a person has in specific areas. They may be designed to determine the basic capacity of a person for clerical, mechanical, or other work regardless of the present skill of the applicant. For example, girls may be tested for manual dexterity and ability to do repetitive, monotonous work. Those who score high would be hired and trained to do whatever tasks required such talents. Tests may also be prepared to measure the current skill of an applicant. Prospective stenographers, for example, may be given tests to measure their skill in typing and taking shorthand.

Physical Examination

Good health is as important as intelligence in most jobs. To determine whether a person is physically qualified, employers are increasingly requesting new employees to provide a certificate from family physicians. Large companies generally employ doctors to make physical examinations at the plant or office.

A person may be in good health but have a physical handicap, such as the loss of an arm or eye or partial deafness. Such persons used to have great difficulty in finding jobs. The scarcity of labor during World War II led to the discovery that such persons could become very useful workers. There is still some prejudice in many companies against hiring such persons, but it is decreasing.

GETTING THE EMPLOYEE STARTED

The first few days or weeks on a new job are critical for the recently hired employee. It is helpful to the employee and good business sense for the employer to take steps to make the adjustment as smooth as possible. This can be done by seeing that each employee gets a good start on the job, and by following this up with progress checks.

ORIENTATION FOR NEW EMPLOYEES

The process of introducing a new employee to his position varies widely. In small companies, it is usually very informal, with the manager taking the recruit to the place where he is to work, introducing him to the foreman or office supervisor, and assigning an older employee the responsibility of showing him how his work is to be done. Larger companies have formal programs of orientation, and give each person hired a booklet describing the company and the rights and responsibilities of employees. The booklet contains information such as the following:

History of the company
Products and services of the company
Hours of work, holidays and vacations, when and where wages are paid
Rules covering absences, sickness, and tardiness
Parking regulations
Stock-purchase plans, retirement benefits, and hospitalization provisions
Employees' credit union
Company policy on promotions and dismissals

New employees may be taken on a tour of the plant, so that the relation of their jobs to the whole company effort may be seen. Each new group of employees may listen to a series of talks by officers from different divisions of the company and be given an opportunity to ask questions.

RECHECK OF NEW EMPLOYEES

It takes time for a new worker to become settled in his job. His surroundings are new, the faces around him are different, the work routine strange, and he is apt to be uncertain of his success. As time passes, the surroundings will become familiar, strangers will become acquaintances and friends, and he will become more confident in his work. During this period of adjustment, the supervisor and the personnel department should keep in closer touch with the employee than is necessary later on. If no inquiry is made by the company officers to see how the new employee is getting along, it will appear to the employee that the company is little interested in him as a person. First impressions are important. Both the employee and the company must make favorable first impressions if the adjustment is to be satisfactory.

The first recheck is usually made a few days after the employee begins work. By this time it can be seen whether he is adjusting to his work easily or not. If not, some special training may be advisable. If it appears that the worker is unsuited to a particular job but possesses basic qualities of value to the company, he may be transferred to another job. The cost of selecting a worker may be small or large. In any case, each new worker represents an investment by the company. Such an investment should not be wasted by firing a new employee after a few days' trial unless no other course appears practical. Furthermore, the human side of the issue should not be forgotten. If an employee who does not fit quickly into a new job is given a chance at another, it will show that the company is considerate. The best of tests and interviewing techniques cannot always determine which job will use the talents of a worker to greatest advantage. For this reason, some companies try a new worker on three or four different jobs, if necessary, before deciding that his capabilities are of no use to the company.

After the first recheck, later ones are made from time to time during the first months of employment. During this time, the employee is more or less on probation. The performance and progress of each new worker are evaluated, and serve as the basis for wage increases and promotions. The probationary period varies from job to job and from company to company. In some, it may be a few months; in others, it may be several years. After the probationary period is ended, the performance of each worker is still reviewed, but less frequently. Some companies review the record of each employee once a year to determine what salary increases or changes in responsibility are warranted. The review may be made by a single individual, usually the employee's immediate superior, or by a committee.

TRAINING PROGRAMS

Concert performers do not stop practicing because they are world renowned. Baseball players spend as much time improving their techniques after they reach the major leagues as before. Physicians continue to read and study even though they have a well-established practice. Successful men never stop learning. As a matter of fact, it is probably no exaggeration to say that to stop learning is to stop living. Learning is not necessarily formal, of course. An intelligent person can learn a lot through conversation, observation, casual reading, and experience.

The most important source of learning on a job is probably experience. In general, the longer one performs a task, the better he becomes at it. He learns what movements to avoid and what techniques improve his output. Some people learn faster by experience than others, but we all learn from experience to some extent. Time on a job, however, does not invariably result in improvement in performance. Some jobs are routine and repetitive. They can be mastered quickly, and once learned, there is little room for improvement. In such cases, improvement in performance is sometimes achieved by having workers exchange jobs periodically. Workers sometimes do this informally among themselves. In other cases, such exchanges are encouraged by the management and controlled by them. More and more, however, the simple repetitive tasks are being done by machines. The application of automation has upgraded the skill of workers, requiring a higher degree of training and judgment than was required of factory workers in an earlier period. As the years pass, more and more training is being required for almost any kind of job. Not only is a higher level of education needed to secure the first job today, but training and education after being hired are becoming important for advancement.

Learning after being hired can be classified as job training and education. *Job training* is concerned with the skills needed for a particular job. *Education* is concerned with learning in a broader sense, beyond the immediate skills necessary for a particular job. Naturally, it is not always easy to draw a sharp distinction between job training and education. Where the distinction is made, the division is usually one of arbitrary judgment.

JOB TRAINING   The skills of a particular job can be learned in a number of ways. The most common method of learning a job is by doing it. This is called *on-the-job training*. Most routine or semiskilled jobs are learned in this way. It is generally wise to appoint an older employee who is both competent and sympathetic as an instructor for new employees on the job.

If the job is more than routine, a relatively long period of training might be required. In such a case, *apprentice training* may be used. A new worker is apprenticed to a skilled worker who teaches the apprentice for months or years while himself working on the job. This type of training is very ancient and is still used extensively in the building trades, such as bricklaying and carpentry.

If training the worker on the job interferes with production or if there is a relatively large number of workers to be trained for the same or similar jobs, *vestibule training* can be used. Also known as the company school, the training is conducted away from where the job will later be performed. By this means, many workers can be trained by a single instructor. The pace of the learners does not interfere with regular production, and they can concentrate on the learning process. Learning with other beginners, they are less likely to feel overwhelmed by their inadequacy at the beginning. Beginners' mistakes are not as costly as they would be in the shop or office. In large companies, the stream of new workers is so heavy that company schools are operated almost continuously and full-time instructors are employed.

COMPANY EDUCATION PROGRAMS   The primary purpose of education after appointment to a job is to prepare an employee for greater responsibilities with the company. In general, the higher a person rises in the company, the broader is the knowledge and experience required. The employee who continues his education has a better chance for promotion than one who stops studying after getting a job. Many companies encourage their workers to expand their education. This is done in a variety of ways. Frequently, a company will arrange to have courses taught during or after working hours. These may be narrow in content and directly related to a job, such as a course in blueprint reading, or they may be as broad as a course in economic principles. Where the courses are job-related, the instructors are usually company personnel; the broader courses are often taught by college instructors.

EXECUTIVE-DEVELOPMENT PROGRAMS   In large companies, executive positions become vacant regularly, and there is continuing need for replacements from lower ranks. Some companies maintain a pool of executive talent from which executive positions are filled. To maintain the pool, executive-development programs are instituted by some companies. Other companies send their promising young officers back to college for periods of 2 weeks, 3 months, or a year. Many universities set up executive-development courses designed specifically for the junior officers of a company. A few universities direct their program toward middle management levels, and, in exceptional cases, design programs as refreshers or broadening courses for men who have already reached top levels of management.

TRANSFERS, DISCHARGE, AND PROMOTION OF EMPLOYEES

TRANSFERS

A *transfer* is a change from one job to another at the same level. There are many reasons for transfers. A division or department may be eliminated or a branch plant liquidated. On the other hand, expansion frequently requires transfers in order to staff new departments or plants. An employee may request a transfer to another plant for family or health reasons. Employees being groomed for management positions might be shifted from one department to another several times in order for them to become broadly acquainted with company operations. Older workers may be shifted to jobs less demanding physically.

While a transfer may be made at the request of an employee, usually it is initiated by his superiors. In some cases, however, he is required to make the transfer if he wishes to remain with the company. One variation is to permit an employee to reject the first request to transfer, but not subsequent ones.

DISCHARGES AND LAYOFFS

When the volume of work falls below that necessary to keep the workers busy, a *layoff* is frequently used to reduce company expenses. Layoffs are temporary, implying later rehiring, and are most common among production workers. Office work does not fluctuate as much as production, and layoffs of office workers are less frequent. Layoffs impose a considerable hardship on workers. Family expenses for rent, food, clothing, and other necessities continue regardless of employment. Irregularity of employment makes budgeting of family expenses almost impossible, and an unexpectedly long layoff can deplete savings. Stabilizing production so as to eliminate layoffs is not only the humane thing for an employer to do; it is also beneficial to the company. If regular employment can be offered to prospective employees, a better type of person can be attracted. Furthermore, when a company lays off some of its workers, it will frequently find that only the poorer ones wait to be rehired. The better ones may have secured employment elsewhere. Recognizing the hardship involved in recurring periods of layoff, labor unions during the 1950s stressed regularity of employment in their bargaining with companies. The United Automobile Workers spearheaded the drive. Some companies have a policy of guaranteeing a full year of work to all employees with a minimum number of years of service. To reduce fluctuation in employment, many companies engage in intensive planning to reduce variations in production volume and make liberal use of transfers from job to job in order to provide steady work for their employees.

Occasionally, it is necessary to *discharge* an employee. This is never pleasant for the person discharged. Consideration for the employee dictates that the process of discharge should be as painless as possible. Separating an unwanted employee from the company may be achieved in a number of ways. The simplest is to call the employee into the supervisor's office and announce to him that he is no longer employed by the company. Another method, commonly used in the past, is to place a printed notice in the pay envelope. The above two methods are used chiefly in firing production workers, maintenance men, and so on. In large factories, several hundred men may be discharged at one time.

When office workers or executives are discharged, the persons are usually permitted to resign. Frequently, advance notice of a week or month is given, to permit the person to hunt for another position. Sometimes, indirect pressure is used to secure a resignation. This can take many forms. To secure the resignation of a company officer, his duties may be assigned one by one to others until he is left with almost nothing to do. He may be informed that he has no chance of further promotion. His salary increases may stop. He may be transferred to a less desirable position or reduced in rank.

In the past, discharges were made on spur-of-the-moment decisions by the employer. They are still made in this way, particularly in small concerns, but less frequently than before. Before a decision to discharge a person is made, his record should be carefully reviewed. Generally, a person is not fired for a single mistake, unless it is of colossal magnitude. To avoid the possibility that prejudice may be the cause of discharge, many companies do not give the authority to fire an employee to his foreman or supervisor alone. If a supervisor develops an unreasoning dislike for an employee, the employee (sometimes the supervisor) is transferred to another department. When the decision of more than one man is required before an employee can be fired, there is less likelihood of a worker being discharged unfairly. In many types of employment, a discharged person finds it extremely difficult to secure the same type of position with another employer. For that reason, if for no other, extreme care should be taken by an employer to avoid unfair dismissals. Besides, an unfair dismissal can injure employee morale.

PROMOTIONS

The opportunity for advancement is an important attraction of any job. If the selection of new employees has brought men and women of high caliber, they will be ambitious. If vacancies for higher positions are filled from the ranks of those below, persons are more likely to work hard at their jobs. But if a job carries no opportunities for promotion, it will be difficult to find capable, energetic persons to fill it.

There is a problem, however, since not every deserving person can be promoted. The number of foremen is small compared to the number of production workers; the number of division heads is small compared to the number of foremen; and there is normally only one president in a company. Although the majority of workers will never be promoted, the possibility is still an incentive. For that reason, the promotion policy of a company has an important bearing on worker morale and efficiency.

A promotion policy should be prepared with care, as reflected by the promotion chart shown in Figure 12-1, and exceptions should be made only with good and sufficient reason. Favoritism and nepotism, while common, are damaging to morale. The workers should know the qualifications on which they are judged for advancement. While any promotion leaves a number of persons disappointed, an undeserved promotion leaves not only disappointment but bitterness.

There are two basic factors considered in selecting a person for promotion: ability and seniority. Ability should not be defined narrowly. A person might be an excellent salesman and yet be a miserable sales manager. A bookkeeper might be very successful at keeping books, but prove a failure when promoted to office manager. Promotions broaden responsibilities, and these responsibilities call for talents of a higher order than are called for by positions at a lower level. When a worker is at the lowest rank, he is usually responsible only for his own work. But when he is promoted, he is generally responsible for the work of several employees.

FIGURE 12-1 A promotion chart.

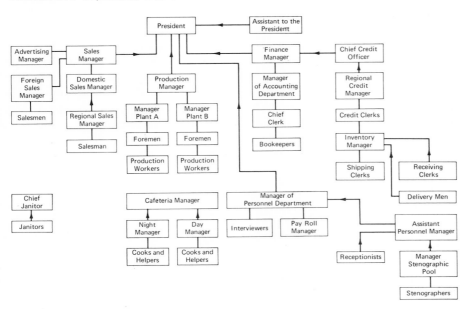

Persons who supervise the work of others must have tact, patience, persuasive powers, and other attributes of leadership.

If there are two persons of approximately equal ability, the person with greater seniority normally should be chosen for the promotion. A person with greater seniority has more company experience, which will help him in his new job, and will be less resented by his subordinates than will a recently hired person.

Selecting the Executive

The use of standardized procedures for selecting executives has developed more slowly than for the selection of foremen, section heads, and other lower-rank supervisors. The turnover of executives is smaller than the turnover at lower levels, so that selection of an executive occurs less frequently, and the process of selection is more apt to vary from case to case.

Some companies develop a file of information on each person considered for possible promotion to executive status. These files provide the company with an *inventory of executive talent*. They go beyond the information on lower-rank employees kept in the personnel files of the company and make it less likely that important characteristics may be overlooked in selecting executives. Furthermore, such an inventory reduces the likelihood that a promotion to executive status will be given to a person because he is located at the main office of the company instead of at a remote branch office.

In addition to the data in the personnel folder of each potential executive, the inventory of executive talent will contain information secured from a special questionnaire filled out by each person considered for promotion. As changes in the status or performance of each person occur, notations are made, so that the inventory is kept constantly up to date. Psychological tests are used by a number of companies in selecting executives. A few companies give considerable attention to such tests in determining promotions, but other companies that use these tests give them little weight. It appears that the consensus is that psychological tests are useful, but that their value is limited for the following reasons:[1]

Tests can err.

Tests cannot determine key qualities like loyalty or industry.

Executives cannot be cataloged exactly.

The mental caliber of executive candidates permits them to outwit psychological tests, give the "right" answers.

Not being businessmen themselves, psychologists may not detect or properly evaluate business judgments.

Psychological tests do best in singling out the patently impossible candidate—the easiest also for the president or his aides to eliminate.

[1] *Bulletin*, American Institute of Management, vol. 6, no. 13, March 1957, p. 3.

In order to select the best persons available for job openings in a company, it is essential that the job requirements be carefully analyzed so that persons best able to meet the requirements will be recruited.

SUMMARY

The sources of job applicants are many, including government and private employment agencies, newspaper advertisements, schools, and recommendations of persons already employed by the company.

In screening applicants for jobs, application forms may be filled out by each applicant, interviews may be used, letters of reference requested, and tests given. Good judgment must, however, be exercised in the use of these devices, because these means alone do not cover all factors needed in making a good selection.

In some jobs, a trained employee can start work as soon as he is hired. In others, a period of training is necessary. The training can be informal or formal, on the job or in special training departments, restricted to a specific skill or broadly educational, brief or lasting more than a year. Although training is common for newly hired employees, educational programs for persons already employed are frequently used to increase the skills of company workers.

Educational programs for persons considered to be of executive caliber are quite common. Such programs are also becoming ever broader in their educational content.

Efficient management attempts to schedule work, as far as it is possible, to eliminate or minimize seasonal hiring and firing. Where it is necessary to discharge a worker permanently, consideration for his welfare and that of his family should be made. Where promotions are given, the person best qualified is usually chosen. The selection should, of course, be fair, and be done in such a manner as to limit the disappointment or resentment of those not chosen. This is particularly important in selecting executives for a company, since a poorly chosen executive can do the company much more harm than a poorly chosen foreman.

1 What was a common method of hiring workers in the last century? Is it different today? Why?

QUESTIONS FOR REVIEW

2 If an employee is unsuited to a job for which he was hired, he can be fired. Why, then, should an employer use care in hiring new employees?

3 "Analyze the job and then seek a worker to fit the job." Is this a good policy in seeking workers? Explain.

4 An employment agency does the preliminary screening for an employer who has a job to fill. What does this mean, and how does it help an employer?

5 To what sources may an employer turn in seeking new employees?

6 "Successful interviewing requires tact." Why should an employer worry about tact? He has a job to offer and the applicant is seeking a job. The applicant should worry about tact and making a good impression, not the employer. Do you agree? Why or why not?

7   It is common for employees to suggest friends or relatives when a job opening exists. Is this useful to an employer, or should an employer refuse to consider such suggested names? Explain your answer.

8   Of what use are letters of recommendation written by friends of an applicant for a job?

9   Why is it important for the personnel department of a company to keep a check on each new employee during the first few months of employment?

10   For what purposes are training programs instituted by company management?

11   Contrast on-the-job training with vestibule training, giving the advantages and disadvantages of each.

12   Education or training after employment benefits the employee. Why then do companies often offer to pay for all the costs of such training programs?

13   The right to fire an employee rests with the employer. Why should such a decision be carefully weighed, and perhaps be decided only on the recommendation of two or more supervisors?

14   Outline the advantages and disadvantages of a policy of promotion from within a company as compared with opening executive positions to outsiders as well as to company employees.

15   What factors would you look for in selecting a foreman from among factory workers? An office manager from among office workers?

SELECTED READINGS

Haimann, Theo: *Supervision: Concepts and Practices of Management*, South-Western Publishing Company, Cincinnati, 1972.

Hegarty, Edward J.: *How to Succeed in Company Politics*, McGraw-Hill Book Company, New York, 1964.

Jucius, Michael J.: *Personnel Management*, 7th ed., Richard D. Irwin, Inc., Homewood, Ill., 1971.

Pigors, Paul, and Charles A. Myers: *Personnel Administration*, 7th ed., McGraw-Hill Book Company, New York, 1973.

Name	Section	Date

COMPLETION SENTENCES

1 In modern factories, physical effort has been largely replaced by

machines .

2 The first step in selecting an employee is job _analysis_ .

3 A _job specification_ lists in detail the requirements needed by an

applicant for the job.

4 People in the personnel department must exercise _____

in the selection of employees.

5 Unemployed workers must register with _____ to qualify

for unemployment compensation.

6 One of the most important means of locating new employees is by

_____ in newspapers.

7 Generally, the types of positions for which school graduates are sought are career positions with opportunities for advancing to _____ levels.

8 Frequently, information can be gotten from an _____ that cannot be secured easily from an application form.

9 _____ and _____ tests attempt to measure the talent a person has in specific areas.

10 The most important source of learning on a job is probably

_____ .

11 Vestibule training is also known as _____ .

12 A _____ is a change from one job to another at the same level.

13 _____ are temporary, implying later rehiring, and are most common among production workers.

14 When office workers or executives are discharged, the persons are usually permitted to _____ .

15 There are two basic factors considered in selecting a person for promotion:

_____ and _____ .

TRUE OR FALSE STATEMENTS

1 The first step in selecting a new employee is job analysis.

2 A job specification lists in general rather than precise terms the requirements needed by an applicant for the job.

Name   Section   Date

T **3**   No deficiency of an applicant for a job, no matter how minor, should be ignored in considering the applicant.

T **4**   If an employer wants the best workers available, he cannot wait for applicants to come to him.

T **5**   Workers with higher skills are more apt to be found through private employment agencies than through government employment agencies.

F **6**   The use of application forms is not intended to permit unqualified applicants to be rejected before being interviewed.

T **7**   The interview of a job applicant can precede or follow the filling out of an application form.

F **8**   The job interview requires tact and judgment on the part of the applicant, but these are of minor importance on the part of the interviewer.

F **9**   Letters of recommendation are more commonly used now in considering applicants than they were many years ago.

F **10**   Tests are more likely to be used to screen applicants for jobs in small companies than in large companies.

F **11**   An aptitude test attempts to measure the talent a person has in specific areas rather than his general intelligence.

T **12**   Good health is as important as intelligence in most jobs.

T **13**   The process of introducing a new employee to his job varies widely from company to company.

T **14**   The first recheck on how a newly hired employee is getting along in his job is usually made a few days after he is hired.

F **15**   Experience is no longer the most important source of learning after a worker has been hired.

T **16**   Most semiskilled jobs are learned by workers through on-the-job training.

T **17**   If a fairly large number of workers are to be trained for the same type of job, vestibule training can be effectively used.

F **18**   Even in large companies, executive positions become vacant irregularly.

F **19**   Transfers from one job to another at the same level are usually made as a result of requests by employees.

20 Layoffs are about as common among office workers as among production workers.

EXERCISES

1 Prepare an application form for a sales clerk in a retail store, specifying the type of store, such as shoe store, camera store, grocery store, or toy store. Include in the form whatever questions you think would be useful to an employer in evaluating the qualifications of applicants, such as age or experience.

2 Outline an orientation and training program for a new sales clerk in a retail store or for a stenographer or bookkeeper in an office. Specify the type of store or office. In preparing your report, remember that training programs are costly to employers in terms of the time the trainer and new employee spent on the training and the wages paid to the new employee while he is being trained.

3 *Case Problem for report or class discussion.*
Joe Irwin, a Vietnam veteran, has applied for a job as salesman for the Wintergreen Automobile Company, a dealer in new and used cars. During the war, Joe lost his right arm and his right eye. Otherwise he has no handicaps. After discharge, he went to college, earned average grades, finished 3 years, and then left to take a job. The reason he gave for quitting school was that he was married, and the approaching birth of a child made it necessary for him to spend full time earning a living. Since leaving school he has worked as a door-to-door salesman of brushes, a position he still holds. His personality is pleasant, he appears intelligent, and his references are favorable. His reason for wanting the job with the Wintergreen Automobile Company is that he prefers selling cars to selling brushes.

Put yourself in the position of the manager of the Wintergreen Automobile Company. Assuming you needed another salesman, how would you appraise Joe Irwin? Would his physical handicap be a reason for not employing him? How important is the fact that he did not finish college? Would this fact be important as a factor in promotion at a later date? Would you hire Joe Irwin?

CHAPTER

13

EMPLOYEE COMPENSATION AND MOTIVATION

One of the most important reasons for working is to earn wages. This chapter discusses the compensation given to an employee in return for the time and effort he expends for his employer. It must be kept in mind, however, that wages are not the only reason a person seeks employment or prefers one job to another, as the last part of this chapter emphasizes. Such things as work conditions, friendliness of employers and fellow workers, opportunities for advancement, and job satisfaction are also important.

There are two fundamental methods by which wages are determined: they can be awarded for (1) the number of hours spent on the job or (2) the number of units of work produced. After reading this chapter, you should be able to determine the advantages of each method for each type of job. Remember, however, that certain types of jobs may not be easily classifiable as to method of payment but might be more suited to a method combining features of both.

During the past few decades, there has been an increase in the use and variety of fringe benefits in compensating employees. This is particularly true for the higher classes of employees, chiefly the officers of a corporation. Try listing reasons for this development.

Personnel management deals with the effective utilization of the labor resources of a company. Take particular note of the concept of "job enrichment." This concept is likely to be given much attention in factories and offices in the coming years.

If it were not for the attraction of wages, few people would work. They demand wages partly because they would rather be doing something else and because money is needed to meet living expenses. From the employer's standpoint, inducements have to be offered to get people to spend most of the daylight hours in factories and offices, and the most effective inducement in most cases is money. Without such inducements, few people would come to work. There is nothing sadder than the man who has dragged himself out of bed, dashed down to the office, and discovered that the day is Saturday.

Wages play a dual role. They are the price management must pay to secure the labor needed for production. Because they are a cost of production—frequently the most important cost—management's interest is in keeping a "lid on wages." But wages are also a source of income for the wage earner—in most cases the chief source. They enable him to buy the goods and services he enjoys. Wages are thus a cost of producing goods and services and a means by which they can be sold.

FORCES DETERMINING WAGES

Wages and salaries are the money payments given to employees. Although the two are used interchangeably, the word *wage* implies payment at the lowest level of company organization and *salary* implies a higher status. A manager is paid a salary; a toolmaker is paid a wage. The two words also imply different types of work. A worker in a factory or on a farm is paid a wage; a worker in an office is paid a salary. For the sake of simplicity, however, the word "wage" will be used here to cover payment in money to employees in general, while "salary" will refer to the wages paid to office and management employees in particular.

Although in this chapter "wages" will refer to money wages, a distinction should be made between money wages and real wages. *Money wages* are the dollars received by a worker. *Real wages* consist of what the worker can buy with his money wages. If the price level rises by 10 percent and the money wages of a worker rise by the same percentage, his real wages are unchanged. Or, to put it another way, the worker's money wages had to rise by 10 percent to keep his real wages from falling.

What are the basic forces that determine wages? Why does a popular singer make $230,000 a year while a dentist makes $47,600? Why does a steelworker make more than a farm laborer? Why were wages higher in 1968 than they were in 1941? Why are wages lower in India than they are in Canada? Such questions have been intriguing scholars for a long time. The basic forces affecting wages have been examined by many social scientists and a number of wage theories have been developed. While it will not be possible to list all of the forces and theories, the more prominent ones will be discussed.

SUPPLY OF LABOR

If the supply of labor increases, wages tend to go down, or at least the pressure for wage increases diminishes. More workers mean more competition for the available jobs, making it more likely that employers will not have to offer higher wages to get the number of workers they want. Conversely, if the supply of labor decreases, the scarcity of workers exerts an upward pressure on wages.

At any given time the supply of workers of each type is fixed. If there are 150 electricians in a town, that is the supply of electricians on the day the count was made. About the only way that this supply can be increased immediately is to ask the men to work a longer day and to offer extra pay as an inducement. If a period of several days is considered, the supply of electricians might be increased by bringing in workers from other towns, or it might be decreased by electricians leaving the town for better jobs elsewhere. If a period of several months or years is considered, the supply of electricians may be increased by new craftsmen being trained, or it may be decreased by the retirement or shifting of workers to other types of jobs. In other words, the greater the period of time considered, the more elastic is the supply of labor. Furthermore, the supply of labor influences wage rates and is itself influenced by wage rates. If wage rates are good in a particular trade, apprentices are attracted to that trade and the supply of workers with that skill increases. As the supply of workers increases, it becomes less necessary for employers to offer inducements.

Employers tend to increase the number of workers in their employ as long as it is profitable to do so. If they can "afford" to hire more workers, they generally do. Since labor is a cost to employers, employers can afford fewer workers at high than at low wage rates. But the ability of an employer to absorb wage costs depends on the demand for his products. If he can sell his products in large volume and at a comfortable profit, he can generally afford to hire more workers to expand production, and he can offer higher wages to keep them. To sum up, there are three basic forces that interact with each other: demand for labor, supply of labor, and wages. An increase in the supply of labor exerts a downward pressure on wages which tends to stimulate the demand for labor. An increase in wages tends to reduce the demand for labor but tends to increase the supply of labor. A decrease in wages stimulates the demand for labor but tends to decrease the supply. It must be remembered, however, that these basic forces are obscured or controlled by such factors as labor organization, employer cooperation, and wage legislation.

THE DEMAND FOR LABOR

Since 1938, the trend of wages in most fields of activity has been up. Wages have risen more rapidly in some fields than in others as can be seen in Figure 13-1, but an upward direction is found in nearly all wages. Where unions have been strong, the rise has been greater than where unions have been weak or absent. In manufacturing, the rise has been quite marked. Because the rate of business activity influences the amount of overtime work done per week, the average weekly earnings fluctuate from month to month. Hourly wage rates have moved upward steadily. On the other hand, the length of the workweek, which declined from the time of the Civil War to the First World War, has in recent years shown little change in either direction. A 40-hour workweek is standard in most manufacturing com-

TRENDS IN WAGES AND HOURS

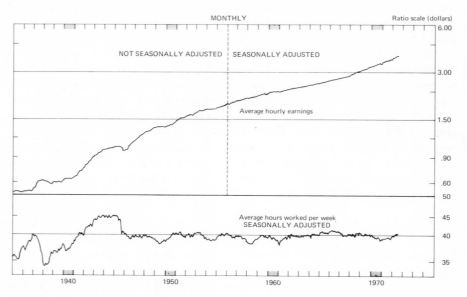

MONTHLY   Ratio scale (dollars)

NOT SEASONALLY ADJUSTED   SEASONALLY ADJUSTED

Average hourly earnings

Average hours worked per week
SEASONALLY ADJUSTED

1940   1950   1960   1970

FIGURE 13-1 Hours and earnings of production workers in manufacturing. (*Federal Reserve Chart Book*, Board of Governors of the Federal Reserve System, 1972, p. 84. Data from Bureau of Labor Statistics.)

panies. Thus the average workweek has remained at around 40 hours since the end of World War II, as shown in Figure 13-1. There have been some predictions, however, that the remaining years of the present century will see a marked decline in the length of the workweek, largely resulting from the expanded use of automation in factories and of computers in offices.

PAYMENT METHODS Payment methods for work done vary according to the industry, the job, and other factors. The more common are salary, hourly wages, piece-rate wages, commissions, and incentive payments. Sometimes these methods are used singly, sometimes in combination.

SALARY Salary is a payment based on time spent in an office or plant, stated in terms of a number of dollars per week, month, or year. It is the method of payment for almost all office jobs, executive positions, and work of a routine, regular nature. Salary schedules for low-ranked office workers often involve deductions for tardiness or absence from the office and overtime payments for working after hours.

Where it is difficult to measure the output of work, hourly or daily wages are generally used. They are also used to pay workers on a production line or in any type of job where machinery sets the speed of work. Still another use for such a method of payment is in precision work. Where errors are costly and workers must not be rushed, payment according to the time worked is logical.

The major weakness of hourly wages is the reduction of the incentive to increase production. If two workers are paid the same hourly rate, neither can be expected to raise his volume of production above the other's. This problem can be met in a number of ways. Close supervision and frequent rating of workers may distinguish the energetic from the laggard, and a suitable reward may be given to the former. Pride of work is enough incentive for some, while the chance of promotion may spur others.

Where a plant operates on two or three shifts, the day shift is the most popular. In order to get workers to work on the late afternoon or night shift some means of assignment is necessary. Seniority may determine the choice of shift, or all workers might be transferred periodically from one shift to another. In order to make unpopular shifts more palatable, companies frequently pay a shift differential. The differential might be 50 to 75 cents an hour above the day-shift rates.

Where output can be measured in units, piecework wages can be used. The worker is paid an amount for each unit produced rather than for the number of hours worked. If the rate is 6 cents for every unit and a worker produces 500 units in a day, his wage for the day is $30. This type of pay is useful for repetitive operations of a routine nature. But what if a machine breaks down? In such a case, management frequently provides some means of preventing the worker's wage from suffering. One is to put a worker on an hourly basis for the time spent at his machine when he is prevented from producing for reasons not his own fault.

The chief advantage of piecework pay over hourly pay is the incentive to increase production. The fast worker is induced to work to the capacity of his speed, while the slower worker is given an incentive to develop greater speed. The chief disadvantage is in its emphasis on production rather than quality. In many cases, this is not a serious problem. Where the operation is a simple one, quality standards can be maintained in spite of the desire of workers to work fast. But where speed reduces quality, the piecework wage may not be wise to use. Rejects can, of course, be charged against the worker in determining his volume of production. Rejects, however, waste material, and the desire of workers for speed may increase the number of rejects. Supervision can help to keep up standards of quality. One difference between supervision of workers on piece rates and on hourly rates is this: under piece rates, supervision is concerned with protecting quality; under hourly rates, supervision is concerned with stimulating volume.

COMMISSIONS

Piecework payment plans applied to salesmen are called *commissions*. For every unit sold, the salesman receives a certain amount of money or is paid a percentage of the selling price. The latter is more common. If the commission is 15 percent of the selling price and the salesman makes a $10 sale, his commission is $1.50. The salesman and the worker on piece rates have the same type of incentive: increase "production" to increase wages. Salesmen paid on a basis of commissions only will receive no pay if no sales are made. Hence, salaries of salesmen are apt to be highly unstable. To make salesmen's incomes more regular, companies sometimes pay a salary plus commission. However, employers generally set the salary low enough so that there will still be the incentive of the commissions to spur selling.

INCENTIVE PAYMENT PLAN

In addition to piece rates and commissions, other incentive payment plans are used in business. The basic payment method in a factory may be hourly wages. If an executive determines that 100 units per day is the standard output per worker, an additional payment may be made to all who exceed the standard. If the daily wage is $20 and if a worker produces 120 units, his incentive payment would logically be set at $4. Incentives are sometimes put on a group basis if the work is performed by teams rather than individually.

SUPPLEMENTAL COMPENSATION

THE BONUS

A bonus is an added payment to workers above their salary, generally paid at the end of the year. Unlike the incentive plan mentioned above, the bonus is not directly related to individual effort. To a small degree, the bonus is an incentive payment since, in most companies, the size of the bonus depends on the profit for the year. For most companies, however, the profit depends as much on the level of business activity as on the effort of employees. Bonuses are distributed to office personnel, salesmen, and executives for the most part and are usually related to seniority and rank. They are generally presented as a gift from the company and not as an additional salary payment. To emphasize the gift characteristics, the bonus is generally given just before Christmas. The office Christmas party is frequently the occasion for the distribution of bonuses.

PROFIT-SHARING PLANS

Profit-sharing plans permit employees to participate in the prosperity of the company for which they work. In addition to regular wages, each employee eligible for the plan is given a payment from the profit-sharing fund. The amount of profits set aside for profit sharing depends on the profitability of the company during the year. The amount in the fund is then divided among the employees eligible to receive shares of the profits. Most plans are restricted to executives. Those that include lower levels of employees generally base each employee's share on his annual salary. Sometimes the basis for distribution includes not only the salary of each employee but seniority, merit, and other considerations as well.

STOCK-PURCHASE PLANS

Stock-purchase plans permit the employee to become an owner of the company. As an owner as well as an employee, he will share the point of view of stockholders in general. According to proponents of stock-purchase plans, owner-employees will strive to be less wasteful, more diligent, and more responsible in their work. The influence of ownership of stock on employee attitudes is difficult to measure. However, the number of shares that the lower-ranked employees are able and permitted to buy is so small in most plans that it is difficult to see that it would make much difference in their attitudes.

One of the first stock-purchase plans was instituted by Pillsbury Mills in 1882. During the 1920s several hundred plans were put into operation, and most of them were abandoned in the collapse of the stock market. It is generally conceded that while the effects on employee attitudes during prosperity are inconclusive, the effects are quite evident during a decline in the stock market. At such times the influence of stock-purchase plans on employee morale is uniformly bad, because many employees do not understand the risks of stock ownership. Many blame the company for the drop in stock prices. For a plan to be successful, education of the employee concerning the risks, rewards, and responsibilities of stock ownership should be undertaken. Another factor in the success of a plan is the degree of fluctuation of prices of the company's stock. Where prices fluctuate over a wide range, stock-purchase plans should probably not be used or should be restricted to executives, who presumably are aware of the risks of ownership. If the price of the company stock is stable, there is greater likelihood that employee attitudes will benefit from ownership.

To make the purchase of company stocks attractive to employees, the shares are offered at a price below the market price. The method of payment is usually a deduction from the pay check of each employee signing for the purchase plan.

PENSIONS

Company pensions for retired employees have existed in the United States for more than 100 years. However, a vast expansion in company participation in pension payments to retired workers has occurred since the enactment of the Social Security Act in 1935. A large number of workers became eligible in 1935 to receive pensions from the social security fund to which they and their employers had contributed equally. This act brought many companies into pension planning for their employees for the first time. Some companies have gone beyond the requirements of the law by setting up plans for pension payments to supplement those of social security. Unions have also bargained for pension payments, and some pension plans have been established under joint union-company sponsorship.

Company pension plans can be considered a deferred compensation for employee services. They permit an employee to continue to receive pay from the company for which he worked but from which he has retired. Rather than receiving all of the compensation, the employee receives only part, although a major part. A portion is held back, to be paid to him when he is too old to work for the company, or it will be paid to his widow or children if he should die before retirement.

The amount held back from the employee and the amount added by the employer are sometimes invested in the stock of the company. If the stock enjoys a relatively stable price, the employee may receive very handsome payments when he reaches retirement age, particularly if there has been an appreciation in value over the years.

FRINGE BENEFITS

Employees are compensated not by money wages alone. Other types of compensation, called *fringe benefits*, are given the worker. These pay for various types of personal expenses, provide services for which an employee might otherwise have to pay, or make working conditions more pleasant. Although a complete list would have more than 100 items, the examples below illustrate the variety of fringe benefits found among United States companies:

Free lunch	Coffee breaks	Family allowance
Health insurance	Welfare fund	Support of credit union
Life insurance	Suggestion awards	Legal aid
Beauty parlors	Company country club	Company housing
Company stores	Educational assistance	Discounts on company products
Laundry services	Parties and picnics	
Income tax services	Reading room	Company publications
Music while working	Nursery	Medical exams
Showers and steam room	Wedding gifts	Free magazines
		Travel expense

Some of these items can be secured by the company at considerably less cost than would be possible for employees, since the company can furnish the items in large volume. Various types of insurance, for example, are available at lower cost on a group rather than an individual basis. Other benefits make work more enjoyable, such as background music or occasional coffee breaks. An important advantage of fringe benefits, however, is the tax advantage. To the company, the cost of these services is a business expense. At 1974 corporation tax rates, about half of the money spent on fringe benefits would otherwise go to the tax collector; or, stated in another way, about half of the cost of fringe benefits is borne by the government. This assumes that money not spent for fringe benefits would not be spent on other business purposes. If the money spent on fringe benefits were given to the employees as added wages, the employees' taxable income would rise. Because the income tax laws have been written to exclude most of the fringe benefits from taxable income, the employee does not usually pay tax on the compensation he receives in the form of fringe benefits. This is the chief reason that fringe benefits are widely used for executive compensation, where money incomes are subject to high rates of taxation.

COMPENSATION FOR EXECUTIVES

The objectives of executive compensation and the means by which these objectives can be achieved can be summarized as follows:

Objective	Means

Hire and hold management and technical people of high competence	Job satisfaction
	    The work itself
	    Opportunity to advance and grow
	    Ownership participation
	 Job security
	    Group insurance (life, health, accident)
	    Individual insurance
	    Pensions
	    Deferred payment contracts
	    Profit sharing for retirement

Obtain a high level of current individual performance	Salary Incentive bonus Fringe benefits
Build a strong and profitable business	Profit sharing Stock options

Plans for compensating executives are made with care, partly because there is usually great competition for managerial talent of a high caliber and partly because of the search for means to avoid high income tax rates. There are as many ways of compensating executives as there are of compensating lower-rank employees. In most cases, the means are the same, differing only in detail and amount. We will discuss in greater detail salary, bonuses, deferred compensation, stock options, and fringe benefits.

SALARY

The primary method of payment of executives, as of employees, is salary. This may remain steady over a number of years, increase regularly each year, or vary with the profit margin of the company.

BONUSES

An executive bonus is a payment in addition to salary or wages given to an executive or worker for superior achievement, the amount of the bonus being related to his performance. In theory, the executive bonus is a reward for excellent performance. In practice, however, bonuses in most cases fluctuate with the profits of the company, whether profits result from superior executive accomplishment or from a rising level of business activity. Bonus payments rise during prosperity and fall during recession. If bonus payments are a measure of the level of executive performance, it would appear that managerial competence rises and falls with the business cycle.

DEFERRED COMPENSATION

Deferred compensation is a means of increasing an executive's compensation in the future rather than in the present. Like a pension, it provides for payments by the company to the executive after his retirement from the company. Deferred compensation, however, frequently requires some concession from the executive. For example, to receive deferred compensation, the company might require the executive to sign a contract requiring him to continue employment with the company until normal retirement age, to serve as a management consultant for a specified number of years after retirement, and not to engage during retirement in any business activity of a nature competitive with the company. It is quite apparent that deferred payment plans serve to hold executives who might otherwise stray to competitors.

STOCK OPTIONS

The purpose of stock-option plans for executives is the same as for other employees: to identify the interests of the worker with those of the owner. In the case of management personnel, however, it can be argued that performance more directly affects company profits. The stock-option plan permits executives to purchase a certain number of shares of stock of the company at a stated price for a stated number of years in the future. For example, if the stock of the company is selling on the market at $20 a share, an executive might be given an option to buy up to 5,000 shares a year during the next 10 years. If the stock rose in market price to $30 the following year, the executive could buy 5,000 shares at $20, sell them later for $30, and make a profit of $50,000 on the transaction. If the price of the stock fell below $20, the executive, of course, would not exercise his option to buy stock.

FRINGE BENEFITS

The list of fringe benefits for employees may be applied to executives, since those benefits companies give to their employees they give to executives also. Executives, however, enjoy additional fringe benefits not available to lower employee ranks, some of which include: free use of automobile, sometimes with chauffeur; free use of city apartment; company-owned hunting lodge for executives; company-paid membership in private country clubs; liberal expense accounts while traveling;

company-owned yacht and airplane for executive use; company-owned vacation resort for executives; and entertainment allowances.

It is difficult to measure what proportion of executive compensation is paid in the form of salary and what is paid in other forms. There is such a bewildering variety of deferred compensation plans, stock options, and fringe benefits that a statistical measurement would be virtually impossible. Furthermore, it is almost impossible to compare the total compensation. On the matter of deferred compensation alone, measurement and comparison are difficult:

> However, the growing trend toward various types of deferred compensation plans makes comparisons (of executive compensation) between companies risky. Many now spread bonus payments out over three, four, or five years.
>
> Deferred cash bonuses are not the only complication. Tax considerations also have led to a host of more intricate deferred payment techniques, including contributions to pension plans, "share units," "dividend units," and "contingent units." Often these are tied to stock option plans. Some of them are so complex the beneficiaries themselves must have a hard time explaining to their wives just how much they earned during the year.[1]

PERSONNEL MANAGEMENT

Personnel management is that aspect of management having as its goal the effective utilization of the labor resources of an organization. At one time, the mission of a personnel department was keeping all jobs in an office or factory filled. The inducement of wages and the fear of discharge were thought to be all that was necessary to bring out the maximum effort of each employee. Today it is recognized that the function of personnel management is not that simple. Wages and layoffs are not the only factors that influence a man's effectiveness at work. Man is a complex being, and his behavior and responses are conditioned by acquisitiveness, worry, love, hate, prejudice, joy, amusement, and the desire for status. These aspects of personnel management are being given increasing attention in the 1970s, as we shall see later in this chapter.

EMPLOYEE MORALE

Morale is a state of mind. It is the reflection of individual attitudes toward the job, one's fellow workers, and the employer. High morale and good performance on the job are usually found together. Low morale is associated with absenteeism, grievances, and high labor turnover. Because morale has a bearing on the quality and quantity of work, it is of concern to management.

How can morale be improved? Can it be raised by putting everybody on a first-name basis, having executives eat with workers in the company cafeteria, and sponsoring an annual company picnic? Possibly, but such tactics alone cannot ensure good morale. If it is apparent to the employees that management has

---

[1] *Business Week*, May 21, 1960, p. 8.

concern for their welfare, that it strives to be fair, that working conditions and salaries are as good as the company is able to provide, and that the demands on employees are reasonable—in short, if the company shows loyalty toward its employees—it will usually receive loyalty in return.

Good morale is largely based on adequate wages, careful selection and training, fairness in promotion, and safe working conditions. These are fundamental to good working relations in any plant or office. There are, however, additional areas in which morale can be improved:

Health services
Handling grievances
Special privileges for workers
Team spirit
Individual recognition
Discipline
Attractive surroundings
Recreational facilities

Health Services

The absence of a worker often necessitates a reassignment of jobs. The absence of an executive may cause a more serious disruption of work. Good personnel planning can reduce the disruption caused by absences, but absences will always be costly. Partly to reduce the number of absences and partly to increase the effectiveness of persons on their jobs, many companies provide health services ranging from very limited to very extensive. The most common type of health services are the following: sanitation control, hygiene education, physical examinations, first aid rooms, registered nurse, and company physician.

Sanitation Control

For the protection of the workers, a company must maintain sanitary surroundings. There must be adequate rest rooms and drinking fountains. The rest rooms must be kept clean at all times and drinking fountains must be inspected to eliminate the possibility of transmitting colds and other diseases. Towels and soap should not be used by more than one person. This usually means that liquid soap and paper towels are provided. Well-managed companies provide such facilities as a matter of course, but many small places of work are extremely primitive in this respect.

Hygiene Education

Just as safety education is important, so is hygiene education. If a worker is careful about his hygiene, he is less likely to become ill. A company may require all production workers to wash their hands when they leave their work stations for lunch. Talks on hygiene and publicity on bulletin boards are other means of promoting individual responsibility.

Physical examinations are very commonly required as a condition to being hired. However, a person may be in good health at the time he first begins working for a company and later fall into poor health. For this reason, some companies require all of their employees to submit to periodic physical examinations. These are usually provided without cost to the employee, frequently by putting a physician on full-time employment or by retaining the part-time services of a panel of physicians. Some companies provide periodic examinations for all of their employees, while some provide them for only certain classes of persons. Some provide simple physical checks by the company physician for lower-level employees and extensive examinations for executives.

Physical Examinations

To provide medical attention for emergencies, companies maintain first aid rooms. If a doctor is employed by the company for physical examinations, the first aid room is usually located adjacent to the room where the examinations are conducted. First aid kits may also be provided at strategic locations around the plant.

First Aid Rooms

A registered nurse is frequently employed by a company so as to be available for emergencies. She also usually has time to treat minor ailments, such as colds, headaches, cuts, and bruises. In some companies, the nurse visits the homes of employees absent because of illness, giving what aid she can to speed recovery. Some companies provide flu shots free or at nominal cost for their employees.

Registered Nurse

While the primary responsibility of most company physicians is to conduct physical examinations, some companies offer services of a physician for consultation and treatment. The treatment is usually restricted in extent, so as not to increase the cost to the company and also so as not to compete with the business of private physicians.

Company Physician

A *grievance* is a complaint of a worker against the company. Even in the best-run companies there will be grievances. The importance to employee morale is

Handling Grievances

not that grievances exist from time to time, but how they are handled by the company. If complaints are rejected by supervisors or executives without a fair hearing, the effect on morale will be bad. Many complaints are not legitimate, but the fact that employees may complain and that management will listen helps to raise morale.

Methods of handling grievances differ. A company may have a policy of referring each complaining employee to his immediate supervisor. If he is dissatisfied with the disposition of his case by the supervisor, he may appeal successively to higher levels of authority all the way to the president of the company. If the worker is a member of a union with which the company has a bargaining contract, grievances may be handled by negotiation between the shop steward of the union and the supervisor in the plant. If these cannot agree, the contract may provide that the business agent of the union and the director of industrial relations of the company attempt to reach an agreement. If the grievances cannot be resolved by negotiation, the contract may call for arbitration to settle the issue.

Special Privileges for Workers

It is human nature to enjoy privileges. It is also human nature to resent the unfair granting of privilege. The granting of privileges can be used to provide an incentive if it is done with discretion. The most common basis on which privilege is granted is *seniority*. For example, all workers with 10 years of service may be given 3 weeks of vacation instead of 2. The choice of vacation dates may also be given according to seniority. Choice parking locations may be given according to seniority or may be based on the record of attendance or some other basis.

Team Spirit

Where companies make a conscious effort to build morale, the fostering of a team or family spirit is almost always a part of the effort. A company newspaper or magazine makes liberal use of photographs of employees and personal as well as company news. An annual open house for families of employees is held by some businesses to enable the members of workers' families to get a better appreciation of the job done by the workers. For office personnel, a company banquet or annual reception in the supervisor's home serves to foster the group spirit. The office Christmas celebration, usually held on the last working day before Christmas, is another expression of the family spirit.

Individual Recognition

As the size of a company grows, there is a danger that the employee will feel that he is being considered more and more a part of a machine rather than an individual. To a considerable extent, the purpose of employee morale programs is to counter this feeling. There are some specific actions that companies can take, however, that help to emphasize the worker as an individual. A few examples are given below:

Listing names of all employees on the reception room wall
Putting office employees' names on office doors wherever practicable
Mentioning each employee in the company paper at least once a year
Liberal granting of awards, with appropriate ceremony and photographs for the company newspaper

Associated with individual recognition is the desire for status. There is, of course, the obvious status associated with different levels of company authority, and it is here that status symbols must be awarded with care so as not to create resentment. The size of the office, a carpet on the floor, the size of the desk, and the location of the office are all considered indications of status within the company. Awarding of status symbols can boost morale but—if not awarded with care—they can damage morale more than boosting it.

Company rules and standards of work must be maintained, and discipline is one means of accomplishing this. In severe cases, discipline may mean a fine or other punishment, but mostly it means criticism. Criticism can be either a stern reprimand or a gentle rebuke. In any case, the kind of reprimand should be determined not only by the severity of the offense but also by the character and personality of the employee. Some employees are "thick skinned" and can accept a stern reprimand. In fact, to some types of persons, a gentle rebuke is meaningless. On the other hand, some people are highly sensitive. To them stern language would do more harm than good. Employees who are highly emotional usually need to be treated with gentleness.

Whenever possible, scolding should be avoided. Rather than criticism for shortcomings, praise for good performance should be emphasized. Praise where deserved is an important morale builder, and opportunities for giving it should not be overlooked. It is a good tactic for a supervisor to couple criticism with praise.

Discipline

Attractive surroundings improve morale. This does not mean merely providing good light and clean rooms. Many other things can be done to make the factory or office a pleasant place in which to work. Companies can provide music as a background for office work. They can landscape the grounds around their buildings. They can provide acoustical tile for ceilings. They can make factory interiors more pleasing by the use of color. A lounge, snack bar, patio, and cafeteria will increase the attraction of the factory or office. One insurance company in Houston, Texas,

Attractive Surroundings

provides a swimming pool adjacent to its office. More and more, offices and plants are being air-conditioned. The consensus is that money spent on making the place of work comfortable and attractive is more than returned in better performance by employees.

Recreational Facilities

Recreational activities are often supported by companies. Many companies support athletic teams composed of employees. Bowling is very popular, and some companies support many teams, so that practically any employee can qualify for a team. Basketball, tennis, and baseball are other supported sports. Frequently, the end of the season for a sport is the occasion for a banquet paid for by the company.

Many less strenuous activities are supported by companies. Choruses, orchestras, drama groups, and camera clubs are examples.

An annual picnic is traditional in many companies. This is most often sponsored by companies small enough so that the number of employees does not overwhelm the picnic site.

A few companies maintain country clubs for their workers. In many cases, these compare favorably with private country clubs in the area, even though the charge to the employee is small or nothing.

COMMUNICATING WITH EMPLOYEES

Communication with employees was once considered a one-way affair. Companies were often managed in a military manner—orders were given and workers were not encouraged to express opinions. It is more common now for communication to be a two-way process, up from the employee ranks as well as down to them. Enlightened managers know that they can better put their ideas across if they know what is in the minds of their employees. This implies, of course, that the idea is clear in the mind of the manager in the first place, unlike the idea in the mind of Napoleon Bonaparte when writing to General Murat, "You will so manage that the Spaniards may not suspect the course I intend to pursue. This will not be difficult, for I have not fixed upon it myself."[2]

There are many ways to stimulate the flow of communications in both directions. Among them are: periodic conferences, private talks between supervisor and subordinate, an open-door policy on the part of executives, and suggestion systems.

Periodic Conferences

Each supervisor may bring together all of his employees for 10 or 15 minutes each week. The employees are encouraged to bring up any matters they wish. If there are any announcements affecting the workers attending the meeting, they will be presented there. If any worker has done outstanding work, he may be compli-

[2] *The Royal Bank of Canada Monthly Letter*, vol. 35, no. 12, p. 1, October 1954.

mented at the meeting. The main purpose of the conference is to make workers feel that their opinions are appreciated by management and that they are considered not merely wage earners but members of a common cause.

Private Talks between Supervisor and Subordinates

Every worker should be called in occasionally by his supervisor for a private talk. His weaknesses can be pointed out in friendly fashion, he can be given encouragement, and his adjustment to changes in the work routine can be made easier. Most employees have problems that can be handled to some extent by the supervisor, but often an employee is reluctant to bring a problem on his own initiative to the supervisor. The private talk furnishes the opportunity to bring any latent problems to the surface. After such a talk, if it is handled capably by the supervisor, the employee is able to give fuller attention to his work.

Open-Door Policy

Most executives probably feel that they are willing to see subordinates whenever subordinates have a problem. There is considerable variation, however, in the actual freedom subordinates have to "drop in" whenever they feel the need. There is risk in too liberal a policy as well as in too restrictive a policy. If so much time of supervisors and executives is taken up in chatting with employees that their other work suffers, the open-door policy is too liberal. On the other hand, if subordinates are fearful of asking for time to see an executive unless the problem is acute, they will probably wait until all problems become acute before taking them to him. Where is the ideal point between the two extremes? This will vary with the type of company, the rank of the executive, his work load, his personality, and his experience with different degrees of open-door policy.

In order to control the use or misuse by subordinates of the privilege of taking the time of an executive, the following devices have been used:

Admittance to an executive's assistant first, particularly at the presidential level. The assistant screens the visitors, passing only those with problems of a relatively serious nature.

Specific hours for seeing the executive. At other hours, the executive may or may not grant an interview, depending on the critical nature of the problem and the press of his other work.

Open door limited to subordinates immediately below the executive. All other employees request appointments.

Suggestion Systems

The purpose of soliciting suggestions from employees is to get the benefit of their thinking on improvements in operations, working conditions, safety, and morale. The conventional means of procuring suggestions is the placement of suggestion boxes at various places in the plant or office. These boxes are emptied periodically and the contents are reviewed by a company officer or a suggestion committee composed of company officers and elected employees.

Both suggestions and complaints are found in suggestion boxes. Complaints are usually referred to whatever officer or department has jurisdiction so that correction can be made if warranted. Employees must not be penalized for submitting complaints in this way or this channel of communication will cease to operate. Because of the natural fear of an employee of offending his immediate supervisor, most companies do not require that the employee sign a communication placed in the suggestion box.

Suggestions that may reduce company costs, reduce waste, save machinery or tools, speed production, improve product quality, reduce work hazards, or improve morale are eagerly sought by management because the workable ones can increase company profits. Not all suggestions are practical, but all suggestions should be acknowledged gratefully whether they have merit or not. Those that are not accepted should be acknowledged, and the reason that they are not practical explained. Those that are adopted should be rewarded, if the company wishes to continue the flow of suggestions. The rewards in most cases should be tangible, such as a cash award, particularly if the suggestion results in a clear improvement in production methods or a reduction in waste. Suggestions of a relatively minor value can be rewarded with an invitation to a monthly "Suggestion Award Banquet" or similar recognition. Publicity in the company magazine and notations in the employment files should be given for all suggestions adopted by the company.

> **CHAMPION SUGGESTER:** Dean Kinsman, a body layout man at Ford's Allan Park, Michigan, plant last year won three new cars and three bundles of $6,000 each for his suggested improvements in car assembly operations. In eight years with Ford, he's won more than $32,000 for his ideas. *Wall Street Journal*, Feb. 21, 1967.

EMPLOYEE ALIENATION AND JOB ENRICHMENT

In 1972 the production workers at the Lordstown, Ohio, plant of General Motors expressed their discontent with the hard-driving, high-speed (101 cars assembled per hour) operation by chronic absenteeism, shoddy work, sabotage, and a bitter 22-day strike. The plant had been constructed only a few years before, incorporating the latest in high technology. It used automated production techniques, and all facilities were modern. Hours and wages were the same as in similar plants. But the workers felt that the machines controlled them, rather than the reverse. There was little chance to exercise judgment, to think, to create. The workers felt dehumanized.

The modern factory has eliminated much of the dirt and sweat of earlier times. Machines do the work. But, instead of increasing job satisfaction, the opposite has resulted in many factories. A survey conducted by the Department of

Health, Education, and Welfare, released in December 1972, entitled **Work In America**, concluded that millions of workers are bored, frustrated, and increasingly bitter with "dull, repetitive, seemingly meaningless tasks, offering little challenge or autonomy." The growing discontent with routine, mechanical work is particularly evident among young workers, and is not confined to factories. It is found in clerical work as well. A 1968 study reported that 56 percent of college students "would not mind being bossed around on the job," but a repeat study in 1971 showed the percentage dropping to 36.[3] Efforts to reduce chronic unemployment in decaying urban areas by giving brief training to uneducated, unskilled persons and setting them to work at monotonous jobs have also failed. Such workers felt they were losing their self-respect, even their identity.

Although worker alienation is not new, only recently is it being recognized that something more than higher pay, shorter hours, and music on the job is needed to bring out the best in workers. Much study is currently being given to this problem. The answer of the 1970s appears to be **job enrichment**, which may be defined as giving the worker more authority to plan his work and to decide how it is to be done, having him learn new skills or trade jobs with others, and an emphasis on participation in management rather than on following orders. In short, job enrichment is designing work to serve human needs as well as corporate needs.

A 1972 survey by the University of Michigan of a sample of workers who were asked to rank 25 work characteristics in order of relative importance gave the following ranking:

1 Interesting work
2 Enough help and equipment to get the job done
3 Enough information to get the job done
4 Enough authority to get the job done
5 Good pay
6 Opportunity to develop special abilities
7 Job security
8 Seeing the results of one's work[4]

The relatively low rank given to good pay and job security is very significant. Workers are no longer satisfied to put in 40 hours a week and collect a weekly pay check. If they are to spend half their lives in a factory or office, they want the time spent in a rewarding manner. They want to look forward to coming to work with anticipation, not dread.

In a factory making pet foods in Topeka, Kansas, General Foods Corporation planned the production process with job enrichment in mind. Workers are free to schedule their own hours to start and stop work. Organized into teams, they arrange the tasks among themselves, with committees of workers to handle safety, welfare, recreation, and disputes. Each team member is encouraged to learn as

[3]David Jenkins, "Democracy in the Factory," **The Atlantic Monthly**, April 1973, p. 78.
[4]Michael Putney, "Work and Enjoy It," **The National Observer**, Mar. 17, 1973, p. 16.

many of the team jobs as he can, so that job assignments can be interchanged. Workers judge the performance of their fellows, which in turn determines each man's pay scale. Undesirable jobs, such as loading materials, are rotated, so they do not become one man's monotonous task. There are no executive parking spaces, no executive washrooms, no executive dining room. There are also no custodians, as each man keeps his own work area clean. The results in terms of production: product quality is higher, operating costs lower, absenteeism negligible, and productivity per worker 40 percent above that of conventional plants.

Similar developments are taking place in other areas. In the automobile factories of Sweden (Saab and Volvo) production processes are grouped, even the final assembly of cars. At the Corning Glass Company plant in Medfield, Massachusetts, workers have been reassigned from doing single repetitive tasks to completing assemblies involving several tasks, with a resulting increase in productivity. At a plant of Procter and Gamble Corporation in Lima, Ohio, workers participate in decisions on hiring, firing, and pay scales. Salaries from bottom to top are known to everyone. The pay scale is higher than for similar jobs, but the costs of production are approximately half those found in conventional factories.

Job enrichment programs are still relatively rare and have been instituted mostly in comparatively small plants. To what extent they can be adapted to very large production units is uncertain, although experience in foreign factories is favorable. Job enrichment will undoubtedly spread, with modifications and changes dictated by experience. In fact, some enthusiasts predict that, like automation in the 1950s and 1960s, job enrichment will be the standard of industrial progress in the 1970s and 1980s.

SUMMARY

Wages are payments for work. Usually they are in money, but to some extent they are paid in other forms. Money wages are measured in dollars; real wages are measured in terms of what the money will buy. If prices rise, money wages may remain stable but real wages will fall.

Two basic methods of paying wages are: (1) time—payment according to hour, day, or other period spent on the job, and (2) piecework—payment according to the number of units of work done or the value of the work done. Salesmen, for example, are often paid a fixed percentage of the dollar amount of sales they make.

In addition to the basic payment for work done, employers frequently make supplementary payments. Such payments are usually offered to stimulate greater care and effort on the part of employees. In addition to supplementary payments, employers furnish fringe benefits such as group life insurance and travel expenses. Fringe benefits are often preferred by an employee to an increase in money payments, because many fringe benefits escape the personal income tax.

Because executives are usually in high income brackets, methods of payment for their services are carefully designed, with the income tax the most important single factor determining the method of compensation. The object, of course, is to pay the executive in such a way as to reduce to a minimum his income tax liability.

Personnel management seeks the most effective use of the skills of workers in the plant and office. To accomplish this requires careful selection of workers, proper training, and good pay. But it also requires treating the worker as a human being, giving him respect, consideration, and understanding. Management must be fair, and it must be concerned with the health and safety of its employees. And it should try to make the office or plant a pleasant place in which to work.

Job enrichment is designing work assignments and schedules to serve human needs of workers as well as production needs of employers. Job enrichment seeks to counter worker alienation by making jobs interesting as well as productive, by developing workers' skills, and by giving employees responsibility.

QUESTIONS FOR REVIEW

1 "Wages are a cost of producing goods and also a means by which they can be sold." Explain this statement.

2 What effect does an increase in the supply of labor have on wage rates? An increase in the demand for labor?

3 What is the difference between salaries and wages?

4 For what types of work are piecework wages generally used? For what types of work are hourly wages used?

5 Why do companies sometimes pay their salesmen a salary plus commission on sales rather than pay them a straight commission on sales?

6 Should factory workers be paid a bonus in addition to salary? Should office workers? Give reasons for your answer.

7 Why should a company be cautious in offering stock purchase plans to its employees?

8 Name some typical fringe benefits given to employees. Why do companies offer fringe benefits?

9 Is there any distinction between an employee bonus and an executive bonus? Explain.

10 Describe some means of compensating executives other than by salary and bonus.

11 What are the attractions to an executive in being given a stock option? What are the benefits, if any, to the company?

12 What is morale? Why should management be concerned with the morale of its workers?

13 Free physical examinations are provided by some companies for their workers. Is there any benefit to the companies in offering such examinations?

14 Should special privileges be given to workers with 10 years of service with a company? Defend your answer.

15 How can a company newspaper or magazine help foster a team spirit within a company?

16 Of what importance is individual recognition in raising a worker's morale? What forms can individual recognition take?

17 Should a worker ever be scolded for making a mistake? Would your answer make a difference if the worker were female?

18 How do periodic conferences with employees help a supervisor better manage his subordinates?

19 Should suggestions from employees be encouraged by management? If so, what form of compensation, if any, should be given?

20 Explain what is meant by the term *job enrichment*.

SELECTED READINGS Dunn, J. D., and Frank M. Rachel: *Wage and Salary Administration*, McGraw-Hill Book Company, New York, 1971.

———— and Elvis C. Stephens: *Management of Personnel*, McGraw-Hill Book Company, New York, 1972.

Megginson, Leon C.: *Personnel*, rev. ed., Richard D. Irwin, Inc., Homewood, Ill., 1972.

Sutermeister, Robert A.: *People and Productivity*, 2d ed., McGraw-Hill Book Company, New York, 1969.

Name   Section   Date

COMPLETION SENTENCES

1 _____ are a cost of production and a means by which

what is produced can be _____ .

2 "Real wages" are what a person can buy with his _____

wages.

3 If the supply of labor increases, wage rates tend to go

_____ .

4 An increase in the demand for labor stimulates a _____

in wages, which tends to _____ the supply of workers

seeking jobs.

5 Where _____ have been strong, the rise in wages has

been weak or absent.

6 The hourly or daily wage is based on _____ spent in the plant or office.

7 The major weakness of hourly wages as a means of payment is that it reduces the incentive to _____ production.

8 The chief disadvantage of the piecework wage is its emphasis on _____ rather than on quality.

9 About half the cost of fringe benefits is borne by _____ rather than by the company.

10 Stock purchase plans permit the employee to become a _____ of the company.

11 The primary responsibility of most company physicians is conducting _____ .

12 Criticism can be either a stern reprimand or a gentle _____ .

13 Growing discontent with routine, mechanical work is particularly evident among _____ workers in a plant.

14 Job enrichment is designing work to serve _____ needs as well as _____ needs.

15 Every worker should be called in occasionally by his supervisor for _____ .

Name	Section	Date

TRUE OR FALSE STATEMENTS

1 If it were not for the attraction of wages, few people would work.

2 There is no difference in status in the implications of the words "wages" and "salary."

3 If the supply of workers increases, the tendency is for wages to rise.

4 The ability of a company to absorb wage increases does not depend upon the demand for the company's products.

5 The average length of the workweek declined substantially from the Civil War to World War I, and continued to decline after World War I and again after World War II.

6 The major weakness of wages based on the number of hours worked is the reduction of the incentive to increase production.

7 To get workers to work willingly on a night shift, some companies offer a higher hourly wage than that for the day shift.

8 Piecework payment plans for salesmen are called commissions.

9 The bonus is an added payment to workers above their regular wage, generally paid monthly.

10 Where bonuses are given, they are usually given equally, not varying according to years of service or rank.

11 Most of the stock purchase plans instituted during the 1920s were later abandoned.

12 The passage of the Social Security Act in 1935 brought many companies into pension planning for their employees for the first time.

13 An important advantage to the company and to the employee of using fringe benefits in addition to wages is the tax advantage for both.

14 Plans for compensating employees of executive status are usually made with care, partly as a result of searching for means to avoid high income tax rates.

15 Deferred payment plans for executives help to keep them from straying to other employers.

16 Morale is a state of mind.

17   It is human nature to enjoy privilege.

18   The most common basis on which privileges within rank are based is seniority.

19   Job enrichment programs are still relatively rare and are found mostly in small plants.

20   In the modern factory, where machines do most of the work, the result has been substantially increased job satisfaction.

EXERCISES

1   Select a job with which you have some familiarity, either through experience or through observation, that is routine and repetitive. Examples are reading utility meters from house to house, driving a city or school bus, and acting as a teller in a bank.

   a   Identify any stimulating or interesting elements of the job.

   b   What elements tend to make the job dull?

   c   What similar or associated jobs might be combined or alternated with this job?

   d   Suggest how job satisfaction could be increased for this type of job.

Name   Section   Date

2 *Case Problem for report or class discussion.*

     The office manager of the Raybardo Manufacturing Corporation, Joseph Fenouk, became concerned with the length of the coffee break taken by some of the workers in the office. The policy of the office had been to permit the workers to take one break in the morning and one in the afternoon. There was no formal scheduling of the periods when the workers could be away from their desks, but it was understood that each worker was responsible for taking his break at a time when it would least interfere with his work. Furthermore, it was understood that only a few would leave from each section of the office at a time. Fenouk had believed, and the top executives had agreed, that informality regarding the coffee break would contribute to employee morale in contrast to scheduling formal, rigidly scheduled breaks.

     When Fenouk noticed that some of the employees remained away from their desks for as long as a half-hour, he wondered if the coffee break privilege were not being abused. Furthermore, he noticed that some workers took their break only 30 or 40 minutes after they had arrived at their desks in the morning. He learned that in some cases workers made a virtual habit of taking their breakfast during their morning break.

     Should Fenouk do anything about this situation? If not, why not? If so, what should he do?

3 *Case Problem for report or class discussion.*

     Robert Breuner, executive vice president of a manufacturing company located in a Midwest town of 100,000, is disturbed by the discovery that the rate of turnover of employees during the first half of 1973 was greater than the rate for the same period in 1972. In addition to the increased difficulty of holding employees, he finds that there is increased difficulty in finding qualified workers to fill vacancies, and that in some cases vacancies have remained unfilled for several weeks. The company has maintained a policy of paying only wages or salaries, and fringe benefits have not been offered except for the company's pension plan. Both the pension plan and the level of wages offered by the company have been roughly equal to what other companies in the industry have offered. As far as Breuner can determine, the workers are satisfied with their jobs. The fact that an attempt to organize a union in the plant failed because of an adverse vote among the company employees indicates that employee compensation must be satisfactory.

Some time ago Breuner was invited to a dinner attended by the top executives of the five other manufacturers in town. After dinner, one of the executives suggested that all of the companies form a common front with respect to employees. Specifically he suggested that no company raise wages without consultation and agreement with the other companies and that the executives of all companies agree not to "hire away" workers from other companies of the town by offering better salaries or other inducements. This merely encouraged shopping for jobs and increased labor turnover for all employers, he said. The other executives seemed to agree. Breuner felt that an agreement between the executives of the other companies would probably be concluded, and would remain highly confidential.

As Mr. Breuner, you are to prepare a report to the executive committee of your board of directors. Your report should give the reasons you assign for the increase in labor turnover during the first part of 1973. You should suggest means for reducing the rate of turnover. Also you should recommend what action, if any, is to be taken on the suggestion of uniform policy by all manufacturers in the town with respect to labor.

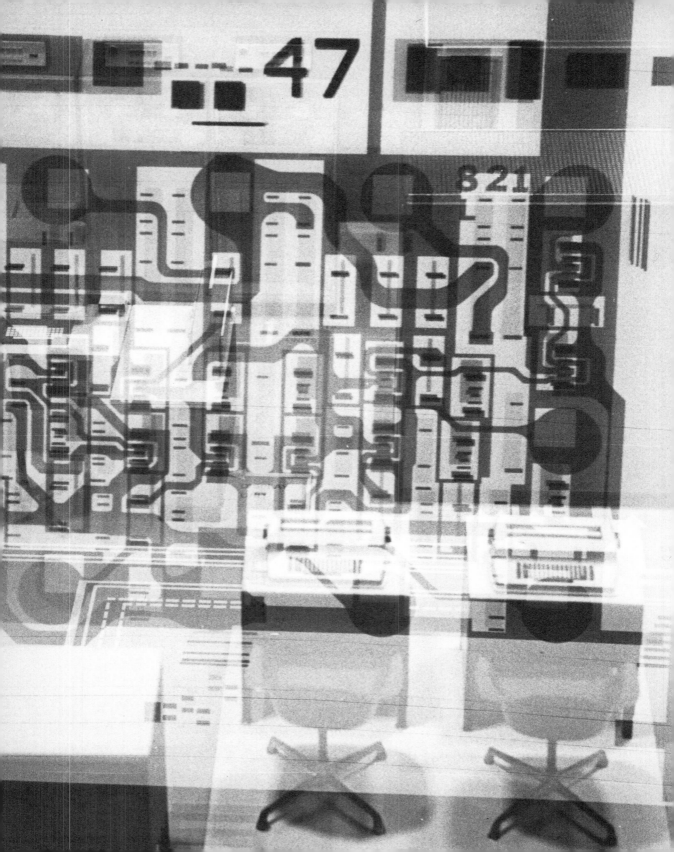

PART 5

INFORMATION
FOR
CONTROL AND
MANAGEMENT
DECISIONS

In order to make decisions, managers must have information. The next three chapters will indicate the types of information needed.

The function of accounting is to record the business transactions of a company. All income and expense items, whether they involve cash or not, are recorded. It is also the function of accounting to arrange the record so that it can be understood easily by managers. The two most important forms in which accounting information is presented are the balance sheet, which shows the financial condition of a business on a particular day, and the profit and loss statement, which summarizes the transactions over a period of time.

In order to make informed decisions, a manager needs much more information than is provided by the transactions of his own firm. There is plenty of information of all kinds available, but until it is presented in a form that can be grasped, it will be of little significance to him. Statistics summarizes, correlates, and simplifies information that is otherwise a mass of meaningless numbers.

Planning for the future is such an important part of management that forecasting is given considerable emphasis in business. The techniques of forecasting may be simple or complex, and many different forecasts may be made by a company. Without forecasting, businessmen would be forced to make decisions almost blindly on a day-to-day basis.

Handling today's volume of paper work in business would be impossible without electronic data processing. Modern computers are fast and versatile, and they have large capacities. They give businessmen information, do clerical work of all kinds, and make routine decisions, permitting businessmen more freedom for creative thought.

CHAPTER
14 ACCOUNTS AND BUDGETS

Many of you will take a course in accounting; some will take several courses. However, others will have no other formal exposure to accounting than what is in this chapter. Therefore, the usefulness of this chapter will vary considerably from one student to another. For those who expect to take accounting courses, it will serve as a broad picture of the accounting field and as an introduction to some of the principles to be studied in more detail in special accounting courses. Those students not expecting to take any other business courses should study this chapter with particular care.

The most important concept in the theory of accounting is double entry bookkeeping. You must understand the advantages that double entry bookkeeping gives in providing accuracy and completeness in accounting. Be sure you understand how balance sheets, profit and loss statements, and surplus statements are made and how they are used in financial analysis.

The balance sheet and profit and loss statements that you see are detailed down to a penny even where the amounts involved are in the hundreds of millions. Nevertheless, the dollar figures represent many accounts that are estimated. The amount representing depreciation, for example, depends on the type of calculation used and on the judgment of the accountant. Therefore, it is vital for you to understand that two accountants of equal ability and equal accuracy can prepare balance sheets for the same corporation that differ from each other by a considerable margin. The use of accounting techniques, in other words, does not supplant the judgment of the accountant. It is merely an aid in more effective application of his judgment to financial analysis.

ACCOUNTING

Lack of adequate accounting records is one of the important causes of business failure, especially in small businesses. As a group, small businessmen are notoriously negligent about keeping adequate records. They put too much reliance on memory or on a simple record of receipts and expenditures similar to the records a housewife might keep. Although a small businessman might remain solvent in spite of inadequate accounting records, a large business could not hope to do so. The decisions a manager makes depend on a constant flow of information. He must have records of purchases of goods, of expenditures for salaries, supplies, and advertising, of sales made, of taxes due, and of hundreds of other transactions involving income and expense for the company. *Accounting* is defined as the function of recording, classifying, summarizing, and interpreting business transactions in terms of dollars and cents. From the data that are collected accountants prepare reports on the financial condition of a company, so that the managers may make informed, intelligent decisions.

The primary function of accounting is to produce these reports, but it is not the only function. The federal, state, and local governments depend on accounting records to determine the taxes payable by businesses. Banks and other lending institutions depend on accounting records to determine how much a business can borrow. Investors depend on financial statements prepared by accounting departments to get information with which to make investment decisions.

The field of accounting is generally divided into three divisions: *cost accounting*, *auditing*, and *general accounting*.

THE DIVISIONS OF ACCOUNTING

Cost accounting is concerned with the measurement of costs involved in doing business. This includes distributing overhead costs, such as management salaries, heat, and light, to different products produced by the company. This branch of accounting is highly specialized and requires special training. A system of cost accounting is expensive to maintain. If a business is large enough, a cost system is generally installed using company personnel. If the business is small, outside accounting firms are frequently retained to fulfill this function.

COST ACCOUNTING

Cost accounting aids in control of production. It helps to determine the unit cost of each line of products manufactured by a company. If the unit cost of an item changes with a change in the volume of production, cost accounting will indicate the extent of such a change in cost. It will show the relative cost of different manufacturing methods so that the least costly can be chosen. It can be used to discover any variation of costs at different seasons or in different years.

A simplified expression of the cost accounting process can be made by the use of equations. It is the work of a cost accountant to gather the information on which the following equations are based:

Direct material cost + direct labor cost = prime manufacturing cost.
Prime manufacturing cost + factory overhead cost = factory cost.
Factory cost + administrative expense = cost of manufacture.
Cost of manufacture + selling expense = cost of product.
Cost of product + markup or profit margin = selling price.

AUDITING   Auditing consists of the examination of a firm's accounts to determine their accuracy. This is of considerable concern to executives, owners of businesses, and government regulatory and tax agencies. Every accountant and bookkeeper strives for accuracy in his work. But accountants are human, and it is human nature to make mistakes. Auditing procedures are designed to uncover such mistakes before they damage the company. Dishonesty is also present to some degree in human nature. The existence of a well-designed auditing program serves to reduce the opportunities for theft and embezzlement.

There are two types of auditing, *internal* and **external**. Internal auditing is done by employees of a company. Where cash is received and disbursed or where items of unusual value are kept in inventory, two sets of records might be kept, each independent of the other. If the two records do not agree, the discrepancy must be explained. Periodically, the accounts of each bookkeeper will be examined for accuracy by a company auditor. A count may be made from time to time of the number of each item in inventory to determine the accuracy of the inventory records on the company books.

Even though the auditing function appears to be adequately served by company employees, a periodic examination of accounts by an independent firm of accountants is used by companies of any consequence. Although the methods used by the independent auditor are generally the same as those used by the company auditors, the impartiality and freshness of viewpoint of the independent auditor lend greater objectivity to his report. After completing the review of company records, the independent auditor frequently prepares a separate set of financial statements with comments and recommendations where appropriate. Then a statement is signed by the officers of the accounting firm and is attached to the auditor's report, with wording similar to the following:

> In our opinion the accompanying financial statements present fairly the position of .... Company as of December 31, 19....., and the results of their operations for the year, in conformity with generally accepted accounting principles applied on a basis consistent with that of the preceding year. The examinations were made in accordance with generally accepted auditing standards and accordingly included such tests of the accounting records and such other auditing procedures as were considered necessary in the circumstances.

GENERAL ACCOUNTING   General accounting consists of recording facts for the general records of the company. It also includes the preparation of the usual financial statements such as the profit and loss or income statement and the balance sheet or statement of condition. In a small business, the accounting statements can be simple, particularly if the manager is able to handle personally most of the daily affairs of his company. A large company must maintain a complete system of records. Of necessity these records will be voluminous. To prevent the vast accumulation of detailed information from smothering managers in paper, a well-designed accounting system will classify and summarize the information contained in company accounts, preparing statements in such form as to be easily comprehended by busy executives.

It is the responsibility of the accountant to prepare the financial statements. They are usually prepared quarterly, semiannually, or annually. Before the statements are prepared, certain adjusting entries are made in the accounts. For example, machinery wears out with use, and as it does, its value decreases. This decrease in value must be shown by an adjusting entry in the journal, which is posted to the machinery account.

FINANCIAL STATEMENTS

The three principal statements are the *balance sheet* or *statement of condition*, the *profit and loss statement* or *income statement*, and the *statement of surplus*. These statements present in concise form the overall financial picture of the business. In essence, they are a summary of the financial information compiled by the accounting department since preparation of the previous statements.

In the preparation of financial statements, one policy is basic: conservatism. The accountant by nature avoids any overstatement of profits or property values. If two methods of estimating the value of an item are available, the accountant generally uses the method that results in the lower value. Inventories, for example, are generally valued at cost (price paid when inventory was purchased) or market (present market value)—*whichever is lower*. In some cases, the values assigned are purely nominal. Patents, goodwill, or other intangibles may be carried on the financial statement at $1. In bank accounting, it has become the custom to carry certain tangible properties at a nominal value. The balance sheet of a bank often lists furniture and fixtures at a value of $1, while real estate owned will also often be valued at $1.

THE BALANCE SHEET

The *balance sheet* shows the condition of the company at a particular instant of time. For example, the balance sheet given in Table 14-1 shows the condition of a company at the close of business, December 31, 1973. For this reason it is sometimes called a "snapshot" of the business. If we take a snapshot of a child on his birthday for 5 successive years, we can see his physical growth more readily. Similarly, if we compare balance sheets for 5 past years, we can see the changes in the financial structure of the business.

The balance sheet is divided into three parts: assets, liabilities, and net worth. The sum of the assets equals the sum of the liabilities and net worth.

TABLE 14-1   BALANCE SHEET OF DUNBAR, INC.

Assets, Liabilities, and Stockholders' Equity			Explanation
Assets	Dec. 31, 1973	Dec. 31, 1972	
Current Assets	*Million*		**The Company Owned**
Cash	$ 9.0	$ 6.2	Cash and United States government se-
U.S. government securities	—	2.0	curities, the latter generally at either cost or market value, whichever is lower.
Accounts and notes receivable	12.4	11.4	Amounts owed the company by its customers and others.
Inventories	27.0	24.6	Raw materials, work in process, and
Total current assets	$ 48.4	$ 44.2	finished merchandise.
Other Assets			
Surrender value of insurance	0.2	0.2	Miscellaneous assets and advance pay-
Investments in subsidiaries	4.7	3.9	ments for insurance. Investments in non-
Prepaid insurance	0.6	0.5	consolidated subsidiary companies.
Total other assets	$ 5.5	$ 4.6	
Fixed Assets			
Buildings, machinery, and equipment at cost	104.3	92.7	
Less accumulated depreciation	27.6	25.0	Land, buildings, equipment, and deduc- tions for wear and tear on these proper-
Bldg., mach., equip. (net)	$ 76.7	$ 67.7	ties.
Land	0.9	0.7	
Total fixed assets	$ 77.6	$ 68.4	
Total Assets	$131.5	$117.2	
Liabilities and stockholders' equity			
Current Liabilities	*Million*		**The Company Owed**
Accounts payable	$ 6.1	$ 5.0	For materials, supplies, wages, and sal-
Accrued liabilities	3.6	3.3	aries to employees, and such things as
Current maturity of long-term debt	1.0	0.8	dividends declared, real estate, social security, income taxes, etc.
Federal income and other taxes	9.6	8.4	
Dividends payable	1.3	1.1	
Total current liabilities	$ 21.6	$ 18.6	
Reserves	3.6	2.5	May be either a liability of a more or less definite nature, such as provision for possible inventory losses, or a part of earnings not available for dividends and segregated so as not to be included in surplus available for dividends.
Long-term debt			
5% sinking fund debentures, due July 31, 1981:	26.0	20.0	For money borrowed (excluding portion due in next 12 months shown as a current liability).
Stockholders' Equity			
5% cum. preferred stock ($100 par)	6.0	6.0	Amount originally invested in the busi- ness by the stockholders. Additional
Common stock ($10 par)	18.3	18.3	capital received from sale of capital
Capital surplus	9.6	9.6	stock above par value.
Earned surplus	46.4	42.2	Retained earnings reinvested in the
Total Stockholders' Investment	$ 80.3	$ 76.1	business.
Total Liabilities and Stockholders' Investment	$131.5	$117.2	

All the properties owned by a business are listed as the assets. The assets are by custom listed first and are usually classified. One classification is as follows: current assets, fixed assets, investment assets, and intangible assets. The management problems of different types of assets require different treatment, and classification is an aid to management in grouping similar assets together.

Assets

Current assets consist of cash, accounts receivable, inventories, and any other assets that will be converted into cash during one cycle of business operations, which is normally one year or less. These assets are valued usually at the price paid at the time they were acquired. However, some inventory items might be bought at different prices during a year. For example, suppose a flour miller purchased wheat during the year at prices ranging from $1.80 to $2.60 a bushel, and he has a year-end inventory of 10,000 bushels. What value shall be assigned to the wheat inventory? One of two methods is commonly used to value inventory in such cases: LIFO and FIFO.

FIFO (first in, first out) assumes that the items acquired earliest are withdrawn from inventory first. This is the method of inventory valuation generally used by retail stores. LIFO (last in, first out) assumes that the items most recently purchased for inventory are used first. In periods of inflation LIFO has the advantage of making the cost of goods sold higher than it would be using FIFO, thus making reported net income lower. Since income taxes are based on net income, any increase in costs on an income statement reduces the amount of taxes payable. These two methods are shown diagrammatically in Figure 14-1.

Current assets are in a continual process of change. In manufacturing, assets start as cash and change in form (raw materials, finished products, etc.), increasing in value until finally they become cash again. This circuit of flow can be represented diagrammatically as shown in Figure 14-2. While the cycle of operation differs from one business to another, a rule of thumb used by accountants identifies current assets as those that become cash within 1 year.

Fixed assets are those items on the balance sheet that are not "consumed" during each cycle of business activity. Where it is necessary to fix an arbitrary time period to distinguish current and fixed assets, 1 year is generally considered the dividing line. Assets with a life greater than 1 year are therefore considered fixed assets. Examples are land, buildings, machinery, trucks, and fixtures.

Although fixed assets are longer-lived than current assets, it must be recognized that, except for land, they are used up in the course of business operations, although at a slower rate than current assets. This consumption of fixed assets is an expense of doing business, and is called *depreciation*. The amount of depreciation for each accounting period is generally determined by one of several formulas used by accountants. A simple formula frequently used is called the "straight line" method. To illustrate, suppose a truck costing $5,000 is expected to be used for 4 years, after which it will be sold or traded in for a new truck. If the trade-in value is expected to be $1,000, the depreciation expense for the 4-year "life" of the truck is $4,000. This expense is charged to each year's operations at the rate of $1,000 each year. Furthermore, depreciation is used to determine the value

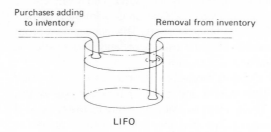

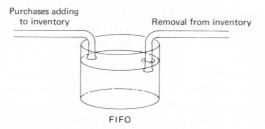

FIGURE 14-1   Pictorial representation of two concepts of inventory control for ac-
counting purposes.

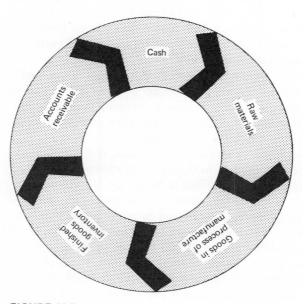

FIGURE 14-2

of the truck on the balance sheet each year. For example, after 2 years of use, the truck would be carried on the balance sheet as follows:

```
Truck . . . . . . . . . . . . . . . . .   $5,000
Less:  Accumulated depreciation  . . .   $2,000
                                                    $3,000
```

Investment assets consist of bonds, stocks, and certificates of other companies or governmental units. The purpose of such investment by a company might be to exercise control of other companies through stock ownership, since corporations are permitted to own voting stock of other corporations. If, on the other hand, the purpose is to put idle cash to work earning interest, securities are bought that have an active market. They can then be readily sold for cash. Accountants generally place such investments under current assets and call them *marketable securities*.

Intangible assets include items such as patents, copyrights, formulas, franchises, mailing lists, licenses, models, and goodwill. If such an asset were acquired by purchase, it would usually be carried at that value on the balance sheet. If the asset has a useful life limited in time, its original cost is absorbed by the company as if it were a truck or a building that was slowly wearing out. Goodwill is the intangible asset most often found on the balance sheet. Where the earning power of the assets of a company is greater than normal, goodwill exists and has value. It is difficult, however, to measure such value. If a company is sold and the price paid for it is greater than the estimated net value of all the individual assets of the company, the excess is assumed to measure the value of the goodwill. In the absence of a sale of the company, the valuation of goodwill is arbitrary. In such cases, companies frequently list goodwill, if it appears at all, at the nominal value of $1.

Liabilities

A liability or debt is an amount owed by the company to anyone who has a right by law to collect. Payment is generally required in cash. The liabilities are classified on the balance sheet according to the length of time before they are due to be paid. The shortest may become due or payable within 1 day.

Bonds are formal certificates of indebtedness and may last for a century or more. Siemens & Halske, A. G., for example, distributed a bond issue payable in the year 2930. There have been a few bond issues that have carried no due date. The holder of such a bond, like a holder of a share of stock, sells it to some other investor when he wishes to liquidate his investment.

Current liabilities are those debts that must be paid within a short time. For purposes of classifying the liabilities of a company, a "short time" is generally defined as less than 1 year. Examples are taxes due, wages due, interest due, accounts payable, and notes payable. A *note payable* frequently represents a bank loan made to the company. *Accounts payable* are usually created when a company buys goods on credit with payment to be made in 30 days, 60 days, or some other period. There is a reasonably close association between current assets and current liabilities. The sale of items in the inventory and collection of payment on credit sales of the company generate the means of meeting the current liabilities as they fall due. Cash receipts and payments due, however, cannot be perfectly coordinated. Whenever payments due threaten to exceed cash receipts temporarily, a short-term bank loan is very helpful.

Long-term liabilities are those that do not fall due for a year or more. Because of the length of time involved, interest is almost always a feature of debts in this category. This is not true of current liabilities. A creditor is frequently willing to accept a delay of 30 or 45 days in payment for goods delivered, with no increase in price, in order to make a sale. Furthermore, a long-term debt is nearly always evidenced by a formal written document signed by the debtor, unlike the informality associated with a sale of goods on credit.

Examples of long-term liabilities are bonds, long-term notes, and mortgages. There is an association between the fixed assets and the long-term liabilities corresponding to that between current assets and current liabilities. Frequently, a long-term note is created as a means of paying for a particular machine. Or a bond issue might have been sold to investors to raise money to purchase a building. Good financial management dictates that the characteristics of a long-term note or bond be tailored wherever possible to suit the characteristics of the fixed assets financed by them. A 10-year note would hardly be used to finance the purchase of machinery expected to be scrapped in 5 or 6 years.

Net Worth The net worth represents the investment of the owners in the business. It is the difference between the total assets and the total liabilities. If a business is not incorporated, the term ***proprietorship*** is generally applied to the investment of the proprietor or partners. It might be recorded as follows:

A. F. Jones, capital	$48,000
M. A. March, capital	64,000
G. S. Lee, capital	32,000
Total Proprietorship	**$144,000**

If the owners wish to show the difference between the original investment and the share of each in the retained earnings of a growing business, it can be shown in this manner:

	Capital	Share of Profits	Total	
A. F. Jones	$42,000	$6,000	$48,000	
M. A. March	56,000	8,000	64,000	
G. S. Lee	28,000	4,000	32,000	
Total Proprietorship				**$144,000**

Where the business is organized as a corporation, a stock record is kept, showing the name and address of each stockholder and the number of shares owned by each. On the balance sheet, however, the names of stockholders are not shown, even where there are only three or four. The original investment of the stockholders and that portion of earnings retained by the company are indicated separately, as shown below:

Capital stock $10 par	$40,000
Surplus	23,465
Total Capital and Surplus	$63,465

THE PROFIT AND LOSS STATEMENT OR INCOME STATEMENT

In contrast to the balance sheet, which shows the financial condition of a company at an instant of time, the income statement shows the changes in financial condition over a period of time. The example shown in Table 4-2 covers a period of 1 year. Income statements are frequently prepared four times a year, covering 3-month periods, in addition to the annual statements. Where a balance sheet is by analogy a snapshot, an income statement is a motion picture. Every time a sale is made, income earned, cost incurred, or other change made in the condition of a company, a new balance sheet could be prepared to indicate the change in the accounts affected. This being obviously impractical, the changes are recorded as they occur, and a summary of such accumulated changes over a period of time is prepared. Such a summary is the *income statement.*

The income statement will show the source of income, the expenses incurred, and the amount of profit earned or loss sustained. With the income statement—or, better still, the income statements for several periods—the executive can determine reasons for the changes shown on the statements. If profits have declined, the income statement will help him spot the reason. Perhaps sales have dropped. Perhaps costs have risen. Whatever the reason, the income statement is an aid in analysis.

Sales

The income statement begins with the source of income. For a commercial bank, it would be interest earned on loans to borrowers and interest on bank investments. For a laundry, it would be the sale of laundry services. For a retail store, it would be the sale of goods bought from a wholesaler or manufacturer. For a manufacturer, it would be the sale of goods produced by the company. For most firms, the starting point in a statement of income is sales. Frequently, a distinction is made between gross sales and net sales. *Gross sales* is the figure representing all sales for cash or credit. Deductions are then made for discounts for prompt payment, allowances for returned merchandise, for defective merchandise, and so on. The resulting figure is known as the *net sales figure*.

TABLE 14-2 STATEMENT OF INCOME OF DUNBAR, INC.

	Year Ended Dec. 31, 1973	1972	Explanation
	Million		
Sales	$115.8	$110.0	Amount received or receivable from customers.
Less:			
Costs and expenses:			
Cost of goods sold	74.8	73.2	Part of income used for wages, salaries, raw materials, fuel and supplies, and certain taxes.
Selling, general, and administration expenses	14.2	13.0	Part of income used for salesmen's commissions, advertising, officers' salaries, and other general expenses.
Depreciation and depletion	4.2	3.5	Provision from income for the reduction of the service life of machinery and buildings and the use of minerals in mines.
	$ 93.2	$ 89.7	
Operating profit	$ 22.6	$ 20.3	The remainder after deducting the foregoing expenses from sales, but before providing for interest charges and taxes.
Interest charges	1.3	1.0	Amount required for interest on borrowed funds.
Earnings before income taxes	$ 21.3	$ 19.3	
Provision for federal and state taxes on income	11.4	9.8	Amount paid or payable for taxes.
Net income for the year	$ 9.9	$ 9.5	This amount was earned for stockholders.
Dividend on preferred stock	0.3	0.3	Amount paid to preferred stockholders
Balance of Net Income Available for Common Stock	$ 9.6	$ 9.2	Amount remaining for common stockholders.

Cost of Goods Sold   The cost of producing or acquiring the goods sold is subtracted from net sales. For a manufacturing company, this consists of the cost of materials used in production plus transportation costs and the cost of preparing the finished product. The amount of materials used may be determined by taking the inventory at the beginning of the period, adding purchases during the period, and subtracting the inventory on hand at the end of the period.

The cost of goods sold subtracted from net sales gives *gross income* or *gross profit*. Frequently, this is small compared to the net sales figure. If the cost of producing goods is a large percentage of the net sales figure, even a small decrease in production cost may substantially increase the gross profit. In a competitive industry, companies are extremely cost conscious. Ways to reduce waste, to increase the efficiency of labor, to locate and use lower-cost materials where possible—these and other means of cutting the cost of goods sold, as long as they do not injure sales, are sought by management. The gross profit figure must be large enough to cover all of the other expenses incurred in doing business.

Generally, operating expense consists of the sales expenditures and administrative expenditures of the firm. Salesmen's expenses, advertising, promotional expenses, and delivery expenses are frequent items of selling expenses. Administrative or general expenses include office salaries and expenses, depreciation on buildings and equipment, heat and light, insurance, and provisions for unpaid customer debts. Property and other taxes are usually included here, but taxes on income are shown separately because income taxes are levied on net income. After the operating expenses are deducted, the remainder is called *net operating income*, or *operating profit.*

Operating Expense

Those revenues and expenses not related to the normal business operations of the company are called nonoperating income and expense, or a similar name. For some businesses, this item is unimportant. For some, it is of considerable significance.

Nonoperating Income and Expense

The most important source of nonoperating income is investments. This income may be received as interest, dividends, royalties, or rents. Ths most common nonoperating expense is interest expense. Other expenses include losses on unpaid customers' debts and sales discounts. While accountants value uniformity, there is still variation in treatment of expense and income items from one company to another.

The income statement of a corporation will usually show two net income figures. The first will show the *net income before income tax*. After all income has been recorded and all expenses accounted for, the net income or profit is the amount on which the income tax is based. The tax is expressed as a percentage of the net taxable income. While this tax is an expense of doing business, the amount cannot be determined until all other expenses and receipts have been included in the income statement. When an income statement for a year is prepared, the income tax liability may be determined with accuracy because the tax is based on yearly income. But where an income tax for a quarter or half-year is prepared, the tax liability can only be estimated.

Net Income

After the provision for income tax is deducted, the remainder is *net income after taxes*. This is the amount added to the surplus of the corporation, from which dividends to stockholders are distributed.

THE SURPLUS
STATEMENT

A third statement is prepared by accountants for a corporation, the surplus state-ment. This shows the changes in the surplus accounts over the period covered by the statement. Accountants may divide the surplus of a corporation into several accounts, but generally only two types of surplus are found on a statement: *paid-in surplus* and *retained earnings*. Most banks and some nonbank corporations sell their stock at prices above the par value of stock (the amount printed on the stock certificate). The difference is called paid-in surplus. When a corporation makes a profit on its regular operations, sells an asset at a price higher than that carried on its books, receives a refund of taxes paid, or receives a gift, the result is retained earnings.

The beginning balance of the surplus statement is the same as the closing balance of the previous surplus statement. The net profit after taxes from the income statement is added to the beginning surplus balance. Other additions to surplus are also made if earned or paid in as explained above. The chief deduction from surplus is dividends declared by the directors. Other deductions are operating losses, uninsured damage to buildings or equipment, court claims levied against the company, and expenses of organizing the corporation. Where the surplus statement is simple, it is frequently prepared as a supplement to the income statement. Frequently, as in Table 14-3, a separate statement may be prepared.

RESERVES

Reserves refers to certain accounts found on a balance sheet that do not contain cash. Their use is to reduce the possibility of overstatement of income or net worth. There are three classes of reserves: asset reserves, liability reserves, and net worth reserves.

Asset reserves, also called valuation reserves, offset the original value of certain assets to reflect the wastage caused by time. Two examples are given below. Accumulated depreciation is an estimate of the amount of depreciation since the

TABLE 14-3 **STATEMENT OF EARNED SURPLUS OF DUNBAR, INC.**

	Year Ended Dec. 31, 1973	1972	
	Million		
Balance at beginning of year	$42.2	$37.6	Surplus or retained earnings rein-vested in the business. Usually not all of the year's earnings can be paid out in dividends, a part being retained in the business for expan-sion or other purposes.
Add—net income for year	9.9	9.5	
	52.1	47.1	
Less dividends paid on			
Preferred stock	0.3	0.3	
Common stock	5.4	4.6	
Balance at End of Year	**$46.4**	**$42.2**	

asset was acquired. The allowance for bad debts estimates the probable amount of existing accounts receivable that will not be paid.

Building and equipment	$400,000	
Less: accumulated depreciation	126,000	
		$274,000
Accounts receivable	$114,600	
Less: allowance for bad debts	2,292	
		$112,308

Liability reserves represent debts the company owes. These are sometimes carried as reserves if the actual amount is not known at the time the balance sheet is drawn up. The most common liability reserve is reserve for taxes. Another example is reserve for employee pensions. The extent of this liability depends on the life expectancy of retired employees.

The *net worth reserves* merely earmark portions of the surplus for particular purposes. A reserve for dividend equalization sets up an account from which dividends out of past earnings may be declared even though current earnings do not justify such a declaration. A reserve for contingencies sets aside part of the surplus for whatever contingencies the management thinks might occur in the future. By reducing the amount remaining in the general surplus account, the directors will be in a better position to resist demands for larger dividends than they think advisable.

ANALYSIS OF FINANCIAL STATEMENTS

Financial statements are prepared to permit executives, stockholders, and others to receive financial information in summary form. Accountants strive to prepare the statements in as understandable a form as possible. But there is a limit to the extent to which condensation can be undertaken without serious distortion to the financial "picture" of a company. If the financial affairs are complex, the financial statements are likely to be complex. An extremely simplified balance sheet of a corporation could be understood by the stockholders, most of whom would not be accountants. But such a statement would not serve the needs of the creditors, government regulatory agencies, or the corporation management. A balance sheet prepared for them would have to contain considerable detail. To aid in the process of understanding and interpreting financial data, the techniques of financial statement analysis have been developed. This is a specialized area of study and is offered as a separate course in many schools of business.

The chief tool of analysis is the *ratio*, which greatly facilitates comparison of the condition of different companies. Dun and Bradstreet, the credit-reporting firm, publishes ratios of various types to permit a company to compare its financial condition with the rest of industry.

The **current ratio** measures the debt-paying capacity of a company. It is expressed as follows:

$$\frac{\text{Current assets}}{\text{Current liabilities}} = \text{current ratio}$$

A popular rule is that the current ratio should be at least 2 to 1. If a company has current assets of $68,432 and current liabilities of $29,648, the current ratio would be greater than 2 to 1. Special situations will require exceptions, and the popular rule should not be substituted for critical judgment in analyzing data.

The **acid test ratio** serves a purpose similar to the current ratio. From the current assets, it selects only the cash and receivables, making the equation appear as follows:

$$\frac{\text{Cash + receivables}}{\text{Current liabilities}} = \text{acid test ratio}$$

The popular rule in this case is a minimum ratio of 1 to 1.

The **ratio of equity to debt** shows the relative importance of these two sources of funds in a company. It is derived by dividing the equity or net worth accounts, such as proprietorship, partners' capital, capital stock, and surplus, by total liabilities. If the equity is large relative to debt, the danger of insolvency in times of difficulty is lessened. If the debt is large relative to equity, the danger of insolvency in difficult times may be increased, but the earnings expressed as a percentage of net worth may also be increased.

The **ratio of income to equity** is found by dividing the net income of a company by the net worth. If a company has a net income of $15,000 and a net worth of $200,000, the ratio would be:

$$\frac{15,000}{200,000} = 0.075 = 7\frac{1}{2} \text{ percent}$$

The **ratio of income to sales** is found by dividing the net income by sales and is usually expressed as a percentage. If total sales are $500,000, and net income $20,000, the ratio would be:

$$\frac{20,000}{500,000} = 4 \text{ percent}$$

Among grocery supermarkets, where volume of sales is high and price competition strong, a ratio of income to sales of 1 percent can yield a ratio of income to equity much higher.

The *merchandise inventory turnover* is obtained by dividing the cost of goods sold by the average inventory. A common method of computing average inventory is to add beginning and ending inventory and divide by 2. If the beginning inventory is $30,000, ending inventory $42,000, and cost of goods sold $108,000, the inventory turnover is computed as follows:

$$108,000 \div \frac{30,000 + 42,000}{2} = \frac{108,000}{36,000} = \frac{3}{1}$$

Thus, the inventory turnover is 3 to 1. The ratio varies from industry to industry. It is higher for grocery stores than for hardware stores. It also varies from season to season. But it is one measure of efficiency of a company that allows comparison with other companies or with the industry average. A high ratio is a favorable indication, whereas a low ratio serves as a danger signal.

BUDGETS

A budget is a formal quantitative plan of operation for a future period. It sets up a schedule of expected operations and serves as a guide to daily activities. Although budgets for business are more complex and varied than for an individual, they serve the same end: a more systematic and intelligent use of resources. A college student's budget for a year might allocate $1,200 for tuition, $320 for room, $680 for board, $80 for books and supplies, and $200 for miscellaneous. If the student were required to buy his meals individually, he might find $24 a week necessary and would prepare his budget accordingly. In any case, he would have to limit his planned expenditures to his expected income from scholarship, stipend from parents, or salary from part-time work. A company, too, must plan its expenditures for a coming period with due regard for its financial resources.

Budgeting in a business provides a systematic plan to guide the future operations of a company. Although a company may prepare a budget for a span of 5 years or more (in addition to an annual budget), the usual period is for 1 year.

A particularly important part of an annual budget is estimating the timing and amount of cash receipts and cash disbursements. Such an estimate enables company officers better to arrange for borrowing from the bank or other sources. If the replacement of a machine or truck or a major repair of a building is anticipated, the process of budget preparation provides better planning to pay for such needs. Furthermore, preparing a budget helps the development of performance standards for the company. For example, if the company budget for the coming year indicates a 10 percent increase in sales over the previous year, the sales quota of each salesman is adjusted to meet the expected increase (usually a 10 percent increase for each salesman). The performance of each salesman can then be measured against his quota established in the budget. If the budget for the production department calls for a 10 percent increase in production with existing equipment and no use of overtime wages, the performance of the production department manager and production workers can similarly be measured against the budget figures. Any budget, to be useful, must be reasonable, of course. Nevertheless, budgeting is a necessary tool of business in planning for orderly operations and measuring performance.

Budget preparation requires careful planning. The company must have a good accounting system. It must also have a good organizational structure, so that authority and responsibility under divisions of the overall budget can be clearly understood. It is necessary to establish basic policies as a guide before delegating the responsibility of budget preparation, usually to an officer of the company. Because of the close association of budgeting and accounting, the chief budget officer is often the company controller. It is his responsibility to collect the estimates of future operations from department heads and to coordinate them. Frequently, a company will have a budget committee. It may consist of the president, the controller, and several vice presidents or department heads. The committee may have power to determine policy, or it may serve as a body to arbitrate differences, modify departmental budgets, and carry out the policies established by the board of directors.

After the budget preparation has been completed, it is the responsibility of department heads to operate within the terms of the budget. But an important fact must be remembered: Any estimate of the future is based upon conjecture. Nobody knows exactly what the future has in store for him, and perhaps it is just as well. In any case, it is important that the budget be considered a guide, not a straitjacket. If conditions during a budget period change, it may be advisable to change the terms of the budget. Any budget program should make allowance for the possibility of changing conditions. On the other hand, the budget should not be changed without good reason, or it will lose its disciplinary effect and therefore its reason for existence.

BUDGET PREPARATION

The overall company budget generally is a summary of departmental budgets and special forecasts. These include the following:

Sales budget	Labor budget
Sales expense and advertising budget	Office-expense budget
Production schedule	Cash budget
Materials budget	Pro forma statements

Because of the vital importance of sales in creating profits, budget preparation frequently begins with the *sales budget*. To estimate sales for the forthcoming period, several factors must be included. The state of the nation's economy, whether depressed or prosperous, must be considered. Since many projections of the nation's future economic performance are made by government and private agencies, such information is readily available. The economic state of the industry must be considered. Again, studies of particular industries are available. It is also necessary to know the volume of sales in the past year. And it would also help preparations to have an estimate of sales by each salesman for each sales territory. The help of an economist or market analyst could be sought. After all pertinent information is received, the sales manager must interpret the information and prepare the figures for the sales budget. The projected total sales will ordinarily be broken down into estimates for each district and for each product. A budget closely associated with sales is the *sales expense and advertising budget*. This estimates advertising, publicity, and promotional expenses, and those expenses incident to securing sales. These will include salesmen's salaries and commissions, entertainment expenses for the purpose of procuring orders, and sales office expenses.

The *production schedule* determines the number of units of each product that will be produced and the rate of production monthly, weekly, or daily. This rate would not necessarily be scheduled to match the expected rate of sales. The demand for a company's products might be highly seasonal. The sales forecasts for August might be double those for April. If such a pattern were scheduled for production, additional workers would have to be hired temporarily, additional machinery might have to be purchased or leased, and raw materials and supplies would either have to be stockpiled or purchased in widely varying amounts. If a reasonably steady schedule of production can be maintained, a more efficient utilization of labor and machinery can be had.

After the production schedule has been set, the *materials budget* and *labor budget* can be determined. Materials must be available when needed, and work stoppages due to shortage of a needed material must be avoided. The labor budget will indicate the number of workers with various skills needed and when they are needed. It will aid the personnel department in its plans for hiring workers. If additional workers with special skills cannot be found, it may be necessary to schedule overtime work. If this can be planned rather than being haphazard, it will permit the workers to adjust their personal plans with less inconvenience to their families. The scheduling of vacations must be carefully coordinated so as not to interfere with the production schedule.

The *office-expense budget* estimates what will have to be paid for supplies, postage, clerical salaries, executive salaries, and similar expenses.

It was stated earlier that the overall budget was a summary of departmental budgets, coordinated by the budget officer or budget committee. It presents a forecast of operations and is frequently called an *operating budget*. It is also called a *pro forma income statement*. Table 14-4 shows an operating budget prepared on a monthly basis for a 1-year period. The total figures for the year would be the pro forma income statement or profit and loss statement for the coming year. A *pro forma balance sheet* is also frequently prepared to show the financial condition of the company at the end of the coming year. These statements are, naturally, estimates. If the profit and loss statement and balance sheet drawn up a year later

TABLE 14-4 BURNSIDE MANUFACTURING CO., OPERATING BUDGET, YEAR ENDING DEC. 31, 1974

	Jan.	Feb.	March	April	May	June
Monthly operations:						
Net sales	$ 70,000	$ 70,000	$ 80,000	$ 80,000	$ 90,000	$ 90,000
Less:						
Materials used	35,000	35,000	40,000	40,000	45,000	45,000
Direct labor	7,000	7,000	8,000	8,000	9,000	9,000
Other manufacturing expense	10,500	10,500	12,000	12,000	13,500	13,500
Cost of goods sold	52,500	52,500	60,000	60,000	67,500	67,500
Gross profit	17,500	17,500	20,000	20,000	22,500	22,500
Less:						
Sales expense	15,000	15,000	15,000	15,000	15,000	15,000
General and administrative expense	7,000	7,000	7,000	7,000	7,000	7,000
Operating profit	(4,500)	(4,500)	(2,000)	(2,000)	500	500

TABLE 14-5 BURNSIDE MANUFACTURING CO., CASH BUDGET FOR YEAR ENDING DEC. 31, 1974

	Jan.	Feb.	March	April	May
Cash flow:					
Cash balance (beginning)	$ 20,000	$ 28,000	$ 13,500	$ 4,000	$ 7,000
Receipts from receivables	90,000	70,000	70,000	70,000	80,000
Total Available Cash	110,000	98,000	83,500	74,000	87,000
Less disbursements:					
Trade payables	40,000	40,000	45,000	45,000	60,000
Direct labor	8,000	8,000	9,500	12,000	16,000
Other manufacturing expenses	12,000	13,500	13,000	18,000	24,000
Sales expense	15,000	15,000	15,000	15,000	15,000
General and administrative expense	7,000	7,000	7,000	7,000	7,000
Fixed asset additions	. . .	. . .	. . .	10,000	10,000
Repayment of bank loans	. . .	. . .	. . .	. . .	. . .
Total Disbursements	82,000	84,500	89,500	107,000	132,000
Indicated cash shortage	. . .	. . .	6,000	33,000	45,000
Bank loans to be obtained	. . .	. . .	10,000	40,000	50,000
Cash balance (ending)	28,000	13,500	4,000	7,000	5,000

July	Aug.	Sept.	Oct.	Nov.	Dec.	Total
$120,000	$160,000	$150,000	$130,000	$ 90,000	$ 70,000	$1,200,000
60,000	80,000	75,000	65,000	45,000	35,000	600,000
12,000	16,000	15,000	13,000	9,000	7,000	120,000
18,000	24,000	22,500	19,500	13,500	10,500	180,000
90,000	120,000	112,500	97,500	67,500	52,500	900,000
30,000	40,000	37,500	32,500	22,500	17,500	300,000
15,000	15,000	15,000	15,000	15,000	15,000	180,000
7,000	7,000	7,000	7,000	7,000	7,000	84,000
8,000	18,000	15,500	10,500	500	(4,500)	36,000

June	July	Aug.	Sept.	Oct.	Nov.	Dec.
$ 5,000	$ 10,500	$ 6,000	$ 6,500	$ 12,000	$ 7,500	$ 8,000
80,000	90,000	90,000	120,000	160,000	150,000	130,000
85,000	100,500	96,000	126,500	172,000	157,500	138,000
80,000	75,000	65,000	45,000	35,000	35,000	35,000
15,000	13,000	8,500	7,000	7,000	7,000	8,000
22,500	19,500	14,000	10,500	10,500	10,500	12,000
15,000	15,000	15,000	15,000	15,000	15,000	15,000
7,000	7,000	7,000	7,000	7,000	7,000	7,000
10,000	. . .	. . .	. . .	. . .	. . .	. . .
. . .	. . .	. . .	30,000	90,000	75,000	35,000
149,500	129,500	109,500	114,500	164,500	149,500	112,000
64,500	29,000	13,500	. . .	. . .	. . .	. . .
75,000	35,000	20,000	. . .	. . .	. . .	. . .
10,500	6,000	6,500	12,000	7,500	8,000	26,000

coincided exactly with the figures on the pro forma statements, it would be sheer coincidence.

The *cash budget* is a most important budget and must be prepared with great care. It attempts to predict the inflow and outflow of cash. Accurate prediction will enable the chief financial officer to plan whatever borrowing is necessary to offset an outflow greater than the inflow in any month. It will enable him to determine the length of time for which money must be borrowed, since a period during which cash inflow exceeds outflow permits loans to be retired. Table 14-5 shows a cash budget for a company with a seasonal sales pattern. Because cash receipts and disbursements for this company cannot be equalized, bank borrowing is used to maintain a proper level of cash.

SUMMARY

Basically, accounting is record keeping. But it involves more than just compiling a list of transactions. Accounting principles determine how transactions will be recorded and on what basis values will be assigned to assets, expenses, and other items.

Accounting furnishes a financial history of a company. By presenting transactions in summary form, accounting permits decisions and plans to be made on an informed basis. One summary statement, the balance sheet, shows what a company owns and what it owes at the end of a period of time, such as at the end of a year. Another summary statement, the income statement, is an accumulation of all of the income and expense transactions for a period of time, such as a month or a year.

As part of the planning of company operations, an estimate of future income and expenses is made. Such an estimate is a budget, and is expressed in dollars and cents. The estimated expenses and income for the coming year may be summarized in a statement called a pro forma income statement. Similarly, the financial condition of the company at the end of the coming year may be estimated in a pro forma balance sheet. Pro forma statements are useful in checking current estimates of the future with actual future achievement.

QUESTIONS FOR REVIEW

1 What are the major divisions of accounting? What are the purposes of each?
2 Name the principal financial statements prepared for a business. To what uses are each of these statements put?
3 Why is it important that accounting records be kept by a company?
4 Show how cost accounting helps management in better controlling costs in a manufacturing plant.
5 If a company is large enough to have auditors of its own, is there any need to hire an auditing firm to make an annual audit of the company books?
6 "Accountants are by nature financially conservative." What is meant by this statement? Do you agree with it? Give your reasons.
7 If the purpose of accounting is to provide accurate records of company transactions, why is it that some accountants carry valuable patents at $1 on the records of a company?

8 What is meant by the circuit flow of current assets?

9 What relationship, if any, is there between current assets and current liabilities?

10 Which are more likely to be stated on the company books at their actual value—assets or liabilities? Why?

11 Distinguish between fixed assets, current assets, investment assets, and intangible assets.

12 What is a balance sheet? Explain how it helps to provide information for management decisions.

SELECTED READINGS

Burns, Thomas J., and Harvey Hendrickson: *The Accounting Primer*, McGraw-Hill Book Company, New York, 1972.

Fertig, Paul E., Donald F. Istvan, and J. Mottice Homer: *Using Accounting Information*, 2d ed., Harcourt Brace Jovanovich, Inc., New York, 1971.

Salmonson, R. F., Roger H. Hermanson, and James Don Edwards: *A Survey of Basic Accounting*, Richard D. Irwin, Inc., Homewood, Ill., 1973.

Wentworth, Gerald O., A. Thompson Montgomery, James A. Gowen, and Thomas W. Harrell: *The Accounting Process: A Program for Self-instruction*, McGraw-Hill Book Company, New York, 1963.

How to Understand Financial Statements, The New York Stock Exchange, New York, 1965.

Name   **Section**   **Date**

COMPLETION SENTENCES

1 Accounting is the function of recording, classifying, summarizing, and inter-

preting business data in terms of _____ .

2 Cost accounting aids in control of _____ .

3 Auditing consists of the examination of a firm's accounts to determine their

_____ .

4 The existence of a well-designed auditing program reduces the opportunities

for _____ and _____ .

5 In the preparation of financial statements, one policy is basic:

_____ .

6 The _____ shows the condition of a company at a

particular instant of time.

7 Current assets are in a continuous process of _____ .

8 Transfer of information from the _____ to various _____ accounts is called posting.

9 All the properties owned by a business are known as the _____ .

10 _____ are those items on the balance sheet that are not "consumed" during each cycle of business activity.

11 The "consumption" of fixed assets is called _____ .

12 The net worth represents the _____ of the owners in the business.

13 A _____ is an amount owed by a company to anyone who has the right by law to collect.

14 For most firms the starting point in an income statement is _____ .

15 The chief tool of financial analysis is the _____ .

TRUE OR FALSE STATEMENTS

1 The decisions a manager makes depend upon a constant flow of information.

2 Cost of product + markup = selling price.

3 If a company's accountants are well trained and careful in their work, there is no need for auditing.

4 FIFO is the method of inventory valuation used in most retail stores.

5 In the preparation of financial statements conservative estimate of values is the rule.

Name   Section   Date

6 During periods of rising prices, inventories tend to be valued at market prices rather than cost of acquisition.

7 Total assets equals liabilities minus net worth.

8 Current assets generally increase in value as they change in form.

9 Fixed assets have a longer accounting life than current assets.

10 Investment assets are the stocks and bonds issued by a company to its stockholders and bondholders.

11 Intangible assets include patents and copyrights.

12 Bonds may have a long life, but not more than 99 years.

13 Long-term liabilities are those that require regular installments for repayment.

14 There is no association between fixed assets and long-term liabilities of a company.

15 Net worth represents the investment of the owners in the company.

16 Both the balance sheet and the profit and loss statement show the condition of the business at an instant of time, such as the close of business, December 31, 1974.

17 The income statement begins with a listing of expenses.

18 The beginning balance of the surplus statement is the same figure as the closing balance of the previous statement.

19 Reserve accounts do not contain cash.

20 The acid test ratio serves a purpose similar to the purpose served by the current ratio.

1 The accounting books of the Marvid Davery Corporation show the following information:

Revenue from oil sales	$345,890.65
Revenue from gas sales	55,450.50
Well-operating expenses	74,657.85
Geological field expenses	12,555.60

Depletion	58,980.25
Depreciation	35,500.00
Officers' salaries	11,500.00
Clerical salaries	6,575.40
Travel expenses	5,600.50
Telephone and telegraph	2,050.25
Legal expenses	1,978.40
Auditing expenses	1,400.45
Insurance expired	856.75
Stock transfer expenses	554.60
Bad debts	334.50
Interest expense	19,565.45

Prepare an income statement from the above information.

2 Secure financial statements from the annual report of a company or from data in *Moody's Manuals* or *Standard and Poor Corporation Records*. Prepare the following ratios:

a Current ratio:

b Acid test ratio:

c Ratio of equity to debt:

d Ratio of income to equity:

e Ratio of income to sales:

Name	Section	Date

3 Prepare a budget showing your expected income and expenditures by months for the rest of the current school year or for the next year, using the following form:

PERSONAL BUDGET FOR COLLEGE YEAR 19 __

Item	Months 1	2	3	4	5	6	7	8	9	Total for year
Cash receipts (itemize)										
Total										
Cash expenditures (itemize)										
Total										
Excess of cash receipts + or expenditures −										
Total										

CHAPTER
15
STATISTICS

It is not the purpose of this chapter to make statisticians of beginning business students. In a statistics course, you would learn the mathematical techniques necessary in the gathering and treatment of data. You would learn the different methods of presentation used to make data understandable. What is important to learn in reading this chapter is the usefulness of statistical methods and some understanding of how to read and interpret statistics.

Statistical methods must be used with care and integrity. An experienced statistician presents the information contained in an array of data quite clearly and honestly. But a statistician who is either careless or wishes to misinform can treat data in such a way as to draw unwarranted and even false conclusions. Whether or not you use statistics as a business student or as a nonbusiness student, it is necessary to have some understanding of how statisticians operate. For that reason, it is good to be able to appraise how raw material is collected, how averages are calculated, and how ratios and index numbers are used.

THE IMPORTANCE OF STATISTICS

People work with numbers every day. In conversation, correspondence, and reading, dealing with numbers is basic to understanding. Lord Kelvin, the British scientist, stated that "when you can measure what you are speaking about, and express it in numbers, you know something about it; but when you cannot measure it, when you cannot express it in numbers, your knowledge is of a meagre and unsatisfactory kind."

How we get our numbers and what we do with them after we get them is another matter. We can collect large volumes of data and learn little, or we can collect small amounts of data and learn much—it all depends on the way we collect and handle them. We can list the hat size of every soldier inducted into the United States Army during World War II. It would make an impressive list of numbers running into the millions, but it would not help a supply officer in knowing how many hats of each size to buy. A group of unassorted data does not tell us much. We must arrange the numbers, classify them, and summarize them. This is the function of statistics. Statistics will tell the supply officer the average hat size of soldiers, tell him how many hats of each size to order for every 1,000 men inducted, and tell him this after measuring the hat size of only a relatively few soldiers.

Statistics is the activity of collecting and classifying data on the basis of the relative number of occurrence of the data and of presenting the data in such a form that a businessman, government official, scientist, or other person may draw reasonable conclusions.

Statistics is a necessary tool of analysis in every phase of life. It is used by government agencies, businesses, and schools. Businessmen make plans on the basis of statistics, and then use it to check the progress of their plans. Governmental policies are based on the statistical material gathered by their agencies. College students cannot understand finance, economics, sociology, or psychology without grasping the meaning of such concepts as average, sample, and correlation. Probably H. G. Wells was not exaggerating when he said, "Statistical thinking will one day be as necessary for efficient citizenship as the ability to read and write."

Statistical information is not important in itself; it must serve a purpose. To gather statistics for which no valuable purpose is in sight is a waste of resources. As one writer has put it: "Consider, for example, the blades of grass on a lawn; what a capital fact-finding project they would make! We could use the very best in stratified sampling devices to calculate an unbiased estimate of the number of blades of grass contained in the defined area."[1] The volume of statistics being compiled is tremendous. Most of it is useful. Some is not. Because statistical efforts cost time and money, it would be well for executives controlling statistical efforts to make sure that none of their staff is counting blades of grass.

Statistical thinking is concerned not with the individual as an individual, but as a member of a group. A statistician does not study a particular man, a particular tree, or a particular house. He may conclude from his study that the average height of trees in a park is 30 feet and that the average age is 64 years. But there may be no tree in the park that is just 30 feet high and exactly 64 years old. Yet the conclusion may be valid. It is a violation of statistical thinking to apply unqualifiedly the attributes of the statistical group to a particular unit. Statistical thinking, in other words, is in terms of averages, approximations, and probabilities. The statistician cannot predict when John Jones will die. But he can predict, with a degree of accuracy acceptable to insurance companies, how many men out of 100,000 will die each year.

STATISTICAL PRESENTATION

To permit statistical data to be of maximum utility, they must be presented to the reader in a form easy to understand. Good presentation can bring out significant facts and can facilitate comparison. There are many ways that statistics can be presented. The choice will be determined by the character of the data and the use for which they are intended. The more common methods of presentation are tables, line charts, bar charts, pie charts, area diagrams, maps, and pictographs.

[1] Dr. J. A. Gengerelli, quoted in *The Royal Bank of Canada Monthly Letter*, vol. 37, no. 1, p. 2, January 1956.

A table is a presentation of data in organized columns and rows (see Table 15-1). It presents data in a systematic arrangement, so that the reader can locate quickly any bit of information contained in the data. Table 15-1 illustrates statistical data presented in the form of a table.

TABLES

A line chart relates two types of measurement of data by means of a line. One characteristic is measured vertically; the other characteristic is measured horizontally. The horizontal measurement is most often in terms of time and the vertical in terms of quantity. Frequently, several lines can be plotted on the same chart, as in Figure 15-1. Sometimes, shading is added for emphasis. If the actual amount of change is less important than the *rate* of increase or decrease, the rate of change can be emphasized by using a *ratio chart* (Figure 15-2).

LINE CHART

In a bar chart, amounts are represented by the lengths of bars. The bars may represent percentages, as in Figure 15-3, or amounts, as shown in Figure 15-4.

BAR CHART

A pie chart is a circle divided into sectors. The segments can represent dollars or other units or can represent percentages. If several circles are to be compared, percentages should be used. Otherwise larger totals should be represented by larger circles. Figure 15-5 illustrates the use of pie charts.

PIE CHART

Area diagrams (Figure 15-6) are used to compare two or more quantities. The diagrams may be squares, circles, rectangles, the outline of a state or nation, or some other shape. The area of the shape corresponds to the quantity represented. This means that if the population of one city is four times that of another city, a square representing the larger city would be twice as high (and twice as wide) as the square representing the smaller city, not four times as high. Because of the difficulty most people have in accurately comparing the areas of surfaces of different sizes, quantity figures are usually included to aid comparison.

AREA DIAGRAMS

Statistical maps are useful in showing geographical differences in the data presented. Variations in shading or color are usually used to indicate differences, as shown in Figure 15-7. Sometimes, geographical differences are shown by using dots, varying the number of dots to indicate the degree of difference.

MAPS

Pictures or drawings can be used to represent quantities, as in Figure 15-8. Their use has increased in recent years because they are more likely to be noticed by the

PICTOGRAPHS

TABLE 15-1   BUSINESS EXPENDITURES ON NEW PLANT AND EQUIPMENT

(In billions of dollars)

| Period | Manufacturing | | | Mining | Transportation | | | Public Utilities | | Communications | Other* | Total (S. A. A. R.) |
	Total	Durable	Non-durable		Railroad	Air	Other	Electric	Gas and other			
1968	67.76	14.12	14.25	1.63	1.45	2.56	1.59	7.66	2.54	6.83	15.14	....
1969	75.56	15.96	15.72	1.86	1.86	2.51	1.68	8.94	2.67	8.30	16.05	....
1970	79.71	15.80	16.15	1.89	1.78	3.03	1.23	10.65	2.49	10.10	16.59	....
1971†	81.21	14.15	15.84	2.16	1.67	1.88	1.38	12.86	2.44	10.77	18.05	....
1972†	89.77	16.11	16.50	2.20	1.75	2.42	1.55	14.58	2.86	12.30	19.51	....
1970–IV	21.66	4.26	4.40	.50	.43	.76	.33	3.12	.63	2.81	4.42	78.63
1971–I	17.68	3.11	3.58	.49	.34	.34	.28	2.70	.41	2.50	3.94	79.32
II	20.60	3.52	4.03	.54	.47	.60	.36	3.20	.63	2.81	4.44	81.61
III	20.14	3.40	3.91	.55	.42	.39	.37	3.35	.71	2.62	4.42	80.75
IV	22.79	4.12	4.32	.59	.45	.56	.37	3.60	.69	2.84	5.26	83.18
1972–I	19.38	3.29	3.32	.58	.48	.50	.32	3.19	.44	2.72	4.55	86.79
–II²ʳ	22.01	3.71	3.92	.61	.48	.73	.39	3.61	.62	2.95	4.98	87.12
–III²ʳ	22.56	4.00	4.15	.60	.43	.58	.37	3.62	.84	7.92		90.38
–IV²	25.16	4.69	4.58	.65	.43	.70	.30	4.11	.85	8.86		91.84

*Includes trade, service, construction, finance, and insurance.
†Anticipated by business.
Note: Dept. of Commerce and Securities and Exchange Commission estimates for corporate and noncorporate business; excludes agriculture, real estate operators, medical, legal, educational, and cultural service, and nonprofit organizations.
Source: Federal Reserve Bulletin, October 1972, p. A50.

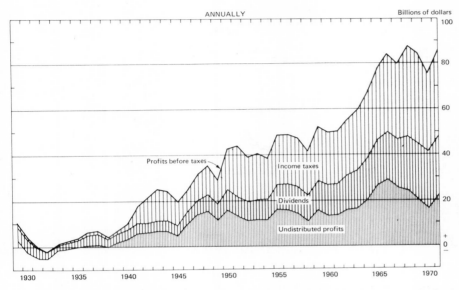

FIGURE 15-1 Line chart showing arithmetic scale of corporate profits, taxes, and dividends. (*Historical Chart Book*, Board of Governors of the Federal Reserve System, 1972, p. 50. Data from Department of Commerce.)

reader than other types of statistical presentation. They are particularly well adapted to general-circulation magazines, newspapers, or publicity brochures, where the contents are destined to be read casually and where eye-catching devices help in maintaining the attention of the reader. Pictographs are usually presented in a form similar to a bar chart. Each picture represents a single unit, 100 units, 1,000 units, or some other number. Fractions are represented by cutting a picture in half, or by showing one-fourth, two-thirds, or whatever the fraction might be.

THE RAW MATERIAL OF STATISTICS

COLLECTING DATA

The first step, obviously, in any statistical study is the collection of data. Sometimes information can be gotten from published sources. Company publications, trade associations, government agencies, universities, colleges, foundations, books, and periodicals are some of the sources of information for business. It is certainly a waste of time and money to collect data that have already been collected by someone else. Therefore a search should be made for the wanted data from published sources. In many cases, it would also be wise to ask trade associations, government bureaus, or university business research bureaus if the wanted data might have been collected but not published.

Frequently, the collection of data cannot be avoided. In such cases how

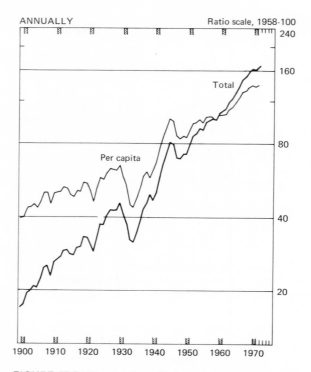

Gross National Product in Constant Dollars

FIGURE 15-2   A ratio chart. (*Historical Chart Book*, Board
of Governors of the Federal Reserve System,
1972, p. 68.)

are they to be collected? In business, the most frequently used methods of gathering data are observation, personal interview, and questionnaire. In **observation**, the gathering of information does not depend on the participation of the subject. For example, learning the number of automobiles passing an intersection at various hours of the day requires merely that they be counted, either by an observer seated at the side of the road or by an automatic counter using a rubber tube laid across the road. The number of persons entering a store can be counted by an electric-eye counter. The high and low daily temperatures can also be secured by observing the thermometer or can be recorded automatically.

In a **personal interview**, an interviewer asks questions either in person or by telephone. The interview can be of a formal questionnaire type or of an informal nature. An informal interview may put the subject more at ease than would a conversation consisting of a series of direct questions. But, to have any value, such an interview requires an interviewer with a high degree of judgment, intelligence, and tact. If handled with skill, an informal interview can uncover information not

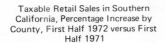

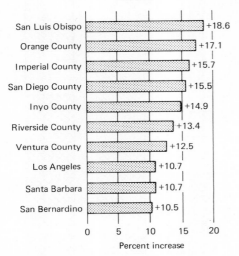

FIGURE 15-3 A bar chart showing percentages. (Monthly Summary of Business Conditions, *Security Pacific Bank*, October 1972, p. 2. *Source:* State Board of Equalization.)

reached by a questionnaire, because of the resistance of persons to unpleasant or embarrassing questions.

If a *questionnaire* is prepared, it can be presented to the subject in person, by telephone, or by mail. Personal presentation is most costly, use of the telephone is next, and mail is least expensive. The telephone can be used only where a few questions are asked. Probably the most frequent use of the telephone in gathering data has been in determining program popularity on radio and television. Here the questions are confined to asking the subject if the radio or television set is on, to what station it is tuned, and how many people are listening or watching. If a questionnaire is sent by mail, personal contact is absent, which may be an advantage in some cases and a disadvantage in others.

SAMPLING

Everybody makes judgments on the basis of samples. A college student is given a sample of two or three razor blades and decides on the basis of the sample his liking for the brand. A tobacco buyer examines a few leaves from a quantity of tobacco and determines how much he is willing to bid for the whole quantity. A college instructor prepares 50 questions covering a semester's work and

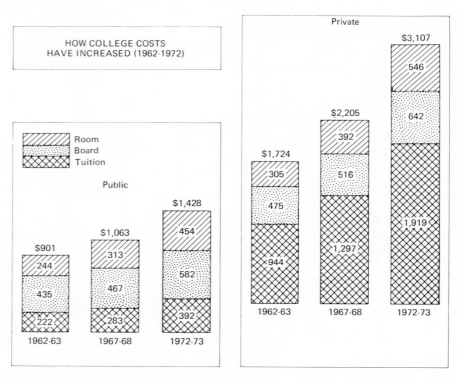

FIGURE 15-4 A bar chart showing amounts. (AFL-CIO, *American Federationist*, November 1972, p. 23.) ***Source:*** Estimated from Office of Education surveys.)

assumes that the answers to those represent a student's grasp of the entire course. A girl has one dance with a boy and decides on the basis of that sample that she has had enough. These are examples of sampling techniques. They are not as refined, of course, as those used by statisticians, but the type of thinking is the same.

The theory of sampling is based on the proposition that the characteristics of the sample are the same as the characteristics of the whole. It does not follow, however, that if 10 college students are asked to identify Shah Jehan, and cannot do so, nobody in the college can. In this case, the sample is too small. If a person sought to learn the racial composition of a city population by interviewing persons in 1,000 houses in a *single* neighborhood, he might conclude that the population is almost 100 percent Irish, or 100 percent Chinese. In representing an entire city, such a sample would be biased. For a sample to represent a whole[2] with reasonable accuracy, it must be carefully drawn so as to be truly representative.

[2]Statisticians call the whole group from which a sample is drawn a *universe*. The statistical universe might be the population of a city, all the students in a college, all of the trucks owned by farmers in Iowa, or all the cattle in Chicago stockyards.

MAJOR OCCUPATION BY SEX 1970

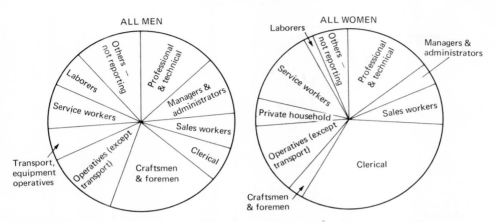

FIGURE 15-5   A pie chart. (AFL-CIO, *American Federationist*, November 1972, p. 19.)

AVERAGES

The average college student makes C's in the courses he takes. The average American speaks only one language fluently, while the average Swiss speaks more than one. The average salary in the X factory is $8,543.21. We use the term "average" every day. What does it mean? To represent a group of persons or a group of numbers, we select one person or number and call the person or number the average. The average may be one of the actual units in the group or it may not. There may be a person in the X factory earning $8,543.21. Probably there is not. The average family in a country may have 2.3 children and a house with 5.7 rooms. In such a case, fortunately, the average is an artificial concept, and every unit would be either above or below the average. Nevertheless, selecting an average is a handy way of looking at the characteristics of a whole group, and the use of averages is very widespread.

There are different types of averages, also known as measures of central tendency, or measures of location. Each one may give a different figure. In some cases, the different averages may be close together; in others, they might be far apart. Each has its uses. A careful businessman will, however, want to know which average is being used in any statistical study he uses. In this chapter, we shall examine the following averages: *arithmetic mean*, *median*, and *mode*.

ARITHMETIC MEAN

The most commonly used average is probably the arithmetic mean. We obtain it by adding a series of numbers and dividing by the sum of the numbers. For example, suppose that a service station has recorded the sale of its most expensive brand of gasoline for a period of time. We first list the numbers in the form shown. Statisticians call the listing of all the numbers used in computing an average an *array*.

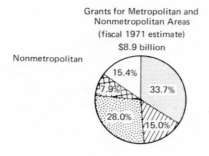

Grants for Metropolitan and
Nonmetropolitan Areas
(fiscal 1971 estimate)
$8.9 billion

Nonmetropolitan

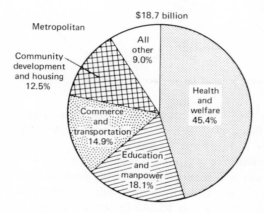

Metropolitan

$18.7 billion

FIGURE 15-6 An area diagram comparing metro-
politan and nonmetropolitan regions.
(*The Federal Budget 1971*, National
Industrial Conference Board, p. 39.
Sources: Bureau of the Budget; The
Conference Board.)

Gasoline Sales by Gallons			
20	15	13	17
14	20	10	20
10	5	16	8
15	20	14	13
16	15	15	14
15	17	12	15
Total: 249 gallons			

It can be seen that some numbers occur more than once. The array can be
arranged into a *frequency distribution* such as the one shown following. To
obtain the arithmetic mean, we divide the total gallons of gasoline sold by the total
number of sales.

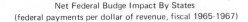

Net Federal Budge Impact By States
(federal payments per dollar of revenue, fiscal 1965-1967)

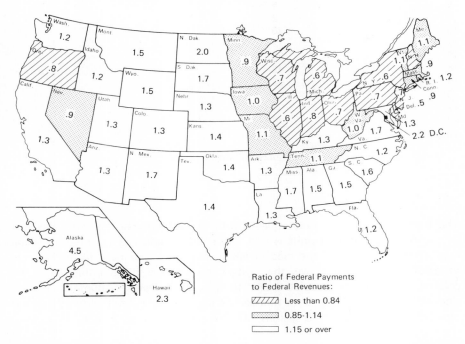

Ratio of Federal Payments
to Federal Revenues:

/////	Less than 0.84
::::::	0.85-1.14
⬜	1.15 or over

FIGURE 15-7 Statistical map of the United States. (*The Federal Budget 1971*, National Industrial Conference Board, p. 45). *Sources:* Library of Congress; The Conference Board.

Revenue Car Loadings of Piggyback Traffic
(1956-1966—class 1 railroads)

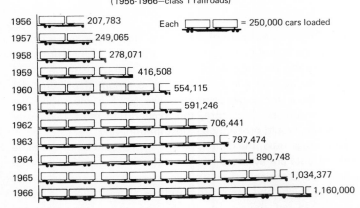

1956	207,783
1957	249,065
1958	278,071
1959	416,508
1960	554,115
1961	591,246
1962	706,441
1963	797,474
1964	890,748
1965	1,034,377
1966	1,160,000

Each ⬜⬜ = 250,000 cars loaded

FIGURE 15-8 Pictograph. (*Railroad Operations in 1966*, Association of American Railroads, Washington, D.C., 1967, p. 25.)

Gallons	Number of Sales	Gallons X Sales
5	1	5
8	1	8
10	2	20
12	1	12
13	2	26
14	3	42
15	6	90
16	2	32
17	2	34
20	4	80
Totals:	24	349 gallons

$$\text{Arithmetic mean:} \quad \frac{349}{24} = 14.54 \text{ gallons}$$

MEDIAN   The median divides the array equally, with the same number of units above as below. If the number of units is odd, the middle number is the median; if the number of units is even, the median falls between two numbers. In the example of gasoline sales used above, the median is computed by counting down the column of number of cumulative sales to 12½, which leaves 12 numbers on each side of the median. Since both number 12 and number 13 fall within the group representing the sale of 15 gallons, the median sale of gasoline is 15 gallons.

MODE   The mode is the value in a series that occurs most often. In the series representing the sale of gasoline, the mode is 15 gallons. In this example, the mode and the median fall at the same point.

SELECTING THE AVERAGE   Although the arithmetic mean is used more frequently than other averages, no single type of average can be considered best for all purposes. For measuring the average income of a corporation for the past 30 years, the arithmetic mean would be used. For measuring the average annual income of a group of persons, the median or mode would be a more representative average. For measuring the average expenditure by consumers at a store, the expenditure most frequently made, the modal expenditure, would probably be most illuminating.

Regardless of the average used, the data to be averaged should be of the same sort. If different kinds of data are averaged, the average will be meaningless. One could measure the height and weight of all college students at a coeducational college and get the average height and weight for students at the college. It would be more useful, however, to get the average height and weight separately for men and women at the college.

A ratio compares one number with another in the form of a fraction or a percentage. **RATIOS**
The purpose is to simplify the comparison. There might be 730 men and 2,120
women enrolled in a college. The ratio of women to men would be 2.9 to 1, or
approximately 3 women to every man, computed by dividing 2,120 by 730. If a
farmer harvests 2,800 bushels of wheat from 70 acres of land, his land yields

$$2,800 \div 70 = 40 \text{ bushels per acre}$$

Sometimes it is more convenient to express a ratio as a percentage than as a fraction
This is especially true where the fraction is less than 2 to 1. In the following
example, the relationship between sales of two different years can be expressed
in three different ways. In this type of relationship, the third way is most commonly
used. The ABC Manufacturing Company had sales of $300,000 in 1973, and
$330,000 in 1974. The relationship can be expressed in the following ways:

The ratio of sales in 1974 to sales in 1973 is 11 to 10:

$$\frac{330,000}{300,000} = \frac{11}{10}$$

Sales in 1974 were 110 percent of sales in 1973.
Sales in 1974 were 10 percent above 1973.

In using ratios to simplify comparisons, one should be careful to avoid certain misuses. The common misuses are as follows:

Suppose a company showed a rise in employment in the office from 50 to
75, an increase of 50 percent, while the number of workers in the plant
dropped from 400 to 200, a decrease of 50 percent. It would be incorrect
to balance the increase against the decline and report the employment position
of the company as unchanged. This is called an ***indiscriminate combination
of percentages.***

If the numbers to be compared are small, no simplification is needed,
and the use of a percentage to express the relationship might distort the
meaning. For example, it was reported that a prominent university that had
admitted only men students prior to World War II allowed girls to enroll
during the first year, 33⅓ percent of the coeds married their
instructors. It would have been more revealing not to have "simplified" the
comparison but to have given the actual figures: Three girls enrolled and one
married an instructor.

If a very large and a very small number are to be compared, percentages
probably should not be used. If the population of a town increased from 20
to 24,000 between the 1960 and 1970 censuses, it would be better to express
the ratio as 1,200 to 1 rather than state that the population in 1970 was
120,000 percent of 1960.

INDEX NUMBERS

CONSTRUCTING
AN INDEX

An *index number* measures changes in groups of data. Most often the changes measured by index numbers are changes over a period of time. One period is selected as the point of comparison or base period and is assigned a value of 100 percent. Change in data before and after the base period are compared to the base-period data by means of percentages. An index number of 133 means that whatever is being measured is 133 percent of the base period, or 33 percent above the base period.

In order to understand index numbers, it is useful to construct one. A simplified example is given below. The price of each item is expressed as 100 percent for the base year, and the change in price of each item is expressed as a percentage of the base year price.

	Base Year Price per Unit	Present-Year Price per Unit	Present Price as Percentage of Base Year
Eggs (dozen)	$0.50	$0.80	160%
Oleomargarine (pound)	0.35	0.45	129
Bread (pound loaf)	0.20	0.40	200
Milk (quart)	0.30	0.55	183
Coffee (pound)	0.55	0.95	<u>173</u>
			845%

Divide by 5 = 169

Or $\dfrac{845}{500} \times 100 = 169$

This reduces the prices of the different items to comparable form. The percentages are then averaged by adding each column and dividing by the number of the items, in this case 5, giving an average rise of 169 percent of the base period.

The example described above gives equal importance to each item in determining the average. Most families, however, consume more loaves of bread than pounds of coffee. To construct an index giving each item approximately the same importance it has in the typical family food budget, one can construct a *weighted index*. To do this, one must first decide how much weight to assign each item. One way is to estimate the amount of each item consumed by the typical family in a week. The weights could then be determined as follows:

	Base Year Price per Unit	Amount Consumed per Week	Cost per Week	Weight
Eggs (dozen)	$0.50	3 dozen	$1.50	1.50
Oleomargarine (pound)	0.35	1½ pounds	0.53	0.53
Bread (pound loaf)	0.20	7 loaves	1.40	1.40
Milk (quart)	0.30	10 quarts	3.00	3.00
Coffee (pound)	0.55	1 pound	0.55	0.55

The calculation of the index of food prices would then be as given below. This shows the index of food prices to be 176.5 for the present year, or 76.5 percent

	Base Year				Present Year			
	Price per Unit	Weight	Percent, Relative	Weighted Percent, Relative	Price per Unit	Weight	Percent, Relative	Weighted Percent, Relative
Eggs (dozen)	$0.50	1.50	100	150	$0.80	1.50	160	240
Oleomargarine (pound)	0.35	.53	100	53	0.45	0.53	129	68
Bread (pound loaf)	0.20	1.40	100	140	0.40	1.40	200	280
Milk (quart)	0.30	3.00	100	300	0.55	3.00	183	549
Coffee (pound)	0.55	0.55	100	55	0.95	0.55	173	95
				698				1,232

$$\frac{1,232}{698} \times 100 = 176.5$$

above the base year. The weighted index in the example above is higher than the unweighted index. If a different set of weights for each food had been used, the weighted index might have been higher than the unweighted one. Two agencies measuring the same price trends may reach different conclusions. The main reason for the lack of agreement in indexes measuring the same price areas, such as food prices, consumers' prices, wholesale prices, raw materials, and so on, is because of differences in the following:

Selection of the base year.
Selection of items in the index.
Selection of weights assigned to each item in the index.

SELECTION OF THE BASE YEAR

If the industrial production of the United States is measured from the year 1950 as a base, the production index for 1972 would be about 200. Measured from the year 1949 as a base, the production index would be approximately 289 because 1949 was a recession year. The index of prices of farm products for the year 1972 was approximately 171 measured from 1944 as a base, but was 320 measured from 1939. The prices look very good compared to 1939, not so good compared to 1944. The selection of the base obviously makes a lot of difference in making an index number look good or bad. How should a base be chosen? If the purpose of the statistician is to inform rather than to deceive—and this should be the purpose of all statisticians—the base selected will be one that is neither unusually high nor unusually low. A "normal" period in the past should be selected. While determining what is a normal period involves some judgment, and judgments can differ, at least we can avoid the extremes. Because it is difficult to choose a single year that can be defended as being normal, statisticians may choose a longer period, such as the average of 3 years.

SELECTION OF ITEMS

The selection of items in an index is determined by the degree of importance of each item. The number of items depends largely on the time and money available for the study. Over the many years that the Bureau of Labor Statistics has measured prices, many changes have been made in the items included. Television sets were not included in the calculation of consumer prices in 1939 since only a few families owned sets. After World War II, however, television sets become a common and important item in the budget of the average family, so they were then included in the index.

Only five items were used in the above examples showing computation of an index. The Bureau of Labor Statistics in 1946 used 61 foods, 39 articles of clothing, 12 kinds of fuel, 21 kinds of house furnishings, 48 miscellaneous goods, and rent in compiling its index of consumer prices. Since 1946, several hundred items have been added. In general, the larger the number of items in an index, the more accurately it will reflect the area it is intended to represent.

SELECTION OF WEIGHTS

The statistician can weight the items in an index by whatever appears to be appropriate. The weights computed in this chapter were determined by multiplying the quantity consumed of each item by the price of the item. Thus eggs were given a weight of 1.50, oleo a weight of 0.53, and so on. An alternative method might assign weights according to the quantity of each item consumed rather than the cost per week. The weights would then have appeared as shown in the table.

	Amount Consumed per Week	Weight
Eggs	3 dozen	3.00
Oleo	1½ pounds	1.50
Bread	7 loaves	7.00
Milk	10 quarts	10.00
Coffee	1 pound	1.00

Index weights may be based on production figures, consumption figures, or distribution figures, to name a few. The weights may be based on quantity or on value.

In the index computed in this chapter, the weights used were the quantity consumed times the price per item in the base year. The prices for the present year could have been used with equal logic. Generally, however, the values for the base year are used in assigning weights. Regardless of the method of selecting weights, care and judgment must be used.

CORRELATION

When two series appear to be related, we can measure the extent of the relationship by a statistical measure known as *correlation*, which compares the observations of one series of data with corresponding observations of the other series. For example, a course in accounting and a course in statistics might be required of all business majors. It might be interesting to determine whether any correlation exists between the grades a student gets in statistics and the grades he gets in accounting. To make a visual determination of the degree of correlation, a **scatter diagram** is prepared, as shown in Figure 15-9. If the dots on the scatter diagram fall in a line, the correlation is perfect. If, for example, the dots in 15-9 fell on the line (called the **line of average relationship** or **the line of regression**), a professor could predict with perfect accuracy the accounting grade of a student if he knew the statistics grade. If a student's grade in statistics were 90, his grade in accounting would be 90. If his grade in statistics were 40, his grade in accounting would be 46. Since the dots do not fall on the line but along it on either side, there is some correlation. This would permit a person to predict with moderate accuracy the grade a student was likely to get in one course after having received a grade in the other course. The degree of correlation can be measured by statistical methods rather than by visual inspection. It is one of the techniques taught in a college course in statistics. If the dots are scattered all over the diagram and do not follow any path, there is probably no correlation between the two series.

If two series measure changes over a period of time, they may be related on a **concurrent basis**. For example, the maximum daily temperatures and the daily water consumption for a city during August might be correlated. High temperatures and high levels of water consumption would occur on the same days. On days with low temperatures, water consumption would also be low. If the two series showed a high degree of correlation, the predicted temperature for the following day could be used to predict the rate of water consumption for that day.

Sometimes two series show high correlation only if one series is shifted in

FIGURE 15-9 Scatter diagram of accounting grades and statistics grades.

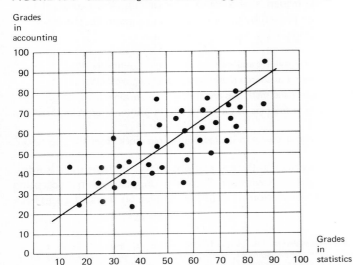

time. For example, the price of beef cattle at a livestock center varies from day to day. Generally this affects the receipt of cattle, but on the following day. If the price of beef cattle rises, farmers and ranchers bring large numbers of cattle to the market on the following day. If the price of beef cattle falls, the next day's cattle receipts fall also. In this case, the price of beef cattle is a *leading series* and the receipts of cattle at livestock centers is a *lagging series*. The lag is 1 day. A daily index of cattle prices, then, would be useful in predicting the next day's cattle receipts. In business statistics, there is a number of series that can be used to predict with varying degrees of accuracy, depending on the degree of correlation, a following series. The index of production of the machine tool industry shows a fair degree of correlation with the index of industrial production several months later. The machine tool index is therefore used to predict business activity during the coming months.

The fact that two series show correlation does not tell us which is cause and which effect. The correlation between daily summer temperatures and water consumption does not indicate the causal relationship. We can safely assume, however, that high temperatures are one of the important factors that increase the consumption of water. We can also conclude that the price of beef cattle is an important factor causing the increase in cattle receipts the following day. Can we assume that an increase in the production of machine tools causes an increase in business activity several months later? Hardly. Leading series do not always cause the changes in a correlated series that follows. If the expectation of future sales is above the level of present sales, businessmen generally react by placing orders for machine tools to expand productive capacity in anticipation of the future rise in sales. Probably business confidence and other factors cause *both* machine tool production and business activity to rise.

A lot of grief has been caused by persons using statistics to "prove" a cause-and-effect relationship where none exists. It cannot be emphasized too often that correlation does not provide evidence of a causal relationship. Any causal relationship that might exist has to be proven by other evidence. For example, the following pairs of series show a surprisingly high degree of correlation:

Increase in inmates of insane asylums and increase in college enrollments, 1920 to 1931.[3]

Increase in bank robberies and in church membership following World War II.

For most years, both suicides and marriages are at their peak in June.

Increase in salaries of school teachers in California and in profits of gambling houses in Nevada.

Increase in bank offices and decrease in United States gold stock from 1951 to 1972.[4]

Which is cause and which is effect in the correlations above? Perhaps the absurdity of pairing obviously unrelated data will put the reader on guard against accepting as proof of relationship the correlation of data that appear on the surface to have some connection.

[3] Harold Larrabee, *Reliable Knowledge*, Houghton Mifflin Company, Boston, 1945, p. 368.
[4] Calculated from the *Federal Reserve Bulletin*, March 1973, p. 198 and the *Historical Chart Book 1972*, both published by the Board of Governors of the Federal Reserve System, Washington, 1973.

A time series is simply the classification of data on the basis of time. Probably most of the charts people see are different kinds of time series. A time series enables a person to compare one period with another, to compare one series with another, and to determine whether any cycle or rhythm appears in the series. In analyzing a time series, a pattern of change is sought. If a pattern can be identified, it will help to predict future movements of the series. For example, a time series of retail sales might show a strong rise every December, a drop in the first 2 months of each year, an increase in March and April, and a drop every August. This would indicate that the pattern is strongly seasonal. There might be other patterns shown by the series, perhaps a rise and fall repeated on the average of every 5 years. To facilitate analysis, the movements of a series covering a long period of time are divided into the following patterns: secular trend, cyclical variation, seasonal variation, and random fluctuation.

TIME SERIES

The long-term movement of a time series is called the **secular trend**. It may increase over a long period, in which case it is sometimes referred to as a **positive trend**; or it may decrease over the years, in which case it is called a **negative trend**. Figure 15-10 shows a positive series and a negative one.

SECULAR TREND

Most time series in the United States show a positive secular trend. This is largely because the population is constantly increasing and because improvements in the techniques of production steadily increase the amount each worker produces.

FIGURE 15-10 Positive and negative series. (**Historical Chart Book**, Board of Governors of the Federal Reserve System, 1972, p. 70.)

Output per Manhour and Hours Worked

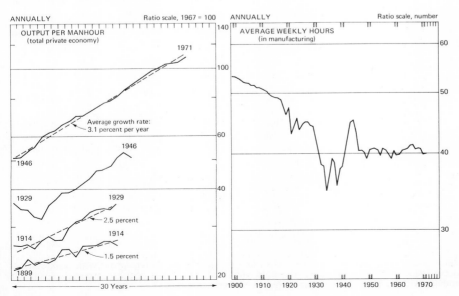

Prices have also increased since 1900, and data measured in terms of prices during the present century have reflected the rise in prices, unless the data have been adjusted to remove the price rise.

CYCLICAL VARIATION

Many business activity time series show a wavelike pattern in which each crest follows the previous one by a few years. These are called **cycles**. For the sake of prediction, it is unfortunate that the waves are not regular with respect to time. Some are long, lasting 10 years or more; others are short, lasting 2 or 3 years. Attempts have been made to classify business cycles into major and minor cycles, but there is little evidence that this has aided in predicting the extent or duration of cycles.[5] Cycles of business activity have shown such irregularity in the past that the best that can be said of prediction is that it is an art, not a science.

Figure 15-11 shows a series exhibiting very marked cyclical variation.

SEASONAL VARIATION

Any activity influenced by changing seasons is likely to show a definite **seasonal pattern**. One example is shown in Figure 15-12. Farm production, of course, shows a strong seasonal pattern. Many businesses are also affected by the seasons, some

FIGURE 15-11   A series showing cyclical variation. (*Historical Chart Book*, Board of Governors of the Federal Reserve System, 1972, p. 101.)

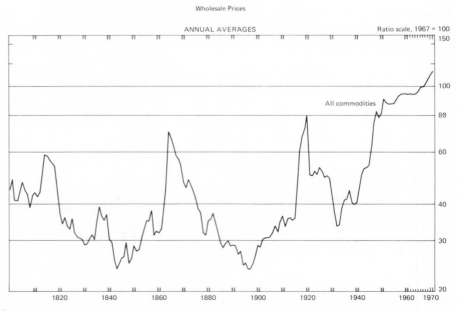

[5]Sunspot activity has shown a cyclical variation of considerable regularity, with peak activity occurring about every 11 years. Attempts were made in the last century to correlate sunspot activity with business activity, but with little success.

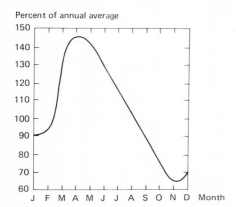

Percent of annual average

FIGURE 15-12 Seasonal variation of egg production in the United States.
(Adapted from *Survey of Current Business*, Department of
Commerce.)

strongly and others slightly. A few show hardly any seasonal variation. Retail sales rise in December and fall in January. Motels in the Northern states are busy during the summer months and suffer a lull during the winter. Ski resorts, obviously, have the opposite seasonal pattern.

Businesses can sometimes use the knowledge of seasonal patterns to their advantage. In the days when iceboxes and coal furnaces were common, companies delivering ice and coal usually took advantage of the seasonal pattern of each. During the warm months, trucks were used to deliver ice. During the winter months, the same trucks were used to deliver coal. In the 1920s, driving in cold weather was not as common as it is today. Consequently, there was a seasonal variation in automobile sales in which a drop occurred during the fall and winter months and a sharp rise during the spring. Partly in an effort to reduce the severity of this seasonal fluctuation, the automobile industry developed the pattern of annual model changes, with styling emphasized to distinguish the current model from that of the previous year. The new models were introduced in the fall to bolster sales during the slack season. This practice, in turn, created another seasonal variation. The annual model changes required partial shutdowns in the automobile plants during each summer to retool assembly lines for the new models.

RANDOM FLUCTUATIONS

After accounting for the secular trend, cyclical variation, and seasonal variation, there generally remain in a time series some movements that resist analysis. These are called *random fluctuations* since they have no pattern or regularity. War might break out, causing a random fluctuation (shown in Figure 15-13). Unusual weather,

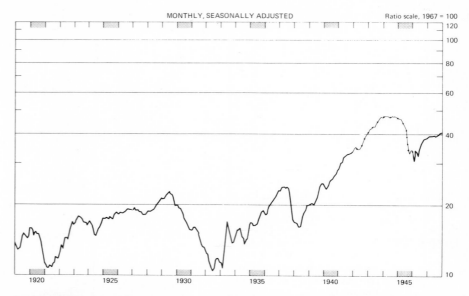

MONTHLY, SEASONALLY ADJUSTED   Ratio scale, 1967 = 100

FIGURE 15-13   Industrial production. Random fluctuation caused by World War II. (*Historical Chart Book*, Board of Governors of the Federal Reserve System, 1972, p. 86.)

a crisis in international relations, or government action of some kind might cause a fluctuation in a series. Random movements may in some cases be explained, but their prediction is difficult.

DECEPTIVE STATISTICS   Two somewhat old bits of humor are, approximately, "Figures don't lie, but liars do figure"; and Disraeli's famous statement, "There are lies, damned lies, and statistics." Statistics, like fire, are highly useful. But statistics, like fire in the hands of a pyromaniac, can be used in a very irresponsible way. A careless but innocent use of the statistical method sometimes results in a wrong conclusion being drawn from the data. More serious damage is done when statistics are manipulated to deliberately lead to a false or unwarranted conclusion. We are confronted with statistical material almost daily, in newspapers and magazines, television, daily conversation, and so on. We cannot all be expert statisticians, but we can be skeptical and we can be on our guard.

One thing that can help is to consider who prepared or published each bit of statistical information we are asked to accept. The source of the information might have a special interest to promote. Labor unions use statistics to prove that labor rates should be raised. Companies use statistics to prove that their profits are low or the industry is highly taxed. Democrats use statistics to prove that Republican policies are damaging the country. Republicans use statistics to prove that Democratic policies are damaging the country. The first thing one should do before accepting statistical "evidence" is to inquire who or what is behind the statistics. Frequently, it is useful to consider statistical presentations from opposing points of view on a controversial point. One of the benefits of a democracy is that it provides the possibility that people may be exposed to "both sides of each question" rather than having to swallow the "official" point of view, as in a dictatorship.

In addition to the misuse of correlation discussed earlier, some examples of misleading statistics are given below. No attempt has been made to distinguish between those that mislead intentionally and those that mislead unintentionally. In either case, the conclusions are unwarranted.

MISLEADING AVERAGE

A corporation was owned by 4,432 stockholders. Two stockholders owned 2,480,000 out of a total of 2,832,000 shares, the remaining stockholders owning 352,000 shares. The announcement was made that the average stockholding was 652 shares (2,832,000 ÷ 4,342). Another misuse of the average is illustrated in Figure 15-14.

BIAS IN SAMPLE

Suppose a questionnaire had been mailed to a large number of people and had contained the question, "Do you object to answering questionnaires?" Perhaps 78 percent of the questionnaires *returned* would be marked "no" to the question. Could one conclude that 78 percent of the population does not object to answering questionnaires? Hardly. Most of those who did object probably threw the questionnaires away. The only conclusion one could draw would be that those who do not mind answering questionnaires are most likely to answer questionnaires.

FIGURE 15-14 An average that does not represent.

"Average annual income here's about $12,000. There's fifty of us clears $2,000 and one fellow makes half a million."

SUSPICIOUS PRECISION

A newspaper a few years ago stated that the average American pays $825 a year in taxes. This included, so the report said, income taxes, state and local property and sales taxes, gasoline taxes, and all of the hidden taxes included in the prices of the things he buys. Much of this, obviously, is based on estimates, and the figure of $825 is not more accurate than "about $800." It merely looks more accurate.

SHIFTING BASES

During the Depression, it was reported that a company had given a group of workers a 25 percent increase in wages, which had restored a 25 percent cut made a few years before. But what had happened was that the wage dollar had been cut to $.75, representing a 25 percent cut. The 25 percent raise (25 percent of $.75, not 25 percent of $1) brought the workers' wages up to $.9375. The percentage in the second case was based on a smaller base, $.75, than in the first case, $1. It would have required a 33.3 percent increase to restore the 25 percent cut.

The above examples of the misuse of statistics are not intended to create distrust of all statistics. There are a great many sources of statistical information that are honest and dependable. Yet, we must be cautious even in using statistics that we are satisfied are unbiased. The *Monthly Letter* of the Royal Bank of Canada puts it this way: "It is not enough to have honest statistics placed in front of us; we need to be intelligent in our interpretation and use of them. Statistical methods cannot be relied upon to take the risk element out of enterprise, nor to create certainty of judgment, nor to predict future events. They are a base upon which to formulate sound business judgment: that is all."[6]

SUMMARY

The data businessmen rely on to make decisions are mostly in the form of numbers, but numbers alone carry little meaning. It is the function of statistics to assemble, arrange, consolidate, and present numbers in a form that can be used in making decisions.

It is often helpful to present a large number of items in the form of an average, in which one item represents the characteristics of a group. The three most common averages are: the mean, the median, and the mode. In some situations, one represents the group more accurately; in others, all three are equally representative.

An index number measures changes, usually over a period of time, in groups of data. The index number may be unweighted, giving each item in the group equal importance, or it may be weighted by giving some items more importance than others in determining the index number.

If two series of data are related, a change in one series might be used to predict changes in the other. The technique of correlation is used to measure the statistical relationship between series of items, but correlation does not prove that changes in one series are the cause of changes in the other. Another aid in prediction

[6] *The Royal Bank of Canada Monthly Letter*, vol. 37, no. 1, p. 4, Jan., 1956.

is the time series, which is the classification and graphical presentation of data on the basis of time.

An important part of statistics is the preparation of charts, diagrams, and graphs, so that statistical data can be presented in such a manner that they can be quickly and easily understood. Statistics thus aids greatly in increasing understanding, but it can also be used to mislead. In preparing statistics to be read by others, and in reading statistics prepared by others, one should be cautious.

QUESTIONS FOR REVIEW

1   If statistics cannot tell an insurance company when a specific house will burn down, what good are statistics to the insurance company?
2   What are the characteristics of a good statistical table?
3   For what types of statistical data is the line chart a useful method of presentation? A pie chart? A statistical map?
4   How does a bar chart differ from an area diagram? For what types of presentation is each useful?
5   Under what circumstances would a mailed questionnaire be a better means of gathering information than using interviews? Under what circumstances would interviews be preferable?
6   What are some of the dangers in using random sampling in gathering information for statistical analysis?
7   Distinguish among the arithmetic mean, the median, and the mode.
8   How does a ratio simplify the comparison between two or more groups of statistical data?
9   What is an index number? How does it help in measuring change over a period of time?
10   What advantage is there in using a weighted rather than an unweighted index?
11   If two statistical series show a high degree of correlation, how does a person tell which is cause and which is effect?
12   Most time series for business data in the United States show a positive trend. Why?
13   What is the distinction between cyclical variation and seasonal variation?
14   What is a business cycle? Why is it difficult to measure in terms of timing of change and extent of movement?
15   How can statistical data be used in a way that misinforms?

SELECTED READINGS

Huff, Darrell: *How to Lie with Statistics*, W. W. Norton & Company, Inc., New York, 1954.
Kazmeier, Leonard J.: *Statistical Analysis for Business and Economics*, McGraw-Hill Book Company, New York, 1973.
Leabo, Dick A.: *Basic Statistics*, 4th ed., Richard D. Irwin, Inc., Homewood, Ill., 1972.
Stockton, John R., and Charles T. Clark: *Introduction to Business and Economic Statistics*, 4th ed., South-Western Publishing Company, Cincinnati, 1971.

Name   Section   Date

COMPLETION SENTENCES

1 Statistical analysis is concerned not with the individual but with

_____ .

2 A statistical _____ presents data in organized columns

and rows.

3 In a line chart the _____ measurement is often in terms

of time and the _____ measurement in terms of

quantities.

4 In a line chart, if the actual amount of change is less important than showing

the rate of change, a _____ chart is used.

5 A pie chart is a _____ divided into

_____ .

6 An area diagram compares different quantities by means of

_____ .

7 The most frequently used methods of gathering statistical data are

_____ , _____ and

_____ .

8 The most commonly used average is the _____ .

9 The average called the _____ has the same number of

units above it as below it in an array of numbers.

10 The _____ is the value in a series that occurs most often.

11 A _____ compares one number with another in the

form of a fraction or percentage.

12 An index number measures changes in data over a period of time compared

to a _____ .

13 By selecting different _____ an index number can be

made to look high or low.

14 If the dots on a scatter diagram are distributed in a random manner, there is

probably no _____ of the two series.

15 A wavelike pattern in a time series is called a _____ .

TRUE OR FALSE STATEMENTS

1 Statistics is a necessary tool of analysis in every phase of life.

2 Statisticians do not study individuals, but groups.

Name   Section   Date

3 A line chart presents measurements by a series of parallel lines of varying lengths.

4 In a bar chart the amounts are represented by the length and width of the bars.

5 An area diagram is a map of a particular region or regions.

6 The purpose of pictographs is to attract the eye to the statistical presentation.

7 To gather information from the general public for statistical use, the telephone can be used effectively only where a few questions are asked.

8 Statisticians draw conclusions based on samples; most other persons do not.

9 A statistical universe is the whole group from which a sample is drawn.

10 The least commonly used average is the arithmetic mean.

11 A statistical survey may show the average income in a community to be $12,056, but with nobody having an income of $12,056.

12 No single type of average is best for all purposes.

13 The median divides the array equally, with the same number of units above as below.

14 The mode is the value in a series that occurs most often.

15 The purpose of a ratio is to simplify comparison.

16 A statistical index number identifies the location of a bit of statistical information.

17 If the number of items to be compared is small, expressing the relationship of the items by a ratio may mislead.

18 If a scatter diagram shows the points falling on a straight line, the correlation is perfect.

19 A high degree of correlation shows that a close relationship exists between two pairs of data.

20 A time series is the classification of data on the basis of time.

EXERCISES

1 Select from a magazine or other nontext source an example of each of the types of statistical presentation discussed in the text, such as line chart, pie chart, times series, arithmetic mean, and index number. For each example, determine whether the material could be presented in any better way, and whether any distortions or unwarranted conclusions are implied by the presentation.

2 The Bureau of Labor Statistics of the United States Department of Labor publishes monthly an index of consumer prices, released in pamphlet form to libraries, newspapers, professors of economics and business subjects, and others. The index lists the price in cents of a long group of food items, representing the average price in the cities of the United States for these items. Select 10 items you consider to be representative and price these items in several grocery stores in your neighborhood. Express the price of each item as a percentage of the price in the Bureau of Labor Statistics release and then average the percentages. Does this indicate that food prices are higher in your community than in the average city of the United States? Is the comparison a fair one in your opinion? Why or why not?

3 Below is the stock of gold held by the Treasury of the United States at the end of each year listed. For each year the total liabilities of the United States owed to foreign nationals is also shown. Make a scatter diagram on graph paper with the gold stock on the vertical axis and liabilities to foreigners on the horizontal axis. By visual inspection draw a line of regression through the dots you have put on the graph. Does there appear to be a correlation? Is it a high degree of correlation or not, or does there appear to be a lack of correlation? What conclusions, if any, can you draw?

Year	U.S. Treasury Gold Stock (millions)	Total United States Liabilities Held by Foreigners (millions)
1959	$19,456	$10,120
1960	17,767	11,088
1961	16,889	11,930
1962	16,978	12,914
1963	15,513	14,425
1964	15,388	15,786
1965	13,733	15,826
1966	13,159	14,896
1967	11,982	18,194
1968	10,468	17,340
1969	10,367	15,998
1970	10,732	23,775
1971	10,132	50,650
1972	10,410	60,977

Name   Section   Date

CHAPTER
16 RESEARCH AND FORECASTING

There are two aspects of business to which businessmen attach more and more importance: research and forecasting. Research attempts to get as much information as possible to make improvements in business methods. Forecasting attempts to determine the events of the future and to make business decisions on that basis. This chapter treats both.

Each of us does research. Every attempt to satisfy curiosity is an exercise in research. The research may be conducted on a scientific basis, it may involve millions of dollars, and it may run for many years before an answer to a problem is found. On the other hand, a person may be curious about the taste of tea and coffee mixed together or the taste of a cigarette lit at the filter end. In both instances, a single test will probably yield a conclusive answer.

Both instances could also be considered research, although at a simple level. It is a common mistake of students to assume that research is the exclusive function of scientists. Research is as useful in business as it is in the scientific laboratory. Many of the same techniques used by scientists in the laboratory are used by businessmen in seeking answers to business problems. This is why the discussion of the scientific method was included in the chapter. It is essential that you understand what is meant by scientific method and how it is applied to research. You should also attempt to cultivate a scientific frame of mind; in other words, you should attempt to solve problems, especially business problems, by applying the scientific method wherever possible.

The expenditure of funds for research by business has increased since World War II. Business is coming to appreciate research as an essential tool of management. Not only is research in business becoming more extensive, it is also becoming more complex. It is not as necessary that you as a student understand the complexities of business research as it is for you to understand that it is becoming more complex. In the future, the development of operations research will probably be given increasing importance in business management. Again, it is not necessary that you understand the mechanics of operations research, but it is necessary that you understand how operations research aids in management decisions.

Students who have found science courses in high school easy and stimulating will find it easier to understand the purposes of this chapter. Those who found science courses difficult will have to read this chapter with particular care and, given time, will have to supplement their study with some of the readings at the end of the chapter.

From the 1940s to the present, research has enjoyed a level of respect it has rarely enjoyed in the past. In industry, government, and universities the amount of research done is considered one of the measures of excellence. The emphasis on research in the last few decades is a recognition of the rapidity of change of modern life, a characteristic that was emphasized in Chapter 1.

What is *research*? It is careful, systematic investigation, undertaken for the purpose of adding to human knowledge. What does it include? Admittedly it covers a wide range of activities, from laboratory experiments to asking questions of customers in a store. It includes investigating the unknown as well as applying the known. The word has been applied to the activities of scientists and to the preparation of a term paper by a college student. It has been applied so often to what might be called "low-level investigation" that research is sometimes defined as follows: "When you copy from one book, it is plagiarism; when you copy from two books, it is research."

Because research means different things to different people, measure of the extent of research activity depends on arbitrary classification. Regardless of how it is measured, however, the amount of money spent on it has grown rapidly. We depend on research for changes in old industries, such as the shift in railroading from coal to diesel-electric locomotives. We also depend on research to create new industries. For example, from 1950 to the 1970s, industries grew from the following research developments:

Antibiotics	Microscopic printed circuits
Jet aircraft engines	Transistors
Radar	Television
Helicopter	Tape recording
Atomic energy	Synthetic hormones
Electronic computers	Long-distance rockets
Lasers	Ocean shipment of liquified gas

What new industries will develop from current research? Prediction is close to guesswork in this area. However, a group of scientists of the Rand Corporation, a research company employed by the Department of Defense and other clients, has compiled a list of predictions for the future (see Figure 16-1). Some of the predicted scientific breakthroughs may be the genesis of new industries.

THE NATURE OF RESEARCH   Research may be divided into two categories: *pure* and *applied*. Both use a process called the *scientific method*, the steps of which are described below.

	One-fourth thought by this date	One half by this date	Three-fourths by this date
Economical desalination of sea water	1964	1970	1980
Ultralight synthetic construction materials	1970	1971	1978
Automated language translators	1968	1972	1976
New organs through transplanting or prosthesis	1968	1972	1982
Reliable weather forecasts	1972	1975	1988
Wide-access central data storage facility	1971	1979-80	1991
Reformation of physical theory	1975	1980	1993
Implanted plastic or electronic organs	1975	1982	1988
Popular use of personality control drugs	1980	1983	2000
Lasers in x ray and gamma ray spectrum region	1978	1985	1989
Controlled thermonuclear power	1980	1986-87	2000
Creation of primitive form of artificial life	1979	1989	2000
Economical ocean-floor mining (other than off-shore drilling)	1980	1989	2000
Limited weather control	1987	1990	2000
Commercial production of synthetic protein for food	1985	1990	2003
Greatly improved physical or chemical therapy for psychotics	1983	1992	2017
General immunization against bacterial and viral diseases	1983	1994	2000
Chemical control over some hereditary defects	1990	2000	2010
Producing 20 percent of the world's food by ocean farming	2000-	2000	2017
Growth of new organs and limbs through biochemical stimulation	1995	2007	2040
Using drugs to raise intelligence level	1984	2012	2050
Direct electromechanical interaction between man's brain and computer	1990	2020	3000 +
Extending life span fifty years by chemical control of aging	1995	2050	2070
Breeding intelligent animals for low-grade labor	2020	2040	3000 +
Two-way communication with extraterrestrials	2000	2075	3000 +
Commercial manufacture of chemical elements from subatomic building blocks	2007	2100	3000 +
Control of gravity	2035	2050	3000 +
Direct information recording on brain	1997	2600	3000 +
Long-duration coma for time travel	2006	3000 +	3000 +
Use of telepathy and ESP in communications	2040	3000 +	3000 +

FIGURE 16-1   Rand Scientists peer into the future. 1963 estimates of when scientific breakthrough would be achieved. (*Business Week*, Mar. 14, 1970, p. 130.)

THE SCIENTIFIC
METHOD

The scientific method is simply a means of bringing order and system into the solution of a problem. It is a form of mental discipline, seeking to eliminate emotion and bias in arriving at decisions, and is thus useful not only to scientists but to businessmen, students, and everybody else. If people used the scientific method more, they would make fewer mistakes in judgment.

The scientific method can be divided into four steps, as follows: *observation*, *explanation* or *hypothesis*, *prediction*, and *testing*. To understand how the scientific method can be used in the solution of a simple problem, we will apply it to a situation in baseball.

1 *Observation:*   A batting slump.
2 *Explanation:*   The batter is standing too far from the plate.
3 *Prediction:*   The batter will make more hits if he stands closer to the plate.
4 *Testing:*   The batter stands closer to the plate, and his batting average improves.

If the batter's average does not improve, the explanation is apparently incorrect. It is then necessary to return to the second step to suggest another hypothesis for testing. A baseball player, of course, would not recognize, and probably not admit, using such formal steps to treat a batting slump. But whether it is consciously or unconsciously used, the scientific method is useful in decision making. Because of its importance, a further discussion of the steps is of value.

Observation

Observation is the essential foundation for scientific inquiry, since our awareness of the universe is based on the wide variety of experience in our daily lives. Most of us probably feel that "normal" experience is not promising material for investigation, but a person with a curious and probing mind would very likely disagree. The average man would overlook a line of ants on a garden path. A man with intense curiosity would see the possible existence of highly developed organization. A falling apple is supposed to have inspired Isaac Newton to investigate the concept of gravity, but, apparently, falling apples failed to inspire people before him. Observation of things and happenings around us is undoubtedly an important starting point for the scientific method in business life. The "keen observer" is a valuable person in industry.

In the examples above, the observer is passive, not affecting or controlling the subject matter observed. Frequently, however, observations are carefully planned and controlled. This is particularly true in the laboratory, or where experiments, questionnaires, interviews, and similar techniques are used to gather data. Information can often be gotten much more quickly and more reliably when the observations are controlled than when they result from unregulated experience. For example, we can learn about the resistance of paper sacks to breaking through experience in overloading the bags, but such observations would be costly in terms of the damaged contents from torn bags. Securing observations through controlled experiments in a testing laboratory would be far quicker and less costly.

After the observations have been made or the data gathered, the observer suggests one or more hypotheses. Some might be eliminated from further consideration almost immediately because of some obvious weakness. The ones remaining would be tested. Even if only one hypothesis appeared to explain the observations, it would be necessary to test it. If the hypothesis did not survive the test, it would indicate that the researcher would have to seek a better explanation.

Explanation or Hypothesis

If the hypothesis is of any value, it must be usable for prediction. The prediction should be stated in terms that can be tested. If the prediction is not fulfilled, the hypothesis is incorrect. If the prediction can be stated in terms of quantity, so much the better, since quantity can easily be measured. For example, let us return to the baseball illustration. The hypothesis explaining the batting slump was that the batter stood too far from the plate. The prediction was that standing closer to the plate would improve the batting average. Fortunately, batting averages can be measured in terms of numbers. If the numbers do not increase, the prediction is not fulfilled, and the hypothesis must be faulty.

Prediction

Testing may be simple, difficult, or impossible. That there is life after death is impossible to test scientifically. That there are fish at the bottom of the deepest oceans is difficult to test, but it has been done. That a coin tossed 1,000 times will fall heads up about 500 times is easy to test. Testing procedures in business research frequently require specialized knowledge. Whether the test is simple or complex, however, care must be taken to ensure that it is an adequate test of the hypothesis.

Testing

Pure research involves exploring the frontiers of knowledge. It is an adventure unlikely to have any immediate applicability. Scientists engage in it to satisfy their curiosity, exploring the unknown for the same reason that Peary sought the North Pole and others seek the peaks of high mountains.

PURE RESEARCH

What good is pure research? If scientists engaged only in investigations that had immediate commercial value, we would be denied the benefit of many scientific achievements we now enjoy. Electricity was once a curiosity that intrigued philosophers, and was hardly worth the time of practical men. The power of steam was studied centuries before it was used in a steam engine. The investigations by Leonardo da Vinci and the Montgolfier brothers of the possibilities of human flight were made long before air transportation was born. Pure research is the foundation on which applied research is built. The dream must precede the reality: The idea must precede the application.

Until recently, however, the findings of pure science lay dormant for decades or centuries before any practical use was found for them. As a result, the practical researcher and the pure researcher did not appreciate their mutual dependence.

Industry did little to support pure research, which was left largely to scientists in universities. Research by business was almost entirely applied research. Each held the other in mild disdain. As *Business Week* puts it, "College researchers continue to think of all industrial research as auto styling or as the process of standing on a street corner counting passers-by to check on the location of a new retail outlet. Industry, on the other hand, continues to think of college research as an elderly professor classifying tropical flies."[1]

A dramatic change in attitude occurred after the Second World War and as a result of the manned moon flights. Albert Einstein's concept of tremendous energy locked in an atom had been translated into practical use by the explosion of the first atomic bomb. Since then, the findings of pure research have been put to practical use at a rapid rate. As a result of grants by the federal government, college professors have engaged in applied as well as pure research. "At the same time, industry —particularly the big chemical, rubber, electrical, and aviation companies—began to get into pure research because development of new products had accelerated to the point where production was pushing against the frontiers of knowledge."[2]

APPLIED RESEARCH

Applied research is adapting existing knowledge to a practical purpose. Designing engines to get more power from gasoline, experimenting with steel alloys to improve the hardness of steel, and striving to discover a better pesticide are examples of applied research. The industrial researcher spends most of his time studying this type of problem. Typically a large industrial corporation will allocate about 80 percent of its research spending to applied research. The importance of applied research in keeping a company competitive is considerable. The attitude of a giant chemical company (E. I. du Pont de Nemours) toward applied research is indicated in this comment: "If anybody can make 4 or 5 percent [producing industrial chemicals in bulk], Du Pont can do much better by building huge plants and using its research to improve production processes—even in commodity chemicals you can make research pay off."[3]

RESEARCH METHODS

The methods used in research depend on the complexity of the problem, the amount of time and money available, and the information existing on the problem. While there is wide variation in techniques and details, there are certain steps common to all business research. These steps are an adaptation of the basic scientific method to business problems. For purposes of illustration, the steps in research in marketing will be discussed as follows:

> Outline of the problem.
> What information is already available?

---

[1] "The New World of Business," a special report, *Business Week*, May 28, 1955.
[2] *Ibid.*
[3] *Fortune* Magazine, January 1973, p. 72.

Collection of the data.

Organization and tabulation.

Interpretation.

Offhand, it might appear unnecessary to outline the problem to be studied. The problem is known, is it not, or else no research would be suggested? However, the problem may be only vaguely known. Outlining may clarify the problem. Furthermore, the persons conducting the research must understand exactly what is being sought so that the investigation will be pointed toward the right goal. The problem should be stated in terms such as the following: What is the best color scheme to use on a toothpaste tube? What proportion of customers would prefer a larger-size package than is now available? How much increase in sales could be expected from a 20-cent reduction in price?

OUTLINE OF THE PROBLEM

Research is undertaken by many agencies. Therefore, the answer to a problem might be already available, so it is wise to check sources of information before proceeding with research. This is particularly true in the field of marketing research. Even if the complete answer to a problem is not available, a partial answer may be. Examining reports of previous research may save a company money by permitting it to limit the scope of new research to be undertaken.

At this point in the procedure, a hypothesis may be stated. Perhaps several hypotheses might be suggested. For example, the problem of selecting a color scheme for a toothpaste tube might be narrowed by reviewing the results of previous investigations indicating that black-and-white packages appear dull, that certain color combinations are unattractive, and that other color combinations are too similar to competitors' packages. In this case, each hypothesis would be a particular color scheme. Preliminary investigations might eliminate all but three of the hypotheses. The remaining hypotheses, then, would be tested by some type of market research.

WHAT INFORMATION IS ALREADY AVAILABLE?

In collecting data, there are several considerations that can be summarized in the following way:

COLLECTION OF THE DATA

Where can the data be secured? From customers, employees, suppliers, the public?

In what way will the investigation be conducted? By interview, questionnaires, or some other means? Should a sample be taken? How should the sample be taken?

How long will the data collection period last? For some types of research, the period should be as short as possible. This would be true in taking a census, for example. In other cases, it might be preferable to spread the collection of data over a period of a year, or possibly to collect data at intervals during the year.

ORGANIZATION AND
TABULATION

Organization is essential to understanding the data. The information should be presented in a table, chart, graph, or some other form that facilitates interpretation. If a questionnaire is used in collecting data, the returns should be edited. Obvious errors and inconsistencies should be eliminated. Frequently, the researcher can transfer the data to punched cards for tabulating by machine, thus speeding up the work considerably and reducing the possibility of errors in computation.

INTERPRETATION

After the data have been tabulated, analysts determine the significance of the results. This requires judgment, since any preconceived notions about the results must be avoided in making evaluations of the data. This is particularly important since interpretation of the data will influence managerial decisions. If the research project was undertaken by the research division of the company for another division of the company, a written report is, in most cases, essential. Obviously, the report should include a statement of the purpose of the research, how it was conducted, and the results. The report might include recommendations for company action, if this is requested by the executives initiating the research.

**KINDS OF BUSINESS
RESEARCH**

We can never satisfy our need for knowledge. In every phase of business activity, our information is incomplete, and research therefore yields useful information. The chief limit to the expansion of research is time and money. Executives should choose with care the possible projects to be studied so that those judged to be more important will be given priority. In order to allocate the research dollars judiciously, it is wise to classify the areas of business research. These classifications will differ from one company to another and from one industry to another. For purposes of illustration, some of the more common categories of business research are: marketing research, product research, human relations research, and operations research.

MARKETING
RESEARCH

Marketing research is useful in answering questions such as the following:

What do customers think about company products?
What is the extent of demand for a new product?
Do customers like the present package?
What is the most profitable price for each of the products sold?
Will premiums help increase sales?
Is magazine advertising better than television advertising for the company's products?

Marketing research is concerned with selling. The purpose of the research is to gain information that will improve the sales position of the company. Since successful selling requires knowledge of the customer, marketing research is directly or indirectly aimed at the customer.

If a company is in a highly competitive industry, marketing research is vital. The attitudes and preferences of customers determine which companies shall survive and which shall not. Consumer attitudes can change, sometimes suddenly; consumer preferences can be influenced by advertising, by styling, or by selling techniques as well as by price and quality. To be successful, a company must know the consumer of its products or services, and marketing research provides this information.

PRODUCT RESEARCH

Products that cannot be sold do not bring profits. The research laboratories devoted to creating new products or improving old ones have as their reason for existence the goal of satisfying the customer better. Product research is directed toward the nature of products and their uses, so that they may be better adapted to customer demand. It involves studying both the customer and the product.

Product research can be aimed at the improvement of existing products or toward the development of new ones. A company can never assume that a popular product will remain popular. Competitors will strive to improve their products, and a company that wishes to remain in competition must do so too. In manufacturing industries, this is particularly true. Products such as automobiles, typewriters, cameras, and locomotives, to name a few, are continually improved. In young industries, the rate of improvement is sometimes staggering, as in the development of transistors to replace vacuum tubes and other electronic components. Where change in an industry is rapid, success in product research may mean spectacular profits and failure may mean a quick end to company existence.

The development of new products is frequently costly; however, it is necessary in an economy of rapid change such as that of the United States. To assume that there will always be a demand for a company's product as long as it is continually improved is to ignore the lessons of history. Not only do products become obsolete, whole industries become obsolete or nearly so. Many companies making carriages went out of business because their managers did not foresee the obsolescence of their product. Research on new products is valuable, in other words, for defensive reasons.

Research on new products is undertaken not only to defend a company's sales position, but with the hope of expanding the market for a company's products. New products that meet consumer acceptance are sometimes fantastically profitable. One example is the pocket-sized calculator introduced in the early 1970s.

RESEARCH ON HUMAN RELATIONS

From the standpoint of company management, labor is an important element in the cost of production, often the most important. Labor must be conserved to avoid wastage. Equally important, a company's labor policies must include human considerations. Our knowledge of human relations and motivation is very imperfect.

We know only imperfectly what induces maximum effort on the part of employees and executives. We know only imperfectly what makes people think the way they do and act the way they do. Our knowledge of phobias, biases, and other influences on behavior is far from complete. To learn more about human nature and how such knowledge can be used in business, research in human relations is undertaken. The manager calls on specialists in personnel relations, psychology, and sociology in an effort to get answers.

For example, what should be the policy of a company president in seeing subordinates? Should it be an open-door policy, encouraging other employees to consult with him at any time? Or should it be a policy of requiring all persons to make an appointment with his secretary? What will be the effect of an open-door policy on the amount of work the president can get done? What will be the effect of a closed-door policy on company morale? Should the president and other executives mingle freely with rank-and-file employees in the company cafeteria, or should there be a separate executive dining room? So much of the art of management has to do with the relations between human beings that any light shed by research in this area is very valuable.

OPERATIONS RESEARCH

Although the subject matter is very old, the name "operations research" and the techniques associated with it are new. This type of research was developed during World War II, first by Great Britain and later by the United States. As a science, it was born of the military operations of the government and was then adopted by industry in the 1950s.

What is operations research? Basically, it is an effort to utilize all the forces operating in a business toward a common goal, to coordinate the operations of various departments, and to allocate resources most efficiently to achieve the common goal. In the military area, for example, operations research attempts to locate the best position for radar installations and determines the extent of repeated bombing of energy positions for maximum military effect. In the industrial area, operations research attempts to reconcile the conflicting aims of different departments. The production department wants to expand production and cut costs, the marketing department wants to expand sales, and the personnel department wants to hire the best workers and keep them in the company. Operations research attempts to give management a scientific basis for solving problems involving different departments or areas of action.

How large should the inventory of a company be? Such a decision affects production, marketing, personnel relations, storage, delivery, and other aspects of the business. Operations research seeks to provide the answer by studying the effect of increasing or decreasing inventory on the various activities of the company. It considers all of the variables that might influence a particular decision. Because of the breadth and complexity of the subject matter and because the problems are treated scientifically, the computations involved are of a high order. Electronic computers are a necessity in this type of research.

Forecasting is an attempt to determine the future by careful evaluation of present knowledge. Decisions affecting the future are made daily by businessmen. It is important therefore that they know as much about the future as possible. For decisions involving the immediate future, such as the following day or the following week, the business manager usually knows enough to decide without formal forecasts. But when the more distant future is involved in making decisions, the manager can benefit from well-prepared forecasts.

In simple terms, a forecast is a statement of expected future conditions. It can be long-range, estimating into the twenty-first century, or short-range, estimating for the next few months or the next year. Both types of forecasts are useful to business planning, since business, to be successful, must make long-range as well as short-range plans. To be specific, forecasts can help in the following ways:

1 *In making decisions that involve budgeting:* Suppose a company needs a certain level of sales to operate profitably, but future estimates of sales do not indicate that the required volume will be reached. Knowing this, steps can be taken to raise sales.
2 *In controlling inventories:* A forecast can help in determining the most efficient level of inventories. If the forecast indicates a rising market, a higher level of inventory can be maintained. If a falling market is forecast, steps can be taken in advance to keep inventories low.
3 *In improving production control:* Forecasting helps to improve scheduling of production. This in turn improves efficiency in the use of equipment, prevents unnecessary overtime work, improves employee morale, and reduces expensive starts and stops in production.
4 *In planning expansion:* Heavy investment in expanded capacity is foolish to meet a short-term increase in sales. Forecasting will help in gauging whether an increase in demand is temporary or long-run.
5 *In maintaining effective financial control:* If interest rates are forecast to be lower in the future, management will postpone borrowing or will borrow on a short-term basis. If interest rates are forecast to be higher in the future, long-term borrowing may be advisable before the rates rise.

THE NATURE OF FORECASTING

THE TECHNIQUES OF FORECASTING

The technique of forecasting selected will depend on the purposes for which the forecast is to be used. We cannot discuss all of the techniques in use in this field. For illustration, however, three methods will be briefly discussed: *trend analysis*, *correlation*, and the *composite estimate*.

TREND ANALYSIS

The assumption on which trend analysis is based is that the activity being forecast changes at a regular rate. If the change has been steady in the past, there is reasonable expectation that it will remain steady in the future. The data for monthly sales, for example, can be plotted on a graph, as is done in Figure 16-2. A *trend line* is then fitted. This can be done by using a transparent ruler to fit the trend line visually. For many cases, this would be accurate enough, and it is certainly the easiest method. The trend line can be fitted mathematically if greater accuracy

Sales, in millions of dollars

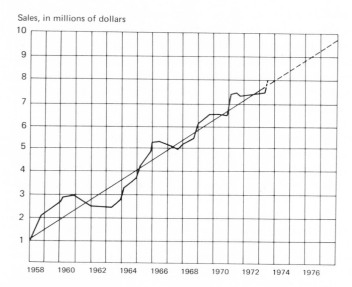

FIGURE 16-2   Trend line for 1958–1974, with trend projected through 1978.

is desired. While most trend lines are straight lines, a curved trend is more appropriate in some instances. Even when the trend line is fitted mathematically, the statistician must decide whether to fit a straight or a curved line. If he decides on a curved line, he must use judgment in selecting the type of curve. After the trend line is fitted, it is extended into the future. This action is called *extrapolation*. A statistician may extrapolate as far into the future as he desires, but the more distant he projects a trend, the less likely it is to prove accurate. The unpredictable occurs and, because it is unpredictable, throws the forecast off. In his second inaugural speech in 1865, Abraham Lincoln predicted a population for the United States in 1930 of 251,689,914. This was far in excess of the number actually achieved. The prediction was inaccurate because the rate of growth since 1900 has been less than the rate of growth from 1790 to 1860, which furnished the basis for Lincoln's prediction. To meet this problem, a long-term prediction will sometimes be made in the form of maximum, minimum, and moderate expectation, as has been done in Figure 16-3.

CORRELATION   If one type of activity can be related to another, the change in one can be used to predict the change in the other. The owner of a grocery store sees a large housing development or apartment building under construction in his vicinity. He expects to get a larger number of customers. He might even decide to enlarge his store or to modernize it. He is correlating his future sales with the population growth expected in his area, a reasonable assumption.

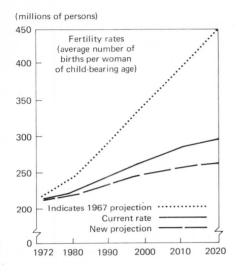

(millions of persons)

Fertility rates
(average number of
births per woman
of child-bearing age)

Indicates 1967 projection ···············
Current rate ——————
New projection — — — —

1972 1980   1990   2000   2010   2020

FIGURE 16-3 Prediction of United States
population 1972 to 2020.
(*The National Observer*, Dec.
30, 1972, p. 2. *Source:* U.S.
Bureau of the Census.)

For the purpose of forecasting, it is most useful if the activity being predicted
can be correlated in advance with another activity that changes. For example, a
building permit must be secured by a contractor from the city government before
beginning construction of a house, factory, or other building. An increase in the
number and value of building permits issued would indicate a later increase in the
demand for house paint, for instance. Building permits would be called a *leading
indicator* because changes in building permits could be used to forecast changes in
business activity associated with home construction, appliance sales, and so on.

If the leading indicator leads at a regular interval, the forecast can be much
more accurate than if the leading indicator leads with a variable lapse in time. The
statistician of a lumber yard might discover that data of past sales of lumber were
closely related, allowing for a 3-months' lag, to the value of building contracts.
For every 10 percent increase in the value of building contracts there was a 7
percent increase in the lumber sales of the firm, after 3 months. In such a case, the
owner of the lumber yard would be in the fortunate position of having a simple
means of forecasting his sales as far as 3 months ahead. For longer projections,
there might be no dependable leading indicator, and other means of forecasting
than correlation might have to be used.

In using correlation, caution should be exercised. A relationship that existed
in the past might not continue to exist in the future. If the relationship continues
to exist, the leading indicator might widen or narrow the time lapse. Periods of
economic stress, unusual weather conditions, labor-management difficulties, and
international complications might upset the normal relationship between series.

COMPOSITE ESTIMATE

In sales forecasting, the composite estimate is often used. The salesmen or branch managers are asked to predict sales in their respective areas. These predictions are totaled to predict the sales for the entire company. This method has the virtue of being simple and easy to understand. The assumption on which it is based is that the persons closest to the customers know best the probable future actions of the customers. Sometimes this method of forecasting is used as a check on the forecasts made by other methods.

ECONOMIC FORECASTS

Economic forecasts are predictions of general business activity. They can be prepared for a state, a region, a nation, or the world. Many state governments use the bureau of business research at the state university to compile the data on which economic forecasts for the state are prepared. Each of the twelve Federal Reserve Banks compiles statistics on which regional forecasts can be made. The most widely used forecasts are the national forecasts made by using the vast array of statistical information gathered by the Bureau of the Census and other federal agencies.

The most important economic series is the **gross national product**, commonly referred to as **GNP**. This measures the value of all goods and services produced in the United States in a year. The United States Department of Commerce publishes the most widely used estimate of GNP, which includes all types of products and services for which a dollar value can be given. Services for which a price cannot dependably be assigned, such as a housewife's services or the work a man does in his garden, are not included. Figure 16-4 shows the changes in GNP over a 40-year period.

Because economic forecasts concern business in general rather than a particular industry, they are of primary interest to those concerned with government economic policy. They are necessary in making government tax and expenditure plans, and they influence the direction of legislation in Congress and the state capitals. However, economic forecasts are also very useful to businessmen. An increase or decrease in GNP during the coming year affects the sales, employment, and profit prospects of each business, large and small. Therefore, forecasts of GNP for future months or years enter strongly into the planning of each company. Economic forecasts for local areas similarly influence the planning of businesses in those areas.

SALES FORECASTING

The American Marketing Association defines a sales forecast as: "An estimate of dollars or unit sales for a specified future period under a proposed marketing plan or program." The benefits to effective budgeting and business planning of preparing a sales forecast are many. A sales forecast helps in financial planning, production scheduling, and inventory control and in establishing sales quotas for salesmen. Sales forecasts may be general or specific. Specific forecasts are more useful in planning than are general forecasts, since a specific forecast might predict sales for each item manufactured, for each sales district, and for each month of the coming year.

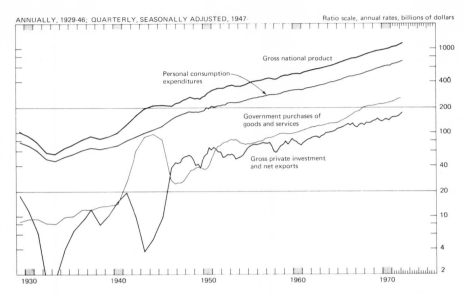

ANNUALLY, 1929-46; QUARTERLY, SEASONALLY ADJUSTED, 1947-   Ratio scale, annual rates, billions of dollars

FIGURE 16-4 Gross national product, 1929–1972, and related series. (*Historical Chart Book*, Board of Governors of the Federal Reserve System, 1972, p. 73.)

Methods of forecasting were discussed earlier in this chapter. These and other methods are used in preparing sales forecasts. Large companies prepare sales forecasts with the highest degree of scientific skill available. Small companies frequently make sales forecasts by guesswork or by using simple techniques. Because production, purchasing, employment, and other activities of business are dependent on sales, the forecast of sales should be prepared with as great a degree of accuracy as possible. The steps used in preparing a sales forecast depend on the forecaster and the demands of his employer; nevertheless, there are certain procedures used in the preparation of most sales forecasts, and these are summarized in the following steps.

The first step is to prepare internal records. They should be broken down by months, customers, sizes, uses, territories, or any other characteristics important to a particular business. All sales figures should be in dollars; this is the common denominator that will make them comparable to external statistics. In developing figures for the first time, one should go as far back as practicable. About 10 to 15 years is a safe period, since it will include several business "swings" in the national economy.

PREPARING THE
INTERNAL FIGURES

The second step is to relate company sales to the total sales of the industry, and thus establish the share of the market the company can expect. To do this, one needs industry statistics to which company figures can be compared.

DETERMINING THE
SHARE OF THE
MARKET

RELATE
INDUSTRIAL SALES

The third step is to relate industry sales to national statistics, which reflect the influences of the national economy on future sales of the industry. Suppose a product is a component used in television sets. A logical starting point would be to analyze future consumer plans for joining cable TV. How are these plans tied to disposable income (money left to spend after taxes)? What will the effect of the national economy be on disposable income? In this way the forecast is not tied just to history, but also to basic causes that are changing our day-to-day economy.

The industry statistics and the national statistics used should have the following characteristics:

> Have been published for years.
>
> Be kept up-to-date and readily available. Some figures may generally be more accurate but are not available frequently enough to be useful.
>
> Be available in useful form. Some statistics require a great deal of work before they can be used.
>
> Be collected by a reliable, nonbiased source.
>
> Be collected by a stable source. Chances should be good that these statistics will continue to be collected and published in the future. Having to convert to a new source can cause a great deal of extra work and uncertainty.

The figures that best fit the above standards are issued by the federal government. The next best are issued by trade organizations, trade papers and magazines, and financial houses.

Company sales should be plotted against industry sales. If sales depart from the pattern formed by the past 3 to 5 years' operations, company executives should try to determine what caused their company to get a larger or smaller share of the total market.

Sometimes it is impossible to find accurate statistics on a particular industry's sales. If this is true, one of the following techniques may be used to get a good approximation: (1) study consumer surveys made by newspapers and trade magazines showing relative positions held by various brands of firms in a particular area; (2) run a sample survey to find out a firm's position in the industry; (3) canvass the firm's salesmen and main accounts as to the total sales of the product being investigated; (4) determine the total from studies showing the consumption per capita and extend this over the entire market.

INTERPRETING
THE FIGURES

The last step is interpreting the figures that have been compiled. The work done to this point can lead to unsound decisions if proper weight is not given to the facts that:

> Prices may change; therefore, a prediction of increased dollar volume could mean an actual decrease in number of units sold. Of course, the opposite holds true for a prediction of a decrease in dollar sales. Some calculations must be made of what prices will be in the future.

Demand may change; a product popular one year may be forgotten the next.

Judgment may be faulty; therefore, the soundness of the forecast should be tested against opinions of salesmen, major accounts, and articles in trade papers and business publications.

Economic conditions may change; therefore, the forecaster must continually keep up to date on what is happening to the economic health of the nation.

SUMMARY

The goal of research is discovery. In business, research is directed toward adding to knowledge about business matters; it may lead to new knowledge, or it may lead to the new application of existing knowledge.

Orderly research uses the scientific method. The order of steps is observation, explanation or hypothesis, prediction, and testing. Each of these steps may be distinct in a complex research study or may be difficult to distinguish in a simple research problem.

Research can in general be classified into two broad categories: pure and applied. Pure research is probing into the unknown. Applied research is devoted to seeking the answer to immediate problems and to giving practical applications to the findings of pure research.

The kinds of business research include marketing research, product research, research into human relations, and operations research. Most of the money and effort of business research are devoted to product research and marketing research.

Forecasting is a technique of predicting the future by evaluating and applying present knowledge. The techniques used are trend analysis, in which past trends are projected into the future; correlation, in which one activity is predicted by studying the changes in another activity; and composite estimates, in which the predictions of several persons or agencies are averaged. Because the estimate of future sales of a business is vital to business planning, sales forecasting is given the most attention and effort in the majority of companies.

QUESTIONS FOR REVIEW

1 Outline the steps in the scientific method of research.
2 If the conclusion drawn from a piece of research is faulty, does the researcher have to begin again at the first step?
3 If the hypothesis is of any value, it must be usable for prediction. Explain.
4 Distinguish pure research from applied research. Of what value to business is pure research?
5 Until recently, those doing pure research and those doing applied research appeared to hold each other in mild disdain. Why? What has brought these two types of researchers closer together?
6 Give some examples of applied research other than those mentioned in this chapter.
7 What are the steps followed in solving a typical research problem in business? Explain each of these steps.

8 What kinds of business research are there? Which ones are given more emphasis in most businesses?

9 In what ways can forecasting help business?

10 To what uses might a business put a short-range forecast? A long-range forecast?

11 Explain how correlation is used in business forecasting.

12 What is trend analysis? How can it help to predict the future?

13 What is an economic forecast? How does it help a business in its planning for the future?

14 How is a sales forecast useful in planning the future operations of departments other than the sales department?

15 What is the GNP? How can a forecast of the GNP help in forecasting sales of a company?

SELECTED READINGS   Brown, R. D.: *Research and the Credibility of Estimates*, Richard D. Irwin, Inc. Homewood, Ill., 1971.

Buzzell, Robert D., and Donald F. Cox: *Marketing Research*, McGraw-Hill Book Company, New York, 1969.

Chisholm, Roger K., and Gilbert R. Whitaker, Jr.: *Forecasting Methods*, Richard D. Irwin, Inc., Homewood, Ill., 1971.

Packard, Vance: *The Hidden Persuaders*, David McKay Company, Inc., New York, 1957.

Plane, Donald R., and Gary A. Kochenberger: *Operations Research for Managerial Decisions*, Richard D. Irwin, Inc., Homewood, Ill., 1972.

Name	Section	Date

COMPLETION SENTENCES

1 The scientific method is simply a means of bringing _____

and _____ into the solution of a problem.

2 The scientific method can be divided into four steps:

_____ , _____ ,

_____ , and _____ .

3 The two types of research are _____ and

_____ .

4 _____ research is adapting existing knowledge to a

practical purpose.

5 The methods used in research depend upon the complexity of the problem,

the amount of _____ and _____

available, and the existing _____ about the problem.

6 Outlining a research problem helps to make it _____ .

7 If a hypothesis is of any value, it must be usable for _____ .

8 Marketing research is concerned with _____ .

9 The attitudes and preferences of _____ determine which companies shall succeed.

10 Product research can be aimed at the development of _____ or the _____ of existing products.

11 Research on human relations in business seeks to understand how _____ can be used to benefit business.

12 Operations research is an effort to utilize all of the forces operating in a business toward a common _____ .

13 Forecasting is an attempt to determine _____ by careful evaluation of _____ knowledge.

14 The assumption on which _____ is based is that the activity being forecast changes at a regular rate.

15 The GNP measures the value of _____ produced in the United States in a year.

Name   Section   Date

TRUE OR FALSE STATEMENTS

1 There has been little emphasis on research in the United States during recent decades.

2 The scientific method is simply a means of bringing order and system into the solution of a problem.

3 Observation is necessary to scientific inquiry.

4 If a hypothesis is to be of any value, it must be usable for prediction.

5 If 1,000 coins are tossed into the air, close to 500 will come to rest heads up.

6 Pure research is adapting existing knowledge to a practical purpose.

7 Until recently, the findings of science and the utilization of scientific theories typically lay dormant for long periods before being put to practical use.

8 Because of the wide variety of types of research, one cannot apply the same steps to all business research.

9 The chief limits to conducting research by a business are time and money.

10 Marketing research is chiefly concerned with buying rather than selling.

11 Product research is confined to studying products.

12 Not only do products become obsolete, but whole industries become obsolete also.

13 Operations research was first developed as an aid in military operations.

14 A forecast is a statement of expected future conditions.

15 Small companies frequently make sales forecasts by guesswork.

EXERCISES

1 Choose a particular problem in marketing research, such as the selection of a site for a restaurant, service station, or apartment building; or take the problem of whether a store should stay open for business until 10 P.M.

or close at 6 P.M. After deciding what you intend to study as a research problem, outline the steps you would take in your research. Are there any ways you can check on the accuracy of your conclusions? What sources of published information are there to help you in seeking answers to your research problem?

2 Below is a listing of the index of industrial production and employment in manufacturing for the years 1954 to 1972. On graph paper present the two sets of figures in the form of a line chart, by connecting for each series the dots on the graph from one year to the next. By visual inspection fit a trend line to each graph line. Extend the trend line to the year 1990. What conclusions can you draw from the information on your graph?

Year	Index of Industrial Production (1967 = 100)	Index of Employment in Manufacturing (1967 = 100)
1954	51.9	89.6
1955	58.5	92.9
1956	61.1	93.9
1957	61.9	92.2
1958	57.9	83.9
1959	64.8	88.1
1960	66.2	88.0
1961	66.7	84.5
1962	72.2	87.3
1963	76.5	87.8
1964	81.7	89.3
1965	89.2	93.9
1966	97.9	99.9
1967	100.0	100.0
1968	105.7	101.4
1969	110.7	103.2
1970	106.7	98.1
1971	106.8	94.3
1972	119.3	99.4

Source: *Federal Reserve Bulletin*, various issues.

Name   Section   Date

17

ELECTRONIC DATA PROCESSING

Although it is useful for you to know what an analog computer is, your primary interest in data processing, as a student of business, is in the digital computer. Your concern should be in appreciating the applications and some of the future potential of electronic data processing in business. Also be aware of the limitations, at least at present, of computer technology.

Since computers depend upon electric current or switches, of which there are two positions, on and off, the binary system of numbers is basic to electronic computation. Although not essential, it might be interesting to you to work a few simple addition and subtraction problems using binary numbers. You might also try a few problems using Roman numerals.

Some input devices are illustrated in Figure 17-2. The next time you use a bank check or a punched card, look at it closely to see how it is adapted to electronic processing.

After reading the list of business applications of computers, see what other uses come to your mind. For example, are the handling of registration for classes and the recording of grades assisted by computers?

> U.S. Banks now clear 22 billion checks a year; by 1980 that figure will jump to 43 billion. It currently [1971] takes the equivalent of 78,000 full time employees just to process checks at those banks with more than $25 million in assets. "The paper float is just too much."[1]

Banks, insurance companies, retail stores, manufacturing companies, refineries—all businesses handle a lot of paper work, and the growth of paper work has been more rapid than the growth of business activity. Some businessmen report nightmares of eventually drowning in paper. Handling today's volume of paper work would be impossible without electronic data processing. Perhaps modern data processing has promoted the growth of paper work. It· is hard to say what is cause

[1] *Business Week*, June 5, 1971, p. 105.

and what is effect—the growth of paper work or the expanding capacities of electronic computers. Both have increased rapidly since World War II.

DEVELOPMENT OF ELECTRONIC DATA PROCESSING

In 1632, Pascal built an adding machine, using adding wheels as the basic unit. In 1693 Leibniz built the first desk calculator. Both machines used the same principles upon which twentieth-century calculators are based, but both were cumbersome to use. During the 1860s, Charles Babbage designed a computer with the versatility but not the speed of modern electronic computers. It was a mechanical monstrosity, but the principles in the design were of value in guiding the design of the early electronic computers.

The first electronic computer was built by the University of Pennsylvania in 1946. Using 20,000 vacuum tubes, it was bulky and slow by today's standards. But it was a tremendous advance over mechanical calculators. It could compute the trajectory of a projectile faster than the projectile could reach its target. The capabilities of the electronic computer drew the attention of scientists, engineers, and businessmen. Improvements came rapidly. The transistor (a tiny crystallized chip that performs the functions of vacuum tubes, does not have to be warmed up, is more reliable, and can be produced at a small fraction of the cost of vacuum tubes) was developed during the 1950s. Computers became ever faster, more reliable, more compact, and versatile. Probably the most spectacular contribution of electronic computers is in space exploration. The landing of two Americans on the moon in 1969 would have been impossible without modern computer technology. Although less spectacular, the business applications of computers have been historic.

The rapid development of computer technology is sometimes divided into stages, referred to as *generations*. The *first generation* used vacuum tubes. The machines were bulky, generated much heat from their thousands of tubes, and were subject to breakdowns. But the speed and volume of work which these computers could produce were such an improvement over the mechanical calculators previously used that their application in business and science increased rapidly. The decade of the 1950s is generally considered the period of first-generation computers.

The *second generation* of computers substituted transistors for vaccum tubes. This reduced the size of computers greatly, virtually eliminated the problem of heat, increased speed and dependability of operations, and reduced the cost of the machines. The use of transistorized computers increased rapidly during the early 1960s.

The *third generation* introduced extremely small transistorized elements, with electrical impulses traveling along printed circuits rather than conventional wiring. These tiny circuits (approximately one ten-thousandth of the size of second-generation circuits) were stamped out by mass production methods. Size of computers was greatly reduced, capacity and speed increased, and cost again reduced substantially. These computers could "read" images printed with magnetic, or printer's, ink on cards, bank checks, or sheets of paper. The period of third-generation computers began about 1965.

Technological improvements, however radical a departure from older technology, usually supplant existing machines gradually. The distinction between a second-generation and a third-generation computer is, therefore, somewhat arbitrary. Many computers built during the mid-1960s contained elements of second- and third-generation technology. Nevertheless, developments of the early 1970s may designate this period as a **fourth generation**. The following new technologies have been applied to computer design and production:

Cryogenics: Circuits operating at close to absolute zero temperature, where resistance to electricity (and therefore power loss) is virtually absent.

Lasers: The use of light beams with coherent wave patterns for storage and other computer uses.

Monolithic circuits: A new type of microminiature component that permits, among other things, a considerable increase in storage capacity with reduction in space.

Fourth-generation computers surpass third-generation computers in speed, capacity, and adaptability to different uses. Size and cost have been reduced still further, permitting computers to be used by business firms that have not used them before. The 1970s also introduced computers that were, for the first time, truly portable.

CLASSIFICATION OF COMPUTERS

The chief uses of computers have been in science and in business applications. This does not mean that only business firms and research laboratories use computers. The federal government operates many computers for tax accounting and other uses. Computers are used by law firms, colleges, and hospitals. Pocket calculators using electronic components are as inexpensive as portable typewriters and are becoming almost as numerous. Sophisticated electronic computers for home use may become common in a few years.

Two general types of computers have been developed: the analog computer and the digital computer. The **analog** computer is used chiefly to solve equations, make scientific calculations, and handle complex mathematical computations. Its operation is similar to that of a slide rule. As with a slide rule, the answers given are not exact, but are accurate to within 1/100 or 1/1,000 of 1 percent. Again, like a slide rule, which has limited use in business but is indispensable in science, the analog computer is used chiefly for scientific research and in engineering.

The digital computer counts numbers. Its accuracy can be carried to as many decimal places as desired. Because it deals with exact numbers and can give exact answers, the digital computer finds wide application in accounting and other business functions. It can prepare payrolls (accurate to the last penny), memorize inventory records (making them available for instant use), and process orders from customers.

CONTRIBUTIONS AND LIMITATIONS OF ELECTRONIC DATA PROCESSING

CONTRIBUTIONS

The four principal attractions of electronic computers are speed, accuracy, capacity, and versatility.

Speed

Calculations that take a person days or weeks to complete can be done in seconds or milliseconds by a computer.

Accuracy

The human brain makes mistakes, particularly when tired. The computer is not subject to fatigue. It works days, nights, weekends, and holidays. And it does not err, although the human beings operating the computer may instruct it improperly. It can solve problems too complex for manual calculation, involving hundreds of variables, and provide quick, accurate solutions.

Capacity

Modern computers can store a staggering amount of information in a very small space. Customer records, inventory records, and even the contents of a library could be stored compactly in the memory section of a computer. Not only does this capability reduce the need for storing paper; it makes possible retrieval of information much more quickly than was possible before the computer.

Versatility

The computer can handle the repetitive, routine work in an office better than a human. It can handle inventory records, check customers' credit, process sales orders, prepare the payroll and type the pay checks, calculate tax liabilities, and balance bank statements. In a meat packing plant the computer can determine daily the ideal mix of ingredients for sausage or dog food, so as to provide the desired proportions of protein, fat, and other ingredients for minimum cost. In a jet engine factory the computer can calculate the best shape, angle, and position of turbine blades—a calculation that would take a mathematician many weeks to make. Businessmen are constantly finding new uses to which a computer can be put. Computers have been programmed to play a respectable game of chess—although in 1973 no computer had yet earned grand master status.

The capability for vast storage of data and for doing routine chores has freed business managers from detail, enabling them to devote their time to planning and innovation. Computers do not have imagination, they do not exercise judgment, and they do not think. But they do give managers the precious freedom from routine that gives managers more time to meditate, to reason, and to hatch new ideas.

The wonders of computer technology have caused some runaway overselling of computer capabilities. Some managers assumed that any decision made by a computer was superior to a decision made by a person, and that more computer use has always meant better management. During the 1970s, there has developed a more cautious attitude toward the ever growing use of computers in business. Some companies have even reduced the business applications of their computers. Some of the limitations of computer use in business follow.

LIMITATIONS

The easy availability of detailed information about a large business has tempted some top managers to meddle in day-to-day decisions formerly made by subordinates. This has caused resentment and mistakes, since most top executives do not make as good managers for day-to-day operations as the men on the spot. Having every piece of information on a company is not useful to intelligent top-level management.

Too Much Data

Computer-generated reports may become a management crutch rather than a management tool. Many business decisions require judgment or intuition—and a computer printout is no substitute.

Too Much Dependence on Decision Making by Computer

Electronic data processing can handle much of the routine correspondence of firms, particularly for large retail organizations. This saves time and money and is satisfactory in most instances. But there are exceptions. A computerized letter responding to a customer's complaint does not always give a satisfactory explanation. Some customers need special attention, and a computerized system does not always identify such cases before the customer is hopelessly antagonized. There are many examples of overreliance on computers and the ignoring of human judgment in any enterprise that uses electronic data processing.

Ignoring the Importance of the Human Element in Business

One of the compelling reasons for using electronic data processing is to avoid mistakes. Humans get tired and they become forgetful or careless. But when a clerk or assembly-line worker makes a mistake, he usually is aware of it and corrects it. An electronic computer processing data can be programmed to make certain types of corrections, such as adjusting the cutting edge of an automatic tool or replacing a drill bit when dull. However, the types of adjustments that cannot be foreseen when the equipment is programmed are not corrected by the machine until detected by the human operator. Even the dullest or sleepiest clerk would not address thousands of magazines of the same date of issue to one subscriber. An automatic addressing machine could—and did. The result was two large mail trucks loaded with one issue of the magazine delivering their load to a subscriber in a remote part of New Mexico.

Mistakes

BINARY SYSTEM OF NUMBERS

The numbering system you learned in school is the decimal system. There are 10 digits, 0 through 9, after which two digits are used. Ten is 10, eleven is 11, and so on, until the 10 digits are all used at 99, at which point three digits are used. This system is not possible with the electronic computer, because the computer works with electrical switches having only two positions: open and closed. Computers use the *binary* system, having only two digits, as illustrated below:

Decimal System	Binary System
0	0
1	1
2	10
3	11
4	100
5	101
6	110
7	111
8	1000
9	1001
10	1010
11	1011
12	1100
13	1101
14	1110
15	1111
16	10000

In the decimal system a digit increases its value 10 times each time it moves to the left: 1, 10, 100, and so on. In the binary system a digit increases its value twice for each move to the left. In the binary code, therefore, 1, 10, 100, and 1,000 correspond to the decimal numbers of 1, 2, 4, and 8. The binary system is used not only to designate numbers, but letters of the alphabet and other symbols, such as + and −. Although the binary system is cumbersome to use on paper, because of the large number of notations required when using only two symbols, it does not slow down a computer, because of the great speed of electric current.

COMPUTER HARDWARE AND SOFTWARE

The chief components of a computer are *input*, *operating unit* (also called *arithmetic unit*), *control*, *memory*, and *output*. The operating unit, control unit (or storage unit) together form the *central processing unit*, commonly referred to as the *CPU*. Their relationship is shown in Figure 17-1.

INPUT

It is by means of the input that data and instructions are fed into the computer (which is sometimes called talking to a computer). The more commonly used input devices are given below, some of which are shown in Figure 17-2.

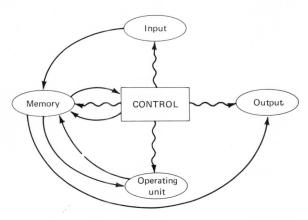

FIGURE 17-1   Relationship of components in a digital computer. Solid lines show paths of information (flow of data). Wavy lines show channels of control. The control unit, memory, and operating unit form the central processing unit (CPU).

An electric typewriter designed for use with a computer is a common means of providing output from the computer. Thus an operator can type data and instructions and, if he chooses, have the solution to a problem or information from the computer memory typed on the same typewriter.

Electric Typewriter

Most persons are familiar with this input device. Payroll checks, college registration forms, and charge account bills use this form. The small rectangular holes in the card permit the passage of electrical impulses. The location of the punched holes determines the information fed to the computer.

Punched Cards

Like punched cards, punched tape has holes to permit the passage of electrical impulses to provide information to the computer. Cash registers and other kinds of business machines may record their operations on tape, which is then fed to the computer.

Punched Paper Tape

Anyone who has seen a tape recorder knows the ability of magnetized tape to record and play words and music. Magnetized tape feeds information to a computer in a manner similar to punched paper tape, except that instead of holes punched

Magnetic Tape

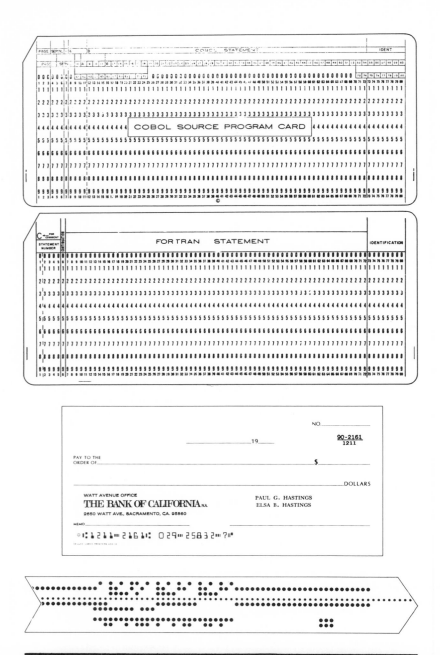

FIGURE 17-2 In/out devices. Punched card, magnetic ink (bank check), punched tape, and magnetic tape.

there are spots on the tape that are magnetized. A tremendous amount of information can be stored compactly on magnetic tape. Furthermore, the tape can feed information to the computer very fast, and it can be erased and reused any number of times. The main risk, usually remote, of recording instructions and information on magnetic tape is the possibility of accidentally erasing a valuable tape.

Look at a bank check. If it is a typical one, there will be a series of oddly shaped numbers and characters on the face, usually at the bottom of the check. A scanner "reads" the check. The information from the magnetized characters is used for check sorting and bookkeeping functions. Electrographic pencils serve a similar purpose. True-false or multiple-choice tests are often given to persons who are required to mark their answers on designated squares on the answer sheet using special pencils. This permits speedy grading.

Magnetized Ink

The optical scanner uses a beam of light to distinguish between light and dark areas on a surface. This input is already being used by the Social Security Administration and the Internal Revenue Service. This device shows promise of rapid development and versatility. Its use will very likely expand rapidly in the future.

Optical Scanner

The operating unit is the "heart" of the computer. It performs mathematical and other operations—whatever treatment of data the computer is instructed to perform. It is sometimes also called the *arithmetic unit* or the *processing component.*

OPERATING UNIT

The control might be called the "brain" of the computer. It interprets the instructions fed into the memory by the input. It gives "commands" to the operating unit and continuously checks to determine whether the commands are accurately carried out. If the human operator feeds incorrect data or instructions to the input, the control can be programmed to indicate the mistake—in the case of one computer, whenever an obvious mistake was made by the operator, the computer printed out the word "dummkopf" three times.

CONTROL

The memory is the storage section of the computer. Data and instructions fed into the computer are lodged in the memory. Data to be processed are taken from the memory and, after processing, are returned to the memory. If a number of successive computations are to be done to the data, the results of each step are recorded in the memory. Data that are completely processed and ready to be "read out" are taken from the memory and transferred to the output.

MEMORY

The memory unit may be composed of disks, like phonograph records, that revolve when the computer is in operation. Memory units are also composed of drums, magnetic tape, or magnetic cores. Although the structure of computer memories differs, the function remains the same: to store data and instructions in the form of patterns of magnetic charges. One measure of the size of a computer is the capacity of its memory. A large computer may have over 2 million magnetic cores, each core a millimeter or two in diameter.

OUTPUT
The output "reads out" the data stored in the computer. When the operator wants information from the memory—either freshly completed computations or data stored for a long time—he usually receives it in the form of typed sheets, called *printouts*. The printer types a line of letters or numbers in a single motion. High-speed printers can type over 2,000 lines a minute.

If the data withdrawn are to be further treated, the data may be read out in the form of magnetic tape, punched tape, or punched cards or typed by electric typewriter. Data can also be read out on a cathode ray tube (essentially a television screen). A stockbroker can get up-to-the-minute quotations on securities prices by punching buttons on a desk-top unit that immediately displays the desired numbers on a small screen. This method of presenting data is particularly suitable for diagrams, graphs, and charts.

COMPUTER SOFTWARE
The programs and program aids used in computer operations are called *software*. A computer *program* is a series of instructions to the computer indicating step by step how the data are to be processed by it. A program may be typed by a programmer and stored in the memory of the computer. Some programs are typed and transferred for storage to a reel of magnetic tape. Others are stored on punched cards or punched tape. Frequently one program is adaptable to the needs of many users, such as handling credit accounts of retailers. In such cases a standardized software package (on tape or cards, usually) can be purchased for use on a computer. Such a program is less expensive than the preparation of a special program. Also, the errors found in any new program are absent from a standardized program (in the words of programmers, the program has been "debugged").

COMPUTER LANGUAGE AND PROGRAMMING
Computers can follow instructions but, as said before, they cannot think. They follow whatever instructions are given to them, no matter how illogical or unreasonable. An early computer, constructed with vacuum tubes, was given the task of dividing a number by zero. It worked on and on until several hundred vacuum tubes burned out. That experience contributed to the practice of programming computers to ignore unsolvable problems.

The instructions given to a computer must be very detailed, very explicit, and in the proper sequence. Programming is a highly regarded skill. To illustrate the nature of programming, a simple illustration is given below:

Enter data.

Divide by 13.75.

If answer is less than 100, read out result; if not, divide by 3.23.

Take square root.

Multiply by 4.81.

Read out result.

When the step-by-step process is represented by a diagram, such as in Figure 17-3, it is called a *flowchart*.

To enable a computer to follow instructions, they must be expressed in symbolic language. Symbolic language expresses data and instructions put in a special form so that the particular computer can understand it. The symbolic

FIGURE 17-3 Flowchart. ("The Corporate Abacus," *Dupont Magazine*, July 1966, p. 14, © OA Business Publications, Inc.)

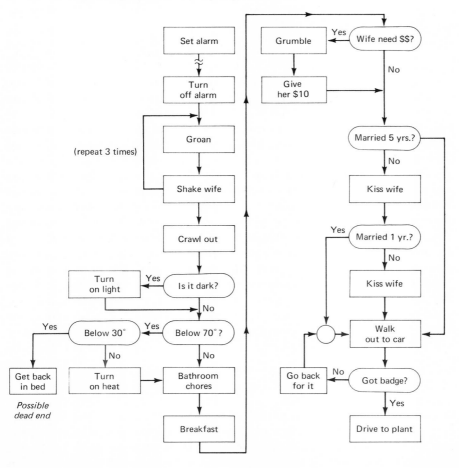

languages used for business are adaptations of English. Terms and symbols vary from one symbolic language to another. For example, in one the term for add is *add*; in another the symbol + is used. If the instructions are incorrectly translated into the symbolic language, the results will be in error or the computer will give the signal for insufficient or incorrect command. Although computers are manufactured by many companies, most are able to receive the computer languages in common use. Examples are given below:

COBOL COmmon Business Oriented Language. Designed primarily for business applications.

FORTRAN FORmula TRANslator. Particularly designed for problems involving complex mathematical compuations. Engineering and scientific uses predominate.

BASIC Beginner's All-purpose Symbolic Instruction Code. Easier to learn than other languages. Sometimes used by students of computer programming as a first step in mastering other, more difficult languages.

PL/I Programming Language I. Recently developed (mid-1960s). Designed as a language flexible enough to be used for either scientific or business uses. It may eventually supplant COBOL and FORTRAN.

Preparing a program and translating it into symbolic language require training and experience. Persons expert in programming are in demand both in industry and in science. Some are trained by the company hiring them, some are trained in classes operated by companies that manufacture computers, some are trained in colleges, and some are trained in commercial schools created to train programmers. Even a trained programmer may take hours or days in preparing a complex program, checking it for mistakes (debugging it), and testing it to make sure nothing has been overlooked.

It is not necessary for users of computers to be trained in the skills of programming. One of the functions of any program is to enable users to get answers by following a relatively simple set of instructions. The airline reservations clerk operating a terminal of a computerized reservations network need not be trained as a programmer. An office worker in an insurance company need not understand the technology of computers to get information from the computer memory about a customer's policy. In both cases the user needs training little more demanding than learning how to operate a desk calculator. Nevertheless, it is true that to understand and fully utilize the capabilities of computers in business, something more than elementary knowledge is required. For this reason some companies provide courses of instruction in computer use for their managers, and colleges offering business curricula increasingly include courses in electronic data processing.

REAL-TIME AND TIME-SHARE

Because computers have a large capacity for work and because they are costly, users make every effort to use them fully. Some operations, such as preparation of a payroll, can be scheduled for night or other times when the computer has unused capacity available. Some operations, on the other hand, require prompt response to the input from the computer. The versatility of modern computers accommodates both types of operations.

REAL-TIME

When computer output follows input sufficiently rapidly to control an activity while the activity is in progress, the computer is said to be operating on *real-time*, a situation that might be described as holding a "conversation" with the computer. Some examples of real-time usage follow:

Oil refining: Computers control the refining process, continuously receiving inputs on temperature, pressure, and composition of crude oil. The computer output adjusts thermostats, pressure valves, and other controls to maintain uniform production.

Airline reservations: A computer is programmed to maintain records of all flights in a system. Passenger agents in widely separated cities can contact the memory unit of the computer to determine the up-to-the-minute availability of seats on a particular flight. The computer adds reservations and subtracts cancellations received in a constant stream from many distant points with a speed and accuracy impossible for human clerks to manage.

Commercial banking and retail credit: A computer maintains records of depositors' accounts, adding deposits and subtracting withdrawals and other charges. Tellers can determine the current balance of a customer, thus providing better service to depositors and reducing the incidence of overdrawn accounts. Retail stores, particularly those chain stores with many outlets, maintain central files of their credit customers. Before completing a credit sale, a clerk can tap a few buttons on a computer terminal and receive immediately a decision from the computer to proceed with the sale or not.

TIME-SHARE

Because the cost of large computers is high, every effort is made to avoid having a computer idle, even for short periods. One result of this effort is the development of *time-share*. This means the common use of a computer by many users. The computer switches from one user to another in a thousandth of a second. Thus 200 or 300 users each have the impression of exclusive use of the computer, since the delay is imperceptible. Furthermore, the computer is programmed to work on payroll preparation, inventory, and other functions to utilize whatever time is not being used by time-share.

Each time-share subscriber has a connection with the computer by means of a terminal appearing somewhat like a typewriter. The charges are similar in nature to those for the telephone—installation fee, monthly subscription charge, and extra fees for special services. Time-share makes available the services of large, sophisticated computers to businesses of moderate size. Time-share is a relatively recent development, but it is expected to expand rapidly. By combining several computers into a network, the number of subscribers to a time-share system can be greatly expanded and the scheduling of computer use can be more efficiently accomplished.

BUSINESS APPLICATIONS

The use of computers by business continues to increase year by year. Large businesses employ 100 or more computers. Smaller enterprises use only one, or share computer use with others. The variety of tasks turned over to the computer by businesses becomes steadily greater, with new applications being found frequently. With computer technology continuing its rapid progress, any listing of computer uses in business is bound to be quickly outdated. Nevertheless, the scope of applications can be suggested by the list below.

Recording purchase orders of customers and transmitting each order immediately to the warehouse nearest the customer, after checking inventory records to ensure that the chosen warehouse has the goods desired in the correct quantities.

Computing payroll, deducting from each employee the correct amount for withholding tax, social security tax, pension contribution, and any others; typing the payroll check for each employee; and making the proper accounting entries for the payroll.

Computing dividend checks on the basis of the number of shares held by each stockholder, making the necessary accounting entries, and typing the checks.

Comparing alternative methods of transportation (for example, truck, rail, and barge) and deciding on the most economical route to follow.

Keeping inventory records constantly up to date, indicating when a shift would be made of an inventory item from one warehouse to another, and when an item is in short supply and should be replenished.

Deciding the most efficient division of advertising funds among different advertising media.

Determining, on the basis of fluctuating costs of raw materials, the most profitable proportions of ingredients to use in production each day.

Preparation of daily financial statements for management.

Recording charges and preparing monthly bills for customers of department stores, light and power companies, and telephone companies.

Probably the most ambitious application of computers in business is the concept of **total systems control**. This means that by use of computers the production, personnel, marketing, and financial operations are subject to unified control, with computers furnishing top management current information on the operation of each department and providing management with comprehensive information presented in digest or summary form. Thus will the operations of each department more nearly conform to the company objectives and be in coordination with the efforts of the other departments. Systems analysis is presented in Chapter 6, and the impact on management of the systems concept is explained in Chapter 7.

The contribution of the computer to the systems concept of management is threefold: capacity, organization, and speed. To consider a business enterprise as a system of interrelated parts, it is necessary to have accurate and complete information on all aspects of the enterprise. It would be almost impossible for a large organization to apply the systems concept in management with the information handling methods (voluminous filing cabinets, interoffice memos, and making computations with desk calculators) of a generation ago. The capacity of modern computers makes the management of an enterprise as a total system feasible.

To determine the effect, if any, of an increase in light in a factory on reduction of substandard output or to determine the relationship of a 5 percent increase in assembly-line speed to an increase in absenteeism, it is not sufficient merely to have a lot of information. The information must be organized, correlated, and summarized. In the systems approach to management an essential ingredient is the effect of an action in one area (for example, the length of the workday) upon another area (for example, rate of wearing out of tools). The computer can organize, correlate, compare, and summarize information in whatever manner it is needed by management.

Finally, total systems control depends upon speed. If it takes days to search, manipulate, and present data on which management decisions are made, the effect of the decisions is delayed, sometimes disastrously. With its incredible speed, the computer can present needed information in time for the management to make prompt adjustments to avoid a crisis or to terminate an action before it becomes damaging.

Computers have been developed that can translate languages, draw blueprints, and compose music. Scientists have pondered the development of computers that can think as humans do. Computers developed so far have been able only to follow instructions, however complex the instructions might be. Computers can make decisions, although only decisions mechanically resulting from the data and instructions fed into them. Computers can learn, in the sense that computers may be programmed to avoid a sequence of steps proven to be incorrect. Thus a computer programmed to play chess will avoid being beaten a second time by the same set of moves made previously by its human opponent. But computers have no imagination, no initiative. And they can probably never be endowed with inspiration.

A LOOK INTO THE FUTURE

Some uses of computers predicted for the 1980s are illustrated in Figure 17-4. Other predictions for that decade include the following:

> By the late 1980's computer prices will be about one fiftieth to one hundredth of the prices in 1970.
>
> The development of smaller, faster computers will continue. Computers no larger than a briefcase will appear before 1980 and pocket size before 1990. Although of moderate capacity, the small computers will be linked to large central processing units.
>
> Central processing units will have vastly greater storage capacity. In the 1980's a memory capacity of 1,000,000,000,000,000,000 bits will be available.
>
> Computers capable of reading handwritten instructions or accepting data by voice will be commonplace. In 1971 the Department of Defense made plans to develop a computer that would respond to a spoken vocabulary of 1,000 words, regardless of who did the speaking.[2]

As computer technology progresses, it will continue to affect business operations. With faster, cheaper computers possessing larger capacities, the variety of tasks given to computers will grow. Practically all routine or repetitive tasks can be accomplished by computers. With smaller, more compact computers, not only will small businesses use computers much more than they do today; some experts pre-

[2] *Business Week*, Oct. 30, 1971, p. 91.

'Intelligent' machines will find jobs . . .

. . . making decisions on the production line

. . . taking the place of man in hostile environments

. . . analyzing results in medical laboratories

FIGURE 17-4 Potential future uses of computer technology. (*Source: Business Week*, Oct. 30, 1970, by Ted Hanke.)

dict the computer will become as ubiquitous as the typewriter or telephone. The increasing use of computers will give business ever more control over its operations. It will relieve the minds of office workers, supervisors, and some managers from routine decisions, permitting them to think less hurriedly on questions the computer cannot decide. Computers will enable government agencies to predict economic trends with more accuracy and to catch errors or fraud in tax returns more readily. Computers will help physicians diagnose more accurately and will aid lawyers in compiling legal precedents. Computers have already increased productivity in the production plant and the office, and of this we can be sure: computers will continue to increase productivity in the future.

SUMMARY

The four principal attractions of electronic computers are speed, accuracy, capacity, and versatility. The computer can handle vast amounts of data, undertake lengthy and complex computations, and operate without fatigue and with few mistakes.

The principal components of a computer are the *input*, by which data and instructions are fed to the computer; *operating unit*, which processes the data; *control*, which interprets the instructions, gives commands to the operating unit, and checks on accuracy; *memory*, which stores data and instructions to be retrieved when required; and *output*, which "reads out" or prints out the data that are requested.

Programming is the function of translating instructions into a form usable by the computer. To aid in this, several symbolic languages have been invented, the principal ones being COBOL, FORTRAN, BASIC, and PL/I.

Some operations, such as payroll preparation, can be processed during the night and at other times when the computer is little used. Other operations require *real-time*, in which a series of prompt answers to questions is required or in which an operator engages in a "dialog" with a computer. In *time-share* a computer with a large capacity provides service for many users almost simultaneously, thus reducing the cost to each user. The computer also makes feasible the concept of total systems control, under which the production, marketing, and other operations of a business are subject to unified decision making.

QUESTIONS FOR REVIEW

1 How does the digital computer differ from the analog computer? Which is preferable for business uses? Why?

2 Explain why a computer is fast and accurate and can store large amounts of data.

3 How can the use of computers allow managers to "do more thinking"?

4 Can all business decisions be made by a computer? What sorts of business decisions should be reserved for human judgment?

5 How does the binary system differ from the decimal system? Why is the binary system used in designing electronic computers?

6 What are the chief components of an electronic computer? What is the function of each?

7 Distinguish between computer "hardware" and "software."

8 What is a symbolic language? Which ones are designed for business uses?

9 Should all office personnel who deal with computers in any way be required to take some training in programming? Explain.

10 Explain how time-share can make available the services of computers to relatively small businesses.

11 What is total systems control? How can it improve the operations of a large company?

12 Does the computer tend to decrease or increase the amount of paper work of a business office? Explain your answer carefully.

SELECTED READINGS   Boyes, R. L., R. W. Shields, and L. G. Greenwell: *Introduction to Electronic Computing*, John Wiley & Sons, Inc., New York, 1971.

Cashman, Thomas, and William J. Keys: *Introductory Data Processing*, Harper & Row, Publishers, Incorporated, New York, 1971.

Desmonde, William H.: *Computers and Their Uses*, Prentice-Hall, Inc., Englewood Cliffs, N.J., 1971.

Martin, E. W., and William C. Perkins: *Computers and Information Systems: An Introduction*, Richard D. Irwin, Inc., Homewood, Ill., 1973.

Vazsonyi, Andrew: *Introduction to Electronic Data Processing*, Richard D. Irwin Inc., Homewood, Ill., 1973.

Name	Section	Date

1 The two principal types of computers are _____ and

_____ .

2 The four principal attractions of computer use are _____ ,

_____ , _____ , and

_____ .

3 Computers lack the _____ and

_____ that human minds possess.

4 In the binary system the decimal system number 5 is _____ .

5 The input feeds _____ and _____

into a computer.

6 The main risk in using magnetic tape to store data is the accidental

_____ of the magnetism.

7 The _____ is sometimes called the brain of the computer.

8 Computers are usually programmed to ignore _____ problems.

9 A flowchart shows the step-by-step process of a program in the form of a _____ .

10 To reduce the time a computer may be idle, the concept of _____ was developed, enabling several users to have access to the same computer.

11 Under total systems control, various operations of a company are brought under _____ control.

12 The speed, capacity, and organization of data possible with computers make management of an enterprise as a _____ feasible.

13 Computers can make _____ , although only on the basis of data and instructions fed to them.

14 Computers can learn, in the sense that a sequence of steps _____ will not be repeated.

15 With faster, cheaper computers, the variety of tasks given to computers will _____ .

Name	Section	Date

TRUE OR FALSE STATEMENTS

1 The first adding machine was built around 1890 in New York.

2 No electronic computers were used before World War II.

3 The analog computer, used in science, provides exact answers.

4 Any decision made by a computer is superior to one made by a person.

5 Having every piece of information about company operations is not necessary for top management in making decisions.

6 An electric typewriter is a common means of feeding data into a computer.

7 Punched cards permit the passage of light through the holes, thus activating the computer.

8 The oddly shaped numbers at the bottom of a check are printed with magnetic ink.

9 Although the structure of computer memories differs, the function is the same: to store data and instructions.

10 Most symbolic languages for programming computers have no relation to the English language.

11 To translate data into symbolic language requires very little training.

12 To make efficient use of a computer, it is necessary that a business executive be trained in the skills of programming.

13 Because of its importance, preparation of the payroll should not be scheduled for nighttime or weekend processing by a computer.

14 Each time-share subscriber is connected to a computer by a terminal.

15 Time-share is a development that began with the early vacuum tube computers.

EXERCISES

1 In Figure 17-4 and in the accompanying text computer uses in the 1980s are predicted. For the uses or developments listed plus others you may have read about in other sources, list the advantages or benefits of each development. List also the disadvantages or possible abuses that might result.

Advantages   *Disadvantages*

2 Watching a computer in operation can be interesting as well as educational. With the increasing use of computers by business, government, and other agencies, you are probably not far from one. Arrange to visit (in a group if possible) the place where a computer is used. If your school uses one, visit it. Prepare a report covering the following points:
a Manufacturer of the computer
b Model or series number
c Type of memory (disk, core, etc.)
d Inputs used (tape, punched card, etc.)
e Outputs available (printout, cathode ray tube, etc.)
f Speed of printer
g Comments and observations

220
ROAD TAX
26058
W. VA. - 63
19 OKLAHOMA 61
BF-25426
MD. ROAD TAX
43030
1962
1962
16996

PART 6
MARKETING

Business activity is often divided into two major functions: production and marketing. The next six chapters are concerned with marketing. The United States is renowned for its mass-production techniques which have made possible a tremendous volume of goods produced with relatively few workers. To market these goods has required transportation, storage, and other aspects of marketing to match the large-scale production.

Since our economy is basically free and competitive, pricing is a reflection of the supply of and the demand for an article. Where competition is weak or where producers are able to combine their efforts, prices of articles are not determined by free market forces and are controlled—either to benefit the producer or to aid the consumer.

Part of the chain of marketing is wholesaling, where a company receives goods from producers and distributes them to retailers. Another part of the chain is retailing, where a company receives goods from wholesalers or producers and distributes them to consumers. There are many different types of wholesalers and retailers, and not all goods follow the chain of producer to wholesaler to retailer to consumer. These aspects of marketing change continuously.

For people to buy goods, they must know that the goods exist. This, basically, is the function of sales promotion and advertising. In these areas of marketing, the efforts of United States businessmen have been aggressive and pioneering.

To a considerable degree, the quality of the transportation network of a nation measures its economic advancement. The United States has an extensive network of railroads, highways, pipelines, waterways, and airlines. Each of these has its advantages and disadvantages. To some degree, each is specialized; but, to some extent, all are in competition.

Just as specialization of production within the United States has given us a high standard of living, so international specialization of production raises our living standards even higher. International marketing is the function of international trade, similar in many respects to marketing within the United States but having characteristics that make it different from domestic trade.

CHAPTER 18

THE NATURE OF MARKETING

Marketing is the process of moving goods from the producer to the consumer. In reading this chapter, try to appreciate the fact that as production units have become larger, their markets have expanded geographically. This means that as production becomes more concentrated, marketing must be over a wider area for each producing plant. Mass production thus requires mass marketing.

Many people assume that there is little to be done in the way of applying the inventive spirit to the process of marketing of goods. Marketing, however, can change as rapidly as methods of production or the design of products. As a matter of fact, one can point to periods in the recent past where the change in methods of marketing has been so rapid that one could almost speak of these periods as revolutions in marketing. One such period was the 1930s, when the process of marketing groceries changed rapidly from small grocery stores to large self-service supermarkets.

In reading the section on selling, notice that the act of selling is merely the reverse of the act of buying. However, it is assumed that the initiative in making a sale comes from the seller rather than from the buyer, that the buyer is relatively passive.

In this connection, you should be aware that nearly everybody is a buyer, and that the range of things that he buys is very great. Nearly everybody is a seller, but the range of his selling activity is limited. A person either sells a limited line of goods or sells his services, but he buys such a wide variety of services and things that he cannot be familiar with them all. In other words, most persons are relatively expert in what they have to sell and relatively naive in what they have to buy. Hence, it is important for people to attempt to make themselves better informed as buyers and to exercise some caution in buying.

THE CHARACTER OF PRODUCTION AND MARKETING

The character of production in the present century in the United States is a highly interdependent one, in which goods are made in tremendous quantities and shipped all over the country and the world. The difference between present production and that of 100 years ago is explained by the shift from small-scale production for a local market to large-scale production for a national and world market.

To see what effect the specializing of production in large factories and the marketing of that production over a wide area have caused in our lives, let us examine the daily activities of an average man. Mr. Average Man first awakens to a new day with the sound of an alarm clock made at Bridgeport, Connecticut, or a clock radio made in Japan. He then groggily gets out of bed, dons a pair of slippers made in Philadelphia, staggers to the bathroom, turns on a light bulb made in Cleveland, and shaves with a razor made in New York City. He then dresses in a suit made in Chicago of cloth woven in England from wool produced in Australia. He has a breakfast of cereal made in Battle Creek, Michigan, oranges raised in Florida, sugar produced in Hawaii, and bacon packed in Fort Worth, Texas. He goes out to the garage constructed from lumber cut in Oregon, gets into the car made of parts produced in Detroit and assembled in Wilmington, Delaware, and goes to the office. Undoubtedly, Mr. Average Man is too sleepy throughout this process to appreciate the variety of goods he takes for granted, which are produced hundreds of miles away and brought to him as part of the process of modern marketing.

The committee on definitions of the American Marketing Association has defined *marketing* as the performance of business activities that direct the flow of goods and services from producer to consumer. Marketing includes the activities of selling, transportation, storage, standardization and grading, financing, risk taking, packaging, and advertising. The costs of the various marketing services represent about 50 percent of the final sales price—more in the case of some products and less in the case of others.

Although the services of marketing may appear costly, they add value, or, in the terminology of economics, utility. *Utility* is the capability of satisfying human wants. Marketing adds two general types of utility: *place utility* and *time utility*.[1] Moving goods from where they are wanted less to where they are wanted more adds place utility to the goods, as happens when goods are moved from a factory to a wholesaler or from a wholesaler to a retail store. Holding goods from a time that they are less wanted to a time that they are more wanted creates time utility, which explains the existence of warehouses and storerooms. In short, marketing makes goods available to persons where they want them, when they want them.

The costs of marketing may, in the case of some goods, seem high to the average consumer. He should, however, consider these points. The variety of goods, sizes, colors, and range of prices is much greater than it was a few decades ago. To provide the added choice takes money. Furthermore, there are services desired by consumers that add to costs. There are, for example, charge accounts, returns of unsatisfactory purchases, stores in convenient but costly locations, wide aisles, window displays, counseling in shopping, fitting clothing, and dozens of other services. These add value as well as cost to the goods bought. Most consumers want the services and are willing to pay for them.

---

[1] Some marketers distinguish a third utility, *ownership* or *possession utility*, which adds value as title to goods is transferred from one owner to another in the chain of distribution.

THE MARKETING MANAGER

The locus of decision making in a marketing system is the marketing manager, as indicated in Figure 18-1. In making his decisions, he is limited by constraints, the most important being the goals of the enterprise—goals which he likely had a hand in formulating. The primary goal of the company might be rapid expansion of sales, maximizing profit (or minimizing loss), or establishment of a reputation for quality. Secondary goals might be expansion of sales in the teen-age market and the successful introduction of a new product. Whatever the company goals, his decisions must be consistent with them.

MARKETING CONSTRAINTS

The marketing manager is constrained by the allocation in the budget for marketing functions, such as advertising, market research, and salesmen's expenses. Laws and regulations must be heeded. Finally, the shifting attitudes of society must be considered, such as the growing concern of the 1970s for respect for the environment. The marketing manager participates in some degree in the forming of the constraints. In addition to helping shape the goals of the enterprise, he participates in the budget-making process. His influence in shaping laws and regulations and in molding attitudes of society is less, but it does exist.

The marketing manager does not make decisions in isolation depending upon his own intuition. If he did, some of his decisions might be the stroke of genius, but most would probably be disastrous. To be successful, he seeks information and advice. He has many sources of information, some of which are shown in Figure 18-1.

FIGURE 18-1   The marketing manager is the focal point of the firm's marketing system.

CONSTRAINTS

Within the constraints imposed on him and with the information at his disposal, the marketing manager makes his decisions. These are transmitted by telephone, letter, and interoffice memo and in person. The process is one of continuously receiving information and transmitting orders or suggestions. Like the production manager, financial manager, and personnel director, he is a member of a team, cooperating to achieve the company goals and seeing to it that the marketing department acts in concert with the other departments of the company.

THE MARKETING CONCEPT

In recent years the *marketing concept* (also known as the *total marketing concept*) has received increased attention in business, in contrast to the production concept previously dominant. The production concept starts with the product. A product is designed and production begun; then it is the job of the marketing division to persuade customers to buy. The marketing concept starts with the customer. Analyze the customer, determine his desires for a product, and find out how much he is willing to pay and what services he wants the product to perform for him; then it is the job of the production department to design and produce a product that satisfies those wants. Neither the production concept nor the marketing concept exists entirely oblivious of the other. The difference is a matter of emphasis, and the emphasis since World War II has shifted in the direction of the marketing concept.

THE MARKETING MIX

A very important part of marketing management is the choice of a marketing mix. The *marketing mix* is the combination of marketing elements (the product, the price, the channels of distribution, and promotion and advertising) manipulated by the marketing manager to achieve his sales goals. Should the product consist of one model or two, one size or five, one color or ten? Should one price be rigidly adhered to, or should there be special sales and end-of-season discounts? Should the product be distributed by mail order only, through retail stores only, by house-to-house canvassing, or by a combination of these? What sort of advertising and promotion should be used? How would you answer the questions above in selecting a marketing plan for a pocket calculator, a new type of tennis racket, or sports clothing? In deciding on your answer, you are choosing a marketing mix in the same way (although perhaps with different results) as the marketing manager of a large corporation.

THE FUNCTIONS OF MARKETING

In our study of marketing, we can break the subject down in terms of its functions, which are the tasks that marketing performs. These functions are selling (the obverse of buying), transportation, storage, standardization and grading, financing, risk bearing, and marketing information. It is through the exercise of these functions that marketing increases the utility of goods and services. In this and later chapters these functions are discussed.

SELLING   *Selling* is the art of persuading a customer to buy, and guiding the transaction until the sale is completed. Selling can be nonpersonal, as in mail-order selling; it can be personal, as in the activity of salesmen. Selling can be quick and simple, as in the sale of a candy bar; or it can be lengthy and complex, as in the sale of a house or a factory machine (the difference in marketing consumer goods and industrial goods is taken up in Chapter 20).

The process of selling can be divided into four parts: demand creation, finding a buyer, negotiation of the terms of sale, and transfer of ownership (title) of the goods. The capacity of customers to buy—and pay for—goods and services is limited. All products and services are thus in competition with each other for the limited number of dollars available to customers. The essence of selling is competing for the customer's dollar.

DEMAND CREATION

There is competition in most industries between producers of the same type of goods. For example, the General Motors Corporation competes with Chrysler and the Ford Motor Company for the customer's choice of an automobile. In some industries, such as long-distance telephone service, the struggle for the consumer's dollar is only with services and products of a different character rather than with competitors in the same industry. In either case, however, it is necessary for the producer to exert an effort to secure the consumer's dollar. *Demand creation* and the finding of a buyer are ways by which this is accomplished. The former function is also known as *sales promotion*, and the latter is sometimes called *salesmanship*. The function of creating demand, or creating desire on the part of the potential customer to buy, has involved the imagination of experts in the field of marketing for a long time. The techniques that experts have evolved in this area of marketing are very ingenious in the United States, and have been copied by businessmen all over the world. Probably one of the characteristics of American business that appears most striking to foreigners is our method of advertising. Here the imagination of the businessman has been most pronounced, and is such an important aspect of marketing that it will be treated in a separate chapter.

FINDING A BUYER

The function of finding a buyer can be either personal or impersonal. The personal aspect involves the use of salesmen who meet potential buyers and attempt to induce them to buy the products the salesmen are handling. Salesmanship is a highly developed art in the United States, and can be passive or active. Its passive aspect is found in the case of retail sales clerks, whose function is to be available to make sales to customers who voluntarily enter the store. The active phase of salesmanship is one in which the salesman takes the initiative to seek out the potential customers. Many businessmen assume that the process of passive salesmanship is less difficult and therefore they place less emphasis on the selection, training, and holding of such employees, as compared with active salesmen. Many sales clerks are hired at relatively low salaries, they are given rather brief periods of training or none at all, and replacement is not considered a serious problem. As might be expected, the turnover in such establishments is rather high. Perhaps this attitude is shortsighted. Our knowledge of selling derived from experience and research is increasing constantly, and it is quite possible that the future will see more care exercised in the selection and training of sales clerks.

Wherever selling is undertaken, buying is also present, since both terms refer to the same function. The function of selling implies that the initiative rests largely with the seller of the goods. The aim of the seller is to exact the maximum payment for the goods or services he is undertaking to sell, and the aim of the buyer is to purchase the goods for as little as possible. Just as the art of successful selling requires considerable experience and aptitude, the art of successful buying exacts similar aptitude.

The average consumer spends a considerable part of his lifetime engaged in the activity of buying. He is interested in getting as much value for his money as possible. A hundred years ago, the consumer was faced with a small variety of goods and services to buy and was able to exercise more care in the selection of the goods he bought. He could tell the quality of a shoe with reasonable accuracy, or the workmanship of a suit of clothes, or the construction of a wagon, farm tools, or a house. Consequently, he depended more on his own appraisal of the value of goods than on the statements or selling activities of the seller.

The consumer today, however, has been reduced to a state of near helplessness in deciding where best to spend his money. The ingenuity of American inventors and the mass-production genius of present-day Americans have showered him with quantities of goods far beyond the number and variety available to others in the world. The American standard of material comfort is the envy of foreigners, but this abundance has placed a nearly impossible burden on the consumer when it comes to selecting the best buy for his money. The problem is not one alone of discounting the bewildering mass of advertising that confronts him from billboards, magazines, newspapers, radio, television, and other forms of advertising, and that necessarily attempts to portray the product of each manufacturer as superior to its competitors'. It is also a problem of trying to choose from the large number of brands of each article on the market. The problem is emphasized by the fact that a large department store offers several hundred thousand different articles to its customers.

NEGOTIATION OF THE TERMS OF SALE

The terms of sale include such items as price, delivery (time and place), warranty (the extent of the seller's obligation to repair or replace defective goods), and obligation, if any, of the seller to exchange or refund at the request of the buyer. For most items bought at retail, negotiation is virtually absent. A customer enters a store, asks for a tube of toothpaste, gets the brand he has requested, pays the clerk, takes immediate delivery, and leaves. At an auction negotiation is in the form of competitive bidding, and the terms of sale generally include no warranty against defects. In an Oriental bazaar higgling over price is the custom. The sale of a house, a car, or a specialized factory machine usually involves considerable negotiation. There is bargaining over price, date of delivery, warranty, and value of trade-in, if any.

TRANSFER OF OWNERSHIP

The act that consummates a sale of goods is the transfer of ownership. For the many small purchases a person makes, transfer of ownership is upon payment and delivery. For items of infrequent purchase the transfer of ownership is generally set forth in a formal written contract of sale.

STORAGE

The pattern of production and consumption over a period of time is very changeable for nearly all products. Persons buy more iced drinks in the summer than they do in the winter, and buy more soup in the winter than in the summer. They use their bathing suits to a greater extent in the summer and use fur coats in the winter. As far as production of agricultural products is concerned, the very nature of these products prevents their production in a steady flow during the year. Therefore it is necessary to store goods whenever the pattern of production is different from that of consumption. Wherever the pattern has any of the following characteristics, storage plays an important part in the distribution of the goods:

Seasonal production
Seasonal consumption
Irregular or unpredictable production
Irregular or unpredictable consumption
Possible interruptions in supply, making stockpiling necessary
Occasional appearance of bargain prices or discounts for large-quantity purchases
The necessity of aging to improve quality
Irregular or unpredictable transportation

Storage is found in virtually every level of production and distribution. Steel companies accumulate vast mountains of iron ore in the warm weather months during which ore boats can negotiate the Great Lakes waterway from northern Minnesota to Chicago, Cleveland, and other lake ports. In the winter, these mountains of ore are used to feed the steel furnaces that otherwise would become cold for lack of raw material. At almost every level of the process of transforming iron ore into iron, iron into steel, steel into bars, wire, or sheet, and transforming steel stock into finished products, storage is necessary to prevent or reduce interruptions in manufacturing. The manufacturer must maintain a parts inventory, a supplies inventory, a fuel inventory, and an inventory of finished products. Most wholesalers maintain a supply of the goods they sell to retailers. Retailers, of course, stock goods on their shelves and in their storage rooms so as to be able to satisfy the desire of customers to receive immediate delivery of the goods they purchase. Finally, consumers engage in storage, as everyone who has an attic or garage knows.

Some products require very little care in storage because of their resistance to weather, corrosion, or other influences. Coal, iron ore, limestone, and similar products are ordinarily stocked in the open air. But some goods are quite sensitive to temperature, weather, or other influences that result in deterioration. The storage of freshly cut flowers, for example, has so far defied the ingenuity of modern man, and therefore they must be enjoyed as soon as possible after they have been cut. Great advances, however, have been made in the science of storing products that until recently had been difficult to preserve for any length of time. The discovery of food canning as a means of preventing deterioration was one of the greatest storage discoveries of the last century and has wrought an incalculable change in the everyday life of American citizens. More recently, the growth of quick freezing has brought rapid changes in the food storage process. Deterioration by moisture has also been solved to some extent by recently developed techniques. Materials subject to corrosion can be preserved by applying a thin coating of oil or grease to the exposed surfaces. Because the problem of corrosion of materials achieved considerable magnitude in the operations of World War II, intensive research was devoted to discovering more satisfactory methods of preserving materials. One of the most promising developments was the method of coating tools, machines, and even battleships with a plastic substance that effectively sealed the objects treated.

STANDARDIZATION AND GRADING

The development of markets in which thousands of bushels of grains are sold daily has made necessary the establishment of standardization and grading. Whenever large amounts of bulk goods such as grain are marketed, we find it convenient to sort the grain into categories according to the qualities of the grain. When grain is marketed, it is sold according to grade. The standards now used for classifying grain and other staple products were determined many years ago, so that buyers could eliminate the necessity of inspecting the goods bought.

Grading is the process of examining samples of goods and assigning them to the standard or classification their quality or characteristics indicate. Grain is divided into standards on the basis of density, freedom from dirt or other matter, and moisture content. Cotton is classified according to the length of the fiber, strength, color, and freedom from extraneous material. Although the use of standardization and grading is virtually necessary in the bulk distribution of grain and food products from the producer to the retailer, they have many other applications. Whenever large quantities of goods of any kind are handled, the use of standards is apt to be employed. It permits buyers to enter into contracts for the future delivery of goods without the necessity of examining them, secure in the confidence that the goods delivered will be up to standard. It also enables buyers to purchase goods of a given standard from whatever source offers them at the most advantageous price. Banks and other lending agencies make loans on the security of goods, where the goods are standardized or graded, because they know immediately the market value of the goods when standards or grading are employed.

Thus, standardization and grading are largely useful as protection to the buyer. They are not used to any great extent in sales to the individual consumer of goods, who has been too disorganized and weak to secure the benefits that would result from the use of standardization and grading of products bought by him. In a few instances, the necessity of grading has been so obvious that the generally reluctant attitude on the part of producers has been insufficient to prevent its introduction. The lack of government regulation of pasteurization and distribution of milk resulted in considerable hazard to the health of adults and children when low-quality milk and even milk from tubercular cows was distributed. Along with the elimination by action of municipal and state governments of the distribution of dangerous milk, consumers can now buy Grade A regular milk, Grade B regular milk, light cream, and heavy cream with reasonable confidence of getting the quality usually associated with those grades. The federal government inspects and grades, where requested by the distributor, eggs, canned fruit and vegetables, and dried meats. The Dominion of Canada provides for its consumers grading of honey, maple sugar, eggs, fruits and vegetables, and meats; and, in addition, inspects and grades all canned foods distributed across provincial borders.

Occasionally, efforts have been made to secure agreement voluntarily on the part of producers, or by legislation, so that a simple-to-understand system of grading might be adopted for food items purchased by householders, but very little has been accomplished toward that end. Increased use of grading in selling goods such as food might reduce the effectiveness of brand names and advertising, since buyers would probably tend to purchase on the basis of quality indicated by the grade rather than by brand names and advertising. Much of the opposition to the use of standardization in selling to consumers comes from the advertising industry and from those producers who have invested heavily in building up a brand name. As long as much of the productive efforts in the field of consumer goods is devoted to building up and maintaining consumer acceptance of a brand name rather than to improving quality and lowering marketing costs, opposition to the greater use of standardization and grading in the consumer field will be considerable. And this will continue as long as the consumer remains poorly organized and poorly informed.

MARKETING FINANCE

Meeting expenses of operation is a constant problem in any business. The expenses in the marketing of goods are met by many of the same methods as in the manufacturing of goods. In the final analysis, all of the expenses of a business must be met from the funds derived through the sale of the company's goods or services. The problem of financing is one of arranging for the payment of certain expenses prior to the realization of funds from the sale of products or services. In other words, expenses usually precede income.

One method of dealing with expenses is to postpone payment on them. Quite commonly, goods are sold on terms that permit the buyer to receive his goods, and to pay for them after a week, a month, or a longer period. This permits, for example, a retailer to buy from a wholesaler, sell the goods to his customers, and receive the cash before paying his bill to the wholesaler. From the standpoint of the wholesaler, however, the privilege he extends to the retailer of delaying payment might require the wholesaler to borrow money to pay for those of his (the wholesaler's) expenses that must be paid as they arise. Although this extension of credit by the wholesaler to the retailer is a considerable financing aid to the retailer, it frequently causes the wholesaler to borrow, from a bank or other source of credit, more than he would like. He extends credit usually because he has to in order to increase his sales.

It has become common in this country for sellers to induce prompt payment for goods received by offering a discount from the invoice price for early payments in cash. A wholesaler might offer payment terms of 2/10/30. This means that if the customer buys goods invoiced at $100, he can pay $100 to the wholesaler at the end of 30 days or remit $98 at the end of 10 days from the date of the invoice. The $2 the customer pays to retain his $100 for an extra 20 days before sending it to the seller represents the same cost as borrowing from a finance company at the rate of approximately 35 percent per annum. Therefore, the customer is likely to send a check for $98 rather than waiting 30 days and sending one for $100. As a matter of fact, with payment terms such as the example above, the buyer would usually find it advisable to borrow money from his own bank, if necessary, to take advantage of the cash discount terms.

In the United States, a type of financing called **installment credit** has become common. The habit of paying for goods in installments is a very common feature of American buying, and other countries have come to use this method increasingly in recent years. England, for example, calls installment buying "hire-purchase contracts." This method of financing the purchase of goods increased rapidly in the United States during the 1920s, particularly in the field of retail sales. Under most installment contracts, the seller retains the title to the goods until they are completely paid for, or retains a legal privilege of repossessing them in the event of default in the installment payments. If the goods are repossessed by the seller as a result of default in installment payments, the seller can resell the goods to pay for the balance owed him.

RISKS

Risks are an inherent characteristic of doing business, as they are of the process of living itself. The future is largely unpredictable and hazards confront every individual each day of his personal and business life. The types of risks faced in the process of distributing goods are as follows:

Physical loss or deterioration of merchandise

Loss of value due to changes in the supply of goods or changes in the demand for goods

Losses as a result of nonpayment for goods by customers

Losses through pilferage, embezzlement, or theft

Losses through lawsuits brought by employees, competitors, customers, or others as a result of injury caused by the products or business action of a company

Some of the above risks can be reduced through careful business operation, others can be shifted to some extent to companies engaged in the business of bearing such risks, but the remainder must be recognized as one of the inescapable hazards of life. Risks of loss from deterioration or damage to merchandise in the process of distribution can be reduced by careful methods of storage and transportation. Some goods, such as coal and iron ore, are so impervious to the weather that the loss from deterioration is a minor factor. Other goods, such as foods, must be handled with extreme care so as to minimize losses.

Another risk in the field of marketing is the possible loss of value to merchandise due to changes in the nature and extent of demand for the goods, or to changes in the supply of goods available. Where the demand for goods is apt to be very unsteady, as in the case of highly styled clothing, this risk is considerable. Style merchandise not sold during the season for which it was manufactured must often be sold at a considerable price reduction toward the end of the season. Changes in the supply of goods may cause loss where a sudden shortage of goods makes a seller unable to deliver except by purchasing the scarce goods at a higher price than he had expected.

Risks due to the insolvency of customers to whom a distributor sells goods on credit is one of the hazards of business. This can be minimized by careful investigation of customers before granting them credit, but it can never be completely eliminated. Through careful selection of customers receiving the privilege of credit, a seller can reduce the losses from this risk to about 1 or 2 percent of credit sales.

Losses suffered through pilferage or embezzlement by employees or customers are sometimes an annoyance and sometimes a severe loss. Small tools and supplies are very difficult to defend from pilferage because they can be so easily slipped into the pockets of workers on the job. Such things as pencils, pens, and other office supplies frequently turn up in the homes of office workers. It would be impossible to stop all pilferage, but the inculcation of a responsible attitude on the part of the employees and care in issuing supplies liable to be pilfered can reduce the risk of such loss. Goods that are shipped overseas in international trade are particularly subject to pilferage, and efforts to reduce risks from this loss are strenuously made.

Losses caused by injuries suffered by employees while on the job, or suffered by customers while using a company's product, may sometimes be considerable. A worker slipping on an oily surface may injure his back, and his rehabilitation may cost hundreds or thousands of dollars to the company. A customer opening a can of vegetables may find decayed matter in the food and may sue the company for any injury resulting from the use of the food. To reduce risks of legal liability to employees, customers, or others, a company should carefully inspect its operations to improve safety, but the chance that expensive lawsuits might be instituted against it is always present.

Some of the above risks can be shifted to companies or individuals charging a fee for the carrying of risks. The whole field of insurance is one in which the risks of a large number of individuals or companies are borne by an insurance company with the result that the degree of risk is actually reduced through the process of bringing together a large number of similar risks. This principle is explained in the chapter on risk management.

Management on the basis of hunch or intuition is sometimes successful, but more often it is not. In every area of management there is need for information. This is as true of marketing as it is of other areas and is indicated in Figure 18-1. Information for marketing decisions can be gotten from government publications, industry publications, reports from company salesmen, and many other sources. Where information is not readily available, research may provide the answers. Marketing research is discussed in Chapter 16.

MARKETING INFORMATION

⤷

FEEDBACK

SUMMARY

Marketing covers the activities of selling, buying, transportation, storage, grading, and international trade. Selling includes stimulating demand for a product, finding a buyer, negotiating sales terms, and transferring title to goods.

Storage permits a steadier flow of products to consumers, because production can rarely be coordinated perfectly to the time and place where products are consumed. Transportation provides the means by which goods are sent from production centers to where they can be consumed.

In agricultural products, raw materials, and similar goods, the items are graded according to quality so that sellers and buyers can negotiate according to grades with which both sellers and buyers are familiar. Grading is needed where buyers purchase in large quantities.

Buying and selling require the setting of a price. The terms of sale indicate whether cash is demanded on delivery or whether the seller permits postponed payment as an inducement in making the sale.

Under the marketing manager the marketing department supports the company goals, operating within the constraints imposed by law and custom and cooperating with other departments of the company to function as a well-organized team.

QUESTIONS FOR REVIEW

1 How does the system of national and international marketing make life better for consumers?

2 What is meant by place utility? Time utility? How does marketing help to provide these utilities?

3 Is it necessary for a company such as a telephone company to create demand when it has no competitors?

4 Why is it more difficult for the consumer today to measure the quality of goods he buys and to make an informed choice between competing firms than it was for his grandfather?

5 Name some products that require considerable negotiation between buyer and seller on terms of sale. Name some products that involve little or no negotiation. Explain why there is such a difference.

6 Give some examples of goods that require little storage care, other than those mentioned in the text, and give, also, some examples of your own goods that require considerable care in storage.

7 Why are standards and grading of goods so little used in selling to consumers?

8 How does installment selling aid in the marketing of goods?

9 What risks are faced by businessmen in the marketing of goods? How can these risks be reduced?

10 What are the constraints on the marketing manager in doing his job? How does he get information to guide him in making decisions?

SELECTED READINGS   Britt, Steuart Henderson, and Harper W. Boyd: *Marketing Management and Administrative Action*, 3d ed., McGraw-Hill Book Company, New York, 1973.

Buzzell, Robert D., Robert E. M. Nourse, John B. Matthews, and Theodore Levitt: *Marketing: A Contemporary Analysis*, 2d ed., McGraw-Hill Book Company, New York, 1972.

Carman, James M., and Kenneth P. Uhl: *Phillips and Duncan's Marketing*, 7th ed., Richard D. Irwin, Inc., Homewood, Ill., 1973.

Lazer, William, and Eugene J. Kelley: *Social Marketing*, Richard D. Irwin, Inc., Homewood, Ill., 1973.

Wish, John R., and Steve Gamble: *Marketing and Social Issues*, John Wiley & Sons, Inc., New York, 1972.

Name	Section	Date

COMPLETION SENTENCES

1 The services of marketing may be costly but they add

~~what~~ _utility_ to goods.

2 Giving place utility to goods is the function of moving goods from where they

are _less_ wanted to where they are

more wanted.

3 All products and services are in competition with each other for the limited

number of _dollars_ available to

customers .

4 The function of finding a buyer can be either _personal_

or _impersonal_ .

5 Whenever selling is undertaken, _buying_ is also present,

because both terms refer to the same function.

6 The average consumer spends a considerable part of his lifetime in the activity of _~buying~_ .

7 For most items bought in a retail store _~negotiation~_ is virtually absent in determining the terms of sale.

8 Storage is necessary whenever the pattern of _~production~_ is different from the pattern of _~distribution~_ .

9 _~Standardization~_ is the action of determining the specifications of various classes of commodities in which quality, color, size, or other variations are found.

10 _~Grading~_ is the process of examining samples of goods and assigning them to the standard or classification their quality or characteristics indicate.

11 Increased use of _~grading~_ in selling goods such as foods at retail might reduce the effectiveness of brand names.

12 One method of dealing with expense is to postpone _~payment~_ on goods ordered.

13 Expense usually precedes _~income~_ .

14 In Great Britain _~installment~_ buying is called "hire-purchase."

15 Coal and iron ore are so impervious to the weather that the loss in value because of _~exposure to weather~_ is a minor factor.

Name	Section	Date

TRUE OR FALSE STATEMENTS

T **1** All products and services are in competition with each other for the limited number of dollars of the consumer.

T **2** The costs of various marketing services represent about half the final sales price of an article.

F **3** Wherever selling is undertaken, buying is not necessarily undertaken, since the two functions differ.

T **4** Compared with today, the consumer of 100 years ago was able to exercise more care in the selection of goods bought.

F **5** At a typical auction the terms of sale usually include a warranty against defects of articles bought.

F **6** All products require considerable care in storage against weather.

T **7** The establishment of grades for grains has made feasible the buying and selling of large quantities of grains without inspection of each purchase by buyers.

F **8** Standardization and grading are used more extensively in selling to consumers than between businessmen.

F **9** Payment terms of 2/10/30 means the buyer can deduct 2 percent of the invoice if payment is made within 10 days or deduct 1 percent if payment is made in 30 days.

T **10** In most installment contracts the seller retains title to the goods until they are completely paid for.

T **11** It is particularly difficult to stop the pilferage of small tools and office supplies.

F **12** Because of stronger packaging, shipment of goods in overseas trade is less subject to pilferage than in domestic trade.

T **13** For a fee some risks can be shifted to others who, for the fee, are willing to bear the risk.

T **14** The marketing manager operates under a number of constraints that limit the range of his freedom of action.

F **15** Among the sources of information for the marketing manager, information from company salesmen and company customers is not considered valuable.

EXERCISE

1 Make a list of the articles or services for which you feel fairly competent to judge quality. For each article or service outline the points or characteristics to be examined in judging quality. Describe briefly how a person can inspect each article or service on your list to judge whether it is worth the price asked.

Article or Service	Characteristics	How to Inspect

2 There have been many advances in the techniques of storing perishable items, particularly foods. Foods are dried, canned, and frozen. These three methods of retarding spoilage have been used for decades. Can they be applied to all perishable products (e.g., flowers)? Some new methods of preventing deterioration are freeze drying and irradiation with radioisotopes. From the library or other sources, find out what you can about recent advances in storage of perishables. Speculate on what the new methods of preventing deterioration will do to the older methods of storage. What changes in consumer habits of buying foods and other perishables will be caused by these advances?

3 Storage is an important part of the marketing process, and is important in the home as well as in business. List the storage areas of your home, indicating any special features each has, the types of articles stored, and where storage facilities of comparable type are found in business.

19 PRICING

As soon as money came into existence many centuries ago, the problem of pricing became one of the most important economic problems man had to face. Pricing is a yardstick to measure value. When we see that a hamburger costs 60 cents, we learn the value of the hamburger. If the price of a soft drink is 10 cents, we can see that a hamburger has a value six times that of the soft drink. Pricing, therefore, permits us to compare the value of different things.

The yardstick used in measuring price is money. It is something like the inches and feet we use to measure length. In the case of money, however, the yardstick is not a stable one. Money itself changes in value. These changes cause as much difficulty as would be caused by a yardstick that changes in length from year to year. So far, human beings have not been able to develop a yardstick of value that remains steady all the time.

Read carefully the pages covering the factors in price. In order to understand the pricing policy of business, it is necessary that you understand the factors that influence pricing. In the section devoted to outlining the price policy of business, keep in mind that in the United States, unlike many parts of the world, there is relatively little haggling over price in a store. While there is considerable competition at the retail level (much of it in the form of price), the competition takes the form of setting individual prices at the same level competitors are setting rather than attempting to outguess the willingness of each customer to accept particular prices.

At the retail level, prices are most freely set by the store owner. To some extent, however, his freedom is restrained. In times of war, the restraint is usually exercised by the government on behalf of customers. At other times, the restraint by the government is often for the benefit of sellers and at their demand. Resale price maintenance and "unfair sales" laws are examples of this. Remember, of course, that the freedom of a retailer to set his prices is a relative one. His concern in setting a price is dictated by his hope of selling goods at a price high enough to cover his cost. His freedom to set prices is limited in the downward direction by his estimated cost of doing business; in the upward direction, it is limited by the extent of price competition in his industry and by his estimate of the willingness of the customers to pay.

It is impossible to determine when man first put a pirce on the goods and services he offered to others. In primitive societies, goods were exchanged on a basis of barter, which is still found, to some extent, in modern societies. For example, people exchange postage stamps. The classified advertisements section of some newspapers contain a department called "Will Trade," listing items people offer and what they want in exchange. But barter is rare in a complex civilization.

When a society develops money as a medium of exchange, sellers state the number of units of money they demand in exchange for the goods and services they offer. The number of units of money demanded is the *price*. During the early years of American history, people produced for themselves much of what they needed, and prices were not so vital a factor as they are today. As population increased, people specialized in production more and more. Exchange increased in importance and, with it, the problems of price.

Where prices have remained stable, price problems have been relatively minor. But with changing prices, problems increase. In a dynamic economy, individual prices are continually changing. Indeed, the economy would not be very dynamic if they did not. Price changes are necessary to reflect changes in costs of production, changes in demand for products, and the obsolescence of old methods and products. Changing prices are necessary to adapt production to the changing needs of a nation.

However, when most prices rise at the same time or fall at the same time, the matter is of national concern. Most people agree that a stable level of prices in general is beneficial. But we do not know how to achieve such a goal by means satisfactory to all. A look at Figure 19-1 shows how much prices have fluctuated in the past. They will undoubtedly fluctuate in the future.

FACTORS INFLUENCING PRICE

Prices are a rationing mechanism. If a man has $1,000 to spend, a glance at the prices of the things he wants will indicate how he must limit his choices to the amount of money he has available. Presumably, he will try to satisfy his strongest desires first. What money he has left, he will spend on less demanding needs.

INFLUENCE OF DEMAND ON PRICE

In Chapter 3 we examined the relationship of price to demand and supply, noting that as demand increases, price tends to rise. Here we note that the price mechanism serves to channel production to those items and services that people demand. Sometimes people change their living habits, spending less on one item than before and more on another. This tends to lower the price of the article losing popularity and to raise the price of the article gaining popularity, signaling to producers that a shift in production is in order. When radios became available after World War I, people shifted their spending to radios and away from phonographs. Radio manufacture became very profitable and phonograph manufacture relatively unprofitable.

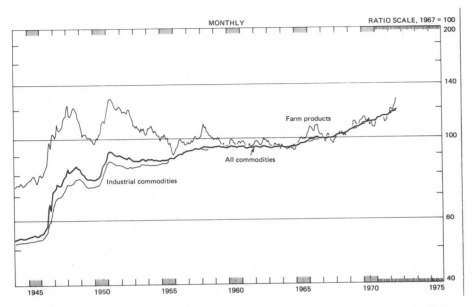

FIGURE 19-1 Wholesale prices. (*Historical Chart Book*, Board of Governors of the Federal Reserve System, 1972, p. 99. Data from Bureau of Labor Statistics.)

To stay in business, a producer must, in the long run, sell his goods at a price high enough to cover all of his costs. If everybody were able to do this, there would be no need for bankruptcy laws. Those unable to do so go out of business. The more fortunate ones continue in existence.

INFLUENCE OF COST ON PRICES

Costs differ between members of an industry, and cost comparisons are frequently difficult to make. Some products, such as golf balls or radios, are different even though similar. Other products differ so much in quality of materials, care in manufacture, and styling, as in men's suits or shoes, that cost and price comparisons are misleading. Some products, however, are sufficiently uniform to illustrate the effect of cost on price. Most farm products are of this type. The influence of cost on prices in the short run is frequently small. If a farmer can sell his wheat for no more than $1.80 a bushel, that is the price he will have to accept. If his costs are $1.50, he will make a profit. If they are $2.10, he will suffer a loss. In the long run, on the other hand, the influence of cost on price is considerable. The farmer will not continue to grow wheat at a loss. If costs rise while prices do not, production eventually falls as some producers leave the industry and others find it less profitable. If demand remains the same, shortages in supply will develop, and the price will tend to rise. If costs fall and demand remains the same, profits will rise. This will attract new producers to the industry, if there is no barrier to entry, and tend to increase production. This in turn will tend to reduce prices.

The study of price determination is complex and cannot be presented in detail here. The relationship of demand, supply, and price can be summarized, however. An increase in demand for an article tends to raise its price; a decline tends to lower it. Demand for bathing suits is high during June, and so is the price. Demand for bathing suits declines sharply as summer ends, and price markdowns are much in evidence. An increase in the supply of an article tends to lower the price; a decline in supply tends to raise it. Changes in price also affect supply and demand, a rise in price stimulating production but tending to reduce the demand. All three, price, demand, and supply, are interacting. A change in any one will affect the other two.

PRICE BEHAVIOR IN MONOPOLY

In a monopoly, there is only one seller to whom buyers can turn. Examples include water, telephone service, and electricity. Although there are many companies in the United States providing electric power, in any given locality, a person can buy from only one. Of course, a person can substitute gas, kerosene, or candles for electricity, and a factory might operate its own electric power plant. A monopoly is rarely complete or pure. But, in the case of electric power, to continue the example, the substitutes are inconvenient for most users. The price of electricity could rise considerably before people would use candles or kerosene.

A monopolist is in the enviable position of being able to choose his own selling price with negligible fear that competition will affect his choice. The price will, however, determine to some extent the amount the monopolist can sell. If the demand for a product is *inelastic*, it is not sensitive to change in price, and a monopolist can raise his price without suffering much of a loss in sales. If the demand for a product is *elastic*, it is sensitive to changes in price. A slight increase in price will result in a substantial decline in sales, while a slight decrease in price will cause a large increase in sales. Therefore, the extent to which a monopolist raises his prices is influenced by the elasticity of demand for his product. In choosing his selling price, he will be concerned with the effect of price on his volume of sales, not with its effect on his competitors, since he has none. In balancing considerations of price and volume of sales, the monopolist will try to choose the magic combination that will give him the largest profit. The choice may be a high price and low volume, low price and high volume, or somewhere in between. Finally, it must be pointed out that in many monopolies, such as water, telephone, gas, and electricity, governmental regulatory bodies attempt to protect the public by restraining to some degree the freedom of a monopolist in setting his prices.

PRICE BEHAVIOR IN COMPETITION

Competition takes many forms—in advertising, styling, research and development, and so on. But we are concerned here with price competition where there are many sellers offering the same product. In pure competition, an individual seller has no control over his selling price. Wheat production is an example of reasonably pure competition. A farmer could not sell any of his wheat if he raised his price above the market price. At the market price he can sell his entire crop, so it would be foolish for him to set his price below it.

Many industries exhibit price characteristics that cannot be explained by simple monopoly or pure competition. Between the two extremes are many degrees of competition that are given different names for the purpose of analysis. Two will be examined here, *monopolistic competition* and *price leadership*. Monopolistic competition applies to a situation where there are several sellers of similar products and where elements both of monopoly and of competition exist. Refrigerators are an example. Westinghouse has a monopoly on the Westinghouse label and if a buyer wants a Westinghouse refrigerator, he can get it from one maker only. But there are many other companies making refrigerators. If one is shopping for a refrigerator rather than a Westinghouse, he has considerable choice. Price behavior of sellers in such a situation is complex. While prices of 12-cubic-foot refrigerators produced by different companies are similar, they are usually not exactly the same. The television sets of different companies are also similar, but again they are rarely exactly alike.

Where a producer can make his product distinctive from other similar products, he can make his price different from his competitors'. But his freedom to set price is limited because the degree of distinctiveness of his product is limited. In the case of aspirin, a simple chemical compound, the degree of distinctiveness is largely limited to the brand name, and consumers are willing to pay different prices for the drug largely because most people are not chemists. In automobiles, the distinctiveness is much greater. Ford, Chevrolet, and Plymouth compete for the same customers, but each car is quite distinctive. The degree of distinction achieved by a producer measures his degree of freedom to dictate price. Where sellers prefer not to compete on a basis of lowering prices, they strive to make their products more distinctive by means of merchandising techniques, product design, and other means. Frequently, when an industry is faced with declining sales the members of the industry will react by spending more money for style design and sales promotion than by cutting prices.

MONOPOLISTIC COMPETITION

PRICE LEADERSHIP

Let us suppose an area is served by four companies making bricks. If one company cuts its price, it will take sales from the other three. But what will the other three do? Obviously, they must match the price cut of the first company so as to regain their lost sales volume. One of them might cut prices even further, starting a "price war." The result would be that the profit per unit of each company would decline. Possibly, the result would be such an increase in total brick sales that the total profit of each company would actually rise. That would depend on the elasticity of demand for bricks. Most likely, the result would be that each company would face a decline in profits. With all four brick makers worse off, it is highly probable that they would get together over a cup of coffee or a steak dinner and decide to compete on a more gentlemanly basis, declaring that price cutting is destructive. Even if the four did not get together, experience would tell them that a price cut by one will bring increased sales for only a brief period.

If one of the brick companies happened to be substantially larger than the other three, it might act as a *price leader*. If an increase in labor costs occurred, the leader would raise prices, and the others would follow suit. If builders started using concrete blocks more and brick less, the leader might cut prices, with the others matching the cut. This type of pricing is found in the steel industry, for example.

PRICE POLICIES IN BUSINESS

"CHARGE WHAT THE TRAFFIC WILL BEAR"

Persons who have been to an Oriental bazaar know that a dealer in brassware may sell identical products to different customers at different prices. American tourists are prized because they are usually willing to pay more than anyone else, and the price quoted to them is higher. In the sale of automobiles, in spite of manufacturers' suggested list prices, this pricing policy has been common, with buyer and car dealer haggling over final price, particularly over the value at which the customer's old car will be accepted in trade for a newer one. Physicians also have used this policy. Those who accept charity patients charge them little or nothing. To other patients, the charge is often determined by estimating the size of the patient's bank account.

ONE-PRICE POLICY

The opposite policy is the one-price policy where the seller establishes a price for each article and sticks with it. No haggling is involved, nor is any distinction in price made between customers except where a customer might buy in large quantities or require extra service. Most retailers in Europe and America follow this policy.

PRICE LINE

Where similar products are offered in a series of grades or qualities, a series of prices will identify each grade. For example, a shoe store might offer five grades of men's shoes at prices of $7.49, $9.80, $12.95, $19.50, and $29.95. Thus, it would offer five price lines. A service station might have three price lines for gasoline, one for regular, one for premium, and one for premium extra. Where price lines are used, price increases or reductions can be made unobtrusively. Rather than raising all prices, the lowest price line can be dropped and a new one added at the top. If sales lag during a decline in business activity, a manufacturer can add a new economy model with a lower price line.

ODD-FIGURE PRICING

Prices such as $.19, $.49, $.95, $1.98, and $9.95 are frequently used instead of even figures. There are two common reasons for employing odd numbers. One is that it forces sales clerks to make change more frequently in accepting payment from a customer. This is thought to reduce the temptation of a clerk to pocket the money paid by a customer instead of ringing up the sale on a cash register. The second reason is that a price of $.98 appears to be much lower to some people than it really is. A price of $4.95 appears to be "over $4" rather than "almost $5." Such pricing probably stimulates the impulse to buy to some extent. Service stations use this policy in advertising gasoline prices to the passing motorist. The approaching driver sees a sign announcing gasoline at 40 in large figures visible at a distance. Not until he enters the station driveway is he close enough to see the small number which indicates the price to be 40.9 cents a gallon.

MARKUPS

An easy method of determining price in wholesale and retail trade is to employ a markup. Because it is mechanical, it obviates the need to exercise judgment in pricing. The markup may be based either on the selling price or on the cost to the seller. In retail trade, the selling price is the basis for markup used by most of the larger stores. If a markup of 33⅓ percent of the retail price is used, as shown in Figure 19-2, an article costing $6 would be priced at $9, or more likely at $8.95.

Some small retailers have been confused in their markup policy when using cost as a base. If the operating expense amounts to 20 percent of retail sales, a store owner might assume that a 25 percent markup would give him an adequate margin of profit above his expenses. Using cost as a base, an item purchased at $8 would be priced at $10. But the markup of $2 on this item would be only 20 percent of the retail price. The retailer would, therefore, not be making a profit at $10 on this item; he would be barely covering his expenses.

DISCOUNTS

A manufacturer or wholesaler frequently sells to retailers and other middlemen by stating the retail selling price and allowing a discount from that price. The retail price is usually called the *list price*, and the retailer is generally expected to sell

FIGURE 19-2 Structure of retail selling price.

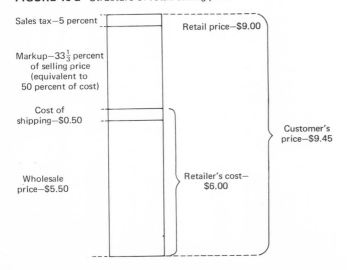

to his customers at that price. The discount to the retailer, however, might be 35 percent. Thus, an item with a list price of $200 would cost the retailer $130.

If a manufacturer wishes to encourage buying in quantity, he can offer *quantity discounts*. A manufacturer may have the following quantity discount schedule:

1 to 9 units	no discount
10 to 49 units	1 percent discount
50 to 149 units	2 percent discount
150 to 499 units	3 percent discount
Carload lots (500 or more)	5 percent discount

Generally, each order must qualify separately for the quantity discount. A seller may, however, permit all orders during a month to be totaled for the quantity discount.

The performance of a specified service for the manufacturer may permit the retailer to take a *functional discount*. Local advertising of the product, window display, special promotion, and stocking of a full line of the manufacturer's products are examples of services for which a retailer may earn a functional discount.

A manufacturer may permit a retailer 30 days in which to pay. To encourage earlier payment, as we mentioned before, a *cash discount* may be offered.

MANUFACTURER'S SUGGESTED PRICES

The control that manufacturers exercise over the retail price of their products varies from negligible to complete. Many manufacturers aim at a particular retail price in designing a product. They may control the price rigidly by retaining title to the goods until sold by the retailer or they may merely suggest the price to the retailer, letting him adopt it or not as he sees fit. The suggested price may be printed on the package or on a label attached to the item. This price may be widely advertised by the manufacturer. Where the suggested price is advertised or is printed on the article, the retailer would hardly attempt to sell at a higher price. He might, however, sell at a lower price, and he often does. In the case of some items, most retailers might adhere to the printed price, which would, therefore, be the "regular" price. But people love to get bargains, and some retailers adopt a policy of pricing their goods below the suggested prices. Sometimes a manufacturer will tag his products with a price substantially above the intended selling price, which enables all retailers to sell at less than the "regular" price and gives the customers the illusion of having saved money on their purchases.

CUSTOMARY PRICES

Many small articles that are purchased frequently are sold at prices designed to be convenient. These prices tend to become customary; for instance, most soft drinks and candy bars are sold at either 10 or 15 cents. The prices of a cup of coffee and a pack of cigarettes in the past were also strongly influenced by custom. The spread of vending machines in selling such items has strengthened the customary price. Custom is difficult to change, and this is as true in prices as in other aspects of society. When rising costs reduce profit margins to the vanishing point, manufacturers will usually resist changing the price until forced to do so. Frequently, the quality or quantity will be lowered instead. During the inflation of prices that followed World War II, the net weight of a 5-cent candy bar was reduced in steps to about half. The size of the package, however, declined more slowly.

GOVERNMENT INFLUENCES ON PRICES

Earlier in this chapter, we examined the influence of demand and supply on prices and touched briefly on the behavior of prices under monopoly and competition. Where the production and sale of a product approach pure competition, the price will remain close to the cost of production of at least some of the producers. Those unable to meet costs will leave the industry, perhaps through bankruptcy. Others will take their place. Buyers are protected automatically by the vigor of competition and by the fact that each producer has such a small share of the total market that he cannot dictate prices. At the other extreme is monopoly. Here prices are set by the monopolist to yield a maximum profit.

In general terms, the influence of government on prices takes two forms. The first includes government attempts to put a floor under prices in those industries where price competition is strong. In such cases, action is taken because producers demand it. Some examples are farm price supports, resale price maintenance, import duties, and production quotas. The second form includes government attempts to put a ceiling over prices in those industries where competition is weak or absent. Such action is taken because consumers demand it. Regulation of rates in telephone, gas, and electricity is an example. In times of depression, the tendency is to strengthen price floors. In times of inflation—particularly during a war—the tendency is to strengthen and extend price ceilings.

RESALE PRICE MAINTENANCE

During the Depression of the 1930s, prices dropped about 40 percent from the 1929 level. Price competition increased in importance while the various forms of nonprice competition became relatively less important. Of all of the forms of competition, a cut in prices by one's competitor is probably resented most by other businessmen. The average retailer, for example, can accept an increase in advertising by his competitor, or the remodeling and enlargement of a store, but a price cut is not so readily accepted. There was a lot of price cutting during the Depression, and there was a lot of resentment.

One reaction to price competition was the effort of some retailers and manufacturers to eliminate competition in prices for the same brand of goods in different stores. The manufacturer already had the power to dictate the retail price of his wares, if he sold on consignment or sold only through those stores that agreed to adopt the manufacturer's price. Most manufacturers, however, were reluctant to do either. Instead, pressure was exerted on the state legislatures to enact laws to hinder price competition. The best-known of such laws are the *resale price maintenance* laws, also known as "fair trade" laws. Forty-five states passed these laws, and the Federal McGuire Act permitted enforcement of such laws where the manufacturer and retailer were located in different states.

Under resale price maintenance, the producer can set the price for each brand of goods he makes and enter into a contract with retailers to sell at not less than that price. The *nonsigner clause*, an essential part of such a law, makes the contract binding on all retailers selling the brand to the general public, whether they signed the contract or not.

These laws have become the subject of considerable controversy, particularly since World War II. The main arguments in support of these laws are as follows:

> Price measures quality. If a store cuts a price, it injures the reputation for quality of the product.
>
> Competition is shifted from price to nonprice competition such as service and quality, which benefits the consumer more than cutting prices would.
>
> "Cutthroat" pricing is prevented and competition put on a more "ethical" plane.
>
> If a manufacturer spends money to build up consumer acceptance of a brand name, he has "property rights" in that brand name. If a product carrying that brand name is sold at less than the price the manufacturer desires, his property rights have been injured.
>
> The use of *loss leaders* is prevented, where a branded article is advertised at a price below the retailer's cost. Loss leaders are intended to lure customers to the store, where it is hoped, they will buy more than enough profitable items to offset the loss on the loss leader.

The arguments against these laws were summarized by the *Wall Street Journal* in an editorial:

> Fair trade laws violate two laws. They violate the first basic law of economics in a free enterprise system, which is that there must be competition.
>
> And they violate the spirit—as well as the fact—of the anti-trust laws which outlaw price-fixing. They do this by a twist of language. "Horizontal" agreements—where manufacturers set the same prices on similar goods—are illegal. But "vertical" agreements—where prices are kept high by agreement of a manufacturer and a retailer—are said to be honest and straightforward and in some states they are legal.
>
> The difference, though, in a number of widget makers putting their heads together to set prices for retailers of widgets and in a number of widget makers getting together with the retailers to set prices, certainly escapes us. Price-fixing, whether it goes sideways or up and down, is still price-fixing and a twist of language cannot disguise the fact.

"UNFAIR SALE" LAWS   In some 30 states, laws have been passed prohibiting retailers from selling goods below cost. These laws have been passed in response to the demand of small retailers and are aimed at chain stores and other mass retailers. *Cost* is generally defined in the laws as invoice cost to retailer plus markup varying from 6 to 12 percent, depending on the state.

Enforcement of these laws has been difficult. Most of the laws permit exceptions to "meet the price of a competitor," to close out perishable goods, to reduce oversupply of an item, and to "relieve financial distress." Furthermore, when one retailer buys in large quantities,and receives a quantity discount, he can legally sell below his competitors not receiving the quantity discount—unless they reduce their prices "to meet the competition." In some cases, little attempt is made to enforce the laws, which remain a potential hazard rather than an actual deterrent in reducing prices.

PRICE INSTABILITY

Since the end of World War II, prices in the industrial nations of the world have risen, almost without interruption. The overall record of the United States has been better than that of most other nations, with a slower rise of prices than the rest of the world. Nevertheless, every year since 1949 has seen higher consumer prices. Not even recessions of business activity have interrupted the upward march of prices. Moreover, since 1967 consumer prices have risen at a rate of 3 to 6 percent each year. Clearly, inflation has become severe, perhaps the most severe domestic problem we face.

We appear to be in a period of increasingly strong upward pressure on prices. Prices of raw materials, responding to heavy world demand, have risen sharply during the 1970s. Labor unions have demanded, usually successfully, substantial wage increases, adding to producers' costs, which are then translated into higher prices. Governmental action on price control has been unpredictable, with the President suddenly freezing prices and wages in August 1971 and removing price and wage controls equally suddenly in January 1973.

The effect on business has been to make planning, particularly long-range planning, more hazardous than before. Businesses that make extensive use of raw materials can reduce the risk of price increases to some extent through hedging (explained in Chapter 26). Labor contracts covering 3 years or more can be negotiated, although in return the union negotiators demand upward annual adjustments of wage rates in anticipation of price rises. Such contracts may lessen the uncertainty but not the cost of labor.

How will inflation affect consumers, and what will be their reaction to constantly rising prices? Of course we are all consumers, whether we are farmers, businessmen, union leaders, or retired people. Inflation affects different groups in different ways, some benefiting, some being injured. But for everybody, a rapid, long-term rise in prices creates an additional hazard, on top of all of the other hazards of economic life. Perhaps we will all eventually adjust to an inflation rate of 3 to 6 percent annually. Perhaps we will be successful in holding price rises to an average increase of 1 percent or less. Perhaps inflation will become even more severe, with prices increasing wildly. Perhaps a severe depression will create a falling price level, as in 1929 to 1933. Such are the possibilities.

As businessmen and as consumers all we can do is to take whatever steps are available to each of us to mitigate the hazards we face, being aware that we live in dangerous economic times and living with the hope that a more stable period will follow soon.

SUMMARY   Price is the number of units of money asked by sellers in exchange for their goods and services. In a dynamic society there are constant changes of prices on individual items, reflecting changes in production and changes in demand. If demand for an item increases, producers can ask for and get higher prices; if demand decreases, producers usually have to lower prices. If costs of production increase, producers sooner or later have to increase prices; if production costs decrease, competition among producers—where price competition is present—forces prices down.

In an Oriental bazaar, sellers "size up" a customer and ask the highest price they think he might accept—then haggle until a price is reached agreeable to both. Identical articles are thus sold at different prices, according to the bargaining skills of buyer and seller. In the United States, such a pricing policy is relatively uncommon. Specific prices are usually quoted for all buyers entering a retail store, for retailers buying from a wholesaler, or for wholesalers buying from a producer.

For the most part, each seller is free to set whatever price he chooses, subject to the influence of whatever competition there might be for his product or service. But there are some restraints imposed by law on price setting. Some laws interfere with setting a low price, generally because producers have demanded such laws. Other laws interfere with setting a high price, usually because consumers have demanded such laws in the absence of competition to control prices.

QUESTIONS FOR REVIEW

1 Why is barter more common in primitive societies than in industrial societies? What types of barter are found in industrial nations?

2 When individual prices rise and fall, it is not of much concern except to the buyers and sellers of the particular products; but if most prices rise together or fall together, the movement is of national concern. Is this a paradox? Explain.

3 "Prices are a rationing mechanism." Explain.

4 How does the price mechanism serve to channel production to those items and services that people demand?

5 If demand for a product, such as potatoes, falls, what tends to happen to production in the long run? Why?

6 What is a monopolist? If a monopolist is free from government laws in setting prices, are there any constraints or forces that limit the levels of the prices he sets? Explain.

7 What is meant by elastic demand? By inelastic demand? What are some examples of articles or services with elastic demand? With inelastic demand?

8 In monopolistic competition there are elements both of monopoly and of competition. What are these elements? How do they influence prices?

9 What types of products are found in monopolistic competition? Give some examples not listed in this chapter.

10 Explain price leadership. In what industries is it found?

11 What is a one-price policy? A price line?

12 What are the reasons for using odd figures, such as 98 cents or $4.95, in pricing?

13 What are the different types of discounts found in business? What is the purpose of each?

14 What is meant by a manufacturer's suggested list price? Are retailers bound to sell at this price? Are retailers more likely to sell above this price or below, if they do not sell at the suggested price? Why?

15 What are resale price maintenance laws? What groups in the United States are responsible for passing these laws?

SELECTED READINGS

Bilas, Richard A.: *Microeconomic Theory*, 2d ed., McGraw-Hill Book Company, New York, 1971.

Harper, Donald V., and William F. Massy: *Price Policy and Procedure*, Harcourt Brace Jovanovich, Inc., New York, 1972.

Howard, John A., and Jagdish N. Sheth: *The Theory of Buyer Behavior*, John Wiley & Sons, Inc., New York, 1969.

Hughes, David G.: *Demand Analysis for Marketing Decisions*, Richard D. Irwin, Inc., Homewood, Ill., 1973.

Walters, S. George: *Marketing Management Viewpoints*, South-Western Publishing Company, Cincinnati, 1970.

Name   Section   Date

COMPLETION SENTENCES

1 If costs rise while prices do not, production eventually _falls or declines_

2 If costs of production fall while demand remains the same,

profits will tend to rise.

3 To stay in business in the long run, a producer must sell his goods at a price

high enough to cover _costs of production_.

4 In a monopoly, there is only one _seller_ to whom buyers

can turn.

5 If the demand for a product is _elastic_, it is not sensitive

to changes in price.

6 If the demand for a product is _inelastic_, it is sensitive to

changes in price.

7 The extent to which a monopolist raises his prices is influenced by the
elasticity of demand for his product.

8 A policy opposite to that of charging what the traffic will bear is the
nonprice policy.

9 In retail trade, the _selling_ price is the basis for markup used by most of the larger stores.

10 Odd-figure pricing forces sales clerks to make change more often in making a sale, thus reducing the temptation for the clerk to _pool the money_

11 The performance of a specified service for the manufacturer may permit the retailer to take a _functional_ discount.

12 In times of depression, the tendency is to strengthen price _floors_.

13 In times of inflation, the tendency is to strengthen price _ceilings_.

14 A brand name article advertised at a price below the retailer's cost is called _loss leader_.

15 The _non-signer_ clause, an essential part of a resale price maintenance law, makes the contract binding on all retailers selling the brand to the general public.

TRUE OR FALSE STATEMENTS

T 1 The number of units of money demanded for an article is the price of the article.

T 2 Changing prices are necessary to adapt production to the changing needs of consumers.

Name   Section   Date

F **3** If a farmer produces a crop of wheat at a cost to him of $2.10 a bushel, he will set his price for that crop at $2.10 or above, in order to be sure of covering his costs.

F **4** A decrease in demand tends to raise the price of an article; an increase in supply tends to lower it.

F **5** If the demand for an article is inelastic, it is sensitive to changes in price.

F **6** In deciding on the price for an article he sells, a monopolist is influenced by the effect of his price decision on his competitors.

T **7** Where sellers prefer not to compete on a basis of price, they strive to make their products as distinctive as possible.

F **8** A price policy of "charging what the traffic will bear" is typically found in Oriental bazaars but not in the United States.

T **9** A price line is a series of prices associated with different qualities or grades of an article.

F **10** The explanation for odd-figure pricing is psychological and is not used to force sales clerks to ring cash sales.

F **11** Applying the same percentage markup to cost or selling price makes no difference provided the retailer applies the markup consistently to all products.

T **12** A quantity discount is used to encourage quantity buying.

T **13** The control producers have over the retail prices of their products ranges from complete to negligible.

T **14** Rather than raise the quoted price of an article, sellers sometimes reduce the quantity or the quality when their costs rise.

T **15** Enforcement of "unfair sales" laws is difficult.

EXERCISES

1 Visit an auction, a secondhand store, a used car lot, a gasoline service station, and a department store. Contrast the pricing policies found in each. How do you explain these differences? Would a different pricing policy be better in any of these cases from the standpoint of the seller? Of the consumer?

2 *Case Problem for report or class discussion.*

Ralph Fouler, president and chief stockholder of Dynamic Motors, Inc., has been wondering if any change should be made in his price policies for the coming season. For example, the price at which he sold a two-year-old station wagon the previous year was $1,990. He knows from experience that there is considerable shopping around by customers before they decide on a car. He also knows that most customers have an old car that they wish to trade in, and on which they seek as high a trade-in price as they can get. At times, Fouler has offered a higher trade-in allowance than he knew the old car was worth to make a sale of a car on his lot. This has resulted at times in shaving the profit margin on the sale closer than he would like.

One of the salesmen suggests that they tag each car on the lot at a price $200 higher than their price policy now dictates. This would put the price of the station wagon in this example at $2,190. The salesman explains that this would permit them to offer a trade-in allowance on old cars of $200 more than the price at which the old cars could be resold. The customer would be happy at the generous trade-in allowance, and there would be no cut in the expected profit margin on each car sold.

What do you think of the idea? Do you think the price policy he suggests would be successful in making sales? Do you think there might be any long-run detrimental aftereffects? Can you suggest any alternative pricing policy?

For the purpose of studying marketing, goods can be classified into two groups: industrial goods and consumer goods. Note that the distinction lies not in the kind of goods, but in what they are used for; not in what they are, but in what they do.

Wholesaling and retailing describe two steps in the process of marketing of goods. Wholesalers buy in large quantities and sell to retailers, who buy in smaller quantities and sell to consumers. Notice that the functions of marketing, such as buying, selling, storage, delivery, bearing risks, and financing, are undertaken at both the wholesaler's level and the retailer's. Some of these functions, such as storage or risk bearing, may be undertaken in a particular instance entirely at the wholesaler's level or entirely at the retailer's. Notice that different types of wholesalers offer varying wholesaling services to their customers.

You should find the section on retailing easy to understand. You are familiar with this aspect of marketing because, as a consumer, you have almost daily contact with retail establishments. In reading this section, however, try to put yourself in the position of the retailer. You will probably get ideas as to how retailing can be improved at particular stores with which you are familiar. This is a useful exercise, but you must remember that methods of improvement that seem simple from the standpoint of the consumer have in some cases very strong drawbacks when considered from the viewpoint of the retailer. Not all ideas for improving retailing, in other words, are practical.

Consumer goods and the environment have been given increasing attention in recent yeasr. Has this attention been overdue, misdirected, useful, or annoying? Judge critically for yourself.

In studying the marketing system of the United States, two general classes of goods are considered: industrial goods and consumer goods. *Industrial goods* are those that are used by enterprises for production purposes or to aid in marketing. *Consumer goods* are those that are intended for the use of the

THE DISTINCTION BETWEEN CONSUMER GOODS AND INDUSTRIAL GOODS

consumer. The distinction lies in who uses the goods and how they are used, not in what the goods are. A station wagon used by a family is a consumer good; an identical station wagon used by a retail store for deliveries is an industrial good. A typewriter purchased for home use is a consumer good; a typewriter purchased for business use is an industrial good. Below are some other examples of consumer goods and industrial goods. Keep in mind, however, that most consumer goods can be used as industrial goods and that many industrial goods can be used as consumer goods.

Consumer Goods	Industrial Goods
Television set	Closed-circuit television
Bicycle	Dump truck
Sunglasses	Safety goggles
Bread	Wheat
Sailboat	River barge
Hammer	Pile driver

THE MARKETING OF INDUSTRIAL GOODS

The purchasers of industrial goods include factories, farmers, trucking companies, retail stores, hospitals, governments, mining companies, prisons, and bakeries.

CHANNELS OF MARKETING FOR INDUSTRIAL GOODS

The channels of marketing for nearly all industrial goods are either from producer directly to user or from producer to wholesaler to user, as shown in Figure 20-1. A large industrial user, such as a big factory, a large university, or a department of the federal government, buys most of its needs directly from the producer. Some producers sell their entire output to one customer, such as the Navy. A small industrial user, such as a small cabinet shop or a restaurant, buys most of its needs from a wholesaler (who in turn buys from producers), but may buy a few items directly from a producer.

FIGURE 20-1 Channels of distribution for industrial goods.

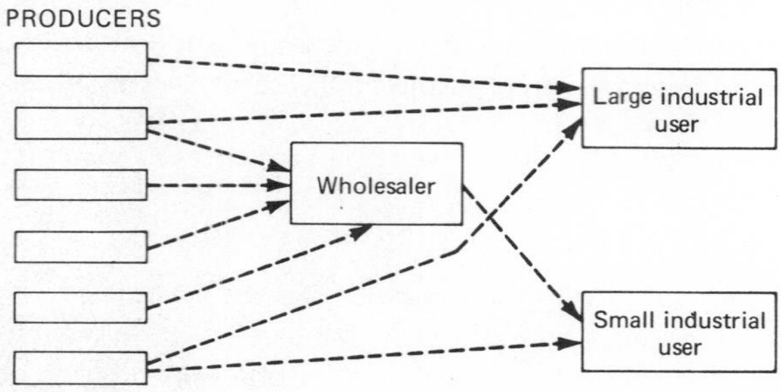

PRODUCERS

From the time a child is first given an allowance, he becomes a consumer buyer. Thus the number of consumer buyers is almost as large as the population. In comparison the number of industrial buyers is small, even though it numbers in the millions. One consequence is the contrast in the size of purchases of industrial goods compared to purchases of consumer goods. Typically the consumer buys one at a time. For some purchases the industrial buyer does also, but typically he makes many of his purchases in large amounts. The industrial buyer will buy not one pencil, but a hundred; not one or two sheets of plywood, but a truckload or a carload. Often an industrial buyer will negotiate a contract with a supplier for delivery of materials over a period of several weeks or months.

The buyer of industrial goods is an informed buyer. Buyers of industrial goods sometimes make mistakes, and sometimes buy on hunch or impulse—but this is much less common than it is in buying decisions of consumers. Industrial goods to a much greater extent than consumer goods are advertised and sold on the basis of grade, specifications, or performance standards. A consumer buying flour makes the decision on the basis of brand name, color and convenience of the package, and similar factors. The milling companies that make the flour buy grain on the basis of grade (grading is discussed in Chapter 18). A consumer buying lumber to make a bookcase selects the wood by looking at what the lumber dealer has to offer; a furniture factory orders lumber on the basis of specification and grade.

In the case of a complex purchase, such as a large machine, or where a considerable amount of money is involved, as in the purchase of a fleet of cars or trucks, the decision may be made by several persons. Large companies have purchasing departments, as is explained in Chapter 10. Some very large buyers put samples of industrial goods through rigid tests before placing an order with the chosen supplier. The Bureau of Standards tests goods that are bought by departments of the federal government.

THE INDUSTRIAL GOODS CUSTOMER

Advertising of industrial goods stresses performance, delivery, and price. Advertising of consumer goods tends more often to emphasize brand names, styling, and prestige. Appeals to emotion and impulse are characteristic of consumer goods; they are comparatively rare in industrial goods.

To a greater extent for industrial goods than for consumer goods, salesmen call at the places of business of buyers. In contrast, a much larger proportion of consumer buying occurs when consumers go to the seller's place of business. The salesmen for most consumer goods are given limited training—sometimes very limited. Salesmen of industrial goods are generally better trained. In dealing with the better-informed industrial buyer, the salesman must know his product thoroughly, explain how it can improve a customer's business, and be able to answer technical questions. For example, the persons hired by E. I. du Pont de Nemours & Company to sell chemicals to industry are selected from among college graduates majoring in chemistry. They spend approximately a year in the company production plants before being sent to visit industrial buyers.

ADVERTISING AND SELLING

RECIPROCITY   Buying decisions based on reciprocity (a steel company buying trucks from the automobile manufacturer that buys its steel) are a common characteristic of marketing industrial goods. Reciprocity is discussed in more detail in Chapter 10.

CHANNELS FOR MARKETING CONSUMER GOODS   Two hundred years ago, it was common for the consumer to meet the producer of goods and make a purchase directly. There was no need for an intermediary in dealing with the butcher, the baker, or the candlestick maker. Production was small-scale and distribution was largely local. It could be represented as follows:

Producer → consumer

Such direct distribution is comparatively rare today. You can still buy a loaf of bread or a cake directly from a baker, a suit of clothes from a tailor, or a bookshelf from a cabinetmaker, but few do. Most of us buy our bakery goods in a supermarket, our clothes ready-made, and our furniture factory-made. Mass production is a characteristic of our economy, and mass production requires mass distribution. To enjoy the lower costs that production in large quantities gives us, it is necessary for distribution to be on a wide scale. In the consumer field, it is the function of wholesalers and retailers to provide the services of distribution. They are intermediaries or middlemen between producer and consumer. The intermediaries in the marketing of goods are collectively known as *middlemen*. They are businessmen or business firms that participate in the distribution of goods from the producer to the consumer. Sometimes there is only one middleman in a distribution pattern:

Producer → retailer → consumer

Often there are two middlemen in the distribution pattern:

Producer → wholesaler → retailer → consumer

Occasionally there may be three or more middlemen. For example, there may be an importer, a wholesaler, and a retailer. The variety of channels is suggested in Figure 20-2. For example, producer A sells to wholesalers and to retailers (perhaps to not more than two or three very large retailers). Producer B sells only to wholesalers. Producer C sells his entire output to one wholesaler. Producer D sells directly to retailers. Producer E sells to retailers and a few consumers. Producer F, perhaps a local manufacturer of ice cream, sells directly to consumers. Wholesaler X sells only to retailers. Wholesaler Y sells mostly to retailers, but also makes some sales to consumers.

The marketing concept (explained in Chapter 18) begins when the final user of the goods, whether a consumer or an industrial customer, determines his wants, and purchases goods to satisfy them. The marketing concept also applies to the choice of channels of marketing. Some customers, particularly large companies, prefer to buy directly from the producer. Some consumers like to shop in small,

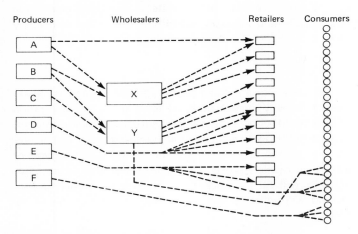

FIGURE 20-2   Channels of distribution for consumer goods.

specialized retail stores. Others prefer department stores or chain stores. Still others prefer mail-order houses. By analyzing the customer who will use the product, the producer can select the marketing channel most likely to meet the desires of most of the users of the product.

The wholesaler generally buys in large quantities and sells in smaller quantities. His customers are mostly other middlemen, chiefly retailers. He also sells to large consumers, such as hospitals, universities, government agencies, and companies buying in quantity. He rarely sells directly to householders.

THE FUNCTIONS OF WHOLESALING

The services provided by wholesalers can be very broad. They may be grouped into three categories: those services facilitating changes in ownership of goods (buying and selling); physical handling of goods; and financing. Not all wholesalers undertake all of the functions of wholesaling, as will be seen later in this chapter.

Wholesalers ordinarily buy directly from the producer, although they may also buy from importers or from other wholesalers. Where production is characterized by many small producers, as in handicrafts and some farm products, the wholesaler may buy the entire season's output of many producers. To be a successful buyer, the wholesaler must *anticipate* the needs of retailers and other customers.

BUYING

The demand of consumers for canned foods, for example, may be fairly regular, but the production is likely to be seasonal. Somewhere along the chain of marketing, storage must take place, and frequently the wholesaler undertakes this function.

STORAGE

This permits the retailer to carry a small inventory of items of seasonal production or with seasonal demand, since he knows he can replenish his stocks from the supply carried by the wholesaler.

DELIVERY   Prompt delivery is one of the important functions of wholesaling and is closely associated with storage. A delivery system designed to attain rapid distribution requires that the wholesaler's stocks be kept at a level sufficiently high to permit rapid filling of retailers' orders. How this is undertaken depends on the character of goods handled, the size of the area served by the wholesaler, the type of customer (small retailer, large retailer, hotels, etc.), and many other factors. For example, a truck wholesaler will fill his truck with a sufficient number of each item he hopes to sell and will solicit orders from small retailers on his route, making delivery on the spot.

FINANCING   Many retailers have limited financial resources. They will buy much of their inventory on credit extended by wholesalers. A successful wholesaler must exercise extreme caution in granting credit to retailers. The failure rate among retailers is high. The wholesaler must keep in close contact with his credit customers, restricting the extension of credit of those whose payment record is poor. The salesmen of the wholesaler can furnish vital information to the credit manager. They can act as bill collectors when necessary. If a retailer fails, the wholesaler generally knows from experience how to salvage as much as possible from the failure so as to reduce his credit losses. Sometimes, the wholesaler will furnish financial aid to set up a new retailer just entering business in addition to selling to him on credit.

The terms of payment extended by wholesalers vary considerably. Common payment terms are listed below:

1 *COD:* Collect on delivery. Payment must be made when goods are delivered.
2 *2/10/30:* Payment of full amount of bill due in 30 days from date of invoice. Two percent discount may be taken if paid in 10 days.
3 *2/15/EOM:* End of month following. Two percent discount may be taken if payment is made within 15 days following the end of the month in which invoice is dated. For example, if the invoice is dated February 12, discount may be taken until March 15.
4 *2/10/30 extra:* The wholesaler may grant retailers 30 days "extra" to make payment. This permits retailers to take 2 percent discount if payment is made within 40 days after date of invoice or pay the full amount within 60 days. The extra period may be 60, 90, or 120 days.

The cash discount is offered as an inducement to prompt payment of bills. Retailers will frequently borrow money from a bank when necessary to pay bills within the discount period. If the payment terms are 2/10/30 and payment in full is made at the end of 30 days, the retailer (as explained earlier) is, in effect, borrowing money from the wholesaler at 36 percent per annum. The failure to pay within the discount period signals to the credit manager of the wholesaler that the retailer may be in financial difficulties.

Risk is inherent in any type of business. Managers must make decisions on the basis **RISK MANAGEMENT** of available data. They gather as much information as they reasonably can, but it will always be incomplete. Although risk cannot be avoided, it can usually be reduced. Wholesalers frequently shoulder some of the risks that otherwise would be borne by retailers. By serving as a ready source of supply, the wholesaler reduces the size of the inventory required by the retailer. He thus assumes much of the loss from price declines and deterioration or obsolescence of merchandise, particularly of style goods. In addition, he bears the other types of risks found in business.

Wholesalers generally sell through salesmen. These may be merely order takers, **SELLING** with little training in the techniques of selling beyond that necessary to quote prices and fill order blanks. A highly capable salesman, on the other hand, may check the retailer's shelves to determine which items are in short supply, help set up attractive window displays, suggest better counter arrangements, and call attention to items that are selling well in other stores. He may bring information of price changes in the industry, new merchandising techniques, and other bits of useful information. In short, a superior salesman can act as a consultant on merchandising problems in addition to pushing the sale of his employer's line of goods.

Attempts to bypass the wholesaler, the retailer, or both are undertaken frequently. **BYPASSING THE** This is indicated by the lines showing channels of distribution in Figure 20-2. The **MIDDLEMAN** lure of eliminating the markup of the retailer and the wholesaler is strong, both for the producer and for the consumer. If some of the functions of the retailer, such as charge accounts or delivery, are eliminated, the consumer may pay a lower price, provided he is willing to pay cash and carry his purchases with him. Similarly, retailers may bypass the wholesaler if they are willing to undertake all the functions of wholesaling. By the same token a manufacturer can bypass the wholesaler or retailer by performing the wholesaling and retailing functions. The vital point to remember is that the wholesaler and retailer can be eliminated from the channel of distribution of a product but the wholesaling and retailing functions cannot.

Wholesalers differ according to the type or extent of services they render. Some **TYPES OF** provide all the services described above. Others limit their activities to a few **WHOLESALERS** services.

MERCHANT
WHOLESALERS

This term is applied to wholesalers who buy and sell goods in quantity. They take title to the merchandise they handle. The wholesalers in this group include wholesale merchants, jobbers, exporters and importers, and cash-carry wholesalers.

Wholesale Merchants

These are also called full-service wholesalers or regular wholesalers. More than half of all wholesale middlemen are of this type. The wholesale merchant generally buys in large quantities and sells in small quantities. His principal customers are retailers. Usually he stocks a large variety of goods. For example, a drug company may carry more than 50,000 different items made by a thousand different manufacturers. Thus, instead of having to deal with several hundred manufacturers, a retailer need deal with only one or a few wholesalers. Other services offered by a wholesale merchant include:

Storage of goods so as to assure prompt shipment to customers
Delivery of goods to customers
Extending credit to customers
Demonstration sales in retail stores
Free mats for local newspaper advertisements by retailers
Suggestions on accounting, personnel, and other management problems

Industries in which the wholesale merchant is particularly strong are foodstuffs, dry goods, hardware, drugs, and electrical appliances. A large wholesaler may place his order with a manufacturer well ahead of actual production, thus enabling the manufacturer better to plan his production schedule. He may alert the manufacturer to shifts in consumer tastes or suggest changes in product design or styling. By distributing his products through a few wholesalers, a manufacturer avoids dealing with thousands of small customers. This enables him better to devote his talents to production, leaving much of the uncertainties and problems of marketing to the wholesaler.

Jobbers

Although the term *jobber* is used synonymously with "wholesaler," it connotes a smaller operation. The distribution may be limited in area covered or in number of articles carried. One type of jobber is the *rack jobber*, also known as a *rack merchandiser*, who supplies items for sideline operations of retailers. Typical products distributed by rack jobbers include drugs, toiletries, magazines, kitchen utensils, stationery, and hosiery. The rack jobber generally installs the display racks or fixtures for his products in the retail outlets he services. On each call he replenishes the rack and bills the store for the amount sold by the store. There is very little expense for the store owner beyond the space occupied by the rack and the cost of checking out the items as they are bought. Small independent stores are the main customers of rack jobbers, but some chain stores and department stores use their services.

Another type of jobber is called a **wagon jobber** or **truck jobber**. The specialty of the wagon jobber is combining selling and delivery. He calls on a customer, makes a sale, and delivers on the spot. Sales are made chiefly to small retail outlets. Typical items include tobacco, cigarettes, candies, bakery goods, automobile accessories, and some food items such as dairy products and potato chips. Some jobbers sell on a cash basis only; others extend credit. A small jobber operates a single truck; a large jobber may have a fleet of many trucks.

In the field of international trade, exporters and importers generally offer full services. The importer usually sells foreign-made goods to retail outlets in the United States, but sells to wholesalers as well. The exporter generally buys from those United States producers who sell in small quantities to the foreign market and for whom the establishment of an export department would be uneconomic. The activities of exporters and importers are described in Chapter 23.

Exporters and Importers

Delivery and credit management are two large items of expense for a wholesaler. To those retailers who wish to buy for less, a cash-carry wholesaler might offer price reductions averaging 5 percent or more. The retailer is required to go to the wholesaler's place of business, pay cash for the goods, and haul them away in his own truck. Some grocery stores buy staple items on this basis.

Cash-Carry Wholesaler

The chief characteristic of this group is that they do not take title to the goods they help to distribute. They help to find buyers for a seller or sellers for a buyer. They help negotiate the terms of sale between buyers and sellers and furnish market information to both. Their compensation is generally in the form of a commission on each sale (usually from the seller, inasmuch as they generally act on behalf of the seller). The most common middlemen in this group are the auction company, commission house, selling agent, manufacturer's agent, and broker.

AGENTS AND BROKERS

Most persons have witnessed auctions and are familiar with this type of selling. In the wholesale field the public is usually not admitted. The rules of bidding are more rigidly enforced than is true of most public auctions. Sales are usually made to the highest bidder, but by prior agreement some sellers reserve the right to reject a sale if the bidding was not high enough. Auction companies are paid by the sellers who bring their goods to the auction, generally in the form of a percentage of the sale price of each item. Fruits, vegetables, tobacco, meat animals, and used cars are among items that are commonly sold at wholesale auctions.

Auction Company

Commission House   The commission house, like the auction company, does not take title to the goods it sells. In other respects, however, it differs sharply from the auction company. Sales are not made by competitive bidding, but through salesmen employed by the house. If credit is extended, the commission house must collect the bills and suffer any losses from nonpayment. It generally has a warehouse and rooms for displaying merchandise. The expenses of operation and the profit earned are covered by the commission charged to the producer whose goods are sold. The commission is usually expressed as a percentage of the price of each item carried and is deducted from the selling price before payment is made by the commission house to the producer. This type of wholesaler operates in the field of foods, textile fibers, and grain.

A commission house sometimes purchases goods for a client. A retailer may ask to have a truckload of potatoes located and purchased at the lowest available price. In this case the commission house collects its commission from the retailer. Whether the commission is collected from the buyer or charged to the seller, the effect is to raise the price the buyer pays by the amount of the commission charged on the transaction.

Selling Agent   The selling agent undertakes to sell the entire output of one or several manufacturers. In effect the selling agent is the sales department of the manufacturer, although the agent is an independent businessman. This is of considerable convenience to small companies in coal mining, textiles, and groceries. Among the services a selling agent offers are the following:

Selling, setting price and terms of sale
Extending financial aid to manufacturers
Furnishing information and advice on packaging, styling, and production
Furnishing information on record keeping

The selling agent receives a commission on each sale. For this reason he is sometimes called a commission man.

Manufacturer's Agent   The manufacturer's agent performs much the same services as the selling agent. But he normally sells only part of the output of a company and sells in a limited geographical area. Also, the price and terms of sale are dictated by the company, not by the agent, although the agent can suggest changes in prices or terms.

Broker   A broker acting on behalf of a seller locates possible buyers. If a sale is made, he collects a commission from the seller. A broker acting for a buyer locates sellers of goods sought by the buyer. If a purchase is made, he collects a commission from the buyer. A broker does not physically handle the goods.

Brokers are found in several fields. Where a distinction is needed, the one described above is a *merchandise broker*. One who specializes in land and buildings is called a *real estate broker*. One who specializes in stocks and bonds is called an *investment broker* or a *stock broker*.

FUNCTIONS OF RETAILING

The retailer is the middleman who sells to the consumer. The average person, therefore, is more familiar with the functions of retailing than with any other part of the distribution chain. Unfortunately, many persons think they know more about retailing than they really do, particularly about what is wrong with retailing. Many a person has invested his savings in opening a store, convinced through his experience as a customer that he knows how to please customers and sell at a profit. A few succeed. Most discover through bankruptcy that there are more problems in running a successful store than they realized. The experience contributes to their education, but this method of learning is rather expensive.

Retailing is typically a small-scale enterprise, although there are, of course, large department stores, chains of retail stores, and supermarkets. About half of the business firms in the United States are retail stores, but only about one-sixth of the labor force is employed in retailing, counting proprietors as well as employees.

A few retail firms are among the giants of industry. *Fortune* magazine's 1972 directory of the 500 largest United States corporations lists the following retail firms among the top ones: Sears Roebuck, Atlantic and Pacific Tea Company, Safeway Stores, Marcor (Montgomery Ward), and J. C. Penney,

BUYING

In order to operate successfully, a retailer must stock his shelves with goods that appeal to his customers. He must search the sources of supply—the wholesale houses, trade marts, manufacturers, importers—to order those goods he thinks will sell. He must study his clientele. He must be familiar with their income status, their level of taste, their prejudices. He must be sensitive to changes in demand. He tries to select those items he thinks will satisfy his customers, in a price range they can afford, in quantities they will buy. If he guesses wrong and his competitor guesses right, he will lose sales to his competitor.

The retailer is sometimes called the buying agent of the consumer. It is certainly true that the buying function of a retailer is of vital importance in determining his financial success. In this function, he is aided by the selling activities of wholesalers. Small retailers frequently depend almost entirely on wholesalers as a source of supply. Large retail outlets, on the other hand, often buy directly from manufacturers, thereby performing the wholesaling functions themselves. Many stores send their buyers on trips to the cities that act as distribution centers, such as New York, Chicago, and San Francisco. Frequently, a buyer will travel abroad, seeking specialties not found in the United States.

A buyer must be a judge of quality, style, price, and dependability of source of supply. At the same time, he must be a judge of consumer taste. Buying is done in advance of the selling season for many consumer items, and must be done with care. The importance of this function is emphasized in the organization of department stores. The head of each department is the buyer. It is his responsibility to buy the items for his department and to see that they are sold. Although primarily a buyer, he is also a department manager.

STORAGE

Most persons buy a considerable proportion of their purchases when they expect to use them. Buying on impulse is common, and to some extent it is promoted by advertising and salesmanship. It is difficult for most persons to plan their needs in advance. For this reason, retailers attempt to anticipate the needs and desires of consumers. Since consumers usually dislike ordering in advance and waiting, retailers order in advance and store the goods until the shelves are cleared of a particular item by sales to customers. The inventories held by retailers are greater than those held by wholesalers. These inventories can be thought of as "storage tanks" in a "pipeline" of distribution through which goods flow from the manufacturer to the consumer. The existence of the storage tanks, particularly at the retail level, reduces the likelihood of an interruption in the flow. Graphically, it can be represented as in Figure 20-3.

SERVICES OF SELLING

The retailer undertakes many activities in order to promote sales. He will place advertisements in newspapers, on television, on billboards, and wherever else he can

FIGURE 20-3 Inventory of goods in stock maintained at various points in the channels of distribution acts as a "storage tank" to permit a more even flow of goods to the consumer.

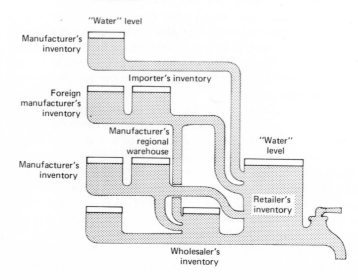

secure the attention of the consumer. This is *sales promotion*. He will display the goods he carries in as appealing a way as possible, grouping together related items. He will make his store as attractive and pleasant as he can, and he will generally have salesmen or clerks available to help the customer with his selection, except in self-service stores. He may extend credit to his customers, offer delivery services, and may provide free parking, free style shows, and a place to leave children while shopping.

Retailing is essentially a business of providing services to the consumer. Since services cost money, a retailer must determine the extent of services demanded by his clientele. Should he provide delivery and credit service, or should he sell on a cash-carry basis? Should he offer free cooking and sewing classes, or should he eliminate such "frills" to keep costs and prices down? The profitability of the store will depend in some measure on the success with which the retailer guesses the "right" answers to such questions in terms of his class of customers.

The retailer must meet the management problems found in any business. He must **MANAGEMENT** raise money, hire clerks and other personnel, delegate responsibilities, and keep adequate accounting records. Retailing is a highly competitive field. It does not permit a retailer to make many errors of judgment and remain solvent. His success depends on how he discharges his general management responsibilities as well as how he serves his customers.

Retail outlets can be classified in many ways, as the following list shows: **TYPES OF RETAILERS**

By ownership:
Independent
Manufacturer's store
Wholesaler's store
Government-owned store
Chain store

By location:
Center of city
Suburban shopping center
Neighborhood
Roadside
Rural

By type of customer:
Luxury trade
Middle income
Industry worker
College or teen-age trade

By type of service:
Credit and delivery
Cash-carry
Sales truck
Catalog store
Door-to-door selling

By legal form:
Proprietorship
Partnership
Corporation
Cooperative

By goods handled:
Hardware
Groceries
Drugs
Cameras
Books

By type of operation:
General store
Mail-order house
Single-line store
Department store
Discount house
Chain store
Specialty shop
Supermarket

We will not attempt to examine all of the above classifications here. However, to provide a better understanding of retailing, a brief picture of some of the types of operation will be given.

GENERAL STORE

The earliest type of store in the United States was the general store. It carries a wide variety of goods, such as groceries, clothing, hardware, drugs, and farm implements. It exists today chiefly in rural communities. Usually, the choices available in clothing, groceries, and other items are quite limited. The general store has declined in importance with the increased mobility of farmers.

DEPARTMENT STORE

The department store, like the general store, carries a wide variety of goods. Here the similarity ends. It is organized by departments. Each department head, usually called the buyer, selects and orders the merchandise for his department, supervises the arrangement and display of goods, and sets the prices. The store is usually located in the central shopping district of a city, and the volume of business is generally large. Because of the rapid growth of suburban shopping centers, however, new department stores or branches of downtown stores are increasingly located in the suburbs and offer a full range of services, such as credit, delivery, alterations, lounges, snack bars, and so on. A few distribute catalogs to permit customers to order by mail or telephone.

A large store may have 100 departments. Some departments, such as the camera department or restaurant, may be leased to independent operators. They bear all merchandising risks, paying the store for space, heat and light, and other services. The heads of the departments controlled by the store are supervised by the merchandising manager, whose area of responsibility is buying and selling goods.

In addition to the merchandising division, there are three main divisions: sales promotion, which includes advertising, window displays, and special promotions; store management, which includes building maintenance, personnel administration, storage, and delivery; and financial control, which includes accounting, credits and collections, and financial planning. The organizational chart of a department store might look like that shown in Figure 20-4.

SUPERMARKET

Although the supermarket existed before 1930, it was not until the Depression that it became an important institution. By dispensing with such services as credit and delivery, by selling in large volume, and by having its customers wait on themselves, it could offer lower prices than other stores. It has always based much of its sales promotion on price, sometimes cutting the price of specially advertised items below cost to attract customers. Although the supermarket originated in the grocery field, it is now possible to buy in supermarkets such items as drugs, magazines, dinnerware, hardware, encyclopedias, and raincoats. The rapid growth of the grocery supermarket has led to the use of this type of selling in other lines. Some variety

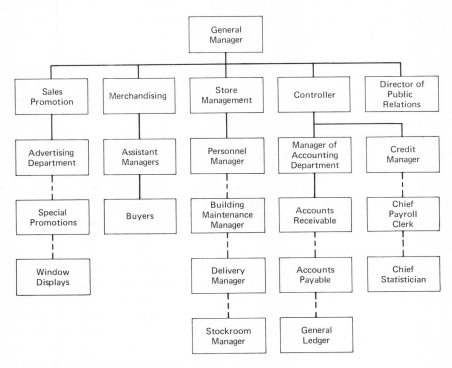

FIGURE 20-4   Organization of a department store.

stores, drugstores, and even shoe stores have arranged their merchandise on counters to facilitate customer selection and have check-out stands where the merchandise is wrapped and paid for as the customer leaves. A few department stores have organized some of their departments for this type of selling. It is evident that the characteristic features of the supermarket will be extended in the retailing field in coming years.

Selling by mail developed in the United States after the Civil War. The growth of railroads, express services, and more extensive parcel post delivery made the mail-order house practicable. Selling by mail permitted the farmer and small-town resident to enjoy as wide a variety of goods as could be found in any large city. The large houses, such as Sears, Roebuck and Company and Montgomery Ward and Company, distributed catalogs the size of a city telephone directory, with color illustrations and page arrangements as attractive as a high-quality magazine. It was with something more than humor that people sometimes said the favorite evening reading of the farmer was his mail-order catalog. However, the advent of good roads and the Model T Ford ended the isolation of country residents. After World War I,

MAIL-ORDER HOUSE

it became easy to drive 50 to 75 miles to do the weekly shopping. Montgomery Ward and Sears opened up a chain of retail stores to meet the changed buying habits of their customers, but found that the demand for buying by mail continued.

Mail-order houses compete largely on the basis of price and variety of products. The delay involved in buying by mail may be offset by a lower price than local stores offer. Where the demand for an item, such as canned fried grasshoppers or polished driftwood for lamp bases, is light, it would probably not pay a local store to handle it. But a mail-order house, distributing its catalogs nationally, would find sufficient demand to stock such items.

A mail-order house generally orders directly from producers in amounts larger than a local store could buy, and can reduce its purchase costs thereby. Furthermore, it saves the expense of salesmen, store displays, and fixtures and the high rent charged for retail store locations. On the other hand, the cost of catalogs, correspondence, clerical expense, merchandise returns, and allowances for defective merchandise and repairs may be high.

CHAIN STORES

A group of retail stores centrally owned and managed and handling the same kind of merchandise is known as a chain store system. The earliest evidence of chain stores is found in Chinese historical records showing their existence prior to 200 B.C. Probably the earliest system on the American continent was the Hudson's Bay Company, founded in 1670, which established a series of trading posts stretching across the continent. Although several well-known chain stores trace their origin to the last century, this type of operation is chiefly a development of the present century.

Chain store operation is most pronounced in variety stores, shoe stores, grocery stores, department stores, service stations, and dry-goods stores. To a lesser extent, it is found in drugs, men's wear, and ladies' wear. Operating many stores under one control permits large-scale techniques to be used in buying, hiring and training of personnel, and sales promotion. Specialists of all types can be hired to help the store manager in store layout, window trimming, stock control, personnel management, and special promotions. Large-scale raising of funds generally reduces financing costs for the chain as compared to the unit store. Some chains act as their own wholesalers and even engage in manufacturing. Partly because of the saving in expenses permitted by large-scale operations, chain stores have relied heavily on price as a competitive tool.

One of the benefits of competitive enterprise is that it permits customers to shift their trade from one seller to another. By this means, the pattern of production and distribution can be constantly changed to increase consumer satisfaction and raise the national standard of living. During the 1920s, customers flocked to the expanding chain stores. Owners of local unit stores subordinated their belief in the principle of free, competitive enterprise to their desire to stay in business. In about half of the states, unit retailers used their political power to get tax laws passed that discriminated against chain stores. The passage of such legislation was aided by the lack of concern shown by the owners of some chains for local charities and community welfare activities. Chain store executives today seek to maintain good community relations, and their store managers are active in local affairs.

Another effort by retailers, in cooperation with manufacturers of brand name **DISCOUNT HOUSE** merchandise, to restrict free enterprise in retailing resulted in the passage of laws curtailing the freedom of a retailer in pricing his wares. These laws, mostly passed during the 1930s, were called "fair trade" laws, apparently under the theory that nobody would be against fair trading. They permitted the manufacturer to use government power to dictate the minimum retail price for his brands. After World War II, many discount houses came into existence, taking advantage of loopholes in the laws or of their lack of enforcement to sell branded goods at prices below those set by the manufacturers.

In order to increase the spread between the "discount" price and the "fair trade" price, these stores opened in low-cost locations, did some of their selling by means of wholesalers' and manufacturers' catalogs, offered little or no credit or delivery, and limited their expenditures on window display and store layout. The future of fair trade laws (renamed "quality stabilization" laws by their supporters in the 1960s) is uncertain.

Retailing has undergone many changes in the United States since the American **CHANGES IN** Revolution. In the early days, the itinerant peddler brought tools, clothing, kitchen- **RETAILING** ware, drugs, pins, and news of the outside world to the isolated farmhouses and small villages, He traveled as he could, by wagon if roads were available, by pack horse if they were not. In the settlements on the frontier, trading posts were established at which furs were bartered for the products of the Eastern cities.

As the territory became more settled, the general store became common. It was the dominant type of retail outlet in the nineteenth century. Sometimes its services were very general indeed, including safekeeping of money and valuables, postal services, barbering, and medical advice. It was the center of community life in many small towns.

After the Civil War, retailing became more varied. With the growth of urbanization and rail transportation, specialty shops became more common, the size of some stores increased greatly, and mail-order selling developed. After World War I, the increased mobility of the automobile permitted the rapid expansion of suburbs and with it the development of suburban shopping centers. The rise of chain stores and supermarkets in the 1920s and 1930s paralleled the growing size of operating units in other sectors of the economy.

Retailing is a dynamic activity. Changes in the pattern of living create demand for new retailing methods. Since the industry is competitive and since there is relatively unrestricted access for newcomers to enter the field, retailing accommodates itself readily to changes in consumer demand or consumer buying habits.

SELF-SERVICE STORES

Cafeterias and grocery supermarkets popularized self-service. During and after World War II, self-service was increasingly used in other retail outlets as well, partly because competent retail sales clerks were difficult to find in most cities, in part because low wages were the rule. The use of self-service, obviously, reduces the number of clerks needed, since the customer requires only occasional help.

Automatic vending machines provide another means of selling without sales clerks, and their use expanded rapidly after World War II. Vending machines are mostly limited to small items of convenience that are bought frequently. Because a machine takes little space, it can be placed anywhere that people are found. Because it does not require an attendant to serve the customer, it can be used at any hour of the day or night. Items sold by vending machines include cigarettes, candy, coffee, soft drinks, ice cream, soup, and other foods, Less frequently, machines are used to sell handkerchiefs, combs, railroad tickets, travel insurance, and postage stamps. Undoubtedly, an increasing variety of goods will be sold in this manner in the future.

TRADING STAMPS

The use by retailers of trading stamps is a selling device that has grown tremendously since World War II. It is not, however, of recent origin. Trading stamps were first used in 1891. They did not become very popular at first, but from 1910 to 1916 their use spread so rapidly that the period might be referred to as a trading stamp boom. After 1916, a decline set in, and by the end of the war they were used by few retailers. Trading stamps remained almost forgotten until after World War II, when another trading stamp boom began.

The cost of using stamps is about 2.4 percent of sales for those retailers using them. This cost must be added to other costs, 'such as heat, light, rent, wages, and cost of goods sold. To operate at a profit, all costs must be covered in the price at which sales are made. Whether prices are raised by stamp-using stores, whether "special sales" are less frequently offered, or whether other services are reduced is difficult to measure. In January, 1959, the United States Department of Agriculture reported a study comparing price of stamp-using and nonstamp-using supermarkets in 21 cities. Prices in stamp-using stores were, on the average, higher by 0.6 percent than those of nonstamp-using stores. According to one report, stamp-using stores have taken 10 percent of the market from their nonstamp competitors.[1] With a higher volume, some of the costs of handling stamps have been absorbed, until such time as nonstamp stores also adopt stamps.

The recent upsurge in stamps has continued longer than the previous stamp boom. Presumably, it will continue for a longer time. Stamps are, of course, not found in sales to industry, where buying agents place orders on the basis of quality, price, and service. Their use in retail trade is an example of the irrationality of consumer buying habits.

[1] Eugene R. Beem, "Who Profits from Trading Stamps?" *Harvard Business Review*, vol. 35, no. 6, p. 127, November–December, 1957.

Concern for the lakes, streams, forests, and the air we breathe is not a discovery of the 1960s, nor is the goal of a better-informed consumer a recent invention. Nevertheless, both these forces showed increased strength in the 1960s and have changed the marketing of goods to some extent. Some examples follow:

THE RISE OF CONSUMER CONCERN FOR THE ENVIRONMENT

In 1972 the State of Oregon required grocery stores to sell beverages only in containers for which a deposit is charged. This eliminates the convenience of cans and no-deposit bottles. It also eliminates, it is hoped, beer cans on beaches, streams, and roadsides.

Beer Cans and Soda Pop Bottles

In the 1960s a federal law required the printing of a health warning on cigarette packages, later extended to cigarette advertisements as well. In 1972 cigarette advertising on television and radio was stopped by law.

Cigarette Packages

It has long been the practice in the retail marketing of perishable foods to mark the containers with either the date of delivery or the date when the food has become stale and should be replaced. This information has generally been in the form of a code understood by the retailer but undecipherable by the consumer. Several grocery chains have begun using calendar dates on their perishables, so that consumers can judge the freshness of what they buy and, more important, determine how many days it is safe to keep foods at home before eating them.

Open Dating

To make comparisons of price and quantities between different sizes of containers and different brands, some grocery stores have posted on their shelves not only the price per package but also the cost per ounce, pound, or other measure.

Unit Pricing

In January 1973 the Federal Food and Drug Administration announced regulations on labeling foods and drugs that would:

Food Labeling

Require uniform labels for different brands of the same food item.
Indicate the number and size of servings contained in the package.
Clearly list the calories, fat, protein, and carbohydrate content.
Permit, for the first time, the listing of cholesterol content on the package.

Although these regulations are voluntary, many businessmen expect them to become mandatory within a few years. The first major food packer to adopt the

Use Unit Pricing and SAVE.

This is where you compare the cost.

This is what you pay.

RETAIL PRICE
34.0¢
BUMB BEE SOLID WHITE TUNA
48/3 1/2 Z
PK/6Z

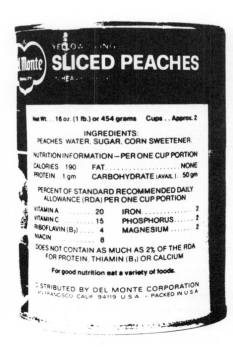

(*Source: Business Week*, Feb. 3, 1973, pp. 42, 44, 45.)

new regulations was Del Monte Corporation, which began labeling the nutritional content of its canned foods in 1973.[2]

SUMMARY

This chapter examines the intermediaries that smooth the distribution of goods between those who produce and those who consume. If the user is an industrial firm, the channel of marketing is generally simple—from producer to user or from producer to one intermediary to user. The channels of marketing for consumer goods, on the other hand, often involve two, three, or even four intermediaries.

Wholesalers and retailers are intermediaries between producer and consumer. Wholesalers ordinarily buy directly from the producer and sell to retailers, large-quantity buyers, and other wholesalers. Wholesalers make it easier for retailers to stock their shelves by providing greater variety, prompter delivery, and better financing terms than most retailers could get by dealing directly with producers. Wholesalers also help retailers, through advertising, sales promotion schemes, and other ways, to increase retail sales.

The retailer sells directly to consumers. Most retailers are small-scale enterprises, have on display the goods they sell, and carry a stock of merchandise they believe sufficient to permit immediate delivery to customers buying from them. There is, however, a great variety of retailer types. Some are large, some small; some carry a wide assortment, some a limited selection; some provide services of credit and delivery, others do not. Retailing is highly competitive. It is also dynamic, with new ideas constantly being developed.

QUESTIONS FOR REVIEW

1 Is a typewriter an industrial good or a consumer good? Explain.
2 The channels of distribution for industrial goods are simpler than the channels for consumer goods. Why?
3 How do salesmen for industrial goods differ from salesmen for consumer goods?
4 Under what circumstances might a producer sell directly to consumers? Give some examples.
5 "Wholesalers make it easier for producers to sell and for retailers to buy." What is meant by this statement?
6 Why are such generous discounts offered by wholesalers for payments in cash for goods shipped to retailers?
7 Explain: COD, 2/15/EOM, 2/10/30 extra.
8 Why is it that many persons believe they know more about how to run a retail store than how to run any other kind of business?
9 The inventories of manufacturers, wholesalers, and retailers can be thought of as "storage tanks in the pipeline of distribution." Explain this statement.
10 Why has the general store declined in importance? Where do persons who used to buy at general stores now purchase their goods?

[2] *Business Week*, Feb. 3, 1973, p. 42.

11 Why is the department head in a department store called a buyer?

12 Why did the growth of the supermarket take place during the 1930s rather than earlier?

13 How can a mail-order house compete with local retailers, since it cannot offer immediate delivery as local retailers can?

14 What are some of the reasons for the development of the discount house?

15 What is meant by "open dating"? Unit pricing?

SELECTED READINGS Duncan, Delbert J., Charles F. Phillips, and Stanley C. Hollander: *Modern Retailing Management*, 8th ed., Richard D. Irwin, Inc., Homewood, Ill., 1972.

Gillespie, Karen R., and Joseph C. Hecht: *Retail Business Management*, McGraw-Hill Book Company, New York, 1970.

Gist, Ronald R.: *Basic Retailing*, John Wiley & Sons, Inc., New York, 1971.

Hill, Richard M.: *Wholesaling Management*, Richard D. Irwin, Inc.: Homewood, Ill., 1963.

Name	Section	Date

COMPLETION SENTENCES

1 A station wagon used by a florist for delivery of flowers is an

~~*industrial*~~ _____ good.

2 A large industrial firm buys most of its needs from *producer* _____,

whereas a small firm buys more of its needs from *wholesaler* _____.

3 Salesmen for consumer goods are generally given *minimum* _____

training; salesmen for industrial goods are given *extensive* _____

training.

4 Wholesalers and retailers are intermediaries or middlemen between

producer _____ and *consumer* _____.

5 The wholesaler generally buys in *large* _____ quantities and

sells in *smaller* _____ quantities.

6   The _____2/,0/30_____ is offered as an inducement to prompt payment of bills.

7   Retailing is typically a _____-scale enterprise.

8   About _____ percent of all the business firms in the United States are retail stores.

9   Agents and brokers do not take _____ to the goods they sell.

10   At _____ auctions the public is usually not admitted.

11   _____ facilitates the comparison of price and quantities between different sizes of containers and different brands of goods.

12   Mail-order houses compete largely on the basis of _____ and _____ .

13   Retailing is essentially a business of providing services to the _____ .

14   The general store has declined in importance with the increased _____ of farmers.

15   _____ provide a means of selling without sales clerks or cashiers.

TRUE OR FALSE STATEMENTS

1   The channels of distribution for consumer goods are simpler than those for industrial goods.

Name   Section   Date

T 2   Typically the consumer buys goods one or a few at a time; the industrial purchaser typically buys in large quantities.

T 3   Making buying decisions on hunch or impulse is more common in consumer buying than in industrial buying.

F 4   Because the consumer market is much larger than the market for industrial goods, salesmen for consumer goods are generally given more training than salesmen for industrial goods.

T 5   Although retailing is typically a small-scale enterprise, a few retail firms are among the giants of industry.

T 6   All advertising of cigarettes on radio and television was stopped in 1972.

T 7   Two hundred years ago it was common for the consumer to meet the producer and make purchases directly.

T 8   Wholesalers sell to retailers, but practically never to consumers.

F 9   Wholesalers always buy directly from producers.

T 10 Payment terms indicated as 2/10/30 mean payment is to be made by February 10 to receive cash discount, with payment in full 30 days from the invoice date.

F 11 It is bad practice to borrow from the bank to get the necessary money to pay bills within the cash discount period.

F 12 The principal customers of wholesale merchants are other wholesalers.

T 13 Retailing is typically a small-scale enterprise.

T 14 Large retailers often bypass the wholesaler, buying directly from the manufacturer.

T 15 The head of a department in a department store is called a buyer.

F 16 Fortunately for most retailers, retailing is not generally highly competitive.

F 17 The department store, unlike the general store, carries a wide variety of goods.

F 18 The supermarket type of store did not exist prior to 1930.

T 19 Mail-order houses are largely a development of the post-Civil War period.

T 20 Most of the state "fair trade" laws were passed during the 1930s.

EXERCISES

1 Many of the changes in retailing since World War II have been in the direction of applying the supermarket principle to goods other than groceries. In addition to the examples mentioned in the text, what other types of goods do you think could be sold on a self-service basis? Give reasons for your answer. What difficulties do you foresee in each case?

2 Vending machines sell candies, hot and cold drinks, pocket combs, handkerchiefs, and cigarettes. How many other goods can you name that are presently sold by vending machines? What additional goods do you think might be sold by them? Write a report on what you consider to be the future development of retailing by vending machines, and how it will change the existing pattern of retailing.

3 Select a type of retail store, such as a hat store, hobby shop, automobile dealership, grocery supermarket, or bookstore. By visiting it (preferably) or by library research, get answers to the following questions:
  a What is the minimum investment to open a new store?

  b What licenses are required and what legal formalities are to be met?

  c What is the minimum number of workers (officers and employees) required to permit proper operation?

Name   Section   Date

d What is the minimum size of store required (including storeroom or any other special facilities such as parking lot, dressing rooms, etc.)?

e Are there any other special requirements?

The United States probably spends more effort on advertising than any other nation. Advertising occupies, in other words, a more important position in our business life than it does elsewhere. It is necessary to be aware of the importance of advertising in facilitating the marketing of goods and to know the functions and media of advertising. In reading this chapter, try to keep in mind what advertising can do and what it cannot do. For the most part, advertising makes the job of the salesman easier, rather than attempting to complete the sale without the services of salesmen. In other words, advertising is supplementary to the efforts of salesmen.

The immediate goal of most advertising efforts is to arouse a favorable attitude on the part of potential customers. This effort involves knowing as much about customers as possible. Advertising to be successful must develop whatever responses are most useful in securing acceptance for the product advertised. This involves appealing either to fear, love, desire for status, patriotism, or some other emotion. If you have studied psychology or plan to study it in college, you will find the information gained in your psychology courses useful in understanding the methods of advertisers. As a matter of fact, psychologists are employed on a regular basis by practically all the major advertising agencies.

In order to put the advertising message across to potential customers, it is necessary to make contact with them in some way. This is the function of advertising media. The advertisement can be delivered to the potential customer by means of television, radio, newspapers, magazines, or other media. Be able to distinguish the advantages and disadvantages and the strengths and weaknesses of each of these media. You will notice each is most useful for certain types of products but unsuited for other types of messages or products.

As in the case of many other aspects of business activity, there is some regulation of advertising by the government and by industry groups. Be able to explain the reason for government regulation. Notice also that advertising is a changing industry, with new ideas constantly being tried.

Before the age of radio and television, advertising was often described as "salesmanship in print." It is probably as old as business itself. Written announcements of slave auctions have been discovered among the ruins of ancient Thebes. But advertising in the modern form is largely a development of the present century. It is also an area of business that has developed most rapidly in the United States, and in which the United States has pioneered in using new techniques. More than any other aspect of business, modern advertising can be called an American contribution to world commerce.

For many decades Hershey chocolate bars were not advertised and yet they outsold their competitors. They were displayed by grocery stores, drugstores, and wherever candy was sold. Why then should a company advertise? One answer is that few products in this century have sold themselves as successfully as Hershey bars. To sell a product or service, the potential buyer must be told of its existence, its uses, its favorable characteristics, and where it can be purchased. Furthermore, the buyer must be told not only once; he must be reminded again and again. It may be true that "if you build a better mousetrap, the world will beat a path to your door." But it may take the world a long time to find out. Some thought should be given to telling the world about your mousetrap as well as to building it better.

The American Marketing Association has defined *advertising* as "any paid form of nonpersonal presentation and promotion of ideas, goods, or services by an identified sponsor." An advertisement can be a colorful, eye-catching container on a store shelf, it can be a handbill stuffed into a mailbox, or it can be a streamer pulled by an airplane flying over a crowded stadium, to name just a few forms that advertising may take.

Over $23 billion is spent annually for advertising by businessmen—a lot of money by any standard. Why did they spend so much? The reason lies in the relation of advertising and selling. Both are intended to persuade customers to buy. In selling, the salesman deals directly with the customer. If he is a good salesman, and many are not, he can "size up" each customer and change his tactics to use the most effective approach on each. Advertising cannot be as flexible as salesmanship, so it is directed toward groups of customers. A salesman usually deals with one customer at a time. An advertiser directs his appeal to many.

THE FUNCTION OF ADVERTISING

What is the purpose of spending money for advertising? In other words, what are the functions of advertising? Basically, there are two: to create demand and to reinforce sales efforts.

CREATING DEMAND

In order for a product or service to be sold, there must be a demand for it. Advertising helps to create this demand. It announces new products or services, so that they will become familiar when orders from customers are solicited. The introduction of the Hewlett-Packard HP-80 pocket computer in 1972 was preceded by a carefully prepared advertising campaign explaining the many uses of the computer.

More frequently, advertising serves to keep reminding people about products that are already being sold. Figure 21-1 illustrates the declining effect on sales of an advertisement. As time passes, people's memories fade, and an advertisement loses its impact. Repeated advertising is necessary to keep a product or service in the minds of persons when they make buying decisions. In the tobacco industry, for example, it is necessary for each company constantly to remind smokers of the brand names of its products. Otherwise customers will be lost to competitors. In consumer products such as soap and canned goods, there are so many brands facing the buyer in the supermarkets that he (or, more likely, she) is apt to make a choice based more on habit than on comparison. In such situations, the brands most frequently seen or heard by the buyer are most likely to benefit from choices based on habit. There has been a rapid increase in self-service stores selling groceries, drugs, and other items and in the number and variety of vending machines. This practically eliminates the salesman in the function of selling. It also increases greatly the importance of advertising in influencing the choice of shoppers.

REINFORCING SALES EFFORTS

The medium is the means by which an advertiser reaches his public. The medium chosen will depend on the type of product or service, the area to be covered, the relative costs of different media, and the characteristics of the public to be reached. A local shoe store would not advertise in a national magazine, but probably would in a local newspaper. A rifle manufacturer might advertise in *Field and Stream* but would certainly not buy space in the *Ladies' Home Journal*. Merchandise sold to teen-agers could be extolled on a radio station specializing in music appealing to young people, but would not likely be mentioned on a program of symphonic music. The selection of the medium must be done with care because the money

ADVERTISING MEDIA

FIGURE 21-1 Effect over period of time of single advertisement contrasted with continuous or repeated advertising.

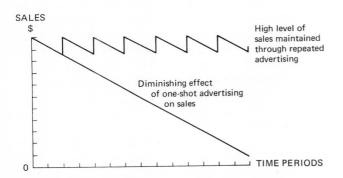

spent on advertising is a cost of doing business. Like any cost, business managers try to get as much value as possible for every dollar spent.

The major advertising media are listed below. In addition, others, used less frequently, will be mentioned.

Point-of-sale	Radio	Outdoor advertising
Newspapers	Television	Handbills
Magazines	Direct mail	Public transportation

POINT-OF-SALE   Probably the oldest form of advertising is point-of-sale advertising. In centuries past, a sign or symbol over the entrance to a craftsman's shop indicated his trade. Perhaps the craftsman might display a sample of his wares in a window. In modern times, point-of-sale advertising has become a well-developed art in retail trade. Window displays are given much thought before being formed. They are intended to catch the attention of potential customers and induce them to enter the store. Counters are arranged to attract shoppers, and demonstrations or samples serve to encourage buying. Indeed, the package itself becomes an advertising tool. Usually the design of a package reflects as much concern for its advertising potential as for its effectiveness as a container to protect the contents.

NEWSPAPERS   The most important medium is the newspaper. Thirty cents of every advertising dollar is spent on newspaper advertisements. Two types of advertisements are found in this medium: *display* and *classified advertisements*. For most newspapers, income from advertisements is greater than income from subscribers. In fact, many newspapers are supported by advertising alone and are distributed free to all addresses in a local area.

Classified advertising, sometimes known as want ads, is usually located in the back pages. A maximum of information is crammed into a few lines, so that the advertisement often reads like a telegram. Frequently, a key word or phrase will be capitalized or set in bold type, to distinguish an advertisement from its neighbors. Such words as "Hurry," "Desperate," and "Last Chance" are common. This device reminds us that advertising—all advertising—must catch the attention of the public to be successful in delivering its message. The insertions in the classified section are cataloged according to kind, such as *Business opportunities, Homes for sale*, and *Sporting goods*.

All other advertisements in a newspaper are known as display. Some are so small as to be in danger of being overlooked. Others cover a whole page. Occasionally, an insert of several pages will be prepared by an advertiser, usually a department store, for distribution with a newspaper. Modern printing techniques permit the use of color, and color displays in newspapers rival those of magazines in quality.

The newspaper is the principal advertising medium of local retailers. Department stores, food stores, druggists, and others make considerable use of it. The newspaper is limited in most cases to a city or town and the surrounding suburbs. Daily papers have the advantage of delivering a company's message to readers within a few hours after receiving the advertiser's copy. This permits prompt announcement of sales, promotions, openings of new stores, and so on.

In many cities, there are weekly regional papers, usually delivered free, to deliver advertising messages to selected neighborhoods. Their names often indicate their limited area, such as *Westside Sun, North Sacramento News,* and *Neighborhood Shopper*. These serve merchants whose trade is concentrated in one part of a city.

MAGAZINES

Magazines are published weekly, biweekly, monthly, or quarterly, the most common being weekly and monthly. Unlike the newspaper, which is read once and discarded, magazines are kept for days. Some, such as the *National Geographic*, are kept for years. Displays in magazines may be seen many times before the magazine is put in the wastebasket. This is particularly so for the back cover of a magazine, for which the cost for a full page may exceed $50,000. Not only does the magazine have a longer impact, but also its message is carried to a wider area, usually nationwide. Although some magazines are printed in black ink on low-quality paper, most are printed in color on high-gloss white paper. Magazines are a valuable medium for companies with a nationwide market.

There is a lapse of time, commonly 6 weeks, between the date that a display is received by a magazine and the date that the copies are distributed to readers. This delay is one of the main disadvantages of this medium. The advertisement may be stale or an unexpected event may make it ridiculous by the time the reader sees it.

Magazines can be divided into two classes: general circulation and special interest. The former are read by all kinds of people. Examples are *The Reader's Digest, Newsweek,* and the *New Yorker*. Products advertised in such periodicals are, naturally, those that appeal to the general public. Automobiles, television sets, drugs, and cigarettes are among the many items found on magazine pages.

Very little geographical selectivity is available in general-circulation magazines. A few magazines with large national circulation, such as *Time* and *National Observer*, offer regional editions, permitting advertisers to pay only for the space in the copies distributed in the Southeast, Midwest, or other region.

The variety of special-interest magazines is almost endless. Some, although written for a special group, are broad in their appeal. *Business Week*, for example, is directed to businessmen in general. Others have a narrow range, such as *Purchasing*, intended for purchasing agents; *Printer's Ink*, for advertising men; and *Today's Secretary*, for women office workers. The list below is a sample of titles intended to attract readers with particular interests:

The Cattleman	*Editor and Publisher*
Popular Photography	*Electrical World*
Control Engineering	*Chemical Week*
Journal of Accountancy	*American Gas Journal*

Journal of Finance   *Electronics*
Sales Management   *Banking*
Journal of Marketing   *Iron Age*
Mill and Factory   *Railway Age*

For a company that sells to a limited group, the special-interest magazine is well suited. Manufacturers of radio and stereo components can be sure, when they place a display in *High Fidelity*, that each copy will be read by persons who are potential customers for their products. People preparing advertising copy for special-interest magazines must keep in mind that the reader is well acquainted with the subject area covered by the magazine. Copy prepared for *Hot Rodder* will be more effective if it is phrased in the jargon of the hot-rod enthusiast. A manufacturer of automobile tires, for example, would use more technical language in *Hot Rodder* than in *Newsweek*.

RADIO The United States, unlike European countries, has no government-operated networks. Except for a few low-budget educational stations, radio is privately owned and the airwaves are devoted to the function of selling. Until the end of World War II, network and local programs were extensively used by advertisers. Since the end of that war, radio has declined in importance relative to television. Radio is now largely a medium for local advertising, although some network programs survive on a national scale. Events of national importance, such as the launching of a manned space vehicle, championship sports, and similar programs, are also carried on network radio.

Spot announcements, either recorded or read by the announcer, are made at frequent intervals to advertise local stores or services or national products available locally. The typical program carries popular music, news, and commercials. Twenty minutes or more of each hour are used for commercials. Radio has an advantage from the advertiser's standpoint over newspapers and magazines. A reader can complete his reading of a news story or magazine article without stopping to look at advertising displays, although this is made somewhat difficult if the reading matter is scattered among pages of displays. The listener to radio, however, cannot skip the portions of time devoted to commercials. He must wait until the advertising message is completed for his program to resume.

Radio is a suitable medium to promote products or services used by all classes of persons. In this respect, it is similar to general-circulation newspapers and magazines. Some selectivity is possible on radio, but it is limited. In cities with several stations, one may specialize in music appealing to teen-agers. Another may program light classical music, with an hour or two of symphonic music in the evenings. Some stations schedule programs appealing to housewives during daylight hours and popular or light music in the evenings. Sport events of major importance, appealing primarily to men, are broadcast usually during the time they are taking place, since some men are able to listen to radio while they work, although professional sports are played most frequently during evenings or weekends. Therefore, if a company wishes to promote shaving cream, it will generally seek to have its commercials used during a sports broadcast. Stores selling to teen-agers will buy time on stations playing teen-age music.

Television commands more attention than radio because it impresses the eye as   **TELEVISION** well as the ear. Products that can only be described on radio can be displayed on television. This medium of advertising has expanded more rapidly than any other since World War II. To advertisers, television offers the same kind of attractions and limitations as radio. National advertisers use television now as they used radio a generation ago, because network programs on television have displaced network radio as the prime evening entertainment medium. So important is television as an advertising medium that companies are willing to pay the high fees ($200,000 and more for a 1-hour network program) for exposure of their products on this medium.

As in radio, commercials on television are placed at the beginning and end of each program and also interrupt programs in progress. The viewer cannot skip the commercials. Television has a further advertising attraction not possible on radio. News, panel, interview, and similar programs not involving dramatic action may display the trademark or name of the advertiser throughout the program, thus carrying the commercial by sight along with the program by sound.

An important attraction of network programs to the advertiser is that the advertiser buys (*sponsors*) the program on which his commercials are used. This permits the insertion of a commercial as part of the program itself. It also makes possible the control of program content by the advertiser, so that nothing will detract from the advertiser's message.

This medium consists of post cards, pamphlets, letters, and packages containing   **DIRECT MAIL** such items as calendars, maps, and samples. The most important part of any direct-mail advertising campaign is the mailing list. Lists are compiled by companies that sell the use of a list to advertisers wishing to use this medium. This list can be general or can be confined to persons having a characteristic desired by the advertiser. A list can be made up of dentists, or of high school teachers, or of importers, or of recently married couples. The list may be nationwide or limited to a state or city. Because mailing lists have a money value, they are guarded jealously by those compiling them. If an advertiser wishes to send a mailing to camping enthusiasts, he delivers a stated number of the advertising items to the owner of the mailing list, who in turn addresses the envelopes to the names on the camping list. A charge in addition to postage is made for the service.

The chief advantage of direct mail is that the selection of the audience can be made to fit the requirements of the advertiser more closely than can be done through other media. It is important to the advertiser, of course, that the lists to which his material is sent be up to date. All of the names on a stamp collectors' list may be true philatelists, but it does the advertiser no good if a fourth of the persons listed are dead. The reputation of mailing-list compilers in maintaining accuracy is important.

OUTDOOR ADVERTISING

This medium is highly selective from a geographic standpoint, but not from an audience standpoint. The displays can be spotted where they will have maximum effect—such as two or three signs spaced a mile apart on a highway east and west of a restaurant or motel. But there is no selection of those viewing the outdoor sign.

Outdoor displays are found in all sizes and shapes. Most are billboards on highways or city streets. A few are known as *outdoor spectaculars*, located usually where pedestrian traffic is heavy. These may consist of flashing electric lights, moving images, "smoke" coming from a gigantic cigarette, or a waterfall. A local advertiser can rent billboard space concentrated in one city, while a national advertiser can buy space on several thousand displays throughout the country.

HANDBILLS

Handbills are limited to local advertising and usually consist of one page. A retailer may hire a group of teen-agers to leave a handbill in the mailbox or on the porch of every house in a residential district. If there is a spot with high pedestrian density, such as a shopping center, stadium, or county fair, handbills may be handed to passing people. Another method of distribution is to leave a copy on each automobile in a parking area. Handbills have the advantage of geographic selectivity, but, like outdoor advertising, have low audience selectivity.

PUBLIC TRANSPORTATION

Companies furnishing local transportation often supplement their income from passenger fares by selling advertising space on their vehicles or in their stations. Advertisements inside buses, streetcars, or subway trains are seen by thousands of passengers. Signs are also fastened to the outsides of buses and taxicabs. Such signs have the same advantages and disadvantages as billboards.

THE PREPARATION OF ADVERTISING

Advertising is prepared either by an advertising agency or by the company selling its goods or services.

THE ADVERTISING AGENCY

An advertising agency plans the campaign and creates the advertising for its clients. Some agencies are small, serving only local companies. Others are large enough to handle campaigns for big clients who are willing to spend millions of dollars annually to promote their products. A typical large agency in New York City employs artists, copy writers (who phrase advertising messages), statisticians, market researchers, and specialists in package design, in addition to officers and clerical workers. In addition, sociologists, psychologists, and economists will be hired as needed to do background research for special projects. Most of the displays found in national magazines, network television programs, and billboards are produced by or with the help of agencies.

The fee an agency receives for its services is usually 15 percent of the advertising bill submitted to the client. For example, for a series of commercial messages on network television the client may pay the agency $300,000. Of this amount the agency keeps $45,000 as its commission and remits $255,000 to the television network.

COMPANY ADVERTISING DEPARTMENTS

As an alternative to the advertising agency, a company may prepare its own advertising. In small companies, this duty may be delegated to the sales manager or some other officer as a part-time duty. In larger companies, an advertising department may be given the responsibility. The department may confine its work to designing packages and preparing counter displays for company products, or the department may be as completely staffed as an independent agency. In the latter case, the department probably would prepare most or all of the advertising of the company. However, advertising bought by company advertising departments normally does not receive the 15 percent discount given to advertising agencies. To illustrate, if a magazine bills a company advertising department $10,000 for a 1-page display, the charge to an agency for the same display would be $8,500.

REGULATION OF ADVERTISING

As stated before, the purpose of advertising is to create sales. It is therefore natural that advertisements call attention to the attractive features of a product and minimize or ignore any weaknesses in the product. Advertising does not tell "the truth, the whole truth, and nothing but the truth." We could not and should not expect it to. But how much variation from this ideal is found in advertising, and how much should be permitted? If a furniture maker states that a product is solid mahogany when in fact it has only a thin veneer of mahogany over cheaper wood, such deceit should be prohibited. On the other hand, if a company claims its product is the best of its kind, such a statement is considered legitimate, regardless of similar claims made by competitors. But suppose a cigarette company pictures a famous opera singer, and quotes him as saying that "X brand cigarettes never irritate my throat," if the statement is true only because the singer never smokes any cigarettes, including X brand, should such advertising be forbidden? Should a line be drawn between "puffing" of goods and deception? If so, where should it be drawn, and by what agency? These questions have been hotly debated for decades, and there is as much disagreement now as there ever was.

One thing is certain. There is more regulation now than there was a generation or two ago. Supervision of advertising is undertaken by the advertising industry, by associations of businessmen, and by the government. These will be briefly discussed.

SELF-REGULATION BY ADVERTISERS

Some members of certain media control the advertising they present. *National Geographic* magazine has several pages of advertising at the front and back of each issue, but none that interrupts the articles in the center section. *Reader's Digest* accepts no liquor or cigarette displays. Most magazines and newspapers limit the extent to which the human body may be uncovered. Radio and television stations prohibit the use of certain words and place other limitations on the commercials that are broadcast.

The National Association of Broadcasters has prepared a code of advertising, which includes a limit of 18 minutes of advertising per hour for radio and 16 minutes, 20 seconds for television stations. The code is voluntary, however, and there is no means of enforcement by the Association. In 1963, fewer than 40 percent of radio stations maintained the recommended limitation, according to a study by the Federal Communications Commission.

THE BETTER BUSINESS BUREAU

Nearly every town of any size has a Better Business Bureau, supported and operated by local businessmen. Each bureau exists to limit unethical methods of competition, to protect responsible businessmen, and to combat dishonesty, fraud, or preying on the gullibility of customers to protect consumers and the reputation of business in general. Much of the activity of these bureaus is directed toward false or misleading advertising. The weapons used are persuasion and publicity. It is useful for any consumer to remember that when he is in doubt about a business transaction or suspects the reliability of a firm, he can often be helped by the local bureaus. It goes without saying that it is advisable, where any large sum of money is involved, to check with the bureau before completion of the transaction rather than after.

STATE REGULATION

As of January 1972, 43 states have passed a model law drawn up by *Printer's Ink* regulating advertising. Because the states are in competition with each other in attracting industry, however, state laws are either loosely enforced or unenforced. State regulation of advertising is practically nonexistent.

FEDERAL REGULATION

Three agencies of the federal government impose restrictions on advertising. The United States Postal Service may bring suit against a company if the mails are used to defraud. Occasionally, this involves deceitful advertising. The Postmaster General also bars the use of the mails to distribute lewd and obscene materials. The application of this authority has depended largely on what the Postmaster General happens to consider obscene. With the frequent changes in the office of Postmaster General, what is barred from the mails one year is sometimes accepted in another year. No clear standards have been published by the Department to guide advertisers and magazine publishers.

The Food and Drug Administration has authority to prohibit false and misleading labeling and advertising of foods, drugs, health devices, and cosmetics. The Federal Trade Commission (FTC) is empowered to proceed against false advertising in general, so long as the advertising is in interstate trade. This exempts most local newspaper advertising and outdoor signs of purely local products. If false or misleading advertising is found by either agency, the action in nearly all cases is to order the offending company to cease the misleading advertising. Two examples are given below:

> The . . . Manufacturing Company of Minneapolis, a seller of seat covers, has been ordered to stop misrepresenting that there are no additional charges on installment purchases of its products. In addition [the company] must discontinue their false guarantee claims. [1]

> The F.T.C. has ordered . . . Products Company of Chicago to stop misrepresenting that merchandise it sells to the public is offered for sale at wholesale prices. [2]

Advertising regulation has been of limited effectiveness for various reasons. Appropriations for enforcement agencies have been small. Opposition to vigorous enforcement has been well organized and powerful, while public support has been spasmodic and disorganized. Finally, as years pass, advertising campaigns and techniques have changed more rapidly than the efforts of regulators to keep pace.

SOME CRITICISMS OF ADVERTISING

The fact that attempts to regulate advertising are made by industry and government is recognition of the possibility of abuse by some advertisers of their power to influence the thinking of people. But what of advertising itself? What contribution does it make to society in return for its cost of over $23 billion annually?

The most obvious contribution of advertising is information—about new products and services, new uses for existing products, new stores, new professional offices, changes in prices, changes in colors, and changes in styles. In a country with a rapidly changing economy, advertising performs an essential service, informing people of the changes produced in the laboratories and designing rooms. Advertising can be used to speed the acceptance of the new, and thus to speed progress.

But the advertising fraternity sometimes exaggerates the benefits of advertising. The claim is often made that if we stop advertising, many factories, stores, and other businesses would close, and that our national standard of living would show a violent decline. This assumes that if advertising were to drop sharply, people would spend less and save more, an assumption that is, to put it kindly, without

---

[1] Order #8565, in *News Summary*, F.T.C., June 5, 1964.
[2] Order #8517, in *News Summary*, F.T.C., May 13, 1964.

any supporting evidence. Statistical studies of consumer spending habits indicate that total spending is determined by income status, level of employment, and other related factors. The effect of advertising is on the direction of spending rather than on the total volume of spending.

One of the sharpest criticisms of advertising is concerned with its influence over radio and television. Except for a very few stations with a limited time schedule, broadcasting is done for the purpose of selling goods. Programs for culture and enlightenment are rare, and are generally restricted to inconvenient hours. Commercial messages incessantly interrupt the programs, destroying the mood of suspense or the flow of entertainment. The test of whether a program will stay on the air is whether it will sell goods, and the goal is to secure as large an audience as possible for the commercial message. The advertiser pays the network for the programs that he selects for the radio and television audiences. The naïve, misleading statement is sometimes made that "advertising pays for our radio and television entertainment."[3] Set owners do not pay *directly* for what they see and hear, but they do pay for the cost of programs in the prices they pay for advertised products.

Another criticism of advertising is directed at highway billboards. Critics contend that the scenic beauty of the countryside is marred by the presence of many billboards. Efforts by state governments to curtail the number of billboards have largely been frustrated by the influence of advertising companies. One state is an exception. Hawaii has no highway advertising. On the country roads of the islands, there is "nothing" to see but mountains, streams, beaches, and greenery.

The reason companies advertise is to influence people's responses. Advertising research constantly improves and strengthens the power to influence. Discoveries in psychological laboratories are put to advertising use, and advertisers seek to influence not only our spending but also our vote. Because advertising is a powerful tool, its use should be under constant public scrutiny. In the hands of responsible advertisers, this tool is beneficial. In irresponsible hands, advertising can do considerable damage. It is up to the public, government agencies, advertising media, and industry to see that it is used for the good of the people.

THE FUNCTION OF SALES PROMOTION

Sales promotion covers those activities that supplement the efforts of the advertiser and the salesman. It includes such activities as stimulating greater enthusiasm in salesmen, securing more cooperation among retailers to push a particular brand, and persuading new customers to give a product a trial. These examples of promotion are discussed briefly below.

---

[3] In complaining of increased advertising costs to comply with government rules on accuracy in advertising, the president of one of the largest advertising agencies says, ". . . and in the final analysis, the consumer pays for everything. There's a kind of unwritten rule that corporate profits are fixed from year to year, so the increased costs [from advertising] get passed on to the public." *Business Week*, June 10, 1972, p. 49.

A common type of sales promotion is the sales contest. Because salesmen are in competition with representatives of other companies for customer orders, it appears logical to extend the competitive spirit between members of the sales force. The prize may go to the person having the largest volume of sales, the greatest improvement over the previous year, or the largest number of new customers. Many years ago one company held a monthly banquet for its salesmen at which the menu for each man corresponded to his performance relative to the others. The top salesman for the month was served filet mignon and vintage wines; the lowest salesman received a plate of beans.

In another example of sales promotion the salesman, perhaps their wives as well, are brought to the company headquarters to examine new company products, learn new advertising and selling themes, and listen to speeches of exhortation. Effectively used, such trips can be valuable for information and inspiration.

STIMULATING THE SALES FORCE

One way to secure greater effort on the part of retailers to sell a company's products is to provide an annual convention in Hawaii, Florida, California, or other resort area to which all dealers meeting a target sales volume are invited as guests of the company. Another common retail sales promotion is the demonstration of the company's products at dealers' stores.

STIMULATING RETAILERS

To introduce a new article or discover new customers for an existing product, samples are frequently distributed. In this case the product does the selling job itself, although descriptive pamphlets or a sales talk often accompany the sample. Obviously such a promotion can be used only for articles of relatively low price, such as cigarettes, candy, foodstuffs, and swatches of cloth.

The coupon is a common device to stimulate sales. A coupon permits a consumer to buy an item at a reduced price. The purpose of distributing coupons is usually to attract new customers, although coupons are also used to retain the loyalty of existing customers. Coupons are attached to newspaper and magazine advertisements, broadcast through the mails (addressed to "resident" or "occupant"), or placed in containers of food and other products. A coupon may usually be redeemed by mailing it to the company or by presenting it to a retail dealer. The coupon may provide a cash refund, the receipt of an article, or the privilege of purchasing an item at less than the regular price.

Frequently where large crowds gather, sales promotions are found. State fairs and county fairs are examples. Exhibits, demonstrations, and contests are useful in bringing products to the attention of possible customers.

Some companies promote their products or the company name by sponsoring (usually with financial support) athletic contests and other events. For example, to promote a brand of cigarettes for women, Philip Morris, Inc., launched in 1972

STIMULATING CUSTOMERS

the Virginia Slims Women's Tennis Circuit, featuring matches between the top women tennis players of the world.

SUMMARY   Advertising is any paid form of nonpersonal promotion of goods or services. It is directed toward groups of people rather than toward individuals, and toward creating demand and reinforcing the efforts of salesmen.

There are many media of advertising. The more commonly used media and examples of thier use are the following:

Point-of-sale	Window and counter displays
Newspapers	Classified advertisements
Magazines	Display advertisements
Radio	Spot announcements
Television	Commercial messages
Direct mail	Letters, cards, and other advertising circulars
Outdoor advertising	Highway billboards
Handbills	Pamphlets distributed at a carnival
Public transportation	Display cards in buses

In order to keep advertising within minimum bounds of accuracy and decency, advertisers are regulated. Regulations are adopted by the private associations to which advertisers belong, but are mostly voluntary with respect to enforcement. Most of the states have regulations regarding advertising, but in most of these regulations, the extent is very limited and enforcement is spotty. Federal regulation of a limited nature is administered by the Federal Trade Commission and some other agencies, but enforcement is mild and punishment rare. What limitations are practiced on advertising policies are largely those that are self-imposed by each advertiser.

QUESTIONS FOR REVIEW

1 What is the relationship between advertising and selling? How are they alike? How do they differ?

2 Why is it necessary to continue to advertise rather than depend for sales upon a one-shot advertisement?

3 What is meant by "demand creation"?

4 How can a well-designed package stimulate sales in a store? Give some examples of goods whose packages attract the shopper's eye.

5 How has the increase in the use of vending machines raised the importance of advertising?

6 How can a sales contest among salesmen stimulate them to greater sales efforts?

7 Give examples of sales contests that have come to your attention recently. How does the use of coupons stimulate retail sales?

8 Newspapers are used mostly for local advertising. They are also used for national advertising to some extent. From a newspaper pick out several advertisements

placed by companies selling nationally. Is the newspaper an effective means of advertising in each of these cases? Does the advertisement catch the eye? Why or why not?

9 Contrast newspapers and magazines with respect to the advantages each has over the other and to the types of advertisements for which each is best suited.

10 To some extent radio and television advertisers can select their audiences through the types of programs they sponsor. Make a list of types of programs, such as sports programs and daytime serials, that are designed to appeal to special groups. To what group does each of these programs appeal? What kinds of products could effectively be advertised on such programs?

11 Much direct-mail advertising is thrown into the wastebasket before it is read. Is there anything that can be done to induce recipients not to throw away advertisements received by mail? What can you suggest?

12 What types of products or services are effectively advertised on outdoor billboards?

13 What does an advertising agency do for its clients?

14 What public and private agencies regulate advertising?

15 What is the Better Business Bureau? Who supports it? How does it benefit businessmen?

SELECTED READINGS

Bender, James F.: *How to Sell Well*, McGraw-Hill Book Company, New York, 1971.

Britt, Steuart H.: *Psychological Experiments in Consumer Behavior*, John Wiley & Sons, Inc., New York, 1970.

Burke, John D.: *Advertising in the Marketplace*, McGraw-Hill Book Company, New York, 1973.

Tillman, Rollie, and C. A. Kirkpatrick: *Promotion: Persuasive Communication in Marketing*, Richard D. Irwin, Inc., Homewood, Ill., 1972.

Wright, John S., Daniel S. Warner, and Willis L. Winter: *Advertising*, 3d ed., McGraw-Hill Book Company, New York, 1971.

Name   Section   Date

COMPLETION SENTENCES

1 Advertising is any _____ promotion of goods or services.

2 The basic purpose of both the advertiser and the salesman are the same—to

_____.

3 Before a product can be sold, there must be

_____ for it.

4 Sales promotion covers those activities that supplement the efforts of the

_____ and the

_____.

5 A coupon permits a customer to buy an article at a

_____ price.

6 In using emotion as a theme, the advertiser takes a

_____ approach or a

_____ approach.

7 The _____ is the vehicle by which the advertising message is transmitted to the public.

8 Impulse buying can be stimulated best by the _____ medium of advertising.

9 The daily newspaper is limited as a medium largely to

_____ advertising.

10 Radio is now largely a medium for _____ advertising.

11 Television has a stronger impact than radio because it catches the

_____ as well as the _____.

12 The main advantage of direct mail is that it gives the advertiser better

_____ of his audience than is possible with magazines or radio.

13 The _____ must give its message at a glance, because it is generally seen by people who are in motion.

14 The _____ is a company that plans and creates advertising for its clients.

15 The most obvious contribution of advertising is _____.

Name	Section	Date

TRUE OR FALSE STATEMENTS

T **1** A common type of sales promotion is the sales contest.

F **2** Demonstration of company products at retail stores is not an example of sales promotion.

F **3** Coupons are a means of attracting new customers, not of retaining existing customers.

F **4** Products with a nationwide demand cannot use magazine advertising effectively.

T **5** Advertising is any paid form of nonpersonal promotion of goods and services.

F **6** Advertising serves more to introduce new products than it does to remind people about products already on the market.

T **7** Classified advertising often reads like a telegram.

F **8** Magazine advertising has a geographically wider impact, but not a longer impact, on the reader compared with the newspaper.

T **9** Except for a few low-budget educational stations, radio is privately owned in the United States

F **10** Unlike magazine advertising, no selectivity of audience is possible for the advertiser who uses the radio.

T **11** In the United States television advertising has expanded more rapidly than any other advertising medium since World War II.

F **12** Direct-mail advertising, like radio advertising, has the disadvantage that it is not selective as to audience.

F **13** Outdoor advertising is not very selective from any standpoint.

T **14** A medium limited largely to local advertising is the handbill.

T **15** The chief function of an advertising agency is to plan and create the advertising for its clients.

EXERCISES

1 For a minimum of 1 hour a day for 7 successive days watch television programs on commercial stations. In addition to the program material itself you will view 30 or more commercials. Record the following information about the commercials.

Day and Time Viewed	Length of Commercial	Appeal Used (Status, Fear, Love, etc.)	Product Advertised	Comments on Effectiveness of Advertisement

2 Among the appeals on which advertising is based are fear, emulation, status, love, and patriotism. Select one advertisement from any advertising medium that appeals to each of the above emotions. Criticize each of the advertisements. Is the appeal in each case effective in promoting the idea or product advertised? Do you think a different appeal should have been used? Is the message subtle or obvious? What improvements could you suggest in each advertisement?

3 Select a product not at present being marketed (for example, self-propelled water skis, an umbrella that can be collapsed small enough to fit into a woman's handbag, or a new food item—use your imagination, but try also to be practical). Devise an advertising campaign for the product, giving attention to the following: type of appeal (fear, status, low price, convenience, etc.); advertising medium or media to be used; type of customers at which advertising appeal is directed; and package design.

In any highly industrialized nation, transportation and communications are highly developed. The United States probably has a more highly developed system of transportation and communications than any other nation. You are probably familiar, at first hand, with most of the transportation media but not, however, all. For example, you may never have seen a pipeline carrying gas or oil. You may never have taken a trip on water in a vessel larger than a ferryboat. In fact, it is possible that you have never ridden on a train. Nevertheless, all the transportation media are important as carriers of freight. In reading the chapter, keep in mind the particular advantages of each of these transportation media for certain types of freight.

From the standpoint of the individual student, railroads are probably the most colorful type of transportation agency. Some of the highlights in the development of the railroad system of the United States are probably familiar to you from courses in history as well as other sources. The railroad system has, during most of our national history, served as the primary transportation medium. The other media have developed mostly as means of supplementing it.

The science of communications has developed very rapidly during the present century. There will probably be even more spectacular advances in this science. The development of satellites as a means of communication will very likely proceed rapidly during your adult life. It is difficult to conceive of business in an era when almost instantaneous communication is not possible. In your reading of the section covering communications, study the services available for business purposes. While not all the many varieties of service can be discussed in the short space in this chapter devoted to communications, this section should indicate to you the extensive nature of communications available.

Physical distribution consists of the movement, handling, and storage of goods. By putting goods at the places they are wanted at the times they are wanted, the utility of the goods is increased. This does not apply alone to finished goods, moving from factory to warehouse, to retail storeroom, and then to the consumer. The contribution of physical distribution also includes the movement, handling, and storage of raw materials, semifinished goods, fuel, and supplies used in the process of creating finished goods.

Our facilities of physical distribution are highly developed. The transportation system, which moves goods and people from one place to another, comprises an extensive network of roads, rails, pipelines, airways, and waterways. Most of the facilities for handling goods in factories, farms, wholesale establishments, and retail outlets are very sophisticated. Storage facilities are similarly well developed to preserve all types of goods.

THE TRANSPORTATION SYSTEM

If all transportation were suddenly to end, food would disappear from grocers' shelves, factories would close down for lack of raw materials and inability to send out finished goods, and the nation would be close to economic chaos. Without a strong transportation system, each household would have to raise its own food, spin its own thread and weave its own cloth, and make its own furniture and tools by hand. In some parts of the world, transportation facilities are so lacking that each family must be self-sufficient, and the standard of living in such cases is very low. In the United States, we live as well as we do and enjoy a quantity and variety of goods that are the envy of the world largely because of our highly developed geographical specialization of production. This specialization could not exist—indeed, could not have developed—until efficient transport was available.

The transportation network of the United States is very extensive. During the nineteenth century, it consisted of railroads and waterways, with wagon roads serving for local transport. During the twentieth century, pipelines, trucks, buses, and air transport were added. The newer forms of transport increased the adaptability of transportation to special needs. Each of the forms of transportation has distinctive advantages and is used for those purposes where such advantages are important.

Transportation facilities are not always available to the public on an unrestricted basis. On the basis of availability, transport is classified as follows:

1 *Private carrier:* This is restricted to the use of the owner of the carrier. A truck or barge owned by a coal company and carrying the company's coal is a private carrier. The government regulations under which a private carrier operates are relatively simple, being confined to traffic and safety rules applying to the public roadway used.
2 *Contract carrier:* The services of a contract carrier are confined to those clients with whom contracts have been made. There is no legal requirement that services be made available to the public in general. In addition to traffic and safety rules, contract carriers are subject to regulation by government. For example, the Interstate Commerce Commission, a federal regulatory agency, has ruled that all motor vehicle contract carriers of property must transport under written contracts, copies of which must be preserved for at least 1 year after the expiration of the contract. A large proportion of truck transportation is by contract carrier.
3 *Common carrier:* Whereas a contract carrier renders a specialized service for a particular customer, a common carrier offers transportation to everyone indiscriminately. Regulation by government is substantial in the case of common carriers and covers not only safety of operation but also rates and services. A large percentage of water transportation, most transportation by air, and practically all rail shipments is by common carrier.

About 15 percent of the domestic freight transportation of the United States is by water. By law, only United States ships and barges may move cargo and passengers when both the origin and destination are within the United States. The geography of the United States permits a classification of water transport as follows: *inland waterways*, *Great Lakes*, *coastal*, and *intercoastal*.

WATERWAYS

The *inland waterways* include such rivers as the Mississippi, Ohio, Tennessee, Missouri, Warrior, Cumberland, and many smaller ones; the Erie Canal, the Illinois and Mississippi Canal, and other inland canals; and the intracoastal waterways along the Atlantic and Gulf coasts. On these waterways, a large amount of barge traffic is found because the barge is an excellent carrier for use on sheltered rivers and canals with limited depth.

The *Great Lakes* combine some of the characteristics of inland and ocean transportation. Because of the vastness of the water area—a shoreline of 8,300 miles and a water surface of 95,000 square miles—the vessels on the lakes must be seaworthy enough to withstand storms rivaling those on the North Atlantic. On the other hand, the vessels must be narrow enough and shallow enough to pass through the canals and locks connecting the lakes. More than 400 ports are found on the shores of the lakes.

The *coastal* shipping of the United States on the Pacific side moves along the West Coast and on the Atlantic side along the East Coast and the Gulf of Mexico. Vessels using these waters are restricted in size and draft only by the port facilities where they call. Some of the vessels, particularly tankers, are quite large. A considerable volume of petroleum moves by tanker from Gulf ports to the population centers of the East. Other products carried include coal, stone, lumber, iron and steel, and sulfur.

Although most of the tonnage in the coastal trade moves by ocean steamers, some moves by barge along the *intracoastal waterways*. This is a system of canals connecting the bays, inlets, and sounds along the coast from Brownsville, Texas, to the New England ports.

Intercoastal shipping connects the two coasts of the United States, mostly by way of the Panama Canal. It is largely west-to-east trade, since 50 percent more tonnage moves east than moves west. The products loaded at the Pacific ports include petroleum, lumber, paper and pulp, canned foods, wine, chemicals, sugar, frozen fruits and vegetables, and wool. On the return trip to the Pacific, cargos include glassware, machinery, chemicals, sulfur, steel products, and textiles. There is much greater variety of cargo in the intercoastal trade than is found on the inland, coastal, or Great Lakes waterways.

As can be seen in Figure 22-1, most of the money spent for freight goes to truck transportation, which rose from less than $30 billion in 1958 to over $60 billion in 1970. Part of this increase has been caused by a shift of some traffic from the railroads to the highways. The short-haul transportation of passengers and freight has particularly been diverted from rail to road, and the trend appears to be continuing.

HIGHWAYS

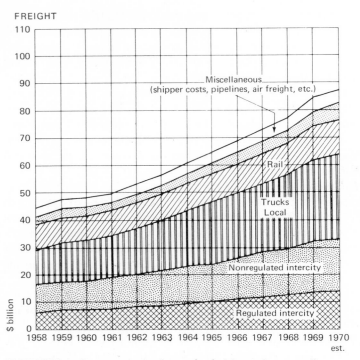

FREIGHT

FIGURE 22-1 Payments by businesses for freight services annually.
(*Fortune*, July 1971, p. 60.)

RAILROADS   The rail network of the United States is about 200,000 miles. It has declined steadily since World War I, while other forms of transportation have expanded. Although the railroads have not increased their freight tonnage at the same rate as the increase in total freight traffic during the past 30 years, the average distance of freight carried has risen. As a result, the **ton-miles**, the tonnage multiplied by the number of miles carried, has risen slightly from 1926 to the present. Passenger traffic, on the other hand, has declined both in total passengers and passenger-miles. To prevent intercity passenger trains from disappearing altogether from the United States, Congress created the National Railroad Passenger Corporation, popularly known as Amtrak. This federal corporation owns no tracks, but operates its trains on the rails of privately owned railroads. Amtrak began operations May 1, 1971.

PIPELINES   Approximately 180,000 miles of pipelines have been built in the United States. Practically all of the lines are used for the transportation of crude oil, petroleum products, and gas. The growth of pipeline transportation, in fact, has closely paralleled the development of the petroleum industry. By means of pipe, oil and gas are transported from the great producing centers of the midcontinent area to the population centers for refining and distribution. The cost is generally considerably less than transportation by rail, but is higher than the cost of shipment by ocean tanker.

To push the oil or gas through the pipe requires pumping stations at intervals varying according to the slope of the terrain, the gauge of the pipe, and the viscosity of the fluid. In exceptional cases, the oil is heated to make it flow easily. Unlike other forms of transportation, the pipeline must be full to be operated at all. The volume of oil or gas transported is varied by changing the rate of flow. Pipelines are not as adaptable as tank cars or tank ships to shifting from one product to another. Partly for this reason, pipe is less extensively used to transport refined petroleum products than to transport crude oil.

The future growth of pipeline transportation is largely dependent on the petroleum industry, since pipe is used only to a limited extent to transport liquids other than oil. It is used to a slight extent to transport powdered coal and wood pulp by mixing the solids with water. By similarly reducing bulk materials to powder and mixing with water, it is possible that the range of substances that may be carried by pipe will be extended in the future.

AIR

Speed has always been the main advantage of air transport. For this reason, it has been used chiefly to transport passengers, mail, and high-value freight. In 1925, the speed in miles per hour was about 100, in 1950 about 300, and in 1960 about 600 in jet airplanes. Speeds of commercial jets have increased very little since 1960; 600 miles per hour is close to the speed of sound (sonic barrier) at high cruising altitude. Future increases in speed are uncertain. The English and French have jointly built and tested a passenger plane capable of a speed of 1,400 miles per hour. The Russians have built a commercial plane of similar speed. But the cost of the planes and the consumption of fuel have been high, making their commercial feasibility doubtful. The extensive use of such planes is dubious.

The main disadvantages of air transportation have been high cost relative to other forms of transportation, more interruptions to schedules by bad weather, and the distance of air terminals from the centers of cities. These disadvantages have gradually been lessened, as the technology of airplane construction and flight control have progressed.

The helicopter, with its power to land and take off vertically, has become increasingly important since World War II. Capable of operating from a small patch of land or a roof top, it has been used to transport passengers, mail, and freight from downtown areas to airports. This flexibility has offset the limited speed, about 100 miles per hour, of which the helicopter is capable.

OTHER FORMS OF TRANSPORTATION

In a dynamic economy such as ours, change is constant. This is fully as evident in transportation as in other fields. New methods of transport are being developed now and will be developed in the future.

A method of transportation that shows considerable future promise is the conveyor belt. This has for a long time been used for short-distance hauling of such bulk goods as coal, stone, ore, and gravel. The conveyor belt, however, is technically capable of operating for considerable distances. A 100-mile conveyor belt system was projected in 1948, running from Lake Erie to the Ohio River and carrying iron ore south and coal north. The project, however, was strongly opposed by the railroads serving the region, and the system never went into service.

Looking into the future, the application of atomic power to submarine propulsion opens up the possibility of building cargo or tanker submarines that could travel between the Atlantic and Pacific under the Polar icecap. Also the possibility of using rockets for extremely rapid delivery of mail or freight has been suggested.

EXPRESS AND PARCEL POST

RAILWAY EXPRESS

The REA Express Agency, previously known as the Railway Express Agency, offers speed and special handling for individuals and industry. Special express cars are attached to trains, and every effort is made to expedite passage. A large fleet of trucks operated by the agency is available to pick up shipments from company premises and to deliver goods to destination addresses. The agency uses trucks, air transport, and rail to provide each shipper with the combination of transport services best suited to his demands.

Although "no article is too large or too small to be handled by express," small packages tend to go by parcel post, United Parcel Service, or other private delivery services; and very large items go by freight. High-value merchandise, style goods, emergency shipments, flowers, and valuable documents are sent by express.

Nearly everything that is accepted for rail express is also accepted for air express. There are some articles, however, that are usually excluded from air express. These include explosives, inflammable articles, dangerous chemicals, and animals. Animals and articles excluded from air express, however, often move by air freight.

PARCEL POST

The parcel post service was inaugurated by the United States Post Office in 1913, bringing to isolated farmers as well as city dwellers the benefits of delivery of packages. Parcel post is extensively used by both industry and individuals, and is essential to the existence of mail-order houses. Many goods can be shipped either by parcel post or by express, and the choice is usually made on the basis of cost, convenience, or habit. Parcel post shipments are limited as to weight and size of package, while express shipments are not. Express rates are frequently lower than parcel rates on shipments to a distant point, while shipments to a near point are generally cheaper by post. If a shipper chooses not to insure his package, it will usually be cheaper to send by post. Also, if the destination is a farmhouse, parcel post is preferable, since express shipments are not delivered beyond the delivery area of an express office.

COMMUNICATIONS

The science of communicating information over distances has progressed during the past 100 years as rapidly as the science of transportation. And, like transportation, communication takes many forms. The forms commercially important today are: postal service, telegraph, telephone, and radio.

POSTAL SERVICES

The necessity for providing a dependable, inexpensive means of communication to help bind the nation together was recognized by the framers of our Federal Constitution. Article I, section 8, authorized Congress to establish post offices and post roads. The office of Postmaster General was created in 1789. The Post Office Department was reorganized in 1970 as the United States Postal Service, with the intention of improving efficiency and removing the service from politics. The director of the service no longer has cabinet rank.

The Post Office has for many years carried certain items for businesses at less than cost "for the purpose of disseminating information." Newspapers, magazines, and other periodicals (second-class mail) are carried at rates considerably below the rate for post cards and letters (first-class mail). Catalogs, books, pamphlets, and advertising pieces (third-class mail) are also carried at less than cost and at rates below parcel post (fourth-class mail) for equivalent weight.

TELEGRAPH

Since the merger of Postal Telegraph Company into Western Union Telegraph Company in 1943, about 99 percent of telegraph revenues have been received by the Western Union company. Many services are offered, including the following:

1. *Telegram:* This is the full-rate standard service. Messages are handled at once, or in the order received if several are received at the same time.
2. *Day Letter:* The transmission of the message is subordinate to telegram transmission in priority.
3. *Serial:* Several messages to the same addressee are sent at different times during the day.
4. *Longram:* This is a type of day letter of at least double the minimum number of words for a day letter, and it is sent at a reduced rate.
5. *Night Letter:* This is receivable up to 2 A.M. for delivery the following morning.

In addition to the above services, which are available to the public, Western Union leases its wires to individual companies for their private use to transmit messages without interruption or delay at any time or for stated hours each day. Corporations with many offices scattered over the United States subscribe to this service.

There is available also, from a number of companies, telegraphic communication by underwater cable to foreign countries. The rates vary according to length of message, distance, and time of transmission.

TELEPHONE Two basic types of telephone service are provided, local and long-distance. The former is limited to a single city and its immediate suburbs, while the latter provides communication with the rest of the country and foreign nations as well. Charges for local service are generally a flat monthly rate regardless of the number of calls made, except in some large cities where a metered charge is made on the basis of the usage each month. For intercity calls, tolls are charged, which depend on the distance and length of the call.

Bell Telephone offers leased wires to business subscribers desiring frequent communication between offices in different cities. Like private leased telegraph services, the telephone channel may be leased for a stated number of hours each day or continuously.

Another business service available is the conference call, which permits three or more persons in different locations to speak together. This is useful to a sales manager, for example, in conferring with his salesmen as a group without the necessity of bringing them back to the home office for a conference.

Where a business office or plant is large, internal communication can be provided by an office switchboard, permitting one office to call another or to be connected to the local exchange.

The development of radiotelephony permitted spoken communication across oceans. The first commercial transoceanic telephone service began in January 1927 and connected New York City and London. The radio has also permitted telephones to be used on trains, ships, and in private automobiles. One of the recent technological advances is a telephone cable with built-in amplifying stations in the cable, which is then strung across ocean floors, the first one being laid on the floor of the Atlantic Ocean in the 1950s. A development of the 1960s is the use of satellites orbiting the earth to relay telephone and television communication across continents and oceans.

REGULATION OF TRANSPORTATION AND COMMUNICATION All of the agencies of transportation and communication are regulated to some extent by government agencies. Regulation has been imposed because of the following reasons:

Lack of competition to protect customers from unreasonably high rates. This characterized the railroads before World War I, the telegraph and telephone industries, and pipeline transmission.

Demand by the particular industry for less competition or the elimination of price competition. This is the reason for certain types of regulations in highway, air, and waterway transportation, and in railroad transportation during the present century.

Safety considerations.

Public consideration. For example, radio transmitters must stay within assigned frequencies, power limits, and transmission periods to avoid the chaos resulting from unregulated transmission.

Regulation of interstate commerce is reserved by the Constitution to the federal government. Intrastate commerce is regulated by the state governments. Local transportation and communication are regulated in some states at the state level and in others at the municipal level.

INTERSTATE COMMERCE COMMISSION

The first attempt to regulate railroads was made by state governments, but it was unsuccessful chiefly because railroad transportation is largely interstate in character. Railroad regulation by the federal government began with the passage of the Interstate Commerce Act in 1887, which created the Interstate Commerce Commission (ICC). The law declared that unreasonable rate discrimination must end, that rates must be published, and that fares must be reasonable. As time passed, the power of the Commission to enforce the law was increased by later acts passed by Congress. In 1906, the Commission was given authority to regulate pipelines. In 1935, highway transportation came under the authority of the Commission and, in 1940, the limited jurisdiction of the Commission over water transport was extended to include all interstate inland waterways.

The authority of the Interstate Commerce Commission is broad. Although considerable control is retained by transportation companies in setting rates and services, Commission authority is found in the following general areas:

1 *Rate setting:* Minimum and maximum rates and publication of rates.
2 *Financing:* Approval of stock and bond issues by the Commission prior to public sale.
3 *Management:* Persons may not serve on the board of directors of competing railroads without permission of the Commission.
4 *Services:* Extension of services, abandonment of services, and change of services.
5 *Mergers:* The merger of competing transportation agencies is regulated.

Commission authority in particular instances is not granted by law uniformly to all transport industries. Generally, authority is most extensive over the railroads and less so over trucks, buses, shipping, and piplines.

FEDERAL AVIATION AGENCY

Instead of bringing air transportation under the control of the Interstate Commerce Commission, Congress created a new agency in 1938, called the Civil Aeronautics Board, now the Federal Aviation Agency. This body was given powers roughly comparable to the powers the Interstate Commerce Commission exercised over contract carriers and common carriers in highway transport.

REGULATION OF COMMUNICATIONS

The ICC was given jurisdiction over wire and wireless communication in 1910. After World War I, the radio industry operated largely without regulation. The first federal regulatory body in the radio field, the Federal Radio Commission, created in 1929, had an inauspicious beginning. One newspaper commented, "The new Radio Commission, intended to bring order out of chaos in the ether, finds itself . . . with two of its five members unconfirmed, offices unprovided, no salaries, and penniless. Herbert Hoover [Secretary of Commerce] will extend it a hand and give it a home . . . the commission has not even office furniture or money for stenographers."[1]

A more comprehensive regulatory agency, the Federal Communications Commission (FCC), was created in 1934. It was given authority to regulate all interstate communications, including telephone, telegraph, radio and television broadcasting, and miscellaneous communications services. Companies subject to FCC jurisdiction are required to furnish adequate service on reasonable request, to provide joint service where necessary in the public interest, to establish fair and just rates for service, and to file rate schedules for approval by the FCC.

Since communication services entirely intrastate, such as local telephone services, are not regulated by the FCC, state agencies, such as a state public utility commission, may regulate rates and services. In some states, regulation of local telephone rates are undertaken by town and city councils. Regulation at this level of government in most cases in tantamount to no regulation at all, since town governments are not equipped to maintain a staff of rate analysts, rate lawyers, and other experts to determine the adequacy of existing rates or the justification for requested rate increases.

COORDINATION OF TRANSPORT FACILITIES

Each of the several forms of transportation available today is superior in some uses to the other forms. As each form develops, it loses those types of traffic for which it is less suited, and it gains those types for which it is better suited. For example, long-distance passenger travel has shifted since World War II from railroads and ocean liners to airplanes. Changes in the pattern of freight transportation are equally apparent.

A combination of two forms of transportation has, in some cases, been found to improve service beyond the capacity of each form acting alone. Prior to World War II, railroads established joint rates and services with steamship lines operating in the coastal trade. The ICC has also encouraged the coordination of rates and services between barge lines and railroads.

A physical combining of truck and rail transportation was achieved in the 1950s by "piggyback" operations. Trailer trucks moved goods from the point of origin to a railroad, where the trailers or trailer bodies were placed on flat cars and secured. The trailers were then removed from the flat cars near the destination of the shipment and proceeded the rest of the way by road. "Piggyback" operations led to the expansion of "containerization," by which goods are packed in large sealed containers for transport by two or three types of carriers. For example, a container the size of a large truck body is packed and sealed at a factory, trucked to a railroad depot, sent by rail to an ocean port, placed on a freighter, unloaded at a European port, and trucked to a warehouse.

[1] *Christian Science Monitor*, Mar. 5, 1927, p. 1.

The speed of handling by means of large cranes designed to lift containers from dockside to ship has reduced shipping times.[2] The sealed containers protect the contents from damage and pilferage, an important consideration at marine terminals. Marine insurance rates have reflected the lower losses. Containerization experienced a rapid increase during the 1960s. New ocean freighters are being built specifically for carrying containers. Furthermore, the principle is spreading rapidly to air freight. Large but light containers shaped to fit snugly in the cargo areas of large jet airplanes are replacing the stowage of individual pieces of cargo. The containers are loaded and unloaded rapidly, thus reducing the time a plane must remain on the ground.

As time passes, each of the major forms of transportation probably will become more specialized. The railroads appear to be developing primarily into an agency for hauling long-distance bulk freight, along with the waterways. Trucks haul more tonnage than all other agencies combined, but it is mostly short haul. Buses and airlines are taking most of the passengers who do not go by private car. Most petroleum and petroleum products move by pipeline or tanker for long hauls and by truck on short hauls. Shippers are in a much better position today to choose the most satisfactory and economical means of transport from among the various forms. And progress in this respect shows every evidence of continuing, perhaps not steadily, but at least making headway.

SUMMARY

Mass production and mass distribution are utterly dependent on good transportation and communication. The United States possesses one of the most extensive networks of railroads and other forms of transportation of any of the industrial nations.

Various types of services are available: (1) private carrier, which is restricted to use of owner or lessee of the carrier; (2) contract carrier, which is restricted to the client or clients with whom contracts for transportation have been made; and (3) common carrier, which offers service to all shippers.

The forms of transportation include water transport, highways, railroads, pipelines, and air transport. Each enjoys advantages over the others in certain respects, such as cost, speed, or adaptability for particular purposes. To some extent, however, each is in competition with one or more of the other forms for certain services. For example, railroads, pipelines, and tankers compete for the transportation of petroleum products.

Progress in communications has been spectacular during the present century. The commercially important forms include the postal service, telegraph, telephone, and radio. As in the case of transportation, each form of communication has advantages for specific purposes and each is in competition with the others for some of its business.

[2] A large crane can unload or load 25 tons of goods in a container from ship to shore in 2½ minutes. The same tonnage by traditional methods of handling takes about 18 hours. Charles Luna, *The UTU Handbook of Transportation in America*, Popular Library, New York, 1971, pp. 125–126.

All of the transportation and communication services are regulated to some degree by government agencies, both to ensure minimum standards of safety and to provide adequate services at reasonable rates. The most important regulatory agency in transportation is the Interstate Commerce Commission, which regulates inland water, railroad, highway, and road transport between states. The Federal Aviation Agency regulates air transport. And the Federal Communications Commission regulates interstate communications.

QUESTIONS FOR REVIEW

1 Explain how an efficient transportation system fosters geographical specialization of production.

2 What is the difference between a private carrier, a contract carrier, and a common carrier?

3 Look at a map of the United States. In what directions do the larger rivers run in the East? In the Midwest? In the South? In the West? What parts of the country are lacking in natural waterways? Could canals be feasibly used in these areas?

4 What characteristics must ships possess for successful operation on the Great Lakes?

5 Are the vessels carrying goods along the coasts small or large? Why? What types of goods are carried?

6 With the development of trucks and buses, some traffic has shifted from the railroads to highway transport. What are the characteristics of the traffic so diverted?

7 What are the advantages and limitations of the pipeline as a means of transportation? What products are carried?

8 What are the attractions of the supersonic airplane for passenger travel? For air freight? What are the disadvantages?

9 Some new or experimental methods of transportation were mentioned in this chapter. Appraise the possibilities of each as a carrier of passengers or freight. What advantages does each offer compared with existing methods of transportation? What disadvantages? Are there any forms of transportation not mentioned in the text that you can think of as holding promise for the future?

10 What are the differences in the services offered by parcel post and by railway express?

11 Should the United States Postal Service be liquidated and the mails carried by private corporations? Argue pro and con.

12 What are the services of interest to businessmen that are offered by Western Union Telegraph?

13 The telephone is one of the fastest means of communication. Does it have any disadvantages compared with telegraph and mail? Explain.

14 What is the ICC? What does it regulate?

15 Why is containerized freight increasing in use? What attractions does it offer in contrast to earlier methods of handling and transporting freight?

Germane, G. E., N. Glaskowsky, and J. L. Heskett: *Highway Transportation Management*, McGraw-Hill Book Company, New York, 1963.

Gray, Carl R.: *Railroading in Eighteen Countries*, Simmons-Boardman Publishing Corporation, New York, 1959.

Locklin, D. Phillip: *Economics of Transportation*, 7th ed., Richard D. Irwin, Inc., Homewood, Ill., 1972.

Pegrum, Dudley F.: *Transportation*, 3d ed., Richard D. Irwin, Inc., Homewood, Ill., 1973.

Taff, Charles A.: *Management of Physical Distribution and Transportation*, Richard D. Irwin, Inc., Homewood, Ill., 1972.

Yearbook Of Railroad Facts, Association of American Railroads, Washington, D.C., (annual edition).

SELECTED READINGS

Name   Section   Date

COMPLETION SENTENCES

1 The services of a contract carrier are confined to those clients with which

_____ for transport have been made.

2 A _____ carrier offers transportation to everyone with-

out discrimination.

3 By law, only _____ ships and barges may move cargo

and passengers when both the port of origin and the port of destination are in

the United States.

4 The growth of pipeline transportation has paralleled closely the development

of the _____ industry.

5 _____ has always been the main advantage of air

transportation.

6 The _____ agency is owned by about 70 railroads.

7 _____ is used by both individuals and industry to ship

goods and is virtually essential to the operations of mail-order houses.

8 Satellites for intercontinental communication began operations in the decade

of the _____ .

9 Railroad rates and services are regulated by the _____ .

10 The Federal Aviation Agency regulates _____ .

11 Most airlines now carry _____ as well as passengers.

12 Articles exluded from air express often travel by _____ .

13 In _____ operations trailer bodies are moved by truck

to rail depots, where they are placed on rail cars for transit.

14 A business service available by telephone is the _____ ,

which permits three or more persons in different locations to speak together.

15 The development of _____ permitted spoken communi-

cation across oceans.

TRUE OR FALSE STATEMENTS

1 Most of the money spent for freight services is spent on truck transportation.

2 Intercity rail passenger traffic is carried by a federal government corporation.

3 The rail network of the United States has expanded slowly but steadily since World War I.

4 Transportation by conveyor belt is possible only for distances under 10 miles.

5 The United States Postal Service was created in 1970.

6 The use of containerization in moving goods has not yet been adapted to air transport because of the rounded cross section of airplane bodies.

Name	Section	Date

7 In the modern world there are no areas where lack of transportation forces each family to be self-sufficient.

8 A private carrier is defined as a carrier that is privately owned.

9 About half of the domestic freight transportation in the United States is by water.

10 Passenger trains declined in number after World War II.

11 A disadvantage of the conveyor belt as a form of transportation is that it is technically incapable of transporting materials except for short distances.

12 The Railway Express Agency offers ground transportation. A separate agency offers air express.

13 The United States Post Office began offering its parcel post service shortly after the Civil War.

14 Progress in the science of communications has lagged in development behind the science of transportation.

15 Authority for the establishment of the United States Post Office is contained in the Constitution.

16 About 99 percent of telegraph revenues are paid to the Western Union Company.

17 Although telegraph cables span the oceans, transoceanic telephone cables have so far not been laid.

18 All the agencies of transportation and communication are regulated to some extent by government.

19 The Interstate Commerce Commission is limited to regulating railroads.

20 The Federal Aviation Agency regulates air transportation.

EXERCISES

1 Prepare a report comparing the cost of one-way and round-trip passenger transportation between your town and either New York or San Francisco, whichever is farther away, by air coach, first-class air, Pullman (roomette), railroad coach, and bus. Are all these forms of transportation available, or is it necessary (for example) to go by bus to a nearby city to get passenger service by rail? Compare the differences in transportation time between rail, bus, and air.

2 Select any one of the following experimental or newly developed means of transport or communication: supersonic airplanes, satellite communications, laser beams, rockets, or any other of your choice. Provide a brief history, and indicate the advantages and disadvantages of the one you have chosen. Suggest its probable use in the future.

a History:

b Advantages:

c Limitations:

d Use in the future:

3 Visit one of the freight terminals (rail, truck, air, or water) serving your town. Make a list of items that are shipped into the town regularly. Make another list of items that are produced locally and shipped out. Comment on the variety

Name	Section	Date

and importance of both groups to your town. Is there any noticeable difference in the characteristics of the two groups? Use the form below:

Principle Items Shipped In	Principal Items Shipped Out

Comments:

23 INTERNATIONAL TRADE AND MULTINATIONAL BUSINESS

For anyone interested in travel, the study of international trade should be of interest. International trade involves dealing with persons of different cultures, living in faraway lands, using a strange language in most cases, using different currency systems, and operating under different business customs.

Be sure you can discuss the advantages of international trade from the viewpoint of the American businessman. Also be sure you understand the natural obstacles to international trade—which are completely independent of any governmental action. This should indicate to you the unlikelihood of any wholesale increase in exports or imports that might result from the absence of such government barriers to trade as the tariff.

One of the most difficult concepts to understand is the principle of comparative advantage in international trade. For this reason, several pages have been devoted to it. Understanding this principle is important not only to economists and government officials but to practical businessmen as well.

Like government interferences in domestic business, tariffs are an interference by the government in business freedom. Also important to a well-educated businessman is a knowledge of the arguments in favor of and against government barriers to trade.

There are many similarities between the techniques of selling to foreign customers and those for selling to domestic customers. When reading the section on exporting, you should notice where differences occur. In the field of advertising, for example, notice how advertising to foreign customers differs from advertising in the domestic market.

International trade is trade that crosses the borders between nations. It is undertaken by private individuals and by governments.

United States exports of goods and services to foreign nations have exceeded imports during the present century. The Depression brought our foreign trade down below $3 billion, but since World War II our exports and imports have increased rapidly, as Figure 23-1 shows.

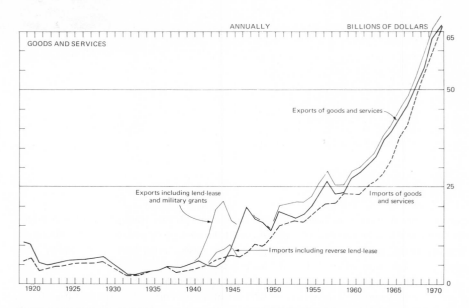

FIGURE 23-1   United States exports and imports, 1920–1971. (*Historical Chart Book*, Board of Governors of the Federal Reserve System, 1972, p. 109.)

BENEFITS FROM INTERNATIONAL TRADE

REGIONAL SPECIALIZATION

People on many isolated islands in the Pacific existed for centuries with no contact from the outside until European sailing vessels visited them. We in the United States could similarly exist without international trade. But we would not live as well as we do. We could grow our own coffee, tea, and bananas—in hothouses if necessary. But few people could afford to buy them. International trade permits specialization of production on a worldwide basis, with each nation producing what it can best and exchanging its products for those that others produce best. We can see the benefits of geographical specialization within the borders of our own country. In fact, one of the important reasons for our high standard of living is that there are almost no barriers between our states, and each region can specialize in what it is most capable of producing. Similarly, national standards of living are raised through international specialization of production. Our already high standard of living could be raised even higher if we removed tariffs and other obstacles to trade.

The United States is remarkably rich in natural resources. However, we do not have all the materials we need in the quantity we need them. During World War II, we used our resources at a rapid rate, and should we have to fight another major war, some of our important resources would probably approach depletion. Our constantly growing population requires ever more minerals and other raw materials, and we have to look more and more to foreign sources for our supplies. In 1971 we imported most of our industrial needs for several important materials, as can be seen in Figure 23-2. More and more items are added to the list as our domestic supplies dwindle and our needs increase.

When one country can produce an item better and more cheaply than another, it has an *absolute advantage* in the production of that item. The United States has a lot of coal. It can produce and sell coal to many countries more cheaply than they can produce it themselves; thus, we have an absolute advantage in the production of coal. Puerto Rico can produce sugar more cheaply than Canada, so we can say that Puerto Rico has an absolute advantage over Canada in the production of sugar. Canada, on the other hand, has an absolute advantage over Puerto Rico in the production of wheat. It is quite apparent that both countries would benefit from the exchange of Canadian wheat for Puerto Rican sugar.

ABSOLUTE ADVANTAGE IN PRODUCTION

The advantages of international specialization do not stop with the exchange of those products which each nation can obviously produce better and more cheaply than others. Suppose a nation could produce everything more cheaply than any nation. Why should it buy anything from abroad? In such a case, even though a nation had an advantage in the production of everything, it could benefit by specializing in those products in which its advantage was greatest. Ricardo, one of the great classical economists, explained the principle of comparative advantage in this way: "Two men can both make shoes and hats, and one is superior to the other in both employments; but in making hats he can only exceed his competitor

COMPARATIVE ADVANTAGE IN PRODUCTION

FIGURE 23-2 Imports as percentage of domestic consumption for 1971.

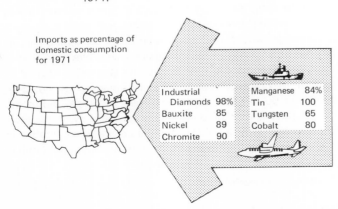

Imports as percentage of domestic consumption for 1971

Industrial Diamonds	98%	Manganese	84%
Bauxite	85	Tin	100
Nickel	89	Tungsten	65
Chromite	90	Cobalt	80

by one-fifth, or 20 percent, and in making shoes he can excel him by one-third or 33-1/3 percent. Will it not be for the interest of both that the superior man should employ himself exclusively in making shoes, and the inferior man in making hats?"[1]

A more colorful illustration of comparative advantage can be found in baseball. Babe Ruth began his major league career as a pitcher, and he was a great pitcher. However, he was also a very capable batter. Because a pitcher cannot play in every game and, therefore, Babe Ruth's batting prowess was available only occasionally, a choice had to be made. Was his comparative advantage over other players greater as a pitcher or as a batter? We know the answer: Babe Ruth gave up a successful career as a pitcher for an even more successful career as a batter.

The principle of comparative advantage can be further explained by a hypothetical example. Suppose the United States and France both make automobiles and bicycles, but the costs of a car and a bicycle are different in each, with the United States having an absolute advantage in the production of both, as shown in the table. Since the costs of production of both items are higher in France than

United States		France	
1 car	$2,000	1 car	$3,000
1 bicycle	$40	1 bicycle	$50
1 car	= 50 bicycles	1 car	= 60 bicycles

in the United States, it would appear that there would be no point in France selling either item here. However, a car "costs" 60 bicycles in France and only 50 bicycles in the United States. So it would be better for Frenchmen to produce bicycles to pay for the cars of the United States rather than making cars in France. In terms of money, France could produce 50 bicycles at $50 each or a total of $2,500, selling them in the United States (where bicycles cost $40) for a total of $2,000. The $2,000 would buy one car in the United States, which could be sold for $3,000 in France. Thus, profit could be made by shipping French bicycles to the United States at a loss to get the dollars to ship American cars to sell in France at a profit. Similarly, American businessmen would find that their profit in selling cars in France would be greater than their profit in selling American bicycles, and that it would be profitable to sell American cars in France even though the profits had to be brought home in the form of French bicycles. Thus, an American car could be sold in France for $3,000 and 60 bicycles could be bought and then sold in the United States for $2,400, for a profit of $400 on the transaction.

At this point, we could ask: Why shouldn't the United States sell both cars and bicycles in France and just bring the dollars home without buying anything?

[1] David Ricardo, *Political Economy*, Everyman's Library, London, 1911, p. 83.

The answer is that there would be no dollars in France with which to pay for the American cars and bicycles and, therefore, no dollars to bring home unless Frenchmen could get dollars by selling something to the United States. In other words, we cannot get paid for our goods and services unless we get paid in the form of foreign goods and services.

BALANCE OF PAYMENTS

Nearly all the transactions involving money between people, corporations, and government bodies in one country and those in other countries are recorded. These transactions constitute the *balance of payments* of a country. The most important in dollar volume of these transactions are merchandise exports and imports. The Department of Commerce publishes the balance of payments for the United States each year. Table 23-1 shows the merchandise exports and imports for the year 1971. A few transactions are unrecorded, and for this reason a balancing item called *errors and omissions* is reported. Smuggling, unreported gifts, losses of money or property while traveling, and similar items explain the lack of balance. The important point brought out by these figures is that to get paid for what we sell we must buy from abroad.

As Figure 23-3 illustrates graphically, our imports are important to us not only because we can enjoy the Swiss watches, French perfume, English bicycles, and Brazilian coffee produced abroad but also because these imports provide foreigners with the means of paying for what we sell them. Foreign trade, as Figure 23-4 shows, is a two-way street.

TABLE 23-1   SELECTED ITEMS OF THE BALANCE OF INTERNATIONAL PAYMENTS OF THE UNITED STATES, 1971

Transactions That Create Payments to the United States	Millions of Dollars	Transactions That Create Payments to Foreign Nations	Millions of Dollars
Merchandise exports	$42,770	Merchandise imports	$45,459
Income earned from U.S. investments abroad	12,898	Income earned from foreign investments in the U.S.	4,903
Transactions in U.S. official reserve assets	2,348	Travel and transportation, net	2,483
		Military transactions, net	2,894
		Unilateral transfers, gifts, pensions, net	1,529
		U.S. Government grants, nonmilitary, net	2,045

Source: Federal Reserve Bulletin, Washington, October 1972.

For our standard of living   For our defense and industry

Bauxite · Cobalt · Tin ·
Diamonds · Manganese ·
Nickel · Rubber · Chromium

For our export industries and agriculture

which employ millions of workers and do a multimillion dollar
business annually—and can
prosper only if other nations—
by selling to us—can earn
enough dollars to buy from us

FIGURE 23-3   The importance of imports to the United
States. (The Twentieth Century Fund, Inc.)

FIGURE 23-4   The interdependence of exports and imports. (The
Twentieth Century Fund, Inc.)

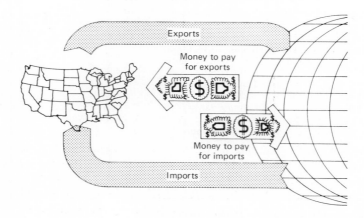

If there were no tariff barriers between nations, the domestic producers of each country would still enjoy a considerable competitive advantage over foreign producers. Even without the government barriers, there are obstacles caused by distance, differences in language, transportation costs, differences in customs, and difference in money systems.

OBSTACLES TO INTERNATIONAL TRADE

Goods travel considerable distances in international trade, much more than in domestic trade. This means delay in filling orders. While it takes almost the same time to send an air-mail letter from New York to Stockholm as it does from New York to Boston, there is a considerable time difference in shipping the goods, unless the shipment is sent by air. Ships travel more slowly than trains, and goods leaving Stockholm would arrive in New York many days later. A supplier far from a market is always at a disadvantage compared with a supplier close to the market.

DISTANCE

A shipment in domestic trade generally travels on one or possibly two transportation media. Manufactured items are sent by rail, truck, or a combination of rail and truck in most cases. In international trade, transportation over water is common, introducing another transportation medium in the shipment. The goods are generally handled more often because of the necessity of transferring packages from railroad car to warehouse to cargo hold and, at the end of the voyage, from cargo hold to warehouse to railroad car. Goods, therefore, must be more carefully packed for foreign shipment. The costs of packaging, freight, and insurance raise the transportation bill for foreign shipments in most cases well above the typical domestic shipment.

TRANSPORTATION COSTS

Misunderstanding between seller and buyer commonly occur in domestic trade where both speak the same language. Where different languages are involved in international trade, the chances of misunderstanding are multiplied.

LANGUAGE

One of the pleasures of engaging in international trade is the contact it affords with customs and cultures different from our own. But this imposes an obstacle as well. One cannot use the same selling techniques or advertising that one uses in domestic selling. Even the product itself may have to be changed to conform with local custom or law. For example, British cars manufactured for the American market have the steering wheel on the left side; for the domestic market, it is on the right. In some countries, the fins, sharp ornaments, and other protuberances that delight the designers of Detroit cars must be removed or modified to conform with local safety regulations.

CUSTOMS

DIFFERENT MONEY SYSTEMS   In domestic trade, the money the seller uses is the same as the buyer's. In international trade, the money of the seller and that of the buyer are usually different. This means that the inconvenience and risk involved in exchanging one currency for another must be borne either by the buyer or by the seller.

GOVERNMENTAL BARRIERS   Governmental barriers are those interferences with the freedom of choice of consumers that are imposed by the government at the demand of domestic producers. The most obvious ones are tariffs, but there are others, as Figure 23-5 shows. These include quotas, subsidies, and preferences for domestic producers, and tariff administration and import regulations.

Tariffs   A tariff is a tax levied on goods imported into a country. The purpose is either to gain revenue or to curtail imports. If the primary purpose is to gain revenue, the tariff is set low enough so that goods will be imported in spite of the tariff duty paid on them. If the purpose is to curtail imports, the rates are set high. Since

FIGURE 23-5   United States barriers to imports. (The Twentieth Century Fund, Inc.)

OUR TRADE BARRIERS

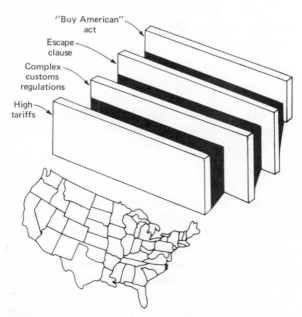

"Buy American" act

Escape clause

Complex customs regulations

High tariffs

1920, rates have been set in the United States for the purpose of curtailing imports, and any income derived has been incidental.

A quota imposes a limit to the quantity of an item that may be imported. An *absolute quota* limits the total number or amount of a commodity that may be imported during a period, usually a year. A *tariff quota* levies a low rate on the imports of an item during a period until a specified quantity has entered; all additional imports of the item during the period are subject to a higher rate. Items such as petroleum, dairy products, potatoes, and fresh fish are subject to quotas.

Quotas

A subsidy is a payment to a domestic company by the government ostensibly to permit the company to offer its products or services to the public at a lower price than would be possible without the subsidy. The shipbuilders in the United States, for example, have received subsidies of 40 percent or more of the cost of construction for the building of an ocean liner. Airplane manufacturers, producers of minerals, magazine publishers, and many others have received subsidies, generally hidden. Direct subsidies, visible to the public, have been proposed from time to time as a substitute for protection by tariff.

Subsidies

The height of a tariff wall is not measured only by the rates officially published. Interpretation, arbitrary valuations, and other administrative practices are of considerable importance in determining the extent of a country's trade barriers. These impose a risk in international commercial dealings quite apart from the ordinary hazards of trade. Studies of American tariffs indicate complex customs procedures, involving uncertainty of tariff classification of goods, delays by customs officials in making decisions, and arbitrary rulings. The result is to make the importation of many items, particularly the introduction of new items, especially hazardous to the American importer.

Administration of Tariffs

Free competitive markets are one of the essential characteristics of a capitalistic society. Tariffs and other governmental barriers to trade restrict the freedom of the market and reduce the extent of competition. They are an interference with free enterprise. In some cases, however, it is advisable for the government to intervene in the nation's economy. Is the restriction of imports a useful function of government? The argument on this question has continued from the founding of the nation to the present day.

TARIFF REDUCTION

International trade was brought nearly to a standstill as the world slid into a depression from 1929 to 1932. In an effort to reduce the barriers to trade between nations, the United States passed the Reciprocal Trade Agreements Act of 1934, which was extended with modifications into the 1960s. By this act, Congress granted authority to the President to bargain with other nations for a mutual reduction of tariff barriers. Many agreements have been negotiated under this program, some on the basis of bilateral bargaining and others on the basis of multilateral bargaining.

Many industry groups support the goal of freedom in international trade. Support for reduction in tariff barriers has been generally more widespread since World War II than it was before. One association of businessmen expresses the position for tariff reduction in these words:

> A free flow of trade is one of the major competitive pressures for improving productivity throughout the American economy. To impose severe import restrictions would almost certainly touch off a spirit of retaliatory restrictions by other countries. The results would be a loss of real income in the United States as a consequence of higher costs and prices, and also a loss of jobs resulting from a lower volume of exports of both goods and services. Even today, the high cost of living of the American consumer is due in part to restrictions, especially "voluntary" and other quotas, on imports into the United States. It is hard to see how a policy of more restrictions can be justified as being in the interests of American workers, since their real income depends fundamentally on the productivity of the whole economy. Moreover, foreign retaliation for increased U.S. import restrictions results in job losses for many U.S. workers in export or export-related industries that are more extensive than the jobs that may be provided by import restrictions.[2]

INTERNATIONAL ECONOMIC COMMUNITIES

Following World War II several nations organized into groups to reduce tariff barriers and other obstacles to trade in the group and to achieve the benefits of specialization of production that unfettered markets larger than any one of the member nations would permit. The groups worthy of mention because of their trade with the United States are the European Economic Community (also called the Common Market), the European Free Trade Association, and the Latin American markets.

THE EUROPEAN ECONOMIC COMMUNITY (EEC)

France, West Germany, Italy, Belgium, the Netherlands, and Luxembourg signed a treaty in Rome March 25, 1957, creating a unified trading area known as the European Economic Community. The goal of this community was to achieve a full economic union, with elimination of government barriers to the movement of goods, workers, and money within the community. The elimination of tariff barriers among the members was completed July 1, 1968, and on that date a uniform tariff was adopted by the member countries against goods from outside nations. Other barriers have been eliminated and the goal of full economic union

[2] *U.S. Foreign Economic Policy and the Domestic Economy*, The Committee for Economic Development, New York, 1972, p. 11.

has been steadily approached. The grander goal of political union has advanced more slowly.

On January 1, 1973, Great Britain, the Republic of Ireland, and Denmark joined the EEC. This has created a nine-nation industrial region exceeded only by the United States in value of industrial production. The existence of the enlarged EEC creates both opportunity and obstacle to United States producers. United States agricultural exports to Great Britain now are subject to the higher EEC tariff rather than the lower British duty. On the other hand American multinational firms (discussed later in this chapter) having plants in the EEC enjoy a duty-free market of almost 250 million persons. In bargaining for mutual tariff reductions, American negotiators face the negotiators of a united bloc of nine nations. The gold and foreign currency reserves of the EEC have increased rapidly during the early 1970s, while those of the United States have dwindled. Clearly, creating a common market of Western European nations has been a success, one that the United States must deal with on a basis of equality of bargaining power.

THE EUROPEAN FREE TRADE ASSOCIATION (EFTA)

This association, comprising Great Britain, Denmark, Sweden, Norway, Switzerland, Austria, and Portugal, was organized as a less closely knit group of nations than the EEC. The goal was to create a *customs union* (the elimination of tariffs between members) rather than an economic union. Each nation maintained its own tariff barriers against goods of nonmember nations. With the entry of Denmark and Great Britain into the EEC, EFTA has become a relatively minor association.

LATIN-AMERICAN ECONOMIC ASSOCIATIONS

Two groups of nations in Latin America have organized to reduce trade barriers. The Latin American Free Trade Association was organized in 1961 with the goal of eliminating trade barriers. The pace of tariff reductions depends upon the success of mutual bargaining sessions among members. The member countries include Argentina, Brazil, Chile, Colombia, Ecuador, Paraguay, Peru, and Uruguay.

In 1962 the Central American Common Market was organized by Costa Rica, El Salvador, Guatemala, Honduras, and Nicaragua. Some progress toward the goal of customs union and a common monetary system has been achieved, but progress has been slow.

MULTINATIONAL BUSINESS

The term *multinational business* is generally applied to those corporations that have manufacturing, refining, or distributing operations in several nations. Like a domestic firm that operates in many states and can take advantage of regional variations in labor, raw materials, and climate to reduce its costs, so can a multinational business take advantage of differences between nations in raw materials prices, interest rates, and other factors to increase its competitive position. A company with facilities in Europe, Latin America, and Asia can more easily expand operations in one part of the world and reduce them in another than can a competitor with operations confined to one nation. If skilled labor is plentiful and relatively cheap in Formosa, a multinational company with production facilities on that island can shift or expand its hand assembly operations there and reduce similar operations in its plants in the United States or Europe. If personal incomes are rising more rapidly in European countries than in Latin America, a multinational company can reduce its operations in Latin America (or change to a different type of product) and expand production in European plants of its line of consumer goods.

A multinational company can train its technical and managerial personnel in one location. It can shift its officers from one country to another as the need arises, much as the United States government moves its consular officers around. Where resentment against foreign-made goods is present in a nation, a multinational firm can produce from raw material to finished product (to the extent that it is feasible) within the nation's borders, using local employees and officers. A multi-national company can borrow money wherever interest rates are lowest, and can shift its funds from one country to another to take advantage of different money rates.

Although American corporations have had far-flung operations for many decades, the rise in the number of multinational companies has been particularly rapid following World War II. Some examples are General Motors, Ford, International Telephone and Telegraph, Sears Roebuck, International Harvester, National Cash Register, Gulf Oil, Shell Petroleum, and Exxon (formerly Standard Oil).

EXPORTING

When a firm wishes to enter the markets of the world, it may do so by engaging in the direct or indirect distribution of its products. A decision to enter foreign markets is not to be taken lightly. The obstacles to success we have already discussed pertain to American companies entering foreign trade as well as to foreign companies trading here.

INVESTIGATING EXPORT POSSIBILITIES

American companies not engaging in foreign trade receive from time to time unsolicited orders from foreign buyers. If the frequency of such orders increases, it suggests the existence of potential foreign demand, which can expand the sales of the company. Regardless of what stimulates the interest of an American producer in foreign selling, the decision to enter the world market should be taken only after careful investigation. This investigation should be concerned with the extent of existing competition in the world market, which products of the company are best for foreign selling, which foreign nations appear to be most likely markets for the company products, the extent to which the company products might have to be redesigned or modified to be acceptable to foreign customers, and which marketing channel to use.

The investigation need not be made entirely with the resources of the company alone. Nor is it necessary for an officer of the company to visit foreign countries in the course of his investigation, unless he wishes to take a foreign tour that can be charged to business expense. There are many sources of information helpful to a businessman considering foreign selling or buying. Included among them are the following:

U.S. Department of Commerce
U.S. Bureau of the Customs
Banks in New York, San Francisco, and other port cities
National Trade Council
Chamber of Commerce of the United States
Foreign Chambers of Commerce
The American Exporter (monthly)
Journal of Commerce (New York, daily)
Universal Commerce (monthly)

U.S. Department of State
New York State Department of Commerce
Dun and Bradstreet (particularly its publication *International Markets*)
Commerce and Industry Association of New York
Consulates of foreign nations in American cities
Embassies of foreign nations
Exporter's Encyclopedia

Of particular help to a person or company wishing help in selling to or buying from abroad is the United States Department of Commerce. This department, created to aid businessmen, has a substantial group of bureaus and offices devoted to supporting exporters and importers. Books, pamphlets, and periodicals are available free or at a low cost. If a businessman has a special problem, a letter to the department will provide information. The bureaus and offices of the Department of Commerce concerned with international trade are shown in Figure 23-6.

MARKETING CHANNELS

The marketing channels can be divided into direct and indirect. In the first, exporting is carried out by the manufacturer. In the second, foreign sales are made through marketing middlemen who specialize in foreign sales. Frequently, a company will enter the world market through indirect channels. If sufficient volume of foreign sales is built up, the company may decide to do its own export selling, at least for those products in which foreign sales are substantial.

Direct Selling

In addition to large volume of foreign sales, there are other reasons for engaging in direct selling. They are: (1) when repair services and replacement parts must be obtained for overseas customers; (2) when intensive sales promotion is required; and (3) when close control over selling efforts or close contact with foreign customers is deemed advisable.

If the volume of foreign sales is not particularly large, the export function may be the part-time responsibility of the sales manager or some other officer. In such a case, the officer may be assisted by one or more export salesmen, a full-time or part-time translator, and a full-time or part-time foreign billing and marine insurance clerk. As a general rule, however, it is not advisable for a company to engage in direct exporting unless the volume of sales is sufficient to support the full time of a company officer and staff.

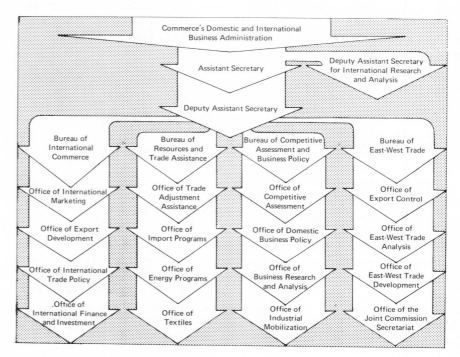

FIGURE 23-6 The business bureaus and offices of the United States Department of Commerce. (**Business Week**, Nov. 18, 1972, p. 65.)

If the volume of exports to a particular country is very large, the American exporter might set up his own retail outlets, as has been done by Sears, Roebuck and Company and by the Woolworth Company. Most American exporters, however, do not sell directly to the foreign consumer.

Branch Offices and Branch Plants

One of the means of direct selling abroad is the establishment of a branch office or a branch plant. If the sales in a particular region of the world are sufficiently high or have the potential of becoming high, the establishment of a branch office or plant may be warranted. Such an office, however, is usually considered a subsidiary by the laws of the foreign country. The laws of some countries are quite restrictive with respect to the operation of subsidiaries of foreign companies. For example, the law may require that a certain percentage of the employees in the office be citizens of the country, or that the office or plant be incorporated under local laws and a majority of the stock be held by citizens of the country.

Direct selling puts the foreign exchange risk on the American company. If exchange control, revolution, or currency devaluation should occur, the American company might be unable to bring home the number of dollars from foreign sales that it considered necessary to make a profit from foreign operations. This can be avoided, of course, by requiring payment in American dollars, but such a requirement might lose sales to competitors.

Indirect Selling

    In distributing goods to foreign markets, American manufacturers can sell through middlemen either in foreign countries or in the United States. The foreign middlemen are wholesalers, brokers, import houses, and agents. Domestic middlemen are export merchants, agents, commission houses, and resident buyers.

If an American company sells to foreign wholesalers, it must offer a substantial discount from the retail price. In addition, such inducements as exclusive rights within a foreign country may be offered provided the wholesaler maintains a reasonably large stock of goods on hand and pushes the company's line with vigor.

Foreign Wholesalers

Like domestic brokers, these do not take title to the goods they handle, but negotiate with producers and sellers to bring about a sale. A foreign broker is located in a foreign country and collects a fee or commission for his services. The products sold by brokers are commodities, such as wheat, wool, and cotton.

Foreign Brokers

These middlemen generally buy in fairly large quantity from American producers. They resell to wholesalers or to retailers.

Foreign Import Houses

The foreign agent is the sales representative of the American company and handles manufactured goods. The orders he obtains in his country are forwarded to the American manufacturer for acceptance. He does not take title to the goods. The goods are shipped directly to the purchasers, and credit losses are borne by the American company. The agent is paid a commission for the sales he makes.

Foreign Agents

These middlemen buy directly from American manufacturers, pay in dollars, package the goods for ocean shipment, transport them abroad, and absorb any risks of nonpayment. Often they have branch offices in the principal cities of the world. Selling to an export merchant is about the same as selling to any domestic customer.

Export Merchants

Export Agents

The export agent is a sales representative of the American manufacturer, and is paid a commission for the sales made. The agent generally bills foreign customers on the agents' own invoices, paying the manufacturer for all orders shipped and in turn collecting from the foreign customer.

Export Commission House

These middlemen act on behalf of the buyer located in a foreign country. An importer in Buenos Aires may write an export commission house in New York to secure prices and terms for water well-drilling equipment. The commission house then secures prices and terms from several American manufacturers of such machinery. The Buenos Aires importer (or the commission house) selects the American company offering the most attractive terms and instructs the commission house to place the order for the machinery. The commission house arranges the placement of the goods on the ship to Buenos Aires, the purchase of marine insurance, the preparation of the necessary documents, and the other details of the shipment. The commission house pays the American manufacturer and bills the importer for the cost of the goods, the shipping expenses, and the buying commission (about 5 percent of the cost plus charges, for example).

Resident Buyers

Foreign companies that purchase from the United States in fairly large volume often employ buyers residing in New York and other American cities. The resident buyer usually takes the initiative in making the purchase, pays the American producer in cash, and handles all the details of the foreign shipment of the goods.

SALES PROMOTION AND ADVERTISING

Advertising and sales promotion in foreign countries cannot be conducted on the same basis as it is in the United States. Although an exporter can appeal to the same emotions of foreign buyers as American buyers, he cannot appeal in the same way. Foreign advertising is traditionally more reserved than our own. Furthermore, customs, taboos, and prejudices differ from ours. In preparing advertising copy or planning a sales promotion campaign aimed at the foreign consumer rather than the foreign merchant, it is particularly important that local customs be considered. Some ludicrous, or even offensive, results are sometimes obtained by the literal translation of an American advertisement into a foreign tongue for insertion in a foreign magazine. Where the American exporter is not well versed in the customs of a particular country, it is advisable for him to have the advertising campaign prepared by an advertising agency in the foreign country or by an American agency with a capable foreign department.

The advertising media in foreign countries are the same in most cases as in the United States. Advertising may be prepared for billboards, car cards, magazines, newspapers, radio, television, calendars, blotters, trade fairs, and many other media. The use of these media varies. In Great Britain, for example, no advertising is permitted on the radio, and advertising on the commercial television network is controlled to prevent it from debasing the quality of the program. In many countries, advertisements are shown in motion picture theatres to a greater extent. Where bullfighting is found, billboards are used as they are in American baseball stadiums. In some countries, advertisements are found on the front pages of newspapers and the front covers of magazines.

Trademarks and brand names are important in selling overseas, and, in some parts of the world, are more important than in the United States. In those lands where illiteracy is high, an easily recognized trademark or brand name is essential to the sale of many consumer products. The trademark, of course, should be registered in each of the foreign countries where selling is planned. In some cases, it is advisable that the trade name or mark be changed because of similarity with an already established product or because the name or mark is either meaningless or offensive in the foreign country. For example, the Colgate deodorant Veto is sold as Tact in Australia.

IMPORTING

A person or company wishing to buy from abroad can take the initiative in the transaction by writing the foreign producer directly or by writing one or more of the foreign middlemen described above. There are always new products and variations of old products being created in other parts of the world, and the alert businessman will keep in touch, to the extent that he has time, with foreign developments and products. Many foreign products are available in domestic stores. Many others, however, are not. The introduction of a new foreign product to the domestic market holds the possibility of considerable profit, as well as considerable risk.

In dealing with foreign sources of supply, the possibilities of delay and misunderstanding are increased. Furthermore, the total cost of an imported article is not realized until after the order has been placed, the goods sent through customs, and delivery made to the buyer. Unless a company expects to import in fairly large volume, it probably should consider buying from a commission house or other middleman. If a small businessman wishes to get into importing, he can get valuable aid from the Small Business Administration or the Bureau of Foreign Commerce of the Department of Commerce. Most important to an importer is the body of import regulations governing the products he is interested in. He should familiarize himself with these and with the import duties he must pay before buying.

FINANCING

Financing is more complicated in foreign trade because there is greater risk in extending credit to foreign buyers and because of the different monetary units involved. With different monetary units there exists the problem of transferring one unit to another. If an American exporter demands payment in dollars from a French importer, the burden of transferring French francs into American dollars is put on the importer. If the American exporter quotes his prices in terms of francs, the burden of transferring francs into dollars is put on the exporter. The transferring of one money into another is *foreign exchange*. The term is also used to designate foreign currencies and credit instruments (trade drafts, bank drafts, and others) in foreign money. If an American importer needs to pay a British supplier 100 pounds sterling, he buys foreign exchange to make his payment.

FINANCING EXPORTS

The principal means of financing exports are cash with order, open-book credit, trade draft, and bank credit.

Cash with Order

Where the credit of the foreign buyer is weak or is unknown, cash with order might be necessary. Another occasion for requiring such terms is in the manufacture of equipment to the specifications of the foreign buyer. In such a case the equipment would presumably be of little use to any other buyer, and the manufacturer might wish to protect himself by requiring cash in advance. The importer required to pay cash with order generally obtains from his local bank a draft in American dollars drawn by the bank on its account in a New York bank. This draft is then sent to the American manufacturer.

Open-Book Credit

If the foreign buyer has a good credit rating and is a regular customer, the American exporter may extend open-book terms. The advantages of this method are convenience and simplicity. The foreign customer is charged the amount of the order on the books of the exporter, and an invoice is sent to the customer indicating the amount of payment, when the payment is due, and the money in which the payment is to be made. Common payment terms are CRM (cash by return mail), CRS (cash on return ship), and 10 EOM (10 days after the end of the month in which order was made). The terms may require payment by draft drawn on an American bank or a check drawn on a foreign bank. In the latter case the check is in a foreign currency and will be "sold" by the exporter to his bank for dollars.

Trade Draft

The common method of financing foreign sales is by use of a trade draft. The use of the draft in domestic transactions is discussed in Chapter 24. Its use in foreign trade is essentially the same, except that foreign exchange is involved. When an order is received from a foreign customer, the American exporter draws a draft (calling for payment either in dollars or in the foreign currency) against the importer, prepares the shipping documents to accompany the draft, and takes them to his bank. The goods are shipped by the exporter and the shipping documents are sent by the bank to its correspondent bank in the importer's country.

Since World War II, the shipping documents have usually been sent by air mail with a duplicate set sent by ship or by a later plane. Upon receipt of the shipping documents, the foreign bank notifies the importer. The importer goes to the bank, where he must accept the draft (paying for it in his own currency or obligating himself to pay it upon maturity if it is a time draft) before the bank will release the shipping documents to him. With the documents in hand, the importer can take physical possession of the goods. The accepted draft is called an *acceptance*. If it is drawn in the money of the importer, the foreign bank generally credits the account of the exporter with the equivalent number of dollars. If the exchange rate should change unexpectedly, the American exporter would receive an unanticipated profit or loss, depending upon the direction of the change. To avoid the exchange rate risk, the exporter can draw the draft in American dollars. In this case the foreign bank generally sends the acceptance to its American correspondent bank (a bank in which the foreign bank has a deposit account in American dollars), where the account of the foreign bank is debited and the account of the exporter is credited.

A less troublesome method of payment is through a *commercial letter of credit*. The foreign importer arranges with his bank to have a document (the letter of credit) issued, authorizing the American exporter to draw a draft against the foreign bank rather than against the importer. This substitutes the bank's credit for the importer's credit, thereby reducing the risk to the exporter. The letter of credit can be prepared for a single shipment and a single draft, or it may authorize the exporter to draw drafts over a period of time on orders for goods placed by the importer. The letter of credit may authorize drafts to be drawn in dollars or in the importer's currency.

Bank Credit

The methods by which an American importer finances a purchase are implied in the description of financing exports. However, because individuals in addition to business firms make occasional purchases from foreign sellers, some further discussion may be useful. There are four methods an individual can commonly use in making payments for goods ordered from abroad. They are the bank check, the bank draft or bank money order, the express money order, and the postal money order.

FINANCING IMPORTS

Some foreign exporters, magazine publishers, and others advertise that payment may be made by check drawn on any American bank. This is quite common in buying from Canada, for example. To the American buyer the transaction is scarcely different from placing an order with a domestic supplier. The check is enclosed with the order in an envelope, dropped in the mail, and some time later the goods or magazine subscription is received.

Bank Check

Bank Draft or Bank Money Order

These instruments can be bought at any bank, and are used in both domestic trade and foreign trade. In either case the seller, upon receiving the buyer's order and the bank draft or money order, may cash the draft or money order at his bank or leave it for collection and deposit to his account. The buyer pays the bank a fee for the draft or money order.

Express Money Order

The American Express Company sells money orders to enable purchasers to make payments for purchases (usually small) either at home or abroad. These money orders may be purchased at any office of the company and at many banks. These are acceptable as payment for goods almost anywhere in the world, and they may be sent by mail safely. Another company providing money orders acceptable abroad is Thomas Cook and Son.

Postal Money Order

A postal money order in dollars may be bought at a post office and sent to the foreign seller to pay for goods ordered. In most cases the foreign seller is willing to receive an order payable in American dollars, which he can exchange for his own currency when he cashes the order at his bank. If the seller demands payment in his own currency, the American purchaser may buy a *foreign currency order* from the post office. These are available in the currencies of the more important commercial countries, such as Great Britain and West Germany. In such a case the American buyer usually is given a receipt by the post office rather than the money order itself. The money order is sent by the post office to the postal money order exchange office, which sends an advice to the foreign post office. The foreign post office notifies the seller to call for the money, which is paid him in the currency of the country. The United States Postal Service settles balances arising out of foreign currency orders with the post offices of other countries through normal banking channels.

FINANCING FOREIGN TRAVEL

There are four methods in general use of paying for the hotel rooms, restaurant meals, transportation, and other services an American buys abroad. They are American dollars, travelers' checks, travelers' letters of credit, and credit cards.

American Dollars

In many parts of the world, hotels and stores in the larger cities are willing to accept American dollars at approximately the current rate of exchange. In some cases even personal checks drawn on American banks are acceptable. In Canada and Mexico coins and bills of the United States are used wherever tourists are found. The danger in carrying a large sum of money to pay for travel, however, is as great abroad as it is in the United States. For this reason this means of financing travel is not to be recommended.

These may be purchased at banks, express companies, and some hotels. When the checks are purchased, the buyer signs his name in the upper left-hand corner of each check. When he wishes to cash a check, he signs again at the bottom in the presence of the person cashing the check. The money in local currency is then given him. Nearly all hotels, railroads, restaurants, theatres, and stores dealing with tourists will cash travelers' checks.

Travelers' Checks

The travelers' letter of credit is similar to the commercial letter of credit discussed above. The letter is a printed form issued by an American bank and addressed to its correspondent banks (banks in which the American bank has deposits or banks which have deposits in the American bank) in foreign countries. This letter authorizes the traveler to draw drafts on the American bank, which the correspondents cash in local currency. As each draft is drawn and cashed, the amount of the draft, the date it was cashed, and the name of the correspondent bank are entered in an appropriate space on the back of the letter of credit. Before cashing a draft, the correspondent bank checks the back of the letter of credit to make sure that the funds authorized by the letter have not been exhausted by previous drafts. The bank also checks the expiration date of the letter of credit and the authenticity of the traveler's signature and requires identification.

Travelers' Letters of Credit

A credit card enables a traveler to purchase services and merchandise from sellers honoring the card. As the purchase is made, the traveler signs a bill for the purchase, and the bill is sent to the issuer of the credit card for payment. The company issuing the card submits a statement periodically, usually once a month, to the person in whose name the card was issued, requesting prompt settlement. The issuer of the card charges the participating retailers a fee for collecting payment. The attraction to the retailer is that the convenience of buying by means of a credit card attracts customers to the participating stores, hotels, and so on. Some credit cards are honored by hotels, transportation agencies, and stores in the larger cities throughout the world. Examples of credit cards are American Express Credit Card, Diners' Club Card, and Carte Blanche.

Credit Cards

During the late 1960s items creating payments to foreigners in the United States balance of payments increased more rapidly than the transactions creating payments to the United States (see "Balance of Payments" earlier in this chapter). In 1971 for the first time in this century the merchandise exports dropped below merchandise imports, and in 1972 they dropped still further. By 1973, the dollar balances held by foreigners had increased to over $80 billion, compared with $30 billion in 1966 and $47 billion in 1970. In response the United States government reduced the value of the dollar by 7.8 percent in 1971 and by an additional 10 percent in 1973. Although the mechanics of the devaluation are too complex to

DEVALUATION OF THE DOLLAR

be treated here, the result was to make foreign currencies more expensive in dollars and, conversely, the dollar cheaper in terms of foreign currencies. For example, the German mark was exchanged for 28.7 cents in 1971, 31.3 cents in 1972, and 33.7 cents in 1973. It was hoped that making the dollar less expensive for foreigners to buy would encourage the purchase of more American products abroad, and that the increasing cost of foreign currencies to Americans would discourage the purchase of foreign goods and also discourage foreign travel by Americans. If successful, this would curb the increase in dollar balances held by foreigners and perhaps encourage the spending of the balances for American goods and services, thus helping to stimulate American sales abroad.

SUMMARY International trade is commerce that crosses national boundaries. As in the case of domestic trade, international trade expands the benefits of specialization of production and service to a world level. The people of all nations could enjoy the benefits of worldwide specialization to the fullest extent economically possible, except for barriers to international commerce. The most important barriers imposed by governments are tariffs and quotas. Tariffs raise the price of imports by the amount of the tariff, and quotas limit the amount of a commodity that may be imported annually. Both types of barriers are a form of government aid to the companies in the specific industries "protected" by the tariff or quota and impose a burden (in the form of higher prices) on businesses in other industries and on consumers in general.

If a company decides to expand its market by selling in foreign countries, it will encounter problems peculiar to international trade—problems in addition to expanding sales within a country. Distances for delivery may be greater, language may be different, currencies may fluctuate, and the customs of the people may require modification of the product. Selling to foreign customers can provide profitable opportunities, but the decision to enter foreign markets should be made by management only after careful consideration.

Buying from foreign companies is usually easier than selling to foreign customers. The foreign seller is generally eager to make a sale and will usually shoulder all or most of the problems and perhaps some of the costs associated with transactions that cross international borders.

Making payments across international borders involves exchanging one currency for another, with the risk that exchange rates might change. The exporter can accept payment in the currency of the importer or require the importer to make payment in his (the exporter's) currency. Banks assist in making payments in international trade.

QUESTIONS FOR REVIEW

1 Since it is technically possible to produce coffee, tea, cocoa, and bananas within the continental United States, why do we import these items from foreign nations?

2 Name several raw materials for industry of which we import more than three-fourths of our requirements from abroad.

3 Define absolute advantage in production.

4 Explain the principle of comparative advantage in international trade. Distinguish it from absolute advantage.

5 We often hear that we should encourage exports because production for export provides jobs for Americans, and that we should restrict imports because imports take jobs away from Americans. Discuss the merits of this argument.

6 "If all tariff barriers were removed, we would be flooded with imports of foreign goods." Examine and evaluate this statement.

7 Why do not the debit and credit figures in the balance of international payments balance exactly?

8 What are the arguments in favor of and against government restriction of imports by tariffs and other measures? Who is benefited and who is burdened by such restrictions?

9 What are the nongovernmental obstacles to international trade? Give examples of each barrier you name.

10 What is the Reciprocal Trade Agreements Act? Why and when was it inaugurated?

11 What is a multinational business? How can it take advantage of differences in labor and other costs between nations?

12 What steps can you suggest that a businessman take before embarking on a program to enter foreign markets to expand his sales?

13 What are some of the differences in advertising in foreign countries as contrasted with advertising in the United States?

14 What are some of the ways the Department of Commerce can help a firm begin a program of exporting to foreign countries?

15 Why is the business of importing generally less complex, and often less risky, than exporting?

SELECTED READINGS

Adams, John: *International Economics*, St. Martin's Press, Inc., 1971.

Cateora, Philip R., and John M. Hess: *International Marketing*, Richard D. Irwin, Inc., Homewood, Ill., 1971.

Kindleberger, Charles P.: *International Economics,* 5th ed., Richard D. Irwin, Inc., Homewood, Ill., 1973.

Kramer, Roland L.: *International Marketing*, 3d ed., South-Western Publishing Company, Cincinnati, 1970.

Leighton, Richard I.: *Economics of International Trade*, McGraw-Hill Book Company, New York, 1970.

Piquet, Howard S.: *Aid, Trade, and the Tariff*, Thomas Y. Crowell Co., New York, 1953.

Name	Section	Date

COMPLETION SENTENCES

1 One of the reasons for our high standard of living in the United States is that

there are almost no _~~barries~~_ between the states and each

region can _~~specialize~~_ in production.

2 When one country can produce an item better and more cheaply than another,

it has a _~~absolute advantage~~_ in the production of that item over the

other country.

3 To get paid for what we sell abroad we must _~~buy~~_

from abroad.

4 The inconvenience involved in changing one currency into another must be

borne either by the _~~buyer (imports)~~_ or by the

~~seller (exports)~~

5 A tariff is a tax levied on goods _~~imported~~_ into a country.

6 Imports and exports of _~~merchandise~~_ constitute the largest item in our balance of payments.

7 One of the pleasures of international trade is contact with

customs and _cultures_ different from our own.

8 A _quota_ imposes a limit to the quantity of an item that may be imported.

9 A free flow of trade is one of the major competitive pressures for improving

productivity in the American economy.

10 The rise in the number of multinational companies has been particularly rapid

since _WWII._.

11 Direct selling abroad puts the foreign exchange risk on

exporter.

12 Of particular help to American exporters and importers in providing information is the Department of _Commerce_.

13 Foreign advertising is traditionally more _restrained_ than advertising in the United States.

14 In those lands where illiteracy is high, an easily recognizable

trademark is essential.

15 The common method of financing foreign sales is the use of a

trade draft.

Name   Section   Date

TRUE OR FALSE STATEMENTS

1 If the United States wished, it could grow its own coffee, tea, and bananas.

2 An examination of balance of payments statistics shows, among other things, that to get paid for what we sell abroad we must be willing to buy abroad.

3 In the 1971 international balance of payments income earned from United States foreign investments exceeded income earned by foreigners from United States investments.

4 If it were possible for a nation to produce everything more cheaply than all other nations, there would be no advantage to that nation in engaging in foreign trade.

5 If there were no tariff barriers between nations, the domestic producers of each country would have no competitive advantage over foreign producers.

6 In international shipments goods are generally handled more times than in domestic shipments.

7 There are several governmental obstacles to international trade in addition to the tariff.

8 Tariff rates in the United States are set primarily for the purpose of yielding revenue.

9 Tariffs on foreign goods are an example of free enterprise.

10 If a company has manufacturing, assembly, refining, or distribution facilities in more than one nation, it is called a multinational company.

11 Although the Department of Commerce is of considerable aid to businessmen in general, it does not contain bureaus or offices designed particularly to aid exporters and importers.

12 Most American exporters do not sell directly to the foreign consumer.

13 Selling to an export merchant is about the same as selling to any domestic customer.

14 Trademarks are unimportant in selling goods overseas.

15 If an American wishes to buy an article from Canada, he commonly can pay for it by sending a check drawn on his American bank, just as in a domestic transaction.

EXERCISES

1 Pick out a foreign product not commonly used in the United States (for example, maté, a beverage common in Brazil). Describe how you would import, advertise, and distribute it. What prejudices might have to be overcome to gain acceptance for it in this country? What other problems might have to be met?

2 From the library or other sources of information make a list of products we import, indicating the principal country or countries from which we buy each product. Make another list of products we export, indicating the principal countries to which each product is shipped. Are there any notable differences in the characteristics of the products in each group?

IMPORTS

Product	Principal Countries of Origin

EXPORTS

Product	Principal Countries of Destination

Name	Section	Date

3 *Case Problem for report or class discussion*

The Scottford Manufacturing Company had for many years produced a portable electric generator fueled by gasoline. Although not one of the largest producers, it enjoyed a reputation for quality. From 1951 to 1960, it sold a larger volume each year than the year before. Mason, the sales manager, noticed that from 1957 to 1960 the number of generators bought by export merchants and export commission houses increased substantially and that orders for parts and requests for service information directly from foreign countries indicated that the Scottford generator was attractive to foreign customers. In fact, during the recession of 1957–1958 when sales of the Scottford generator in most parts of the United States fell below previous years, sales to export middlemen were responsible for total sales in 1958 slightly exceeding those of 1957 and so maintaining the record of sales increases each year.

During a conversation at lunch with some top executives of the company, Mason suggested that the company should consider the active exploitation of the apparent foreign market for the Scottford generator. The president of the company considered the suggestion a good one, but cautioned that careful examination of the suggestion be made before any action be taken. Therefore, he asked Mason to secure as much information as he could that would be helpful in deciding whether Scottford should push into foreign markets and to appear before the board of directors at its next meeting with a report and recommendations for action.

Where can Mason go for information? One of the other executives at the lunch had stated that he felt the company should welcome all orders from abroad, but should not actively seek orders outside the United States. Foreign customers were too undependable and collecting payment from purchasers in foreign lands was too hazardous, he said.

Do you agree? As Mason, prepare a report recommending the action that should be taken with respect to entering into the exportation of Scottford generators. The report should cover the following:

The type of marketing channel that might be used
The foreign countries that might be entered first in any export program
The advertising that should be undertaken in foreign countries

The risks of nonpayment for foreign sales that might arise, and what, if anything, might be done to minimize these risks

Keep in mind that the report would have to be defended before a meeting of the board of directors of the company and that the recommendations might be subject to searching questions from members of the board.

PART 7
FINANCE

Finance is the art of raising money and of spending it wisely. It is also defined as the management of the monetary affairs of a company.

Short-term finance deals with the commercial bank, trade credit, and other sources of funds that have to be repaid within a year or less. Trade credit is the privilege extended by suppliers to their customers of delaying payment for goods purchased, sometimes for periods of a month or more. The commercial bank is the chief source of cash loans for businesses. In addition, the commercial bank provides many other financial services for its business customers.

Long-term finance covers the sources of long-term funds, such as retained earnings, the sale of stocks and bonds, and the investment of money by the owners of businesses. It also covers the uses to which the funds are put, such as purchase of machinery, land, or buildings.

There are many institutions that provide specialized financial services. Among these are securities exchanges (also called stock exchanges), investment bankers, the Federal Reserve System, and others. Each provides services essential to business as it is conducted today.

Every business faces risks. Some risks can be avoided, some can be shifted to others, and some must be accepted as a part of business life that cannot be avoided. Those risks that can be shifted are usually shifted to insurance companies. By accepting for a fee similar risks of many clients, insurance companies can calculate their probable loss for each type of risk, and can periodically charge each client a small sum to cover the total losses of each type expected for their many clients.

CHAPTER 24

SHORT-TERM FINANCE

Short-term finance concerns paying for current assets. Notice the variety of ways that current assets can be financed, and distinguish between promissory notes, drafts, acceptances, and open-book purchases. You will read and hear more about these in advanced business courses.

Everybody has to deal with commercial banks. If you become a businessman, your contacts with banks will be frequent, since they are the prime source of short-term loans. The material of the chapter will become more meaningful to you if you put yourself in the position of a businessman.

In many aspects of business operations a choice between conflicting goals has to be made. Notice how the goals of liquidity and profitability are to some degree in conflict. A compromise has to be effected, just as you have to make compromises in many areas of your personal life.

It takes money to make money. A machine to make paper clips may cost $40,000, a factory building $1,000,000, and an office calculator $700. To pay for all of the things needed to operate a business requires money. Finance is the aspect of business operations devoted to the many arrangements by which payments may be made. To state it in other terms, finance is the management of the monetary affairs of a company. It includes determining what has to be paid for and when, raising the money on the best terms available, and devoting the available funds to the best uses.

If the repayment of money borrowed or the payment for goods and services is not due for several years, the financing is long-term. If the payment is due soon, the financing is short-term. The distinction between the two is arbitrary but useful. The dividing line between the two is generally put at one year, and we shall use this point of division in discussing the subject.

Short-term financing is associated largely with paying for those business assets that change constantly in form and that are used up or consumed in the course of operations. Such assets are called *current assets* or *working assets*. Examples are raw materials, accounts receivable, finished goods inventory, and supplies. The means by which such assets are financed include open-book accounts, promissory notes, drafts, and borrowing from the bank.

THE CIRCULAR FLOW OF CURRENT ASSETS

One of the characteristics of current assets (cash and those assets that will be turned into cash in a short time) is that they are in a state of continual change. A manufacturing business, for example, changes its cash into raw materials, supplies, and other elements needed for production. A retailer changes cash into inventory and inventory back into cash.

During the process of production in a manufacturing business, raw materials are changed into goods in process of manufacture, and goods in process of manufacture are in turn completed into finished goods. Some of the inventory of finished goods is sold to customers on credit. To put it another way, finished goods become accounts receivable. The collection of accounts receivable creates cash. Thus there is a cycle of change in the form of current assets. The rapidity of change depends upon what is manufactured, the methods of manufacture, and the season of the year. For some businesses the complete cycle starting and ending with cash requires only a few days; at the other extreme are those processes that require several years. If aging is necessary in transforming raw materials into finished products, as happens with some beverages and cheeses, the cycle of current assets will last for months or years. In any case the cycle, as diagrammed in Figure 24-1, is present in virtually every business.

One of the foremost skills of business management is that of operating in such a way as to create a smooth flow from one stage to another over a period of time. At any given moment there will normally be some current assets in the forms of cash, raw materials, goods in process of manufacture, finished goods, and accounts receivable. If there is not a smooth flow in the manufacturing cycle, there will be shortages of some current assets and an overabundance of others, both

FIGURE 24-1 The circular flow of current assets.

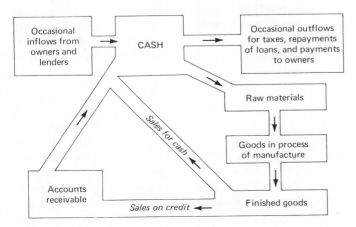

conditions being inefficient. Furthermore, if management can speed the cycle of change of current assets without sacrificing quality of product or service to customers, it will help to increase profits.

The current assets, of course, cannot by themselves be transformed from one form to another; machinery, equipment, and other fixed assets must be applied to the current assets. In the process the fixed assets are gradually used up. All fixed assets, except for land, are slowly "consumed" in the process of adding value to current assets. In the successful management of a business, a larger amount of cash will be generated at the end of a cycle than was present at the beginning. This is essential to profitable operations. This is necessary to offset the drain on cash that is found in any enterprise. The circuit flow of current assets must generate sufficient cash to purchase additional raw materials to continue the cycle and to pay for all the other expenses of business operations.

SOURCES OF SHORT-TERM FINANCING

Short-term financing is generally used for current assets. Since current assets are turned into cash normally within a year, short-term credit can be liquidated from the cash generated by company operations. The principal sources of short-term financing for most businesses are open-book accounts, promissory notes, drafts, and bank loans.

OPEN-BOOK ACCOUNTS

Credit is one of the important elements of modern business, and without it, it would be impossible to support an industrialized society. The principle is simply defined. It is "buy now and pay later" or "borrow now and repay later." Credit can be either informal or formal, using either an oral agreement or a written form. The use of credit is familiar to all, as practically everyone is involved in credit transactions of an informal nature throughout his adult life. For example, he will borrow a dime from a friend to buy a candy bar, promising to repay in a few days. In such an instance, the lender depends on the integrity of the borrower, and the borrower is likely to consider friendship more important than the 10 cents he would gain by neglecting to repay. Where credit is extended by oral agreement, the transactions are apt to be as informal as the example, even though such transactions may involve thousands of dollars, on the New York Stock Exchange, at organized auction markets, and in other areas of business.

Open-Book Credit

If a person buys regularly from a retail store, the store will often extend him the privilege of paying for his purchases at the end of the month. Although some stores require the customer's signature on a sales slip, the use of oral credit is quite common. A customer well known to the store might select an article, ask the clerk to wrap it up, and simply tell the clerk to charge the purchase to his account. Similarly, businesses sell goods to wholesalers and other business customers on the same basis that a retailer sells to his customers. Where one company sells to another company (wholesaler to retailer, for example) on the basis described above, the arrangement is known as *open-book credit* or *trade credit*. A large volume of sales are made in this way.

The most important element in trade credit is the length of time permitted to the customer before making payment. A common period is 30 days from the date of the invoice (the itemized statement sent by the seller, indicating the amount of goods shipped, prices, and terms of payment), although 60 days and longer are found. It is also common for a seller to offer a *cash discount*, a discount from the amount due if payment is made in advance. For example, credit terms of 2/10/30 means that 2 percent may be deducted from the amount billed if payment is made within 10 days from the date of the invoice. The full amount is payable if payment is made after 10 days. If payment is delayed beyond 30 days, the account is overdue. For a $100 invoice the terms require payment of $100 within 30 days but allows the buyer to pay $98 if the payment is made within 10 days. Some examples of credit terms are shown in Table 4-1.

In retail trade, stores sell expensive items such as television sets, major appliances, and automobiles on a time-payment basis lasting months or years. Payment terms are in installments, usually monthly, covering interest and reduction of principal during the payment period. The interest in such a transaction is often higher than the customer is led to believe. For example, a customer might buy a radio priced at $100 with payment to be made in 12 monthly installments of $9 each. The amount paid over the 1-year period is $108. The customer might assume that the $8 he pays above the cash price constitutes interest at 8 percent on his credit purchase. This is not so. The actual rate of interest he pays is approximately 16

TABLE 24-1 SAMPLE CREDIT PAYMENT TERMS EXTENDED
BY WHOLESALERS

Goods	Credit Payment Terms
Tobacco and tobacco products	Net 7 days
Candy	2% 30 days
Drugs	1/10/EOM (1% deductible up to 10 days after *end of month* in which invoice is dated
Dry goods	3/10/EOM or 2/10/60
Electrical supplies	2/10/30
Hosiery	10 days EOM or net 30 days
Building materials	2/10/30
Knitted outerwear	8/10/EOM
Plumbing supplies	2/10/30
Woolen goods	1/10/60 or net 30 days

percent. The original amount of the loan, $100, is reduced by the monthly payments of $9 until it reaches $0 at the end of the year. The average amount of the loan during the year is $50, and $8 is 16 percent of $50.

PROMISSORY NOTES   Borrowing money by means of a written form and the use of a written promise to pay for goods received are common business practices in all commercial countries. One common form of written credit is the ***promissory note***. To illustrate, a person borrowing $100 gives the lender a piece of paper that looks like the accompanying illustration.

April 8, 1974

I promise to pay to the order of David Jonathan Craig, three months from the date of this note, for value received, the sum of $100, with interest at 6 percent per annum added.

Lee Patrick Guiler

Lee Patrick Guiler

The note could be held by Craig until maturity (July 8, 1974), at which time he would collect $100, the principal amount of the note, plus $1.50, the interest for three months at the rate of 6 percent per annum. If Craig needed money before the maturity date, he could sell the note to somebody else for the maturity value ($101.50) less the amount of interest at 6 percent still to be earned on the unexpired life of the note. Craig could transfer the note by endorsing it, usually on the reverse side. Sometimes a promissory note will pass from one person to another several times before it is presented to the signer (Guiler) for payment.

An individual well known in his community might be able to use promissory notes for many purchases. His ability to use promissory notes without inconvenience would depend on how well he was known, his past record of payment, the extent of his financial resources, and his general character. These considerations are sometimes called "the three C's of credit." They are: ***character, capacity***, and ***collateral***. Character is self-evident. Capacity means the borrower's financial resources and general business capability. Collateral means the assets he can use as security for ensuring payment. The better the qualifications of the borrower with respect to these considerations, the easier it will be for him to get credit and the lower will be the rate of interest he is likely to pay.

The average individual businessman is not in a position to use promissory notes frequently. Large, well-established corporations, on the other hand, make considerable use of promissory notes in their short-term financing. A corporation, for example, will raise several millions of dollars by printing 100 or more promissory notes (in the case of corporations, such an issue of notes is called ***commercial paper***). These notes are sold to investors by ***commercial-paper houses***, which are financial institutions specializing in such notes. Purchasers of commercial paper are mostly banks, insurance companies, and corporations with a temporary excess of funds over immediate needs.

The proceeds of the sale of commercial paper (promissory notes) minus the expenses of distribution is received by the corporation in cash. The interest rate at which the corporation can borrow funds through commercial-paper houses is usually very low, frequently lower than the interest rate that would be charged by a bank.

Another form of written credit instrument is the *draft*, which is an order by a person or company to another person or company ordering him to pay to a designated payee a certain sum of money. An example of a draft is shown in the accompanying illustration.   **DRAFTS**

New York, May 4, 1974

On August 4, 1974, pay to the order of Margery R. Christina and Company the sum of three hundred sixty-five dollars and twenty-eight cents ($365.28) for value received.

To William Jones
448 Market Street
Hastings, Nebraska

John Rita Brewster

John Rita Brewster

Such a draft might be sent by Brewster (the drawer or maker) to a bank in Hastings, Nebraska, along with a bill of lading authorizing Jones to pick up a shipment of goods that will arrive at the railroad station in Hastings. When the bank receives the draft and bill of lading, it would notify Jones. Jones would then go to the bank and accept responsibility for payment of the draft by writing "accepted" on the face of the draft and signing his name below. The bank would then give Jones the bill of lading permitting him to pick up the goods at the railroad station. The accepted draft, now called an *acceptance*, would be forwarded to Margery R. Christina & Company to hold until maturity, or to be transferred by endorsement of Margery R. Christina to another holder prior to maturity. At maturity, the holder would present the acceptance to Jones for payment. The above is an example of a *trade draft*.

A more common type of draft is one drawn on a bank. The simplest form is a bank check, in which the drawer orders the bank, the drawee, to pay the payee a certain sum of money. This amount is then charged against the account in the bank of the drawee.

The average individual is often a little careless in his use of bank checks. Without reasonable caution, the amount on the face of the check can be raised. Although bank tellers exercise ordinary care in trying to notice evidence of raising of check amounts, the bank is not liable for the difference in payment, unless the maker can prove that he used reasonable care in writing the check. The paper used to print checks is designed to show evidence of erasures or other tampering, and this undoubtedly helps to keep down fraud.[1]

[1] For special occasions and for publicity purposes, bank checks are made with unusual materials or written on unusual surfaces such as birch bark, coconut shells, planks of wood, and similar materials. Checks have been embroidered on cloth. They have been written on the sides of footballs and presented to coaches of winning school football teams. A check was once etched on the surface of a watermelon and cashed by the Fort Worth, Texas, bank on which it was drawn.

COMMERCIAL BANKING

When a person speaks of a "bank," he generally has in mind a commercial bank, although there are different kinds of banks, savings banks, investment banks, and commercial banks. Banks serve a very useful purpose in modern business; they lend money, accept deposits, rent safety deposit boxes for keeping valuables, provide convenient means of transferring funds to distant points, and serve as a source of financial counsel. Practically all commercial banks are corporations. Both the federal and state governments issue corporation charters to organize banks. In either case, the requirements are stricter than the requirements for securing business charters. The intent of the law—although not always the result—is to give only experienced and responsible persons a charter to do a banking business.

Banks confine most of their lending to businesses to short-term loans. If a retailer, for example, wants to buy $100,000 of goods that he expects to resell within 6 months, he would probably find a bank loan a useful means of paying for the goods. If he were unknown to the bank, a careful investigation of his credit would be made before the loan would be granted. His record of prompt payment of debts, the amount of debt he already owes, his success in managing his retail store, and even his personal habits might be investigated. The loan officer of the bank probably would want a schedule showing how the money was to be spent and might retain the right to seize certain property of the retailer in the event of his inability to repay the loan.

If the loan application is approved by the loan officer (and, in the case of large loans, also approved by the bank loan committee or the board of directors of the bank), the retailer would receive a deposit of $100,000 minus whatever amount is deducted by the bank for interest, credit-investigation fees, and other costs. Most borrowers prefer to leave the money borrowed from the bank in their checking accounts. This is fortunate, since nearly every bank insists that a borrower leave a minimum, commonly 20 percent of the loan, on deposit at all times until the loan is paid back. On repayment of the loan, the bank returns to the retailer the promissory note he made when the loan was first extended.

The United States has a banking system that differs sharply in some respects from those of other industrial nations. All banks in the United States, except for a very few, have their deposits insured by the Federal Deposit Insurance Corporation, an agency of the federal government. The insurance guarantees payment to each depositor of each bank, if the bank should fail, to a maximum of $20,000 of their deposit. Other nations do not provide such insurance, probably because it is not needed. In the United States, a few banks fail nearly every year, and from 1929 to 1933 more than 5,000 became bankrupt. By contrast, Canada had its last bank failure in 1924 and Great Britain its last failure in the 1890s.

The United States is also unique in not having a nationwide branch banking system. Canada, for example, has 10 banks, and these together have more than 4,000 branches throughout the Dominion. Practically all of the banking business in Great Britain is done by only five banks, again with many branches. By contrast, branch banking is severely restricted by law in the United States. Of the more than 13,000 independent banks in the country, only a few have any branches. One result of the localized banking structure in the United States is that large companies doing a nationwide business maintain deposit accounts with many banks. Also when large companies borrow from banks, they often must borrow from several banks at once, in order to raise the amount of money they need.

Banks do not keep on hand an amount of money equal to the total deposit accounts of their depositors. They make loans and invest in bonds and other securities, both bringing interest income to the banks. They must, of course, keep some cash ready to pay out to depositors wanting to withdraw money from their accounts, but the amount is normally much less than 10 percent of the deposits of customers.

Because of the small reserves of cash maintained by banks, a sudden and widespread demand for cash withdrawals may be difficult to meet. A bank can borrow cash temporarily, for a period as brief as 1 day if that is all that is needed, from other banks, unless other banks are experiencing a similar sudden demand for cash withdrawals. Wholesale withdrawals have not occurred in recent years, but in past decades there have been some memorable money panics. Faced with withdrawals beyond their capacity to pay immediately, banks have usually closed their doors and refused to pay. After a severe panic in 1907, Congress created the Federal Reserve System in a bill passed in 1913. One of the important functions of the Federal Reserve Banks is to lend money to commercial banks when necessary to meet large withdrawals. For example, a bank in Fort Worth, Texas, was faced with a run of depositor withdrawals in 1933. This was successfully met by borrowing cash from the Federal Reserve Bank of Dallas, 40 miles away. While a police escort led the way to Fort Worth for the armored truck loaded with cash, a band was hired by the Fort Worth bank to play music to the long lines of depositors slowly working their way to the tellers' windows. The bank stayed open until late at night and paid in full all demands from its depositors.

CIRCUMSTANCES REQUIRING BANK BORROWING

One of the factors determining the ability of a company to pay for its purchases of current assets is the degree of stability of activity of the company. The volume of operations of any business fluctuates from time to time. The fluctuation is small for electric light companies, larger for manufacturing firms, and very high for the owners of most resort facilities.

In order for a business to operate, some minimum investment in current assets is necessary. This minimum is called the *permanent* or *primary working capital*. If the directors of a business estimate that the investment in current assets cannot fall below $1 million without curtailing operations altogether, that figure would represent the investment in primary working capital. Since this investment is permanent, it can advantageously be financed by common stock, bonds, or some other kind of "permanent" financing.

To meet the fluctuating seasonal requirements for raw materials, supplies, and other current assets, short-term financing is used. The extra current assets for seasonal operations requires an additional investment above the primary level, and is called the *variable working capital*. A company might have primary working capital (during the slack season) of $1 million and variable working capital (during the busy season) of $2 million. Thus, the investment in current assets would vary from a low of $1 million to a high of $3 million.

Because the investment in current assets of $3 million is needed for only a short period each year, it would be unwise to finance that amount of working assets by any of the long-term financial instruments. The $2 million of current assets required for peak operations during the busy season can better be paid for by funds raised through short-term loans. Such borrowing is obtained largely from commercial banks and by postponing payment for materials bought from suppliers.

BORROWING FROM THE BANK

As stated before, commercial banks do most of their lending to business borrowers in the form of short-term loans, usually for less than a year. Banks lend money to business borrowers under a wide variety of requirements. If the credit of the borrower is good and his relationship with the bank is long-standing, securing loans will be simple and quick. Where the credit standing of the borrower is not high or is not well established, the bank will make a much more extensive investigation. In the case of newly established concerns, a loan application may be delayed for weeks before the bank accepts or rejects the application.

In order to decrease the possibility of nonrepayment of a loan, the bank might insert a clause in the loan contract giving it the right to foreclose on certain property of the borrower, if he fails to pay interest or the principal of the loan. Such loans are called *secured loans*. Almost anything of value can be used as security for a loan, for example: raw materials, supplies, merchandise, accounts receivable owed by customers to the borrower, and even fuel supplies.

The interest paid by the borrower will vary considerably. The cost to the bank of setting up the ledger cards, preparing the necessary bookkeeping forms, and making the credit investigation on a loan will come to at least $5 on the simplest, routine loans. Where the credit investigation is lengthy or where the loan contract is complex, the cost of the office work alone will be much higher. For this reason, small loans frequently cost more per dollar than large loans. In this respect, the high cost of borrowing small amounts of money compared with borrowing large amounts is similar to the greater cost of buying goods in small quantities compared with buying in large quantities. Furthermore, a small borrower is in a weaker position to bargain with a bank officer for better loan terms than a large borrower is. A small borrower might have to pay a rate of 10 percent interest per annum on a loan of $200 while a large corporation might borrow from a bank at the rate of 5½ percent on a loan of $5 million.

A businessman should choose a bank carefully because, like other industries, the banking industry has many types of banks. The owner of a small business usually finds it advantageous to borrow from a bank close to his place of business, and he might prefer to deal with a small bank rather than a large one. Some banks specialize in loans to particular types of borrowers, such as farmers, and might have officers more sympathetic with and informed of the particular problems of borrowers in that industry. The smaller banks usually operate under the authority of a charter granted by the state government in which they are located, whereas the larger banks usually have charters issued by the federal government. State-chartered banks generally are less restricted in the type of loans they can make, and to the small borrower this is frequently an advantage. Large borrowers usually find the more extensive interbank connections of large banks more suited to their needs, and they require the greater capacity for lending of large banks.

CREDIT RATINGS

Business firms that can defer payment for the goods they buy are less dependent on banks and other lenders of short-term funds. But, to receive the privilege of postponing payment, the buyer must have shown responsibility in making payments. It is vitally important to a new company to establish as early as possible a record of prompt payment of bills, and it is equally important for older companies to maintain a good record of payment.

Before a supplier will extend credit to a new customer, he may demand references from which he can determine the credit worthiness of the customer. Once a record of credit payments has been established, a credit-rating agency generally gives a rating to the customer. A company given a low credit rating will naturally try to raise it, and a company given a high rating will strive to maintain it.

For businesses that buy on credit, there are many credit-rating agencies, most of them confining their ratings to a particular industry, for example, the Lyon Furniture Mercantile Agency. The oldest and most extensive credit-rating agency is Dun and Bradstreet, Incorporated. This company compiles credit information and publishes ratings on retailers, wholesalers, and manufacturers in a large number of industries, as well as rating service industries. By means of symbols and abbreviations, a rating and condensed financial information on more than 3 million firms is contained in the *Reference Book*, a volume of more than 4,000 pages. The *Reference Book* and additional services of Dun and Bradstreet are bought by subscription by companies selling to business customers on credit. Banks also make use of the services of Dun and Bradstreet in deciding on business loans.

LIQUIDITY VERSUS PROFITABILITY

In setting the financial policy for the operation of a business enterprise, two prime considerations are present: liquidity and profitability. To some extent each is in conflict with the other. *Liquidity* is the measure of the capability of a firm in meeting debt payments, payroll, taxes, and other financial obligations promptly. *Profitability* measures the success of a firm in using assets in creating income and in keeping expenses low.

The operations of a business firm generate an inflow of cash (from cash sales, customers paying their bills, and other receipts) and an outflow of cash (payment of company bills, cash purchases, wage payments, and others). This is shown graphically in Figure 24-2.

The cash budget (explained in Chapter 14) aids the company financial manager in anticipating cash inflow and outflow. However, it is not possible to coordinate perfectly cash receipts and cash disbursements. The unexpected happens

POOL OF AVAILABLE FUNDS

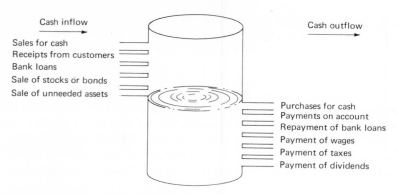

FIGURE 24-2 Cash inflow—outflow chart

and upsets the best-laid plans. Because of this uncertainty, there must be a "cushion," which generally takes the form of a cash balance in the bank in excess of the anticipated needs. The size of this cushion (the "pool" of available funds in Figure 24-2) will vary according to the accuracy with which cash receipts and cash expenditures can be predicted and the speed with which money can be raised in an emergency. If the firm has investments, such as government bonds, that can be quickly sold, the firm's cash balance can be held at a lower level than would otherwise be safe. However, any investment that can be quickly sold usually does not pay a high yield.

A cautious business policy dictates a comfortably large cushion of cash or low-yield but quickly marketable securities. Obviously cash in the bank (checking accounts) and cash on hand earn no income. They provide security but not profit. To earn income, money must be put to work. Hence there is a conflict of goals: liquidity versus profitability. Liquidity (safety, peace of mind) dictates a large cash balance to meet every conceivable contingency; profitability dictates a low cash balance (cut down on idle funds and money invested in low-yield securities—put money to work in the business).

There is no easy resolution to this dilemma. A compromise of the two goals is the answer. But what sort of compromise? Whether the compromise is in the direction of liquidity and safety or in the direction of more profit with more risk depends largely on the temperament of the owners. This is a policy decision so important that it should be resolved at the highest policy-making level of the firm. The executives of some companies are noted for their willingness to accept a high degree of risk; managers of other companies have a reputation for financial conservatism and caution. The comment of one of the patriarchs of the famous banking family of the Rothschilds is illuminating in this context. A young man asked Baron Rothschild whether he should invest his inheritance in high-yield but risky ventures or in conservative investments. The baron thought for a moment, then asked, "Young man, do you want to eat well or sleep well?"

The current assets of a business are constantly changing in form in the course of business operations. One of the most important management skills is ensuring that the flow of assets from one form to another is smooth.

Short-term finance is the means by which current assets are provided for a business. The more important means are the following:

SUMMARY

1 *Open-book credit (or trade credit):* Materials purchased are paid for later, such as in 10 days or a month.
2 *Promissory note:* A written promise to pay a sum of money at a later date.
3 *Draft:* A written order by one person or company to another, instructing him to pay a sum of money to a person or company on the date named.
4 *Bank loans:* Money provided by which goods and services can be bought for cash, repayment to the bank being made when the loan falls due.

The United States has many banks (over 13,000), most of which are small and without branches. The other commercial countries of the world have a few banks, each with many branches. A businessman should choose a bank with care, because it is better for his business if he stays with one bank rather than shifting frequently.

A compromise of two conflicting goals, liquidity and profitability, must be made in operating a firm. This is determined by deciding the degree of risk the managers are willing to accept in order to increase profits. Liquidity means security; profitability means accepting risk.

1 Describe the circular flow of current assets. What, if anything, is accomplished by a business in starting a cycle with cash, changing the cash into other assets, and then ending with cash again?

QUESTIONS FOR REVIEW

2 What is credit? Why is it so important in modern society?
3 Show by means of an illustration how one can approximate the cost in interest per annum of installment credit.
4 What is a promissory note? For what purposes is it used?
5 What differences are there in the use of promissory notes by small businesses and by large corporations?
6 Describe a trade draft, explaining how it is used in business.
7 In what respects does the banking system of the United States differ from those of other nations?
8 Banks do not keep on hand an amount of money equal to the total deposit accounts of their depositors. Does this not make it hazardous for a person to deposit money in a bank? Explain.
9 Describe the steps in a typical loan transaction between a bank and a business borrower.
10 What is the Federal Deposit Insurance Corporation? What does it do? Why is such a corporation not found in other countries?
11 If a businessman wishes to borrow from a bank, what information about the businessman would the bank seek before granting the loan?
12 What is meant by variable working capital? How does it differ from primary working capital?

13 Why is it that a loan in a small amount for a bank will usually be charged a higher rate of interest than a loan in a large amount?

14 Why is it important to maintain a good credit rating?

15 Why is there a conflict between the goals of liquidity and profitability?

SELECTED READINGS   Beckman, Theodore N., and Ronald S. Foster: *Credits and Collections*, 8th ed., McGraw-Hill Book Company, New York, 1969.

Curran, Ward S.: *Principles of Financial Management*, McGraw-Hill Book Company, New York, 1970.

Dauten, Carl A., and Merle Welshans: *Principles of Finance*, South-Western Publishing Company, Cincinnati, 1970.

Fisher, Douglas, *Money and Banking*, Richard D. Irwin, Inc., Homewood, Ill., 1971.

Name	**Section**	**Date**

COMPLETION SENTENCES

1 One of the characteristics of _Current assets_ is that they are in

a state of continual change.

2 All fixed assets, except for _land_, are slowly "consumed"

in the process of business operations.

3 If a person buys a refrigerator priced at $300, without a down payment but

with payments of $30 a month for 12 months, the approximate rate of interest

he is actually paying is _40 %_ percent per annum.

4 Payment terms of 2/10/30 means that on a $100 invoice the buyer may remit

$_98.00_ if payment is made within 10 days or he

remits $_100.00_ if payment is made after 10 days.

5 A common form of draft is a _bank check_ drawn by a deposi-

tor on a commercial bank.

6 When a trade draft is endorsed by the person on whom it is drawn, it is called

a _*acceptance*_ .

7 Both federal and state governments issue _*corporate ch*_ to

organize new banks.

8 Banks confine most of their lending to _*business*_ customers

to short-term loans.

9 The Federal Deposit Insurance Corporation insures depositors in each insured

bank up to a maximum of $_*20,000*_ per depositor.

10 There are more than _*13,000*_ separate bank corporations

in the United States, Canada has _*10*_ , and most of

the banking business of Great Britain is done by _*5*_

banks.

11 It is vitally important to a new company to establish as early as possible a

record of _*prompt payment*_ of bills.

12 The minimum investment in current assets required by a business for operation

is called the _*permanent*_ working capital.

13 There are many credit rating agencies, most of them confining their ratings

to _*a single industry*_

14 The oldest and most extensive credit rating agency is _*Dun & Brad.*_ .

15 The cash budget aids the financial manager of a company in anticipating

*Cash inflow* and _*cash outflow*_ .

Name   Section   Date

TRUE OR FALSE STATEMENTS

T **1** Current assets are in a state of continual change.

T **2** The cycle of transformation of current assets in some businesses requires years.

F **3** In the process of business operations all fixed assets are gradually consumed or used up.

F **4** To be valid credit must be in the form of a written instrument.

T **5** If a person borrows $100 and repays $18 a month for 6 months, the rate of interest on the loan is about 32 percent per annum.

F **6** If a depositor suffers loss because a check he wrote was raised in amount and the alteration was not noticed by the bank personnel, the bank must refund the difference to the depositor.

T **7** When a person uses the word "bank," he generally means a commercial bank.

F **8** About half of the commercial banks in the United States are corporations.

T **9** Unlike Canada and Great Britain, the United States does not have a nationwide branch banking system.

T **10** Large, well-established corporations make considerable use of promissory notes for their short-term financing needs.

T **11** Almost anything of value can be used as security for a loan from a bank.

T **12** Small companies generally pay more for loans than large companies do.

T **13** Large banks are generally chartered by the federal government. Most small banks are chartered by state governments.

F **14** Interest charges by a bank on the loans it extends are fairly uniform.

T **15** Cash in the bank and cash on hand earn no income for a company. Cash provides security but not profit.

EXERCISES

1 Get information on securing a loan (for example, a loan of $1,000 to pay tuition and fees) from a commercial bank, a personal finance company, a credit union (if possible), and any other sources you can think of or that your instructor suggests. Cover the following points and arrange the information for easy comparison:

a Interest (percent per annum)

b Term (length of time for repayment) and method of repayment

c Fees, in addition to interest

d Security required, if any

2 From Moody's *Manual of Investments* or a similar source of information on corporations, secure the following information from the balance sheets of five corporations:

a Dollar amount of accounts payable

b Amount of total debt

c Ratio of current assets to total debt

d Dollar amount of cash

e Dollar amount of commercial paper outstanding or bank loans outstanding

Businesses need money for periods of different lengths. These could be divided into categories as long-term financing, intermediate-term financing, and short-term financing. Long-term financing refers to funds permanently invested in a company or needed for a long period, such as 10, 15, 20 years, or longer. Although in this chapter the discussion on long-term finance is confined largely to corporations, you can apply most of the principles to the financing of proprietorships and partnerships. The long-term financing of unincorporated businesses is less complex than for corporations. But notice the greater degree of flexibility in financing corporations have because of their capability of issuing stocks and bonds to raise money. In connection with long-term financing for corporations, the business of investment banks is discussed. Be sure that you do not confuse an investment bank with a commercial bank. The two institutions are entirely different, and, since 1933, undertaking both types of banking by the same institution has been prohibited by federal law.

Commercial banking deals largely with short-term lending to businesses. Investment banking is not really banking at all: it is selling. In this case, the "product" sold is the issue of securities prepared by the company wishing to raise money.

Many people rent the place they live in rather than buy. Many businessmen rent their places of business rather than buy. A lease is similar to a rental agreement but is more formal and generally runs for a year to several years.

About one out of every eight families in the United States owns some stock in corporations. The average student taking business courses today will probably be a stockholder and a bondholder when he becomes an adult. The description of stocks and bonds in this chapter will help you become acquainted with them. If your parents or friends of your parents have any stock or bond certificates, it would be useful for you to examine them in detail.

In this chapter we study long-term finance. This is the area of finance that has to do with acquiring and paying for land, buildings, and equipment. Because the assets acquired have a life measured in years and are often very expensive, careful planning is required in this field of financial management.

CAPITAL BUDGETING Just as a businessman plans his needs for raw materials, fuel, labor, and other items for the approaching season, so most large companies and some small ones plan their needs for machinery, factory expansion, and similar items. For many companies, this planning is made formal by preparing a *capital budget*. A capital budget lists the purchases of capital goods, the date each will be acquired, the amount of bonds, stocks, long-term promissory notes, and other instruments issued to raise funds, and the dates each will be issued. A capital budget is prepared for as long a period in the future as the company directors wish to plan. It may be for 5, 10, or some other number of years. Generally, the budget is reviewed, and perhaps revised, annually. An example of a simplified capital budget is shown in Table 25-1. A surplus resulting from capital transactions would not remain idle in the company's checking account. It would either be used to pay current expenses or be invested in an investment that could be liquidated easily when needed, such as government bonds. Any deficit in the capital budget can be met by short-term borrowing, usually from a commercial bank.

USES OF LONG-TERM FUNDS Long-term funds, or *capital funds*, are raised by means discussed below. They are used to pay for capital goods such as buildings, machinery, land, trucks, and furniture.

It is a rare man who "has everything he wants." It is also a rare company that has all the capital goods its officers think it should have. Most companies have to

TABLE 25-1 CAPITAL BUDGET OF THE MARVID COMPANY

	1975	1976	1977	1978	1979
Expenditures					
Enlargement of factory building		$50,000			
Paving of parking lot	$ 2,000				
Air-conditioning of factory			$ 8,000		
Purchase of new machinery				$14,000	
Repayment of 5-year bank loan					$10,000
Receipts					
20-year loan on mortgage of addition to factory		40,000			
5-year loan from bank	10,000				
Sale of unneeded land			15,000		
Sale of common stock				10,000	
Difference	+$ 8,000	−$ 2,000	+$ 5,000	+$ 1,000	−$ 9,000

set up a system of priorities in making capital expenditures. Air-conditioning the factory or office may have to wait until old machinery has been replaced with new. A company cafeteria or employee lounge may be put far down on the list, unless the company is losing good workers because of the lack of these facilities. To make the best use of long-term funds, a well-managed enterprise will prepare the priority list of capital needs after careful deliberation. In this way, the funds will be devoted to the most pressing demands first.

The largest amount of funds for long-term uses is derived from retained earnings and depreciation allowances. As more money comes in from sales than is paid out in expenses, the excess is available for investment in the business. Part of this excess is earmarked for replacement of machinery, buildings, and similar items that wear out during business operations. This amount is indicated by the account called **depreciation allowances**. It is not income, because its purpose is eventually to replace buildings and machinery. But, until it is so used, it is available for temporary, reasonable long-term uses. The balance of the excess is determined by what is credited to **retained earnings**, or **surplus**. The payment of dividends reduces surplus. It is the policy of most businessmen to hold some of the surplus for expansion, emergency, or similar purposes. A common policy is to devote half of the earnings to payment of dividends, the other half being retained permanently in the business. A rapidly growing company may enjoy a high rate of earnings, but the directors may allocate all of the earnings to speed expansion and thus may pay no dividends at all for several years.

SOURCE OF LONG-TERM FUNDS

Most of the long-term funds of small enterprises are contributed by the owners. This is true whether the enterprise is a proprietorship, partnership, or corporation. Some long-term funds may be gotten by borrowing from commercial banks, insurance companies, or mortgage banks, frequently by mortgaging the real estate owned by the enterprise. Since 1958, **small business investment companies** have been a source of long-term financing. These companies are privately owned but receive money both by selling stock and by borrowing from the federal government. This money is, in turn, loaned to small businesses for terms of 10 years or longer.

In most cases, a large corporation has an advantage over a small company in raising long-term funds. Corporations can sell common stock, preferred stock, or bonds, all of which are known as corporation **securities**. These may be sold directly to large investors such as insurance companies, pension funds, investment companies, and endowment funds of colleges, hospitals, and other institutions. This is known as "private placement." Alternatively, the securities can be distributed to the investing public through **investment bankers.** The dollar volume of securities sold to investors by corporations wanting to raise money is shown in Figure 25-1.

An investment banker—who is not a banker in the usual sense of the word—is a merchant. What he sells, however, is not merchandise but securities. If a company wants to spend $160,000 to expand its plant, it may raise the money through the services of an investment banker. The banker in such an example would probably investigate the company's past record of earnings, the capability

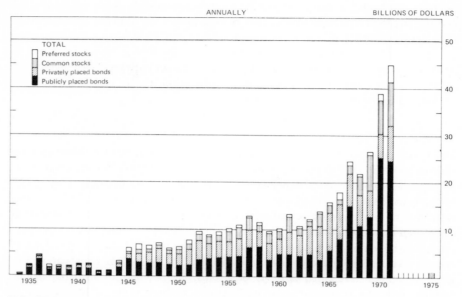

FIGURE 25-1 Corporate security issues. Gross proceeds by type of issue. (*Historical Chart Book*, Board of Governors of the Federal Reserve System, 1972, p. 47.)

of the management, the quality of its products, its reputation among its customers, and its credit standing. If the banker is convinced that the proposed expansion will be financially successful, an agreement will be proposed to the company officers. While the terms of the agreement may be complex, the important parts to the agreement would state the type of issue to be sold, the number of securities to be sold, the price to the public, and the amount to be paid to the corporation. To raise $160,000 for the company, the banker might offer to sell 10,000 shares of the company's stock to investors at $20 a share. A typical contract would provide that the banker buy 10,000 shares from the company at $16 a share, giving the corporation a check for $160,000. The banker in turn would sell the shares to investors at $20 each. If the sale were successful, the banker would receive $200,000 and have $40,000 to cover the expenses of distribution and give him a profit. If the sale proved unsuccessful, the banker would be unable to sell all of the shares at $20, and might have to cut the price sharply to sell the stock. In any case, the banker, in a typical contract, would be bound to give the corporation $160,000.

If the issue is small—$1 million or less—only one investment banker would probably be involved. If the issue is large, many bankers probably would form a group, called an **underwriting syndicate**, to buy the securities from the corporation and resell them to the public. Although this spreads the profit, it also spreads the risk of loss. An issue of common stock distributed for the Ford Foundation in 1955 raised more than $600 million. The number of investment bankers in the syndicate was 728. The price per share paid by investors was $64.50 and the amount paid to the Ford Foundation was $63. The entire issue was sold the first day it was offered.

Corporation securities are divided into three types: *bonds, preferred stocks*, and *common stocks*. A tabular comparison of the three is given in Table 25-2. A stock certificate is shown in Figure 25-2.

TYPES OF LONG-TERM SECURITIES

BONDS

A corporation bond is a promise by the corporation to pay the holder of the bond a stated sum of money at a stated time, usually several years in the future. It is part of the long-term debt of the corporation. The formal statement of the features of a bond issue are in a document called an *indenture*. Bonds are issued with so many different characteristics that for every characteristic usually associated with bonds, a few issues can be found without the characteristic. A bond issued many years ago by the Third Avenue Railroad, for example, gave the bondholders the right to elect one director to the board annually by mail ballot. We shall not delve into the features of unusual bonds, however. Most bonds have the following characteristics:

If a corporation fails to pay the interest and principal when due, bondholders can sue the corporation. If the corporation cannot pay, the court can declare the company bankrupt, dissolve it, and pay the bondholders.

Definite Promise to Pay

When bond certificates are prepared, the date that the corporation agrees to redeem the bond by paying the amount stated on the face (the par value) assures payment to the holder. This is usually a single date, such as June 30, 1984.

Definite Maturity Date

TABLE 25-2 FEATURES OF CORPORATION SECURITIES

Bond	Preferred Stock	Common Stock
Debt	Equity	Equity
Interest is an expense	Dividends are distribution of profit	Dividends are distribution of profit
Interest must be paid to avoid bankruptcy	Dividends declared at discretion of directors	Dividends declared at discretion of directors
Interest takes priority over dividends	Dividends take priority user dividends on common stock	Dividends payable only after interest and preferred stock dividends
Interest a fixed, stated amount, payable at regular intervals	Dividends a fixed, stated amounts, payable at regular intervals	Dividends usually variable
No power to vote for directors	Usually no power to vote for directors	Vote for directors
Maturity at stated date	No maturity date	No maturity date
Usually retired through regular, periodic purchases of bonds by company	Sometimes retired through periodic purchases of stock by company	Rarely purchased by company except to reissue later to officers or investors

FIGURE 25-2 A stock certificate.

Some bonds, such as certain government bonds, have a maturity period, such as May 31, 1993–1998. This allows the issuer to redeem the bond at any time during the years stated.

Definite Interest Payments

Since a bond is debt, the company must pay interest for the use of bond purchasers' money. Interest, unlike dividends, is considered an expense. Like other expenses, interest expense reduces the net income on which the corporation pays income taxes. A company may raise $10 million by issuing securities on which it pays 6 percent, or $600,000 a year. If the securities are preferred stock, no reduction in income tax is made. If the securities are bonds, the net taxable income is reduced by $600,000. If the corporation income tax is 48 percent, the reduction in tax paid is $600,000 × 0.48, or $288,000 per year.

Failure to pay interest when due has the same consequences as failure to pay principal. The amount of interest is definite, usually expressed as a percentage of the principal, such as 6 percent per annum. The payment dates are stated on the bond certificate, most commonly being twice a year. If a $1,000 bond pays 6 percent interest on April 1 and October 1, each of the two payments is $30. The payment may be made by check to the registered holders of each bond (called *registered bonds*), or by the holders sending to the company or a designated bank a coupon clipped from the bond as each coupon date falls (called *coupon bonds*).

The corporation is liable to pay interest regardless of whether a profit or loss is made. It is also required to pay the principal when due. To ensure that this is done, a bond issue may be secured by a mortgage on the property of the corporation, the bond being called a *mortgage bond*. Failure of the corporation to pay its bond commitments when due may result in loss of the mortgaged property, which by law can be liquidated to pay the bondholders. If the bond issue holds no mortgage on any specific property of the corporation, it is called a *debenture bond*. The corporation, however, is no less liable to meet payments than before. Failure to pay will not liquidate any specific property, but will give the bondholders the right to sue for payment.

Security

The most common face value (denomination) on a bond is $1,000. Other denominations are $500, $100, $5,000, and $10,000. Occasionally denominations above $10,000 or below $100 are offered.

Denomination

PREFERRED STOCK

Preferred stocks are so named because they have certain preferences over common stock. The nature of these preferences is detailed in the corporation charter and summarized on the stock certificate. The variety of preferred stocks is great. We shall, however, consider only the more common characteristics.

Like common stock, preferred stock indicates ownership in the company. Payment of dividends is made only from profits (either current profits or profits retained from the past). In the event of liquidation of the company, preferred stockholders must wait until all creditors and other claimants are paid before receiving any return on their investment. They do, however, enjoy preference over common stock to the extent of the principal amount of the stock investment plus any dividends due.

Commonly found features of preferred stocks are discussed below. A particular preferred stock may have all, some, or none of the features discussed.

Most preferred stocks pay a stated dividend, expressed either as a percentage or as a dollar figure. A stock issued at $100 a share paying $6 annually would be called a 6 percent stock or a $6 stock. The dividend is often divided into four quarterly payments. Before any dividends may be paid to holders of common stock, dividends must be paid to holders of preferred stock.

Regular Dividends

If a preferred stock is *noncumulative* and the corporation directors do not distribute the regular dividend during any year, no dividend may be paid on the common stock either in that year. But the holders of preferred and common stock in such a case will lose their expected payment for that year, whether the reason is failure to make a profit or a decision of the directors to retain the earnings to use in the

Cumulative Dividends

company. Most preferred stocks, however, are cumulative. The cumulative feature protects the stockholder from failure to distribute dividends. If any part of the regular preferred dividend is not paid in the year it is payable, it must be paid later, along with the current dividend, before the directors may distribute dividends to the common stock. Sometimes, a preferred stock may fail to receive dividends for many years. The full amount of dividends in arrears on the preferred stock must be settled before resumption of dividends on the common stock is permitted.

Participating Stock

As in the case of bonds, stocks sometimes are given features to enhance their salability. A participating preferred stock has a regular dividend, as does a regular preferred stock. In addition, it shares with the common stock any extra dividends as defined in the corporation charter. For example, a preferred stock issued at $100 per share may be given a regular dividend of $5. Common stock issued at $20 per share, with a dividend of $1 per share, would yield the same return (5 percent). The preferred dividend of $5 is, of course, paid prior to any payments on the common. If an amount greater than $1 is paid the common, the participating feature gives proportionately the same additional amount to the preferred. If the common stock is paid $1.20, the preferred is given $6; if the common is paid $1.50, the preferred is paid $7.50.

Convertible Stock

If a preferred stock is convertible into common, the number of shares of common into which it may be converted, the life of the conversion privilege, and any limitations on the right of conversion are stated in the charter of the corporation.

Voting

Nearly all preferred stocks have no privilege of voting for directors of the corporation, as long as the regular preferred dividends are paid promptly. Preferred stocks, however, often are given by the corporation charter the right to vote for the directors if, for example, more than two regular dividend payments have been missed. The exact nature of this voting right is described in the charter. Furthermore, a vote of approval by the preferred stockholders is usually required before an issue of bonds may be sold, a change in the charter made, a merger fulfilled, or the corporation dissolved.

Par or No Par

Preferred stocks are found in both forms. The difference between par and no par is explained in connection with common stock below.

COMMON STOCK

Although preferred and common stock both are ownership instruments, the rights and risks of business ownership rest mostly with the holder of common stock.

Common stock receives dividends only after bond interest is met and regular dividends are paid to preferred stockholders. Holders of common stock are last to receive the proceeds of liquidation of the corporation.

On the other hand, the holders of common stock elect the directors of the corporation, usually on the basis of one vote per share. Furthermore, the common stockholder is paid dividends according to the profits earned, subject to the decision of the directors to hold the profits for reinvestment or to distribute them. In good years, the dividends may rise sharply. If the company expands, the holder of common stock may expect an expansion in earnings and dividends.

The corporation charter gives the common stock a par value of $10, $50, or any other figure. This is the amount printed on the face of each certificate and represents the minimum value for which the stock must originally have been issued by the corporation. The par value has no significance after original issuance, since the amount of earnings retained and the prospect of future profits are largely responsible for the market price of shares, regardless of the dollar figure printed on the face of the stock certificate.

Since the par value of stock has no bearing on its market value after it is first issued by the corporation, why print the par value on the certificate? Most states allow corporation charters the right to issue *no-par* stock, which bears no monetary figure on the certificate. Unlike par stock, no-par stock may at original distribution be assigned whatever figure the directors decide. This gives the directors greater freedom in deciding the offering price of an issue of stock. It should be emphasized that stock traded after it is first issued is bought and sold at prices determined by market forces, and not by any figure printed on the certificate.

Two or more different classes of preferred stock may be issued by a corporation. This is found frequently in corporation finance, but it is rare in the case of common stock. In those cases where a corporation does issue two classes of common stock, generally labeled class A and class B, the usual difference is that A carries no vote for directors. The corporation is therefore controlled by holders of class B common stock.

LEASING

If a business firm has money to buy a machine or a factory building, it usually does so; if it does not have funds available, it can usually borrow them. There is, however, a third alternative, one that has grown in importance during the last 20 years. This is leasing. Almost anything can be obtained by means of a lease, although land, equipment, and transportation vehicles are the most common items provided through a lease.

The essential feature of a lease is the separation of ownership from use. A *lease* is a contract in which the property or equipment owner, known as the *lessor* (or landlord), transfers possession of the leased item to a person or company, known as the *lessee* (or tenant). In return for the use of the leased property, the lessee agrees to pay a rental to the lessor. The lease of an office machine may be for a few months; the lease of a piece of land may run for 99 years. The contract may be between a single lessor and a single lessee or it may involve several persons or companies.

The principal attractions of leasing rather than buying are these:

If a person does not wish to pay in full for a truck or other item, he can sign an install-ment contract, making a down (initial) payment of between one-fifth to one-third of the purchase price. If the item is leased instead, no down payment is required.

In the case of items such as computers, technological advances in design are rapid. A firm using such equipment can reduce the risk of owning obsolete equipment by leasing it rather than buying.

In lease contracts, the maintenance and repair of equipment are commonly done by the lessor. Thus the lessee is freed of the burden of maintenance and repair. This is a convenience in the case of trucks, machinery, and buildings; it is almost essential in the case of electronic computers.

There is a tax advantage in leasing. If an item is bought outright, only the expense of maintenance, repair, and depreciation can be deducted from income in computing income tax liability. In an installment purchase, that part of the installments repre-senting interest may also be deducted. In a lease, the full lease payments may be deducted.

A lease does not appear on the balance sheet of a company as a liability. Thus leasing, rather than borrowing money to buy needed items, may make the balance sheet of a company appear more favorable. However, since a lease requires a company to make the lease payments, this obligation is sometimes placed as a footnote in financial statements.

The main disadvantage of leasing in contrast to buying is the cost, which in most cases is higher than financing by means of installment purchases. However, leasing may be the only way to secure the use of certain items. Many owners of land in choice downtown locations refuse to sell their property but permit use on a lease basis. Some industrial machinery and office equipment is available either for sale or for lease. But if the terms of sale are prohibitive, the only practical alternative is leasing.

A popular means of raising money is *sale and leaseback*. If a businessman owns land and a factory building valued at $1 million, he can borrow money on the security of the factory or he can sell it and lease it back for a period of, for example, 50 years. The maximum loan on such a piece of property is generally $600,000 to $750,000. However, in a sale and leaseback contract, the businessman would receive $1 million from the purchaser-lessor (so named because he then leases the land back to the businessman). In both methods of raising money the businessman has the use of the land for 50 years.

Now suppose the businessman builds an office building at a cost of $1 million on the land. What happens to the property at the end of 50 years? The purchaser-lessor then gets full use of it, along with the land. Assuming the building is kept in good repair and property values remain the same, it is equivalent to making a $1 million payment at the end of 50 years. However, this is not as much of a loss as it appears, because the "payment" is postponed for 50 years. The present value of a $1 million payment made at the end of 50 years discounted at 8 percent is only $21,000. In other words, if $21,000 is invested at 8 percent compounded annually, it equals $1 million in 50 years.

SUMMARY

Long-term finance covers the means of paying for land, buildings, machinery, and other items with a relatively long life. Since it is a rare business that has all of such things that it can use, good managers will list the priority of items needed and plan for the purchase of those in an orderly way. Such a plan of purchasing needed equipment, factory additions, and so on, is called a capital budget. A carefully prepared budget will see that the company's money is spent for the most-needed items first.

Money to pay for long-term assets can be gotten from earnings retained by the business or from sources outside the business. If the business is not incorporated, the money from outside sources is usually contributed by the owner or owners. A corporation can raise money by selling stocks or bonds, or by borrowing from private or government agencies. A bond is a formal promise by a corporation to pay a stated sum of money to the bondholder at a future date, the maturity date. Usually a series of many bonds are sold at the time of issue, and the certificates are engraved. A stock certificate represents a "piece" or part ownership of the corporation. Bondholders receive interest; stockholders receive dividends.

A lease permits a company or person to have the use of property without owning it. A lease contract may be for a few months or for as long as 99 years. Equipment, machinery, trucks, land and buildings, and many other types of property can be leased.

QUESTIONS FOR REVIEW

1   What is a capital budget? How does it differ from an ordinary budget?
2   What are the sources of long-term funds for a company?
3   How are long-term funds for small businesses raised?
4   What is a small business investment company? In what activities does it engage?
5   Describe the activities of an investment banker. How does an investment banker differ from a commercial bank?
6   What does an underwriting syndicate do?
7   What are the typical characteristics of a bond issue?
8   What is a bond indenture?
9   What is the distinction between interest and dividends?
10   What is a registered bond? A coupon bond?
11   What is cumulative preferred stock? What is participating preferred stock? What is the attraction of each to the investor?
12   Preferred stockholders usually do not have the right to vote for the directors of a corporation. Does this mean they have no voting rights? Explain.
13   If a corporation issues common stock without par value, how does the investor know what the stock is worth?
14   What are the principal attractions of leasing rather than buying a factory building? A truck?
15   Explain by means of an example what a sale and leaseback transaction is.

SELECTED READINGS   Dobrovolsky, Sergei P.: *The Economics of Corporation Finance*, McGraw-Hill Book Company, New York, 1971.

Hastings, Paul G.: *The Management of Business Finance*, Van Nostrand Reinhold Company, New York, 1966.

Husband, William H., and James C. Dockeray: *Modern Corporation Finance*, 7th ed., Richard D. Irwin, Inc., Homewood, Ill., 1972.

Prather, Charles L., and James E. Wert: *Financing Business Firms*, 4th ed., Richard D. Irwin, Inc., Homewood, Ill., 1971.

Name	Section	Date

COMPLETION SENTENCES

1 The long-term instruments of corporate finance are _____ *Stocks* _____,

which are an evidence of ownership, and _____ *Bonds* _____, which

are an instrument of debt.

2 A _____ *Capital Budget* lists the planned purchases of capital goods,

the date each will be required, and how they will be financed.

3 The largest amount of funds for long-term finance is derived from

_____ *retained earnings* _____ and, _____ *depreciation allowance* _____

4 Small business investment companies have been a source of investment funds

or loans for _____ *small business* since 1958.

5 _____ *investment banker* is a marketing organization specializing in the

distribution of stocks and bonds.

6 A corporation bond is a formal promise of a corporation to pay the bond-

holder _____ *stated sum* _____ of money at _____ *stated time* _____.

7 An indenture states the features of a _bond issue_ .

8 The value stated on the face of the bond certificate is the
par value .

9 A debenture bond holds no _mortgage_ on any specific
property of the corporation.

10 A callable bond gives the _issuer_ the option of retiring
the bond before maturity date.

11 Convertible bonds may be converted at the option of the
bond holder into _stock_ .

12 In cumulative preferred stock if a regular dividend is not paid when due, it
must be _paid before_ any future dividend
paid.

13 Holders of common stock elect the directors of a corporation, usually on the
basis of _one_ vote per _share_ .

14 The essential feature of a lease is the separation of _ownership,_
from use.

15 A lease does not appear on the _balance sheet_ of a company
as a liability.

TRUE OR FALSE STATEMENTS

F **1** A capital budget lists the estimated income and expenses of a company for
the coming year.

F **2** The largest amount of funds for long-term use by companies is derived from
the sale of stocks and bonds.

Name	Section	Date

T 3 An investment banker is a marketer of securities for corporations.

T 4 Bonds are a long-term debt instrument of a corporation.

F 5 If a corporation that issues bonds fails to pay interest on the bonds, in order to secure payment of the interest it is necessary for all of the bondholders jointly to sue the corporation.

F 6 The par value is the market value of a bond or stock.

T 7 Interest paid on bonds of a corporation is an expense of the corporation, but dividend payments on stock are not.

F 8 A corporation bond with a mortgage on specific property of the corporation is a debenture bond.

T 9 An income bond pays interest only when the corporation earns enough income to cover interest.

T 10 Preferred stocks are simply stocks that have certain preferences over common stocks.

T 11 Payment of dividends to preferred stockholders is made only out of corporation profits.

F 12 Most preferred stocks are noncumulative.

F 13 If a preferred stock is convertible, it is usually convertible into a bond.

F 14 Only one class or kind of preferred stock may be issued by a corporation at one time.

T 15 Some types of assets desired by a business are available only by leasing them.

EXERCISES

1 From a brokerage office or your library secure a prospectus describing a stock or bond issue. In the space provided below list briefly the items of information contained in the prospectus that you consider important to an investor contemplating the purchase of stocks or bonds. Is there any information you think should have been included that is not in the prospectus? Explain.

Name of company: _____

Date securities offered for sale:_____

Name of distributor of securities: _____

Price to purchasers:　$_____

Total amount of issue:　$_____

Amount received by corporation for each stock or bond sold:

　　$_____

Comments:

2 Using the chart below, list the short-term and long-term instruments used in business financing.

Instrument	Principal Source of Funds	Principal Uses of Funds	Advantages in Raising Funds

3 *Case Problem* for report or class discussion.

The Roban Lumber Company was incorporated under Texas law in 1967 for the purpose of selling lumber and all complementary materials (both wholesale and retail), and to construct and sell houses.

The capital stock consisted of 500 shares with a par value of $100 each, all in the form of common stock. All corporate business is conducted within the state of Texas. A life of 50 years was granted by the secretary of the state of Texas, the maximum life permitted a Texas corporation at that time. This, however, may be renewed on application for extension.

The promoters of the corporation were R. M. Rogers, L. M. Jones, and C. U. Dougall. These promoters, who had been familiar with the lumber business for many years, decided not to sell common stock to the general public, but rather to issue all of the authorized shares to themselves. Rogers was issued 250 shares, Jones and Dougall 125 shares each. One of the bylaws of the corporation bound the three stockholders not to sell stock to outsiders without first offering it for sale to the other two stockholders.

The initial capitalization was sufficient to purchase the land, construct the buildings, and provide a beginning inventory to start the business. The balance sheet of the company at the end of 1967 is given at the end of this case.

One of the immediate problems of the corporation was that of expansion,

Name   Section   Date

to enable the corporation to serve satisfactorily the growing number of customers the business attracted. After considerable examination of various alternatives, Rogers, Jones, and Dougall, who constituted the stockholders, directors, and principal officers of the corporation, narrowed the possibilities to three. These alternatives were as follows: (1) an increase in bank borrowing; (2) an increase in authorized stock so that additional shares could be sold to the stockholders; and (3) stockholders' loans to the corporation. The relationships between the three men and the commercial banks prior to the establishment of the corporation had been excellent, but there was a question in the minds of the men as to whether the bank already holding the notes of the corporation would be willing to increase considerably its loans to the corporation directly. In order to use the second alternative, it would be necessary under Texas law to apply for an amendment to the charter authorizing the issuance of additional stock. The third possibility would, of course, make the stockholders also creditors of their company.

The financing required for expansion was intended to be used largely for the purpose of increasing the inventory and accounts receivable of the company, both of them being current assets. It was expected, however, that the need for additional financing to finance an expansion of these two assets would continue for several years, to bring the investment in cash, accounts receivable, and inventory up to an average level of $100,000.

Examine critically the three alternatives considered by the officers of the corporation. Indicate which one, in your opniion, is best, giving the reason for your choice.

ROBAN LUMBER COMPANY
Balance Sheet as of December 31, 1967

Assets		
Current		
Cash	$10,000	
Inventory	19,000	
		$29,000
Fixed assets		
Land	$15,000	
Building	30,000	
Equipment	3,000	
		48,000
		$77,000
Liabilities		
Notes payable to bank	$15,000	
Mortgage loan	12,000	
		27,000
Net worth Common stock		50,000
		$77,000

26 SECURITIES EXCHANGES AND OTHER FINANCIAL INSTITUTIONS

The financial institutions discussed in this chapter are treated in much greater detail in specialized courses in finance. If you should take a course in money and banking, you will find this chapter a useful introduction to part of what you will study there.

The stock exchange is one of the most interesting financial institutions in the United States. If there is a stock exchange close enough for you to visit, it would be very useful to do so. There is nothing that substitutes for a personal visit to the stock exchange in understanding the process of trading in stocks and bonds.

The Federal Reserve System is the central bank of the United States. Notice that the United States has a decentralized central banking system. This is unique. Other countries have a single central bank, usually with many branches.

It is sometimes difficult to understand a hedging transaction. If you do not understand the operation after reading about it, read the section over again. If you still do not understand, go to the library and read further on this subject.

Although commercial banks and investment banking are important financial institutions, they are not the only ones. There are many financial institutions aiding businessmen in their domestic operations and in their foreign activities as well. The institutions we shall discuss in this chapter are the following: securities exchanges, Federal Reserve System, deposit insurance, savings institutions, commodity markets and hedging, financial agencies of the federal government, and international financial institutions.

SECURITIES EXCHANGES

Persons who have stocks and bonds may wish to sell them from time to time to get money. Except for Series E federal government bonds and a few other exceptional issues, the investor may sell to anyone he chooses. Most investors, however, do not want to go to the trouble to hunt around for buyers of the securities they want to sell. They find it more convenient to engage the services of a *brokerage house* to sell their investments. Most brokerage houses with which the public deals are members of the New York Stock Exchange and some other exchanges as well. The New York Stock Exchange provides a convenient place for the buying and selling of securities during its working day from 10:00 A.M. to 3:30 P.M., five days a week.

Although the stock exchange provides an auction market, it is not like a conventional auction at which farm products or used furniture are sold and where there is one seller with many competing buyers. The stock exchange provides a two-way auction market, in which there are many competing buyers and many competing sellers. For example, the owner of 100 shares of Dow Chemical Company stock can have the shares sold for him on the New York Stock Exchange in a few minutes after he enters a brokerage office in Portland, Oregon. The Portland broker will send the order to sell 100 shares of Dow Chemical to his New York office, which will transmit the order to the floor of the stock exchange, where it will be delivered to the member of the exchange that executes orders for the broker. The member walks to the trading post where Dow Chemical stock is traded (the one of 18 U-shaped trading posts to which the stock is assigned, and the only one at which that stock may be traded). He may find very active trading of the stock. If he feels the trend of the bidding is downward, he will make his offer to sell immediately. If the trend is upward, he will probably wait a few moments, so as to get a higher selling price for the customer. If there is no activity in Dow Chemical Company stock at the moment, the member will sell 100 shares to the specialist at the highest price then attainable. The specialist is a stock exchange member who stays at one trading post to maintain a continuous and orderly market in the stocks he specializes in.

If the Portland, Oregon, customer had placed an order to buy less than 100 shares of Dow Chemical Company stock, the order would have been relayed to the floor of the exchange as before. However, the shares would have been purchased from the inventory of the odd lot trader (a member who maintains an inventory in various securities and is ready to buy or sell in lots of one to 99 shares) dealing in Dow Chemical stock. The price per share in this case would be fractionally higher than the price per share for a round lot (multiples of 100 shares) transaction.

When a round lot transaction is completed on the exchange, the price is reported by the ticker tape to the Portland office a few minutes later. The ticker tape is a transparent tape projected on a screen at brokerage offices, reporting transactions completed on a stock exchange a few minutes after each one takes place. A segment is shown in Figure 26-1. Within a few days the owner of the Dow Chemical stock will deliver his stock certificates to the Portland broker, and will receive a check from the broker representing the sale price of the stock minus brokerage commission and transfer tax.

Stocks and bonds have been sold at the New York Stock Exchange every year since its founding in 1792. It was first organized as an unincorporated association somewhat like a country club, but was incorporated in 1971. The present membership is limited to a maximum of 1,375 members. In order to become a member, a person must buy the membership of an existing member and be accepted by the membership committee of the exchange. The price of a membership (also called a *seat*) in recent years has fluctuated from $80,000 to $300,000.

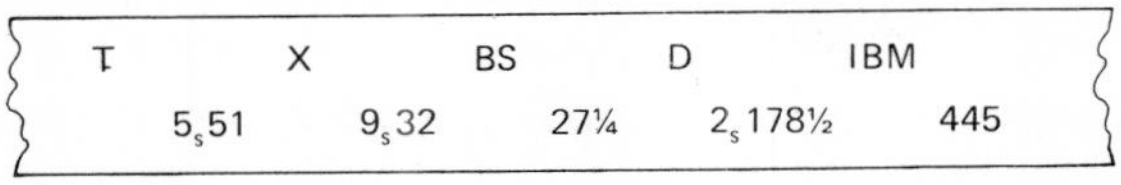

```
   T        X        BS       D        IBM
      5ₛ51     9ₛ32     27¼    2ₛ178½     445
```

Stock sales recorded

T   American Telephone and Telegraph 500 shares
at $51 per share

X   United States Steel 900 shares at $32 per share

BS   Bethlehem Steel 100 shares at $27.25 per share

D   E. I. du Pont de Nemours 200 shares at $178.50
per share

IBM   International Business Machines 100 shares at
$445.00 per share

FIGURE 26-1. Section of ticker tape with explanation.

The stocks and bonds of almost all of the large well-known corporations are listed on the New York Stock Exchange. While corporations receive no direct benefits from having their stock bought and sold on the New York Stock Exchange, they do receive some important indirect benefits. The following are the advantages to a corporation of having its stocks and bonds listed on the New York Stock Exchange or, to a somewhat lesser extent, on the smaller American Exchange:

The advertising value of trading on the exchange makes the marketing of securities by corporations easier. Many prospective purchasers of securities are reluctant to buy stocks and bonds of companies not listed on one of the exchanges in New York.

The active auction market in corporation securities gives the corporation executives an up-to-the-minute knowledge of the market price of their stocks and bonds, making it easier to determine the price at which future issues might be sold.

The laws of some states restrict the purchase of securities by banks, insurance companies, and other financial institutions to certain selected stocks and bonds listed on the New York Stock Exchange. The listing of the stock of a corporation on the New York Stock Exchange makes it more likely that the stock will be bought by financial institutions.

Stocks and bonds that are not listed for trading on one of the major exchanges may be sold by securities dealers in the over-the-counter market. This market exists anywhere that stocks and bonds are sold in the United States. It consists of dealers who maintain an inventory of unlisted (not listed on a stock exchange) stocks and bonds and who are ready to buy and sell securities, making a profit on the difference between the buying and selling prices. In this respect dealers in the over-the-counter market are somewhat like dealers in used cars. Both maintain inventories and both stand ready to buy and sell. In the over-the-counter market the number of securities that are actively traded is about 3,000. Many more are traded intermittently, perhaps between 30,000 and 40,000 issues. Dealers in these securities furnish their buy and sell prices to a centralized computer system that in turn provides instantaneous quotations of stock and bond prices to brokerage offices anywhere in the country.

A person who has 10 shares of common stock of the Delhi Oil Company can sell the shares by taking them to any dealer in securities or to a brokerage office, who will then contact a dealer. The dealer will either sell the securities for a commission and hunt for a buyer, or he may buy the securities himself, hold them as an investment, and perhaps sell them at a later date. The price at which a dealer will buy shares is, of course, lower than the price at which he will sell shares. For example, on April 16, 1973, the price at which the common stock of Reliable Life Insurance Company could be sold by the investor to a dealer was $19 a share, and the price at which the same stock could be bought from a dealer was $20 a share. On the same day the quotations for Allied Van Lines were $6.75 and $7.25 per share. In the above examples the dealers charge no commission for the stocks bought and sold, but cover their expenses by the difference between the price at which they buy and the higher price at which they sell.

THE FEDERAL RESERVE SYSTEM

The United States had a central bank from 1791 to 1811 and from 1816 to 1836, but from 1836 to 1913 there was none. Experience, particularly the disastrous financial panic of 1907, proved the need for one. Congress, responding to the need, established the Federal Reserve System by an act passed in 1913, thus restoring the services of central banking to the country.

CENTRAL BANKING FUNCTIONS OF THE FEDERAL RESERVE SYSTEM

A central bank furnishes the following services: bankers' bank, bankers to the government, credit control, and issuing of paper money.

Bankers' Bank

All of the national banks and some of the state banks are members of the Federal Reserve System. The services we receive from a commercial bank, the commercial bank receives from the Federal Reserve bank. The Federal Reserve banks lend money to commercial banks on the security of government bonds or other assets. The member banks of the system have deposit accounts in the Federal Reserve banks. Whenever cash is needed, the member bank can withdraw its deposit from the Reserve bank and borrow more from it if needed.

The Federal Reserve banks clear checks for member banks. If a bank in Milwaukee receives from a customer a check drawn on a bank in Camden, New Jersey, the Milwaukee bank can deposit the check for collection with the Federal Reserve bank in Chicago, which in turn will send it to the Federal Reserve bank in Philadelphia, which will collect it from the Camden bank.

If a customer of a member bank needs to send money immediately to a distant city, the Federal Reserve System facilitates the transfer by means of its Teletype connection among all Federal Reserve banks. By this means, a customer of a member bank in Forth Worth, Texas, can have funds transferred to, for example, an individual in Seattle, Washington. Delivery can be made within an hour, and the individual will be notified by telephone.

The Federal Reserve banks aid the federal government in borrowing money by helping to sell government bonds and notes. In addition, the Reserve banks invest in government securities. Government agencies keep their deposits mostly in Federal Reserve banks, making payments by checks drawn on these accounts.

Bankers to the Government

More than four-fifths of the dollar amount of business payments are made by drawing checks on checking accounts; less than one-fifth are made by cash. Checking accounts therefore represent the money we use for most of our payments and, if the amount of checking amounts increases rapidly, prices tend to rise; if the amount decreases rapidly, prices tend to fall. The Federal Reserve System attempts to prevent inflation and deflation of prices by preventing the total amount of deposit accounts in banks from increasing or decreasing too rapidly. An explanation of the means used is beyond the scope of this book.[1]

Credit Control

Examine a dollar bill. You will notice on the face "Federal Reserve Note." Most of our money in circulation is issued by the Federal Reserve banks. At the end of January 1973, for example, the total amount of paper money and coins in circulation was $64,312 million, of which $56,428 million was in the form of Federal Reserve notes. In addition to issuing paper money, the Federal Reserve banks collect and retire worn-out bills and coins, replacing them with new ones.

Issuing Paper Money

The Federal Reserve System differs somewhat from systems used by many countries.

THE STRUCTURE OF THE FEDERAL RESERVE SYSTEM

Other countries with central banks have a single bank with a number of branches to serve the needs of the country. In establishing a central banking system for the United

Federal Reserve Districts

[1] A simplified explanation can be found in Edwin W. Kemmerer and Donald L. Kemmerer, *The ABC of the Federal Reserve System*, 12th ed., Harper & Row, Publishers, Incorporated, 1950.

States, however, Congress chose to establish 12 central banks, each serving a region. The districts were originally established roughly according to population and trade, with the geographically smaller districts serving the Northeastern states with their high density of population and industry. The more sparsely settled states in 1913 were put in the ninth, tenth, eleventh, and twelfth districts, as shown in Figure 26-2. The largest district is the twelfth, which now includes Hawaii and Alaska. The district boundaries may be changed by the Board of Governors (described below), but only Congress may change the number of districts. For example, the line dividing the tenth and eleventh districts originally followed the border between Oklahoma and Texas. The banks in the southeast corner of Oklahoma, however, requested that they be put in the eleventh district. Granting the request, the Board of Governors changed the boundary, placing southeast Oklahoma in the eleventh district, served by Dallas. Ten of the districts have branch banks to provide better service to the commercial banks in the area.

Ownership and Management of Each Bank   Each of the Federal Reserve banks is organized as a corporation. The capital stock is entirely held by the member banks in the districts. Each Federal Reserve bank

FIGURE 26-2 Federal Reserve districts and branch districts. (Board of Governors of the Federal Reserve System).

THE FEDERAL RESERVE SYSTEM

has a board of nine directors, who appoint the president, vice presidents, and other major officers of the bank and decide policy matters for the bank. Six of the directors are elected by the member banks and three, including the chairman of the board, are appointed by the Board of Governors. Only three may be bankers; the other six are usually businessmen.

The Board of Governors is composed of seven men appointed by the President of the United States with the consent of the Senate. Each term is for 14 years, arranged so that one of the seven terms expires every second year. The length of the terms, adequate salaries, and a tradition of nonpolitical appointments has made the Board of Governors a highly respectable body. The functions of the Board are to coordinate the activities of the 12 Federal Reserve banks and to outline the policies to be carried out by the banking system so as to serve the monetary interest of the nation. For example, the Board usually acts to raise interest rates to counter inflation and to lower interest rates to combat a decline in business.

The Board of Governors

There are several institutions that provide a safe place to deposit money. The sums deposited are reinvested in real estate, mortgages, bonds, and similar investments. The emphasis is on safety of principal and the interest paid to depositors is below that of riskier investments.

SAVINGS INSTITUTIONS

Most commercial banks provide savings accounts as well as checking accounts for their customers. Deposits and withdrawals may be made at any time during banking hours or by mail, although banks reserve the right (rarely exercised) to require advance notice of a week to a month for large withdrawals. Interest is credited semiannually or quarterly. It is necessary, however, to leave money in the account until the quarter or half-year is completed in order to receive interest for any part of such period. For example, a deposit left in a savings account from April 1 until June 15 receives no interest at all. If left in the account until June 30, it would receive interest for a quarter of a year.

SAVINGS DEPARTMENTS OF COMMERCIAL BANKS

Mutual savings banks are banks that do not offer checking privileges or the other services associated with a commercial bank. The services offered are essentially the same as those offered by the savings departments of commercial banks. Mutual savings banks are owned by their depositors. The boards of directors, however, are not elected by the owners; rather, they are self-perpetuating. Operation is subject to the laws of the state from which the charter is received and to regulations of the FDIC, if the bank is insured.

SAVINGS BANKS

A similar type of savings bank is the ***stock savings bank***. It is similar in operation to the mutual savings bank. The difference is in organization, since the stock savings bank is owned by stockholders who may or may not be depositors of the bank. The bank is operated for profit, and the directors are elected by the stockholders.

SAVINGS AND LOAN ASSOCIATIONS

Savings and loan associations, also known as *building and loan associations*, accept deposits or sell "shares" to persons wishing to save money. Although a few are organized as corporations with stockholders, most are owned by the depositors. If a person wishes to have the interest on his account acuumulate, he opens a deposit to which interest is credited, usually four times a year. If he wishes to have the interest sent by check to his home, he purchases shares in denominations of $100 or some other round number. If the association is insured, both the share accounts and the deposits are insured up to $20,000 per depositor.

The deposits received are invested in house mortgages, house improvements, and, to a limited degree, business real estate. The associations are created by either Federal or state charter. The former must be owned by the depositors and must be insured by the Federal Savings and Loan Insurance Corporation (FSLIC). The latter may or may not be insured and may have stockholders investing for profit as well as depositors.

CREDIT UNIONS

Credit unions are organized to serve people with a common bond of some kind, such as a membership in a labor union, employment by a company, or membership in a church. Persons wishing to save money purchase shares, on which dividends are paid at about the same rate as or slightly higher than savings and loan shares, but they are not insured. Persons wishing to borrow money to buy a car, pay physicians' fees, or take a vacation can secure a loan of the funds at rates of interest in the neighborhood of 12 percent per annum or less. A credit union organized by employees of a company often receives free office space from the company.

MUTUAL FUNDS

A financial institution of growing importance is the *mutual fund*, also known as an "investment company." Mutual funds pool the savings of a large number of small investors to form a large fund for investment. This is done by selling shares of the mutual fund in conveniently small dollar amounts and using the money to buy securities of corporations in large blocks. The activity of mutual funds helps businesses by providing an additional market for the stocks and bonds of corporations. Millions of small investors who would otherwise put no money into corporation securities directly do so indirectly by buying shares of mutual funds.

The number of mutual funds runs into the hundreds, providing a variety of funds suited to almost every type of investor. Some funds invest only in bonds, some in stocks and bonds, some only in stocks. Some funds invest only in stocks of large, well-known corporations. Others invest in stocks of small, little-known companies, where the possibility of rapid growth is present but the risk of failure is high. The retired person can invest in a fund with a policy of buying stocks providing generous dividends but little prospect for growth in price. A young investor can buy shares of a fund investing in companies providing little or no dividend payment but with the expectation of substantial growth in the price of the stock.

Mutual funds provide several attractions, of which the principal ones follow:

1 *Diversification:*   The fund purchases the securities of many companies, thereby reducing the risks of investment.
2 *Management:*   The investment portfolio of each fund is managed by professional investment managers, with greater knowledge and experience than are available to the small investor.
3 *Convenience of acquisition:*   A person can buy mutual fund shares from time to time as he has money available, or he can sign up with a mutual fund to buy shares on a basis of regular monthly or quarterly payments. Most funds (called *load funds*) charge a sales fee of 8 to 9 percent each time mutual fund shares are bought. A few funds (called *no-load funds*), employing no salesmen and not aggressively sold, make no sales charge.
4 *Convenience of liquidation:*   If an investor wants to cash in his fund shares, he can do so at any time by ordering the fund to redeem his shares. The redemption price is determined by the market value of the securities held by the fund and is calculated daily. No charge is made to the investor in redeeming his shares.
5 *Government regulation:*   The Investment Company Act of 1940 requires investment companies (with a few exceptions) to register with the Securities and Exchange Commission and provide detailed information regarding their operating policies, investments, contracts, loans, and other aspects of their business.

FEDERAL SAVINGS INSURANCE

THE FEDERAL DEPOSIT INSURANCE CORPORATION

One of the first acts of Congress in combating the Depression in 1933 was to restore the shaken confidence of depositors in banks. To do this, the Federal Deposit Insurance Corporation (FDIC) was created. Congress intended to protect the small depositor, believing that large depositors protected themselves by investigating the banks in which they placed their money. For this reason, the insurance covered a maximum of $5,000 (now $20,000) per depositor in each insured bank. The cost of the insurance is covered by premiums paid by each insured bank, amounting to 1/12 of 1 percent per annum of the amount of deposits in each bank.

When an insured bank fails, the FDIC assists in the liquidation of the assets or in the reorganization of the bank. Each depositor is paid the full amount of his deposits unless they exceed $20,000. For that portion over $20,000, the depositor receives a settlement dependent on the liquidation value of the bank's assets. All member banks of the Federal Reserve System are required to join the FDIC. Other banks are invited to join but are not required to. Such has been the demand of depositors for insurance, however, that of the 13,669 commercial banks in the United States on July, 1972, only 206 were not insured.[2]

OTHER FEDERAL DEPOSIT INSURANCE CORPORATIONS

The popularity of bank deposit insurance has led to federal insurance of savings in other forms. In each case, rather than including the savings media under the FDIC, a new federal corporation was created, patterned after the FDIC. Thus savings in all federally chartered and most state-chartered savings and loan associations are insured to $20,000 for each depositor by the Federal Savings and Loan Insurance Corporation (FSLIC).

In 1970 two additional insurance corporations were created by Congress. The Federal Credit Union Insurance Corporation (FCUIC) insures depositors of all federally chartered credit unions and most state-chartered credit unions to a maximum of $20,000. The Securities Investor Protection Corporation (SIPC) insures each customer's account in a brokerage house against losses resulting from embezzlement or theft of securities, bankruptcy, or financial distress of the brokerage firm. Losses to an investor resulting from a drop in the market price of the stocks or bonds held in his account are not covered. All brokerage houses having memberships on an organized stock exchange are insured by the SIPC. Each customer having securities and cash on deposit in a brokerage firm is insured up to $50,000, although the cash in the account is insured only to a maximum of $20,000.

COMMODITY MARKETS AND HEDGING

A commodity exchange is organized for the purpose of buying and selling commodities in large lots for immediate or future delivery. Like a stock exchange, it is owned by its members, who are limited in number, and only members may buy and sell on the trading floor. Some exchanges handle several commodities, each of which is traded at a separate *ring* or *pit*. Hand signals are generally used to communicate between buyers and sellers, and sales are made in units such as 5,000 bushels of wheat, 100 bales of cotton, 50 tons of sugar, or 15,000 dozen eggs. The following are examples of commodity exchanges: Chicago Board of Trade, New Orleans Cotton Exchange, Winnipeg Grain Exchange, New York Coffee and Sugar Exchange, and Memphis Board of Trade.

As stated above, commodity sales are made either on *spot* (delivery within a short period or immediately) or in *futures* (delivery during a specified month in the future). Dealing in futures permits a company to reduce the risk of future price changes by means of *hedging*. This practice is mostly engaged in by flour millers, coffee roasters, and others requiring the purchase of commodities for their operations. For example, suppose a flour miller contracts in October to deliver flour to a buyer on January 25 at an agreed price. The miller does not know what price wheat will be selling at in January, when he must secure wheat to be milled into flour for

[2] *Federal Reserve Bulletin,* March 1973, p. A22. If a person has deposits in several banks, each deposit is insured up to $20,000.

delivery January 25. He therefore buys wheat futures for January delivery. Spot prices and future prices tend to rise and fall together in the commodities markets. When the miller needs the wheat for his flour, perhaps about two weeks before January 25, he will buy spot wheat at whatever price prevails. If the prices of spot wheat and wheat futures have risen 10 cents per bushel between October and January, he will be forced to buy the wheat (spot) at a higher price than in October. Such a rise in raw materials might wipe out his expected profit. However, when the miller buys the spot wheat for his mill, he will sell his wheat futures. The 10-cent rise will give him a 10-cent-per-bushel profit on his futures contract to offset the 10-cent rise in the cost of raw material for his mill. Had the price of wheat fallen between October and January, he would have suffered a loss on his futures contract equivalent to the gain he would receive through buying spot wheat at a lower cost than he had expected when he made the flour contract in October. Hedging (by dealing in futures) enables the miller to enter into commitments for delivery of flour in the future, and to concentrate his energy and talents on flour milling and selling rather than speculating on fluctuating commodity prices.

We have discussed the Federal Reserve System (a quasi-public institution), the Federal Deposit Insurance Corporation, and the Federal Savings and Loan Insurance Corporation. There are many other agencies of the federal government providing financial aid through insurance of deposits, lending of money, or guaranteeing loans made by private agencies. The following is a partial list:

FINANCIAL AGENCIES OF THE FEDERAL GOVERNMENT

> Federal Land Banks
> Federal Intermediate Credit Banks
> Federal Regional Banks for corporations
> Farmers' Home Administration
> Federal Crop Insurance Corporation
> Commodity Credit Corporation
> Rural Electrification Administration
> Public Housing Administration
> Federal Housing Administration
> Home Loan Bank Board
> Veterans Administration
> Small Business Administration
> Federal National Mortgage Association
> Export-Import Bank

Three of the above agencies will be described, as representative of the activity of the federal government in the field of credit. They are: the Federal Housing Administration, the Small Business Administration, and the Export-Import Bank.

The Federal Housing Administration (FHA) was created by Congress in 1934. It makes no loans, since its purpose is to insure private lenders against loss through the default of loans they make to home owners and apartment owners. The FHA

THE FEDERAL HOUSING ADMINISTRATION

was created to induce private lenders to make loans to home buyers and apartment owners at lower rates of interest, for longer terms, and for a larger percentage of the appraisal value of the house or apartment than private lenders had been willing to do before. During the FHA's first 25 years, more than 5 million loans were made to house buyers, and the volume of insured loans reached almost $40 billion.

The FHA, as stated before, does not lend money. If private lenders are unwilling to lend at the legal maximum for FHA-insured loans, the house buyer must secure an uninsured (conventional) loan at whatever rate of interest is available at the time. Furthermore, if a lender makes a loan under FHA insurance, he often requires a discount in addition to the stated interest. For example, a house may be sold for $20,000 with a $600 down payment from the buyer and $19,400 (insured by FHA) "lent" to the buyer secured by a mortgage on his newly purchased house. Interest may be stated as 8 percent. However, the mortgage banker will not lend the full $19,400. He will discount the loan, at 5 percent or some other figure. For example, the amount paid to the builder or seller of the house may not be $600 from the house buyer and $19,400 from the mortgage banker, but $600 from the house buyer and $18,250 from the mortgage banker. The mortgage banker, however, collects interest on $19,400. By this means, the true rate of interest charged by lenders is in excess of the maximum fixed by Congress on loans insured by the FHA. The seller, aware of the discount, will consider it a cost of selling and will raise the price of the house to offset the discount.

SMALL BUSINESS ADMINISTRATION

The Small Business Administration (SBA) was created by Congress in 1953. The purpose of its creation was to accomplish the following: (1) to provide management aids and counseling to small firms, (2) to help small firms in competing for government orders, and (3) to make loans to small businesses.

The SBA has organized management classes or conferences in cities throughout the United States, usually in conjunction with universities and colleges. It also publishes a large number of management aids in pamphlet form.

In consultation with the Defense Department, the SBA participates in the designation of those government orders that are to be placed with small businesses. It also helps small businesses in preparations for bidding on government contracts. Where contracts are given by the government to large concerns, the SBA aids small concerns in negotiating subcontracts for supplies and materials for the large concerns.

The loan program of the SBA has two parts: *business loans* and *disaster loans*. The disaster loans are made to business concerns that have suffered damage from storms, floods, and similar catastrophes. The business loans are made to small, independently owned enterprises that are unable to get satisfactory accommodation from private lending agencies. The maximum maturity is 10 years for a business loan and 20 years for disaster loans. The interest rate is 6 percent on business loans and 3 percent on disaster loans.

The Export-Import Bank was established by Congress to finance exports and imports of the United States, and to assist and support United States firms doing business in international trade. Like the SBA, it extends credit to American concerns "where credit is unavailable on reasonable terms through private financial institutions." The interpretation of what constitutes "reasonable terms" is up to the judgment of the officers of the Export-Import Bank. The credit may be extended in several ways. Direct loans can be given to American companies to help finance export or import transactions. Loans extended by private lending agencies may be guaranteed by the Export-Import Bank. In some cases, the Bank participates in loans made jointly with private lenders.

EXPORT-IMPORT BANK

The Export-Import Bank has made extensive loans to foreign importers to enable them to buy goods from the United States. Loans are made both to private foreign companies and to foreign governments. The size of loans ranges from a few thousand dollars to several million.

Toward the end of World War II, representatives of the Allied Powers met at Bretton Woods, New Hampshire, for the purpose of planning the means by which international trade could be restored upon the resumption of peace. Out of this meeting two international institutions were born, the International Bank for Reconstruction and Development (popularly known as the World Bank) and the International Monetary Fund (IMF). Later several other international financing agencies were created. We shall not discuss all of them here. Rather we shall confine our attention to the World Bank, the IMF, the International Finance Corporation, and the International Development Association.

INTERNATIONAL FINANCIAL INSTITUTIONS

The World Bank was created for the purpose of promoting the international movement of long-term funds. This is accomplished by the direct loan of funds, the guarantee of loans made by other agencies, and participation in loans with other agencies. The earliest loans were made to European nations for reconstruction of facilities destroyed by war. Later loans were made to nations in all parts of the world and have been principally for the purpose of developing the economies of the countries. Typical loans are made to construct or improve railways, irrigation projects, port facilities, and electric power. Funds for lending are derived from subscriptions of the member governments and from the sale of World Bank bonds to investors.

THE WORLD BANK

The IMF was created to help maintain stable exchange rates between nations, reduce restrictions on the free flow of funds, and provide the machinery for consultation and collaboration on international monetary problems. The funds of the IMF are derived from the payment quotas from the more than 100 member nations.

THE INTERNATIONAL MONETARY FUND (IMF)

If a member nation is short of a particular foreign currency, the central bank of that country can borrow the currency from the IMF, thus preventing the foreign currency from rising in price relative to the money of the country. If France finds United States dollars in short supply, as was common during the early 1950s, the Bank of France may borrow dollars from the IMF, depositing French francs as security. When the loan is repaid, the Bank of France repays United States dollars to the IMF, and the IMF returns the francs to the Bank of France. The resources of the IFM are intended only to counter temporary shortages of foreign exchange. If the shortage of foreign exchange in France were chronic, other means than a loan from the IMF would have to be taken. In such a case the usual corrective action is devaluation of the currency, a step that many nations have taken since World War II, including the United States. The United States devalued the dollar with an announcement in December 1971, and devalued it a second time with an announcement in February 1973. The first was a devaluation of about 8 percent; the second was a devaluation of 10 percent.

THE INTERNATIONAL FINANCE CORPORATION (IFC)

The IFC was organized in 1956 with capital subscribed by 55 member nations of the World Bank. Its purpose is to further the economic development of nations in undeveloped parts of Africa, Asia, and other areas of the world. The IFC invests only in private enterprises, in association with private capital, and finances no more than half of the total costs of an enterprise.

THE INTERNATIONAL DEVELOPMENT ASSOCIATION (IDA)

The IDA was created in 1960 by member nations of the World Bank to aid depressed areas of the world to build housing, purify water supplies, construct sanitation facilities, and provide the other essentials of development. Although a charge of about 1 percent per annum is made to service the loans, no interest is levied. Installments to repay the principal usually begin after 10 years. Loans are made for periods of 50 or more years.

SUMMARY

Financial institutions are organizations created to accomplish a particular goal or to furnish a financial service. Some are privately organized by the federal government. The ones discussed in this chapter and their principal functions are listed below:

1 *Securities exchanges:* Provide a place for members to buy and sell stocks and bonds for themselves and their customers.
2 *Federal Reserve System:* Created by the federal government to act as "bankers' banks," to be banker for the government, and to aid in combating depression and inflation.
3 *Federal Deposit Insurance Corporation:* Insures depositors having money in commercial and savings banks. Other federal insurance corporations insure deposits in

savings and loan associations, credit unions, and accounts in securities brokerage houses.

4 *Savings institutions:* Provide a place to invest savings and earn a moderate interest, with emphasis on safety; they include savings departments of commercial banks, savings banks, savings and loan associations, and credit unions.

5 *Commodity markets:* Provide a place to buy and sell, in large units, wheat, corn, cocoa, coffee, and other commodities.

6 *Government financial institutions:* Agencies of the federal government created to provide a specific financial service or a broad range of financial services to a specific class of persons or businesses.

7 Several international institutions were created after World War II to provide funds to restore the world economy. The two principal institutions are the World Bank, which makes long-term loans, and the International Monetary Fund, which makes short-term loans for the purpose of stabilizing exchange rates.

QUESTIONS FOR REVIEW

1 Suppose you want to sell 200 shares of Ford Motor Company stock. Outline the steps through which the stock is sold and transferred to the new owner.

2 What is a stock exchange ticker tape? What information does it reveal?

3 What are the advantages to the corporation of having its stock listed on the New York Stock Exchange? To the stockholder?

4 If a stock is not listed for trading on a stock exchange, is there any way an investor can buy or sell shares of the stock?

5 The Federal Reserve banks are called "bankers' banks." What is meant by this term?

6 How does the Federal Reserve System aid in the transfer of money between distant points in the United States?

7 What service does the Federal Reserve System provide for the federal government?

8 Examine a dollar bill. What assurance do you have that people will accept this dollar if you offer it in payment for a purchase?

9 What is the Board of Governors of the Federal Reserve System? How are the members appointed? What is their function?

10 Compare the different types of savings institutions available to persons in the United States.

11 If an insured bank becomes bankrupt, what actions does the FDIC take to protect depositors?

12 What is the amount of insurance per depositor of a bank today? If a person wants to have more than that amount on deposit covered by insurance, what can he do?

13 How are commodities traded on a commodity exchange?

14 What services does the Small Business Administration provide for businessmen?

15 Distinguish between the functions of the World Bank, the International Monetary Fund, the International Finance Corporation, and the International Develment Association.

SELECTED READINGS Clendenin, John C., and George A. Christy: *Introduction to Investments,* 5th ed., McGraw-Hill Book Company, New York, 1969.

Hastings, Paul G., and Norbert J. Mietus: *Personal Finance*, McGraw-Hill Book Company, New York, 1972.

Lorie, James H., and Mary T. Hamilton: *The Stock Market*, Richard D. Irwin, Inc., Homewood, Ill., 1973.

Smith, Paul F.: *Economics of Financial Institutions and Markets*, Richard D. Irwin, Inc., Homewood, Ill., 1971.

Annual Report; New York Stock Exchange, New York (annual edition).

Life Insurance Fact Book, Institute of Life Insurance, New York (annual edition).

Name   Section   Date

COMPLETION SENTENCES

1 The creation of the Federal Reserve System in 1913 restored the services of

_____ to the United States.

2 If the amount of dollars in checking accounts of banks in the United States

increases rapidly, prices tend to _____.

3 Most of the money in circulation is issued by _____.

4 A dealer in the over-the-counter market for securities will buy at a

_____ price than the price at which he sells.

5 All banks that are members of the _____ are required

to join the Federal Deposit Insurance Corporation.

6 The Federal Reserve banks are owned by _____.

7 Stocks of most of the larger corporations are listed for trading on the

_____.

8 _____ are savings institutions organized to serve people

having a common bond, such as membership in a labor union or club.

9 The SIPC does not insure a brokerage customer's account from losses resulting

from _____.

10 Dealing in futures permits a company to reduce the risk of future price changes

by means of _____.

11 The FHA does not _____ money to home buyers. It

insures _____ against loss resulting from defaults on

home mortgage loans.

12 The International Monetary Fund was established to help maintain stable

_____ among nations.

13 The International Finance Corporation invests only in

_____.

14 The maximum length of time for a business loan (not a disaster loan) extended

by the Small Business Administration is _____ years.

15 The _____ was created for the purpose of promoting

the international movement of long-term funds.

TRUE OR FALSE STATEMENTS

1 Most investors buy and sell corporation securities through brokerage houses.

2 The New York Stock Exchange is a corporation owned by its members.

Name   Section   Date

3 A dealer in the over-the-counter securities market stands ready to buy and sell securities but does not maintain an inventory of the securities he deals in.

4 Prior to the Federal Reserve System the United States had no central banking system.

5 Although most national banks are members of the Federal Reserve System, a few national banks are not members.

6 Checking accounts represent the kind of money we use in terms of dollars for most of our business payments.

7 Member banks can borrow from the Federal Reserve banks.

8 Most of the hand-to-hand cash in circulation in the United States is Federal Reserve Notes.

9 There are 12 central banks in the United States.

10 The Board of Governors of the Federal Reserve System has power to change the number of Federal Reserve districts.

11 The Federal Reserve banks are owned by the federal government.

12 The Board of Governors is composed of seven men elected by the member banks.

13 The Federal Deposit Insurance Corporation was created during the depression of the 1930s.

14 If an insured bank fails, each depositor is paid $20,000 by the FDIC.

15 The FDIC insures deposits in banks, savings and loan associations, and some credit unions.

16 All commercial banks are required to belong to the FDIC.

17 The Chicago Board of Trade is a commodity market.

18 The Federal Housing Administration makes loans to home buyers.

19 Loans extended by private lending agencies are sometimes guaranteed by the Export-Import Bank.

20 The World Bank derives some of the funds it lends from the sale of its own bonds to investors.

EXERCISES

1 Make a list of the features you observe comparing the major savings institutions in your area with respect to the following:

	Bank	Savings and Loan Association	Credit Union	Other
Minimum deposit				
Interest credited per annum				
Conditions that must be met to receive full interest				

	Bank	Savings and Loan Association	Credit Union	Other
Restrictions, if any, on withdrawals				
Deposit insurance, if any				
Special services, if any, provided to depositors				

2 If a stock exchange or commodity exchange is near your community, visit it. Prepare a report describing your visit and outlining the operations of the exchange. If it is not possible to visit an exchange, prepare a report on the operations of an exchange by getting information from the library and by writing the New York Stock Exchange or other exchange.

3 List the financial institutions discussed in this chapter. What types of loans, if any, are available from each? Are all businesses eligible for loans from each institution? If not, which are? What is the purpose for which each institution exists?

Name	Section	Date

Financial Institution	Types of Loans Available	Types of Businesses Eligible for Loans	Purpose of Existence

CHAPTER

27 RISK MANAGEMENT

There are risks of all kinds in life, and particularly in business. Some of these risks cannot be covered by insurance; many, however, can. These insurable risks, and the many different kinds of insurance available to cover them, are discussed in this chapter. Be sure you understand that the principle of insurance is not merely the shifting of risks from the businessman to the insurance company. Rather, it is reduction of total risk, since bringing together a large number of individual risks permits an insurance company to predict with reasonable accuracy the degree of risk in the aggregate of all of the individual risks.

The descriptions of the major types of insurance are intended to give you a broad picture of the variety of insurance available. If you are interested in more detailed information about any of these types of insurance, a textbook devoted to insurance or library reading will give you the information you need.

Today Marvin Miller's house burned down, Robert Fong was killed in a traffic accident, and Jorge Miranda was injured at his factory job. The above names are fictitious, but the occurrences are real. They happen every day. We live in a world full of hazards, and we do not know when or where misfortune will strike. Risk is part of our existence. We cannot eliminate it, but we can reduce it, and we can to some extent shift it to others.

In addition to the physical dangers to which everybody is exposed in varying degree, businessmen are exposed to the risks inherent in a business economy. It is the purpose of this chapter to study these risks and to investigate the means by which businessmen meet them.

TYPES OF BUSINESS RISKS

Business risks may be classified in a number of different ways. The following list does not include every hazard of doing business, but it does include the more common ones: economic risks, property risks, risk of death, risk of employee dishonesty, risk of injury to the public, risk of injury to employees, and credit and title risks.

ECONOMIC RISKS   Some of the risks of doing business are the result of actions of competitors or of the economic forces affecting the economy as a whole. In either case, the individual businessman has little control over such developments. As stated in this book, ours is a dynamic economy, an economy of change. Change brings with it risks. Some examples of economic risks are the following:

Change in
Consumer Demand   Consumer demand changes rapidly in some fields, such as style goods. In other areas, it changes more slowly. In any case, the direction of change is largely unpredictable.

Replacement of Old
Products by New
Developments   The amount of funds committed by a business to a particular product may be very large. At any time, this investment might be endangered by the introduction of a new product by a competitor.

Changes in the Price
Level   Prices do not change uniformly. The risk to the businessman in price changes is that the prices he pays may rise more rapidly than the prices he receives. When this happens, profits are reduced or eliminated.

Changes in Production
and Marketing   The discovery by a company of a more efficient method of manufacture or a more profitable means of distribution can take business away from competitors. In an industry where competition is intense, this risk can be great.

PROPERTY RISKS   Property is always subject to damage or deterioration. Buildings may burn down or be injured by lightning, flood, earthquake, or wind. Trucks may be involved in collisions. Inventory may deteriorate. Goods may be damaged in transit.

RISK OF DEATH   Death is a certainty. The uncertainty is in the timing, and therein lies the risk. From a business point of view, this risk involves the untimely death of a key executive. The injury to a business from such a death is great in the case of small businesses where the judgment of one man may be a vital factor in the success of the enterprise.

Employees are exposed to temptations that a few are unable to resist. Losses from employee dishonesty range from a few dollars to hundreds of thousands of dollars in exceptional cases.

RISK OF EMPLOYEE DISHONESTY

A customer in a store may fall on a staircase or get his hand caught in a door. A visitor to a factory may hit his head on an overhead pipe. The wiring in an electrical appliance may be faulty, causing severe shock to the purchaser. These and many other accidents may result in costly damage suits against a company.

RISK OF INJURY TO THE PUBLIC

The health of employees while at work is the responsibility of employers. The employer is liable even for injuries where the primary cause is the carelessness of the employee.

RISK OF INJURY TO EMPLOYEES

One risk in the purchase of real estate is that the title received may be defective, and the defect may not be discovered until long after the purchase. The extension of credit to customers also involves risk, the risk of nonpayment for goods delivered or services rendered.

CREDIT AND TITLE RISKS

Some of the risks a businessman faces can be easily handled. Others, such as a change in consumer demand, defy attempts at control. Wherever possible, effective management requires that a businessman analyze his risks and control those that can be controlled. This can be done by hedging, self-insurance, removal or reduction of hazards, and buying insurance.

HANDLING RISKS

The principle of hedging was discussed in connection with commodity markets in Chapter 26.

Hedging

If a company owns many trucks, it may decide to act as its own insurance company. Rather than paying premiums to an outside insurance agency, the premiums can be paid into a fund owned by the company. When a claim involving one of the trucks must be paid, it is paid out of the fund. Obviously, this can be done only where the number of units insured is large enough to spread the risk. A railroad owning a large number of cars or a grocery chain owning a large number of retail stores can use self-insurance effectively. If risks cannot be spread over a large number of units, a company may establish a *reserve for contingencies*. This is not, however, self-insurance.

Self-Insurance

Removal or Reduction of Hazards

Good management can eliminate or reduce many risks. Machinery can be shielded and adequate railings can be put on stairs. Buildings can be designed to prevent crowding of equipment and to provide plenty of light. Truck tires and brakes can be inspected regularly. Safety education can be instituted in the plant. Protective clothing can be required for employees while on hazardous jobs. Fire extinguishers can be placed in strategic locations and a sprinkler system can be installed to reduce the hazard of fire. These and many other things can be done to reduce risks. Even where insurance covers some of these risks, it is good management to reduce risks in the plant, office, and store. Insurance rates are dependent on the number of claims and the size of each claim. Anything that contributes to reduction of insurance claims helps to reduce the costs of insurance.

Buying Insurance

Insurance is a device by which one party (the insurance company, or *insurer*) collects payments (premiums) from another party (the *insured* or *policyholder*), in return for which the insurer compensates the insured for designated losses up to a stated maximum. The purchase of an insurance policy permits a company to shift a risk to the insurance company, the service for which the premium is charged. Many types of risk can be insured. Since this is one of the most important means of handling risks, most of this chapter is concerned with insurance.

DEVELOPMENT OF INSURANCE

An insurance company is frequently called a *carrier* because it bears the burden of risk of those persons or companies it insures. The person or company insured pays a small amount (the *premium*) periodically. The receipt of premiums from many persons and companies furnishes the funds out of which the insurance company is able to pay the losses suffered by the insured. Starting from humble beginnings, insurance has become one of the largest industries in the world.

THE INSURANCE PRINCIPLE

Many events that are individually uncertain are predictable in large numbers. A person can predict only with 50 percent accuracy the toss of a coin. But he can predict with a much higher degree of accuracy the number of heads and tails from 1,000 tosses of a coin. An insurance company cannot predict the year a thirty-year-old person will die, but it can predict with reasonable accuracy how many thirty-year-old persons out of 100,000 will die this year, the next year, and so on, until all are dead. Thus, whenever the number of similar events (tosses of a coin, or deaths) under study is increased, the accuracy of prediction is increased. This phenomenon is called the *law of large numbers* or the *law of averages*. Using large numbers, statisticians (called *actuaries*) for life insurance companies can predict accurately the life expectancy of various age groups, and so can determine the premium that should be charged at each age level to cover the risk of death.

Large numbers are used in fire insurance, collision insurance, and other types of insurance as well, but prediction cannot be made with as high a degree of accuracy as in life insurance. Nevertheless, prediction is sufficiently high to permit premiums to be set with reasonable confidence that they will cover losses. In some types of coverage, the insurance principle can hardly be applied at all since there are not sufficient cases in the group on which to base a prediction. "Insuring" a famous dancer's legs, a violinist's hands, or a comedian's voice cannot be done on the insurance principle. There are so few famous dancers, violinists, and comedians that no one, not even a statistician for an insurance company, can do more than guess when an injury to such a person will occur and what the amount of the injury will be.

In spite of the unpredictability of certain types of hazard, coverage can be bought for almost any type of risk.[1] One of the most interesting types of coverage is weather insurance. If rain would cause loss to the promoter of an outdoor event, such as a fair, the payment of a premium to an insurance company would compensate the promoter in money for part of the loss suffered.

THE ORIGIN OF INSURANCE

The origin of insurance is found in the attempts to cover the hazards of shipping. The spreading of risks of loss of cargo at sea by contributions from many merchants was undertaken by the Greeks before the Christian Era. When shipping on the Mediterranean recovered from the downfall of the Roman Empire, the roots of modern insurance were established in Italy. For a premium paid in advance, a shipowner received a contract under which he could collect a stated sum of money in case his ship was lost at sea. Such a contract was called a *polizia*, from which our modern word "policy" is derived. The contract was generally signed by a number of persons, each one specifying the amount of risk he was assuming under the contract. In England, such persons came to be known as *underwriters*, a term still used today. From Italy, the practice of insurance spread to the northern coast of Europe, during the fourteenth century. In the sixteenth century, it was introduced into England.

TYPES OF INSURANCE COMPANIES

Although insurance companies are organized in a number of different forms, there are two types that are dominant in the United States. These are: the *stock company* and the *mutual company*.

The Stock Company

A stock company is a corporation owned by stockholders who are not necessarily policyholders of the corporation. It is organized for profit. The board of directors is elected by the stockholders. If losses are higher than expected, the stock company

---

[1] Lloyds of London has insured such risks as the outbreak of war and the results of elections.

does not assess the policy holders, but puts the burden on the stockholders. On the other hand, stock companies sometimes share profits with the policyholders, who participate with the stockholders in dividends when earnings are good. This has been largely the result of competition from mutual insurance companies. The companies are known as *participating stock companies*, and the policies issued are called participating policies.

The Mutual Company

The mutual company is dominant in life insurance in the United States. More than two-thirds of the life insurance in force is written by mutual companies. There are many life insurance companies, however, that are organized as stock companies. Although the number of stock companies exceeds the number of mutual companies in this field, the stock companies are mostly small and localized.

THE INSURANCE COMPANY

Every insurance policy covers a specified risk. The risk must be an occurrence which would cause loss to the person holding the policy. This is the principle of *insurable interest*. A man has an insurable interest in his own life or in that of his wife, children, or business partners. He does not have an insurable interest in any person not associated with him through family or business, since the death or injury of such a person would not be considered a loss to him. A man does not have an insurable interest in property, the damage to which will not cause him any loss. If a man is discovered to have taken insurance where he did not have an insurable interest, the laws of some states declare the insurance contract void.

An insurance policy generally contains the following information:

The identity of the person insured or a description of the property insured
A definition of the kinds of risk covered and a statement of the risks not covered
The amount of the premium
The basis of payment of the premium
The amount of insurance
The method by which claims are paid

In addition, a policy may contain clauses relating to special characteristics associated with particular types of insurance. A common clause found in automobile insurance covering collisions is the deductible clause. This states that the first $50, for example, of the damage suffered by an insured car in a collision will be paid by the owner, with the insurance company paying any amount of damage in excess of that sum. The deductible clause is also found in health insurance and other types of coverage. A clause often found in fire insurance is the coinsurance clause. Since most fires do not destroy buildings completely, owners are often tempted to reduce the cost of insurance by carrying a policy for less than the value of the building. To counter this, insurance companies include the coinsurance clause, which, in its simplest form, states that if a building is insured for substantially less than its value, the owner must bear part of the loss of a fire. For example, if a company requires that an owner carry insurance of at least 90 percent of the value of his house, this transaction may result after fire damage:

Appraised value of house	$30,000
Insurance of 90 percent of appraised value required	27,000
Insurance carried by owner	21,000
Therefore, company is liable for 21/27 of any damage, or 78 percent, but not to exceed $21,000	
Fire damage	20,000
Company pays 78 percent of damage	15,600
Owner pays	4,400

LIFE INSURANCE

As we have stated before, death is a certainty; the only uncertainty is the time. Some of us will live to be 70 or 80, while others will die before reaching retirement age. If a man dies prematurely, his death may mean hardship for his widow and children, who depend on his income for their livelihood. His death may also mean hardship for his business associates, who depended on his judgment, knowledge, and skill. Life insurance protects the widow and children by substituting payments from the insurance company for the salary payments they would have received had the man lived. Insurance also protects a man's business associates by making a payment (usually in a lump sum) to cover the estimated damage to the company from the man's death.

CHARACTER OF LIFE INSURANCE

In life insurance, one is not guarding a loss that can be partial, as in the case of fire insurance. Death is total, and payment is made in the full amount of the policy. Another distinguishing characteristic of life insurance is in the amount of insurance that can be carried. If a house appraised at a value of $30,000 is destroyed, an insurance company cannot be held liable for more than that amount. But what is the value of a man's life? That can never be measured by an appraiser as can the value of a house. In general, a man can carry as much insurance on his life as he can pay for, and the insurance company will pay in full on his death. A person may take insurance of $175,000 on his life to cover a trip on an airplane. His regular insurance policy may be for only $10,000. If he should die as a result of an accident on the plane, his family would be paid $185,000 from the two policies. If he should die under other circumstances, his family would be paid only $10,000.

TYPES OF LIFE INSURANCE

The number of different types of life insurance is large, and new types are designed constantly. Only the more common types will be treated here.

Term

The least costly coverage can be obtained through term insurance. The insurance is payable if death occurs within the term stated in the policy. When the term expires, the policy is without value. Term insurance can be purchased for periods up to 20 years. It can also be purchased for a 5-year term, renewable at a higher premium for successive 5-year terms. Generally, the privilege of renewal stops at age 65.

Straight Life

Straight life, also known as ordinary life, is issued for the whole life of the insured, being payable at death. Premiums are paid throughout life. Unlike renewable term insurance, in which premiums are raised each time the policy is renewed, straight life provides a level premium throughout.

Three variations of straight life are: *single payment life, limited payment life*, and *joint life*. Single payment life provides a single premium payment. After the payment is made, no other payments are made on the policy. Limited payment life provides for 10, 15, 20, or some other number of annual payments. After the required payments have been made, the policy remains in force with no other payments required. A joint policy covers the lives of two or more persons, and matures on the first death in the group.

Group Life Insurance

A company may cover all of specified classes of its employees under a single contract. This is called group life insurance. The policy is generally a term policy. In some cases, the premiums are paid entirely by the company; in others, the cost is shared by employer and employee. Some plans cover each employee at the beginning of his employment, while others require a waiting period. Physical examinations may or may not be required, according to the policy. The amount of insurance provided generally varies according to the salary of the employee. Group life insurance is one of the attractions in addition to salary offered by companies, and its popularity has increased in recent years.

Industrial Life Insurance

Industrial life insurance is insurance designed for persons of limited means, such as unskilled workers in industry. Medical examination is usually not required. The premiums are collected weekly or monthly by the agent of the company. Straight life and endowment (explained below) are the two types of insurance most commonly written. The size of the policy is small, usually below $500.

Annuities do not insure the hazard of dying too soon but rather the hazard of living too long. In a strict sense, they are not insurance at all. No payment is made on the death of the annuitant (the person whose life is covered). The annuity provides retirement income of a certain number of dollars a month, beginning at the age specified in the contract and ending with the death of the annuitant.

Annuities

Two variations of the annuity should be mentioned. One is the *joint and survivor policy*. This policy provides retirement income during the life of the primary annuitant, usually the husband, and the same or a reduced monthly payment to the wife should she outlive her husband. The second variation is the *variable annuity*. This provides a monthly retirement income determined by the income the company earns on its investments. The investments in this case are mostly common stocks of large, well-known corporations, and the dividends received from them determine the amount paid monthly to the annuitants. The variable annuity represents an attempt to provide retirement income that rises with the cost of living, a point on which regular annuities are vulnerable. The theory of the variable annuity is that the income from common stocks varies with the price level, rising and falling as the price level rises and falls. Therefore, while the number of dollars received each month by the annuitant varies, the purchasing power of the monthly payment remains fairly constant.

Endowment is a combination policy. It combines life insurance and investment in one contract. There are many forms in which an endowment policy can be written. Two examples will be given for illustration. A father may want to ensure that his son will receive a college education. He can take out a 20-year endowment policy for $20,000 at the birth of his son. If the father should die before 20 years are over, the policy would be paid on his death. Otherwise, the $20,000 would be paid at the end of 20 years. If a man wishes to provide for his retirement at age 65, he can, at age 35, take a 30-year endowment policy for $50,000. If he should die before he reaches 65, the beneficiary named in the policy will be paid $50,000. When the man reaches 65, he will be paid according to the terms of the policy. The terms chosen by the policyholder might call for a lump sum payment at 65 of $50,000, or they might call for a monthly payment of a stated amount from age 65 until death.

Endowment

Life insurance is based on averages, as are other forms of insurance. While prediction of the life expectancy of an individual cannot be made with accuracy, the prediction of the life expectancy of a large number of individuals can. Since life insurance companies insure large numbers of persons, they can determine the amount of premium to charge to individuals of various ages, because they know how many persons out of 100,000 will die each year. This information is derived from a mortality table, which indicates the number of persons expected to die

LIFE EXPECTANCY

each year. This number is based on records of deaths in the past for large numbers of persons. It is usually expressed in terms of 100,000, 1 million, or other round number. Beginning at age 0 (birth), it states how many persons will die each year. Part of a mortality table is shown in Table 27-1.

FIRE INSURANCE

A fire insurance policy indemnifies (pays for loss or damage) the insured (the policyholder) for the actual amount of loss, up to the full amount of the policy,[2] in the event of damage to insured property by fire or lightning. Fire insurance contracts commonly include an endorsement covering damage from tornado, hurricane, or other wind; damage by aircraft, automobile, or other vehicle; and damage from hail, riot, or explosion. Policies are written for periods of 1 to 5 years.

A fire insurance contract generally contains a description of the building or buildings included in the coverage, the kind of damage covered, the causes of damage covered (fire, wind, etc.), how the extent of damage will be appraised, and the responsibilities of the policyholder in the event of damage. Fire insurance contracts may be canceled before expiration either by the insurance company or by the policyholder. In either case, the insurance company refunds a portion of the premium paid. The rates of insurance vary according to the degree of risk estimated by the insurance company. Fireproof materials (brick, concrete, asbestos siding) will reduce the premium. If fire-fighting facilities are close and efficient, the rates will be less than for a building with obsolete fire-fighting equipment or where a building is far from fire-fighting services. The installation of an automatic sprinkler system will reduce insurance rates. If the record of fires has been bad in a locality, the rates will be increased. If the record has been good, the rates will decline.

A fire insurance policy covers only losses directly caused by the fire. Those losses that are incidental, even though they may be large in amount, are not covered. For example, the loss covered by a fire insurance policy on a factory building will cover only the immediate damage by fire and will not cover the loss of income to the company because the factory is idle. For such a loss, however, insurance can be had. It is called *business interruption insurance*, and covers the loss of income from the interruption of business operations resulting from any cause stated in the contract.

AUTOMOBILE AND TRUCK INSURANCE

In Massachusetts and New York, automobile insurance is required before the owner may register his car. Several other states require insurance or evidence of financial responsibility from those persons involved in automobile accidents where injury to persons or property has occurred. Even where legal compulsion is absent, responsible citizens carry insurance on their vehicles.

---

[2]Unless there is a coinsurance clause. This clause was explained earlier in this chapter.

TABLE 27-1 MORTALITY TABLE

Age	Combined or Actuaries' Experience	Annuity Table for 1949— Male	Annuity Table for 1949— Female	Age	Combined or Actuaries' Experience	Annuity Table for 1949— Male	Annuity Table for 1949— Female
	Expectation of Life Years	Expectation of Life Years	Expectation of Life Years		Expectation of Life Years	Expectation of Life Years	Expectation of Life Years
0	41.30	73.18	78.69	50	20.18	26.23	30.81
1	47.76	72.48	77.94	51	19.50	25.40	29.91
2	49.97	71.59	77.05	52	18.82	24.58	29.01
3	50.79	70.65	76.10	53	18.16	23.78	28.11
4	51.02	69.70	75.14	54	17.50	22.99	27.22
5	50.93	68.75	74.17	55	16.86	22.20	26.33
6	50.62	67.78	73.19	56	16.22	21.44	25.46
7	50.17	66.82	72.21	57	15.59	20.68	24.59
8	49.63	65.85	71.23	58	14.97	19.93	23.72
9	49.01	64.89	70.25	59	14.37	19.20	22.87
10	48.39	63.92	69.26	60	13.77	18.48	22.02
11	47.68	62.95	68.27	61	13.18	17.76	21.18
12	47.01	61.98	67.29	62	12.61	17.06	20.36
13	46.33	61.01	66.30	63	12.05	16.37	19.54
14	45.64	60.04	65.32	64	11.51	15.68	18.73
15	44.96	59.07	64.33	65	10.97	15.01	17.94
16	44.27	58.10	63.35	66	10.46	14.36	17.16
17	43.58	57.13	62.37	67	9.96	13.71	16.39
18	42.88	56.17	61.39	68	9.47	13.08	15.64
19	42.19	55.20	60.41	69	9.00	12.46	14.90
20	41.49	54.23	59.43	70	8.54	11.86	14.18
21	40.79	53.27	58.45	71	8.10	11.28	13.47
22	40.09	52.30	57.48	72	7.67	10.71	12.78
23	39.39	51.33	56.50	73	7.26	10.15	12.11
24	38.68	50.37	55.53	74	6.86	9.61	11.45
25	37.98	49.41	54.55	75	6.48	9.09	10.82
26	37.27	48.44	53.58	76	6.11	8.58	10.20
27	36.56	47.48	52.61	77	5.76	8.10	9.60
28	35.86	46.52	51.64	78	5.42	7.63	9.02
29	35.15	45.56	50.67	79	5.09	7.17	8.47
30	34.43	44.61	49.70	80	4.78	6.74	7.93
31	33.72	43.65	48.73	81	4.48	6.32	7.42
32	33.01	42.70	47.77	82	4.18	5.92	6.93
33	32.30	41.75	46.80	83	3.90	5.54	6.46
34	31.58	40.80	45.84	84	3.63	5.18	6.01
35	30.87	39.85	44.88	85	3.36	4.84	5.58
36	30.15	38.90	43.92	86	3.10	4.51	5.18
37	29.44	37.96	42.97	87	2.84	4.20	4.79
38	28.72	37.02	42.01	88	2.59	3.90	4.43
39	28.00	36.08	41.06	89	2.35	3.62	4.09
40	27.28	35.15	40.11	90	2.11	3.36	3.77
41	26.56	34.22	39.17	91	1.89	3.12	3.47
42	25.84	33.30	38.22	92	1.67	2.88	3.19
43	25.12	32.38	37.28	93	1.47	2.67	2.92
44	24.40	31.47	36.35	94	1.28	2.47	2.68
45	23.69	30.57	35.41	95	1.12	2.28	2.45
46	22.97	29.68	34.48	96	.99	2.10	2.24
47	22.27	28.80	33.56	97	.89	1.94	2.05
48	21.56	27.93	32.64	98	.75	1.79	1.87
49	20.87	27.07	31.72	99	.50	1.65	1.71

Source: Institute of Life Insurance.

The types of risk covered by an automobile policy include fire, theft, collision, injury to the property of others or to other persons in a collision, and injury to persons riding in the insured vehicle.

FIRE AND THEFT   Originally, a policy covering this risk was limited to fire and theft of the car alone. Now most policies cover comprehensive risks, such as hail, windstorms, riot, theft of articles from a locked car, damage to glass from flying stones, flood, and lightning. Where damage to the car is sustained, the insurance covers the value of the car at the time of damage, not the value at the time the insurance was purchased.

COLLISION   This insurance pays for damage to the insured car resulting from collision with either a moving vehicle or a stationary object. The insurance company can choose any of three settlements:

> Replacing the automobile and its equipment
> Repairing the vehicle
> Paying the policyholder an amount equal to the damage

Because such a large number of collisions are minor, involving scraped fenders and dented bumpers, the cost of collision coverage for total damage is high. Most persons prefer to pay lower premiums by excluding minor damage from coverage. This is accomplished through the use of the deductible clause, which was explained earlier. The amount of deductible damage varies according to the contract; the larger the deductible amount, the lower the premium. For example, if a person has a collision contract with a $50 deductible clause and suffers collision damage amounting to $87.60, the policyholder pays $50 and the insurance company $37.60.

LIABILITY   Liability insurance is of two types: *bodily injury liability* and *property damage liability*. The first type covers injury caused by the car of the insured to pedestrians or persons in other vehicles. The second covers damage to other cars or property caused by the car of the insured. Bodily injury liability is usually stated as $5,000/$10,000, $20,000/$40,000, or some other pair of amounts. The first amount is the maximum the company will pay for the injury or death of one person. The second amount is the maximum the company will pay for death or injury in one accident. Property damage liability is stated in one amount, such as a maximum of $5,000.

If the insured or any occupant of the car driven by him is injured, medical payment insurance covers the hospital and physicians' fees up to the maximum amount stated in the policy.

MEDICAL PAYMENT INSURANCE

The oldest type of insurance is marine insurance. Originally, it covered loss of vessel and cargo at sea, but gradually the term has come to include insurance of other types of transportation as well, including transportation on land. Coverage at sea is now called *ocean marine insurance*, while coverage on land is known by the somewhat contradictory term *inland marine insurance*.

MARINE INSURANCE

Ocean marine contracts cover all sorts of hazards to the vessel and cargo while at sea and in port. There is very little standardization of rates or coverage. Each contract is custom-made. Some policies cover indemnity for earnings lost to the owner if his vessel is damaged or lost. A policy may be written for a single voyage, covering hazards between port of origin and port of designation, or for a period of time, such as 1 year. In the latter case, the vessel is generally covered regardless where it sails. Some policies cover a number of vessels.

OCEAN MARINE INSURANCE

Inland marine insurance includes coverage of all forms of transportation over land, in the air, and on rivers, lakes and canals, and along the coast. The hazards covered are fire, wind, lightning, hail, theft, collision, and flood. Both the vehicle and the goods carried can be covered.

One variation of inland marine policy is called the *personal property floater*. This policy covers the household goods and personal effects of the insured while in the home or away from home, whether in transit or not.

INLAND MARINE INSURANCE

A casualty is any unfortunate occurrence. Traditionally, casualty insurance has meant all forms of insurance other than life, marine, or fire. We have discussed one type of casualty coverage under automobile insurance. In this section, we shall discuss a few of the many other forms.

CASUALTY INSURANCE

This is available both to the home owner and to the businessman. It usually does not cover theft by customers or employees, since most policies specify that there must be evidence of breaking and entering.

BURGLARY INSURANCE

LIABILITY INSURANCE   Liability insurance protects the insured from damage suits resulting from injury to others caused by negligence of the insured or one of his employees. This insurance protects a golfer from a damage suit arising from his hitting a person with a golf ball. It protects a home owner from a damage suit arising from a person being bitten by a pet dog, or from a guest falling down the stairs. It protects the business-man from a suit arising from injury to a customer in his store. A specialized form of liability coverage is the **product liability policy**. This covers the manufacturer in the event of injury to property or person where the product is to blame. Another special form is **malpractice insurance**. This covers suits against physicians charged with incompetence and negligence.

WORKMEN'S COMPENSATION INSURANCE   All states have workmen's compensation laws which require an employer either to have insurance or financial responsibility to cover the cost of injuries to his employees. Farm laborers are conspicuously exempted, as are domestic workers and workers for employers having less than a certain number of employees.

The states differ in the extent of coverage, but the following are required to be covered in most states: accidental death, temporary or permanent disability, and disease caused by work done for the employer. The payments are made according to the requirement of the law. Payment covers hospital and physician's charges and loss of income, and may be paid in a single payment or over a period of time. Where loss of income is provided for, the amount paid is generally one-half or two-thirds of the income of the injured person.

ACCIDENT AND MEDICAL INSURANCE   An accident policy is taken out by a person for his own protection. If he falls off a ladder at home, the policy will cover his medical bills and loss of income. An accident policy is usually combined with a health policy, which indemnifies the insured for loss of income while ill.

Medical insurance covers the cost of hospital and physician's fees. Policies either have a deductible clause or are scheduled. Where the deductible clause is used, the first $50 (or some other figure) of each illness is paid by the insured, the balance being paid by the insurance company up to the stated maximum. If the policy is scheduled, a list of payments is stated in the contract, giving the maximum payment the company will make for hospital room, tonsillectomy, blood trans-fusion, or special treatment. In most cases, the insured is indemnified only if the medical service is rendered in a hospital. This has resulted in persons seeking hospital admission in cases where they might be as well off at home. Medical insur-ance covers only a part—usually a small part—of the total cost of health to the individual. If the policy is scheduled, the insurance rarely covers the total cost of the physician's fees or the hospital bill.[3]

[3]Physician's fees are usually based on ability to pay. There has been some evidence that a num-ber of physicians have considered medical insurance as indications of increased ability to pay, and have raised their fees to insured patients accordingly.

There are many specialized casualty policies available. Some examples are boiler insurance, elevator insurance, and plate-glass insurance.

MISCELLANEOUS FORMS

Fidelity and surety bonds guarantee the reliability of persons. If the person who buys the bond suffers a loss as a result of an action covered by the bond, he can recover payment from the bonding company.

FIDELITY AND SURETY BONDS

The fidelity bond is most commonly used to protect an employer form the dishonesty of an employee. It can cover a single employee or several, provided that all employees covered are listed in the bond. Bonds can also be bought that list the titles of positions in a company rather than the names of employees. In such a case, the bond covers whatever person holds the position. Bonds are usually used to cover employees who handle money for a company. If a bonded employee steals money or property from his employer, the bonding company pays the employer the amount of the theft, up to the maximum amount of the bond. The bonding company may then attempt to locate the employee and collect from him.

FIDELITY BOND

A surety bond indemnifies a person or company for loss caused by nonperformance under a contract. A corporation contracting for the erection of a factory building might require the contractor to furnish a surety bond indemnifying the corporation if the building is not built to specifications and completed within the time limit of the contract.

SURETY BOND

Title insurance protects the purchaser of real estate from losses due to any defects in the title to the property. With title insurance, the purchaser finds it unnecessary to hire a lawyer to make an exhaustive search through the records of previous ownership to determine the possibility that anyone might claim the property as rightfully his. Title companies have lawyers on their staffs who specialize in making title searches. The insurance may protect the person for a stated period, such as 20 years, or may protect the purchaser until he resells the property. If the protection is for a stated number of years, the sale of the property before the expiration of the period of years ends the insurance.

TITLE INSURANCE

Credit insurance protects a businessman from losses through the default on debts owed by the customers. Although policies can be purchased that cover losses from unpaid debts, the premium is high. In order to keep the premium down, the

CREDIT INSURANCE

insurance usually is restricted to losses in excess of normal credit losses. The insurance contract will define normal losses, and pay whatever extra losses are suffered by the company during the year.

SUMMARY

Insecurity is an integral part of business life. There are different kinds of uncertainties that must be faced: economic, property damage, death, dishonesty, injury to employees and customers, and nonpayment of debts owed to the company. Any of these occurrences can damage a company. But risks may be lessened by avoiding those dangers that can be avoided, such as providing safety measures where possible. Those risks that cannot be avoided can be offset by insurance. There are many types of insurance policies, each suited for a particular need. An understanding of the principle of insurance and of the types of policies available to businessmen enable them to shift insurable risks to insurance companies. This permits a businessman to concentrate on the problems of pricing, product and service improvement, competition, and general business conditions. It is in these problems that sound, considered business judgment is required, since insurance is not feasible to cover such uncertainties.

QUESTIONS FOR REVIEW

1 Give some examples of economic risks that business faces. Can any of them be reduced by insurance? Why or why not?

2 Can self-insurance as a means of reducing business risks be used by all types of businesses? Explain.

3 Define insurance. Why is an insurance company often called a carrier?

4 What is meant by the law of large numbers? Of what benefit is it to insurance companies?

5 Distinguish between a stock company and a mutual company in the field of insurance.

6 Illustrate by means of examples the meaning of insurable interest.

7 What are the general features found in an insurance policy?

8 How can life insurance be used to reduce business risks?

9 What is the least costly type of life insurance? What do the more expensive types of life insurance offer to offset their greater cost?

10 What is an annuity? A variable annuity? What types of uncertainty are they designed to cover?

11 If fire insurance is carried on a building and its contents, is there any inducement to management in reducing fire hazards in the building? Explain.

12 What types of risk does business interruption insurance cover?

13 Name the types of risks found in various automobile insurance policies.

14 How does casualty insurance help reduce business risks?

15 Explain the purpose of product liability insurance and malpractice insurance.

Bickelhaupt, David L., and John H. Magee: *General Insurance*, Richard D. Irwin, Inc., Homewood, Ill., 1970.

Gregg, Davis W., and Vane B. Lucas: *Life and Health Insurance Handbook*, 3d ed., Richard D. Irwin, Inc., Homewood, Ill., 1973.

Mehr, Robert I., and Emerson Cammack: *Principles of Insurance*, 5th ed., Richard D. Irwin, Inc., Homewood, Ill., 1972.

Williams, C. Arthur, Jr., and Richard M. Heins: *Risk Management and Insurance*, McGraw-Hill Book Company, New York, 1971.

SELECTED READINGS

Name   Section   Date

COMPLETION SENTENCES

1 The purchase of an insurance policy permits a company to shift a risk to

_____ .

2 Self-insurance is feasible for a company if it has a _____

number of similar risks.

3 It is good management to reduce risks even though they are covered by insur-

ance, because this reduces the cost of _____ .

4 Losses resulting from actions of competitors or from forces affecting the

economy as a whole are called _____ .

5 Whenever the number of similar events studied is increased, the accuracy of

_____ is increased.

6 Two types of insurance company are dominant in the United States: the _____ company and the _____ company.

7 In _____ insurance the loss is not a partial one, and payment of claims is for the _____ of the policy.

8 _____ does not insure the hazard of dying too soon but rather the hazard of living too long.

9 An endowment policy combines _____ and _____ in one contract.

10 If a man carries $50,000 of fire insurance on his house, which has an appraised value of $35,000, and the house is destroyed by fire, the maximum amount for which the insurance company is liable is $ _____ .

11 The oldest type of insurance is _____ insurance.

12 _____ insurance covers suits against physicians and other professionals charged with incompetence and negligence.

13 An indemnity bond indemnifies a person or company for loss caused by _____ of persons.

14 Title insurance protects the purchaser of _____ from losses due to defects in the title.

15 _____ insurance protects a businessman from losses through the default on debts owed by customers.

Name   Section   Date

TRUE OR FALSE STATEMENTS

1 The average individual businessman has little control over the economic risks he faces.

2 Death is a certainty; therefore, it is not a risk.

3 Establishing a reserve for contingencies is the application of the principle of self-insurance.

4 A person can predict with a higher degree of accuracy the outcome of 1,000 tosses of a coin than he can predict 50 tosses.

5 The life expectancy of groups of persons at various age periods can be predicted with only the same degree of accuracy as that of one person following careful physical examination.

6 One cannot apply the principle of insurance to cover injury to a violinist's hands or to a comedian's voice, so insurance for this type of hazard is unavailable.

7 Historically, the earliest insurance was life insurance.

8 Although mutual life insurance companies are found in the United States, most life insurance is sold by stock companies.

9 To be collectible an insurance policy must cover an occurrence that would cause loss to the policyholder.

10 A deductible clause exempts the first $50 (or other amount named) of loss from payment by the insurance company.

11 Fire insurance does not cover loss of income for a business resulting from a fire. For this (loss of income) a businessman can get business interruption insurance.

12 In general a person can buy as much life insurance as he can pay for, and the insurance companies will pay the full amount of the policies on his death.

13 When term life insurance expires, the policy can be renewed, if done promptly, at the same premium payment as before.

14 In a joint life policy the policy matures on the last death of the persons named in the policy.

15 Group life insurance covers a number of persons, for example, the employees of a firm, under a single policy.

16 Industrial life insurance covers the lives of employees but is paid for by the employer.

17 An annuity covers the "hazard" of living too long.

18 A fidelity bond is used most commonly to protect an employer from the dishonesty of an employee.

19 If a purchaser of real estate buys title insurance, it is still necessary for him to have a lawyer search the title to make sure it is valid.

20 Inland marine insurance covers risk of damage or loss of goods transported over land.

EXERCISES

1 The Regal Office Machine Company sells typewriters and other office equipment both in the United States and in foreign countries. Under the shipping arrangements used by Regal, the title to each shipment remains with Regal until it reaches the city in which the customer is located. Make a list of the risks associated with each shipment to a designation within the United States. Make a similar list for shipments sent across oceans. Who bears each of these risks? To what extent can each of these risks be covered by insurance?

2 Use the chart below to list the types of insurance available to businesses, the hazards for which the insurance provides protection, and the types of businesses that probably don't need such insurance.

Type of Insurance	Hazard Protected	Types of Businesses Not Needing Such Insurance

PART 8

BUSINESS
AND SOCIETY

The relationships between businessmen as a class and the rest of the citizens of a nation have been the subject of much attention from businessmen, labor leaders, economists, and many other groups. Nearly everybody is willing to express an opinion concerning the rights and responsibilities of businessmen. There is, however, little agreement as to what these rights and responsibilities should be.

During most of the last century, the prevailing attitude of people in the United States was one of giving businessmen a large measure of freedom of action. During the present century, the general attitude has been one of placing restraints on the conduct of business. During both centuries, businessmen have succeeded in securing government aid of a wide variety of types for themselves.

Every society of human beings has laws. Chapter 28 takes up the laws in the United States that are of particular importance to business. Chapter 29 discusses in broad outline the ways in which government, particularly the federal government, aids business and the ways in which government regulates business. The services of government must be paid for. The chief means of raising revenue for this purpose is taxes, although there are other sources of income for the government. Chapter 29 examines the taxes that are the concern of businessmen.

Chapter 30, the last chapter of the book, examines the position of the businessman in the society of which he is a part, a society which the businessman helped to create and which, in turn, has shaped the attitudes and actions of the businessman.

CHAPTER
28   BUSINESS LAW

You will not be able to remember all the laws and all the information contained in this chapter. You should consider the chapter as a compendium of some of the most common legal aspects of our business system, referring to it when necessary. As in other aspects of business life, you should be aware of the changing nature of laws, since law is not a static thing. It changes at a slow pace, steadily, slowly, through time.

Laws define the "rules of the game" in business transactions as they do in other areas of life. While a businessman does not need to be a lawyer, he does have to know law, and it is advisable for him to learn as much of the law concerning his particular occupation as he is able.

Law is an obligatory rule of action prescribed by the government. It identifies what is permissable conduct and prohibits what is defined as *wrong* conduct. The origin of law lies in the social habits or customs of the people. Those customs that become strong and remain fixed for generations become precedents, which act as guides or models of conduct. Gradually, some precedents become so strong that any deviation from them is regarded as undermining society and is prohibited. Precedent hardens into law.

OUR LEGAL SYSTEM   The system of laws developed in the English-speaking countries is derived from two main sources. They are *common law*, which is peculiar to Anglo-Saxon heritage, and *statute law*, which is found in all civilized nations.

COMMON LAW   Common law is a body of principles on which judges decide cases. These principles rest on custom rather than legislation. Because common law is built directly on custom, judges support their decisions by citing rulings of courts in similar cases in the past. These prior decisions are called *legal precedents*. In some cases, precedents dating to the twelfth century in England are used to prove the firmness of the custom. Although precedents are broken from time to time, judges are reluctant to do so. A precedent, once established, becomes stronger after each decision reaffirming it. The adherence to precedent is called *stare decisis*.

English common law was, naturally, incorporated into the judicial system of the colonies of Great Britain. After the American Revolution, the former colonies retained the English common law, adding to it and modifying it as the passage of time and changing conditions warranted. From these roots, each state has developed its own common law, following a roughly similar pattern but differing in particular areas. One exception is Louisiana. This state, with its French historical background, has a legal system founded on the French Civil Code.

STATUTE LAW

Prior to the seventeenth century, law in England was primarily custom. Social conditions, however, sometimes change rapidly. Custom changes very slowly. Where customs interfered with the changing needs and demands of the people, they sought their relief in legislation by Parliament. Law by legislation is *statute* or *written law*. The laws enacted by Parliament took precedence over the common law. By the time of the American Revolution, the precedence of statutes enacted by legislatures over common law had become well established. In other words, written law became superior to custom wherever there was conflict between the two.

The written law of the United States consists of the three types shown in the accompanying table.

Because of the lack until recently of uniformity among state laws, efforts were made to reduce the variation. Some success has been achieved in getting state legislatures to adopt uniform laws. The Uniform Negotiable Instrument Law and the Stock Transfer Act have been adopted by 50 states. Many, but not all, states have adopted the Uniform Partnership Act, the Bill of Lading Act, the Sales Act, and the Uniform Small Loan Law.

Federal Law
Constitution of the United States, the supreme law of the land
Treaties ratified by the United States Senate
Statutes enacted by Congress
Rules and regulations of federal regulatory bodies acting under the authority of statutes

State Law
State constitutions
Statutes enacted by state legislatures
Rules and regulations of state regulatory bodies acting under the authority of state statutes

Local Law
Corporation charters of municipalities, issued by the state
Municipal ordinances
Rules and regulations of local bodies acting under the authority of municipal charters

---

A significant step toward uniformity was taken in 1957 by the National Conference of Commissioners on Uniform State Laws and the American Law Institute in drafting the *Uniform Commercial Code (UCC)*, which simplified and brought up to date state laws governing business transactions. During the 1960s nearly all the states adopted the UCC. The UCC absorbed the more specialized uniform codes mentioned above and expanded into other areas of business as well. The scope of the UCC can be inferred from the fact that it is often referred to simply as "the Code." Among the many areas of business conduct that the UCC encompasses are stock transfers, bills of lading, trust receipts, warehouse receipts, warranties, sales transactions, and negotiable instruments. Unless otherwise indicated, the discussions in this chapter follow the UCC.

The volume of statute law has grown tremendously in the United States since the adoption of the Constitution. In deciding a case, the court will base its decision on written law if there is one that applies to the case; if not, the court will use the common law to guide the decision.

COURTS

There are two systems of courts in the United States, one established under the authority of the Federal Constitution and one established under state authority. The federal courts decide cases involving violations of federal laws and the Federal Constitution. The state courts hear all cases not involving any federal issue. Most of the disputes brought to court by persons or corporations are tried in state courts.

State Courts

The state courts may be classified into:

1 *Inferior courts:* These courts are known by a variety of names, such as municipal courts, police courts, and corporation courts.[1]
2 *Superior courts:* These courts have jurisdiction over a county. They might be called county courts, probate courts, land courts, or surrogate courts. While most cases tried by these courts originate with them, they do in some instances act as courts of appeal to hear cases originally tried in municipal courts.
3 *Courts of appeal:* Each state has courts of appeal. While these may be courts of original jurisdiction for certain cases, they confine most of their activity to hearing appeals from lower courts. They may be called district courts or circuit courts. All states have a state supreme court, which is the court of last resort for all cases not involving federal jurisdiction.

Federal Courts

For those cases involving federal jurisdiction, such as bankruptcy, patents, interstate commerce, and internal revenue, suit is brought in federal courts. The courts of original jurisdiction are the federal district courts. There are more than 80 of

---

[1] A municipal court is sometimes called a corporation court because the municipal government under which it operates receives its authority from the state in the form of a corporation charter.

these courts, each having jurisdiction over the area of a state or part of a state. The appellate courts are the United States Courts of Appeals, formerly known as Circuit Courts. The highest court of appeals is the Supreme Court. In addition to the district courts, there are special courts established by Congress to hear cases confined to a particular body of law. The jurisdiction of these courts is indicated by their name. They are the United States Court of Claims, United States Tax Court, United States Customs Court, and United States Court of Customs and Patent Appeals.[2]

The best way to settle a dispute is usually to keep it out of court. Court cases are costly; they involve delay, both before they are brought to trial and while they are being heard; and their outcome is uncertain. While disputes involving as little as 50 cents have been taken to court, and even appealed to higher courts, it is generally wiser to avoid recourse to litigation unless the issue is important in terms of principle or money. A number of devices exist to settle disputes outside of the courts. The dispute may be referred to a mutual friend for settlement. Disputes between labor unions and companies are often resolved by arbitration. Because of the legal risks involved in commercial dealings between persons living in different countries, contracts in international trade frequently specify that any dispute arising from the contract be settled by a person or agency named in the contract and that the decision shall be binding on both parties.

Initiation of a Court Case

Where an issue is taken to a court, the person initiating the suit is called the *plaintiff*. The person against whom the suit is brought is the *defendant*. The defendant is notified of the suit by an order called a *summons*. The summons states the name of the action, the name of the court, and the time and place of the hearing. A *complaint*, stating the nature of the dispute, is usually attached to the summons. The defendant is given a certain length of time to answer the complaint. He may deny the charges, deny any knowledge of the existence of the incident in question, or set forth the facts on which he intends to base his defense. If the defendent does not answer the complaint, the court usually awards judgment to the plaintiff by default.

If the defendent wishes to contest the case, he generally hires a lawyer for his defense. Often, before the case comes to trial, the lawyers representing the two contestants attempt to reach a settlement outside of court. This frequently takes place in suits involving damage claims. A company will often settle a claim by a customer for damages by agreeing to an out-of-court settlement, even where the customer's case is weak, simply to avoid unfavorable publicity.

Cases are tried either by a judge or by a jury. If a jury tries the case, the members of the jury, being ordinary people and not experts in the law, weigh the

---

[2] There have been suggestions from time to time for the establishment of additional specialized federal courts. In 1954, a bill was drafted to create a United States Bankruptcy Court, which would have complete jurisdiction over every phase of bankruptcy. This bill had the support of the National Bankruptcy Conference, an organization composed of lawyers and others concerned with bankruptcy proceedings. It did not, however, receive sufficient support for passage.

facts brought out in the trial, apply the law bearing on the case, and render a verdict. The judge presides in the courtroom, instructs the jury on matters of law, and makes specific legal rulings as needed in the conduct of the case. If both plaintiff and defendant waive a jury trial, the case is tried by the judge. Whichever party is the loser in a case may appeal the verdict to a court of appeals on the basis that an error of law was made in the lower court. The appellate court may affirm the decision, reverse it, return it to the lower court for retrial, or refuse to consider the case.

CONTRACTS A contract is an agreement between two or more parties. However, not all agreements are contracts. A contract is an agreement of a type that is enforceable by law. To meet this requirement, it must have the following elements: *mutual assent, capacity to contract, valid consideration, compliance with required form*, and *legality of object and purpose*.

A contract may be oral or written. Because of the greater possibility of misunderstanding when the agreement is oral, it is wise to put contracts in writing wherever possible.

MUTUAL ASSENT Mutual assent generally consists of an offer and an acceptance on terms agreed to by both parties. The first step in a contract is an *offer*. It may be made in a variety of ways. It may be conveyed by writing or by speaking. At an auction, it may be made by raising the hand, nodding the head, or holding up a numbered card.[3] The offer may be revoked at any time before acceptance; and if acceptance is not forthcoming within a reasonable period of time, the law considers that the offer has expired. Advertisements and announcements of prices are not offers; rather, they are considered to be invitations to the public to make an offer to buy.

When the person to whom the offer is given assents to all of the terms, an *acceptance* has been made. An acceptance may be made by any of the means of communication ordinarily used. The customs of the trade indicate what constitutes a valid acceptance. On the New York Stock Exchange, an offer to sell is accepted by a member saying "sold" or a similar term in a clearly audible voice. If an offer has been communicated by mail and does not specify the method of acceptance, acceptance is completed and the contract is born when the letter of acceptance is placed in the mailbox properly addressed and with sufficient postage. It may, of course, be difficult to establish the fact that an acceptance has been placed in the mails should a letter go astray. If that fact can be established, however, the person

---

[3] A friend of the author once attended a livestock auction as a spectator, not as a participant. To get the attention of an acquaintance seated below him, he waved his hand. This was unfortunate, since the auctioneer was calling for a higher bid at the moment. As a result, the friend found himself high bidder on a prize pig for which he had no possible use. The moral for those who attend auctions for amusement is obvious.

making the offer cannot seek to withdraw from the contract by stating that he did not receive the letter. For this reason, an offer transmitted by mail sometimes specifies that acceptance is not valid until the letter is received. The relationship of the main elements of a contract is sometimes expressed as follows:

Offer + acceptance = contract

A contract does not exist where one of the parties to the contract is not competent to make a binding contract. In general, drunks, convicts, persons of feeble mind, those acting under duress, and infants do not have the capacity to contract. In past centuries, slaves and women were added to the above list. If a corporation exists under a charter that limits the authorized activity of the corporation, contracts beyond the authority of the charter are not binding against the corporation. Where a contract has been concluded between two parties both of whom are incompetent, neither is bound. If only one party is incompetent, he may accept or reject the contract as he chooses. If he chooses to accept the contract, it is binding on the competent party. Noncompliance with the contracts by the incompetent party, however, releases the competent party.

CAPACITY TO CONTRACT

An infant (also known as a minor) becomes an adult at the midnight that signals the beginning of his twenty-first birthday. Prior to that time, he is protected by the law as an infant. If he should buy a guitar, he may have to return the guitar to the seller. He would, however, recover the full purchase price less an amount representing reasonable depreciation of the instrument while in his possession. If the guitar were broken and thus worthless, the minor could void the contract, and loss would be borne by the seller.

There are certain exceptions to the right of a minor to avoid liability under a contract made by him. Some examples are given below:

1 *Contracts for necessities:* If a minor is unable to obtain the necessities of life except by making contracts for them, these contracts are held to be binding against him. If, however, the seller of such goods and services has charged more than their reasonable value, the minor is liable only for the reasonable value.
2 *Engagement in business by a minor:* Some states will bind him to reasonable terms of contracts made by him.
3 *Where the marriageable age is less than 21 years:* The marriage contract is held to be binding on minors of marriageable age. Some states give full capacity to contract to all married minors of marriageable age.
4 The enlistment of a minor into the armed forces: This is considered a binding contract.

The purpose of making voidable the contracts entered into by legal incompetents is to protect them from the consequences of their immaturity or mental incapacity. A person signing a contract while intoxicated, deluded, or under duress may repudiate it later. If a person is legally insane, any contract by him is completely void.

VALID CONSIDERATION

Consideration is something of value given in exchange for a promise. Some courts may refuse a token payment as constituting valid consideration, but most will not inquire into the amount. A token payment of a dollar for something of great value is usually considered to be valid consideration.

Although consideration is most often money, it may be a promise to do something, a promise not to do something, the rendering of a service, or the transfer of an article. If a college student agrees not to play football while in college in return for a sports car at graduation, his promise is a valid consideration.

COMPLIANCE WITH REQUIRED FORM

Where the law requires that certain contracts be in a prescribed form, they must be in that form to be binding. The most common requirement is that certain contracts be in writing. The contracts that must be written are commonly found in the *Statute of Frauds* in each state. The following are examples of contracts required by some states to be in writing:

> A contract made in consideration of marriage (except for mutual promise to marry, which need not be in writing to be a contract)
>
> A contract that cannot be fully performed within a year
>
> A contract for the sale of real estate, or the lease of real estate for more than a year
>
> An agreement to be held liable for the default of another person to a contract
>
> An agreement that a person discharged from liability for a debt by bankruptcy proceedings agrees to pay the debt later
>
> A contract to make a will
>
> A contract to submit an issue to arbitration
>
> A contract for sale amounting to $500 or more

LEGALITY OF OBJECT AND PURPOSE

The purpose of a contract must be lawful, and the means of accomplishment must also be lawful. A contract to commit a crime is void. A contract to borrow money is valid, but not if the interest charged is in excess of the legal maximum. An agreement in restraint of trade is unlawful. In some states, a contract made on Sunday or a contract to be performed on Sunday is not valid.

BREACH OF CONTRACT

The total or partial nonperformance of a contract is a breach of contract. In such an event, the injured party may: exercise his right of rescission, sue for damages, or secure a court order compelling performance.

Right of Rescission

If one party to the contract is guilty of a minor breach, such as making one payment late on an installment contract, which causes little demonstrable injury to the other, the courts will generally hold the contract still in force. A court may, however, grant the injured party compensation equal to the amount of injury. If the breach is substantial, the injured party may use the right of rescission. In effect, rescission cancels the contract, and the injured party is excused from performance of his obligations.

Suit for Damages

The injured party may sue for damages under a breach of contract. If the injury is minor or negligible, he may demand *nominal damages*, such as $1. If the injury is substantial, the injured party may sue for *compensatory damages* in an amount equal to the extent of the injury. In many cases, it is very difficult for the court to measure in terms of dollars the amount of injury actually suffered as a result of breach of contract. If damages are awarded, the person guilty of the breach of contract may not be able to pay, particularly if he is a wage earner. The court may then order that his wages be *garnisheed*, which requires the employer to withhold a certain amount from the pay check of the wage earner to apply against the damages until the entire claim is paid.

Suit to Compel Performance

Courts are usually reluctant to compel performance, preferring instead to award damages. Particularly if performance will work an undue hardship, courts will seek a different remedy. If the payment of damages will not compensate the injured party, the courts will sometimes compel performance of a contract. When a court so orders, it usually supervises the performance.

THE STATUTE OF LIMITATIONS

Each state has a statute of limitations, restricting the length of time within which a suit may be brought. An important use of the statute is to bar a creditor from suing for nonpayment of the old debt. The period varies from one state to another and also varies according to the type of contract. For nonpayment of a promissory note, the most common period is 6 years, but it varies from 3 years in the District of Columbia, Maryland, and North Carolina to 15 years in Kentucky and Ohio.

PROPERTY

Anything that is subject to ownership is property. This includes land, buildings, automobiles, clothing, house furnishings, and steamships. Before the Civil War, it included human beings, if they were slaves. In general, a person may do with his property what he wishes, provided that his use of property does not injure others. The right of private ownership and use of property is one of the most important foundations of a capitalistic society. The Constitution protects the right of private ownership by stating that no one may be deprived of his property without due process of law. The ownership of property is also important to the tax system of our nation. Although the federal government levies no taxes on property, the states and local governments do. In fact, municipalities depend on the property tax for most of their revenues.

Property may be divided into real property and personal property. *Real property* includes land, buildings, and anything permanently attached to land or buildings, such as fences, heavy machinery imbedded in concrete, doors, and trees. The ownership of real property may be complete or partial. If a person has *title* (ownership) to land on which no one else has a claim, he holds the land in *fee simple*. This gives him ownership of everything below the land and that portion of the air space above his land that he is able to use. When selling land, a person will sometimes sell only the surface rights, and retain the rights to the minerals below the land, or he may retain a percentage of the mineral rights. A house or piece of land may be owned by a single person, a husband and wife together, or by several persons, or by a corporation, government body, college, or other institution. Because of the permanent nature of land and the importance of establishing ownership to real property, the title to real property is recorded in the official records of the county in which the property is located. When property changes ownership, the transfer of title is recorded on the county records. Title may be transferred by a *quitclaim deed*, which does not guarantee that the seller owns the property, or by a *warranty deed*, under which the seller warrants that his title to the property is clear and that he will defend the title in case of dispute over the validity of his ownership. The use of property without ownership can be transferred by means of a lease (see Chapter 25 for uses of a *lease*). During the period of the lease, which may run for nearly a century, a person may act as though he were the owner as long as he does not violate any of the terms of the lease. At the expiration of the lease, the property plus any permanent improvement made by the user is returned to the owner.

Personal property is any property that is movable. It includes automobiles, trucks, inventories, airplanes, refrigerators, books, sewing machines, stocks, bonds, and money. Ownership of some items of personal property is recorded by county or state governments and may be transferred only in writing. Examples are automobiles and trucks. Personal property is further subdivided into *tangible* and *intangible property*. Tangible property includes merchandise, materials, and things directly usable. Intangible property refers to claims or interests in property, such as stocks, bonds, promissory notes, and money. One reason for making a distinction between real and personal property and between tangible and intangible personal property is that property taxes are frequently levied at a different rate and collected in a different manner for the various classes of property.

In order to ensure the payment of a loan, a lender may require that certain property of the borrower be mortgaged. The terms of the mortgage generally permit the lender to foreclose and sell the property mortgaged in order to recover whatever part of the loan was defaulted by the borrower, any excess usually going to the borrower. Mortgages must be in writing and, in some counties, are recorded at the county courthouse. Mortgages on real property are known as *real estate mortgages*, and mortgages on personal property are called *chattel mortgages*.

AGENCY   An agency is created when one person, the *agent*, is authorized to act on behalf of another, the *principal*. When an agency is established by a formal written document, it is known as a **power of attorney**. Agency relationships, however, are often formed informally. An agency may also exist by implication. If a person knowingly and without objection permits another to act on his behalf as an agent, a legal agency is considered to have been established.

An agent can bind the principal to all business dealings and actions not only within the scope of the actual authority conferred on the agent by the principal but also within the apparent scope of the agent's authority. A customer has the right to assume that a clerk in a store is the legal agent of the store owner and has all of the authority to make sales, quote prices, or effect delivery that is usually associated with retail clerks. If the clerk's authority is not as extensive as that of clerks in similar stores, the limitation of authority must be made clearly known to all with whom the clerk may deal. Otherwise, the courts will hold the principal to all actions that clerks of similar stores are authorized to perform.

A **negotiable instrument** is a written obligation that can be transferred from one person to another. It is usually used as a more convenient substitute for money. Two common forms of negotiable instruments are the promissory note and the bank check. To be negotiable, an instrument must conform to the requirements of the law.

Under the Uniform Commercial Code, an instrument to be negotiable must:

NEGOTIABLE
INSTRUMENTS

Be written.
Be signed.
Be payable to the order of a designated person (the payee) or to bearer (whoever holds the instrument).
Be payable in money only.
Be for a stated amount of money.
Be payable absolutely (if payable only from a particular fund, it is not negotiable).
Be payable at a stated and certain time.

The purpose of negotiability is to make instruments pass from one owner to another easily. To have valid rights in a negotiable instrument, it is necessary that a person acquire the instrument as a holder in due course. To be a **holder in due course**, the following conditions must be fulfilled:

The instrument must be complete and regular on its face.
It must have been acquired before the maturity date (the date of payment).
It must have been taken in good faith.
It must have been received as payment for valuable consideration rather than as a gift.
There must be present no notice of defect in the instrument or defense against payment.

An instrument is usually negotiated by endorsement and delivery. If the instrument is made to the order of an individual, it must be endorsed by him. If it is made to the order of several persons, every one named must endorse it unless one of them is empowered to act for the others. A refund check on a joint husband and wife income tax return or a dividend check on stock jointly held by the husband and wife would require that both the husband and wife endorse in order to receive payment. The principal kinds of endorsement are: *blank*, *special*, *qualified*, *restrictive*, and *conditional*. Endorsements are usually found on the back of the instrument.

Blank   A blank endorsement is merely the signature of the endorser. It is the most commonly used endorsement, but a major disadvantage of it is that it does not designate the next holder. If the check should be endorsed in blank, placed in an envelope, and lost on the way to the mailbox, any person finding it could endorse it and cash it at a store or bank. It is wise not to use this endorsement except at the moment of delivery of the instrument to the next holder.

Special   If the person to whom delivery is made is designated in the endorsement, it is known as a special endorsement. The instrument can then be negotiated only by the person designated. An example of such an endorsement is given below:

Pay to the order of Henrietta McChesney

Marc Mulberry

Qualified   A person who endorses and presents a check or other instrument in payment for a debt is liable to the creditor for the amount of the instrument if the maker of the instrument should default in payment when it is due. If a person uses a qualified endorsement, however, he assumes no liability as a result of default by the maker. Such endorsements are not often used. The wording is similar to that below:

Without recourse

Dwight D. Martin

Restrictive   The most common type of restrictive endorsement is that used when sending a check to a bank for deposit. Because this type of endorsement ends further negotiation, it protects the depositor in the event the check is lost on the way to the bank or to the person to whom it is being sent. Two restrictive endorsements are shown below:

For Deposit Only.
Harry S. Boyd

Pay to Richard Monde
D. Ray Lentil

A conditional endorsement is dependent on the condition stated in the endorsement being fulfilled. An example of such an endorsement follows:

Conditional

Pay to the order of John Arch
upon completion of construction
of wooden desk at 4221 Elva
Way, Sacramento, California.
Herbert Rovere

When an instrument is made payable to **Cash** or to **Bearer**, it may be transferred by delivery and no endorsement is needed. If the last endorsement on an instrument is an endorsement in blank, it also may be transferred without further endorsement. Obviously, the same care should be taken of such an instrument as of a piece of paper money.

A sale is a contract requiring the seller to transfer title to property to the buyer in exchange for payment of a stipulated price. In most sales, the transfer of the property (cigarettes, candy, shoes) is simultaneous with the sales agreement and payment is made immediately. A sale, however, may be made for future delivery of property or for future payment. The body of law that governs sales in about two-thirds of the states is the Uniform Sales Act.

SALES

In ancient times, the law of Rome fixed delivery of the property as the time of transfer of ownership. English law followed Rome in this respect, but the passage

TRANSFER OF TITLE

of centuries modified the law. At the present time, title is held to be transferred at the time when the buyer and seller intend that it shall pass. If there is dispute as to when title passed, the customs of the trade will guide the court in fixing the time. This is important, because goods may be damaged during delivery, and because there may be disagreement as to whether the seller or buyer is required to pay for transportation and unloading. For example, if a person buys a trayful of food at a cafeteria and drops it, the law holds that the loss is borne by the purchaser, if the cafeteria owner wishes to insist on it.

In general, the person who owns the property at the time any damage occurs is the person who bears the loss. There are some exceptions, however. If a refrigerator is bought on a time-payment plan, the title remains with the seller until the last installment is made. If the refrigerator is damaged, however, the loss is borne by the buyer. If a television set is delivered to a railroad for transportation, the title may remain with the seller until delivery, but damage will be the responsibility of the buyer (who will endeavor to recover from the railroad).

Some examples of the timing of transfer of title are given below.

Consignment　If goods are sold by a manufacturer to a retailer on consignment, the title remains with the manufacturer until the retailer sells the goods to a customer.

Goods Sent on Approval　When goods are sent on approval, the title remains with the seller until the buyer has indicated his intention to buy. If no word has been sent by the buyer, the passage of a reasonable period of time indicates the intention to buy.

Auction　Title passes when the auctioneer's hammer falls or he shouts "Sold."

FOB　If the terms of the sale are *free on board* Dallas on a shipment to New York, the title passes when the goods are loaded on the train or other common carrier at Dallas, and the buyer pays the freight. If the terms are FOB New York on a shipment from Dallas, the seller pays the freight, and title passes to the buyer when the shipment arrives on the railroad at New York.

If a person does not have title, he cannot pass title to someone else. If an innocent person buys goods that were stolen, he has not acquired title to them. They still belong to the rightful owner.

WARRANTIES　Warranties are of two kinds: *express* and *implied*. An express warranty is a statement, in writing or oral, by the seller that the goods sold have certain characteristics. Express warranties may be made by the owner of a store, by the clerk making the sale, or by the manufacturer. If a painting is stated to be by a famous artist, the buyer can recover damages if it is not.

The Uniform Sales Act binds the seller to an *implied warranty* containing the following elements:

1 *Valid title:* The seller has valid title to the goods or has a right to sell them.
2 *Free and clear:* There is no mortgage or legal encumbrance on the goods except what is made known to the buyer.
3 *The goods are reasonably fit for the purpose intended:* For example, there is an implied warranty at a restaurant that the plates are clean and the food fit for consumption. A seller may, however, remove this implied warranty by warning the customer that the goods are being sold "as is." This is commonly the basis of sale of secondhand goods.
4 *The goods sold are as described:* If a catalog describes articles offered for sale, they must be as described. This refers to measurable descriptions such as weight, color, size, resistance to shrinking, type of fabric, and so on. A statement such as "these articles are world renowned" or "best on the market" is not a warranty.
5 *The articles are of merchantable quality:* Although the principle of *caveat emptor* (let the buyer beware) should still guide the buyer, he is protected against quality grossly under that usually associated with the article in question. The term "merchantable" is variously defined by the courts as "standard," "average quality," or "salable."

If an article appears to be substandard according to express or implied warranty, the purchaser may retain the goods and either sue the seller for damages or seek a refund of part of the price paid; or he may return the goods and demand a full refund, or refuse to accept the goods.

BAILMENT

Where one person (*bailor*) transfers personal property to another person (*bailee*) temporarily, the contract is called *bailment*. The contract usually states the purpose for the transfer and requires that the property be returned to the bailor or to a third person designated by him at the end of the temporary period. For example, a person might turn over household furniture to a storage company for safekeeping until he builds a house. When goods are shipped by railroad or truck, the shipper is the bailor and the railroad or trucking company is the bailee.

A bailee must use reasonable care to prevent damage to the property entrusted to him. Thus, the operator of a parking lot must have his attendants exercise care to prevent the fenders from being scratched while cars are being moved, and a hotel owner must use reasonable care to prevent luggage of guests from being damaged or stolen. A railroad is liable for damage or loss of goods carried on its trains, unless the loss or damage is caused by acts of God (e.g., lightning), war or insurrection, acts of a governmental agency (e.g., confiscation), or irresponsibility of the shipper (e.g., careless packing of the goods in boxes).

GUARANTY AND SURETYSHIP

Guaranty and suretyship are primarily concerned with loans, and involve three persons: the *debtor*, the *creditor*, and the *guarantor* or *surety*. The guarantor pays whatever part of a debt is unpaid by the debtor after the creditor has endeavored to collect from the debtor and has been unable to do so. The surety pays the money owed by the debtor if the debtor fails to make the payment. A creditor is not required to make the formal collection effort from the debtor in the case of a suretyship that he is in the case of a guaranty. The cosigner of a promissory note is a surety. The creditor may demand payment from the cosigner rather than from the signer, although he usually presents the note to the signer first. The difference between guaranty and suretyship is largely one of degree and, in some states, the two are considered the same.

BANKRUPTCY

The purpose of bankruptcy legislation is to permit a debtor to rehabilitate himself and to provide the means of an equitable distribution of the debtor's assets among the creditors. The Constitution gave to Congress the authority to establish uniform laws on the subject of bankruptcies throughout the United States. Under this authority, such laws were passed in 1800, 1841, and 1867, each one being repealed shortly afterward. An act passed in 1898, however, has remained on the statute books, although it has been extensively amended in the years since it was passed.

When a person or corporation is unable to meet its debts, the creditors may agree to an *extension agreement* (extension of the payment terms) in hope that the debtor will be able to meet the obligations if given enough time. The creditors may also agree, by means of a *composition agreement*, to accept a reduction of the amount due each creditor. Under either agreement, the creditors often engage in the management or supervision of the debtor's business until the creditors have been paid. For example, during the life of the agreement, the creditors' committee may require the debtor to reduce the amount of money he takes from the business for living expenses, make no increases in employees' salaries without committee approval, contract no additional debt without committee approval, and make no large or unusual purchases without committee approval. If the debtor refuses to accept such restrictions, the alternative is bankruptcy proceedings in court. Both the creditors and the debtors are usually anxious to avoid a court suit, since court actions are costly and time-consuming. Furthermore, the outcome of court cases is uncertain.

Bankruptcy may be either *voluntary* or *involuntary*. Voluntary bankruptcy is initiated by the filing of a petition of bankruptcy in the United States District Court by the debtor, who declares that his liabilities exceed his assets and that he wishes the court to dispose of his assets equitably among the creditors and to relieve him of further burden from his debts. An involuntary bankruptcy is initiated by the filing of a petition from the creditors in the District Court alleging that the debtor has committed an act of bankruptcy. Common acts of bankruptcy are:

Transferring property with intent to hinder, delay, or defraud creditors
Transferring a portion of assets to one creditor to defraud others
Failure to pay interest when due

Failure to pay principal when due

Concealment of property

Admitting in writing inability to pay debts

When bankruptcy proceedings are started by petition from the creditors, the court notifies the debtor of the action. The debtor must answer the court, either denying or admitting that the alleged act of bankruptcy has occurred. The court may investigate whether the debtor is guilty of the act of bankruptcy. If the court finds that the debtor is bankrupt, it appoints a **referee** who notifies all of the creditors to submit their claims to the court. The assets of the debtor are turned over to a **trustee**, who administers the assets or operates the business during the bankruptcy proceedings. The trustee may liquidate the assets of the debtor and distribute the proceeds to the creditors.

The priority of claims against the assets of the debtor are:

Court costs, including expenses of the trustee, lawyers, and other persons approved by the court

Wages of employees earned within 3 months prior to the start of the proceedings, but limited to $600

Reasonable expenses of creditors opposing the plan for disposition of assets finally approved by the court. Reasonable expenses of creditors in securing evidence resulting in the conviction of any person violating the Bankruptcy Act

Taxes

Debts, in the order of priority determined by law

If a large corporation is bankrupt, the court may prepare a plan of reorganization rather than of liquidation, particularly if liquidation would work hardship on the general public. The liquidation of a railroad, for example, would end the transportation services of the railroad, since the locomotives, cars, and other assets would be sold for cash. This might cause so much disruption of trade as to cause chaos in a region. The liquidation of a corporation employing thousands of people and providing essential services would similarly cause hardship. The trustee in such a case would be instructed by the court to prepare, with the help of a reorganization committee, a plan of reorganization that would keep the company in active operation while satisfying in an equitable manner the claims of creditors. The creditors would then be paid not in cash, but in bonds and stocks of the reorganized corporation. The result frequently would be that the creditors would become owners of part or all of the corporation as a result of receiving stock under the reorganization plan.

A reorganization plan must be approved by a vote of two-thirds of each class of creditors and by one-half of each class of stockholders before being put into effect by the court. If a particular plan is rejected by vote, another must be prepared. A company might remain in court for 20 years under the operation of a trustee before a plan is worked out acceptable to all classes of creditors and stockholders. During long bankruptcy proceedings, the trustee may have to raise money several times to continue the operation of the business. To do this, he may issue and sell *trustee certificates*. In order to make them salable, they are given priority over existing indebtedness of the corporation.

The final act in a bankruptcy proceeding is the order of the court putting the plan of reorganization (if one is required) into effect and discharging the debtor from the liabilities that brought him into bankruptcy. The debtor (person) is then free for a new start, or the debtor (corporation) begins existence as a reorganized company.

TORTS

An action that causes injury to a person or his property is a tort, for which a court may award damages to the injured person. Examples of torts that may occur in business dealings are: conspiracy to defraud, negligence, libel, slander, malicious prosecution, combination in restraint of trade, and inducing breach of contract. Not only are individuals subject to prosecution for torts; corporations may be sued as well. One of the areas in which cases involving torts are frequently brought to the attention of the public is the alleged infringement of copyrights, trademarks, and patents. It does not matter whether the infringement is innocent or intentional. If the court finds that injury has been sustained by infringement, damages may be awarded.

SUMMARY

Law is the set of rules that govern the actions of individuals in a society and that are enforced by courts of law. The legal system of the United States is a continuous development of the English system of law, transplanted to the colonies and modified through time to its present form.

Our laws are derived from two sources: common law and statute law. Common law is the body of past decisions of courts made in accordance with custom. These customs become precedents, on which lawyers depend in arguing their cases. Statute law is the body of law resulting from legislation passed by Congress, state legislatures, and county and municipal governments. To decide cases, we have two sets of courts, federal and state. Federal courts decide cases involving federal laws. All other cases are decided by courts established under state legislation. A decision of a state court can, however, be appealed to federal courts (up to the Supreme Court of the United States) if a constitutional issue or other federal jurisdiction is shown to apply.

Among the elements of law of importance to business are contracts, property, negotiable instruments, sales, bankruptcy, and torts. Throughout practically all of the United States, the state laws on business transactions have been uniformly codified under the Uniform Commercial Code (UCC). A contract is an agreement between two or more parties, enforceable at law. Property is anything that is subject to ownership. Negotiable instruments are written obligations transferable from one party to another. A sale is a contract obligating the seller to transfer title to the buyer at a stated price. Bankruptcy permits a debtor unable to pay his debts to have them discharged by court order, enabling the debtor to make a fresh start in business. An action causing injury to a person or his property is a tort, for which a court can award damages in the amount of the injury.

1 Distinguish between common law and statute law.
2 What is the difference between the legal systems of the Anglo-Saxon nations and those of other countries?
3 If common law and statute law conflict, which take precedence? Does this seem reasonable? Explain.
4 What is meant by the Uniform Commercial Code? Discuss its importance in business transactions involving persons in different states.
5 What is the distinction between inferior courts, superior courts, and courts of appeal?
6 What types of cases are heard first in a federal court?
7 Outline the steps in a court case, from initiation to decision.
8 What are the advantages to settling a case out of court?
9 For a contract to be valid it must have certain elements. What are these elements?
10 To what extent can a minor be bound by the contracts he makes?
11 Some contracts must be in writing to be binding. What are they?
12 In the legal sense what is meant by "personal property"?
13 Illustrate by means of an example each of the types of endorsement: (*a*) blank, (*b*) special, (*c*) qualified, (*d*) restrictive, and (*e*) conditional.
14 What is the difference between an express warranty and an implied warranty?
15 List the priority of claims against the assets of a bankrupt company.

Anderson, Ronald A.: *Social Forces and the Law*, South-Western Publishing Company, Cincinnati, 1969.

Corley, Robert N., and Robert L. Black: *The Legal Environment of Business*, McGraw-Hill Book Company, New York, 1973.

Goodwin, John R.: *Business Law*, Richard D. Irwin, Inc., Homewood, III., 1972.

Jones, Harry W.: *The Courts, the Public, and the Law Explosion*, Prentice-Hall, Inc., Englewood Cliffs, N.J., 1965.

Name   **Section**   **Date**

COMPLETION SENTENCES

1 _____*law*_____ is an obligatory rule of action prescribed by the

government.

2 Common law rests on _____*custom*_____ rather than legislation.

3 A significant step toward uniformity of state laws governing business was

taken with the adoption of the _____*Uniform Comm. Code*_____.

4 The highest court of appeals is the _____*Supreme Court*_____.

5 The person against whom a suit is brought is notified by means of a

_____*summons*_____.

6 The person initiating a court suit is called the _____*Plaintiff*_____

and the person against whom the suit is brought is called the

_____*Defendant*_____.

7 If both plaintiff and defendant waive a jury trial, the case is tried before a

judge .

8 Each state has a statute of *limitation* restricting the length

of time within which suit may be brought.

9 Municipalities depend on the *Property* for most of their

revenues.

10 The use of property without ownership to it can be had by means of a

lease .

11 A minor can be held legally liable for a contract for goods or services that are

necessary to him.

12 A contract for sale amounting to $*500.00* or more must

be in writing.

13 Warranties are of two kinds, *express* and

implied .

14 In order to ensure payment of a loan, a lender may require that certain property

of the borrower be *mortgaged* .

15 If a check is made out to both husband and wife, *both*

must sign in order to receive payment.

TRUE OR FALSE STATEMENTS

1 The origin of law lies in the social habits or customs of the people.

Name   Section   Date

F **2** Following the American Revolution, the United States abolished the common laws that had previously existed in the colonies.

F **3** Where the two conflict, common law takes precedence over statute law.

F **4** Superior courts are also known as courts of appeal.

T **5** Every state has a state supreme court.

F **6** As a general rule the best way to settle a dispute is to take it to court, because the dispute is then most likely to be settled impartially.

T **7** A company will often settle a damage suit against it out of court, even though the plaintiff's case is weak, simply to avoid unfavorable publicity.

T **8** If a defendant who has been properly served by a legal complaint does not answer the complaint, the judge usually awards the decision to the plaintiff.

T **9** A contract is an agreement enforceable at law.

F **10** A contract must be in writing to be legally binding.

T **11** Consideration (in law) is something of value given in exchange for a promise.

T **12** Even though a person is under legal age (a minor), if he enlists in the armed forces the act of enlistment is a legally enforceable contract.

T **13** A contract to commit a crime is not enforceable at law.

T **14** A partial nonperformance of a contract is a breach of contract.

T **15** Courts are generally reluctant to compel performance in a breach of contract, preferring instead to award money compensation.

F **16** The statute of limitations is uniform in length of period among the various states.

F **17** When real property changes ownership, the change is recorded in records kept at the state capital of the state in which the property is located.

F **18** Although corporations are subject to many taxes, they are not subject to personal property taxes.

T **19** Two common forms of negotiable instrument are the promissory note and the bank check.

T **20** A blank endorsement is merely the signature of the endorser.

EXERCISES

1 Attend a trial involving a commercial dispute, if possible, in one of the local courts of your community. Afterward write a report covering the following aspects of the trial:

    a Nature of the dispute

    b Outline of arguments for the plaintiff

    c Outline of arguments for the defendant

    d The law bearing on the case

    e The decision

2 Pick out any recently enacted law not mentioned in this chapter. This may be a law recently passed by Congress, by the legislature of your state, or even a measure enacted by the municipal government serving your town. Discuss the following aspects of the law:

    a Why was the law passed?

Name	Section	Date

b What was the need for the law?

c What results have been achieved by the law?

3 What limitations on your individual freedom are imposed not by law but by other kinds of regulations? To what extent does custom limit your freedom of action? One of the customs that has changed during the past 30 years is the custom of gentlemen relinquishing their seats on a subway or bus to women passengers. Another custom that has changed is that of men removing their hats in a business elevator. Are these changes for the better or for worse? What other changes in custom do you notice? Do you think any customs should be made into laws? If so, which? Give reasons for your answer.

a Limitations on my freedom imposed by regulations other than law:

b Limitations on my freedom imposed by custom:

c Customs I think should be made into law:

29

GOVERNMENT AND BUSINESS

Government in a complex society must be given more power than government in a simple society. We have learned through experience to do things by means of our government. The extent of government activity is far greater today than it was when your grandfather was born.

You can study this chapter by attempting to classify the activities of government into two categories. In one, list those government activities that are intended to aid business. In the other, list all other government activities that restrict business freedom for one reason or another. Where the restriction of business freedom is intended to protect the general public, there will be opposition on the part of some segments of business. On the other hand, you should notice that some restrictions of business freedom are imposed at the demand of businessmen themselves. After reading this chapter, you should be able to give examples of each of these types.

Where the government attempts to aid business, the aid may be direct or indirect. Most regulations designed to aid business will provide indirect aid. Where the government attempts to give direct aid to business, it usually does so in the form of a subsidy. After reading this chapter, see if you can give examples of each.

Taxes are levied by many governmental units on income, property, estates, sales, imports, and many other things. Because of the wide variety of government services, the need by government for raising money is considerable. It is not possible to discuss taxation at length; this chapter merely attempts to give you an understanding of the varieties of taxes in existence and their effects on business decisions.

There are a large number of taxing agencies. It is unlikely that you or your parents are aware of the number of taxes you bear and the number of taxing agencies collecting them, because in many cases they are imposed indirectly rather than directly.

Indirect taxes are those that are paid by one individual and passed on in the form of higher prices for goods or services to a customer, or as lower wages to an employee, or as lower dividends to a stockholder. Because many taxes are indirect, it is difficult to determine their burden on each person. Nevertheless, you should appreciate the fact that the total burden of taxes is not the same thing as the taxes an individual pays directly.

Many taxes are levied on businesses. Except for certain classes of corporations, such as municipal governments and charitable foundations, all corporations pay a tax on income. Notice that the income of corporations is directly taxed, but the income of unincorporated businesses is not directly taxed. Remember, however, that the income of a proprietorship or partnership becomes the personal income of the owners, who are then subject to income tax with respect to that income.

COMPLEXITY OF MODERN BUSINESS

An officer of the Philadelphia Federal Reserve Bank was invited to give a speech before an association of businessmen in 1954. The speaker immediately preceding him castigated those members of the association who were using price competition to increase sales. These men were "chiselers," he said, and should be made to stop cutting prices before they ruined the industry. His talk was loudly applauded. The bank officer had written a speech extolling the virtues of free enterprise, especially price competition. Unable to change his speech at the last minute, he read it as written, but felt certain his praise of freedom in setting prices would be unwelcome, coming right after the previous talk. But he, too, was loudly applauded. Pondering this inconsistency, he concluded that most businessmen favor freedom from regulation in theory but deplore the absence of regulation that permits intense competition.

Such an attitude can be largely explained by the rapid pace of industrial change and the lag in the habits of thought of most people, businessmen and others. Before the Civil War, business enterprises were small, numerous, and competitive. They were also largely unregulated. Purchasers of a wagon, a load of bricks, or a suit of clothes nearly always dealt directly with the maker. The variety of goods available was small compared with today, and buyers could determine quality in most cases by simple examination of the items for sale. Except for banking, the public could protect itself without government help.

Business has changed greatly during the past 100 years. Consumers today rarely buy directly from manufacturers. The variety of goods is so great that the average man can determine quality by inspection in only a small percentage of the goods he buys. In most industries, manufacturers are no longer small, numerous, and competitive—at least, not competitive in the same degree as a century ago.

Although government activity in business has increased considerably, and is accepted by most people, many businessmen cling to the philosophy of their grandfathers. They are in favor of the principle of limited government, and they want as little government regulation—as distinct from government aid—as possible. But most businessmen realize that more regulation is needed now than in times past. An automobile cannot be examined for quality as easily as a farm wagon could be in 1850. Government must be more active in business at present than in the past. But how much government regulation and aid should there be? On this there is a sharp disagreement. For the purpose of this chapter, we can only state that this is an issue involving different philosophies, points of view, and strong emotions.

The activities of government in the sphere of business are many and varied. We shall pursue our examination of government and business by dividing it into the following categories:

Regulations to increase competition
Regulations to decrease competition
Patents, copyrights, and trademarks
Protection of the consumer
Subsidies and other aids to business

Until the Civil War, there was little public concern about declining competition. After that war, in several industries, many small companies disappeared, leaving one giant dominating each industry. Competition gave way to monopoly, and the customers of these industries were at the mercy of the dominant firm. This occurred in petroleum, tobacco, sugar, whiskey, explosives, and others. Railroads combined into large networks, taking advantage of their power by raising freight rates to those towns served by only one line and using other discriminatory practices.

REGULATIONS TO INCREASE COMPETITION

First farmers and then small businessmen and the public in general became alarmed. They demanded government action to curb monopoly power. Both major political parties, Republican and Democrat, promised relief. Bipartisan support in Congress resulted in establishment of the Interstate Commerce Commission in 1887 to regulate railroads. In 1890, Congress passed the Sherman Antitrust Act to prohibit "combinations in restraint of trade." Since 1890, many laws have been passed to limit monopoly and promote competition. The chief ones are listed below:

Clayton Act	1914
Federal Trade Commission Act	1914
Robinson-Patman Act	1936
Wheeler-Lea Act	1938
Celler Antimerger Act	1950

It is not possible here to explain these laws in detail. A brief description of each act follows:

1 *Clayton Act:* Prohibits exclusive agreements between sellers and buyers. Prohibits interlocking directorates, a device by which two or more companies in the same industry are controlled by a group of men serving on the boards of directors of both. Prohibits one corporation from owning the shares of a competing corporation. The above prohibitions apply when the result "may be substantially to lessen competition or tend to create a monopoly." Specifically exempts labor unions from antimonopoly legislation.
2 *Federal Trade Commission Act:* Created the Federal Trade Commission to investigate unfair methods of competition and to issue "cease and desist" orders to offending firms when such methods are found to exist.

3 *Robinson-Patman Act:* Forbids companies' giving allowances, discounts, and other concessions in price to large buyers unless small buyers receive proportionately the same concessions. Any discrimination in favor of large buyers must be limited to the saving in cost resulting from buying in large volume.

4 *Wheeler-Lea Act:* Forbids unfair methods of competition that injure consumers, such, for example, as advertising television tubes as new when they actually are reconditioned used tubes. Until 1938, unfair methods of competition were unlawful only where they injured competing businesses, not the consumer.

5 *Celler Antimerger Act:* The Clayton Act prohibits concentration by means of one company acquiring stock in a competing corporation. The Celler Act forbids mergers that may substantially lessen competition.

REGULATIONS TO
DECREASE
COMPETITION

As mentioned before, competition forces businesses to "keep on their toes." When this happens, consumers can benefit through improved quality, better service, or lower prices. Competition, however, is a potential threat to the profits and even to the existence of firms. Few businessmen welcome competition in their own industry. By various means, they seek to reduce competition, or at least to channel it into weaker forms, such as competition in the guise of advertising. In spite of their advocacy of freedom from government interference in business, businessmen have sought government action to restrict competition for their benefit.

One of the most important, and certainly the oldest, governmental interferences with competition is the large number of laws restricting the importation of foreign goods into the United States. These restrictions include tariffs, quotas, exchange restrictions, and many others.

In 1931, California passed the first resale-price-maintenance law, which gave the manufacturer of brand name goods the right to dictate the minimum price at which any retailer in the state could sell the brand goods to the consumer. Forty-five state legislatures passed such laws, promoted by small retailers, drug manufacturers, and other businessmen under the appealing label of "Fair Trade" laws.[1] Since World War II, decisions of state and federal courts and the actions of some state legislatures have reduced the range of coverage and the enforceability of such laws.

Three-fifths of the states have passed laws prohibiting the sale by retailers of goods "below cost." Owners of small retail stores have pressed for passage of these laws. Enforcement has been spotty because cost to the retailer is often different when goods are bought in small quantities compared with large quantities, and because many exceptions are permitted (close-out sales, reducing oversupply, or to "relieve financial distress").

The minimum price of some commodities is regulated by laws pushed through legislatures at the demand of producers. Milk and alcoholic beverages are examples. In such cases, the members of the industry use the government to restrict competition in price. The price-support legislation of the federal government achieves the same end indirectly in agricultural staples.

[1] A bill debated in 1965 in Congress to strengthen such laws was named the "Quality Stabilization" bill.

Patents are among the oldest devices to limit competition. The United States patent law provides exclusive rights to the inventor of a new device to make, license, or otherwise use it for a period of 17 years. Granting a monopoly for 17 years is intended to encourage invention. In some other countries, the patented article must be produced and distributed to continue the existence of the patent. In the United States, the patent holder may withhold use of the patent for the full 17 years, if he chooses not to exploit it. During the life of a patent, the person or corporation owning the patent may license others to produce under the patent, collecting royalties for the right.

A copyright indicates ownership of a book, musical composition (including recordings), play, work of art, or photograph, giving the owner of the copyright exclusive authority to sell, license, or otherwise use his creation. A copyright (good for 28 years, renewable for one additional period of 28 years, for a total of 56 years) can be obtained by sending two copies of the work to the Copyright Office of the Library of Congress, completing a copyright form furnished by the Copyright Office, and making payment of $6. Notice of the copyright is printed or otherwise indicated on the material. An example of such a notice can be found on one of the first pages of this book.

The trademark of a company, distinguishing its product from its competitors', may be registered at the patent office. Registration is denied to marks that are immoral, that closely resemble existing trademarks, that represent the flag or insignia of the United States or that of a state, or that discredit public institutions.

PATENTS, COPYRIGHTS AND TRADEMARKS

There are many ways that the government protects us. Indeed, it is probable that the idea of government itself derived largely from the need for organization in protecting primitive man from marauders and other hazards. Much of the protective activity of government, such as national defense, policing, and traffic laws, does not affect business directly. We are concerned here with those laws that are primarily directed toward business. We shall discuss the following:

Antifraud legislation
Food and drug laws
Securities regulations
Regulation of public utilities and transportation
Deposit insurance
Weights and measures
Small-loan laws
Zoning laws
Licenses

PROTECTION OF THE PUBLIC

Of the many examples of government antifraud activity, one is the United States Postal Service, which bars the use of the mails to defraud. It is up to the postal

ANTIFRAUD LEGISLATION

inspectors to investigate possible frauds either on their own suspicion or on a complaint made to the Postal Service by a citizen.

FOOD AND DRUG LAWS   Although some people produce a small amount of the food they eat, nearly all of the food each family consumes is raised, processed, and packaged by food companies. Practically all of the medication we use is produced by drug manufacturers and distributed by drug companies. There are more than 80,000 plants producing foods and drugs in the United States. It is obvious that individual families are unable to protect themselves from foods or drugs that are unsafe or that are prepared under unsanitary conditions. Efforts to control quality and cleanliness in the food industry and in the production of drugs by government regulation are moderately successful. Federal laws provide that new drugs be adequately tested before being marketed, that, in most cases, the quantity and chief ingredients be stated on the container, and that foods and drugs be produced, stored, and distributed under sanitary conditions. The inspectors of the Food and Drug Administration may visit food or drug plants, but only at "reasonable times and on written notice." The number of inspectors permitted from appropriations by Congress in recent years allows an average of one inspection for each plant every five years.

Although the inspectors of the Food and Drug Administration visit plants infrequently, when unfit conditions are found, action is taken. The following examples were taken at random from recent "Notices of Judgment under the Federal Food, Drug, and Cosmetic Act":

1 *Flour:* Sixty-four 100-lb bags of flour . . . contained rodent excreta and rodent hairs, also held under insanitary conditions. Disposition—destruction.
2 *Rice and azuki beans:* . . . contained rodent urine, also held under insanitary conditions. Owner pleaded guilty. Fine: $150.
3 *Trout filets:* Thirty-six cases containing four 15-lb cartons each . . . contained decomposed fish while held for sale. Disposition—destruction.
4 *Raisins:* Eighty-nine 30-lb boxes . . . contained insects while held for sale. Disposition—destruction.

Control of quality in the production of milk is done by state or local governments. In some parts of the country, the inspections are frequent and rigid. In other areas, inspections are lax.

SECURITIES
REGULATIONS   Distribution of stocks and bonds is regulated by state and federal laws. The state laws, however, are either weak or poorly enforced. The federal laws, beginning with the Securities Act of 1933, are administered by the Securities and Exchange Commission (SEC), a body of five men appointed by the President. The consensus is that this Commission, aided by the cooperation of the securities industry, provides a reasonably high degree of protection to the investor in stocks and bonds. It must be emphasized, however, that the Commission's chief function is to see

that the buyers of securities are provided full and accurate information. The regulations do not—and should not—prevent investors from purchasing risky, speculative securities. The SEC requires merely that the facts of the nature of the risks be available to them.

REGULATION OF PUBLIC UTILITIES AND TRANSPORTATION

Public utilities are privately or governmentally owned companies furnishing an essential service. They include the following industries: telephone, telegraph, natural gas, local public transportation, electric power, water service, sewers, and trash collection.

Those companies doing business across state boundaries (interstate) are subject to regulation of rates and services by the federal government. Services rendered entirely within a state (intrastate) are regulated either by the state government or by local city or county governments. The regulations generally cover rates and services. The following tabulation shows the regulatory activity of the levels of government:

Industry	Regulatory Agency
Telephone (interstate calls)	Federal Communications Commission
Telegraph (interstate)	Federal Communications Commission
Natural gas (interstate pipelines)	Federal Power Commission
Electric power (interstate transmission)	Federal Power Commission
Natural gas (intrastate transmission)	State or local government
Electric power (intrastate transmission)	State or local government
Telephone service (local calls)	State or local government
Local public transportation	State or local government
Water service	County or city government
Sewers	County or city government
Trash collection	County or city government

The regulation of transportation companies carrying goods and passengers in interstate commerce (this includes nearly all except transit lines) is divided among three federal agencies. Rates, services, and safety of the following are regulated by the Interstate Commerce Commission: railroads, pipelines, inland and coastal shipping, and highway transportation.

The rates and services of air transport are regulated by the Federal Aviation Administration. Safety rules, licensing of aircraft and pilots, and controlling air traffic are also the responsibility of the Federal Aviation Administration.

DEPOSIT INSURANCE

More than 5,000 commercial banks in the United States failed from November 1929 to March 1933. In each failure, depositors lost a small or large part of their savings. Hoarding became widespread as people considered it safer to keep money in a teapot or under a mattress than in the local bank. To restore confidence in banks, the federal government created in 1933 the Federal Deposit Insurance

Corporation. Other federal insurance corporations were later formed to protect depositors in savings and loan associations, credit unions, and stock brokerage firms. The opeation of these federal corporations is explained in Chapter 26.

WEIGHTS AND MEASURES

When you pay for 10 gallons of gasoline or 5 pounds of meat, how do you know you get full measure? The policing of measuring devices such as scales, gasoline pumps, and the like is undertaken by state governments. Inspection is infrequent in most states and punishment for violations rare. It is a credit to the honesty of businessmen that most measuring devices used in business are accurate and that the minor deviations reported appear to be as often in favor of the buyer as the seller.

SMALL-LOAN LAWS

It costs roughly the same to negotiate, credit investigate, record, and handle a $10,000 loan as a $50 loan. In other words, the handling expenses of lending $10,000 in 200 loans of $50 each is about 200 times as high as lending $10,000 on a single loan. Small borrowers must obviously pay more for money than large borrowers. But small borrowers are not often as sophisticated in financial matters as large borrowers. Advantage is taken of their lack of knowledge by some lenders to charge exorbitant rates of interest. Such lenders are called *loan sharks*, since they prey on people in financial distress. Thirty-four states, however, have small-loan laws providing some protection to borrowers by placing maximum limits on the rates of interest that may be charged on loans of different sizes. Lenders often make charges in addition to interest. These charges are subject to varying degrees of regulation by the state governments. In 1968 the federal Consumer Credit Protection Act became law. Part of this law, Title I, is the Truth in Lending Act. This act requires companies making cash loans and companies selling goods on credit to express the cost in terms of dollars and in terms of simple annual interest. Thus, persons borrowing to buy a car, for example, can more easily compare the cost of loans from different lenders.

ZONING LAWS

People owning real estate do not have unrestricted rights to its use. Where people live closely together, one man's use of his property may injure his neighbors. To protect the public from unrestrained use of property, zoning laws are found in nearly all cities and residential areas. These laws specify which parcels of land may be used only for single-family houses, which for apartment buildings, and which for service stations or stores. The laws may limit the size or location of a house or building on a plot of ground. In Santa Fe, New Mexico, all construction must be uniformly of Spanish Colonial adobe style. Thus, the city preserves its antique appearance, so attractive to tourists, who constitute its largest single source of income.

In certain businesses, a license is necessary before beginning operations. The original purpose of licensing was to protect the public from incompetent operators. All of the states require proof of competence, by examination usually, before a person may practice law, accounting, medicine, pharmacy, or dentistry. Licensing has also been used to reduce competition by restricting the number of firms. In New York, California, and some other states, the number of liquor stores is limited by the number of licenses issued. In some cases, the fortunate applicant for a license may make a small fortune by selling the license granted him even before it is used. In some states, more than 100 kinds of businesses require a license to operate. Licenses are issued not only by state governments, but by counties and towns as well.

LICENSES

Government has subsidized and otherwise aided business throughout the history of the United States. In some cases the aid has been direct, by payments of cash, reduction of tax burdens below those paid by others, and the furnishing of services free or below cost. In such cases the government aid has been paid for by the taxpayers as a whole. In other cases the aid has been indirect, by sheltering enterprises from the force of competition. In these cases the aid has been paid for by customers in the form of prices higher than would exist under free competition. The principle of promoting the economy through public aid to private enterprise was the basis of Alexander Hamilton's recommendation to Congress for tariffs to reduce competition from abroad. The principle has been the foundation of government relations with business ever since.

GOVERNMENT SUPPORTS FOR BUSINESS

Agriculture and transportation have been recipients of government subsidies for many years. The cost of supporting agriculture amounts to a few billion dollars each year, through a variety of loan programs, price supports, and other services.
    Railroads were heavily subsidized in the last century through grants of land and cash to encourage railroad building. As other forms of transportation developed, they have also received subsidies. Some examples follow:

SUBSIDIES

Dredging of channels, building and maintaining canals, and traffic controls have been provided free or at low charges to users of the inland waterways.

Barge Lines

The construction of ocean vessels in the United States has been supported since World War I by construction subsidies from the federal government. Operating subsidies have also been paid to shipping lines to offset the higher seamen's wages and other costs that are higher than those of foreign operators.

Ocean Shipping

Road Transport   The Interstate Highway System and other major highways are built to support heavy trucks. The cost of maintenance and construction of such roadbeds is borne by all highway users. Whether the cost is fairly allocated among trucks, passenger cars, and other users of the highways is a matter of controversy.

Air Transport   The air transport industry uses airports, traffic controls, instrument landing systems, and navigation aids provided by the government. Some payment for these services is made through landing fees and the tax on aviation gasoline, but it does not cover the total cost. Cash subsidies have been paid to airlines in the past, most recently to helicopter companies, to encourage the more rapid development of air transport services. The design and construction of new airplanes are sometimes financed by the federal government and in other instances adapted for civilian use from military aircraft designs. One example is the supersonic transport plane, for which the federal government spent several millions of dollars out of a projected total of over a billion dollars for design and production. Construction of the prototype airplane stopped in 1972 when Congress balked at continuing the financing.

SPECIAL TAX TREATMENT   Businesses are taxed on a different basis from individuals, as indicated in the latter part of this chapter. In some instances businesses are taxed more heavily than individuals; in other cases, more lightly. However, some businesses enjoy tax treatment not received to the same extent by other businesses. One example is the depletion allowance, particularly for production of oil and gas. Companies extracting oil and gas may deduct from their income before calculating their income tax liability an amount equal to 22 percent of their gross income. This is in addition to the deductions for business expenses enjoyed by all businesses.

LOANS   The federal government makes loans directly to businesses, participates with private lending agencies in making loans, and insures private loans to reduce costs to businesses of borrowing money. Loans are extended by the Small Business Administration (discussed in Chapter 5 and Chapter 26), by the Export-Import Bank (Chapter 26), and by other departments and agencies of government.

MISCELLANEOUS BUSINESS AIDS   Business aids of a variety of types are offered at every level of government, from local to federal. For purposes of illustration, however, we shall confine our examples to the federal government. The federal government finances a considerable amount of research useful to business. All patents of a business nature owned by the government are available free to business.

The Fish and Wildlife Service provides fishing companies with information on fish and fishing techniques. The United States Forestry Service provides lumber companies with the results of studies on trees. The Bureau of Mines is virtually a government-financed laboratory for the mining industry. All of the departments of the federal government, from the Department of State to the Department of Health, Education, and Welfare, furnish information and services to business.

The Department of Commerce was created to aid businessmen. It provides a wide range of information and services. The chief bureaus of this department are the following:

THE DEPARTMENT OF COMMERCE

> Bureau of Foreign and Domestic Commerce
> Bureau of Standards
> Bureau of the Census
> Small Business Administration
> Weather Bureau
> Patent Office

In addition to the main office in Washington, the Department has field offices in the major cities of the United States. Each office is a storehouse of information useful to businessmen. Books, pamphlets, statistical material, and periodicals are in abundance. Some must be used in the office, particularly statistical data. But many of the books and pamphlets can be bought for a nominal charge, and others are free for the asking. Each office is staffed with experts available for consulting on almost any type of problem found in business. The services of the field offices are particularly valuable to small businesses. Small enterprises are also aided by loans, direct and indirect, extended by the Small Business Administration.

Taxes are the payments exacted to pay for the services rendered by the government to its citizens. The level of taxes is determined to a considerable extent by the cost and extent of the services the government undertakes to give the people. In connection with the extent of the services rendered by the government, a fundamental question is always raised: How many services and which services should the government undertake to do for the people, and how many services and which ones should the people receive from privately owned companies or do for themselves? To answer this question is obviously more difficult than raising it. Opinions differ considerably concerning the legitimate extent of governmental activity. During the early part of the United States' history, the extent of services rendered by the federal government, except in time of war, was so limited as to make that government hardly more extensive in its operations than a large business corporation. The present century, however, has seen a considerable increase in the amount of services rendered by the federal government, and a smaller increase in state and local services. A strong body of opinion argues for a severe limitation of govern-

TAXATION AND BUSINESS

mental activity, while an equally strong body of opinion argues that an increase in the scope of governmental activity beyond the present level would be beneficial. Perhaps the difference between these opposing viewpoints could be reduced if the philosophy of Abraham Lincoln were more rigorously applied in seeking the answer to the above problem. Lincoln's viewpoint was that people should do through their government those things they could not do as well through private agencies for themselves.

There are some services on which there would be no serious question as to the necessity of government provision. Only through their government can citizens effectively and efficiently protect themselves from outside enemies and from the possibility of armed assault. Only through their government can people adequately maintain internal peace and order, and seek for themselves freedom of religion, assembly, speech, and thought. Only through their government can they adequately control criminal conduct and administer justice through courts of law. Only through their government can people maintain a dependable system of currency. The functions mentioned above are essential functions of government, functions that few persons would advocate being undertaken by agencies other than the government. Most governments, however, undertake services in addition to essential or minimum services. They undertake the distribution of letters, books, and packages, although that service is also undertaken to some extent by private agencies. Most governments today provide educational services, although the principle of public education for all children was fought with intensity and bitterness in the last century. Most governments undertake recreational services for their citizens in the form of public parks, picnic grounds, camp sites, and other facilities.

Modern governments have undertaken a wide variety of miscellaneous services for their citizens. The federal government of the United States, for example, in recent years has operated two small railroads, manufactured synthetic rubber, built and operated steamships, generated and distributed electricity, sold life insurance, made or guaranteed loans to corporations and individuals, and operated a number of small businesses confiscated from enemy nations during the two world wars. The services provided by federal spending are indicated in Figure 29-1.

The extent of activity of the federal government explains the level of taxation imposed by the people's representatives. Not all of the services rendered by the federal government are paid for by taxation, of course. The cost of some of the services, such as the postal, are covered by charging the users of these services for the benefits received. Most of the services, however, are paid for by means of taxes, and, because such a great increase in the extent of the services of national defense has been required by the existence of powerful potential enemies, the level of taxes has in recent years reached record heights.

By what authority does the government levy taxes? Municipalities gain their authority in the city charter granted by the state government. State governments in turn derive their authority from the state constitution. The federal government derives its taxing power from the Federal Constitution. Article I, Section 8 of the Constitution gives Congress the right to levy and collect taxes, duties, imposts, and excises—terms that covered every known method of collecting revenue by

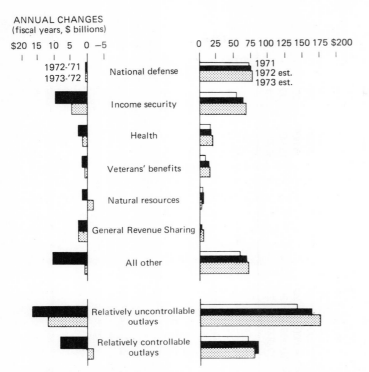

ANNUAL CHANGES
(fiscal years, $ billions)

FIGURE 29-1   Budget outlays by function for 1971, 1972, and 1973.
(*Source: The Federal Budget*, 1973, The Conference Board,
New York, 1973. Data from the Office of Management
and Budget.)

means of an exaction on its citizens. The Constitution provided, however, a number
of limitations on the taxing power of Congress, the chief being that the purpose of
any federal tax must be "to pay the debts and provide for the common defense
and the general welfare of the United States." The general welfare limitation has
been interpreted very broadly by the Supreme Court and has not offered a serious
limitation on the taxing power of the Congress.

TAXATION PRINCIPLES

Taxes may be divided into three classes according to their effect on different levels
of income. A tax that takes a larger percentage of a small income than of a large
income is called a *regressive* tax. One that takes the same percentage from large and
small incomes is called a *proportional* tax. A *progressive* tax takes a larger percentage
of large incomes than of small ones. Table 29-1 illustrates the effect on income of
the three types of tax. Notice that in all three examples the amount of the tax rises
as income rises. The distinction lies in the proportion of each income that is taken
by the tax. Most taxes on consumer goods, such as sales taxes, are regressive. A
proportional tax is the corporation income tax. Except for the first $25,000 of
income, which is taxed at 22 percent, corporation income is taxed at a uniform rate

TABLE 29-1   PROGRESSIVE, PROPORTIONAL, AND REGRESSIVE TAXES

Income	Regressive Tax		Proportional Tax		Progressive Tax	
	Tax	Percent of Income Taken	Tax	Percent of Income Taken	Tax	Percent of Income Taken
$ 1,000	$ 300	30%	$ 200	20%	$ 100	10%
2,000	560	28	400	20	220	12
5,000	1,300	26	1,000	20	800	16
10,000	2,000	20	2,000	20	2,000	20
20,000	3,600	18	4,000	20	5,000	25
50,000	7,000	14	10,000	20	15,000	30
100,000	10,000	10	20,000	20	35,000	35

of 48 percent. The federal tax rates on personal income are progressive, rising from 14 percent on the first $1,000 of taxable income to 70 percent on taxable income above $100,000. The science of transforming large incomes into forms that escape the high rates, however, reduces the effective progressivity of the income tax.

TAXING AGENCIES

It must not be forgotten by the student that wherever he lives in the United States, he is a citizen of several governments, each of which has the power to levy taxes. In descending order, these taxing authorities are the federal government, the state government, the county government, the city or town government, and various taxing districts that might have jurisdiction over areas still smaller than a city. Examples of such taxing agencies are school districts, fire-prevention districts, water districts, light and power districts, and sewer districts. Thus, a person or a company might pay taxes to federal, state, county, and city governments, and also to a school district, a water district, and a light and power district. Each of these taxing authorities provides services to companies and individuals for which taxes are collected in payment. It has been suggested by a number of authorities on taxation that some elimination of the number of taxing agencies or at least a coordination in the process of tax collecting by the various taxing agencies would reduce the cost of the services rendered and raise the efficiency of tax collections. Improvements in this area, however, are slow in achievement.

Although people and businesses cannot escape federal taxes except by emigration from the United States, they can to some extent escape the burden of state and local taxes by moving to less heavily taxed areas. One of the important elements in reaching a decision on the location of a new plant or factory is the extent of taxes imposed by various communities to cover the cost of the services rendered by them to their citizens. Taxes are an important element of cost in doing business. Therefore, business executives are interested in choosing a location where the tax expenses are low. As a result, state and local governments are in competition with each other in making their tax program most attractive to the location of new businesses within their areas. Some cities have made agreements with new corporations locating within their city limits not to levy property taxes for a period of 10 years. Other cities have obligingly drawn their city limits in such a way as to exclude the area on which a new factory is to be built, thereby eliminating city taxes on the property. State governments have remodeled their tax structure from time to time to make it more attractive for businesses to locate within their borders. The above is a partial explanation of why state and local taxes are very low compared with federal taxes and also why the services provided by states and municipalities are less extensive than federal services.

TAXES ON CORPORATION INCOME

Corporations as well as individuals pay income taxes. Corporations are artificial beings created by the government that gives them a charter authorizing business activity, and they are entities separate from their owners. Corporations may own property, enter into contracts, and earn income. Ever since the income tax was reintroduced on the federal level in the present century, corporation income has been subject to taxes. The rate of taxation has been levied according to the philosophy of the majority of congressmen in Washington, and according to the financial needs of the federal government. The federal income tax on corporations is in two parts. All taxable income earned by a corporation was taxed at 22 percent in 1974. All income above the first $25,000 was subject to an additional tax of 26 percent, making a total tax of 48 percent on all income above $25,000.

Many state governments levy taxes on corporation income, but these taxes are levied at a very low rate. This is due to two factors: the smaller financial requirements of state governments and the knowledge that a higher rate levied by one state than a neighboring state might induce corporations to transfer their operations to the state levying the lower tax.

Because of the difficulty of determining in some instances what is a legitimate expense of business operations and what is really a cloak for the evasion of taxes, the Internal Revenue Service has examined very carefully the accounts of corporations where unusual expenses deducted from income have been reported. The general philosophy of the courts of law in adjudicating disputes connected with tax liability has been to interpret tax law in lavor of the taxpayer wherever the wording of the law or the intent of Congress is unclear. That does not mean, however, that corporations have a field day in creating emergency expenses to reduce their liability to income taxes. The Internal Revenue Service has determined a reasonable depreciation schedule for the various categories of buildings and equipment, and has set standards for certain other types of business expenses where the amount of the expense depends on the judgment of the financial officers of the corporation. It is in the area of selling expenses, developmental expenses, and compensation to executives that the job of the Internal Revenue Service and the courts in determining what is legitimate is made difficult.

TAXES ON PROPERTY   Corporations, like individuals, own property. Therefore, they are subject to those taxes on property that are assessed by state and local governments. There are two kinds of property taxes, taxes on real property and taxes on personal property. Corporations are subject to both. Real property is generally defined in the tax law as land, buildings, and all machinery or installations that are permanently attached to the land or buildings. This includes, for example, heavy generators embedded in a concrete base. It may seem odd that corporations are subject to a personal property tax. But personal property, defined in tax law, includes all property not permanently attached to the ground or to buildings. For example, business property subject to the above definition includes trucks, movable machinery, raw materials, supplies, and furniture. The tax on real property of businesses is ordinarily stated as a certain percentage of the assessed value of the property. The assessed valuation is that valuation determined by estimate of the *tax assessor*, an individual whose responsibility is to examine the property of taxpayers to determine valuation for tax purposes. Such determination is relatively simple in the case of residential houses for which there is an active market, but is sometimes very difficult to determine in the case of industrial property, which is infrequently bought and sold. For this reason, the assessment of some industrial property is very low compared with residential property. Furthermore, the fact that the position of tax assessor is frequently filled on a basis of political considerations rather than capability and is sometimes subject to partisan pressures causes the burden imposed by the property tax frequently to be inequitably distributed among citizens.

The property tax constitutes the main source of revenue of local governments. The rates vary considerably from town to town and from one section of the country to another. This variation is an important factor in the location of new businesses and constitutes in some cases a reason for the rapid development of towns having low taxes on business property and the slow development of towns having high taxes on business property. While the promoters of a new business are in the fortunate position of being able to select a town with low taxes on property, the owners of businesses that have already made a heavy investment in real estate in a particular town usually find it very difficult to move from a town where tax rates on business property have increased. For this reason, the selection of a community for a new business operation should take into consideration not merely the present tax rates on business property but the probable future trend of tax rates on business property in various communities.

EXCISE TAXES

An excise is a tax levied on the movement of goods from the manufacturer or producer to the consumer. Excises may be levied on the manufacturer of the goods, on the wholesaler or jobber, on the retailer, or on the consumer. All three levels of government, federal, state, and local, levy excise taxes. State governments, however, may only tax the movement of goods confined within their borders, and local governments may not tax the movement of goods not in their own jurisdiction.

One of the most important taxes of the excise type is the tariff. The federal government, since the first Congress, has levied taxes on imports. These taxes have been levied on a wide variety of goods, and the tariff has become exceedingly complex. The purpose of the tariff has been primarily to inhibit American consumers from buying foreign products, and this has been accomplished by raising the price of foreign goods to such heights as to induce many Americans to buy goods produced at home. This interference with the freedom of choice of the American consumer is, naturally, imposed by the government at the demand of American producers, who are generally more powerful in their influence over Congress than are consumers. In a few cases, however, such as newsprint and farm machinery, the consumer has been sufficiently well organized and potent to counter the power of the domestic producer and, as a result, has prevented the establishment of tariff impediments to trade in these items.

The taxes levied by the federal, state, and local governments on the manufacture and distribution of goods within the United States are not primarily for the purpose of interfering in trade but to secure revenue. The excise tax imposed on alcoholic beverages may have some effect in reducing the consumption of such beverages, but the taxes on cigarettes, gasoline, automobiles, electric light bulbs, jewelry, sugar, and other items are levied for revenue. The federal excise taxes are generally levied at the wholesale and retail levels. Many states levy a sales tax, as do some cities. The sales tax is usually collected from the consumer when he purchases an article from the retailer. Most states require the retailer to furnish evidence of all taxable sales made, and to pay a certain percentage of the retail value of such sales. In such instances, the store owner ordinarily increases the price of taxable articles by the amount of the sales tax, and thus endeavors to pass on to the customer the burden of the tax.

MISCELLANEOUS TAXES   In addition to income taxes, property taxes, and excise taxes, a number of taxes are levied on particular businesses and on particular activities of businesses. Although it would be beyond the scope of this chapter to discuss in detail all the taxes imposed on various businesses, a few of them deserve mention.

The federal government levies a tax on payrolls imposed jointly on the worker who receives wages and the employer who pays them. This tax is used for old age and survivors benefits under the social security program inaugurated during the 1930s.

State governments levy on corporations taxes called by a variety of names but all based on the amount of capital stock corporations use to raise funds. These taxes on capital stock are, for the most part, at very low rates.

Many states levy taxes on public utilities, which include power and light companies, street transportation companies, gas companies, and communication companies. These states have found that, in many instances, it is relatively easy to levy taxes on these companies, since they generally pass the burden of the tax to their customers in increased rates charged for their services.

Every state levies special taxes, called business and occupation taxes, for the privilege of conducting operations in particular industries. Business and occupation taxes are those levied on specific businesses or occupations. They include licenses purchased before a businessman can open for business, such as a license to open a restaurant. They also include periodic levies (usually annual) on the privilege of continuing in a specified business or occupation. The number of occupations or business activities subjected to special taxes varies considerably from state to state. In some Southern states, the number of occupations and businesses subject to license taxes is very large. For most states, however, such taxes are restricted to a relatively few types of businesses, and the rates are modest. Recently, local governments have increased the number of businesses and occupations subject to license taxes imposed at the local level. License taxes on the manufacture and distribution of alcoholic beverages have been imposed by states and municipalities from the earliest years of the Republic. Generally, the rates imposed have been high enough to furnish considerable income to the taxing governments. As a matter of fact, the level of liquor license taxes in some states has been so high that it is evidence of the intent of those governments to restrict such activity by means of taxation.

Severance taxes form an important part of the revenue of many states. These are taxes imposed on the extraction of minerals from the ground and the cutting of timber in the forests. The purpose of these taxes is for regulation and revenue. The regulatory aspect of severance taxes is, in theory, a means of controlling the depletion of forests and minerals, in order to utilize this wealth most efficiently.

Most of the burden of miscellaneous taxes mentioned above is passed on to consumers in the form of higher prices. Although it is probable that some of the burden is absorbed by the owners of business, it is evident that most of the added costs of doing business resulting from the imposition of these taxes is reflected in the higher prices that consumers pay. In many instances, the intent of the legislators imposing the tax is that it shall be an indirect tax on the ultimate consumer.

WHO BEARS THE BURDEN OF TAXES?

There is a wide variety of taxes that people pay either directly by sending in the check for tax payments or indirectly by paying a higher price for the goods or services bought from individuals or businesses who must cover their tax expenses in the price they charge for their services. The tax burden of an individual, therefore, is not measured by the amount he pays to the tax collector. That represents only the visible tax burden. The invisible taxes are just as much of a burden. But, because most invisible taxes are included in the price he pays for goods and services, the individual does not always realize the amount of that burden.

Tax payments to federal, state, and local governments by incorporated and unincorporated businesses are very large. The burden of all business taxes, however, is borne by individuals. It would be fine if an inanimate corporation could be made to shoulder the costs of the services rendered by the government to its citizens in the sense that physical burdens might be placed on noncomplaining machines, but, unfortunately, this cannot be done. Tax payments are one of the expenses of doing business. They may be passed on to the customer of a company in the form of higher prices, they may be passed on to the employee in the form of lower wages, or they may be passed on to the owner of the business in the form of lower dividends or profits. As a matter of fact, the burden of business taxes is shared in varying degrees by all three groups. That is not to say, necessarily, that business taxes should not be levied, but it is important to remember that the burden of such taxes is borne by individuals, and that individuals cannot escape paying for the cost of government services by levying taxes on business.

One of the goals of business owners and operators is to increase profits as much as possible. As far as taxes on business are concerned, business operators attempt, as far as possible, to shift the burden to others. However, this cannot always be easily accomplished. A business cannot generally increase the price of its products without suffering a decline in sales. In the case of a few products, such as table salt, this can be done. A tax of 2 cents a pound on the sale of table salt could be passed on to the consumer by raising the price of salt from its former price to a price 2 cents higher. Such an increase would hardly affect the volume of sales. But an increase in the price of theater tickets of 10 percent, to offset a 10 percent admissions tax, would probably induce some theatergoers to watch television a little more and to go to the theater a little less. In such a situation, the theater owner might discover a considerable decline in attendance after the 10 percent increase in admission price. He might find that the profit would be greater by reducing the price of the admission slightly. By increasing the admission price after the imposition of the tax to an amount less than 10 percent above the previous price, and thereby absorbing part of the burden of the tax, he might find his profits greater than they would be if he increased the admission price by the same amount as the increase in the tax. In other words, by absorbing part of the burden of the admissions tax, the theatre owner would suffer a smaller reduction in profit than he would be trying to pass the whole burden on to the consumer.

From the above examples, and from the investigation of many other instances, a general principle emerges: Where the demand for an article is very insensitive to changes in price (price inelastic), the producer can pass on almost the full burden of a tax to the customer in the form of higher prices. Where the demand for an article is very sensitive to changes in price (price elastic), the producer cannot pass on the full burden of a tax to the customer, because an increase in the price of the article would cause a decline is sales. Price elasticity is explained in Chapter 3.

The size and complexity of modern government are, to some degree, a consequence of the spectacular advances in mass production and distribution. Big government reflects, also, an attempt by the people through their government to find solutions to the problems created by modern technology. Furthermore, the size of government is, to a considerable extent, an expression of the insecurity of the present age. As long as government is large, in terms of the size of its expenditures and the extent of its services, the problem of sharing the cost of those services will remain acute. A fuller appreciation of the extent of shifting of tax burdens from the person or agency taxed to others will make possible a fairer distribution of the cost of government.

EFFORTS TO CONTROL THE BUSINESS CYCLE

One of the characteristics of an industrialized, competitive economy is the business cycle, defined as a succession of periods of prosperity alternating with periods of recession. Because of the economic suffering involved in recessions, the attention of business and government leaders has generally been focused on this phase of the cycle.

From 1790 to 1940 we have had 27 recessions of moderate to severe intensity, periods lasting from several months to several years, during which business activity declined substantially from the periods immediately preceding, unemployment rose, and bankruptcies, both personal and business, increased sharply. Until 1930 it had been assumed by practically everyone that the best action government could take in a recession (or in a depression, which is a more severe recession) was not to interfere. The economic theory taught in colleges stated that if businessmen, farmers, and other producers found they could not sell all their products, they would cut prices; if workers became unemployed, they would offer to work for lower wages; if buildings stood unoccupied, landlords would cut rents. Although it might take a while for such readjustments to take effect, they would in due time bring about a reversal of the recession and a return to prosperity. In short, unemployed workers and idle factories were a temporary occurrence, and according to theory could not last long.

Then came the stock market collapse of 1929 and the Great Depression of the 1930s (see Chapter 2). Instead of reversing itself promptly, conditions became worse. Most economists—at least, those who were still working—counseled patience. In the long run things would turn out all right, they said. To this attitude one economist, John Maynard Keynes, reacted, "In the long run we shall all be dead."

In a 1936 book entitled *The General Theory of Employment, Interest, and Money*, Keynes postulated a new theory, generally referred to as the *Keynes theory* or *Keynesianism*. Keynes argued that businessmen did not always cut prices if they could not sell their planned production; they tended to cut production instead. And workers did not always accept lower wages to get scarce jobs; many of them, through their unions, held out for higher wages even if this meant unemployment for large numbers. Keynes believed that full employment and full production were not necessarily normal, interrupted only by occasional recessions. Rather he felt that an economy operating at less than full employment and full production could continue for many years, and that therefore a "slack" economy could be considered normal, albeit unwelcome.

The remedy suggested by Keynes was government action. He recommended that government should actively combat a recession, principally through deficit spending (increasing government payments, reducing taxes, and increasing the federal debt). There was more to his theory than this, of course, but government action was the principal ingredient of the theory. The return of full employment and production, he felt, was the time to reduce government debt in anticipation of a future recession. His conviction that government action was necessary to combat recessions is one that has been accepted by most economists, by most businessmen, and by Republican and Democratic administrations alike.[2]

The Employment Act of 1946 established in law the responsibility of the federal government to counter the instability of the business cycle. It was a formal statement of policy rather than a mandate of specific powers. The law did not dictate what measures the government must take to combat a recession or dampen an inflationary boom. But it did remove from the arena of partisan politics, because the act was supported by both parties, the issue of whether any action by government should be taken. As such it signified acceptance of the Keynesian doctrine of government intervention to achieve and maintain a high level of economic activity.

The Employment Act created a three-man (the first woman economist took office in 1972) Council of Economic Advisers to the President. This Council advises the President on steps to be taken to maintain the economic health of the nation, "to foster and promote free competitive enterprise, to avoid economic fluctuations or to diminish the effects thereof, and to maintain maximum employment, production, and purchasing power." The Council prepares an annual economic

---

[2] President Richard Nixon, Republican, in a nationally televised conversation in 1971 with a news reporter, classified himself as a Keynesian.

survey for the President, which becomes the basis for the President's annual Economic Report to Congress. A Joint Economic Committee of Congress was also established, composed of both representatives and senators, to investigate economic conditions and to recommend action to Congress. Contacts between members of the Joint Economic Committee and the Council of Economic Advisers have been frequent.

From 1945 to 1973 the United States has experienced seven recessions. Government action has been applied, sometimes hesitantly, sometimes vigorously, to combat them. The degree of success is debatable. But it is true that the recessions since 1945 have been milder and shorter than those in our earlier history. It is also true that we have suffered a continuous rise of consumer prices since 1950. Perhaps 30 years is too short a span of time in which to affirm or deny the validity of an economic theory. Nevertheless, the Keynes theory, modified and brought up to date, and the principle of affirmative government action to combat recessions are likely to be national policy for years to come.

SUMMARY   Most government activity in the area of business can be divided into the following spheres: regulations to increase competition, regulations to decrease competition, protection of the consumer, and subsidies and other aids to business.

There are several laws passed by Congress for the purpose of increasing competition by preventing the development of monopolies and by prohibiting unfair methods of competition and collusion among members of an industry that "substantially lessen competition."

Regulations to decrease competition are almost always imposed by government because of the demand of businessmen. These laws are enacted at all levels of government, federal, state, and local. These laws are very numerous and take many forms. Enforcement in some cases is strict; in others, it is weak.

Laws to protect the consumer also have been passed by all levels of government. They have been passed under the conviction that the activities of persons are so interdependent and that the variety of goods and services available so numerous and complex that consumers need the help of government in some aspects of their lives.

All levels of government have aided business since the beginning of the Republic. Direct subsidies of cash, loans on easy terms, vast amounts of information, and a wide variety of services are made available to businesses. A few businesses are aided handsomely; all are helped in some measure.

Government services are paid for through taxes, although fees, fines, sales of goods and services, and other types of collections are also used. Local governments levy taxes by authority of city charters or other delegation of powers from the state government. Each state levies taxes by authority of its state constitution. Congress levies taxes under the authority of the federal Constitution.

Taxes are levied on businesses as well as on individuals. One of the most important business taxes is the corporation income tax, levied on the net profit of corporations by the federal government and most state governments. Businesses are also subject to a property tax, levied by state and local governments, on the real and personal property they own.

Business activity continually fluctuates from prosperity to recession. Efforts to control this instability are made chiefly at the federal level, by government action to combat inflation during a business boom and by combating unemployment and sluggish economic activity during a recession.

1   Why were businesses largely unregulated before the Civil War?
2   Describe how you as an individual determine the quality of the goods you buy.
3   Since there are laws aimed at increasing competition, why are there other laws designed to reduce or eliminate competition?
4   What is the period for which a patent is good? A copyright? A trademark? Do these periods seem reasonable in each case? Discuss.
5   How does the federal government help protect the public against dangerous drugs and foods?
6   Why is the public utilities industry regulated as to rates and services by the government when most other industries are not?
7   When you buy 10 gallons of gasoline at a service station, how do you know that you have received 10 full gallons?
8   What is the purpose of the small-loan laws enacted by the states?
9   How does the federal government give protection to investors?
10 List some of the services rendered by government for which taxes pay.
11 By what authority does each of the following levels of government levy taxes: federal, state, municipal?
12 Explain the differences between a regressive tax, a proportional tax, and a progressive tax.
13 What are tariff duties? Are they imposed to satisfy the demands of producers or consumers? Explain.
14 What remedy did Keynes suggest as a cure for economic depressions?
15 What are the functions of the Council of Economic Advisers to the President?

Bunting, John R.: *The Hidden Face of Free Enterprise*, McGraw-Hill Book Company, New York, 1964.

Scitovsky, Tibor: *Welfare and Competition*, Richard D. Irwin, Inc., Homewood, Ill., 1971.

Smead, Elmer E.: *Government Promotion and Regulation of Business*, Appleton-Century-Crofts, New York, 1969.

Stelzer, Irwin M.: *Selected Antitrust Cases: Landmark Decisions,* Richard D. Irwin, Inc., Homewood, Ill., 1972.

Wilcox, Clair: *Public Policies toward Business*, 4th ed., Richard D. Irwin, Inc., Homewood, Ill., 1971.

Name	Section	Date

COMPLETION SENTENCES

1 Until the Civil War, there was little public concern about declining

Competition .

2 Until 1938 unfair methods of competition were unlawful only if they injured

Competitors Injured

3 The United States Postal Service prohibits the use of the mails to

defraud .

4 Control of quality in the production of milk is done at the

state a local level of government.

5 Companies, either privately or governmentally owned, furnishing an essential

service are called _public utilities_ .

6 Rates, services, and safety on the railroads are regulated by the

ICC .

7 To protect the public from the unrestrained use of property,

Zoning laws are found in nearly all towns and counties.

8 The _Air Transport_ industry probably receives the most bountiful subsidies from the federal government.

9 The agency of the federal government devoted principally to aiding businessmen is the Department of Commerce.

10 The federal government derives its taxing powers from the

Fed. Const. Art. I Sec. 8.

11 There are two kinds of property taxes, those on _real_ property and those on _personal_ property.

12 The _assessed_ valuation is the valuation determined by the estimate of the taxing authorities.

13 The _Property Tax_ constitutes the main source of revenue of local governments.

14 American producers are generally more powerful in their influence over Congress than are American _Consumers_.

15 _Severance_ taxes are taxes imposed on the extraction of minerals from the ground and the cutting of timber in forests.

TRUE OR FALSE STATEMENTS

T1 Before the Civil War, American business was largely unregulated by government.

F2 In United States history there has always been a high degree of concern over the problem of declining competition.

Name	Section	Date

T 3 The Clayton Act was intended to promote competition.

F 4 Competition may be a threat to the profits but not to the existence of businesses.

T 5 One of the oldest and most important interferences with competition is the tariff on imports.

F 6 Patents are among the most recent of government limitations on business freedom.

F 7 In the United States the holder of a patent must use it in order to keep it "alive."

F 8 The inspectors of the Food and Drug Administration may visit a food canning plant unannounced to check on sanitation and safety in preparing foods.

F 9 Health standards in the production and distribution of milk are uniformly and strictly enforced throughout the United States.

T 10 Even though a person has full title to a piece of land, he does not have unrestricted rights to its use.

F 11 All the services rendered by state governments are paid for by taxation.

T 12 The Federal Constitution limits the purpose of any federal tax only to paying debts and providing for defense and the general welfare of the United States.

F 13 The level of local taxation is not considered an important factor in selecting a location for a new plant or office, because local taxes change frequently.

F 14 Only a few states levy a tax on corporation income.

F 15 The general philosophy of the courts in tax cases is to resolve uncertainties in favor of the government rather than the taxpayer.

T 16 Taxes on real property and taxes on personal property are generally levied at different rates.

F 17 Property taxes have become relatively minor sources of revenue for local governments.

F 18 The import taxes levied by state governments are low.

F 19 A severance tax is a form of estate tax.

T 20 The burden of all business taxes is borne by individuals.

EXERCISES

1 Federal, state, and local governments provide services to businessmen. Choose one service to businessmen provided by each of these levels of government. Make a report covering the following items with respect to each service:

a Need for the service—is it needed or not, in your opinion?

b Which businesses benefit from the service?

c How are the costs of the service met?

d Who bears the burden of the cost?

2 Investigate through the library or other source of information one of the governmental regulatory agencies, such as the Pure Food and Drug Administration or the Federal Communications Commission. Describe its history, the types of business it regulates, and the types of activities over which it exercises control. Also indicate whether the scope of the agency's regulation should, in your opinion, be expanded or contracted, giving reasons for your opinion.

3 Select a local business, such as a retail store, service station, or manufacturing plant. List below the municipal, county, state, and federal taxes the business must pay. List also the services to the business rendered by each of the levels of government. What conclusions do you draw?

Name   Section   Date

Type of business:

	Municipal	County	State	Federal
Taxes				
Services				
Comments:				

CHAPTER
30
ETHICS, SOCIAL
RESPONSIBILITIES,
AND
THE CHALLENGE
OF THE FUTURE

Two of the subjects treated in this chapter are public relations on the one hand and ethics and social responsibilities on the other hand. Each is intimately associated with the other, but each has its own emphasis. Public relations is concerned with projecting a favorable image of the company in the public mind. Business ethics is the concept of a business conscience. Be able to explain why each of these is associated with the other.

It is useful to consider different types of publics, such as employees, customers, owners of the business (stockholders usually), and the general public. The efforts of a company to maintain a favorable image in the minds of each of these publics will require different techniques. In some cases, an action by the corporation will improve its image with employees but will damage its image with another group, perhaps the stockholders. The point to keep in mind is that any business must attempt to maintain a favorable public image with a number of different types of people, having different ideals, aspirations, and relations with the company. After reading the chapter, you should understand the difficulty of maintaining a favorable image with all groups at all times.

The development of a business conscience is more difficult to examine. Compare business management with such professions as the law, accounting, medicine, and teaching. Try to appraise the progress in developing a social conscience in the area of business as compared with other professional groups. Also try to judge the extent of need for a social conscience in the business area as compared with the professions mentioned above.

In June 1969 two Americans stepped onto the surface of the moon. As a triumph of technology and human daring, this accomplishment stands alone. The pictures of men walking on an alien planet were exciting. But probably of greater significance were the photographs of the earth, taken from thousands of miles away. These showed the earth to be rather small, somewhat fragile-looking, and very much alone in the blackness of space. This has made the more perceptive among us less insular in our concerns. We appreciate that what we do to our environment we do to ourselves. There appears to be a growing sense of responsibility, with notable exceptions, of course, of understanding that our actions affect our neighbors and that, as we approach the twenty-first century, we are all neighbors. Our world is our home, and it is the only one we have.

Responsibility to society is not what we expect of any one group. We expect it from politicians, businessmen, labor union leaders, farmers, professionals, everybody. However, this book is about business. Therefore we shall focus on the responsibilities and ethics of businessmen. Business has a responsibility toward various groups, as indicated in Figure 30-1. Business owes employees decent working conditions and decent wages, for example. But the responsibility works both ways. Employees owe the business that employs them an honest day's work. Each is dependent upon the other. Each must be concerned with the welfare of the other, for in doing so each will contribute to his own welfare. Enlightened businessmen strive to build good relations with those groups with which they deal, an activity that is referred to as "public relations." But business has concerns that are broader than its relations with individual groups. These are the areas of public responsibility of business, as illustrated in Figure 30-1. These are not alone the responsibility of businessmen; they concern us all. But again, since this book is about business, our attention is directed to the role of business in these problems.

There are many definitions of **public relations**. It has been called the management of the asset "goodwill." It has been defined by Paul Garrett, public relations director of General Motors Corporation, as follows: "Public relations is a fundamental attitude of mind, a philosophy of management, which deliberately and with enlightened selfishness places the broad interest of the public first in every decision affecting the operation of business." A more homely definition is "being good and getting credit for it."

FIGURE 30-1   The social groups and the social concerns of business.

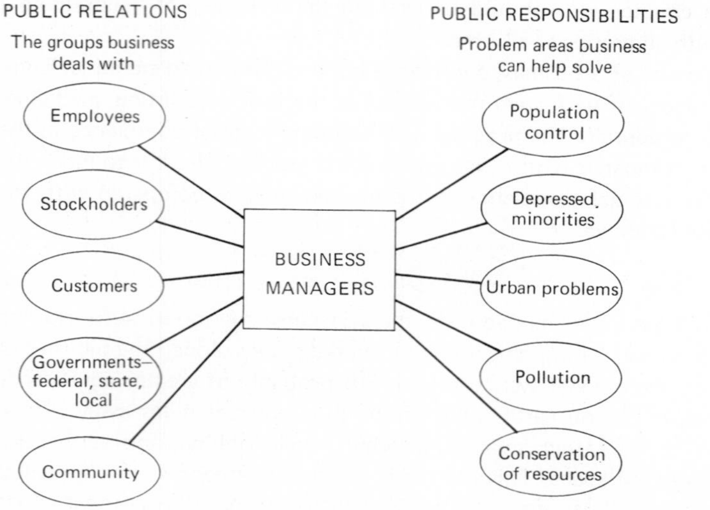

PUBLIC RELATIONS

The groups business deals with

PUBLIC RESPONSIBILITIES

Problem areas business can help solve

- Employees
- Stockholders
- Customers
- Governments—federal, state, local
- Community

BUSINESS MANAGERS

- Population control
- Depressed minorities
- Urban problems
- Pollution
- Conservation of resources

Fundamentally, public relations is not a program. Rather it is a philosophy. It is a frame of mind that conditions the activities of a business. It recognizes a continuing responsibility toward every institution and person who is directly or indirectly related to the business. The ideal of public relations is to win deserved confidence and respect. Public relations is not publicity. The latter does not inquire into business responsibility, but is merely a tool by which goods or ideas are promoted, be they good or bad. Through publicity, businessmen buy public support; through public relations, they earn it.

Public relations considers many different groups; it studies the relation of a company to each of these groups, the aspirations of each group, and the responsibilities of the company toward each.

EMPLOYEE RELATIONS

General Electric Company has more than 200,000 employees, General Motors more than 300,000, and the Bell Telephone System employs more than half a million. One of the grave problems created by the growth of businesses into giant corporations is the loss of personal contact between management at the top and workers at the bottom. An important goal of employee relations is the reestablishment of the contact that existed when the company was small. Obviously, such contact cannot be established in the same form as might have existed at the beginning of the company's history. The president of a large corporation cannot call everybody by his first name. Contact cannot be personal between top management and the worker at the lathe or typewriter. But there are other means of communication than personal contact. The company magazine is one. Bulletin boards, open houses, and public address systems are others.

In a classic experiment made from 1927 to 1932, a group of women in the Western Electric plant at Hawthorne (near Chicago) were subjected to a series of changes in their work environment to determine the effect of different conditions of work on output. Rest pauses were introduced, lengthened, increased in number, and reduced in number; pay was shifted from an hourly basis to piecework and back to hourly pay again; the workweek was changed in length; and free hot lunches were provided and later taken away. During all of this, the women were watched by a representative of management, counseled, asked to give their opinion on changes, and told the reason changes were made. The results of the experiment were perplexing. No matter what changes were made, the output of the group went up in almost every case. Even when working conditions were returned to what they were originally, the output increased.

Until this experiment, management had accepted as self-evident that the way to improve the rate of production in a plant was to improve the machinery, reduce unnecessary hand motions, provide better light, reduce fatigue, and so on. In other words, only the physical characteristics of the worker were considered. The Hawthorne experiments proved the importance of considering the emotional makeup as well. The only explanation of the increasing output of the test group regardless of the changes in environment was that the women were made to feel more than just cogs in a machine. It was obvious to them that management realized their importance. They were even asked for their opinions on working conditions. Management was no longer impersonal, and they were no longer just "hired hands." They had achieved status and some degree of respect. The experiment proved that the road to more effective worker effort lay in recognizing the emotional as well as the physical well-being of the employee, explaining to him the reasons for management decisions, and making him aware that management appreciated the importance of his work.

Having recognized that the employee is a complex being, progressive management studies him in all his complexities. Employers have found that money is not the only compensation for which men work. There are other factors that influence the quantity and quality of a worker's output, such as desire for status, pride in accomplishment, approbation of the group to which the worker belongs, the desire to be appreciated and noticed, and the need for respect. Having recognized man's complex nature, management can better direct its employee relations program. With a better insight into the wants and fears of their employees, managers can attempt to satisfy those wants and reduce those fears insofar as this can reasonably be accomplished.

The mechanics of employee relations are largely those of providing effective two-way communication between employee and management. The methods of maintaining communication and raising employee morale were discussed in Chapter 13. The main point to emphasize here is that a better understanding of the employee as a human being rather than as merely a factory hand or a member of the office help must be the foundation on which effective communication and personnel policies must be built. Speaking for his company, one corporation president has said: "We conceive of communications essentially as a way of working with people. Good communications with us results from having something to communicate, sound policies, beliefs, and principles of operation."[1]

STOCKHOLDER RELATIONS

The American corporation is managed by executives chosen by a board of directors. Each director is elected by the stockholders, who own the corporation. However, each person elected by the stockholders to fill a vacancy on the board of directors is typically selected not by the stockholders but by the remaining directors. The board room is the seat of power in the modern corporation. Chapter 1 mentioned the lack of control by scattered stockholders over the corporation they own. The relationship between the directors of a corporation and the stockholders is not the relationship of a hired manager to the owner of a store. The owners of a large corporation are not active in the affairs of their company. Their contact with the directors is largely through the mails, when stockholder meetings are announced, quarterly statements of financial conditions are sent, and annual reports are distributed.

Stockholder relations in the past were notable in many instances for the

[1] Neil McElroy, of Procter and Gamble, quoted in John W. Hill, *Corporate Public Relations*, Harper & Row, Publishers, Incorporated, New York, 1958, p. 103.

absence of any attempt by the directors to cultivate the owners of the business. Information about the company was rarely sent to them except for financial statements, and these were prepared with little thought of making them readable to persons unfamiliar with accounting. Attendance at stockholders' meetings was not solicited, although announcements of time and place were usually sent. Stockholders visiting the offices of the company were given a reception indistinguishable from that given any stranger.

Stockholder relations, like employee relations, are largely a matter of maintaining effective two-way communication between the stockholders and the management of the corporation. There are two means of contact between the management and the stockholders that are commonly used. They are the announcements, statements, and letters sent through the mails and the annual meeting.

Some corporations send letters to their stockholders only once a year. These are likely to contain financial statements in summary form and a proxy for the stockholder to sign, delegating an officer of the company or a member of the board to vote the stockholder's shares as the management sees fit. Most of the large corporations, however, send a letter to their stockholders at least four times a year. It is also common for them to mail quarterly financial statements, announcements of the annual meeting, and information of interest about the company from time to time. When dividend checks are sent out, companies frequently enclose a pamphlet containing news about the company.

Some corporations with a large number of stockholders publish magazines specifically prepared for company owners. Examples of such magazines are the following:

Avco Stockholders News Letter

Westinghouse Stockholders Quarterly

Du Pont Stockholder and *Du Pont Magazine*

U. S. Steel Quarterly

JM Stockholders News (Johns-Manville Corporation)

News and Views for Stockholders (Consolidated Edison Company of New York)

The size, frequency of publication, and scope of information contained in these magazines vary considerably. Quarterly publication is probably most common. The articles will commonly include news about new products, changes in management, and information about the industry the company is in.

The annual financial report to stockholders has in recent years changed considerably. For many years, it was confined to a statement of condition (balance sheet) of the company at the end of the year and an income statement. For many companies, these reports have become magazines in themselves, running to 50 pages or more. They are printed on good-quality paper and are often in full color. They contain financial information presented not only in the traditional form prepared by accountants but also in charts, diagrams, and tables. Every effort is made to present the data about the companies' past year of operations in a manner as easy to understand and as attractive as possible.

The annual meeting of stockholders presents an opportunity for the owners to meet those who run the corporation. The primary purpose of such a meeting is to elect the board of directors. It is very rare that this is anything more than a formality, since the existing board of directors has in nearly every case most of the votes of absent stockholders by means of proxy forms signed by the stockholders. Although attendance runs less than 1 percent of total stockholders for many large companies, the effort of the owners to attend meetings has shown a remarkable increase. Attendance is encouraged by managements, and shareholders' questions at most meetings are answered courteously and fully. The great advantage of annual meetings in the field of stockholder relations is that they provide a face-to-face meeting between shareholder and management. The give-and-take between the two groups during the question-and-answer period provides a spontaneity impossible in communication by mail.

Because most stockholders are not able to attend the annual meeting, some corporations publish postmeeting statements. One of the best of these is published by the Standard Oil Company of New Jersey (now Exxon). It contains a verbatim report of the meeting, the number of shares represented (in person or by proxy), the result of the balloting for directors, and pictures taken at the meeting.

CONSUMER RELATIONS

Goods and services are produced in order that they may be consumed. This means that the goods must be offered at a price at which they will sell, that the quality must be acceptable, and that the goods must be advertised and made available for purchase. Executive decisions are made to a considerable degree with the consumer in mind. Because of this, the attitudes of consumers are investigated and analyzed probably more than those of any of the other various publics with which management has to deal.

In any consumer relations program, a company is concerned with its reputation. Primarily, this is built on good quality, reasonable price, prompt delivery, and a fair policy for return of defective merchandise. If a company does not have these qualities in its production and marketing, no amount of publicity will save its reputation in the long run. One of the benefits of competition, as stated before, is that it keeps each competitor on his toes in his relations with consumers.

Consumer relations, however, go beyond the narrow concept of price and product. The enormous increase in the variety of goods and services and the number of brands of each available to consumers today make consumer choice difficult and exploitation of consumer ignorance easy. If public relations is defined by a company in the way it is used in this chapter, the responsibility of the company will go beyond merely refraining from exploiting the consumer's ignorance. It will support those means by which consumers can become better informed and by which they can be protected from unscrupulous producers. The goals of consumer relations are twofold: to help consumers become more intelligent and discriminating buyers, and to become more responsive to the needs and desires of consumers.

One of the evidences of responsibility toward the consumer is the creation and support by businessmen of the Better Business Bureaus throughout the country. These bureaus exist to protect the consumer and, by so doing, to protect reputable businessmen from the destructive competition of unscrupulous sellers. The bureaus examine local advertising and selling methods, using publicity and persuasion to effect reforms.

As in dealing with its other publics, business recognizes that effective consumer relations must seek to maintain and improve channels of communication between producer and consumer. This can be accomplished by a variety of means. Retailers can solicit suggestions and criticisms about store policy from their customers. Manufacturers can solicit criticisms from purchasers of their products and invite letters from customers, satisfied or dissatisfied. The Ford Motor Company makes available to the purchaser of a new Ford a general-interest magazine called **Ford Times**. Plant tours and open houses are other means by which customers in the vicinity of a plant may become acquainted with the company.

COMMUNITY RELATIONS

The responsibilities of a business toward the community go beyond merely paying taxes. A community is the place where people have their homes, where they work, bring up their children, and enjoy most of their leisure hours. Good communities make for pleasant living. To make a community a good place to live requires the cooperation of all who live in it or own property in it. Because business managers generally have more power and prestige in a community than the average person, their responsibility is greater in community affairs. It is this responsibility that is the subject of community relations.

Effective community relations is not a matter of giving money to worthy causes, although such contributions from business are always welcome. It is found in the participation of business leaders in community affairs. And it is found in the recognition of management that nearly all of their business decisions affect the community in some way, and that community welfare should be given consideration in making decisions. The areas in which community relations can be promoted include education, health, cultural activities, and community attractiveness.

EDUCATION

The primary support for education comes from the taxes paid by businesses and individuals. But there are other ways of supporting education in a community, and enlightened management will participate in such support. Businessmen can furnish speakers or participate in forums and round table discussions. This will help enrich the educational program of the schools in a community. Plant tours may be arranged to permit students and teachers to see how products are made and distributed. Businessmen in some towns hold a joint Business-Education Day, during which local banks, offices, and plants guide groups of teachers through their places of work, describing the processes seen. During lunch, the guests meet the top executives of the companies and have a chance to ask questions about business operations.

HEALTH

As in the case of education, the health of a community is the primary responsibility of the local government. However, business has the power to injure or enhance the health of the residents by the degree of responsibility it exercises in this area. Streams and rivers have been polluted, explosions have destroyed residential property, and smoke and fumes from factories have menaced the health of the community. These are examples of irresponsibility, of which no *enlightened* businessman would be guilty. Good community relations include not only refraining from endangering the health of the community but influencing others to cooperate as well. Furthermore, enlightened management will actively support those activities that contribute to raising the health of the residents.

CULTURAL AND
RECREATIONAL
ACTIVITIES

Art museums, symphony orchestras, legitimate theater, and similar cultural efforts generally exist through private support. Businesses can give financial aid to supplement that of individuals. Some companies make their auditoriums or large rooms available for drama presentations or music rehearsals. Others publicize cultural events on their plant bulletin boards or in company newspapers. One of the most common evidences of business support in the field of recreation is the sponsorship of Little League baseball teams; businesses purchase uniforms, provide equipment, and furnish playing fields. Company personnel, from employees of the lowest rank to executives, are found as umpires and coaches.

AN ATTRACTIVE
COMMUNITY

The industrial section of a city can be a depressing sight. Gaunt factory buildings, blackened with smoke, squatting among weeds or surrounded by asphalt pavement are found in nearly all cities, particularly the older ones. Such surroundings are unpleasant to work in and to live near. People generally avoid them if they can. Recently, however, businessmen have become aware that industrial buildings can be attractive as well as practical. Some recently built factory and office buildings show the keen aesthetic sense of the architect and, instead of detracting from the beauty of the surroundings, enhance it. Even where a factory building is old and ugly, it can usually be made to look better with a new coat of paint, For example, the storage tanks and pipes of an oil refinery on San Francisco Bay are painted in a variety of pastel colors, transforming a cluttered industrial landscape into a view pleasing to the passing motorist.

Landscaping improves any area. A modern company, sensitive to its community relations, will make use of whatever opportunities for landscaping there are.

Green grass, trees, and flowers can make an area parklike. The dividends in community goodwill, while difficult to measure, will usually be worth the cost.

URBAN PROBLEMS

The older sections of many of America's cities, usually the central areas, are places where buildings are in decay, crime is rampant, and unemployment is high. Families that can afford to move have left. Department stores and other businesses have abandoned their downtown locations in favor of the suburbs. The people who remain are those who cannot afford to live anywhere else.

Can the urban areas be saved? Some efforts are already being made. Federal and state governments have provided financial incentives for urban renewal projects which clear areas of abandoned and unsafe buildings to make way for newer, more attractive residences, office buildings, and stores. A few cities have transformed some sections of downtown streets into attractive malls with trees, shrubbery, and fountains—and where pedestrian traffic only is allowed.

Business has aided in the efforts to revive urban areas. Some retailers have chosen redeveloped downtown locations for their new outlets. Businessmen in the downtown locations of some cities have subsidized low-fare or no-fare bus transportation to attract customer traffic. A few banks have encouraged, through lending programs, the establishment of new enterprises located in older urban areas. Much more needs to be done, for the problem of the cities is monumental. But the problem is recognized, and a start, through cooperation of government and business, is being made.

AID TO MINORITY GROUPS

In the generally prosperous times since World War II, some groups have not shared to the same extent as others. Unemployment has been higher, wages lower, and opportunities for advancement less for the following groups: women, blacks, teenagers, American Indians, and Chicanos (persons of Mexican origin). Other groups are sometimes included, but the above have been most often mentioned.

In an effort to improve the economic and social position of these groups, the federal government has responded with legislation and money. An Equal Rights Amendment, requiring equality of treatment for men and women, passed Congress in 1972 and was sent to the state legislatures for ratification. Several laws have been enacted by Congress and regulations have been imposed by federal agencies to provide more employment and improve opportunities for advancement for women and minorities. The Small Business Administration, through its MESBIC program (see Chapter 5), has channeled funds to enterprises started by minority groups, particularly in older urban areas.

The Ford Motor Company and other corporations have initiated programs to train and employ members of disadvantaged minorities. Most of the larger companies and many smaller ones have opened up positions formerly the exclusive preserve of males. To some extent the reverse is evident, with the recent appearance, for example, of stewards on the airlines. The Bank of America and other banks make special efforts to encourage, through advice and financing, members of minority groups to organize enterprises.

SAVING THE ENVIRONMENT

In 1973 smog was so severe in Los Angeles that the Federal Environment Protection Agency gave serious consideration to imposing rationing of gasoline in southern California.

In 1973 Lake Erie was in danger of becoming a dead lake, choked with sewage and other wastes.

The major river of Cleveland, the Cuyahoga, has become so oily that it has caught fire on occasion.

Our environment is in danger, and not just in the United States. Persons in Japan have been reduced to imbecility through eating fish from streams contaminated with industrial mercury wastes. Lake Baikal, in Siberia, the deepest and one of the clearest large bodies of fresh water in the world, is endangered by sewage and other untreated discharges from industrial plants near the lake.

Twenty years ago there was almost complete apathy regarding care for the environment. Abundant resources and a smaller population made us careless and wasteful. In recent years, however, apathy has been replaced by growing concern. Young people in particular have voiced alarm, possibly because they realize they are the ones who will live to see the results of our current practices as they affect life at the end of this century.

Theodore Roosevelt described conservation of our environment as "the fundamental problem which underlies almost every other problem of our national life."[2] To save our environment, we must all help. But business, because so many of its activities are devoted to transforming our resources into goods, can provide leadership. Without the cooperation of businessmen of all countries, the environment cannot be saved; with their support, it can.

The immediate problem areas of the environment are population control, conservation of natural resources, clean air, pure water, and disposal of wastes. To these we shall turn our attention.

POPULATION CONTROL

Population figures for the United States and the world are shown in the table for selected years. Most of this growth was made possible by declining death rates,

[2]Editors of *Fortune, The Environment, A National Mission for the Seventies,* Harper & Row, Publishers, Incorporated, New York, 1970, p. 12.

Year	1650	1800	1900	1947	1970	1985 (estimated)
			(millions of persons)			
United States		4	80	145	205	253
World	470	919	1,571	2,317	3,632	4,933

particularly infant mortality. But what is the consequence of adding more and more people, particularly as the surface of the earth remains constant in area? Can constantly rising numbers of people and constantly rising per capita consumption of the world's resources continue? For how long?

These questions are not easily answered. However, they are being asked, and increasing concern is being shown over implications of these questions. What is the position of business on this matter? There is no one position, since businessmen have as diverse opinions on population control as the general population itself. Nevertheless, there are some recent trends visible. Fifty years ago it was unthinkable for business groups in a city or a state not to encourage rapid growth of population and industry. Now, however, businessmen and others in a few municipalities no longer push the goal of ever-increasing size. Businessmen and others are giving greater support than before to family planning. The theme that economic prosperity requires constantly increasing population is being preached much less frequently by businessmen and economists. In short, population growth is being examined critically as never before.

CONSERVATION OF NATURAL RESOURCES

The growth in world population and the growth in per capita income have combined to produce a rapid increase in the consumption of natural resources. This raises two serious questions: How soon will the consumption of renewable resources, such as breathable air and drinkable water, exceed the capacity of nature to regenerate them? How rapidly will nonrenewable resources, such as fossil fuels and ores, become so scarce that a decline in per capita standard of living becomes inevitable? A large part of the answer to such questions is conservation of natural resources. This is a goal, of course, that everybody supports in principle. But how can businessmen in particular help attain this goal?

To some extent we are forced to practice conservation. As some materials become scarce, their prices rise; and with the rise in prices, substitutes are used. Competition forces manufacturers to use less of those materials that increase their costs and, where possible, to use other materials.

Increasingly, businessmen are moving away from urging ever-increasing consumption of their products, advocating instead a more careful pattern of consumption. Electric power companies and gas companies until recently urged their customers to "use more electricity, burn more gas." Now the accent is less on trying to sell more electricity or gas and more on urging careful, conservative use to avoid waste. Oil companies are making more effort to inform motorists how to get more miles per gallon. Such actions will very likely increase in the future, as resources become depleted. Business, with the power to persuade that it has developed in marketing products and services, can use that power to promote the awareness of our limited global resources and to instill a pattern of careful rather than wasteful consumption.

CLEAN AIR   More than 200,000 tons of smoke particles and other pollutants are released into the atmosphere each year. Most of the pollutants are created by burning fuel, and nearly all of the fuel burned is coal, oil, and natural gas. These fossil fuels, that took hundreds of millions of years to create, are being converted to waste at a rate in the United States that doubles every 20 years. Moreover, in the process of burning any fuel, the air that we breathe is consumed. It may be that we are consuming oxygen in the atmosphere more rapidly than it can be regenerated by nature. We do not really know. In our cities the quality of air has declined to the point that it is at times an active cause of lung diseases. Industry smokestacks, incinerators, and automobiles contribute to the smog (a smoky condition of the air that cuts down on visibility and causes eye and nose irritation), but the automobile is the worst offender. One ponders the question whether it is possible to be urbanized and motorized and still be civilized.

The three major sources of air pollution are transportation, industry, and heating. Because the automobile exhaust is a major contributor, the Clean Air Act of 1970 mandates that cars manufactured in 1975 (postponed in 1973 to take effect in 1976) and later must provide a 90 percent reduction in nitrogen oxide in automobile exhausts. Burning of leaves and the use of backyard incinerators are banned in many cities and towns. The electric utility industry by 1970 had spent over $1 billion for air filters to remove ash and other precipitates from the stacks of its coal-burning generators and to remove sulfur from its fuel (sulphur particles combining with water in clouds has been found to create sulfuric acid). Exxon Corporation has spent $200 million constructing a plant in the Caribbean to remove sulfur from oil, and plans to construct additional such facilities. President Nixon has proposed a discriminatory tax on sulfur-rich coal and oil to spur research to remove sulfur.

Concern with air purity recognizes that pollution in one country affects other countries. Sulfuric acid in snow and rain showers in Sweden have been found to be caused by the burning of sulfur-rich coal in England. International cooperation to save our atmosphere will eventually come—hopefully before we are all smothered. At present, actions to clear the air are undertaken in varying degrees in the industrial nations. The high level of industrial production and the large number of internal combustion engines in the United States makes us one of the worst offenders. But we are also foremost among nations in making a start, through governmental regulations and voluntary industry effort, in restoring breathable air.

About 95 percent of the world's water is in the oceans. Less than 5 percent is in lakes, rivers, the ground, and the air. Although we dare not dismiss the oceans as being so vast that we cannot destroy them with pollution, the critical concern of our time is with use and abuse of fresh water.   **PURE WATER**

A sample of water taken from the Ohio River near Cincinnati yielded the following:

Coliform bacteria (from raw sewage)
Viruses (including polio and hepatitis)
Cyanide
Pesticides (DDT, dieldrin, heptachlor, toxaphene, and others)
Arsenic
Phosphorus
Zinc
Strontium 90

Over 100 million Americans get their drinking water from rivers and lakes that may contain pollutants. Although the water is chlorinated or otherwise treated before it is piped to homes and factories, the treatment has little effect on many of the pollutants.

The problem of clean water cannot be divorced from the problem of sewage treatment. In the 20-year period since 1952, more than $15 billion has been invested in municipal and industrial sewage treatment facilities. And yet thousands of communities, including Memphis and other cities, dump raw sewage into rivers and waterways. Many cities give only superficial treatment, and most give no treatment at all to water from storm sewers. In 1970 over 300,000 industrial plants dumped their untreated wastes into lakes and rivers or into municipal sewage systems incapable of removing industrial pollutants.[3] As population increases and industry expands, the volume of pollutants will continue to rise. But the natural supply of fresh water will not. We cannot depend any longer on nature to cleanse our water supplies. We shall have to do it ourselves.

Some progress, slow to be sure, is being made in cleaning up fresh-water supplies. Under the Water Quality Act of 1965, the Clean Water Restoration Act of 1966, and the Water Quality Improvement Act of 1970, federal and state officials establish water quality standards, set timetables for compliance by municipalities and industry, and plan surveillance programs.

Some companies have taken steps to eliminate impurities from their waste water, and more will undoubtedly follow in the future. Paper processing companies are spending some $200 million a year on equipment to cleanse water. In some areas there is planned "cross cycling" between plants, by which one plant disposes of its hot water by piping it to another plant that uses hot water, and where certain wastes of one plant become the raw material of another. Investigating the many

[3] Ibid., p. 20.

possibilities of "cross cycling" is in its early stages. Its use will very likely spread.

The insistence of the public through its government and the ingenuity of industry will result, we hope, in a cleaner water future. This will be most evident in newly designed plants of paper, chemical, refining, and other industries. A top executive of Dow Chemical Company says, "From an operating man's standpoint, the emphasis on waste control is one of the better things that has happened to us. It sharpened up our whole operation. We will not accept a plant today that doesn't have its pollution control in hand before it's built."[4]

DISPOSAL OF WASTES

As we have seen above, most liquid waste is dumped into waterways. Sewage contains solid wastes, too. Both must be removed before the water is clean. However, there still remain the problems of disposal of solids such as ashes, garbage, bottles, cans, slag from steel furnaces, paper, old rubber, and junked automobiles. True, some of these are dumped into our waterways. But better solutions can and must be found.

One answer is recycling. During World War II, it was a patriotic duty to save the empty toothpaste tube to be collected for reuse. Some communities sponsor paper drives, at which bundles of old newspapers are collected for reprocessing. A few communities urge homeowners and businesses to sort their trash into different categories (paper, bottles, aluminum cans) for easier reuse by industry. Recycling undoubtedly will expand. Already over half of the lead used by industry is derived from scrap, and close to half of the copper and brass is also. About one-third of the aluminum and a fourth of the steel is reclaimed from scrap. Research into ways of economically compacting automobiles and separating the glass, sheet steel, and other components may cause the disappearance of abandoned cars from fields and roadsides.

The disposal of used atomic fuel, dangerous chemicals, and other deadly wastes will probably require special handling. Such contaminants cannot be dumped into streams or fields where they can do damage. They cannot even be safely dissolved in the waters of the oceans. Abandoned salt mines, deep in the earth, have been suggested as garbage dumps for such wastes. Eventually some of these materials may be rocketed into space, to circle the sun endlessly or disappear into its interior.

The challenge of environmental deterioration is one we all face and must solve together. But business, through industrial technology, can provide the means of accomplishment, if we are willing to meet the challenge. A statement read by President Nixon says,

> Man has applied a great deal of his energy in the past to exploring his planet. Now we must make a similar commitment of effort to restoring that planet. The unexpected consequences of our technology have often worked to damage our environment; now we must turn that same technology to the work of its restoration and preservation.[5]

[4]The Editors of *Fortune, Challenges for Business in the 1970's*, Little, Brown and Company, 1972, p. 153.
[5]Editors of *Fortune, The Environment, A National Mission for the Seventies,* Harper & Row, Publishers, Incorporated, New York, 1970, p. 13.

ETHICS AND BUSINESS

It is axiomatic that businessmen have power. Their stewardship of the productive and distributive resources of the nation gives them a large degree of control not only over the economic aspects of the nation's existence but over its cultural and social aspects as well. Businessmen are human beings, and human character has weaknesses as well as strengths. What checks exist to prevent or limit the abuse of power held by businessmen? The checks we have depended on include competition among firms in an industry; competition among industries; the development of countervailing blocks of power such as labor unions, large retail organizations, and large manufacturers;[6] and the growth of government regulation and government ownership of industry.

Businessmen must first strive to make profits, a fact that should be recognized by business critics as well as by businessmen. Without profits a firm does not long survive and thus cannot serve society. But beyond the drive for profits are other forces affecting business actions. One of these is the conscience of the businessman, giving him an increasing awareness of his social responsibilities. Another is the force of public opinion, to which large corporations are particularly exposed. Paul Samuelson, Nobel laureate in economics, has commented, "A large corporation these days not only may engage in social responsibility; it had damn well better try to do so."[7]

Business executives discharge their social responsibilities to different degrees and in different ways. A prime example of long-term dedication to involvement in community problems is the Polaroid Corporation of Cambridge, Massachusetts, which for many years has used company resources to aid disadvantaged persons. The company's accomplishments in 1973 included the following:

> Of the 10,000 United States employees of the company, about 300 are disadvantaged physically or mentally or with a poor command of English.
> Over 150 ex-convicts have been hired, with only two having failed to remain law abiding.
> From 1968 to 1973, 243 "unemployable" workers were trained by Polaroid to become useful workers in its own and other plants.
> In Boston and nearby towns Polaroid supported 143 community projects, including camera loans and family planning services.
> Two dozen Polaroid officials were assigned to projects to rehabilitate prison inmates.[8]

The record of Polaroid has been largely due to the impetus of the founder and first president, Dr. William H. Land. "Land has always felt that your job and your company should be things you can take pride in. He has always encouraged employees to do things on their own. People know this and they realize Polaroid has a tradition of being concerned with more than the balance sheet."[9]

What will develop of the concept of social responsibility is hard to say. There

[6]The theory of equilibrium attainable through the existence of powerful economic groups is presented in John K. Galbraith, *American Capitalism: The Concept of Countervailing Power,* Houghton Mifflin Company, Boston, 1956.
[7]Gilbert Burck, "The Hazards of Corporate Responsibility," *Fortune,* June 1973, p. 115.
[8]"How Social Responsibility Became Institutionalized," *Business Week,* June 30, 1973, p. 74.
[9]Ibid., p. 74.

is considerable skepticism that the business community can rise above the habits hardened by generations in which self-interest was considered not only a permissible goal of conduct but the sole responsibility of businessmen. The benediction of self-seeking was given by Russell Conwell, a nineteenth-century preacher who reported earning $8 million by 6,000 deliveries of his sermon, "Acres of Diamonds." In this sermon, he said, "To secure wealth is an honorable ambition, and is one great test of a person's usefulness to others. . . . I say, get rich, get rich!"[10] Until the present century, it was evident that if the decisions of businessmen were to be guided toward the general welfare, the guidance had to come from outside the businessmen, not from within. The present century, however, is one of profound change. We have lived through the two most devastating wars of all time and the worst depression of our history. We have also recovered from that depression and achieved a prosperity unmatched in previous times. During these upheavals, we have come to understand our mutual dependence, and to realize that our decisions do not affect us alone and, therefore, are not ours alone to make. We live in a world becoming ever smaller, and in a nation becoming constantly more closely knit.

A sense of social responsibility is developing, perhaps slowly, but developing nevertheless. Young people, more exuberant than their elders, have become more assertive. Consumers have become more vocal, particularly where they have uncovered real or imagined abuses. Businessmen increasingly are listening to both. Business management is exhibiting some of the characteristics of a profession, like medicine or the law. Both physicians and lawyers have a professional code of ethics to which the responsible members of those professions adhere. While no formal, simply stated code of ethics exists to guide businessmen, since they do not have a professional organization of the type that serves law and medicine, professional standards of conduct are nevertheless being expected of businessmen increasingly as time passes. And progress is likely to continue. M. A. Wright, Chairman of the Board of Humble Oil and Refining Company (now Exxon Corporation), expresses a common concern of businessmen in these words:

> If businessmen hope to merit a central position in our society, we must work at helping solve society's social problems with the same energy and imagination that we apply to the nation's economic problems. This challenge demands the best of every American leader.[11]

SUMMARY   Public relations includes all of the activities of a business devoted to improving the public image or reputation of the business. Public relations is directed chiefly toward the following people:

> **1** *Employees:*   To instill a spirit of loyalty toward the company, and a recognition by officers of company responsibility toward employees.

[10]Quoted by Marquis W. Childs and Douglas Cater, *Ethics in a Business Society,* Mentor Books, New American Library of World Literature, Inc., New York, 1954, p. 137.
[11]M. A. Wright, *The Business of Business,* McGraw-Hill Book Company, Inc., New York, 1967, p. 24.

2 *Stockholders:* To recognize that stockholders, even those with a single share, are part owners of the company and that company policies should be selected to benefit them as owners.

3 *Consumers:* To improve the reputation of the company's products and services and to refrain from taking unfair advantage of customer ignorance.

4 *Community:* To operate the company as a "responsible citizen" of the community, participating with individuals and other companies in efforts to improve the community.

Professional organizations of physicians, dentists, lawyers, professors, accountants, and others have individual codes of ethics. There is no single professional organization representing businessmen comparable in authority to the professions mentioned above. Nevertheless, business management is increasingly considered a profession as time passes. Although professional codes of conduct for businessmen are not yet as strong as they are for physicians and lawyers, improvement is seen as each decade passes. The concept that a responsible businessman is a "trustee for society as a whole" is gradually gaining acceptance.

The crisis of long-term damage to our environment has three parts: clean air, fresh water, and harmless disposal of wastes. Industry can lead, with technology and management, and government can regulate in the interest of a healthier environment, but we must all do our share. If we succeed, our planet will be a pleasant place for our children and our grandchildren.

**QUESTIONS
FOR REVIEW**

1 What is the distinction between publicity and public relations?

2 Why is it useful to management to consider the emotional welfare of employees as well as their physical welfare?

3 Describe the Hawthorne experiments. What did management learn from them?

4 What factors other than money wages influence the quantity and quality of a worker's output? How important are these, in your opinion?

5 What influence do stockholders have in a large corporation over the policies of management?

6 Why should the directors of a corporation having many stockholders encourage attendance at stockholders' meetings? Discuss.

7 Why do some corporations send postmeeting reports to their stockholders after each annual meeting of stockholders?

8 What is the difference between public relations directed toward the customers of a company and the advertisement of company products?

9 What is the Better Business Bureau? Who supports it? What does it attempt to accomplish?

10 Businessmen support education by paying taxes. Do businessmen have any further obligation to education? How can they support education by means other than paying taxes?

11 What are some examples of business irresponsibility in the field of health of the community? Some examples of responsibility?

12 Does a company benefit by supporting a city symphony orchestra in the

community in which the company is located? A zoo? A children's museum? A local art gallery?

13 If a company sells to customers who almost never visit the company's place of business, why should the company be concerned with the appearance of its place of business?

14 Why does there appear to be more concern for the quality of the air we breathe and the water we drink today than there was 30 or 40 years ago?

15 The problem of clean water cannot be divorced from the problem of sewage and the disposal of waste water. What are the reasons why the two are parts of the same problem?

SELECTED READINGS   Bohm, Peter, and Allen V. Kneese: *The Economics of Environment,* St. Martin's Press, Inc., New York, 1972.

Brownlee, Oswald, and John Buttrick: *Producer, Consumer, and Social Choice,* McGraw-Hill Book Company, New York, 1968.

Childs, Marquis W., and Douglas Cater: *Ethics in a Business Society,* Mentor Books, New American Library of World Literature, Inc., New York, 1954.

Galbraith, John K.: *American Capitalism: The Concept of Countervailing Power,* Houghton Mifflin Company, Boston, 1956.

Harter, Lafayette G.: *Economic Responses to a Changing World,* Scott, Foresman & Co., Glenview, Ill., 1970.

Nader, Ralph: *The Consumer and Corporate Accountability,* Harcourt Brace Jovanovich, Inc., New York, 1973.

Nickson, Jack W. Jr.: *Economics and Social Choice,* McGraw-Hill Book Company, New York, 1971.

Name	Section	Date

COMPLETION SENTENCES

1 All groups in a nation owe it to society to act _responsibly_ .

2 The ideal of _P. R._ for a business is to win confidence

and respect of the public.

3 One of the grave problems of businesses that employ large numbers of employ-

ees is the loss of personal contact between _rank, file, + top employees_

4 The Hawthorne experiments proved the importance of considering the

emotional makeup as well as the physical characteristics of

the worker.

6 The _board of directors_ is the seat of power in the modern corpo-

ration.

6 Most of the large corporations send a letter to their stockholders at least

_four_____ times a year.

7 The primary purpose of the stockholders' annual meeting is to

elect a board of directors

8 A company's reputation among its consumers depends largely upon the

price quality [and] service

9 Better Business Bureaus exist to protect _consumers_ and

business men from the destructive competition of unscrupu-

lous sellers.

10 The attitudes of _consumers_ are investigated and analyzed

more than the attitudes of the other publics that management deals with.

11 Effective community relations involve the participation of

business leaders in community affairs.

12 The primary financial support for education comes from

local taxes.

13 The health of a community is the primary responsibility of the

local level of government.

14 The immediate problem areas in environmental damage are

air, _water_, and

disposal of.

Name	Section	Date

15 Nearly all the pollutants in the atmosphere are caused by

_____.

TRUE OR FALSE STATEMENTS

1 Public relations can be defined as the management of the asset goodwill.

2 Public relations is synonymous with publicity.

3 Business owes employees decent wages, and employees owe the employer an honest day's work.

4 Money is not the only lure by which to achieve greater production from employees.

5 There are two means of contact in common use between the corporation and its stockholders: information distributed by mail and the annual meeting.

6 Some companies have magazines prepared specifically for their stockholders.

7 Even though most stockholders of large corporations attend the annual meetings in person, many corporations distribute postmeeting reports to their stockholders.

8 The attitudes of consumers are investigated and analyzed probably more than any of the other groups with which a company deals.

9 The responsibility of a business toward the community goes beyond paying taxes.

10 Factory buildings, being built for utility, cannot avoid detracting to some extent from the beauty of their surroundings.

11 Businessmen exercise a large degree of control over the economic aspects of the nation, but not the cultural and social aspects.

12 Business management is exhibiting some of the characteristics of a profession, like medicine or the legal profession.

13 Twenty years ago there was almost complete apathy toward care for the environment.

14 In some cities the agent that contributes most to the creation of smog is the automobile engine.

15 Although some cities do not give sufficient treatment to sewage to purify it for immediate further use, all cities give primary treatment to their sewage.

EXERCISES

1 The social responsibilities of businessmen are to some extent discharged through such organizations as the local chamber of commerce, the Rotary club, the Kiwanis club, or the Lion's club. Compose a statement of objectives for a businessmen's organization, indicating the types of community responsibilities such an organization might undertake.

2 Select a business, such as banking, a small retail store, a department store, lumbering, furniture manufacturing, or magazine publishing. Prepare a proposed public relations program for the business, stating the activities you recommend in each of the following areas:

a Employee relations

b Customer relations

c Relations with local schools

d Support of cultural and recreational activities

e Relations with the local government

APPENDIX

CHOOSING A CAREER IN BUSINESS

It has been said that the two most important choices a person makes in his life are the choice of a career and the choice of a mate. So far as it is possible, the choice of a career should be made early. The amount of preparation required for various careers increases as time passes. This means more time must be spent in school studying for one's life work than was necessary half a century ago or even a generation ago. Ideally, every student should know what his career will be before he graduates from high school. Then he would know exactly what courses to take in college and how else to prepare himself for his first position. This, unfortunately, is not possible. Many persons are quite uncertain what they want to do after graduation from high school. Even after graduation from college, people often change their minds about their choice of a career. W. Somerset Maugham was trained as a physician, and later became a world-famous novelist. Nevertheless, it is better if a person can make his choice early and plan the preparation for his career accordingly. The information in this appendix is offered as an aid to those interested in making a career in business.

BASIC OBJECTIVES IN THE CHOICE OF A CAREER

Success in choosing a career requires investigation of two kinds. A person must investigate himself and the career in which he is interested. In investigating himself, he must answer the questions: What do I want? and What can I do best? In answering the first question, a person generally has in mind three things: satisfaction, some degree of security, and an opportunity for advancement.

Satisfaction in one's work depends mostly on the place of work and what one does there. The place of work can be thought of as some part of the country. Personal preferences differ, some people enjoying the Atlantic coast, some the Pacific Northwest, some the Midwest or Southwest, and some the Southeast. Some prefer to work in a large city or near one, while others like small towns. The place of work cannot always be chosen by a person, but it is one of the factors in satisfaction on a job.

What one does at his place of work is probably more important in contributing to satisfaction than where one works. This is partly a matter of making a happy choice of a profession. Partly, it is a matter of choosing the right kind of job within the chosen field of work. There are many different kinds of work in the field of selling, as there are in the fields of medicine, business management, and law. A man might be happy selling chemicals to industrial buyers but be miserable selling advertising space to local retailers. Some prefer a job with a chance to travel; others prefer to remain in one place. It is not that one job is more interesting than another; rather, it is that one mind is more receptive than another mind to a given job.

Security is an obsession to some and relatively unimportant to others. Everyone places some value on security, and it should be considered in the choice of a career. Security, however, can never be absolute. And, frequently, a high degree of security can be had only with the sacrifice of other desirable qualities, such as opportunity for advancement.

Every person with ambition wants to advance to positions of more responsibility. Although few will rise to the top, the fact that the way is open serves as a stimulus to better work. Often, the opportunity for advancement is a stronger inducement in selecting a job than the size of the starting salary.

In searching for the "right" job, it is useful to prepare a list of employment sources. The following should be helpful in indicating where to look for job possibilities.

College and university placement offices.

College Placement Annual, listing over a thousand companies, with the names and addresses of those who do the hiring.

Moody's Manuals. These are large volumes giving financial information about corporations in industrial, transportation, public utility, banks, and other companies. Although prepared primarily for investors, these volumes list addresses of corporations and names of principal officers and describe the business of the companies. These annual volumes are found in many college libraries and public libraries.

Trade journals, such as *Today's Secretary*, *Mill and Factory*, *Electrical World*, *Food Industries*, and *Electronics*, are particularly useful if your interest lies in a particular field.

Careers in Business, Careers, Inc., 635 Madison Ave., New York, N.Y. 10022. Most college libraries and placement offices have a copy. Revised annually.

Annual reports of corporations. Prepared primarily for stockholders, these reports also contain information about company progress and company activities and names of chief officers.

Careers for the Seventies, Dow Jones Books, Box 60, Princeton, N.J. 08540.

Careers in Business Administration, Regents Publishing Company, 200 Park Avenue South, New York, N.Y. 10003.

CHARACTERISTICS OF OCCUPATIONS

If a person is interested in business as a career, there are many occupations from which he may choose. There is not space to discuss all of them here. Only the more common ones will be briefly described.

Accounting is a type of work in which a person records and analyzes the financial transactions of a company or institution and prepares and interprets financial statements. The field of accounting can be divided broadly into two categories: private accounting and public accounting. In private accounting, a person keeps the books of a company or supervises bookkeepers who do the routine work. The accountant prepares statements for the executives, makes analyses when necessary, and may advise on financial matters. If a person is employed by a large concern, his job may be a highly specialized one. If he is employed by a small concern, he is likely to do a wide variety of accounting operations.

ACCOUNTING

A public accounting firm is somewhat like a law office in that work is done for clients. The more common services provided by public accountants are: auditing the accounts of client companies to determine their accuracy, designing and installing bookkeeping systems for new companies or revising accounting systems in use, and preparing tax returns or advising clients on tax matters. Whether one wishes to engage in private accounting or public accounting or to teach accounting, a Certified Public Accountant (CPA) certificate is a valuable document. The certificates are issued by the state governments to candidates passing CPA examinations. The examinations are difficult. Successful completion indicates a high level of attainment in the study of accounting.

The field of marketing includes retailing, wholesaling, advertising, and salesmanship. The job opportunities in this field are extremely varied. In general, a person must enjoy selling, even though the actual solicitation of orders is only one part of this field, because the basis of marketing efforts is to make sales. He must also be willing to deal with the public, and must have a pleasing personality.

MARKETING

If one chooses to become a salesman, the opportunities for advancement are limitless and the financial rewards for success are high. The pay is often a commission for each sale made or a combination of commissions and salary. If a person succeeds in securing a large number of orders, his income will be high. This field, however, is less secure than accounting, banking, or personnel work. While clerking in a retail store is part of the field of selling and is sometimes the "breaking in" job offered by a company to college graduates, the type of selling that offers the most opportunities is calling on customers at their places of business. This usually involves a considerable amount of travel, although the territory of some salesmen in New York City is confined to a section of the island of Manhattan. The salesman must have an intimate knowledge of the products he is selling and must be acquainted with the characteristics of his competitors' products and the needs of his customers. It is highly competitive work, but it is vital to a company's existence.

Retailing is one of the few fields in which women may rise to the top levels of management. For both men and women, retailing offers excellent opportunities. One may begin with a large organization, working up to the position of buyer (in a department store, this is the equivalent of department head), advertising manager, or store manager. Executive positions in retailing often require knowledge of finance, personnel relations, and public relations in addition to buying and selling.

Retailing is a field in which small units and large units can thrive together. A young person interested in operating his own store can get experience in retailing as an employee, and then open his own retail outlet. While the risks are great, the rewards for success are equally great.

A person interested in advertising can find employment in the advertising department of a company or in an advertising agency. In the larger departments or agencies, the positions may be highly specialized. The following is a partial list of the positions one may find in a large agency:

Layout (sketching an advertisement in rough form)
Copy writing (writing advertisements)
Account executive (supervising a program for a client)
Advertising sales
Artwork
Media specialist (newspaper, radio, television, billboards)
Production (supervising preparation of advertisements or radio and television commercials)
Research

The purpose of advertising is to influence people's buying habits. A person choosing advertising should have an interest in psychology. He should be a student of people. And he should be able to express ideas effectively through both the written and the spoken language.

FINANCE

Finance is largely office work, although some positions (securities salesman, promotion of banking services among business customers, and handling oil, mining, or agricultural loans) may involve considerable time away from the office. Integrity and responsibility are essential to success in this field. Close attention to detail and accuracy in handling reports are also necessary.

Finance positions in a corporation are relatively few. They are usually found in the treasurer's department and are concerned with means of raising money for company operations. Commercial banking is one of the largest sources of jobs for persons interested in finance. There are several thousand bank corporations in this country, some of them having many branches, most of them having none. Before World War II, banking had developed a reputation as a career in which prestige substituted for salary and where advancement was slow. Since the war, however, starting salaries have compared with salaries in the community for similar positions. Advancement has been more rapid, and promotion to officer status has not been delayed for the promising young employee.

Because investment banking is concerned with the selling of securities, a person entering this field should have an interest in sales as well as finance. In the brokerage field, a young employee may be handling the orders of customers to buy and sell stocks and bonds. Ability to work with the public and inspire clients' confidence are valuable traits.

There are many opportunities in government work for persons interested in finance. The Treasury Department, the Federal Reserve banks (semigovernment institutions), government lending agencies, and the Securities and Exchange Commission have frequent openings.

PRODUCTION

The beginning positions for college graduates in production frequently are on machines in a factory. As supervisory talent is evidenced, the young man will be promoted to foreman, supervisor, or plant manager. Other positions include time-and-motion study, quality control, inventory management, and purchasing. As much technical knowledge as one can get in college is useful to a career in this area. Sometimes a person will combine an engineering degree with one in business. Or a graduate with a major in business will take courses in engineering before and after graduation in order to enhance his chances for advancement.

PERSONNEL

For success in this field, one should be a good judge of character, enjoy working with people, and understand the factors that raise or lower morale and how diverse human natures can be made to work cooperatively toward a common goal. In personnel work, a person deals with such problems as hiring, firing, promoting, transferring, handling complaints of workers, bargaining with union representatives, and suggesting improvements in the working conditions at a plant or office. Sympathy, tact, and patience are highly desirable traits for persons in this field.

TRANSPORTATION

The railroads, airlines, bus and truck companies, and shipping lines offer opportunities of interest to the college graduate. Young men and women may become airline host(esse)s, work in ticket offices or travel agencies, or be employed on cruise ships. Scheduling, dispatching, and other clerical work is available and may lead to executive positions. One of the fringe benefits often is the opportunity to purchase transportation at privileged rates.

FOREIGN TRADE

Many young persons have conceived of a career in foreign trade as involving travel to exotic foreign lands, where one lives in luxury, surrounded by servants, and makes trips back to the United States frequently. At times this is a reality—for a few. For most, however, a career in foreign trade does not provide any more opportunity to travel than most other careers. Nevertheless, jobs in foreign trade often permit a person to become acquainted with foreign peoples and customs. Even though one may not travel abroad, a considerable amount of correspondence with foreign persons is found in the business of exporting and importing. Knowledge of one or two foreign languages is useful, as is knowledge of commercial and social customs in other parts of the world.

The activities in foreign trade are similar in most respects to domestic trade. There is buying, selling, advertising, packaging, arranging for transportation and insurance, financing, and accounting. A good background in general business is needed. Experience or training in a specialty, such as finance, advertising, or selling, is also useful. A person might begin working for a company in its domestic operations, later transferring to the export department as an opening occurs.

INSURANCE

Selling insurance is one of the most common positions offered to college graduates. The salesman earns commissions not only when a policy is sold, but for years afterward. While the work may be hard at times, the financial incentive is good and the position carries prestige in the field of selling. Freuqently, the agent representing a life insurance company is looked on by customers as not merely a salesman but a counselor as well.

An underwriter decides on applications for insurance. If the information furnished by the agent in preparing the application indicates that the risk is high, the underwriter has the responsibility of disapproving the application. Underwriting is a position requiring sound judgment. Insurance is a field in which study after receiving the initial job is characteristic. Agents selling insurance are encouraged to study for and pass the examinations qualifying for Chartered Life Underwriter (CLU) or Chartered Property Casualty Underwriter (CPCU).

PERSONAL PLANNING

Choosing a career is a job in itself. To make the best possible choice requires careful thought, considerable study, and planning. Those who plan their careers with care will be in a better position to take advantage of circumstances that may help them. Those who do not have a clear idea of their goals in life will be less likely to recognize opportunity when it presents itself. According to Confucius, "In all matters success depends upon preparation; without preparation there will always be failure. When a line of conduct is previously determined, there will be no occasion for vexation."[1]

After a person has chosen a career, he should become as well prepared for it as possible. Some careers require a lot of training, while others require little. In some, the training must be largely secured before beginning work; in others, training can in part be deferred until securing the initial position after graduation, and can be continued on a part-time basis. As the decades pass, most careers require a higher degree of training. To keep abreast of changing developments in one's field requires continuous study. Commencement speakers are fond of saying that the graduation ceremonies mark not the end but the *commencement* of learning. What one has learned soon becomes stale. The mind must be constantly refreshed. It must be alive to new ideas and receptive to change. Therein lies the key to success, regardless of the career one chooses for himself.

[1] Quoted from *The Royal Bank of Canada Monthly Letter*, vol. 34, no. 4, April 1953, p. 2.

GLOSSARY

Accountability: A person's responsibility in completing an obligation.

Accounting: The recording, analysis, and interpretation of business transactions in financial terms.

Accounts receivable: Payments due from customers but not yet received.

Administration: The officer class of a company. Also the functions of an executive.

Ad valorem: According to the value (Latin).

Advertising: Any paid form of nonpersonal presentation of goods or services for an identified sponsor.

Advertising agency: A company that prepares and places advertising for a client.

Advertising medium: The channel through which the sponsor's message is presented to potential customers. Examples are radio, billboards, and newspapers.

Agency shop: In labor relations, the provision of a labor contract requiring all employees covered by the contract to make payments to the union, but not requiring all employees to join the union.

Agent: A person authorized to act on behalf of another.

Amortization: Repayment of a debt through installments.

Analysis: In production, the process of making several end products from a raw material. For example, breaking up crude oil into gasoline, kerosene, fuel oil, and asphalt.

Antitrust laws: Laws designed to prevent concentration of an industry in one or a few firms. Also called antimonopoly laws.

Applied research: The application of scientific inquiry to solving a practical problem.

Arbitration: The act of settling a dispute—for example, in labor—by submitting it to a third party, with a prior agreement by each party to abide by the decision.

Array: In statistics, the arrangement of numbers in rows and columns.

Asset: Any piece or item of property that has value. It may be tangible, as in a building, or intangible, as in a patent.

Audit: In accounting, the examination and verification of accounting records.

Automation: The process of using machines to control other machines. Self-regulating machinery.

Balance of payments: In international trade, the compilation of all of the transactions involving money between one nation and all other nations.

Balance of trade: In international trade, the record of transactions in goods and services between one nation and all other nations. Does not include investment transfers, gold movements, and other items in balance of payments.

Balance sheet: A statement of financial condition showing a company's assets, liabilities, and net worth on a specified date.

Bank acceptance: A draft drawn on a bank, accepted by the bank. See *Draft*.

Bar graph: The representation of data by bars of differing lengths.

Bill of lading: A receipt for goods shipped by a transportation company.

Binary system: A system of mathematics using only two digits, 0 and 1. Used in electronic data processing.

Black list: In labor relations, a list of union organizers or workers supporting union activity used by employers to withhold employment from such persons.

Board of directors: A group of persons elected by the stockholders of a corporation that sets policies of operation and appoints the officers of the corporation.

Bond: A certificate of long-term indebtedness of a corporation.

Book value: The value of an item owned by a company as shown by the accounting records. *Book value* of a company is the difference between the assets and liabilities shown by the accounting records.

Boycott: The refusal by one group to engage in commercial transactions with a company or agency; for example, the refusal of union members and their families to patronize a particular store.

Break-even point: The point at which the volume of sales is just sufficient to meet all expenses. The point at which neither profit nor loss is incurred.

Broker: An agent who negotiates a purchase or sale for a client and for which purchase or sale a commission is paid.

Budget: A financial plan, showing income and expenditure, to guide business operations for a specified period in the future.

Business: An organization created to produce or distribute goods or furnish services for profit. The general activity of furnishing goods and services.

Business cycle: The rhythmic expansion and contraction of business activity.

Buyers' market: A condition in which sellers are more eager to sell than buyers to buy, with prices tending to fall.

Capital: In economics, the productive facilities of a nation used to produce consumer goods and services. In accounting, the amount of long-term funds invested in a business.

Capital goods: The buildings, machinery, and other relatively long-lasting goods used to produce other goods.

Capitalism: The economic system of a country that has the following characteristics: private ownership of property, freedom of enterprise, production for profit, free competition, limited government activity in business, and extensive use of capital.

Cash discount: A reduction in the sales price, such as 2 percent, if payment is made immediately or within the number of days specified by the seller.

Casualty insurance: Coverage of risks in fields other than life, fire, and marine insurance.

Caveat emptor: Let the buyer beware. (Latin)

Charter: The document containing the terms under which government grants authority to a business to operate as a corporation. Also called a *certificate of incorporation*.

Check: A written order directing a bank to pay a specified sum of money to the party specified in the order.

Checkoff: In labor relations, a clause in a labor contract requiring the employer to collect union dues from each union employee's pay check.

COBOL: COmmon Business Oriented Language, a computer language designed for business applications.

Collateral: An asset that is pledged as security for a loan.

Commercial paper: Short-term promissory notes used by large corporations to raise money.

Common carrier: A transportation company offering services to the general public, such as a railroad or an airline.

Common law: Law originating from long-held custom rather than enactment by a legislature.

Common stock: Shares of ownership in a corporation usually carrying the right to vote for corporation directors and receiving dividend payments after payments to preferred stock.

Conciliation: In labor relations, the efforts of a third party to persuade an employer and a union to negotiate their differences in good faith.

Consumer foods: Products used by individuals and households for their own satisfaction.

Containerization: Placement of goods in large containers that are kept sealed from point of origin to destination.

Contract: An agreement between two or more parties, enforceable at law.

Contract carrier: A transportation carrier confining its services to those clients with whom contracts have been made.

Convenience goods: Goods that consumers purchase frequently, usually in small quantities; for example, cigarettes.

Cooperative: A private business, organized as a corporation, owned by its customers through stock ownership, and distributing profits on the basis of the amount of patronage of each stockholder, rather than the amount of stock owned.

Copyright: The exclusive right to publish a manuscript or make and distribute copies of a work of art.

Corporation: A form of business organization, created under state or federal law, in which ownership is in the form of stock (also called *shares*), with power to make contracts and do business in its own name and with liability of owners limited to the amount of their investment in the company.

Correlation: The degree to which two variables rise or fall together.

Cost accounting: The branch of accounting that identifies, measures, and records the costs of specific activities of a business.

Cost of goods sold: The direct material costs of production.

CPA: Certified Public Accountant.

Craft union: A labor union that organizes workers according to a particular skill or craft; for example, the American Federation of Teachers, or the Bartenders Union.

Credit union: A cooperative that promotes savings and makes loans to members.

Current assets: Cash and assets, such as accounts receivable and inventories, that will be turned into cash within one accounting period (usually 1 year).

Current liabilities: Obligations to pay, falling due within a period of 12 months.

Current ratio: Current assets divided by current liabilities.

Customs duty: A tax levied on the importation of goods from a foreign country.

Customs union: An association of nations, usually contiguous, among which customs duties have been eliminated so that goods may move freely between the associated nations.

Data processing: The operations, generally by mechanical or electronic devices, involved in recording, manipulating, and presenting information.

Debenture bond: A long-term debt not secured by a creditor claim on any specific property.

Debugging: The search for and correction of errors in a computer program.

Deficit: The net loss resulting from the excess of expenses over income.

Demand: In economics and business, the desire by customers for a good or service coupled with ability to buy.

Demand schedule: The quantities of a good or service that will be bought at each price of a range of prices.

Depreciation: The decline in the value of an asset, such as a machine or building, over a period of years.

Digital computer: A computer that deals in discrete units rather than approximations. This is the computer used in business applications.

Discount: Interest on a loan deducted at the time the loan is made rather than collected at the time the loan is repaid.

Dividend: The payment, usually in cash, to stockholders, representing a distribution of earnings.

Draft: A negotiable order in writing directing the payment of money from one party to another. A bank check is one example of a draft.

Entrepreneur: A person who organizes and directs a business, receiving the profits and accepting the risks of loss.

Equity: The owner's share in a business. The difference between total assets and total liabilities (also referred to as *net worth*).

Excise tax: A tax levied on the production, distribution, or consumption (use) of goods within a country.

Extrapolation: Extension of a past trend into the future.

Fabrication: In business, the processing of materials into products.

Fair trade laws: State laws enforcing the authority of manufacturers of branded goods to dictate the prices at which retailers may sell the goods.

Featherbedding: In labor relations, a requirement imposed by a union forcing an employer to use more workers than he needs. The forced use of unneeded workers.

Feedback: In production, the capability of a machine to control its own operation, making adjustments as necessary to keep output within specified standards.

Fixed assets: Business property with relatively long life, such as land, buildings, and machinery.

Fixed costs: Costs that do not rise and fall with the rise and fall in the volume of business; for example, rent, property taxes, and office salaries.

Flow diagram: A diagram showing the sequence of operations in a business. In production, a flow diagram also shows the type and location of each operation.

Foreign exchange: Orders to pay in one currency paid for in another currency. For example, a draft in Indian rupees payable in Bombay purchased from a bank in New York and paid for in American dollars.

Foreign exchange rate: The price of one unit of currency expressed in terms of another currency. For example, the rate of the German mark may be 43 cents in American dollars.

Foreman: A man at the first level of supervision.

FORTRAN: FORmula TRANslator. A computer language designed principally for scientific applications.

Franchise: The right granted by one firm to other firms to distribute the first firm's products, use its name, or benefit from its promotion and advertising in return for fees paid to the first firm.

Fringe benefits: Items of value given to employees or executives in addition to salary. Examples are expense accounts, pensions, and paid vacations.

Goodwill: In accounting, the value of a business above the value of other assets. The increased value of a business resulting from its reputation and good name.

Gross income: Net sales minus cost of goods sold. Also called gross margin or gross profit.

Gross National Product (GNP):   The total market value of the goods and services produced for sale by a nation during a given period (usually 1 year or one quarter-year).

Hedging: The purchase of a contract for the future delivery of a commodity for the purpose of minimizing business losses resulting from price fluctuations.

Holding company: A corporation the principal function of which is to control the operations of one or more other corporations (called "subsidiaries") through ownership of a controlling block of stock in each subsidiary.

Income statement: An accounting statement summarizing the revenues and expenses of a company over a period of time, such as a year or a month. Also called *profit and loss statement.*

Incorporate: To form a corporation.

Industrial union: A labor union that organizes members according to the industry that employs them rather than the craft or skill of the members. Examples are the United Auto Workers and the United Mine Workers.

Injunction: The order of a court directing a person, corporation, or group to do a specified act or to refrain from doing a specified act.

Installment buying: A purchase contract obligating the buyer to pay a stated sum of money periodically (usually monthly) until a stated total is reached.

Insurance: A service in which one party (insurer) contracts for a sum of money (premium) paid by another party (insured) to pay the second party a stated amount of money if the second party should suffer a specified loss.

Intangible asset: Any nonphysical asset, such as a patent or goodwill.

Interest: The amount paid for borrowed funds.

Inventory: The stock of goods used by a business or available for sale by a business.

Investment banker: A person or company that markets an issue of bonds or stocks for a corporation.

Invoice: A detailed, descriptive statement of goods shipped by a seller to a buyer.

Job analysis: A detailed analysis of the essential elements of a job including duties to be performed, equipment to be used, physical and mental requirements of the worker, conditions of work, and relations to other jobs.

Job description: A statement, based on job analysis, of the duties to be performed and the worker qualifications needed for a job.

Job rotation: The planned shifting of a worker to a sequence of related jobs, sometimes used to relieve worker boredom, sometimes used to acquaint a management trainee with the types of work which he will later supervise.

Laissez faire: To leave alone (French). In economics, the form of capitalism in which there is no government regulation or support of business activity in any degree.

Liabilities: In accounting, the debts owed by a business.

Limited partnership: A partnership in which at least one partner (general partner) is personally liable to pay all partnership debts unpaid by the partnership and in which the other partners (limited or silent partners) are liable only to the extent of their investment in the partnership. Limited partners may not participate in the management of the partnership.

Line and staff organization: An organization structure that modifies the line organization by adding staff specialists at each level to provide guidance to the line officers.

Line of credit: An agreement under which a lender, such as a commercial bank, stands ready for a given period to make loans at an agreed rate of interest up to an agreed maximum to a borrower.

Line organization: An organization structure in which authority flows from top executives to lower ranks in a straight line, a structure in which each worker is subject to the direction and authority of a single supervisor.

Lockout: The refusal of an employer to permit workers to enter a plant, so as to force workers to agree to the terms of the employer. The opposite of a strike by workers.

Long-term liability: Financial obligations of a company with a life greater than one year.

Management: The activity of directing the work of others and coordinating their efforts so as to achieve a common goal. The persons who direct and coordinate the work of others. The group of executives of a business firm.

Marketing: The function of moving goods from producers to consumers, in the process providing time, place, and possession utility to the goods.

Market research: Research devoted to learning the demands of customers and how to apply the findings to improve the sales of a company.

Markup: In retailing, the difference between the price paid by the retailer for goods and the price at which he sells them to customers.

Mass production: A method of production using specialized machines to produce standardized products in large quantities.

Maturity date: In finance, the date on which the principal of a loan is due to be repaid.

Mean: In statistics, the average found by adding a group of numbers and dividing by the number comprising the group. For example, adding the ages of 20 children and dividing by 20 to get the average age. Also known as *arithmetic average* or *arithmetic mean*.

Measure of central tendency: In statistics, the number that is taken as being representative of a group. Measures of central tendency include the *mean*, *median*, and *mode*.

Median: In statistics, the midpoint of a series of numbers arrayed from lowest to highest.

Mediation: In labor relations, the effort to resolve a labor dispute by using a neutral party to participate in negotiations between union and management.

Memory: In data processing, that part of a computer that stores information and instructions.

Merchant wholesaler: A wholesaler who buys goods from producers for resale to retailers.

Merger: In everyday business conversation, the combination of two or more corporations into one. In strict financial terms, the absorption of one or more companies by another company, with the absorbing company retaining its identity. Thus company X merges into company Y.

MESBIC: Minority Enterprise Small Business Investment Company. Private corporations, subsidized by the federal government, extending loans and providing management assistance to businesses operated by ethnic minority persons; businesses that are, for the most part, located in the older neighborhoods of larger cities.

Middlemen: Wholesalers, retailers, and others who facilitate the movement of goods from producer to consumer.

Mode: In statistics, the most frequent number in a series of numbers.

Monopoly: In everyday business conversation, the domination of an industry by a firm, with the result that competition in the industry is stifled. In economics, there is only one producer in a monopoly industry (a single company *is* the industry).

Motion study: The analysis of a worker's movements in a particular task to determine the most efficient sequence of movements in accomplishing the task. Also known as *motion-and-time study*.

Multinational business: A large company having operations in several nations.

Mutual company: In insurance, a company owned by the policyholders in which any distribution of net income is made on the basis of the amount of insurance held by each policyholder.

Mutual fund: An investment institution that sells its shares to investors and, with the money received, purchases bonds and stock of corporations. A mutual fund typically sells its shares in small units and buys corporation securities in large blocks.

Negotiable instrument: A written promise to pay or order to pay in which the right to receive payment may be transferred from one party to another.

Net profit: The amount that remains after all expenses have been deducted from revenues. Often stated as *net profit before* (income) *taxes* or as *net profit after taxes*. Also called *net income*.

Net sales: Total sales minus returns of goods for credit and discounts for prompt payment of sales.

Net worth: Total assets minus total liabilities. Also called *owners' equity*.

No-par stock: Stock that does not contain a statement of value on the face of certificates. Sometimes called *nonpar stock*.

Note: In finance, a written promise to make a payment in money. Also called *promissory note*.

Objective: In business, a specific goal of a business firm.

Odd figure pricing: The practice at the retail level of pricing merchandise slightly below round numbers, to create the illusion of a lower price. For example, 49¢, 95¢, $4.95, $298.

Oligopoly: A market condition in which an industry is controlled by a few sellers that account for either the total industry sales or a dominant portion of industry sales.

On-the-job training: Instruction given to a worker at his assigned work station. Learning while doing.

Open dating: A statement on the package of a consumer item indicating the date of production or date of receipt by the retailer, intended to indicate to the shopper the freshness of the item.

Open shop: In labor relations, a condition that permits workers in a plant to hold employment whether joining a union or not.

Operations research: The analysis of all the forces and consequences of a given business activity done for the purpose of achieving the most efficient method of operation.

Organization chart: A formal diagram showing the lines of authority of an organization.

Overhead: Those expense items not chargeable to a particular product or line and not varying directly with volume of sales; for example, executive salaries, telephone and electric utility expenses, and office equipment expense.

Partnership: A form of business organization comprising two or more persons who share ownership of a business.

Par value: In finance, the monetary value printed on the face of a stock certificate or bond certificate. The par value of a corporation bond is typically $1,000.

Patent: The exclusive right to make and sell an invention. The right, good for 17 years, is granted by the federal government.

Per capita: Per person (Latin).

Personal property: In business and taxation, all movable property, such as equipment, inventories, and supplies. Property taxes are generally levied at a lower rate on personal property than on real estate.

Personnel management: Those management functions covering selection, training, supervision, and motivation of workers in a plant or office.

Piggyback: In transportation, a railroad freight service in which loaded truck bodies or trailers are secured to flat cars for shipment by rail.

Place utility: The value added to goods by moving them to where they are most wanted by potential buyers.

Plaintiff: In law, one who initiates a court action.

Policy: A rule or guideline, usually established at the supervisory levels, that sets the boundaries within which business decisions must be made.

Preemptive right: The right of a stockholder to purchase the number of shares in any additional issue of stock of his corporation that is necessary to maintain the same percentage ownership of the corporation that he previously held.

Preferred stock: A class of stock having priority, usually in payment of dividends, over the common stock. Preferred stock ordinarily does not vote for directors and is usually limited as to amount of dividends regularly paid.

Price fixing: Collusion among industry members to set price higher than they would be under competition.

Price index: In statistics, a number or series of numbers representing changes in prices compared with a base period.

Primary boycott: In labor relations, the refusal of the employees of a company to buy the products of the company in the hope of exerting pressure on management in a dispute.

Private enterprise: A business system characterized by production and distribution through privately owned business enterprises with limited government regulation.

Productivity: The amount of output per unit of input; for example, the amount of output per hour of manufacturing labor.

Profit: The remainder left after deduction of all expenses from revenues.

Profit and loss statement: See *Income statement.*

Programming: In data processing, the setting up of a problem in a series of steps that can be entered into a computer.

Progressive taxation: A tax that takes a larger percentage of a high income than of a low income.

Promissory note: A written promise to make a payment in money.

Promotion: In marketing, those activities undertaken for the purpose of influencing customers to ask for a company's products or of improving the image of the company in the minds of the public.

Proportional taxation: A tax levied in such a way that it collects the same percentage of income from the low-income person as from the high-income person.

Proprietorship: An unincorporated business owned by a single owner, who is called the proprietor.

Protective tariff: A tax on imports levied not for the purpose of raising revenue but to reduce competition by restricting foreign goods.

Proxy: A written form signed by a stockholder appointing another person or persons to represent him and vote his shares at a stockholders' meeting. Also the person appointed to represent the absent stockholder.

Public relations: The activity devoted to creating a favorable public image of a company, trade association, labor union, university, or government agency.

Purchasing agent: The officer designated to place orders for goods and supplies for a company or institution.

Quality control: The process that, through inspection and testing, seeks to ensure that production will meet designated standards.

Real time: In data processing, the use of a computer in applications where the output follows the input sufficiently promptly to control an activity while the activity is under way. For example, the making of airline passenger reservations, where an entry by a ticket agent into a computer terminal gives an indication whether a seat is available, and if so, immediately notifies the clerk that the reservation has been made, while at the same time keeping track of the number of seats still available.

Regressive taxation: A tax that takes a larger proportion of a small income than of a large income. A sales tax is a regressive tax.

Retailer: A business firm that sells goods to consumers.

Sales promotion: See *Promotion*.

Sample inspection: Determining the quality of output by analyzing or examining a small number of items, under the assumption that the small number is representative of the larger group.

Scientific management: Principles of management developed by Frederick W. Taylor and his followers that, among other ideas, emphasize the use of motion-and-time study to improve worker performance.

Seasonal variation: In statistics, the pattern of fluctuation in a time series that is repeated yearly.

Secondary boycott: The refusal by members of one organized labor group to buy from, make deliveries to, or otherwise deal with an employer engaged in a dispute with a labor group different from the first labor group.

Security: In finance, the stocks, bonds, and other financial instruments that give evidence of ownership or debt of corporations and financial institutions. Also, any item of value that is held, actually or through a lien, by a lender as guarantee of repayment of a loan.

Sellers' market: A market in which buyers are more eager to buy than sellers are to sell, with the result that prices tend to rise.

Seniority: A worker's status relative to other workers as measured by the number of years of service. Often used in deciding relative wage scales, promotions, and length of annual vacations.

Share: In finance, the unit of stock into which ownership of a corporation is divided.

Shopping goods: Those goods for which a customer spends time in comparing price and quality at different stores, rather than choosing on the basis of habit. Examples are clothing, furniture, and sports equipment.

Short-term debt: Those financial obligations of a company that must be repaid within 1 year.

Sight draft: A draft payable upon presentation or demand. Also called a *demand draft.*

Sinking fund: A fund into which a business borrower makes periodic payments to build up an amount needed to pay off a long-term debt.

Socialism: An economic system in which the government owns all the major industries.

Sole proprietorship: See *Proprietorship.*

Span of control: The number of workers that a supervisor can effectively supervise.

Specialty goods: Goods for which a customer has a strong brand preference and to obtain which he is willing to undertake extra effort.

Speculative buying: A policy of buying raw materials or other items by forecasting future prices and buying heavily when prices are down, so as to profit from price rises.

Staff executive: A specialist serving to provide advice and counsel to a line executive.

Standardization: The establishment of precise production criteria to which units of production must conform (with respect to weight, dimensions, color, etc.).

Statutory law: Federal and state constitutions, laws, and legal codes enacted by legislative bodies.

Stock certificate: A certificate of ownership in a corporation, giving the name of the owner, the number of shares owned, and the class of stock (common or preferred, usually).

Stockholder: A person who owns stock in a corporation. Also called a *shareholder.*

Strike: Workers acting together in refusing to work for a company in an effort to force concessions from the company.

Subsidiary: A corporation that is owned or controlled by another corporation (called the *parent company*).

Subsidy: Support, usually in the form of money, given to a business firm by government.

Surety bond: A guarantee given by the first party to the second party that a third party will fulfill a contract.

Surplus: In accounting, the portion of net worth in excess of the capital stock account of a corporation. Surplus results mainly from two conditions: the sale of stock for a price greater than par value (*capital surplus*), and retention of earnings (*earned surplus*).

Surtax: An additional tax levied on top of a tax already levied.

Synthesis: In production, the creation of a product by bringing together different elements, such as the manufacture of paints and varnishes.

Tariff: A tax levied on the importation of goods into or their exportation out of a country. In the United States the federal constitution forbids the levy of a tax on the exportation of goods from the country.

Term loan: A loan extended by a bank or other lending institution to a business firm having a duration of more than 1 year and with repayment made in installments.

Time-and-motion study: See *Motion study.*

Time draft: A draft payable at a specified time in the future.

Time series: The classification of statistical data on the basis of time, showing the changes (such as business activity) that take place from one time period to another.

Time sharing: The utilization of a computer by several users simultaneously through terminals at different locations.

Top management: The highest level of management. For example, the president and vice presidents of a firm.

Trade association: An association of businessmen in the same industry or having common interests.

Trade credit: Credit extended by sellers to business firms for payment of goods purchased. For example, the privilege extended by a supplier to customers to pay for goods 30 days after shipment.

Trade discount: A reduction from the published retail price extended by a manufacturer to retailers, interior decorators, and other businessmen.

Trade journal: A periodical specializing in news of a particular industry or profession. Examples are *Railway Age*, *Textile World*, and *American Gas Journal*.

Trademark: A name, symbol, or design that distinguishes one company's products from those of its competitors.

Trend line: In statistical presentation, a line that identifies the general, long-run movement of a time series.

Ultra vires acts: In business, actions taken by directors or officers of a corporation not granted in the corporation charter (Latin).

Underwriter: In finance, a person or firm that guarantees (and usually participates in) the successful sale to the public of securities of a corporation. In insurance, a person or firm that undertakes to guarantee a person or firm against loss resulting from a specified hazard. Also an officer of an insurance firm who examines applications for insurance.

Union shop: In labor relations, a contract between a union and an employer requiring a newly hired worker to join the union within a specified period (usually 30 days) to keep his job.

Unit pricing: The marking on packages in retail stores of prices (in addition to total price) on a cents-per-ounce (or other unit) basis to facilitate price comparisons by shoppers.

Unlimited liability: The liability of a person to the extent of his personal wealth to pay the business debts of his firm. Proprietors and general partners have unlimited liability. Limited partners and corporation shareholders have limited liability.

Unsecured debt: A debt that does not have any specific collateral to increase assurance of repayment.

Variable costs: Costs that vary closely with the volume of production. For example, costs of raw materials and wages of production workers.

Vestibule training: Training of production workers with machines and under conditions that simulate actual work but in an area separated from the production plant.

Warehouse receipt: A receipt for goods stored in a warehouse, sometimes used as collateral for a loan.

Warranty: A guarantee of quality, title, or other characteristic specified.

Wholesaler: A business firm that sells to or arranges sales for other business firms, generally retailers.

Working capital: Assets that are generally converted into cash within 1 year. Also called current assets. Net working capital is the dollar value of current assets minus current liabilities.

Workmen's compensation insurance: That type of insurance required by state law and financed by employers that compensates workers injured while on the job.

INDEX